Truman's Crises

Books by Harold F. Gosnell

Boss Platt and His New York Machine: A Study of the Political Leadership of Thomas C. Platt, Theodore Roosevelt, and Others
Non-Voting: Causes and Methods of Control (co-author)
Getting Out the Vote: An Experiment in the Stimulation of Voting
The American Party System (co-author)
Why Europe Votes
Negro Politicians: The Rise of Negro Politics in Chicago
Machine Politics: Chicago Model
Grass Roots Politics
Democracy: The Threshold of Freedom
Champion Campaigner: Franklin D. Roosevelt
American Parties and Elections (co-author)

TRUMAN'S CRISES

A Political Biography of Harry S. Truman

60093

Harold F. Gosnell

CONTRIBUTIONS IN POLITICAL SCIENCE, NUMBER 33

GREENWOOD PRESS

WESTPORT, CONNECTICUT • LONDON, ENGLAND

Library of Congress Cataloging in Publication Data

Gosnell, Harold Foote, 1896-
   Truman's crises.

   (Contributions in political science ; no. 33
ISSN 0147-1066)
   Bibliography: p.
   Includes index
   1. Truman, Harry S., Pres., U.S., 1884-1972.
2. Missouri—Politics and government—1865-1950.
3. United States—Politics and government—
1933-1945. 4. United States—Politics and government—
1945-1953. 5. Presidents—United States— Biography.
I. Title. II. Series.
E814.G67   973.918'092'4 [B]   79-7360
ISBN: 0-313-21273-2

Library of Congress Catalog Card Number: 79-7360
ISBN: 0-313-21273-2
ISSN: 0147-1066

First published in 1980

Greenwood Press
A division of Congressional Information Service, Inc.

51 Riverside Avenue, Westport, Connecticut 06880

Printed in the United States of America

10 9 8 7 6 5 4 3 2 1

ACKNOWLEDGMENTS

Grateful acknowledgment is made to the following sources for permission to reprint:

The Man of Independence, Copyright, 1950 by Jonathan Daniels, Copyright renewed ©, 1978 by Jonathan Daniels. Reprinted by permission of Brandt & Brandt Literary Agency, Inc.

Laurin Henry, *Presidential Transitions,* Brookings Institution, 1960. Copyright © 1960, by Brookings Institution.

George E. Kennan, *Memoirs 1925-1950*, Little, Brown and Company, Copyright © 1967, by George E. Kennan.

Elmo Roper, *You and Your Leaders,* William Morrow and Company, Copyright © 1957, by Elmo Roper.

Harry S. Truman, *Memoirs, Year of Decisions,* Doubleday & Co., Inc., Publishers, 1955, used by permission of Harry S. Truman Estate.

Harry S. Truman, *Memoirs, Years of Trial and Hope,* Doubleday & Co., Inc., Publishers, 1955, used by permission of Harry S. Truman Estate.

Margaret Truman, *Souvenir,* McGraw-Hill Book Company, Inc., Publishers, 1956, Copyright © by Margaret Truman.

Margaret Truman, *Harry S. Truman,* William Morrow and Company, Inc., Publishers, 1972, Copyright © by Margaret Truman Daniel.

Selections from *Mr. President* by William Hillman and Alfred Wagg. Copyright 1952 by William Hillman and Alfred Wagg. Reprinted with the permission of Farrar, Straus & Giroux, Inc.

CONTENTS

PART II   ACCIDENTAL PRESIDENT

PART III   PRESIDENT IN HIS OWN RIGHT

Contents   ix

MAPS

PREFACE

The curious may ask, Why another book on Truman? Although the books and materials on Truman and the Truman period have been increasing at a rapid rate, there is a scarcity of general scholarly biographical works on Truman's entire political career. Most biographies on Truman have been written by journalists or by leftist revisionists, and they contain information that is not available elsewhere and would have been lost forever if it had not been obtained when it was. What is still lacking is a book based on newly available documentation and social science analysis covering Truman's entire career. The more than sixty doctoral dissertations on various phases of the Truman period have seldom been used by the journalists who have written about Truman.

This book analyzes and assesses Truman's leadership and political career. He served at three levels of government—ten years at the local level, ten years as a U.S. senator from Missouri, and nearly eight years as president. His decision-making processes, staffing, relations with fellow administrators, legislators, and top officials, his economic, social, and foreign policies and their formulation, budget making and administrative management practices, speech making, his relations with mass media, his role as a party leader, and his techniques for winning elections are discussed.

In my many years of teaching and research, I have been concerned with the subject of political leadership and have asked many questions. What accounts for the rise of some people to positions of political leadership? Do events make leaders, or do leaders influence the course of events? Are leaders born to rule, or are they made to rule by social circumstances? Are leadership qualities inherited, or can they be learned and improved upon by training? This book ponders whether leadership is an individual matter or the product of group activities. What is it that makes certain people willing to follow the guidance of others? Is the rise of a given person to a position of leadership inevitable, or is there a large element of good fortune in the picture?

Some years ago I considered the possibility of undertaking a thorough study of presidential leadership. I am still revising a schedule on characteristics of successful and unsuccessful candidates for elective office. Teaching duties, government service in the Bureau of the Budget and Department of State, and the pressure of other responsibilities and circumstances have delayed the fruition of this plan. My first book, *Boss Platt and His New York Machine*, recently republished, dealt in part with some phases of the leadership of Theodore Roosevelt. My *Machine Politics—Chicago Model*, *Negro Politicians*, *Grass Roots Politics*, and *Champion Campaigner—Franklin D. Roosevelt* deal with some phases of Franklin D. Roosevelt's career and the four men who ran against him.

Another question frequently asked of me is whether I am pro- or anti-Truman. Was Truman one of the great presidents, or will he go down in history as one toward the bottom of the list? There are two diametrically opposed schools of thought about Truman and his record. One school puts him in the class of the great, pointing to the ratification of the United Nations Pact, the Truman doctrine of containment of communist aggression, the Marshall Plan for saving the economies of Western European nations, the stopping of communist aggression in Greece, Turkey, Iran, and Korea, the building of NATO, the strengthening of America's military defenses, the holding of the line on social reforms, and their advancement in spite of hostile congressional majorities. An opposing school of revisionists challenges this interpretation. They accuse Truman of starting the unnecessary cold war, promoting a wasteful and dangerous arms race, needlessly permitting the slaughter of civilians by approving the dropping of atom bombs on two Japanese cities, threatening the Soviet Union with atomic blackmail, bypassing Congress and ignoring the United Nations in the Korean crisis, mismanaging the control of inflation on the domestic front, and following a policy of trying to balance on a tightrope and going no place—a policy of stalemate that counted on problems to solve themselves.

The two schools also present sharply contrasting views of Truman's personality characteristics. To one he was decisive, intelligent, modest, discreet, farsighted, a good judge of men and measures, and a sturdy fighter for the public interest. To the other, he was indecisive, dumb, inept, cocky, indiscreet, vulgar, shortsighted, second rate, poorly educated, a poor judge of men, a man of low moral standards, and a poor champion of the public interest. Obviously, these two views cannot both be correct. As images, they can exist side by side, their acceptance or rejection depending upon one's ideological orientation. The aim of this book is to search for the truth, which, I hope to show, lies somewhere between the extremes.

In addition to my great debt to the Truman, Roosevelt, and Eisenhower presidential libraries, I have been aided by the staffs of the National Archives in Washington, the Library of Congress, the Kansas City Public Library, University of Rochester Library, Howard University Library, American University Library, Columbia University Oral History, University of North Carolina Library, Princeton University Library, Washington, D.C., Public Library, Bethesda Public Library, and the interlibrary loan system.

In preparing the maps, I have been aided by my niece, Deborah Tucker. The Dan Daniels Printing Co. has been helpful in reducing the maps to manageable size.

Countless persons have been consulted in the preparation of this book. I am especially grateful for the information furnished by the following people in personal interviews, telephone conversations, or correspondence: Charles Aylward, Richard Bolling, Walter Bowers, Philip C. Brooks, Henry Bundschu, Oscar Chapman, Marquis Childs, Clark Clifford, William G. Colman, Robert Cook, Jonathan Daniels, Donald Dawson, Lewis Dexter, Paul H. Douglas, J. William Fulbright, Ken Hechler, Herbert Emmerich, Sue Gentry, John W. Godbold, Alonzo Hamby, Joseph P. Harris, Jerry Hess, Harold Ickes, Roger Jones, Richard Kirkendall, Philip D. Lagerquist, David Lloyd, Samuel Lubell, Curtis MacDougall, Charles Murphy, Samuel Rosenman, Harold Seidman, Herman Miles Somers, Elmer Staats, Alfred Steinberg, James Sundquist, Stuart Symington, Harry S. Truman, Henry Vaughan, Margaret Woodson, and Raymond R. Zimmerman.

My and my wife's visits to Independence were made very pleasant by our friends, the A. T. Hancocks, who extended cordial hospitality to us in their well-appointed home. They introduced us to their friend, May Wallace, sister-in-law of Truman's wife, who entertained us in her home next to the famous Gates-Wallace-Truman house on Delaware Street.

I have been very fortunate in having the manuscript read in part or in its entirety by my wife, Florence F. Gosnell, Gladys Baker, Ronald O. Burnett, Sydney Connor, Thomas E. Cronin, Fred Greenstein, Fred Howell, Carol Howell, Theodore Lowi, Dexter Perkins, Jane Porter, and Lawrence Yates. The comments of these persons have been most helpful, but they in no way are to be held responsible for anything appearing in the book.

During the Truman years, I worked for the Office of Price Administration, the Bureau of the Budget, and the Department of State. I had access to classified material during most of that time. My personal contacts with President Truman date back to 1950, and they continued until the mid-1960s.

PART I | FROM LAMAR TO THE WHITE HOUSE

chapter 1 | EARLY INFLUENCES

It was a bizarre celebration. Newsmen by the score poured into the little town, and all southwest Missouri turned out to hear "Harry" say yes. . . . Merchants who lacked buying sense and advertising skills were over supplied. Hotdog stands wound up with a stock they could not sell; barrels of lemonade and bottles of pop were still on the shelves. . . . An estimated twelve thousand persons jammed and crowded into the little town. . . . There was no longer much doubt where Lamar, Missouri, could be found. It, like Harry Truman, had arrived.

> —Frank McNaughton and Walter Heymeyer, *This Man Truman*

Harry S. Truman's beginnings were modest. He was born on May 8, 1884, in the tiny village of Lamar in southwestern Missouri of parents whose families had been farmers for generations. He was christened with just a middle initial; his parents could not decide whether to use the name of Solomon after his maternal grandfather or Shippe after his paternal grandfather. Lamar proved to be only a temporary home site. It was certainly not selected as the location of a future ceremony for the acceptance of a vice-presidential nomination. Physically it was totally unsuited for that purpose; it lacked facilities, sanitary and otherwise, for handling a crowd of some fifteen times its population. Sentimentally, it was something else. It indicated that the tiny baby had come a long way from humble beginnings to this impressive occasion. It was proof of the fulfillment of the American dream that any native American boy could aspire to the highest office. It was a symbol of the importance of luck in American politics.

ANCESTRY

Was Harry Truman born to political leadership? Did he possess inherited traits that helped him achieve a position of leadership in which he attracted and influenced followers? These are difficult questions to answer in view of the present state of our knowledge regarding the inheritance of mental and temperamental characteristics. Psychologists have not yet developed ways of separating these characteristics. They are also still working on operational definitions of leadership and on methods of testing for traits significantly related to specified leadership types.

The literature on the personality characteristics of an individual and the way he or she behaves or is perceived to behave in a group situation involving leader-follower relationships shows that there is some positive correlation between leadership and intelligence, extraversion, and interpersonal sensitivity. There is also some tendency for dominant personalities to become leaders.[1]

Another question can be asked about Truman's ancestry. Did he come from a family with a tradition of a high level of political activity? Did he have forebears who achieved high political positions? In American history, certain names have reappeared in the higher political posts—John Adams and his son and later progeny; William Henry Harrison and his son and grandson; Theodore Roosevelt and his son; Franklin D. Roosevelt and his sons; Robert M. La Follette and his sons; and most recently the Kennedy brothers, John, Robert, and Edward. I do not intend to imply that the impulse to enter politics may be in the blood. Rather, the question is raised whether a son or daughter or a sibling possessing some of the characteristics of the blood relative who has achieved political distinction is influenced to think that he or she also might achieve a position of political leadership. Potential followers might also recognize these traits. Of course, many children of famous parents fail to achieve any great political distinction, but this cannot be blamed on their ancestry.

Harry Truman, however, had no record of an immediate direct-line ancester who achieved high political position. On his father's side, he was remotely related to President John Tyler (Tyler's brother was the father of his great-grandmother), but Truman's opinion of John Tyler was not high.

If leaders are not born, how are they made? Of what importance are early influences? Some answers may be apparent if we first turn our attention to the parental influences upon the development of Harry S. Truman.

Maternal Influences

Psychologists agree upon the importance of a mother or surrogate mother in providing physical and affectional satisfactions for children from their earliest years. If a normal child's needs are met, the chances are good that he or she will develop a well-adjusted personality. A child who is deprived of such wanted delights may develop anxieties, insecurities, and a warped personality.

In turn, a mother's ability to provide for the needs of a child so that he or she will develop a stable and well-balanced personality depends in part on her own upbringing. Truman's mother, Martha Young Truman, came from a family that had provided her with happiness and security. Her father, Solomon Young, was a farmer, a prosperous freighter with huge wagon trains that plied between Independence and the West Coast, and a successful real estate operator.[2] Truman was proud of his grandfather, and shortly after becoming president, he paid tribute to him. After coming by airplane from San Francisco to Kansas City in some five and a half hours' flying time, he told his listeners in Kansas City: "My grandfather made that trip time and time again from 1846 to 1854, and again from 1864 to 1870, and when he made that trip it took him exactly 3 months to go, and 3 months to come back."[3] Grandfather Young seems to have been something of a hero to his grandson, and Harry was delighted when the distinguished old adventurer took him to the Belton Fair to watch the races from the judges' stand. In 1892, Grandfather Young ended his strenuous and exciting life at the age of seventy-seven on a six-hundred-acre farm near Grandview, now part of the Kansas City metropolitan region. His wealth was estimated at $150,000 at the time of his death, a large estate in the last half of the nineteenth century. Most of this was left to his bachelor son, Harrison Young, after whom Harry was named, and to his daughter, Martha Ellen Young Truman. The other eight children fought the will in the courts, and as Truman's brother, Vivian, ruefully put it, "The lawyers got most of it. All we got was debts."[4]

Martha Ellen was the youngest of the Young children and apparently was in good favor with her father. He sent her to the Baptist Female College in Lexington, Missouri, where she studied literature, art, and music and occasionally indulged her taste for dancing. She called herself a "light foot Baptist," because dancing was frowned upon by some Protestant fundamentalists. Her lifelong interest in music she passed on to her son, Harry, her daughter, Mary Jane, and her granddaughter, Margaret Truman. It was she who gave her son his first lessons in both reading and piano playing. Later she hired Mrs. E. C. White (who had been a pupil of Fannie Bloomfield Zeisler and also Zeisler's Viennese teacher, Theodor Leschetizky, who taught Paderewski, Rubinstein, and Josef Lhevinne) to continue Harry's piano instruction. A friend, who later became a foe of Harry, said: "Vivian did all the hard work in that house. His mother wanted Harry S. Truman to be a piano player, and he did what his mother wanted him to."[5]

Martha Ellen Young was known for her wit, bluntness, and intense loyalty to the Democratic party. While women's suffrage did not arrive until 1919 and voting was denied her until she was over seventy years of age, she expressed her pro-Confederate views on politics long before she had the franchise. Abe Lincoln was not her favorite president. Positive in her opinions and outspoken, she kept up on national affairs by reading news-

papers and the *Congressional Record* and, later, by listening to radio
newscasts. One of Truman's associates found her very discerning in sizing
up the feeling of strangers about her son.[6] One of Senator Truman's colleagues in the Senate put it this way: "No one who ever saw his late mother,
or even a photograph of her, can forget the strength in her face, the kindli-
ness, the spirituality, the simplicity and, withal, the wholesome twinkle of
good humor in her eyes."[7]

She was a person of great courage. Biographer Jonathan Daniels, when
told by Truman's brother how seriously ill Harry was with diphtheria in
1894 (he was almost totally paralyzed) and how he gradually recovered,
commented: "It must have frightened your mother." Vivian grinned, "She
didn't scare easy."[8]

As the first-born son, Harry had the full attention of his mother during
those most formative early years. The effect on Harry's character was not
unlike the effect of Sara Delano Roosevelt's loving care upon the character
of her son Franklin Delano Roosevelt.[9] Both Harry and Franklin became
oral optimists.[10] It is true that Martha Young was no Sara Delano and that
Grandview lacked the patrician air of Hyde Park, but both mothers made
their sons feel loved, secure, happy, trusting, and optimistic. Psychologist
J. F. Brown states that an infant obtains great satisfaction through nursing,
and vital impulses hence become first localized in the mouth. He contends
that "unwarranted optimism is typical of individuals strongly fixed in the
oral sucking stage." Adult continuations of this fixation are to be found in
drinking, eating, chewing, speaking, smiling, joking, laughing, kissing, and
in attention to oral hygiene.[11] Both Harry and Franklin demonstrated these
characteristics.

Harry was a dutiful son. Referring to his mother, he noted that "she
taught us the right thing to do and made us do it." After praising his father
for his integrity, Truman wrote: "My mother was the same sort of person.
She taught us the moral code and started us in Sunday School. She was
interested in our school progress, and our place was always the gathering
place for all the kids in the neighborhood because my mother liked children
and liked to see them have a good time, and liked to help them have a good
time."[12] Elsewhere, he said: "My mother was very patient with us and our
pals and always came to our defense when we went too far and the various
fathers decided to take a hand."[13]

Possessed of a strong personality and given to exercising considerable
influence in the family councils, Martha Young Truman's potential inheritance from her father put weight behind her words. Her husband left the
upbringing of the children largely to her, and she ruled with firm affection.
Regarding the punishment she meted out for misbehavior, Harry reported:
"We finally wound up at the mudhole with a neighbor boy about our age

and I loaded Vivian and John Chandler into the little wagon, hauled them into the mudhole—and upset the wagon. What a spanking I received, I can feel it yet.''[14]

His mother instilled in him the simple rules of Christian morality and taught him to become a faithful student of the Bible. Not surprisingly, his later public addresses and papers are studded with biblical references. Herself a Baptist, she saw that he went to a Protestant Sunday school, which, when they first moved in Independence, was Presbyterian. The Ten Commandments were a sacred code, and young Truman observed them as he understood them. He also believed in the Golden Rule and tried to live up to that high standard to the best of his ability. He closed his opening address to Congress on April 17, 1945, five days after becoming president with a reference to King Solomon's prayer.[15]

Always a dutiful son and brother, Truman helped his mother with the cooking and dishes, helped take care of his younger sister, Mary Jane, sang lullabies to her, and put her to bed.[16] Later on, when he was away from Missouri, he wrote to his mother and sister or called them on the telephone two or three times a week.

Martha Young Truman denied any favoritism but was closer to Harry than to her second son, Vivian, who took after his father. But when Harry became president and she was asked if she was not proud of her son, she said she was just as proud of Vivian and Mary Jane. When it became evident that nearsightedness would keep Harry out of strenuous sports, Truman's mother suggested that he learn to play the piano. A boy who carried a music roll rather than a baseball bat was regarded by the other children as a sissy, yet so strongly did Harry identify with his mother that her wishes were more powerful than the scorn of his peers. He practiced on the piano instead of playing rough games with the other boys, even considering at one time making a career as a musician. He decided at the age of fifteen, though, that he was not good enough. His brother, Vivian, states that his mother tried to get him to take piano lessons too, but ''she couldn't get a lasso long enough.''[17]

Truman loved to shock male companions with off-color stories. In 1971 this story about his choice of a career appeared in *Esquire*: ''My choice early in life was either to be a piano player in a whorehouse or a politician.'' Taking the old joke teller's practiced beat, he laid in the punchline: ''And to tell the truth there's hardly a difference.''[18]

His early decision not to choose piano playing as a career was not a decision between music and politics but between music and a military career. The Spanish-American War stirred the youths in Independence High to drill with air rifles in the woods. Harry was too young to enlist in the army, but he began planning to attend West Point. Truman was going through the identity crisis of adolescence. Branded a sissy because of his music roll, he wanted to assert his manliness. His reading in the library was directed toward the exploits of military heroes.

His mother also had a strong influence on Harry's personal habits. He did not smoke, was very neat in his personal appearance, and was usually careful of his language in the presence of women. Merle Miller, in *Plain Speaking: An Oral Biography of Harry S. Truman*, presents some alleged Truman quotes in earthy, rough, gutsy, and vulgar language, but Clark Clifford has told me that he never heard Truman use such language in mixed company.[19] Truman's language used in informal conversation with men reflected his experiences in early life. It was the product of the way men talk in a railroad section gang, in an army barracks, on the farm, and in the precinct politics of a city ruled by a tough political boss who had ties with the underworld.

Truman also showed moderation in his drinking. The Christian code of sexual morality was also stressed in his family life. Divorce was unthinkable for a Truman or a Young. A member of Congress from Missouri, recalling how shocked Truman was when he learned that the congressman was getting a divorce, remarked: "Truman was puritanical. The bosses sometimes want an honest man. Truman did not like divorce. He was shocked, but he got over it in my case."[20]

Gambling, though not looked upon as a dreadful sin, seemed evil enough to deter Harry from acquiring a mania for it such as wrecked the career of Kansas City's political boss, Tom Pendergast. When Harry was a young man, he once "hit the jackpot." Jonathan Daniels reports that Truman "was seventeen years old, and he had eighteen silver dollars. With a cousin and three young fellows he went to the horse races which were then going strong in St. Louis. He had never been to a race track before. He never bet on a horse again, though sometimes in later years he had to go to the tracks in Kansas City to talk politics with Tom Pendergast. That day they bet $5.00 on a horse named Claude. It rained just before the race and Claude not only came in ahead; he paid twenty-five to one."[21]

Truman's mother had some influence upon him in his choice of a profession. For a year after graduation from high school, he worked successfully as a bank clerk in Kansas City until, in response to his parents' urging, he returned to the farm. He stayed for eleven years, even though he was not satisfied with farming as a profession. Returning from World War I service overseas in 1919, he got financial help from his mother in starting a haberdashery store in Kansas City. When the business failed, he entered politics. Evidently his mother did not oppose his running for elective office in 1922, and she was at his side when he launched his campaigns for the Democratic nomination for U.S. senator in 1934 and 1940. Although she was not in favor of his seeking the vice-presidency in 1944, thinking he could do more good as senator, once he was nominated, she loyally supported him.

When Truman was elevated to the presidency by the death of President Roosevelt, his mother's comment pleased him immensely. He said that it could not have been better had it been prepared by the best public relations man. She had said:

I cannot really be glad my son is President because I am sorry that President Roosevelt is dead. If he had been voted in, I would be out waving a flag, but it does not seem right to be very happy or wave flags now. Harry will get along. I knew Harry would be all right after I heard him give his speech this morning. I heard every word of it but Mary, my daughter, is going to read it to me. Everyone who heard him talk this morning will know he is sincere and will do what is best.[22]

A few weeks later, President Truman sent the presidential plane, the "Sacred Cow," to bring his mother and sister to Washington for Mother's Day. When his mother saw a group of thirty or more photographers and newsreel cameramen at the airport, she turned to the President and in a voice that could be heard above the airport din, said, "Oh, fiddlesticks! If I had known this I wouldn't have come." The President beamed when she admonished him to "be good." She did not seem to be affected by the new status of her son. Her praise and criticism were characteristic of her forthright common sense. When she died, Senator Alben Barkley of Kentucky in a tribute delivered in the Senate described the ninety-four-year-old Martha Truman as "one of the finest characters in the history of the United States, and one of the finest mothers. . . . She was totally unspoiled by the honors that came to her distinguished son."[23]

Harry showed strong tendencies toward identification with his mother. He engaged cheerfully in such activities as cooking, washing the dishes, washing his own socks, caring for his younger sister, and nursing his sick father, and he employed diplomacy to accomplish his ends rather than fighting with his fists. When greatly provoked, Truman's anger took the form of verbal abuse. Of modern political leaders, Truman most clearly resembled Woodrow Wilson in his identification with his mother. While Wilson worshipped his father, he tried to behave more like his mother, as indicated by his love of words, his belief in persuasion rather than in hard materialistic bargaining, and his avoidance of physical violence.[24] Franklin D. Roosevelt also showed some of these characteristics.

No affair of state, no obligation imposed upon him by the presidency, took precedence over Truman's responsibility to his mother when she needed him. Even in stormy, icy wintry weather, he would risk his own life and the lives of some correspondents to fly from Washington, D.C., to her side in

Grandview when she was seriously ill. No matter how busy, he always took time to write to her or talk with her on the telephone.

Paternal Family Influences

On his father's side, Harry Truman traced his ancestry to great-grand-mother Nancy Tyler, who was related to President Tyler. Nancy wore a lace cap on her head to cover the scar of a scalping wound inflicted during an Indian uprising in Kentucky in 1788. The account handed down relates that Nancy pretended she was dead and made no noise or motion while being scalped. The story is a proud tradition among the Trumans.

Of the twenty-seven major party presidential candidates since 1896, only five had fathers who were farmers. In the twentieth century, agriculture has lost prestige to business and the professions. Thus, the fact that his father was a mule trader did not help Harry Truman very much in his political career except, perhaps, among rural voters.

According to Geoffrey Gorer's theory of American characteristics, the father, as a model and an authority figure, is the rejected member of the family group.[25] The theory does not fit the Truman family. Harry's father was accepted by his offspring; he had a respected place in his home. Although his dream of bringing affluence to his family was never realized, he earned enough during the crucial years to keep them in moderate middle-class circumstances.

Psychologists argue that a son may be a rival of his father for the affection of his mother. The theory is that in some cases this rivalry—an Oedipus complex—leads to antagonism toward the father or paternal substitutes. There appears to be no evidence that during adolescence Harry rebelled at masculine discipline. His father never took the form of a stern authoritarian figure; he was, instead, an easygoing member of the family circle. Harry recalled that when he once fell off a pony, his father made him walk home. Although he cried at the time, he harbored no resentment at the treatment and later thought that it was well deserved.[26] His relations with his father were somewhat like Franklin Roosevelt's with his: friendly, comradely, respectful. Unlike Woodrow Wilson, Harry did not fear his father's condemnation for failure to live up to expectations, nor did he feel frustrated because of impossible demands made upon him by his father.

John Truman's niece said of him: "He loved children—there wasn't anything he wouldn't give up to spend time with us. He liked to tell us stories. I remember his voice—very soft—and how well he could sing." In concluding an interview with the President, Bela Kornitzer observed, "And with it all I could see the President was deeply moved as he added that his father was the happiest man he ever knew."[27]

John Truman had less education than his wife, who, with the children, encouraged him to continue his self-education. To that end the family saved and bought a set of Shakespeare's *Works*, at that time equated with a solid education. Truman's father did not feel that the lack of education handicapped him in the economic struggle. As a self-made man, he did not realize that his failures were in part due to his lack of knowledge of business economics. Rather he blamed them on lack of luck.

Truman did not worship his father as Woodrow Wilson and Winston Churchill did theirs. Wilson deified his father and Churchill placed his on a pedestal that he spent a lifetime trying to reach.[28] Harry had no close relatives who had scaled the heights of American politics. Instead he created his masculine ideal from history books. Andrew Jackson was a rugged figure he genuinely admired: "One thing I always liked about Jackson was that he brought the basic issues into clear focus. People knew what he stood for and what he was against, and 'the friends of General Jackson'—as his supporters called themselves—always knew that he represented the interests of the common people of the United States."[29]

Among his other political heroes were Andrew Johnson, whom he considered much maligned and underrated; Theodore Roosevelt, who, though a Republican, repudiated the reactionary conservatism of his party; Woodrow Wilson, a progressive and fundamentally a man of peace forced by circumstances into an unwanted war; and Franklin D. Roosevelt, champion of the underprivileged and a great commander-in-chief.

As for his own father, Harry admired him for his readiness to take chances in the American game of trying to get rich quick. His father did not succeed in his speculations, but he had a few near misses and some of his real estate deals came out well. His plunge in the grain market, however, caused him to lose money that he had accumulated in various ways.

John Truman was closer to his second son, Vivian, than he was to Harry. Vivian followed more exactly in his father's footsteps and seemed to be more closely identified with his father's interests. When he was still a boy, his father gave him a checkbook and told him to buy and sell stock. Harry was not engaged in this manner.

His father also had an influence upon Truman's choice of occupation. Never fully acclimated to urban life, John Truman, even in Independence, made a living by trading animals and running a farm in the outskirts. The yard and barn on the Crysler Avenue property once contained several hundred animals. He exemplified the rural virtues of independence and shrewdness. He joined his wife in urging Harry to return to the soil.[30]

Although a small man physically—five feet six inches tall—Truman's father had a reputation for physical courage. The story is told of a court hearing at which the opposition attorney, a man physically much larger than

John Truman, accused him: "Now John, you know that's just a damn lie."
John jumped out of the witness chair and chased the lawyer out of the
courthouse. That broke up the lawsuit; it was typical of John Truman's
character.[31] Similar incidents show that Truman's father from time to time
had uninhibited rage impulses, which by example or by genes he transmitted
to his son.

Here is Harry Truman's own tribute: "My father was a very energetic
person. He worked from daylight to dark, all the time. And his code was
honesty and integrity. His word was good. When he told us that something
was a fact with regard to a horse or a cow or a sheep or a piece of land, that
was just what it was. He was quite a man, my dad was. And he raised my
brother and myself to put honor above profit."[32]

From both his parents, Truman learned to act courageously, to prize
honor and integrity, to speak candidly, to have faith in religion, and to
work hard. To his mother he owed his optimism, his tact, his friendliness,
his modesty, his reliance on reasoning rather than violence, and his
fondness for reading and music. To his father he owed in part his sunny
disposition, some of his skill in bargaining, his interest in speculation, his
gregariousness, his impetuosity, his sometimes uninhibited rage impulses,
and his liking for political rallies and discussions. He was brought up to be a
nineteenth-century Victorian in his morals and outlook on politics and
economics. Neither parent made impossible demands upon him, which
might have developed frustrations and rebelliousness in him. He was satisfied to conform to the discipline of the family, the Democratic party (including a local organization of unsavory reputation), and the American
system of government. It could hardly be claimed that Truman became
president because he possessed these qualities—many other Americans have
had similar characteristics. But it can be argued that, given the American
political milieu, these were among the qualities that would make a rising
political figure acceptable to the politicians and the voters. Truman's early
environment and the personality it molded made him attractive to voters
who like to see the embodiment of their own characteristics in political
office.

ENVIRONMENTAL INFLUENCES

In seeking available candidates, major party conventions select persons
from strategic states or regions. Beginning with the election of William
McKinley in 1896, there have been twenty-one presidential elections and
twenty-eight major party candidates, some of whom ran more than once.
Of these candidates, eight were residents of New York State and four were
from Ohio, suggesting that conventions have regarded these two states as

key ones because of their size and relatively even balance between the major parties. Grouping the candidates by regions, eleven have come from the Northeast, twelve from the Midwest, three from the Far West, and two from the South. Although Missouri appears only once during the period—in 1948 when Truman was nominated—the state clearly is in a politically strategic region.[33]

Truman came to represent the Midwest and its deep-rooted antagonism toward the eastern establishment. During the 1948 campaign, he wrote in his private notes: "Dewey synthetically milks cows and pitches hay for the cameras just as that other faker Teddy Roosevelt did—but he never heard of 'turnip day'. I don't believe the U.S.A. wants any more fakers—Teddy and Franklin are enough. So I'm going to make a common sense intellectually honest campaign. It will be a novelty—and it will win."[34]

Place of birth as well as residence is important. Of the twenty-eight candidates since 1896, eleven, slightly more than a third, were born in rural communities with populations of fewer than twenty-five hundred. Truman thus kept company with Warren G. Harding, James M. Cox, Calvin Coolidge, Herbert C. Hoover, Franklin D. Roosevelt, Alfred M. Landon, Lyndon B. Johnson, Hubert H. Humphrey, George McGovern, and James Carter. Rural origins, hinting as they do of a Cincinnatus-like quality, are important in American politics. Presidential image makers are fond of seeking parallels between office seekers and the myth of Cincinnatus, who, in ancient Rome, was called from the plow to save the state.[35] Truman was highly conscious of the Cincinnatus legend. On April 16, 1950, he wrote in a personal memorandum: "This is a Republic the greatest in the history of the world. I want this country to continue as a Republic. Cincinnatus and Washington pointed the way. When Rome forgot Cincinnatus, its downfall began."[36] Philosophers as well as propagandists have ascribed certain virtues such as honesty, integrity, stability, responsibility, patriotic devotion, and morality to rural upbringing.

Truman fitted into the Cincinnatus mystique when he chose to have the notification ceremony for his vice-presidential nomination held in Lamar, Missouri. Located in Barton County in southwestern Missouri, about 130 miles south of Kansas City and on the fringe of the Ozarks, Lamar was an ideally suited location from which to project the image of humble beginnings. When Truman was born in Lamar, its population was about eight hundred, and his parents lived in a simple five-room house for which his father had paid $685. Without plumbing, electricity, or central heating, it was the sort of structure that today would be condemned as inferior housing. In politics, however, it was an asset. Although not a log cabin, it was close enough for public relations purposes.

To celebrate young Truman's birth, his father hung a mule shoe, a sign of hope and optimism, over the door for good luck. People who expect good fortune often find it, but who could have dreamed in 1884 that this farmer's son would one day be president of the United States? Not his mother—she said so frankly.[37] Yet some of Truman's apparent setbacks placed him on the road to the White House. If his oil-well wildcatting had been successful, or if his haberdashery shop had remained solvent, he probably would not have gone into politics. His trials and tribulations kept steering him toward his ultimate destiny. After he became president, Truman hung a mule shoe over the door of his office as a symbol of his hope in the future. Faith was one of his special characteristics.[38]

Missouri is near the geographic center of the nation. In 1868 and 1872, the state had furnished Democratic candidates for vice-president. In 1912, its native son, House Speaker Champ Clark, came close to winning the Democratic nomination for president.

Missouri is bounded by eight other states—more than any other one in the country. Its eastern boundary is the Mississippi River and it shares riparian rights with Illinois, Kentucky, and Tennessee. On the north is Iowa and on the south, Arkansas; the Missouri River marks the western boundary with Nebraska and part of Kansas; and the southwestern tip of the state touches Oklahoma. Truman had close ties with influential politicians in each of these states. During his service in the U.S. Senate, he was befriended by such men as Senator J. Ham Lewis of Illinois, Senator Alben Barkley of Kentucky, Senator Kenneth McKellar of Tennessee, Senator George Norris of Nebraska, Governor Robert S. Kerr of Oklahoma, Works Progress Administrator Harry Hopkins of Iowa, and Secretary of War Harry H. Woodring of Kansas.

Truman was proud of his home state with its strategic place in American history, its role in crucial compromises before the Civil War, and its philosophy of independence. As a boy, he was brought up to admire its military heroes, statesmen, writers, and artists—men like General John J. Pershing, Senator Thomas Hart Benton, and Mark Twain.

Harry Truman was a true son of the West and the westward movement of the nineteenth century. Following Daniel Boone, his grandparents had migrated from Shelby County, Kentucky, to Missouri in the 1840s. Instead of settling near St. Louis, as did Boone, they continued westward to the Missouri River's Great Bend, where the Kaw River joins it and Kansas City now stands. Both of his parents were born in the Kansas City area, and they were married there.

Truman's parents were brought up as farmers. They speculated in land suitable for farming, but they failed to anticipate urban trends and industrial uses of land. All of Harry's grandparents owned land in the Kansas City area. Had their heirs held on to it until the urban explosion produced skyrocketing land values, the Trumans could have become millionaires, and Harry might not have gone into politics.

When his father moved south to Lamar, John Truman grossly misread the future possibilities of the Kansas City area. After spending five lean years in the isolated village of Lamar, he moved north to a farm near Belton, Missouri, some six miles from his father-in-law's farm in Grandview, Jackson County. Here in 1886 the Trumans' second son was born.

At the invitation of his wife's parents, Solomon and Harriet Louisa Gregg Young, John Truman and his family moved in 1888 to the ancestral farm at Grandview. Thus, at the age of four Harry entered the county that was to furnish him a political base. Named after President Andrew Jackson, the county is bounded on the west by the state of Kansas and on the north by the Missouri River, and it covers some six hundred square miles. When Truman was nominated for vice-president in 1944, it had a population of about five hundred thousand, more than triple its 1890 size. Whereas Kansas City made up 65 percent of the total county population in 1890, sixty years later it made up 84 percent.

Toward the end of 1890, when Harry was six, the Truman family moved from the Grandview farm some twenty miles northeast to Independence, a town near Kansas City of some fifteen thousand inhabitants, where John Truman bought a big house with several acres of land. Harry's mother thought that the schools in Independence would be better than those in Grandview, and John Truman's sister, Ella Noland, and her three daughters lived nearby.

Independence has had a fascinating history even though its younger neighbor, Kansas City, has become the center of the metropolitan area situated on the banks of the Kaw and Missouri rivers. During the early part of the nineteenth century, when part of the present Kansas City area was little more than mudflats subject to devastating floods, Independence, on high ground with excellent clear water springs, was a raw frontier town. Joseph Smith had chosen it in 1831 as a site for a Mormon settlement, but two years later he and his followers were driven out. Before and after the Civil War, many of its inhabitants, including Truman's ancestors, had strong southern sympathies, for which they were subjected to some bitter hardships. One writer has described Independence as a "community where the well-springs of character and personality are the traditions of the pioneer, the prairie farmer, and the Southern rebel."[39] Confederate troops occupied it twice for brief periods. In the postwar period, painful memories lingered on, and some former guerrillas—including the James brothers— became notorious outlaws. Along with a tradition of lawlessness, however, a growing tolerance permitted some of the former followers of Joseph Smith to establish a reorganized Latter Day Saints church.

The Trumans became fond of Independence, and Harry later played an important role in securing the improvement of highways connecting it with the rest of Jackson County. Although the community lacked city planning and adequate zoning, it gradually developed into a flourishing suburb of comfortable, middle-class homes and light industry. The Truman house had a large yard and a barn big enough to house horses, mules, cows, goats, sheep, and other animals held for trading. One of Truman's cousins regarded the house as pretentious.[40] It had been built by a wealthy merchant who was not bothered by nearby railroad tracks. Other wealthy persons had built elaborate homes in the area. As far as Harry was concerned, he was thrilled by the passing trains.

Some of John Truman's real estate deals turned out well. He accepted an attractive offer for the house in 1895, and the family moved to another comfortable house, which also had a large yard and a big barn for the livestock. A boyhood friend of Harry recalled that John Truman drove cattle from this house to the stockyards in the bottomlands of Kansas City.[41]

Financial reverses in 1902, resulting from his father's speculation in grain futures, made it necessary for the Trumans to sell their home and move to a far more modest house in Kansas City. Harry had finished his public schooling and soon obtained a job in a Kansas City bank. Now he was in the city's midst and part of its commercial life.

By 1900, Kansas City had become the second largest urban center in Missouri, looking for its trade and culture largely to the West. St. Louis on the opposite side of the state was older and larger, but its economic and cultural ties were with the East. In the political arena, St. Louis was more powerful; Lincoln Steffens had immortalized its notorious boss, Ed Butler.[42] Kansas City had its alderman Jim Pendergast, but he was more of a ward boss than a city-wide leader. His more famous brother, Tom, was to attract attention a quarter of a century later.[43]

At the time that Harry became a resident of Kansas City, St. Louis had a reputation for being open to gambling and vice, an image accentuated by reports from visitors to its 1904 World's Fair celebrating the Louisiana purchase. While Kansas City had had its Jesse James, its political reputation was not notably unsavory. It was a growing city with many transients— cowboys, traveling salesmen, and railroad men. Its industries attracted foreigners of German, Irish, Italian, and Slavic origins and an increasing number of displaced blacks from the South.

Harry knew that it was possible to get drunk, gamble, go to a lewd show, or meet a prostitute in Kansas City, but he was not interested in such diversions. Trained by his mother to look upon such activities as sinful, he spent his leisure time in such innocent pleasures as going to vaudeville shows. He claimed that he attended every show in the two main theaters from the age of sixteen to twenty. He was also a connoisseur of eating places and a charming dinner companion.[44]

In 1906, at the request of his mother and father who needed his help to run the Young farm, where they had moved two years before, Harry left his job at the bank in Kansas City for Grandview, where he spent the next eleven years as a farmer. If his enlistment in May 1917 as an army first lieutenant began the break with the farm, his marriage to Bess Wallace in 1919 completed it.[45] He never returned to the farm, and Independence became his voting residence for his political career.

In his prepolitical career, Truman had experience in three different types of American community life. He spent about sixteen years in a rural environment, fourteen years in the small suburb of Independence, and six years in Kansas City. During four of his Independence years, he worked in the city. Thus his urban experience lasted for ten years. He had wide contacts in these three important areas of American life and grew to understand their problems. He acquired considerable knowledge about agricultural land-use planning and about urban and suburban problems. Like many of his contemporaries, he moved from the farm to the big city. He had lived in a cross-section of the United States and was prepared to be a representative of a variety of interests.

chapter 2 | ORIGIN OF POLITICAL INTERESTS, 1892–1922

My father was a Democrat, my grandfather was a Democrat and my great grandfather was a Democrat. They were all pretty good active and leading Democrats. I am a Democrat by inheritance, conviction and belief and I have never given anybody cause to believe that I am anything else.
—General Hugh S. Johnson, director of the National
Recovery Administration, *New York Times*, August 12, 1933

Most Americans acquire their political preferences during their early home life. The child discovers that his family has specific party identifications, and he comes to regard himself as a member of the political group to which the family belongs. Although party membership is extremely easy to change, a person whose parents have strong partisan convictions may face emotional difficulties encountering parental disapproval. Such a break with tradition might be made with less pain after the young person has left home, but it would take something of a rebel to manage a political departure while still residing at home.

Harry Truman was never a rebel in the family group, nor was he ever a political party insurgent. Since there were no divided political loyalties in his family, the young Truman had no difficulty in making his party choice. Both parents had been consistently and strongly Democratic.

The strong identification of the Truman family with the national Democratic party went back to pre-Civil War days, when Grandmother Young, for instance, judged the financial worth and eligibility of possible suitors for her daughter by the number of slaves they owned.[1] Although Truman's grandfathers were too old, and his father too young, to serve in the Civil War, an uncle fought with the Confederates, and family sympathies were with the South. In Missouri this meant destructive guerrilla raids by Union irregulars and other northern sympathizers in their struggle for control of the state. Kansas Free Soil "Red Legs" raided the Young farm, confiscated all of the livestock, slaughtered some four hundred pigs, and then burned the barns.[2] The raiders were also accused of stealing the Young silver.[3]

Stories like these, repeated so often that they became Truman lore, justified a rabidly anti-Republican bias. Another event never forgotten by Truman's ancestors was their dislocation under the much-hated Order 11, issued by Union General Thomas E. Ewing, which banished them along with other Confederates from Jackson County to neighboring Platte County for three years. Bitter memories lingered on. When Harry, in the blue dress uniform of the Missouri National Guard, visited Grandmother Young, she objected strenuously: "Don't come here again in that uniform."[4]

Eighty years did not erase the rancor that Harry's mother displayed toward the North and the Republican party. Several days before she came to the White House in 1945, her son Vivian teased her by saying that she would have to sleep in the Lincoln bed. She claimed that she would rather sleep on the floor. President Truman stopped the teasing but did not escape a lecture later on when she read that he had laid a wreath before the Lincoln statue.[5]

In a letter to a college student in 1936, Senator Truman wrote: "However, the general principles of the Democratic party are for as little government as possible, and for the government to be as close to the people as it is possible to put it. That is the principal reason I am a Democrat." Hardly an adequate statement of the New Deal philosophy, which emphasized expanding governmental activities at the national level, it reflects rather the influence of Thomas Jefferson and the impact of Justice Louis D. Brandeis on Truman during the early years of his senatorial career. The letter continued: "Another good reason is that I was raised one. My mother and my grandmother and all the rest of my family have all been good Democrats."[6] Truman's emphasis here was on the influence of the Young parentage on his political identification; his father's views are only implied.

Truman's father was an ardent Democrat in national politics and a party activist at the local level as a precinct captain, road overseer, and local postmaster. He owed his appointments to the Pendergast faction of the Democratic party in the country outside of Kansas City. Vivian Truman said that his father "never sought office, . . . but he was always interested in civic life and participating in Democratic party affairs. Cleveland was his idol and when President Cleveland visited Kansas City that year, father was a member of the delegation which welcomed him."[7]

Truman recalled the political picnics held at Lone Jack, a small town in the southeastern part of Jackson County, during the early 1890s. In response to an inquiry about these affairs, his press secretary, Joseph Short, wrote:

The President asked me to advise you that he attended approximately ten of the . . . picnics at Lone Jack between 1892 and 1904. Your letter provoked some very pleasant memories for the President. He recalled that on the picnic days his father, his brother Vivian, and he would hitch two big mules to a spring wagon and the whole family would set out before dawn for a five mile drive to Lone Jack. . . . The President feels that a contribution was made to his early political education at Lone Jack. Although he did not pick up the old school oratory which he heard so many times there, he caught the excitement of politics, something he never has ceased to relish.[8]

Truman remembered in 1892, when he was eight years old, his father was greatly pleased by the victory of Grover Cleveland over President Benjamin Harrison. In his *Memoirs*, Truman wrote: "My father was very much elated by Cleveland's victory. He rode a beautiful gray horse in the torchlight parade and decorated the weather vane on the tower of the northwest corner of the house with a flag and bunting. The weather vane was a beautifully gilded rooster."[9] In a 1949 interview, Truman recalled his father's putting a flag on top of the house in Independence after Cleveland was elected, saying that it was going to stay there as long as the Democrats were in office. As in other elections, his father got into a fight on that election day because of his quick temper and strong feelings on politics.[10] Later on, Truman developed some reservations about President Cleveland's policies. In his *Memoirs*, he wrote: "Cleveland had a lot of trouble with strikes and riots, but the Democratic party, as usual, was on the liberal side during his second administration. But the President was not. He became an ultra-conservative."[11]

The Democratic National Convention of 1896 completely revolutionized the policies of the party, repudiating those advocated by President Cleveland. Truman's father apparently accepted the changes brought by the "boy orator," William Jennings Bryan, of Nebraska, and his inflationary cohorts, although his brother-in-law, Harrison Young, did not. Nebraska was not far from Kansas City, and it was a great honor for a presidential nomination to go to any state west of the Mississippi. Farmers with heavy debts welcomed inflationary monetary policies, and the Trumans were always in debt. The elder Truman did not seem disappointed that Bryan had stolen the thunder of Missouri's favorite son, Senator Richard P. ("Silver Dick") Bland, the outstanding spokesman on the silver issue of the time.[12]

Harry was in high school when Bryan was nominated a second time by the Democratic National Convention, which met in 1900 in Kansas City. It was a memorable time for the city. The building where they expected to hold the convention burned down, and a new structure was built in record time. In the new hall, Harry was greatly impressed with Bryan's oratorical powers. There were no loudspeakers, of course, but Bryan could make himself clearly heard in the huge auditorium, and his words commanded the attention of the milling delegates that other speakers failed to get. Regarding the nomination, Truman said: "I was at the Kansas City Convention when Bryan was nominated for the Presidency. I was a rabid Bryan man—

my father was also—but I had an uncle for whom I am named who was a Gold Democrat.''[13]

Later on Truman added certain details regarding local politics that are significant in view of subsequent events: ''Old man Kemper was a friend of my father's. They had known us in the grain business. He got us in his box. Father never missed a session but I went to several.''[14] William T. Kemper, the man who founded the Jackson County Democratic Club in 1899, which was independent of other Democratic factions, was appointed by Democratic Governor Alexander Docker in 1902 as a member of the Kansas City Board of Police Commissioners over the opposition of Alderman James Pendergast. The latter was called a political boss because he controlled his own ward strongly and helped elect James Reed, a lawyer and political orator, as mayor of Kansas City in 1900. In 1904, however, the Pendergast organization gave strong support to Kemper's unsuccessful campaign for the mayoralty. Kemper's son was later active in Truman's senatorial campaign.

At the turn of the century, Pendergast was not a nationally publicized political boss as were Richard Croker of Tammany Hall in New York, Ed Butler (the king of ''boodlers'' in St. Louis), George B. Cox (the ''thing above the law in Cincinnati''), Albert A. (''Doc'') Ames in Minneapolis, and Abe Ruef, the labor boss of San Francisco.[15] Although this was the period of the muckrakers, a ward boss of Kansas City was not deemed important enough to be written about. Not until three decades later did the Pendergast machine in Kansas City, this time under the rule of Tom Pendergast, Jim's younger brother, command national attention.[16] Jim Pendergast, a saloon keeper who was elected alderman from the West Bottoms of Kansas City in 1892, served continuously in that post until 1910, when ill health caused his retirement. His faction of the Democratic party was called the ''Goat'' faction, a label traceable to some newspaper stories and political legends. Irish-Americans were prominent in the Pendergast faction, and they, including Jim Pendergast, used to keep goats on the rocky Missouri River bluffs in Kansas City. One story has it that an opposition orator called the Pendergast adherents ''Goats,'' and the name stuck. Pendergast was the leader of the faction until 1910, and he liked the symbol, which he thought indicated his faction's devotion to freedom, combat, and clannishness. On the eve of a party convention, Jim roared: ''When we come over the hills like goats, they'll run like rabbits.'' Members of the rival faction, led by Joe Shannon, were called ''Rabbits.''[17]

Truman was working in a Kansas City bank in 1904 when Judge Alton B. Parker ran against President Theodore Roosevelt. A spectator at the Democratic convention in St. Louis, Truman just missed making the age requirement for voting. That same year, Harry Truman saw President Roosevelt and described the event in this way:

The first President I ever saw was Teddy Roosevelt—William McKinley's successor. It was in 1904, after Roosevelt had just about served out the remainder of McKinley's second term and wanted to be elected President in his own right. He was in Kansas City on a trip through the Middle West, and I was working in the National Bank of Commerce at that time. I ran down to the corner of Tenth and Main streets just to see what a President looked like. Roosevelt made an excellent speech. I was disappointed to find that he was no giant, but a little man in a long Prince Albert coat to make him look taller. After I became President I often thought back to that time. I found out that the people usually ran to see the President and not the man. A few decades back I had done exactly the same thing—running to see the President— who was then Teddy Roosevelt.[18]

Interestingly Theodore Roosevelt was one inch taller than Truman. Conscious of his own average height, Truman seemed to expect national leaders to be tall and imposing in stature, as were Washington, Jefferson, Jackson, and Lincoln. This attitude is strikingly clear in the remarks attributed to Truman in 1962 by Merle Miller. In answer to a question about seeing Theodore Roosevelt in 1904, Truman is reported as saying: "They wanted to see him grin and show his teeth, which he did. He was a short man, only about five foot six." Since TR was five ten, Truman had to cut off four inches from TR's height so that it would be below his own five feet nine inches.

Truman was back on the farm in 1908 and registered to vote in Grandview, where he cast his first vote for Bryan for president. There was no hesitation about this choice. From his family conversations and from his study of American history, he had formed a mental picture about the two major parties, which dictated his choice. In his *Memoirs*, he reveals that he thought the Democratic party was the party of the common people, the liberals, the progressives, the small businessmen, the farmers, and the workers. The Republican party was the party of the monied men on Wall Street, the bankers in the East, the special interests that were exploiting the country's natural resources, the conservatively controlled mass media, and the reactionaries.

Harry's vote was also determined by the activist role of his father in the affairs of the local Democratic party. On this point his brother observed: "In 1908 he [father] was very active in the campaign and ended up a delegate to the Missouri State Democratic Convention in Joplin. Two years later, he became an election judge in the Grandview precinct."[19]

The 1908 elections in Jackson County marked the transition of leadership of the so-called Goat faction of the Democratic party from Jim Pendergast to Tom. Jim built a legend in Kansas City politics, which still lives on in spite of the disgrace that later was heaped upon his brother. Although a saloon keeper, Jim was noted for his own abstinence and for his insistence that this customers not overdo their drinking. He was also famous for his many charities and for his backing of the move of the railroad station from the West Bottoms to higher ground. He earned the gratitude of the city for his high sense of duty because this change affected his own interests adversely. Jim Pendergast was ailing in health in 1908, and he began to turn over the reins of power to his younger brother, Tom, whom he had been carefully training for eighteen years. He had persuaded Mayor Thomas T. Crittenden, Jr., to appoint Tom superintendent of streets, a key patronage position in the city government which Tom had held earlier.[20] Harry Truman's father belonged to the Goat faction of the Democratic party and he undoubtedly saw Tom Pendergast at the state convention, which they both attended.

In the 1912 convention in Baltimore, Speaker Champ Clark, a Missourian, came close to winning the Democratic nomination, securing a majority but not the required two-thirds vote. Truman supported Woodrow Wilson, who carried Jackson County in the fall elections, but his father had voted for Clark.[21] This presidential campaign was the last that Truman's father witnessed. He died in 1914.

By 1912, Jim Pendergast was dead and Tom Pendergast was firmly in control of the Goat machine. Tom took over at a most difficult time for the party. The reform Republican governor, Herbert S. Hadley, elected in 1908 for four years, had purged the Kansas City election lists of padded registrations, contributing to a Republican victory in the city elections of 1910. Tom Pendergast lost the key appointive post of superintendent of streets, and his brother, Michael J. Pendergast, also in the organization, lost his post as county license inspector, an important office for those in the liquor business. However, Jim Reed, a Pendergast partisan, was elected U.S. senator by the Democratic legislature.

Boss Tom Pendergast proved very resourceful in preparing for the city elections of 1912. He formed an alliance with the leader of the rival Rabbit faction, Joe Shannon, and had his brother Mike start the Tenth Ward Democratic Club in the residential section of Kansas City. These moves paid off, and the Democrats carried the city elections.

Careful preparations were also made for the county primaries in August and the general elections in November. For the primaries, Tom Pendergast formed an alliance with Tom Marks, a leader of a Republican faction, who was willing to switch some of his followers to the Democratic primaries in order to aid the Goats. This maneuver, plus hard work, secured an important primary victory for the Pendergast faction. The continued alliance with the Shannon faction in the general elections ensured victory for the Goat nominees. Among them was R. D. Mize, candidate for county judge from the Eastern District, a friend of John Truman and Harry, who by 1916 had not only inherited his father's strong Democratic identification but also his minor political and party posts. Because of his friendship with Judge Mize, Harry was made a road overseer and a precinct election official. He was on the first rung of the political ladder, and his connections with the county court made him a logical candidate for president of his township Farm Bureau. His activities in the National Guard strengthened ties with the Democratic party, because the guardsmen from Kansas City were mostly Democratic.

In city and county politics, Boss Tom Pendergast was much stronger in 1916 than he had been in 1912. In the special referendum election in the summer of 1914 on a new franchise for the Kansas City Metropolitan Street Railway, he had strengthened his ties with Republican leader Tom Marks, and he had made important contacts with such business leaders as Conrad Mann, who was later president of the Kansas City Chamber of Commerce. For this special election, he permitted his cohorts to use fraudulent election practices, something that his brother Jim had always frowned upon. In the county elections of that year, he had made alliances with Alderman Miles Bulger, the "Little Czar" of Ward Two, which bordered the North Side, and Municipal Judge Cas Welch, who controlled two central-city wards inhabited by a mixed population, including many blacks. Bulger was supported for the position of presiding judge of the county court in return for aid in the reelection of Judge Mize, who had a good record from his first term.

Elliott W. Major, the Democratic governor of Missouri, had at first favored the Shannon faction in awarding the prize gubernatorial patronage plums—appointments to local election and police boards. But in the Democratic state convention held in March 1916, the Goats clearly showed their superiority over the Rabbits, and Governor Major soon switched his patronage to Pendergast. City elections the following month found the Goat faction working out another bipartisan alliance with the Republicans in order to defeat Shannon's candidate, Mayor John Jost, for reelection. Shannon's desperate use of the city police force who arrested suspected Goat voters in order to keep them from the polls did not suffice to win. At the end of 1916, Boss Tom was in control of the county government and the city police, and the new Democratic governor elect, Frederick D. Gardner, was favorably disposed toward the faction.

At the time of the 1920 election, Truman had established residence at 219 North Delaware Street in Independence, which was to remain his official voting residence for the rest of his life. The war was over; he had married Bess Wallace; he was in partnership with Eddie Jacobson in a haberdashery shop in Kansas City; and he was under no obligation to a political party. In general, he supported the Democratic candidates, including Roger

Sermon, who was mayor of Independence for seventeen years. In 1920, however, when Truman voted for the position of marshal of Jackson County, he voted for the Republican candidate, John Miles, a fellow veteran of World War I and his former commanding officer, an act that brought disapproval later when he was a candidate in a Democratic primary race. Truman had this to say:

> You have heard it said that I voted for John Miles for county marshal. I'll have to plead guilty to that charge along with some five thousand other ex-soldiers. I was closer to John Miles than a brother. I have seen him in places that made Hell look like a playground. I have seen him hold the American line when only John Miles and his three batteries were between the Germans and a successful counterattack. He was of the right stuff, and a man who wouldn't vote for his comrade under circumstances such as these would be untrue to his country. I know that every soldier understands it. I have no apology to make for it.[22]

It was a Republican year, with the voters repudiating Wilson and wartime sacrifices. Warren G. Harding, clearly the least-qualified candidate for president in this century, carried the country, including Jackson County, Missouri, and Arthur Hyde, the Republican candidate for governor of the state, won the election on an anti-Pendergast platform.

In 1920 the Pendergast forces fared poorly. After the 1918 elections, Bulger had turned against Tom Pendergast, trying to assert his own leadership of the Democratic party in the county. This rebellion was crushed in 1920 by another deal with Shannon and a renewed alliance with Republican Tom Marks, but it was done at a cost. The Goat machine acquired an unfavorable image because of the protection of vice and gambling by the police and the favored treatment given to certain contractors, including some in partnership with Tom. The local press also decried the corrupt election practices of the Democrats and helped the Republicans win the state and local elections on reform platforms. Boss Pendergast lost control of both the city police and county patronage.[23]

Truman thus became conscious of politics at an early age, and he conformed to the family pattern of strong Democratic identification. As he grew up, his father's and his own political interests became entangled with the affairs of the Pendergast machine, which was in the process of becoming the strongest Democratic organization in Kansas City and Jackson County. Young Truman never voted in Kansas City where the machine employed the most questionable methods, but the notoriety that the election and subsequent police and administrative scandals attracted in the local press hardly could have escaped his attention. It was Truman's practice to vote the straight Democratic ticket except on one occasion where overwhelming loyalty to a wartime superior officer overran partisan considerations. He also supported the bipartisan deals made by his factional leader, Tom Pendergast.

In national elections, Truman's loyalty to the Democratic party was unswerving. As the party shifted its program and varied the type of presidential candidate it brought forward, he supported each change, and he was loyal to the party platforms determined by Democratic national conventions.

It is difficult to say where among the various group loyalties Truman came to rank loyalty to his party and its leaders, but surely it was high. Some said that Truman held party loyalty too high when it prevented or delayed his taking action against partisans who had betrayed the public trust. To journalist Richard Rovere, Truman was a man full of contradictions and ambivalence, with both "broad and narrow vision," which made it possible for him to dream "the dreams of Woodrow Wilson and also those of old Tom Pendergast—dreams of a world united and dreams of a ward united."[24]

chapter 3 | THE EDUCATION OF HARRY TRUMAN, 1892–1901

Truman's early formal education took place during the 1890s in the public schools of Independence, Missouri, a suburb of some ten thousand inhabitants, which had a better school system than Grandview, where the Truman farm was located. Before the family moved to Independence, Harry's mother had taught him to read before he was five. She also gave him a substantial head start and instructed him in literature, music, art, religion, history, nature, and the social graces, as well as in the moral principles that she thought should guide human conduct. Remarkably, she had provided this instruction at a time when there was no public emphasis on the importance of a stimulating preschool environment. Harry's mother showered him with affection while he was learning, but at the same time, her discipline was firm. Life on the farm was also an education in itself. There was, for example, no need for special courses on sex education. And there were playmates—a younger brother and sister and many cousins.

In 1892, at the age of eight, Harry entered first grade in the Noland School in Independence. Here he learned arithmetic and improved his reading skills with the *New Franklin First Reader*, with which he was favorably impressed. In later years he remembered his first-grade teacher, Myra Ewing, as a "grand woman."[1] Harry was quick in learning how to get along with his peers in school; his earlier experiences with his cousins in Independence had helped him know how to adjust to his contemporaries. It can be assumed that the educational program of the Independence schools was basic, traditional, and conservative. When John Dewey's revolutionary *The School and Society* was published in 1899, Truman's formal education was about complete.

As a second-grade pupil, Truman was out the last half of the school year, paralyzed briefly by an attack of diphtheria. During the following summer, he was tutored. He not only made up the lost time but forged ahead so far that he was able to skip the third grade, fully in accord with the educational theory that pupils should progress at their own pace. His fourth-grade class met in a new school building, the Columbian, on South River Boulevard. He finished elementary school in five and one-half years and graduated with the class of 1898. According to his *Memoirs*, Truman eventually became a favorite with all his teachers: "Whenever I entered a new school room I would watch the teacher and her attitude toward the pupils, study hard, and try to know my lesson better than anyone else."[2]

Truman entered Independence High School in the fall. The school was under the gifted leadership of W. L. C. Palmer, who assembled an excellent faculty, including Maggie Phelps, a history teacher who gave Truman special training, and Matilda Brown, an English teacher, who was especially remembered when he became president. At the time, the high school course lasted three years, its curriculum including algebra, geometry, English literature, rhetoric, logic, music, history, Latin, and science. With the exception of history, this curriculum offered no social sciences. Also absent were practical courses, such as manual training, accounting, and domestic science. After completing the regular course, Truman graduated in the class of 1901—with eleven boys and thirty girls.[3]

The high school offered a number of opportunities for school activities. During his last year there, Truman, Charlie Ross, and two other students organized a school magazine, the *Gleam* (named after Alfred Lord Tennyson's poem, "Merlin and the Gleam"), which has continued until the present. Truman remembered occasional debating activities in the high school auditorium, commenting in 1956 that he considered such experience useful to students, "such as I," who worked on their speeches.[4] In his *Memoirs* he stated that his belief in a low tariff policy began with a debate on the subject in high school.[5]

Truman also gained some familiarity with the Roman orators from his study of Latin. A former Latin teacher wrote in 1958 that she was sure Harry had studied the first four orations of Cicero against Catiline. In 1953 Truman himself stated, "Charlie Ross and I used to translate Cicero's orations from the Latin. I guess I have read almost all of his speeches."[6]

He liked his teachers and enjoyed school. He was spirited when it came to learning, and he was anxious to please his teachers. One of his first acts as president was to telephone his former high school English teacher, Tillie Brown, to announce that Charlie Ross would be his press secretary.[7] Regarding his teachers, he wrote: "I do not remember a bad teacher in all my experience. They were all different, of course, but they were salt of the earth. They gave us our high ideals, and they hardly ever received more than forty dollars a month for it."[8]

Harry was near to the top of his class scholastically. The top student was Charlie Ross, who went on to a distinguished career in journalism. While Ross was press secretary to Truman, Henry Bundschu, a long-time resident of Independence and a contemporary of both men, said to him, "Charlie, don't kid me, You always were smarter than Harry Truman. I know you well enough to tell you what I think." "Well, I'll admit that I might have been smarter in a literary way than Harry," Ross admitted, "but Harry possesses a political sagacity that far surpasses anything that I have ever thought of or could aspire to."[9]

Truman's theory of education was that although teachers can help, the individual is responsible for acquiring his own education.[10] Almost any educator would have succeeded with Harry. He presented no problems arising from a lack of stimulating home environment, a lack of interest, poor motivation, or a low level of aspiration. He wanted to succeed in school, and later in life, he aspired to increase his knowledge and under-standing of national and world affairs. He did not join the other boys in skipping school.[11]

Blurred vision—corrected by thick lenses—kept Truman from participat-ing actively in strenuous sports during his school years. The evidence is conflicting regarding his role in the athletic activities of his day. One report is that he played baseball as hard as any of the other boys when he was so inclined. He was sometimes chosen as an umpire, and he early developed facility as a negotiator and reconciler of different points of view. It would appear, however, that he preferred to read rather than to spend a large proportion of his time playing rough outdoor sports.[12]

Truman's reading covered a wide range of subjects, with special interest in American political history, biography, and world military history. As a student of Caesar, he and his fellow students built a replica of Caesar's bridge crossing the Rhine, which they found described in the *Commentaries*. In an interview in 1934, he said: "I read everything in the Independence Library, including the encyclopedias, before I quit school."[13] One of his favorite sets of books was *Great Men and Famous Women*, a four-volume work. The titles of the four volumes were *Soldiers and Sailors, Statesmen and Sages, Workmen and Heroes*, and *Artists and Authors*. Other favorites were Plutarch's *Lives* and Jacob Abbott's biographies of great men. He was also fond of the King James version of the Bible, Shakespeare, Mark Twain, and other English and American classics. He later wrote to Cyril Clemens (second cousin to Mark Twain): "Before I was 12 years old I had read everything Mark Twain had published up to that time. I have the pur-ported complete set of his works put out by Harper Brothers, and a lot of

other publications of articles which have never been included in his books."[14]
Other books he read included Robert Burns's poems, Lord Byron's *Childe
Harold*, Creasey's *Fifteen Decisive Battles of the World*, Benjamin Frank-
lin's *Autobiography*, and Blackstone's *Commentaries*.[15]

Later Truman testified as to the importance of history in shaping his
career:

My debt to history is one which cannot be calculated. I know of no other motivation
which so accounts for my awakening interest as a young lad in the principles of
leadership and government. . . . I pored over Plutarch's *Lives* time and time again
and spent as much time reading Abbott's biographies of famous men. I read the
standard histories of ancient Egypt, the Mesopotamian cultures, Greece and Rome,
and the exploits of Genghis Khan and the stories of oriental civilizations, the accounts of the development of every modern country, and particularly the history of
America.[16]

Reading serious historical and biographical works became a habit: "I
made it my business to look up the background of these historic events and
to find out who brought them about. In the process I became very interested
in the men who made world history."[17] It is worth noting that Truman
listed none of the available left-wing literature, not mentioning Karl Marx's
Das Kapital, Henry George's *Progress and Poverty*, or Edward Bellamy's
Looking Backward.[18] Nor did he refer to Coin's *Financial School*, the
guidebook of the Populists and later of William Jennings Bryan. In commenting on Truman's knowledge of history, Jonathan Daniels said:
"Truman imagined himself a great historian but actually Truman knew the
kind of history that McGuffey would have put in his readers, and he liked
the historical anecdote that expressed a moral. Roosevelt's mind, intellectually, was far less stereotyped than Truman's, and maybe that explains
why Roosevelt was not as simple and direct as Truman."[19] Richard Neustadt,
later on the President's White House staff, wrote: "Truman often learned a
great deal more than he articulated and his *Memoirs* scarcely show the
sweep of his self-education; but in fact, if not in memory, it was vast."[20]

There is much less evidence concerning Truman's popularity with the
girls in his coeducational classes. He did not dance, nor did he play bridge.
Sometimes he carried Bess Wallace's books home from school, occasionally
studying algebra with her and his cousins, the Noland sisters, who lived
across the street from the Gates. Although he says in his *Memoirs* that Bess
was his sweetheart from the first time he saw her in 1890 in Sunday school,
it does not appear likely that he dated her while at school. She was very
athletic, almost a tomboy, with tennis, track, dancing, skating, and horse-
back riding among her athletic skills. Only one of these—riding—could she
share with Harry. His friend, Mize Peters, recalls taking Bess to a dance.[21]

Indeed she had many beaux who liked active sports. One wonders what chance a boy of average height who wore thick glasses and carried a music roll would have with a girl like Bess. During the 1890s, apparently, Truman admired her mostly from a distance.

Truman makes no mention of any other lifelong female friendships acquired while going to school. In fact, he says that Bess was the only girl-friend he ever had and that he was always afraid of the girls his age and older, a shyness about women that stayed with him throughout his life.[22] As a senator, he liked all-male parties, and when women came into a room, he sometimes excused himself.

Truman said that he wanted to go to college, but his father had financial reverses about the time of his graduation from high school, and the family could not afford to send him. He considered trying to get an appointment to the U.S. Military Academy at West Point. He and his friend, Fielding Houchens, studied with their former high school history teacher, Margaret Phelps, during the summer of 1901 in order to prepare for the examinations. Because he had some fears that he might not pass the physical examination, Truman went to the army recruiting station in Kansas City and was frankly told that he would not pass the physical for the academy. He gave up his preparations and his hopes of trying to obtain an appointment.[23]

Aspiring to West Point may be related to young Truman's struggle for identity. We know that military history was one of his early and enduring interests, and he apparently obtained some vicarious satisfactions from reading about military exploits. Like other youths of that age, he may well have imagined becoming a military hero himself. Certainly his dreams came true when he became commander-in-chief of the most powerful military force in the world.

With West Point out, Truman did not seek a scholarship at any other college or university. His cousins, the Noland sisters, stated that although a college education was not customary for boys at that time, they did not think that Truman's father's financial losses were decisive. Perhaps it did not seem as necessary then to acquire a higher education as it does today.[24]

Although Truman's dreams of going to college faded, his will to learn remained as strong as ever. After his election as judge for the Eastern District of Jackson County Court in 1922, Truman continued his formal education by going to evening classes at Kansas City Law School. He did not need to be a lawyer to hold the position of county judge, since the duties were administrative, not judicial. (In most other counties, the office is called member of the board of county commissioners.) Truman wanted to increase his usefulness to the county by acquiring legal skills that might come in handy even though they were not required. He completed half of the course with good grades.[25] These courses gave him some famil-iarity with business as well as legal practices. Because he lost the election of

1924 and had to seek private employment, which engaged his full energies, he did not finish. In addition, he found that being a father made increasing demands on his time.[26] After he was elected U.S. senator from Missouri, Truman considered continuing his legal education at Georgetown University Law School, but he soon found his Senate duties so absorbing that he abandoned the idea.

After dropping out of law school, Truman's formal education was completed, but his informal education continued without interruption during the rest of his life. He never stopped learning from books, the daily press, radio and television, the flood of official reports and documents, the testimony of witnesses before governmental investigating bodies, the many conferences with officials and party leaders at all levels of government, and also from the stern march of events. He resembled Governor Al Smith, who lacked a college education but learned rapidly from public documents and political activities.

In the Senate, he learned about the history and finance of transportation and communications from the Interstate Commerce Committee hearings, about budget and fiscal problems from the Appropriations Committee hearings, and about wartime mobilization and reconversion problems from his own special committee hearings, meetings, inspections, and report writing.

Whatever his occupation, Truman never stopped his habit of spending every spare moment reading almost everything he could get his hands on that fell within the scope of his broad interests, constantly fascinated by history and biography. Regarding the importance of the political history of the United States, he wrote:

It seemed to me that if I could understand the true facts about the growth and development of the United States government and could know the details of the lives of its presidents and political leaders I would be getting for myself a valuable part of the total education which I hope to have some day. I know of no surer way to get a solid foundation in political science and public administration than to study the histories of past administrations of the world's most successful system of government.[27]

Commenting on the attraction of biography, Truman told Arthur Krock that the best way to understand the world was "to know the people who have lived greatly in it."[28] In preparation for his Senate duties, he examined the biography of every senator.[29] Long before he reached the White House, he had made a careful study of each president—his background, the criticisms he faced, and the way he solved administrative problems.[30] He also read political philosophy and was fond of quoting Plato. In addition to his reading of Blackstone and Coke in law school, he read Montesquieu's *Spirit of the Laws* and the *Federalist Papers*, works that gave him an understanding of American constitutional history. Many were surprised at the breadth of his reading interests. He kept up with the daily press and current periodicals and found time to examine such varied books as William Prescott's *The History of the Conquest of Peru*, Hitler's *Mein Kampf*, the novels of outstanding Victorian writers, and Trollope's parliamentary series.[31]

Although he did not appear to be a very religious man to some, he always came back to the Bible as a guide on moral issues. At the age of fifty, he wrote about the Ten Commandments and the Sermon on the Mount: "I am still, at fifty, of the opinion that there are no other laws to live by, in spite of the professors of psychology." He was so interested in religion that he read the Koran and the Book of Mormon. When asked what books had the greatest influence on him, he replied, "The one that had the most influence is right here—The Holy Bible, then Shakespeare."[32]

His military aide, General Harry H. Vaughan, stated that he admired President Truman's background in American history:

Well, I think it is due to more extensive study and reading on the subject. Harry Truman has always been a very, very intensive student. He's one of the best educated men that I knew. As you know he has no formal education beyond high school, but he certainly is well read and well informed. Even during all the years he was in the White House, he read extensively; I'd say he read six or eight daily papers through, and he read all the periodicals and then a lot of the things he had to read by virtue of his position.[33]

Max Lowenthal, attorney for the subcommittee of the Senate Interstate Commerce Committee, defended Harry Truman vigorously against belittlement because of his lack of a college education. Lowenthal found many college graduates on what he regarded as the wrong side of the battle for the realization of the American creed in the field of civil liberties. In 1949, he wrote to Jonathan Daniels:

Westbrook Pegler laments that Truman became president without having much more education. Is there any better test of the quality and extent of the education Truman did obtain, whether in formal halls of learning or not, to fit him for the presidency and other high public office, than [his] grounding in the American tradition, in the struggle that produced it, and so in Anglo-American history, and by his capacity and readiness to apply the lessons of our history to new forms of old issues.

Lowenthal found that President Truman passed this test much better than did Thomas Dewey, Richard Nixon, Harold Velde, Robert Taft, and Karl E. Mundt. He added:

Will you tell me why so much more about the facts of life, as well as history, should be known to Truman who did not go to college, and to men of a third of a century

ago who did, when presumably our educational process was not as advanced as now
—why they should know what they do and did know, and so many university-bred
men of this day know so little of the past? As one reads their remarks and their
know-nothingism, one may be excused for wondering whether our educational
methods have deteriorated.[34]

Truman's lack of a college education may have hindered him in attracting
members of the so-called intellectual community to his administration—the
sort of individuals who were attracted to Franklin D. Roosevelt and to John
Kennedy, both of whom could call upon sophisticated literary, scientific,
and business specialists for help in writing speeches and in formulating
policy.[35] It also created in him a sense of inferiority which made him sensitive
to criticism from people with advanced formal education. Thus, he tended
to be hostile toward such intellectuals in the Senate as William Fulbright
and Paul Douglas, both of whom had higher degrees and years of university
teaching. In a sense, Truman's education tended to be more factual and less
theoretical, and it made him more reliant on actual data than on philos-
ophical considerations. Unlike Roosevelt or Kennedy, his turn of mind was
to the pragmatic rather than toward the abstract evaluation of pros and
cons. The education that he had, limited though it was, was substantial. His
mother and his schoolteachers had managed to inspire him to pursue his
search for knowledge and understanding throughout his life.

chapter 4 | LEARNING FARMING, 1905–1917

*When tillage begins, other arts follow. The farmers therefore are
the founders of human civilization.*
> Daniel Webster, *Remarks on Agriculture*, January 13, 1840

Of the twentieth-century presidents, Truman had the deepest roots in the soil and was the most deserving of the Cincinnatus image. That his campaign biographers recognized this is shown in their lyric description of his farm days: "He liked to ride along on the Emerson gang plow, holding the levers with his hardened hands, while the earth curled in a black, sweetly fresh ribbon at the side of the shining steel moldboard."[1] Campaign biographers of Calvin Coolidge, Herbert Hoover, Franklin D. Roosevelt, and Thomas E. Dewey had a more difficult time building a valid image of their subjects as farmers. Dewey, a gentleman farmer from Pawling, New York, is a case in point. During his campaign against Truman in 1948, he either decided or was talked into being photographed in a farm costume and setting. Harry looked at the picture and said with deep sarcasm, "He's got his fence upside down."

Harry Truman's earliest recollections were of farm life. In particular, he had fond memories of the Young farm, where he had spent some fourteen years of his life. When he was a boy, he and his brother had the freedom provided by six hundred acres, and there was always something to see or do. Truman records memories of apple and peach pies, fresh preserves, apple butter, pork sausage, souse, and pickled pigs' feet—all homemade. His father, grandfather Young, and Uncle Harrison taught him about farm animals, and he watched wheat planting, threshing, corn planting and shucking, the mowing and stacking of hay, the birth and death of animals and their care, the repair of farm machinery, and other farm operations.

Jackson County, Missouri, was and is a livestock- and grain-growing area. Prairie tableland, used for pasture and some small grain production, is interspersed with rich alluvial bottomland, where corn is grown. The

Young farm was large for this area. The fact that it employed several hired men and had an annual income of $15,000 in good years was further evidence of more than average specialization and commercialization during a period when the average annual cash sales of a U.S. farm's products were $600 to $1,100.

Many improvements were made in livestock production during this time. The Missouri Experiment Station, along with the Texas Experiment Station, worked out methods of dipping cattle for control of ticks carrying Texas fever, giving great impetus to cattle breeding and feeding in the state. Methods worked out for the control of hog cholera greatly stimulated hog production, for which the state was well fitted. At the same time new and improved breeds of livestock were introduced.

Farm machinery also improved during this time. Although the tractor was not extensively used until the 1920s, the horse-drawn grain harvesters, corn harvesters, and haying, tillage, and seeding machinery were much more efficient than machinery used in the 1800s.[2]

When Truman returned to the Young farm in 1906 at the age of twenty-two, the transition from bank clerking to farming was not abrupt. He had been in touch with farm problems during the twelve years in Independence and the four years in Kansas City. During the Independence years, his father had traded in farm animals and had run farms on the outskirts of the city with the help of a farmhand who was married to the Truman maid. During the entire period, Truman had visited the Young farm in Grandview from time to time and had occasionally entertained his friends there.[3] Farm life, nevertheless, required sacrifices. The early rising, the long hours of hard physical work, the hot sun in the summer, the bitter cold in winter, the uncertain income due to variations in weather conditions, and the fickleness of the market meant drastic changes in Truman's way of life. He could no longer go to every vaudeville show. He would have less time for reading although a rumor was circulated on the farm that he spent a lot of time reading in the shade. He vehemently denied this, saying that his father would not have let him get away with that.[4]

Truman wrote that he regarded these years as the best of his life. He plowed, sowed, reaped, milked cows, fed hogs, castrated pigs, performed surgery on cows with the bloat, nursed sick horses and mules, baled hay, and did all other necessary chores. The farm, run by his father, himself, his brother (for a while), and some hired hands, raised corn, wheat, oats, potatoes, and hogs and fed some cattle. Truman said that he set up and operated all sorts of farm machinery and really liked to do it.[5] Actions, however, speak louder than words. As early as 1916, his business ventures in mining and oil leases began to take more and more of his time. For a man who was courting a woman like Bess Wallace, the granddaughter of the founder of the Gates-Waggoner Flour Mill, farm profits were insufficient. In 1917 he left Grandview for soldiering and, except briefly in 1919, never returned to the farm. Agriculture obviously did not satisfy his gregarious habits, his ambitions for quick financial returns, and his longing for self-fulfillment.

On the farm Truman learned to care for his crops and his cattle. He kept books and records showing what farm products would bring the highest returns and what methods would produce the greatest yield per acre for various crops. He developed an active concern for farm accounting procedures, soil conservation, fertilizing methods, weed control, crop rotation, labor-saving machinery, labor management, seed improvement, stock-breeding advances, and better farm management. He learned, in other words, the wide range of responsibilities and skills necessary to make a farm succeed. In his bookkeeping, as in his crop rotation, Truman was ahead of his time.[6] But essentially the Trumans and the Youngs were farmers who clung to traditional methods, which did not yield such rich rewards as scientific agriculture does. (It was in just such scientific agriculture that another American vice-president made not only a fortune but also a considerable reputation as an agrarian. Henry Wallace, graduate of a land grant college, geneticist, farm journal editor, agricultural economist, and statistician, developed a very successful hybrid seedcorn that helped to revolutionize American farming.)

Contour plowing was yet to be developed, but where there were gullies on the Young farm, Truman tossed in bales of straw, and when a layer of soil formed over the bales, he planted timothy. Neighbors called this a "sodden watercourse," but it did arrest erosion. In general, though, the farm was level, and plowing and planting could be in straight lines. In fact, Truman's mother was proud of his ability to "plow the straightest row of corn in the county and to sow wheat so there was not a bare spot in the whole field."[7] The naturally fertile farm with eighteen inches of black topsoil was being constantly improved by manure from the farm barns and from the adjoining towns.

Truman also worked at improving the livestock. In 1912 the American shorthorn herdbooks showed that he owned at least five purebred shorthorn bulls and three registered cows.[8] But when his father died in 1914, he had to sell their black Angus cattle in order to pay the doctor's bills.[9] The Young farm was prosperous, as farms went in those days, but like George Washington, America's first Cincinnatus, Truman was land rich but short of cash. When he sold his stock at auction in 1919, he listed 231 head of stock hogs, all immunized, 18 head of horses and mules, and 23 head of cows and calves.[10]

Banker John Slaughter of Hickman Mills, near Grandview, recalled that

Truman was nearly always the first in the neighborhood to invest in labor-saving farm machinery. Truman used a gang plow drawn by four draft animals:

In those days we had what we called a gang plow, two twelve-inch plows on the same frame with three wheels on it, and the locomotive power was four horses, or four mules, or three mules and a horse, or whatever you could get to pull it. It moved at a rate where it turned over a two-foot furrow, and you could count the revolutions of the big wheel from which you could tell how long it would take to plow an acre or to plow a field.[11]

In addition, the Trumans had a binder, a corn planter, a wheat drill, a derrick and a swing for hay stacking, and many other types of farm machinery. Truman was mechanically minded enough to help keep this machinery in good order.

In handling farm labor, Truman had a reputation for being fair but strict. Brownie Huber, who worked for six years as a farmhand on the Young farm, recalled: "Though Harry was always anxious to get things done, he could be the most patient fellow you ever met." He added, "Harry was always mild tempered, but you couldn't put anything over on him." He mentioned a farmhand who was caught asleep under a tree when he was supposed to be cultivating corn. Brownie said: "Though he wasn't angry, Harry fired the guy right on the spot because he couldn't trust him."[12]

Under Truman's supervision, the production of wheat was increased from thirteen to nineteen bushels per acre and that of corn from thirty-five to seventy bushels per acre, yields (particularly of corn) spectacular for this period.[13] In 1913 when cars were scarce and regarded as luxury items, he was able to buy a second-hand Stafford for six hundred dollars, greatly improving his mobility and lessening the isolation of his farm existence.

When the Trumans inherited the Young farm, other heirs contested the will, and Truman's mother settled claims out of court by heavily mortgaging the property. The farm did not do well enough to carry the heavy interest and amortization charges. In 1940, when Harry was waging one of his toughest political campaigns, the Jackson County sheriff foreclosed on behalf of the school board on whose real-estate loan no interest or taxes had been paid. Senator Truman claimed that he had nothing to do with the making of the original mortgage for the loan. Nevertheless, he was hurt politically and was deeply chagrined that he could not save the farm for his mother.

Interested in improving farm management, Truman in 1912 was active in establishing the Jackson County Farm Bureau, which, with other county farm bureaus scattered over the state, formed the Missouri Farm Bureau. It, together with other state farm bureaus, formed the American Farm

Bureau Federation in 1920. Truman was elected president of his township farm bureau, whose secretary recalls:

Mr. E. A. Ikenberry was our county agent, at that time called a farm adviser much to the disgust of many farmers, and through his direction and cooperation our local work was carried on. In 1914, when time came for the annual election of township officers, Mr. Ikenberry advised us to seek out a progressive farmer who was also a good farmer and one who would also have some political support with the county court of Jackson County as the Farm Bureau work received much of its support from the county court. Harry S. Truman was elected.[14]

Truman's political influence at the time was the friendship that he and his father had for Robert Mize, Jackson County's Eastern District judge—a position that Truman himself later held. At the time he was a loyal supporter of the Farm Bureau and an active promoter of 4-H clubs. When he was president, Truman developed some differences with the American Farm Bureau Federation after it had turned more conservative, and it became the chief opponent of one of Truman's cherished farm proposals.

In 1917, shortly after Harry Truman left the farm to join the army, William Hirth, the publisher of the *Missouri Farmer*, organized the Missouri Farmers Association for the "benefit and advancement of members as producers of agricultural products." It developed nonprofit cooperatives that furnished supplies to its members at cost and marketed all kinds of agricultural products, including livestock. By 1950 the association became the largest business in Missouri and the largest cooperative in the United States. Hirth, who was president of this organization until his death in 1940, was a consistent foe of Boss Pendergast and provided a number of obstacles that Truman had to overcome in his struggle for political advancement. Hirth's paper and his voice were articulate in opposing any candidate backed by the Goat faction of the Democratic party.

Although he was not always able to come up with solutions for farmers' problems, Truman's experience on the farm enabled him to understand their feelings. He farmed most actively during the period of relative prosperity for farmers, the base period used by the Department of Agriculture for calculating the various parity formulas. During this time, the prices of farm products were held to be in line with the prices of other goods, and farmers got what was regarded as their fair share of the national income. After World War II, when farm prices fell drastically, Truman was close enough to his family farm problems to know the problems caused by failing to make production costs on the market. Campaigning in the rural areas of Missouri, Truman stressed the benefits of his road program and the New Deal agricultural policies.

At this point one can ask to what extent Truman acquired the alleged virtues supposedly possessed by sons of the soil. He discovered, certainly, what hard work was. The farm work, plus his military training in the National Guard, moreover, built a rugged physique, which was able to withstand the strain of seven years and nine months in the White House at a time when many crucial decisions had to be made. (The strain of office for roughly the same length of time broke the health of Woodrow Wilson.) In Harry Truman the nation found a man physically able to assume the rigorous schedules imposed on the presidency.

Truman also developed responsibility. He did not shirk his obligations for the health of his farm animals, nor did he neglect his crops. Further, it was as a farmer that Truman made the first demonstration of his capacity for democratic leadership when he was chosen president of his township farm bureau in one of the first counties to have such an organization.

Honesty, as part of the Cincinnatus image, is more difficult to relate to this farm background. Truman's father believed in honest dealings with his customers and apparently set a good example for his sons by living up to his beliefs.

Other presidents and presidential candidates have tried to assume a Cincinnatus posture. Cal Coolidge, a wry native of Vermont, looked ridiculous in his farmer's costume, but this did not stop his campaign biographer from lauding him as the agricultural genius who "could get an exceptional amount of sap out of a maple tree." We can all picture Tom Dewey tending to his cabbages behind his upsidedown fence. General Eisenhower, the gentleman farmer from Gettysburg, may have thought that he looked like General Washington who, after hectic days as president, longed to return to his Mount Vernon, but he acquired his black Angus cattle late in life. And so it goes. In the twentieth century, the only true farmer in the White House was Harry S. Truman.

chapter 5 | BUSINESS AND ACCOUNTING SKILLS, 1898–1935

There are in business, three things necessary—knowledge, temper and time.

—Owen Felltham, *Resolves*

Practical experience rather than university course work was Truman's introduction to the world of business. He did not have the advantage of training in accounting, finance, business management, labor relations, retailing, and the wide variety of courses now offered by modern business schools. And, while the tough lessons he learned did not give him a grasp of economic theory, they did provide a concrete knowledge about economic operations in the mixed American economic system based partly upon the free enterprise system and partly on state regulation of potential economic abuses. Because most of his own small-scale business enterprises did not succeed, he had a populist dislike of huge trusts, mammoth holding companies, investment bankers, and giant corporations. He shared such feelings with others: Andrew Jackson, Woodrow Wilson, and Justice Louis Brandeis.

Like his father, Truman showed an interest in speculative activities. He was willing to assume risks on the chance that he might get rich. Farming is inherently a speculative activity. Every year the farmer takes a chance on the best crops to plant, the prospects of favorable weather for planting, growing, and harvesting, the probable health of his farm animals, the availability of reliable farm labor at wages he can afford to pay, and the prices that his cash crops will bring on a fickle market. The only thing that a farmer can be sure of is a roof over his head—if his mortgage is not foreclosed—and food on his table—if he spends enough time on his garden.

Before he went to Washington, D.C., and settled down to a political career, Harry Truman's gainful occupations other than farming and military service included: drugstore handyman, timekeeper for a railway construction gang, newspaper wrapper, bank clerk, mining stock investor, oil well prospector, partner in a haberdashery shop, solicitor for automobile association memberships, building and loan company official, and bank official. During the period from 1898 to 1935, he held ten different jobs of greatly varying duration and importance. In some, he was a minor employee, and in others he was a proprietor. His job mobility suggests a restlessness, a lack of job satisfaction, a search for identity, and, in some cases, a lack of good business judgment. The proprietary activities would generally be placed in the category of small business, experiences that became part of his economic education, proving useful later in helping him understand the problems of small businessmen, when such an understanding was helpful.

Truman was eleven when he landed his first job—part-time handyman in the Clinton Drug Store. He was responsible for cleaning and dusting before school, and after school he waited on customers at the soda fountain, in those days the social meeting place for youngsters. Harry found the job of dusting the thousands of bottles boring and tedious. He was also bothered by the subtle evidences of local hypocrisy. The drugstore was frequented by church-going drys and Anti-Saloon Leaguers coming in for nips of hard liquor apparently of a nonmedicinal nature. After a year's work, during which he learned something about the value of money and how hard one must work to get so little, he quit the drugstore.[1]

Six years later Truman went to work—temporarily—for a contractor who was building trackage for the Santa Fe Railroad not far from Independence. Trains held a special fascination for him. Now, graduated from high school, he was hired as a timekeeper for the work crews to make up the payroll and pay the laborers every Saturday night. This involved operating a handcar between the three camps and living with a bunch of rough characters who used foul language and dissipated their earnings drinking hard liquor on weekends.[2] Crude though they may have been, they were at least not hypocritical about their drinking. These workers were not unionized and, of course, were ignorant of collective bargaining, so Truman's experience here cannot be regarded as the equivalent of a course in trade unionism and labor management. It furnished, however, practical experience in dealing with men whom he had to convince of his fairness, insuring them that each got what was due him. The foreman said that he "was all right from his navel in all directions." Truman's own observation, while equally simple, suggests a different frame of reference: "That is where I learned about minimum wages."[3] The work ended in June 1902.

In August 1902 he got a job at the *Kansas City Star* wrapping newspapers in the mailroom. He was paid seven dollars a week and, no doubt, learned a bit more about minimum wages. According to the records of the *Star*, he kept this job for only two weeks; the paper wrapping part of journalism held no attraction for young Harry.[4]

Harry's job as clerk in the National Bank of Commerce, at a salary of $35 a month, came after the family moved to Kansas City. He worked in the caged section of the basement, clearing checks drawn on country banks. The work was not challenging enough, but he liked living in the city. (Dwight Eisenhower's brother, Arthur, was one of his boardinghouse companions during this period.)[5]

Dissatisfied with his salary, Truman moved to the Union National Bank at $65 a month, later raised to $135 a month, which he then regarded as good. If Truman so chose, there was a career in banking. At the bank Truman learned fundamental lessons in accounting, which helped him grasp more complicated governmental finance later. Truman felt that he learned more about how to get along with people at the bank: "Because of my efforts to get along with my associates I usually was able to get what I wanted. . . . I gained a reputation in the bank of always finishing the task that was set before me and of helping the others get theirs done as well."[6]

Truman's next change was the return to the Grandwiew farm at the urgent request of his parents in 1906. After his father's death in 1914, Harry, still on the farm, became involved in a number of speculative adventures, none of which paid off even though they had good potentials, which were later successfully exploited by others. Apparently farming was not enough to absorb his restless spirit. Jerry Culbertson, a glib-tongued promoter, persuaded him to invest $7,500 in a lead mine in Oklahoma not far from Joplin, Missouri, where lead mining had at one time been a flourishing business. This mine proved to be unproductive, and Truman lost all of his investment (although a little more capital might have made it pay when the price of lead rose during the war).[7]

Next Culbertson interested Truman in helping to organize an oil exploration company that bought and sold leases and drilled for oil. In 1916 Truman purchased a third interest in the firm by putting up $5,000 in cash and five notes for $1,000 each, all due in ten months and cosigned by his mother. He was made treasurer of the company, known as Morgan and Company, after the president, David H. Morgan, a lawyer from Muskogee, Oklahoma.[8]

The company leased land for drilling rights in Eureka, Greenwood County, Kansas, but did not drill deep enough to strike oil. The company to which they sold the lease when Truman joined the army in 1917 went deeper and struck a highly productive pool, known as the Teeter pool, now owned by Cities Service Company. Truman came very near to striking it rich and perhaps becoming active in the oil business.

During his wildcatting days Truman made a good impression on the auditor for the company, who later praised Truman for his courtesy and affability.[9] The Morgan and Company partnership was not dissolved until 1919, after Truman came back from Europe and was discharged from the army.[10]

Truman did not lose money in his oil ventures, but he did not make the fortune others were in this field. Like his father, he never managed to put together the winning combination. Herbert Hoover, who had had geological training, made a fortune in the mining business, becoming a multimillionaire before he was forty.[11] Alf Landon, wildcatting in Kansas, struck it rich and later combined business success with politics, becoming governor of Kansas and the Republican nominee for president in 1936.[12] Truman, without the training of Hoover or the luck of Landon, was to move toward high office in a more tedious, more arduous manner.

Success in an army canteen venture led former Captain Truman and former Sergeant Eddie Jacobson to believe that in 1919 they could make a success of a civilian men's furnishings store. Jacobson had had experience as a shirt salesman, and Truman thought he could raise sufficient funds to start the venture. In running the store, Jacobson would be the buyer, Truman the bookkeeper, and both would be salesmen. A partnership was established, a site in downtown Kansas City was selected, and the Truman and Jacobson Haberdashery Shop was in business. The location, at 104 West Twelfth Street across from the Muehlebach Hotel, was, as Jacobson put it, "the real white way of wide-open Kansas City. Cater-cornered across in the Dixon Hotel were two wide open gambling houses, one in the basement and the other upstairs."[13]

About $35,000 was invested in the business, and during the first year the partners netted a good profit, selling shirts, collars, underwear, ties, socks, belts, and other small items of male attire. Because they thought times were prosperous, they even stocked $16 silk shirts. The work was not easy; the store was open from eight in the morning until nine at night six days a week. On Sundays both Harry and Bess had to work on the books. The partners also hired a salesman.

The store's first year was prosperous as discharged soldiers bought civilian clothing, but in the spring of 1920 came the swiftest and deepest fall in apparel prices in the nation's history, followed by unemployment in the needle trades.[14] Agricultural prices dropped, and farmers economized on clothing. Although prices inflated by wartime and reconversion demands could not last, Truman blamed his troubles on what he called the "Mellon squeeze." Secretary of the Treasury Andrew Mellon introduced conservative banking policies and discontinued deficit spending, but he can hardly be blamed for inflated wartime prices, which could not last when peacetime demands slackened.

Truman described how these events affected him personally:

We . . . bought $35,000 worth of merchandise and did a thriving business for two years. We sold over $70,000 worth of merchandise in a year and a half and showed a very good profit after all expenses. . . . Our inventory was worth $40,000 one week and the next it was worth $5,000. We went broke. Our creditors drove Eddie into bankruptcy, but I became a public official and they couldn't do that to me. Eddie and I continued to pay and settle our obligations, and after about fifteen years, cleaned them all up honorably.[15]

Because other Kansas City shops survived the depression of 1920-1921, the Mellon squeeze explanation is inadequate. More to the point is the fact that Harry had no prior experience in retail trade. He did have the makings of a good salesman—he was friendly, pleasant, had an engaging smile, dressed well, and knew how to get along with people. And he and Eddie certainly worked hard enough in the store. One explanation of the failure is that the partners did not have enough reserve capital to tide them over the sharp decline in the prices of men's clothes. They could not secure adequate loans to keep them going until they could write off their inventory losses and start at the new price levels. (Legislation providing loans to small businessmen by the federal government did not come until 1953.) Another explanation of the failure is that they were overextended on luxury items, which could not be sold when business declined and unemployment rose. The partners took a chance when they stocked such items in the first place. A third explanation is that although Eddie Jacobson insisted that the business was on a strictly cash basis, in practice it was not. We find hints of likely business practices in one account that states that Harry had a tendency to be softhearted with other veterans regarding loans and credit.[16] A fourth explanation is that the depression created an energy crisis, which prevented the store from staying open the long hours it did at first.

Reverses in the nation's economy, blending with a less than sophisticated approach to running a small business, probably account for the store's failure. Its closing was a terrible blow to Harry, and the unpaid debts hung over him until he entered the U.S. Senate. He might well have followed Eddie's example and declared bankruptcy. That he did not is offered by some as proof of his honesty and high moral principles.[17] If he was trying to avoid the stigma of being declared bankrupt, he did not succeed, since his opponents attached the Jacobson bankruptcy label to him regardless of his refusal to become part of the proceedings. Even his daughter fails to give him credit for not going into bankruptcy.[18] The final settlement was expedited by the failure of the banks that had held their note. In liquidation of the last bank that had the note, the obligation was picked up for $1,000, about one-tenth of its face value as determined by the courts.[19]

The haberdashery experience was important because it made Truman receptive to going into politics. He liked meeting people, and socially the store was a great success. It was a gathering point for veterans, friends, and acquaintances. It also increased his knowledge of the American free enterprise system. Although it was a painful and expensive course in economics, it helped him develop a sympathetic understanding of the problems of small businessmen.

Harry found that he liked politics. Elected to an administrative post as county judge in 1922, he was retired two years later when both state and county went Republican. To meet this financial crisis, he turned to a sales job and became the promoter for Kansas City Automobile Association memberships for two years. He was successful in this and earned over $5000 but did not want to continue. When the Pendergast organization asked him in 1926 to run for the post of presiding judge of the county court, he accepted and won.

The uncertainty of the electoral process led Truman to seek a calling in addition to his official position. He wanted something to fall back upon in case of a political reversal. For this purpose, he chose the building and loan association business and late in 1924 organized the Community Savings and Loan Association of Independence with offices in the Board of Trade Building in Kansas City and in Independence.[20] Truman started out as the general manager and later was listed as president. In 1926 an old army associate, Spencer Salisbury, joined as treasurer, and a young lawyer, Arthur S. Metzger, became secretary. Later on Truman and Salisbury broke up and became foes. In the 1920s, however, relations were generally friendly, and the business prospered along with a building boom. On August 31, 1930, the assets of the company were reported to be $437,703.[21]

In 1934, the institution was converted into a federal savings and loan association. Truman was not shown as one of the officers at this time, but Salisbury was listed as treasurer and manager. By December 1939, an examination by officials of the Federal Savings and Loan Insurance Corporation revealed "impairment of capital" and liquidation proceedings were started in June 1940.[22] Senator Truman reported irregularities, and as a result Salisbury was tried and convicted of concealing litigation and was sent to jail.[23] Salisbury never forgave Truman for his part.

Just before Truman became presiding judge of the Jackson County Court, another business opportunity seemed to open up. He and some of his friends discovered that they could acquire ownership of the Citizens Security Bank of Englewood (founded in 1919) with no money down. The problem soon appeared: what purported to be a bank was not really one but merely a facade to hide the fact that the secretary of state was trying to enrich himself and his friends by means of his power to determine where to deposit state funds. In addition, the institution had some bad paper, and some of its officers had engaged in questionable activities. Truman and his friends, Salisbury and Lou Holland, removed themselves from this scheme quickly. It does not appear, however, that they informed the new owners of the character of the enterprise.[24] Later in the same year it failed, its new president lost everything and committed suicide, and some of the bank officials were indicted for irregularities.[25]

In spite of the failures, Truman's experiences in the business world were valuable training for his political career. He learned how to meet people and how to talk to them persuasively while demonstrating qualities of friendliness, persistence, and loyalty. Jacobson became a lifelong friend who had important roles to play on the national and international scene. To the trials and tribulations of the small businessman, Truman would be able to lend a friendly and sympathetic ear. Truman's business career setbacks did not undermine his optimism. His losses did not make him bitter. Culbertson and Morgan remained his friends. Truman always bounded back after each reverse. Success was just around the corner. His building and loan business was going well while he was still in Independence.

Truman did not have a firm economic base from which to launch a political career. His prepolitical occupations had brought him neither wealth nor distinction. He had no profession and no established business to fall back upon in case of political reversal. Many years ago Theodore Roosevelt wrote that he did not believe any man should make politics his only career: "It is a dreadful misfortune for a man to grow to feel that his whole livelihood and whole happiness depend upon his staying in office. Such a feeling prevents him from being of real service to the people while in office, and always puts him under the heaviest strain of pressure to barter his convictions for the sake of holding office."[26] Truman's career was to show an exception to the rule that a man could not make politics his profession and still withstand pressures. A simple moral code and circumstances helped him to guard his reputation for honesty.

chapter 6 | MILITARY EXPERIENCES, 1905– 1919

"Of all the military heroes," Truman once remarked, "Hannibal and Lee were to my mind the best because while they won every battle, they lost the war, due to crazy politicians in both instances, but they were still the Great Captains of History. I found a lot of heroes were made by being in at the death or defeat of one of the really great. Scipio, Wellington, and U. S. Grant are the most outstanding."[1] Exploits of military heroes fascinated Truman most of his life. It does not seem unnatural for a young boy, especially one denied an active athletic outlet for his energies, to derive vicarious enjoyment from accounts of great military deeds.

In his autobiographical notes, Truman set forth the qualities of leadership that he thought should be admired and those that he thought should be despised. The greatest of all leaders had a special quality of magnetism. Truman was impressed, for example, with Napoleon's ability to win over Marshal Ney, who was sent to bring him back as a prisoner. "When Napoleon got out of his carriage and turned to Ney, Napoleon said, 'My great Marshal.' So strong was Napoleon's magnetism that Ney abandoned the king and joined Napoleon. A fellow has got to have something to be able to do that."[2]

Truman was also impressed with how some great military commanders overcame physical handicaps. Hannibal had but one eye, Caesar was epileptic, and Napoleon was of short stature. Yet each compensated so well for his physical shortcomings that he became an outstanding world leader.[3] Truman, we know, was conscious of his own defective eyesight and of his height, and he wished that he had more charisma.

Truman also had his own ideas of just and unjust wars. He admired unselfish and patriotic warriors who fought for what they thought was right and for their countries and condemned those who fought for conquest and personal glory. Self-discipline and modesty were to be commended, while excessive egotism was to be despised.

During his high school days, Truman's heroes of the Spanish-American War were Admiral George Dewey and General W. R. Shafter. He admired the way General Shafter, who had a serious problem of excessive weight, overcame this disability, moved his troops to Cuba, and won the war. Harry and the other fourteen-year-old boys had great fun drilling with rifles in a nearby woods in order to prepare themselves for active service. If they had been older or if the war had lasted longer, they all might have enlisted. If he had gone to West Point he would have been about ten years ahead of Dwight Eisenhower and Omar Bradley. Truman much admired Bradley, a fellow Missourian, and George C. Marshall, the wartime army chief of staff.

In 1905, when he was still in Kansas City working at the National Bank of Commerce, he joined the National Guard, which apparently did not require perfect eyesight.[4] He enlisted for three years and, after moving to the farm in 1906, continued his drilling and attendance in Kansas City and at summer camps. In 1908 he decided to reenlist for another three years. When this term was up in 1911, he did not reenlist because of his heavier responsibilities on the farm after his brother, Vivian, left to run a farm of his own.

Truman's first encampment was at Cape Girardeau, which was reached by train to St. Louis and from there by steamboat down the Mississippi River. This experience, for a lover of Mark Twain, and the encampments at Fort Riley, Kansas, where he received light artillery training, he found exciting and a welcome change from the loneliness of farm life. In 1911 he ended his six years of National Guard service as a corporal. He did not rejoin in 1916 when some of his former fellow soldiers were sent on the expedition into Mexico.

Truman recalled the tremendous impression made on him by the outbreak of World War I in Europe in 1914.[5] When Germany invaded Belgium, his sympathies were on the side of France, England, and Belgium. After the United States entered the war in April 1917, the army appealed to those with military training to volunteer. In Kansas City, Major John L. Miles persuaded Truman and others to enlist in order to build a field artillery regiment out of two undermanned batteries of the Missouri National Guard. Truman had hesitated at first. He was over the draft age, he was needed on the farm, the government was urging farmers to stay on the land, and he hoped to strike it rich in the oil business. Furthermore, there was strong isolationist pro-German sentiment in Missouri, which opposed U.S. involvement in the European war. Senator Jim Reed, a favorite of the Democratic organization of Kansas City, was one of the "wilful men" denounced by President Wilson for opposing the arming of merchant ships.

Speaker Champ Clark from Missouri, still nursing his defeat by Wilson in 1912, openly opposed the draft bill even after war was declared. Truman was not as yet fully involved in politics, but he was a loyal Democrat and he thought that loyalty should be strongest at the highest level, so he joined the regiment.

National Guard officers at that time were elected by the men. When Battery F was formed, Truman hoped to be a sergeant, but he was elected a first lieutenant. Officers so selected had to prove themselves in officers' training camp, to which he was sent. Because of his lack of a college education, he had to study trigonometry on his own time.[6]

On August 5, 1917, Truman became an officer in the U.S. Army when the Second Field Artillery of Missouri became the 129th Field Artillery of the 35th Division. On September 26, the unit left Kansas City for Camp Doniphan, Fort Sill, Oklahoma, for artillery training. Here Lieutenant Truman won his first army commendation for the efficient way in which he ran the regimental canteen. He selected Sergeant Eddie Jacobson, who had had retailing experience and whom he knew from his days as a bank clerk, as his assistant in managing the canteen.[7] They collected two dollars from each of the eleven hundred men as the original investment to start the canteen; six months later they declared fifteen thousand dollars in dividends.[8] This amazing success was to help him in his army career, and it gave him some false ideas about the ease of making money in retailing.

Success in the army canteen business was not enough to qualify Truman as an artillery officer. Since the 3.2-inch artillery was horse drawn in World War I, Truman's earlier experience with horses helped him to qualify. He also showed aptitude as a firing instructor; in fact, his enthusiasm for firing light artillery was so great that in 1928 he stated that firing a French 75mm gun was his favorite sport.[9] Many years later in 1951, he sent the following letter from the White House to an admirer who had given him a miniature of an old 3.2 artillery piece:

Dear Mr. Cavasin:
    I certainly appreciated the miniature brass model of the old 3.2. I had my first training as a field artilleryman way back early in the nineteen hundreds on a 3.2 cannon. When you fired the old thing it rolled back twenty yards and one of the orders in training was "cannoneers on the wheels" to roll it back into position. Then they furnished us with a 3″ German piece which was used up to World War I, and later we were equipped with the old French 75 mm with high wooden wheels. I commanded a battery of those old 75 mm and they were wonderful guns.[10]

One of these guns is now on display in the Truman Library in Independence. Truman found himself in the midst of important and exciting events. He loved the comradeship of army life.

At Camp Doniphan, Truman showed that he could get along well with his superior officers. Captain Allen wrote a glowing report recommending Truman for promotion, and Brigadier General Lucien C. Berry commented that there was "nobody that good." Berry had the reputation for being highly critical and explosive in his language. Truman remembers that the general, in conducting promotional examinations, tried to find out how much the candidate did not know rather than what he knew. He reported the general as saying: "Ah, you don't know, do you? I thought you were just ignorant rookies. Now you aspire to be officers and gentlemen sure enough by becoming captains in the United States Army. It will be a disaster to the country to let you command men."[11] General Berry's bark was worse than his bite. A tongue-lashing was his way of impressing the men with the seriousness of their responsibilities.[12] Truman passed the examination in February 1918, and his commission as captain was dated in April but he did not receive it or a captain's pay until it caught up with him in France the following October.

Late in March Truman was sent with a group of ten officers and a hundred men for special training in France in the use of French light artillery. It was his first trip outside the Midwest. On the way he got his first view of New York City where an optician ground him several pairs of glasses without asking for payment. The Missouri farm boy found his first ocean voyage a thrilling experience. The men were shipped on the *George Washington*, which later took President Wilson to the peace conference.

Upon arriving in France in April, the men were sent to the Second Corps field artillery school at Montigny-sur-Aube where they were instructed in the use of the French 75mm gun. The school was run by Richard (Dick) Burleson, nephew of Postmaster General Albert S. Burleson in Wilson's cabinet. In 1945 Truman sent Dick, noted for his strong language and aggressiveness, with Ed Pauley to bargain with the Russians over reparations.

After five weeks of schooling, Truman was sent back as battalion adjutant to his regiment, which was then sent to Angers for more training at Coetquidan, the location, Truman noted with a thrill, of one of Napoleon's old artillery camps.[13]

On July 11, 1918, Truman was put in command of Battery D of the 129th Field Artillery, an assignment that would prove to be a real test of his ability to lead men. The battery had been recruited in Kansas City in the neighborhood of Rockhurst College and was composed mostly of Irish-American Catholics who had acquired a reputation for being boisterous and unruly. A high turnover in the commanding officers of this battery had prompted the colonel to consider breaking up the battery and reassigning the men. Captain Truman was given a chance to try to keep the group together and whip it into shape. He later observed: "I won't forget that day. I was never so

scared in my life.''[14] Truman's friend Edgar G. Hinde wrote later about
Truman's assignment: "He was a thirty-third degree Mason in a Catholic
battery and we thought he was going to have a pretty rough go of it but he
made the best success of any of them.''[15]

Truman was given a rough initiation. First the men staged a stampede
with the horses. As a farmer and the son of a mule trader, Truman had seen
a stampede before so he took it calmly and then ordered the men to repair
the damage. Not to be outdone, they started a mild riot in the barracks.
Four men were injured and sent to the infirmary. Captain Truman called
the sergeants and corporals together, telling them that he had not come
there to get along with them—they had to get along with him. He recalled
later saying, "And if there are any of you who can't, speak right up now
and I'll bust you right back now.''[16] They got along.

Firm discipline combined with fair treatment and a willingness to assume
his share of the hardships of combat won the respect of Truman's men. The
evidence indicates that he worked at living up to his ideals as a military
leader and, when the battery finished training, it was notified that the time
of loading, forty-eight minutes, was the best record to date.[17] The loading
accomplishment is early evidence of Truman's ability to weld together a
smoothly working unit out of disparate elements. Battery D served a little
more than two months at the front. The men recalled their first combat on
August 29, 1918, as "the battle of Who Run." They had been assigned to
the Gerardmer sector, supposedly a quiet sector high on Mount Herrenberg
in the Vosges Mountains in Alsace, and were directed to fire a barrage of
gas shells at the German positions. The German reply was devastating. High
explosive and gas shells fell close to the battery position; four horses were
killed. One of the sergeants was quoted as yelling "Run, boys! They've got
a bracket on us!" All but five of the men scattered for cover. Truman,
whose horse had just fallen in a shell hole, recalled that he "got up and
called them everything I knew.''[18] Either his example or the word barrage—
or both— turned the men around. The chaplain, Father L. Curtis Tiernan,
remembers Truman's courage, calmness, and the decisive action on this
occasion. Appropriately, he forgave the language indicating that, at any
rate, the tone was certainly not irreverent.[19] Colonel Karl D. Klemm wanted
Captain Truman to court-martial the sergeant, but Truman decided to
demote him to private and transfer him to another battery, saying that he
did not care for courts-martial and preferred to do his own disciplining. The
episode revealed an ability to make decisive judgments and to handle the
consequent actions.

Marching only at night, the division was then sent to the St. Mihiel sector.
During the day they hid in the forest to avoid enemy air observation. At
4 A.M. one morning, a regimental commander complained about the unmili-
tary appearance of the tired battery and ordered Captain Truman to have
the men march at the double. Truman protested that the men were too

exhausted and as soon as it was diplomatically convenient, ordered them off the road for their daytime bivouac. The grateful men stumbled to their rest more impressed by Truman's leadership than by that of the regimental commander.

When the battle of St. Mihiel finally broke out, Battery D was in reserve, and neither Truman nor his men saw action. Another American did, however: Brigadier General Douglas MacArthur of the Forty-second Division.

Friendships formed during the stress of war have a way of enduring beyond the period of the war itself, and this was the case with Captain Truman. A number of those who surrounded President Truman could date their original acquaintance by the war in Europe—for example, Lieutenant Colonel Bennett Clark later became his colleague in the Senate. More than a million men were being gathered for a drive to smash the Hindenburg line in the Meuse-Argonne sector. Truman's battery, sent there by train, was met by Clark, who decided to have some fun with the newcomers. With tongue in cheek, Clark warned Captain Truman to unload his men as quickly as possible and have them take cover, pointing to two dead horses lying nearby. Battery D scrambled for cover. Nothing happened. Laughing, Clark informed Truman of the joke. There was no barrage expected; the horses were victims of the veterinarian's gun. In its own way, the joke had its ironic turn when Truman asked Clark to nominate him for the vice-presidency in 1944.

At the front Truman saw his share of active service and experienced a number of narrow escapes. He knew, from his own personal involvement, what war was like and how it could affect a man. Once he narrowly missed being shelled by the enemy. He was pinned down by German machine-gun fire on one occasion and on another, when in an advanced position, he found himself isolated, his support having been forced back. An infantry sergeant informed him of his solitary and dangerous position, suggesting that he move back. He did.[20]

Captain Truman said that he was once threatened with a court-martial for firing outside the Thirty-fifth Division sector. The situation was described by the historian of the 129th Field Artillery in this way: "Balancing the importance of effective results against a formal adherence to supposed orders to fire only within our own sector, the guns of D. Battery were quickly turned on it [a German battery], and it as quickly ceased to operate, the effect being directly observed from Captain Truman's observation post."[21] The incident reveals Truman's willingness to exercise independent judgment, a characteristic that followed him to the White House.

Captain Truman was at the Verdun front when the armistice was declared on November 11, 1918. He recalled vividly the events of that day:

Firing stopped all along the line at eleven o'clock on November 11, 1918, and the silence that followed almost made one's head ache. We stayed at our positions all day and then crawled into our pup tents to sleep. That night, however, the men of the French battery just behind our position got their hands on a load of wine which had come up on the ammunition narrow gauge, and every single one of them had to march by my bed, saluting and yelling, *"Vive President Wilson! Vive le capitaine d'artillerie americaine!"* No sleep that night! The infantry sent up all the flares they could lay their hands on, fired Very pistols and rifles and whatever else would make a noise all night long.[22]

Truman found that demobilization involved endless red tape, extended leaves, wasted time, continuous poker games, and strenuous efforts to keep out of mischief. On one of his leaves he went to Paris, where, he reported, the Folies Bergere were "disgusting." Truman had fewer reservations about the spoils of the demobilization poker games. The company used some of the jackpot funds to buy a huge silver loving cup, which they presented to him. (Years later it was proudly placed for display in the Truman Library.) Trouble of a sort did, however, derive from some of the poker playing. Jonathan Daniels reported Roger Sermon as saying that after the armistice in 1918, he and Truman lived in a small chateau near Courcemont where

. . . to keep from going crazy we had an almost continuous poker game—one night [we went] to the quarters of Captain Spencer Salisbury billeted with two French old maids in quarters up a high narrow stair—after a while Sermon's half pint bladder got best of him and let go out of window—HST and others joined—Few days later Colonel got letter of protest from the ladies and ordered Sermon as regimental adjutant to give Salisbury a reprimand before entire mess—He did.[23]

At this time Truman had his first close view of British royalty and of a famous American general who came from Missouri. The young prince of Wales, later King Edward VIII, and still later, after his abdication, the duke of Windsor, reviewed the regiment at Courcemont with General John J. Pershing. One of Battery D's Irishmen was reported as calling out, "Hey, Captain Truman! What did the little so-and-so say about freeing Ireland?"[24] The record does not show whether the prince or General Pershing overheard this.

Truman had his first encounter with air travel while in France, an encounter apparently both memorable and influential. After he became president, a young girl, the niece of his confidential secretary, wrote to him thanking him for her first plane ride on the presidential plane *Independence*. Truman replied:

I am so happy that you enjoyed your first plane ride. My first one was in France in 1918 and I had to do what I was ordered to do. It was in an old "Jenny" and the pilot didn't want me to ride with him any more than I wanted to take the ride. I became very sick, due to all the gyrations he gave the plane. I was sick for many years after that whenever I took a flight in a plane. But I got over that. I'm glad you had a good start in flying. The Independence is tops.[25]

The trip home on the S.S. *Zeppelin* was rough too. Truman lost thirteen pounds from sea sickness. Following a brief view of New York City, Battery D was sent to Camp Finiston, Kansas, for demobilization. Truman had been recommended for a majority, but it did not come in time, and he was honorably discharged as a major in the reserve on May 6, 1919.

For Truman the war brought many experiences that he prized for the rest of his life. It helped fulfill his gregarious longings. It demonstrated his ability to lead men, as well as his modesty and courage. He revealed coolness in crisis, fairness, willingness to share hardship, and a desirable decisiveness. Importantly, it broadened his horizons and brought him in brief contact with European culture. He also made friends whom he never forgot even though it would have been better for his public image later on if he had ceased to be so defensive of some of them (loyalty to wartime friends involved in the so-called Truman scandals cost him dearly). Truman's start in politics was based upon his wartime contacts and on the example of other veterans who ran for public office. He continued service in the reserve after the war, rising to the rank of colonel and helping to organize the Reserve Officers' Association in Missouri. He was also active in the American Legion and enjoyed reunions of veterans (though some critics said that his antics were undignified on these occasions).

chapter 7 | BESS TRUMAN

We made a number of new acquaintances, and I became interested in one in particular. She had golden curls and has, to this day, the most beautiful blue eyes. We went to Sunday school, public school from the fifth grade through high school, graduated in the same class, and marched down life's road together. For me she still has the blue eyes and golden hair of yesteryear.
—Harry S. Truman, *Memoirs*

Recently the former First Lady was asked by an old friend what she considered the most memorable aspect of her life. Her answer was prompt: "Harry and I have been sweethearts and married more than forty years, . . . and no matter where I was, when I put out my hand, Harry's was there to grasp it."
—Marianne Means, "What Three Presidents Say About Their Wives," *Good Housekeeping* (August 1963)

Elizabeth Virginia Wallace was the only daughter and oldest of the four children of David Willock Wallace and Madge Gates Wallace. Both the Wallaces and the Gates were well-known, well-established families in Independence, Missouri. George P. Gates, Bess Truman's grandfather, one of the founders of the Waggoner-Gates Milling Company, which made "Queen of the Pantry Flour," was the man who built the house at 219 North Delaware Street, Independence, which became the home of President Truman. Regarded as the handsomest man in town, David Wallace was interested in politics, and he held various positions. First, he was deputy county recorder in charge of issuing marriage licenses at the courthouse in Independence, then county treasurer, and still later internal revenue collector. At the age of thirty-one, he was elected Eminent Commander of Knights Templar of Missouri. In 1903, at the age of forty-three, having lost his voice through throat cancer and being worried about financial troubles, he shot and killed himself in a fit of despondency.[1] Mrs. Wallace, Bess, and her three younger brothers moved into the Gates house at 219 North Delaware Street, where Bess became a companion and helper to her widowed mother. From 1904 to 1906, Bess attended the Barstow School for Girls in Kansas City where she studied literature and languages and engaged in athletics. She was popular and had many beaux.

In contrast to the prominent Gates and Wallace families the John Trumans had been in Independence for only about ten years, when they moved first to Kansas City and then in 1906 to Grandview in southwestern Jackson County where Harry saw few of his old friends in Independence. In fact, it was about four years before the famous cake plate incident brought Harry and Bess together. Harry had ridden twenty miles from Grandview to visit his Aunt Ella Noland, who lived on North Delaware Street. His aunt said that she had a cake plate that belonged to the Wallaces, and Harry volunteered to return it. When Bess opened the door, Harry made the best of his opportunity to renew an old friendship. Various accounts place this incident around 1910.

According to some versions of the romance, Bess's mother and grandparents were not enthusiastic at first about Harry's courtship. Mrs. Wallace was a proud woman of aristocratic bearing, and some said she was not overly pleased at the prospect of her only daughter's marrying this smiling, bespectacled farmer who did not own his own farm. A friend explained: "Harry was about the most unpromising prospect for a husband we had around here then, a dirt farmer with no money, no college education and apparently no future."[2] Another contemporary put it picturesquely: "We thought Bess was scraping the bottom of the barrel."[3] On the other hand, other observers maintain that Mrs. Wallace liked Harry. He was tactful, considerate, respectful, and good fun.[4] Eventually, part of the Young legacy would come to him, and he was moving away from the profession of farming. Nobody in those days, least of all Harry Truman, thought that he was a future president of the United States.

Harry's mother was once asked why Harry and Bess did not get married sooner. She was quite candid: "Bess wouldn't have him."[5] In all likelihood, Bess, who had grown up as a city girl, interested in city sports, recreation, and urban social activity, was not interested in becoming a farmer's wife. Harry would have to leave farm life and prove himself financially to win her. He was not, however, easily discouraged in his courting, displaying a persistence and tenacity which later became apparent in his political life. He was determined to overcome the objections raised to his marrying Bess. The Young farm was on rich land near a metropolitan center, and he inherited some of this property from his Uncle Harrison, who died in 1916. In addition to farming, he had embarked on various other business enterprises. At the very least, Bess was willing to regard him as a steady suitor and, as their daughter later estimated, they had several hundred dates.[6] The second-hand Stafford automobile he had bought in 1913 made his trips to

Independence much easier; it also afforded him an opportunity to give Bess and her friends a better time. After all, cars were scarce in 1913, and they accorded their owners, who statistically were one out of a hundred, with considerable prestige.

The Trumans' courtship, like their marriage, was characterized by a sense of humor. Since they each knew so much about the other's life, they could and did have fun teasing each other. But Harry was more businesslike in planning the engagement and marriage. Not until he had left the farm and his ties with his mother in 1917 did the two become engaged. Harry refused to get married while still on active duty. He told Bess that he did not want her to be married to a war cripple; only after the war was over and he was safely home would they marry. It was an arrangement about which Truman had no doubts. On the way to Europe for active duty, he decided to telephone Bess. It was four in the morning, but he placed the call anyway. He reports that the railroad switchman, turning the phone over to him, remarked: "Call her. The phone's yours. But if she doesn't break up the engagement at four o'clock in the morning, she really loves you."[7] Bess accepted the call as one would expect a girl newly engaged saying goodbye to her fiancé—graciously. Harry also called his mother and sister, and, as he recalls, they all wept a little. But he thought they would be glad to hear from their overseas lieutenant.[8] Truman was as regular with his letters as he was eager with his phone calls. Eddie Jacobson, who served under him as a sergeant, reports that he mailed Truman's letters to Bess and that they went out daily.[9]

Truman and Bess planned their marriage for six weeks after he was mustered out of the army. Harry left Camp Funston, Kansas, and returned for a brief visit to the farm at Grandview, resuming, for the duration of his visit, the life of a farmer. But he had no plans for any immediate return to the farm following his marriage. At the time he estimated his assets at from $15,000 to $20,000 in cash and eighty acres in land.

In a traditionally picturesque red brick church—the Trinity Episcopal Church in Independence—the Trumans were married on June 28, 1919. It was the church of Bess's mother. Captain Ted Marks, a fellow artillery officer and a tailor, was the best man. Both groom and best man wore Marks's handiwork at the wedding. Bess's attendants were her cousins Louise Wells and Helen Wallace.[10] Some of Harry's wartime buddies came to the wedding, arriving just in time for the services. In a fashion familiar to their former commanding officer, they had first gone to the wrong church. The reception was held at the Gates-Wallace home, and the couple left for a honeymoon trip to Chicago and Port Huron, Michigan.

When the couple returned, they moved into the Gates-Wallace residence with Bess's mother and grandmother. For Harry, this was not the smoothest way to begin married life, but the arrangement worked out well. Bess could fulfill her obligations to her husband and her mother and could also continue the social life she enjoyed. Harry was the one who had to make adjustments. For a while, he held a subordinate position in this new household, but living with his in-laws gave him a cushion while he was seeking to find himself and select a profession. The marriage survived this trial. As Truman's daughter put it, ''I think the secret of his success with my mother was his absolute refusal to argue with her.''

Harry adjusted himself well to the Gates household and became attached to the building itself. When he left the White House, he bought out the other Wallace heirs, and the old house became former President Truman's house. If he did not have fond memories of the rambling old gabled structure where he began his married life, he certainly would not have gone to this trouble and expense. The Gates house, with its high ceilings and fourteen large rooms, was built in the 1860s and is still in excellent condition. The feeling that the Trumans had for this house has been best expressed by their daughter, Margaret:

I wish I could re-create the rhythm of those early days of mine in Missouri, . . . for it seems to me that I was completely happy and that I lived in the center of the world. The house on Delaware Street is nearly a hundred years old and it was built at a more spacious time in history. The rooms are enormous and the ceilings high, wide, and handsome. The long living room runs across the front of the house with a little parlor or music room and a study. The dining room is big and the pantry is huge and the kitchen is a real kitchen, always smelling deliciously of Vietta's cooking. A long porch runs the length of the house in the back and that was where we used to eat supper on summer evenings. The dark trees leaned over the house and you could smell the lilacs and Grandmother's roses.[11]

The Truman marriage was one of mature people in their mid-thirties. During their early married life, they had to endure many hardships. Harry had to work long hours at the haberdashery, and Bess helped with the bookkeeping on Sunday. When the store failed, Bess agreed to Harry's decision not to go into bankruptcy, forcing them to make sacrifices for many years to pay back their creditors. Truman's start in politics was also demanding, requiring long, strenuous days of campaigning. And then in 1924, the year when their daughter was born, Truman suffered his only defeat as a candidate for elective office and had to seek another occupation until a new political opportunity opened.

Margaret Truman was born in the Gates house on February 17, 1924. There were no other children in the household, but Bess saw to it that her daughter was not spoiled. Margaret's recollections of her early life are happy:

I remember only the sound of laughter, for I grew up in a family of jokers and teasers on both sides of the house. In fact, my first connection with political affairs was a joke and occurred when I was four years old. It was 1928 and Herbert Hoover was running for President against Al Smith. My uncles were listening to the election returns on a crystal radio set in the study. Mother and Daddy were upstairs.

"I want you to do something for me, Tuffy," Uncle Fred said, and called me over and gave me detailed instructions.

I entered heartily into the conspiracy and ran upstairs shouting happily, "Hoover was elected! Hoover was elected! Hooray!"

You can imagine how well this went down in a Democratic household. I guess that's the last time I ever rooted for a Republican.[12]

When Bess Wallace married Harry Truman, she could hardly have expected to become the First Lady. As her husband climbed the political ladder, she faced increasing social and political responsibilities, never shrinking from her duty. This does not mean that she enjoyed being in the spotlight, enduring the hardships of campaigning, rising above the slurs cast upon herself and her husband, shaking hands with thousands of strangers, putting up with constant interruptions, living through the terror of assassination attempts, and resisting the persistent attempts of the press to invade her privacy. She summed up her feelings to one inquiring reporter: "If I had a son, I would never wish him to be President."[13]

Harry Truman testified that his wife participated in every important decision that he had to make after they were married. This means that she agreed to his running for elective office on eight different occasions from his first bid in 1922 to his presidential race in 1948. In the beginning, she read and criticized his speeches and listened to some of them. She was always the critic, never hesitating to give an honest opinion about a matter, regardless of Harry's reaction. He had complete confidence in her integrity, and while her opinions might be unwelcome on certain subjects, he never doubted that she expressed them for his good. Her advice was an important factor in his decision not to run again for the presidency in 1952. She was also consulted on such important questions as the dropping of the atom bomb, initiating the Marshall Plan to rebuild Europe, coming to the aid of Korea, and the firing of General MacArthur. Truman said that "her judgment was always good. She never made a suggestion that wasn't for the welfare and benefit of the country and what I was trying to do. She looks at things objectively, and I can't always."[14]

During the first sixteen years of their married life, they lived in the Gates house. In 1935 when they moved to Washington, D.C., for the beginning of Harry Truman's ten years of service as U.S. senator, they had to move into a small apartment where Bess did all of her own housework. Living quarters seemed very cramped after the spaciousness of the Gates house, and Bess's mother was still living with them. Yet Bess took living conditions in her stride and made many friends among the other senators' wives and the parents of Margaret's school friends. During the hot, humid summer months, Bess, her mother, and her daughter trekked back to Independence where the living was more to their liking.

When anyone cast a slur at his wife, Harry's usually inhibited rage impulses came close to the surface. Occasionally, they did surface. The flamboyant congressman from Harlem, Adam Clayton Powell, once aroused Truman's anger in such a way that the resentment never died. It started when the congressman's first wife, Hazel Scott, a pianist, was not allowed to play in Constitution Hall, which is run by the Daughters of the American Revolution. When Bess Truman went to a DAR tea, Powell remarked, "From now on, Mrs. Truman is the last lady of the land." The Powells were never invited to the White House after this. Similarly Truman never forgave Clare Boothe Luce, the acid-tongued wife of Henry Luce, publisher of *Time* and *Fortune*, for remarks she made about Mrs. Truman during the 1944 campaign. On this incident Harry Vaughan reported:

One time Henry Luce came to the White House and asked Truman why his wife was barred. "Mr. Luce," Truman replied, "you've asked a fair question and I'll give you a fair answer. I've been in politics thirty-five years and everything that could be said about a human being has been said about me. But my wife has never been in politics. She has always conducted herself in a circumspect manner and no one has a right to make derogatory remarks about her. Now your wife has said many unkind and untrue things about Mrs. Truman. And as long as I am in residence here, she'll not be a guest in the White House."[15]

In 1935, when she was a senator's wife, Mrs. Truman had occasion to meet the President's wife. She called her meetings with Eleanor Roosevelt "delightful. Never does one hear the slightest criticism of her in the social circles in Washington. Her graciousness, her ability to say the right thing at the right time, made a lasting impression."[16] A decade later it was her turn to perform the duties of White House hostess. The local newspaper wrote about her: "Washington found her modest and retiring, although completely natural and unaffected, friendly and thoughtful. . . . People with whom she comes in contact while she is shopping, find her friendly and pleasant. She has an amazing ability to remember names and place people, despite all of the thousands she has met in recent years."[17] Bess Truman was not easy to know, but her friends maintain that she is friendly, warmhearted, and loyal to those who know her.[18]

For a while Bess worked in Harry's office as an unpaid clerk. When his duties became heavier and his expenses greater, she joined his staff as a full-time salaried employee. He said at the time, "I don't know where I'd get a more efficient or willing worker."[19] Although it has been customary for a portion of members of Congress to put their relatives on the payroll, many carefully avoid this practice, and the Trumans faced some unfavorable publicity during the 1944 presidential campaign when it was revealed that Bess was on the Senate payroll at $4,500 a year.[20] Even though a prominent Republican, Roy Roberts, managing editor of the *Kansas City Star*, came to her defense with the statement that "she earned every penny of it," this did not silence the opposition.[21]

One of the reasons why Senator Truman was reluctant to declare himself a candidate for vice-president in 1944 was his wife's lack of enthusiasm for the added duties that might fall upon her. She attended the Chicago convention that year, and it was not until almost the final day that she realized that the convention might practically force her husband to run. Truman later recalled that the family meeting after the news broke was gloomy.[22]

As wife of the vice-president, Mrs. Truman faced her new duties and responsibilities bravely. Still living in a small apartment, the Trumans could not entertain on the scale that might be expected of a vice-president if this officer were furnished an appropriate residence with an ample expense allowance for entertaining. (It took until 1974 for Congress to provide the vice-president with an official home.) The Trumans, however, entered the social whirl of Washington society with a vigor that astonished society reporters. As *Time* put it: "The amiable Missourian with the touch of country in his voice and manner had conquered a schedule that had . . . Capitol Society writers breathless."[23]

When the death of President Roosevelt suddenly transported the Trumans to the White House, the new responsibilities weighed heavily upon both of them at first. Bess Truman early determined that she would not try to emulate the example of Eleanor Roosevelt. Instead she preferred to operate behind the scenes. She assisted both her husband and her daughter in writing their memoirs but did not choose to do writing for the public on her own. She disappointed the women's press corps by refusing to hold press conferences of the type that Eleanor Roosevelt held. She performed all of her duties as hostess of the White House faithfully with great consideration for the staff, but beyond this she held that her primary responsibilities were to protect and safeguard her husband's peace of mind, to take care of her elderly mother who moved into the White House with them, and to see that her daughter completed her college education and her voice training without too much interference from the complications that face White House living.

One such complication for Truman, as he climbed the political ladder, was his daughter's safety. The Kansas City area was notorious for its kidnappings. The kidnapping of City Manager Henry F. McElroy's daughter was one of the tragic events, and it ultimately led to her suicide. Margaret Truman took the necessary precautions in good grace, got along well with her guards, and did not let them interfere with her enjoyment of life.

The Truman family was a close-knit model American family. Harry Truman was exceedingly proud of his wife and daughter. They saw him through many difficult situations; neither left him alone to fight his battles, did not nag, and let him enjoy his poker parties with his friends.

In the opinion of some of her contemporaries, Bess married beneath her station. Probably at the start of her marriage, even she did not realize Harry's capacity for growth. From Harry's standpoint, he always regarded himself lucky in having Bess for a wife. His loyalty to her was unshakeable. From living with her and her family, he learned tact, diplomacy, forbearance, some of the social graces, and pride. Bess was not destined to be a second Eleanor Roosevelt in the White House, but she exercised a strong restraining influence in favor of dignified behavior and of actions that protected the public interest. As Truman moved higher in politics, she met each new responsibility with grace and consideration for others. Above all she strove to protect the peace of mind of her husband.

chapter 8 | FIRST CANDIDACY, 1922

> *In politics if thou wouldst mix,*
> *And mean thy fortunes be,*
> *Bear this in mind: Be deaf and blind,*
> *Let great folks hear and see.*
> —Robert Burns, "At the Globe Tavern"

Failing in the clothing business, on which he had counted so much—envisioning, perhaps, a repetition of the army canteen success—Truman was faced with the question of what to do next. His savings were gone, he was deeply in debt, and he refused to go into bankruptcy. Whatever else happened, he did not want to return to the farm. The opportunity for some radical change in his life was at hand. The impetus for change came in the form of an offer, or at least encouragement (accounts vary), to file for the Democratic nomination for county judge from the Eastern District of Jackson County.

One story has it that Jim Pendergast, one of Truman's former fellow artillery officers (son of Michael Pendergast and nephew of Tom), took the initiative. Jim came to the Truman store and tried to interest Harry in running for public office. Although Truman claimed that he did not see Tom Pendergast until years afterward, he certainly knew about the Pendergast political organization.[1] His father had attended state party conventions with Jackson County delegations headed by Tom Pendergast. The local press had mentioned Tom prominently since 1900 when he was appointed superintendent of streets by Mayor James Reed. On the other hand, in an interview granted in 1945, Jim Pendergast said that Truman was introduced to Tom in 1922.[2] This account seems correct in view of the procedures that Tom Pendergast followed; he insisted on personally evaluating the men whom his organization backed.[3]

Tom Pendergast in 1922 was not nationally publicized as a city boss. Locally, he was known as the head of a delivery service, ex-saloon keeper, ex-hotel owner, head of Ready-Mixed Concrete Company, obsessive frequenter of racetracks, former alderman in Kansas City, and factional leader of the Democratic party in the depressed residential areas of West Bottoms and the north side of Kansas City since 1910.

The Pendergast Kansas City machine of the 1920s and 1930s was enormously efficient in bringing together diverse groups and keeping them satisfied. Kansas City business magnates wanted franchises, tax favors, deposits of public funds, and a booming city with an ambitious public works program to help attract new business to the city. Underworld interests wanted police protection for their gambling, bootlegging, and vice activities. Underprivileged minority groups wanted jobs, better housing, small favors in the form of food, clothing, and rent money, and protection against police brutality and administrative red tape. Middle-income groups wanted lower taxes and better streets, better police protection, better schools and parks, and more libraries and museums. Tom Pendergast was very effective in his public relations, and he appeared to be rendering these varied and, at times, somewhat contradictory services. He was a worthy contemporary of Boss Frank Hague of New Jersey, Boss Edward J. Kelly of Chicago, Boss E. M. Crump of Memphis, and Boss Edward J. Flynn of the Bronx.[4] In Rogow and Lasswell's classification, he was clearly a gain politician.[5] Pendergast came from a poor Irish family, and in his earliest days he was deprived of various comforts, an adequate income, and economic opportunities. The formula as Rogow and Lasswell put it is as follows: "If the deprivation has been experienced mainly with reference to welfare values, power in corrupt form will be employed in behalf of material advantage." This formula fits Pendergast's case exactly; he used his political power for his well-being, wealth, and skill and that of his family, his friends, and his political constituents. Politics was a form of commercial enterprise, and according to his moral code, he was expected to exploit politics for gain and to acquire a fortune for himself and his family.

In 1922 Tom Pendergast was emerging as a potential leader of the Democratic party in Kansas City. Physically, he was the archetype of the political boss who had thrived in American cities since the middle of the nineteenth century—heavy, like Tweed, with an oversized head, thick neck, and large fists, which he used occasionally when he thought physical violence would make his point. His power over the party had been challenged from time to time by the rival Rabbit faction led by Joe Shannon, who regarded himself as an authority on Thomas Jefferson.[6]

Tom had led the Goats since his brother, Jim, had retired from the city council in 1910. This faction used all of the devices of the traditional American boss system, including patronage appointments, friendly services for the poor, partisan administration, close links with the underworld, assessment of officeholders for campaign funds, special favors for the utilities, and the persecution of businesses that were unfriendly by tax harassment or other methods. The twelve years between 1910 and 1922 had not brought great notoriety to the Pendergast faction except in the local press. It had not been in special favor with the Wilson administration in Washington since Senator James Reed, associated with the faction, had been rabidly isolationist and anti-Wilson. The prohibition era cramped the style of some of the local politicians, but others turned to bootlegging. Tom Pendergast, however, had sold his saloon before prohibition went into effect and was concentrating on selling cement and running his many other business enterprises, which included a racetrack and some racehorses. In contrast to his brother, Jim, he did not hesitate to use corrupt election practices to win votes.[7]

A person going into politics in Jackson County in the 1920s had to face the fact that underworld influences would be active—at least in Kansas City—and that corrupt businessmen and corrupt politicians were doing business with each other. He could enter politics as a crusader as Joseph W. Polk had done in St. Louis in 1900 or as Rabbi Samuel Mayerberg was to do in Kansas City in 1932, or he could make his peace with the party leaders and turn his head the other way when he saw something he did not like. Harry Truman had to make this decision. He did not believe that Jim Pendergast, a young Kansas City attorney and a fellow legionnaire, was corrupt. The most prominent Goat at the time was Senator James Reed, a noted lawyer, orator, isolationist, and a leading citizen of Missouri. Jim Pendergast's uncle, Tom, had a well-deserved reputation for shrewdness; he liked to pick winners in political contests as well as in horse races. The Pendergasts had a mixed record in four decades of politics. Winners among their supporters included Senator Reed, a long list of congressmen who made distinguished records in Washington, and numerous local officials, including Judge Robert Mize, a friend of the Trumans, who had done well on the county court. On the other hand, local scandals marred the picture.

The Pendergast machine did not reach the peak of its power until after 1925, and its decline began only after Tom Pendergast's conviction for income tax evasion in 1939. During the fourteen years of its maximum strength, it suffered a number of setbacks, but in the main it held a tight grip on the affairs of Kansas City and Jackson County. Only in the Missouri statehouse did it suffer reverses when Governor Stark turned on it in 1937 and took a leading role in the anti-Pendergast drive.

In the earlier years, Democratic reform governors and Republican governors had no interest in dealing with the Pendergasts. In Kansas City and Jackson County, also, Goat rule was intermittent. Only in the northern wards and in the bottomlands next to the river was the Pendergast control continuous for some fifty years. In 1922 a Republican reform governor was elected, and the Goats were out of power as far as Kansas City police and the Jackson County court were concerned. City and county patronage dried up, and the gambling, bootlegging, and vice interests suffered accordingly.

Tom Pendergast's control was built on a series of alliances with other Democratic factions and, at times, with some Republican elements that he used in primaries to defeat his Democratic rivals. He was a typical political broker who could deliver favors to Kansas City businessmen, the underworld interests, middle-income groups, and the poor people and minority groups. While the price he asked for favors granted was high, inefficient and costly government, the beneficiaries, many not fully aware of the cost of the services they were receiving, did not complain, at least not too loudly. The city was growing rapidly, and the many new services needed were being provided. Reformers pointed out the irregularities and the enormity of the maladministration, but the businessmen and the modest home owners would not listen. Only when Tom was in prison and no longer held political power did the businessmen and the substantial citizens respond to the pleas of the reformers. Only a few in Kansas City would—or could—condemn Truman for not leading the reform movement.

The city of Independence was a quiet town. It was not regarded as a hangout for underworld characters nor did it appear to Truman that he was making any compromises with his ethical principles when he entered into eastern Jackson County politics. He did not need a large campaign fund, because the electorate was small (around fifteen thousand) and could be reached by energetic face-to-face campaigning. There was no record of election irregularities in eastern Jackson County. Harry, of course, knew that the Goats were not entirely ethical, but he followed the Christian motto, "He that is without sin among you, let him first cast a stone."

The office of county judge was administrative, not judicial, the equivalent to the office of county commissioner in most other American counties. Three county judges were to be elected, with the presiding judge chosen for four years from the county as a whole. The judge from the Western District was chosen for two years from Kansas City and the judge from the Eastern District for the same term from the balance of the county, which was primarily rural. Although the two districts were unequal in population (Kansas City had 85 percent of the total population of the county in 1920), the powers of the three judges were the same, except for certain supervisory duties exercised by the presiding judge.

The support of two other persons was important to Truman in his first try for elective office. One was Colonel William M. Southern, editor and proprietor of the *Independence Examiner*, the local newspaper. Southern was influential in the county, with a large following of readers who were attracted by his weekly Sunday school column. His daughter, May, had married Bess Wallace's brother, George, so Harry felt free to appeal to him for advice. The shrewd editor advised him not to go into politics.[8] As one account put it, the colonel said: "I abused him like a pickpocket for an hour. I told him all the bad effects of life of chronic campaigning could

have on a man. . . . At any rate, Harry Truman went away from the newspaper office as certain as he had been when he went there that he was going
to run for public office."[9] Once the decision was made, the editor went to
Nicholas Phelps, Tom Pendergast's representative in Independence, and
told him that Harry was going to run. Southern must have given a good
recommendation because Phelps backed Truman for the nomination at the
meeting of the eastern Jackson County Goat faction.

Also figuring in the preliminaries to the contest was Colonel Edward M.
Stayton, an active Democrat who had been a fellow artillery officer of
Truman in World War I. At a casual meeting of several former officers at
which Truman was not present, Truman's name was brought up as having
been a splendid officer. Stayton remarked that Truman was too valuable to
be allowed to settle down on a farm and suggested that an effort be made to
nominate him for judge of the Eastern District. Stayton took active charge
of the matter and one account claims that Truman was backed without
either his accepting or declining.[10]

On March 8, 1922, an article appeared in the *Independence Examiner*
relating that a group of some five hundred ex-service men from all parts of
the county had met at Lee's Summit, where Truman was presented by
Colonel Stayton as a suitable candidate. The article added that the Truman
announcement was made without any organization or factional endorsement.

The headline for the local paper on April 21, 1922, ran: "Want the
County Court: Politicians Must Control Judges to Hold County Purse
Strings." Truman, listed as one of the candidates, was described in this
way: "He has consulted no political director and has already announced
and has received much promise of support." Then, on May 12, 1922, the
Independence Examiner reported that the Men's Rural Jackson County
Democratic Club had an enthusiastic meeting at the chamber of commerce
rooms at which some two hundred persons present endorsed Truman for
the nomination as county judge. Frank Wallace, Bess's brother, was the
secretary of the club.

It was not until the June 13 issue of the *Independence Examiner* that it
was made clear that Truman would have Pendergast's endorsement: "Harry
Truman of Independence is credited with the Goat support, although he
came out without consulting either the Goats or the Rabbits. The Jackson
County Democratic Club, which is said to be a Goat organization, has endorsed Mr. Truman."

In the field against Truman were four candidates. His chief opponent,
E. E. Montgomery, a banker from Blue Springs, was backed by the Rabbit
faction, which also had a strong candidate for presiding judge. If the Rabbits
won the eastern and the presiding judgeships, they would take over control
of the county patronage. According to some accounts, Tom had promised

to support Montgomery. The next most important contender was T. W. Parrent, who had the backing of the Bulger faction. Miles Bulger, originally a Goat elected to the county court in 1914 and 1918, was rabidly partisan in his administration, and the county court acquired a reputation for inefficiency, favoritism, and corruption. Bulgerism became synonymous with bad administration of the county roads and institutions. Suffering from delusions of grandeur, Bulger became so arrogant that he tried to set himself up independently of the Goats who had originally backed him. Having had two terms as presiding judge, he was not eligible for another term. He hoped to retain some power through his supporter, Parrent. James V. Compton, running as an independent, had received an appointment to the court but had not been elected to that position. George W. Shaw was also an independent. With so many candidates running, some with fairly strong backing, the race was bound to be close.

While Truman was supported by the rural Jackson County Democratic organization, he never belonged to the Kansas City Democratic machine, which had been attacked on a number of occasions for election scandals and police corruption. The distinction between the two parts of the Pendergast organization is important, because Truman did not regard himself as responsible for what happened inside Kansas City.

Truman desperately sought to win the nomination. His haberdashery business was clearly on the way to failure, and he had to win this nomination or seek some other method for earning a livelihood. As in every campaign he waged later, he put all his energies into winning, rallying his own and his wife's relatives scattered throughout the county, lining up friends of his in the American Legion and the Reserve Officers Corps, and appealing as a former farmer and a member of the Farm Bureau to the rural vote in the county. As a Mason, he quietly pushed his candidacy among his fellow Masons. He also cultivated religious and minority groups. As a Baptist he appealed to Protestant groups, while his war record of friendliness with the Irish Catholics in his company helped him with the Catholics. His position on race relations had not as yet been sharply defined but it did not appear that he had offended any minority group. Jacobson, his business partner, was a Jew, and Truman could not be accused of anti-Semitism. His family had a good reputation for fair dealings with black household and farm employees. Although his ancestors' record on the slavery issue and reconstruction policies was that of southern sympathizers, the question of civil rights was not brought up during the campaign. Kansas City, unlike Chicago, had not had a recent race riot.

During the campaign, picnics were held at various locations at which all of the candidates were invited to make brief speeches. The chief burden, however, was on the individual candidate who had to get around the county, show himself, shake hands, and make friends on street corners and in shops. "Harry is the greatest personal campaigner I've ever seen," Mayor Roger Sermon of Independence said. "He'd go up to the first man he saw in a country town, hold out his hand and say, 'I'm Harry Truman, and I'm running for . . .'"[11] According to the local newspaper, Truman made the briefest of acceptance speeches, saying he was willing to run for county judge.[12] In 1957 Truman told an interviewer, "That was my first public speech," and he called it a complete failure since he felt that he should have said more.[13]

In the middle of July, the big political picnic of the summer was held at Oak Grove, a small town near the eastern border of Jackson County. "The crowd in the afternoon was estimated at two thousand persons. . . . By 9 o'clock it was estimated that at least four thousand persons were present."[14] All five candidates for the Democratic nomination for judge spoke for a few minutes each. Candidates sometimes obtained an immediate response from the audience. Both Truman and Parrent briefly addressed the Mount Washington Democratic Club, and the club then endorsed Truman for the nomination.[15]

On the way home from a political meeting, Truman stopped at Lee's Summit and, as reported by the local paper, "was talking to some friends on the Farmers' Bank corner. Some one suggested a speech, another rushed for a truck and in three minutes Mr. Truman was making a speech to about a hundred men and in five minutes this crowd increased to about two hundred. We did not hear the speech, but all say it was a good one."[16] Truman recalled the campaign in this way:

> I had an old Dodge roadster which was a very rough rider. I kept two bags of cement in the back of it so it would not throw me through the windshield while driving on our terrible county roads. I went into every township—there were seven of them—and into every precinct in the county in the Eastern District. Luckily I had relatives all over the county, and through my wife I was related to many more.[17]

We have no full record of what Truman actually said at these early meetings. The *Kansas City Star* and the *Independence Examiner* carried accounts of the Oak Grove meeting, which are substantially in agreement:

[Truman] then plunged into what he planned to do as county judge. He said water bound macadam roads, good a generation ago, were not good now and the money of the county should not be wasted on them. He favored grading and oiling dirt roads. First of all he favored a budget which would plan the distribution of the road fund and all the other funds and a law which would permit the spending of the taxes collected this year during the next year and thus save borrowing money and running the county into debt.[18]

One report states that Truman spent $524.80 on his primary campaign but did not reveal how this money was spent and how it was raised.[19] The

Independence Examiner implied that money on election day was spent to buy drinks, although prohibition was then in effect and serving drinks to voters was against the Corrupt Practices Act.[20] Truman said about the use of money in elections: "One rule that I did make in the beginning in politics was that I would have nothing to do with money. I just wouldn't handle it. I wouldn't collect it. I wouldn't distribute it. I wouldn't have anything in the world to do with it. And the boss politicians respected me because of this, although they never did understand it."[21]

Truman's strenuous campaigning paid off. With the votes divided five ways, he won by a plurality of 279 votes over Montgomery, his closest rival. His percentage of the total Democratic primary vote was only 35.6. Of the 11,871 votes cast, Truman won 4,230 (35.6 percent), Montgomery won 3,951 (33.3 percent), Parrent gained 2,172 (18.3 percent), Shaw 1,437 (12.1 percent), and Compton 81 (0.7 percent).

The primary was so close that Montgomery considered asking for a recount, but finally decided against it. Rabbit leader Joe Shannon thought that it was an outrage that a respected banker had been defeated by a "busted merchant." Thus Truman started on his political career by a mere handful of votes. By a narrow margin, he had demonstrated vote-getting abilities. Bess did not care for campaigning, but Harry found the social contacts stimulating and exciting. He would now have a chance to show how well he could run in a general election and, if he won that test, he could show how well he could do in public office. His entire political career may well have hung on those 279 votes.

While contemporary newspapers seemed to think that Democratic candidates for local office were in no danger in Jackson County, Truman continued to campaign strenuously, this time against his Republican opponent, Arthur L. Wilson. Nearly every night for about a month before the election, Truman spoke at meetings. He reiterated his promises to provide a businesslike administration of county affairs, reassuring his listeners that there would be "no more county warrants when there was no money to pay, roads by contract to the lowest bidder, enough deputies to do the work and no more, a dollar's worth of work for a dollar."[22]

Truman's Democratic running mates were Elihu W. Hayes, candidate of the Rabbit faction for presiding judge, and Henry F. McElroy, candidate of the Goat faction in the Western District of Jackson county. McElroy was a successful Kansas City real estate operator, who later became the controversial city manager of Kansas City and an important figure in the Pendergast machine. Until the late 1930s, McElroy was to overshadow Truman in the news and in the local party organization. In the end, however, McElroy died in disgrace under charges of misappropriation of public funds and income tax evasion. Truman's association with the Tom Pendergast organization was to present him with problems that would cast a shadow over his subsequent career.

Among the important forces in the campaign was the Ku Klux Klan, whose organizers after World War I appealed with some success to anti-foreigner, anti-Catholic, anti-Jewish, and anti-Negro prejudices in the North as well as in the South. Their appeals were disguised as forms of patriotism and religious fundamentalism. Cross burnings in Jackson County were used as a form of political pressure during campaigns. As a Protestant with a well-established American heritage, Truman was expected to attract nativist votes, but, according to his sister, he tried to dodge the Klan issue.[23]

Truman's alleged relation to the Ku Klux Klan in 1922 was to be brought up twenty-two years later when he was a candidate for vice-president. The Hearst papers claimed in October 1944 that they had affidavits showing that Truman had joined the Klan in 1922.[24] The charge was denied by Truman who said repeatedly that he never took the oath.[25] Edgar Hinde, a close personal friend, asserted that Truman considered joining the Klan, but when he learned that if he did he could not offer jobs to Catholics, he refused to join. Truman's loyalty to the Catholics who had served under him during World War I was such that he could not think of taking such a pledge.[26]

On election day, the Klan in Jackson County distributed sample ballots which in effect urged the voters not to vote for Truman. Opposite his name on the sample ticket appeared the following: "Church affiliation, Protestant, endorsed by Tom and Joe."[27] The two endorsers were Tom Pendergast and Joe Shannon, both Roman Catholics whose recommendations should be rejected by Klansmen.

Hayes, McElroy, and Truman were all elected judges of the county court on November 7, 1922. Hayes won 52 percent of the votes for the county as a whole. McElroy won with 52 percent of the votes for the Western District, and Truman received 59 percent of the votes in the Eastern District. Some 9,063 voters cast their ballots for Truman, and 6,314 voted for Wilson, giving Truman a plurality of 2,649 votes.[28] The aggregate vote for congressional candidates showed that the swing of the political pendulum was back toward the Democrats from the low point in 1920.

Harry Truman, at the age of thirty-eight, had passed the first two hurdles to a political career. Not an effective orator, he had shown, nevertheless, that he had voter appeal. A person who does not have striking political gifts that are clear to all must work hard and take one step at a time. Even sophisticated Americans have made mistakes about public men. For example, it took such a brilliant columnist as Walter Lippmann more than two decades to recognize that Franklin Delano Roosevelt was a great politician with unusual leadership ability. How long would it take for observers less gifted than Lippmann to recognize the potentialities of the modest ex-bank clerk, ex-farmer, ex-soldier, ex-merchant who had just been elected county judge from the least populous district in Jackson County? (As a matter of fact, Lippman was to underestimate greatly Truman's leadership qualities later.)

Enough had been revealed about the operations of the Pendergast machine in Kansas City to warn Truman that he was stepping into a situation that would confront him with moral dilemmas. He regarded his own moral principles and conduct as puritanical. He told the voters he would follow the law about letting contracts on a competitive basis, and he intended to live up to that promise. His campaign had not involved excessive expenditures or any irregular election practices. The Goat machine had not asked him for any favors that he regarded as contrary to the public interest.

What did Truman's nomination and election mean to Boss Tom Pendergast? The boss had been out in the cold as far as county patronage was concerned. At first, under the Bulger regime, he had had patronage and lucrative contracts for his companies and his friends, but Bulger had turned on him and deprived him of both jobs and graft. Under Bulger's own regime the county government continued to acquire a bad image, and people thought of it as inefficient, wasteful, extravagant, and corrupt. McElroy and Truman might improve the popular image of the county government, and Pendergast was willing to forgo certain contracts if he could get the county patronage. His candidates were not all crooks. An officeholder who could build up a reputation for honesty and efficiency was very useful to the machine, particularly when bond issues were coming up for a referendum vote. A boss could not be too greedy and still expect to survive. Francis Wilson, his candidate for governor in 1928 and 1932, insisted vehemently that Tom Pendergast would never make any improper demands on him.[29] So, doubtless, thought Truman in 1922.

chapter 9 | POLITICAL APPRENTICESHIP, 1923–1924

In statesmanship get the formalities right, never mind about the moralities.
                    —Mark Twain, *Pudd'nhead Wilson's New Calendar*

The position Truman was to fill as one of the judges in the three-man county court gave him an opportunity to show what he could do as a budget analyst, an administrator of public works, a personnel director and patronage dispenser for the Eastern District, and an organizer of electoral support for huge bond-issue referenda. It is obvious that Boss Tom Pendergast would come to value the patronage and bond-issue promotion most highly. If the boss could get the public to approve bond issues, he knew what he wanted to do with the money from those issues. He would get jobs and graft for his followers. Judge Truman was not as flexible in administering county affairs as Judge Henry F. McElroy later proved to be in handling city affairs as city manager, but the voters' trust in Truman was to rise while that in McElroy was to fall. Truman could help Boss Pendergast get funds for the city as well as for the county.

Truman and McElroy worked together during their two-year term on the county court. Coming from a larger constituency and enjoying greater prestige as a businessman, McElroy gained the reputation with the *Kansas City Star* as being the "dominant figure of the court and its policy."[1] On some occasions, he took a supercilious attitude toward his younger fellow judge. Jackson County had two courthouses, one in Independence and the other in Kansas City. McElroy tried to move all county business to the Kansas City building but met resistance. As he explained to a reporter, "I tried to get it moved when I was in the county court, but a lot of little fellows around Independence Square made such a howl that the move failed."[2] Later on McElroy was to acquire a reputation for taking despotic, strong-willed action on public matters.

The two-year term was too brief to accomplish great changes, but Judges Truman and McElroy laid the ground for later developments. They had several jurisdictional battles to win before they could make a good public record. One concerned the right of the court to manage county institutions. A state law passed in 1919 had put the control of county institutions in the hands of the circuit judges. Truman and McElroy hired an able lawyer, John T. Barker, to challenge the constitutionality of this legislation. Barker won the case before the Supreme Court, and the county court established its control over county institutions.[3]

Another jurisdictional battle was waged within the state government over the powers of the county court. Miles Bulger, who had been on the county court for two terms and then was elected state senator, had succeeded in sponsoring a bill that provided for the transfer of road work supervision from the county court to the county highway engineer in Jackson County. The Goats waged a strong fight against the bill, and the Republican governor, Arthur Hyde, vetoed it on the ground that it was special legislation and therefore was unconstitutional.[4]

When the new officials took over, county finances were in a deplorable state. The practice of operating on tax anticipation warrants meant that it was difficult to ascertain the exact condition of the finances at any given time. Different experts placed the deficit when Truman and McElroy took office as between $800,000 and $1.2 million, an amount the new court was reported as reducing by half during 1923. McElroy later became known for his dishonest bookkeeping, but as county judge he had practically no opportunity to manipulate the county books. (The county clerk kept the books.) The finances of the county for 1924 were not complete when McElroy and Truman had to stand for reelection.

Since both McElroy and Truman wanted to make records for themselves, they hired two engineers as consultants in order to place county road building on a sound basis. Colonel Stayton, who had had a role in discovering Truman, and L. R. Ash were selected to survey the roads and to make recommendations.[5] They began a survey, which was completed after Colonel Stayton was reappointed in 1927. Truman wrote about his own efforts in this matter:

I also became completely familiar with every road and bridge in the county. About that time the State Highway Commission had begun the construction of a Missouri road system by getting right of ways across the county for the state, and I soon became acquainted with the state system and what the Commission had in view for the western end of the state.[6]

In performing his function as a personnel director, Truman admitted that in making appointments, partisan and factional considerations were of prime importance. In other words, Tom Pendergast passed on appointments made in the Eastern District. Truman insisted, however, that he demanded service of all appointees. Those who failed to render proper service were dismissed.

According to the *Independence Examiner*, the two Democratic factions had agreed to handle county patronage belonging to Kansas City on a fifty-fifty basis, but no such agreement was made for the Eastern District.[7] Other acounts claim that Truman's candidacy and election were in violation of that agreement.[8] When the new court organized in January 1923, McElroy and Truman, both Goats, stood together against Judge Hayes (a Rabbit) and promptly took all of the jobs.[9] This failure to divide the patronage between the two factions was to contribute to the defeat of McElroy and Truman in 1924. When they came up for nomination and reelection, they enjoyed the support of the *Kansas City Star*, most unusual for candidates of the Goat faction.[10] The anti-Pendergast factions in the Eastern District united to support Robert L. Hood, a deputy in the Independence office of the county collector and a member of the Independence City Council. Hood belonged to the Rabbit faction, and he received Bulger's endorsement. Judge Truman received the backing again of the rural Jackson County Democratic Club, a Goat organization. He had proved himself to be a good vote getter, and his performance in office had attracted favorable publicity in the local press, assets of value to his faction of the Democratic party.

The two factions waged vigorous campaigns for their respective candidates. Truman defended the record of the Truman-McElroy court with a detailed account of its economies and improved services, especially in the field of road building and maintenance. The Ku Klux Klan came out openly against Truman in this primary by distributing ballots throughout the district that scratched off Truman's name. The *Independence Examiner* came out strongly for Truman.[11]

In the primary Truman received 6,757 votes and Hood 5,119. Although this was a much larger margin of victory than Truman had won in the 1922 primary, he faced the threat of a bolt in the general election because of the bitterness of the Rabbits at their defeat and their charges of violation of the fifty-fifty agreement.[12]

Opposing Judge Truman in the general election was Henry W. Rummel, an ex-harness maker and a former deputy marshal, who had won the Republican nomination by a narrow margin. According to Henry Bundschu, a friend and neighbor of the Trumans, fellow war veteran John Miles had asked Bundschu to file for Rummel. Bundschu, a Catholic, later regretted his action because Rummel made a deal with the Klan and with the Shannon faction.[13]

In the general election campaign, Judge Truman continued to defend the record of the court. One speech was reported in these words:

Many in the audience called for Judge Truman, who walked to the front and made a few brief statements as to the way the county affairs had been handled, declaring that he had conducted his work from a business standpoint and said if re-elected the county would be out of debt in two years, when it was $1,250,000 in debt when he went in; he said much of the bad road work was due to lack of harmony between the county court and the county engineer; that he could prove that days of time were wasted in poor repair work and the failure charged up to the court.[14]

The hostility between the Pendergast and Shannon factions persisted during the campaign. It extended to city as well as county affairs and involved a reshuffling of factional alliances. Kansas City ward leader Cas Welsh had deserted the Shannon faction and had come over to the Goats. In addition, the Pendergasts had recruited the organizational skills of James Aylward, a prominent Kansas City lawyer and shrewd politician. Disappointed in the primary election results, some Hood supporters announced that they would not vote for Truman in the general election.[15] With the defeat of either McElroy or Truman, the Shannon faction hoped to end the control of the court by the Pendergast faction.[16]

The election of 1924 marked a low point in the fortunes of the Democratic party nationally. Hopelessly split in its national convention between the wets and drys—those supporting Alfred E. Smith and those supporting William Gibbs McAdoo—the party failed to rally much support for its compromise dark-horse candidate, John W. Davis. These conditions were reflected in Jackson County and Missouri as a whole. Both the state and the county went Republican in the presidential election by a wide margin; President Coolidge received 57 percent of the votes cast in the county.

The Shannon faction outdid itself in cutting the Democratic county candidates. Both McElroy and Truman were defeated, and the Republicans took control of the county court. The election was close in the Eastern District; Truman secured about 48 percent of the total votes cast.[17] But just enough Rabbit voters had scratched his name to bring defeat. This was the only election for public office that Truman ever lost. It was a bitter disappointment to go back to private life at the age of forty, just as he was getting a taste for public office, especially so in the year when his daughter was born, but he took it in good spirit. Henry P. Chiles, a neighbor who worked for Rummel, remembered the episode:

We elected Rummel and I hated it because I was in the same precinct as Harry and Harry lost the precinct. So the next morning after election—I was ashamed of it as I could be, but I stuck to my job (they would have fired me if I hadn't of stayed with them, of course)—I saw Harry coming and I said, "Well, I didn't want to see him this morning." So I crossed over the street and then, just down from the square, he saw me and called me over there, stuck out his hand and said, "Now I want you to understand there's no hard feelings."[18]

It was Truman's ability to take setbacks with equanimity, apparently to hold no grudges, that helped him in his political career. He recognized that today's opponent may be tomorrow's proponent—a philosophy that enabled him to pick up support from a wide variety of sources.

Pendergast machine fortunes in Kansas City were improving during these two years. In 1925, Pendergast favored the passage of the proposed new Kansas City charter, which abolished the cumbersome mayor-bicameral council plan and substituted a council-manager plan with a small non-partisan council of nine, five of whom were to be chosen at large. The plan had the backing of the Kansas City Civic Research Institute, which looked upon it as a way of improving the efficiency, economy, and responsibility of the city government. The director of this institute, Walter Matscheck, had had a hand in drafting the charter. Administrative powers were to be concentrated in the hands of the city manager, who was appointed by the council and was responsible for carrying out council policies. The charter provided for a detailed, itemized budget system, competitive bidding on contracts, a thorough system of accounting, and a merit system for appointments. The plan looked good to the reformers and to the Republicans who controlled the office of mayor at the time; reformers regarded the plan as a panacea that would eliminate graft and inefficiency. Joe Shannon was alarmed by the claims of the reformers and opposed the plan as a danger to organization politicians like himself, but Tom Pendergast thought that it had possibilities that he could not afford to miss.

In a referendum vote with a small number of voters participating, the new charter was adopted by a large margin—37,504 to 8,827.

According to the charter, elections to the council were to be on a nonpartisan basis, with a primary election determining the nominees for the final election. The two major parties did not pay much attention to the nonpartisan provision and both backed party or factional slates.[19] There was no active nonpartisan citizen group, as there was in Cincinnati, Ohio, which could recruit qualified candidates and support them vigorously in the two elections.[20] The Goat and Rabbit factions each had its own candidates. In the primary, the Goats won all of the places for the final election contest against the Republican-backed candidates. By a narrow margin, the Pendergast faction won five of the nine seats on the council in the November 1925 elections. Only five hundred votes separated the lowest Democrat and the unsuccessful fifth Republican. Those sincerely interested in carrying out the spirit of the new charter thus lost their opportunity to do so for some fourteen years. It was not until 1940 that the citizens of Kansas City realized that civic groups had to be well organized in order to win in local politics.

When the new council met, the Pendergast majority seized control, brushed aside all pleas to choose a professional city manager from the outside, and, in accordance with the party caucus, selected Henry F. McElroy as city manager. The new administration was frankly partisan, and its personnel policies openly flaunted the charter merit system provisions from the beginning, paying no attention to the requirements for competitive examinations, the time limit on temporary appointments, and the need for efficiency ratings if promotions were to be based on merit. Its budget, fiscal, and accounting policies also ignored completely the charter provisions, but this was not apparent to the general public for several years, even though Matscheck kept charging that there were gross irregularities.[21] An objective observer from the outside also noted that the charter was being flagrantly disregarded by City Manager McElroy and his partisan assistants.[22]

The appointment of McElroy gave Tom Pendergast a hold on Kansas City government, which he used to further his own business enterprises and to build a party organization based on patronage and spoils administration. It furnished him and the party treasury with large sums of cash taken directly from the public till. It was this organization that soon began to manufacture the tremendous electoral majorities that brought further extensions to Pendergast's power. As Matscheck described it later, "The Pendergast organization wanted to maintain itself in power and as years went on they wanted more and more power, more and more money, more and more people working for it, more and more people on the city payrolls, and all that sort of thing."[23] City Manager McElroy fitted into Pendergast's scheme of affairs and soon found himself so entangled that he could not extricate himself from the mire of corruption, which finally led to the collapse of the Goat organization in 1939. At first, however, McElroy enjoyed the support of the press and the business community, since he parried skillfully the thrusts of Matscheck and other critics.

Firmly established in power in the city, Pendergast turned his attention in the summer and fall of 1926 to regaining power in the county. At this time he enjoyed a public image that was not too unfavorable. He and McElroy had deluded the public into thinking that the city government was solvent and efficient. He could afford to be generous with Rabbit leader Joe Shannon in making up the county ticket. An agreement was reached between the two factions before the August primary, and there was no contest for certain key positions.[24]

The swift takeover of the Kansas City government under the new city manager plan by the Pendergast machine astounded the reformers, but it was obvious to all who cared to face the facts. The Kansas City dailies were explicit in their description of the partisan character of the new administration.[25] McElroy's open defiance of the personnel, budget, and accounting provisions of the new charter were all publicized by the Kansas City Civic Research Institute.[26]

Harry Truman faced a serious moral dilemma: should he continue in politics in Jackson County? The Goat organization did not control the county government at this point, but if it did, the Pendergast machine might make demands upon it. His former colleague on the county court, Judge McElroy, was not withstanding the machine pressure in the city. Could Harry Truman do better in the county? Could he serve the public interest as a member of the Pendergast organization? In four years he was compelled to reassess this situation.

chapter 10 | CHIEF COUNTY ADMINISTRATOR, 1927–1934

The whole of government consists in the art of being honest.
—Thomas Jefferson, *Works*, VI

Willing to return to public life in 1926, the forty-two-year-old Truman had his eyes fixed on the position of county collector. The job paid well—about $25,000 in salary and fees. This income looked quite attractive since Truman still had business debts. One of the Pendergasts, Michael, leader of the Goat faction in the Eastern District, was willing to back Truman for the position, but the consent of Michael's brother, Tom Pendergast, was necessary. Truman had seen the Pendergast takeover of the Kansas City government through the actions of his former colleague on the county court, Judge McElroy, and had to decide whether he wanted to be a party to the same subordination of the county government. He felt that he had to take the chance if he wanted to continue in politics.

Truman made the trip to the Democratic headquarters in Kansas City to see Pendergast. He waited his turn to be ushered into the drab office of the party chieftain, who told him the nomination had been promised to another. Pendergast then offered to support Truman for the position of presiding judge of the county court, an office with a salary of $6,000. Mike Pendergast urged him to hold out for collectorship, but Truman decided to accept support for the presiding judgeship. There was no contest in the primary for this position or for the position of county clerk, for which R. L. Hood, Truman's 1924 rival with Shannon backing, was slated. Truman's problem was to accept this support to win the office but not let machine pressures ruin his reputation and to avoid any connection with the unfavorable publicity that the Goat organization was receiving in the city.

In the campaign, Truman defended the record of the county court during the years he was judge and criticized the record of the Republican-controlled court. He cited specific savings that his court had made. The Republicans answered with comparisons of the 1924 and 1925 expenditures of the court. Truman replied that such comparisons were unfair since there were five elections in 1924 costing $400,000 and no county elections in 1925.[1] In the 1926 election the Democratic party carried Jackson County by a comfortable margin of over fifteen thousand for its candidates. Truman was swept in with the tide, defeating his Republican opponent, Don G. Stewart, by some sixteen thousand votes (nearly 56 percent of the total).[2] There were no charges of irregularities in this election since the Republicans still controlled the election machinery under the Republican governor, Sam Baker, but it was clear that the Pendergast vote-getting machine was gathering momentum for the time when the Democrats would control the election board.

As presiding judge with a four-year term, Truman was in a much better position to show what he could do in public office than he had been in 1923. Actually the county court furnished him a better opportunity than the collectorship would have because it controlled some nine hundred jobs and expenditures that in eight years amounted to more than $60 million. Moreover, he was no longer overshadowed by the dictatorial McElroy. He was, instead, the leading man in county affairs.

When the new county court met, Judge Truman made the following comments to the crowd assembled for the proceedings: "We intend to operate the court for the benefit of the taxpayers. While we were elected as Democrats, we were also elected as public servants. We will appoint all Democrats to jobs appointable, but we are going to see that every man does a full day's work for his pay. In other words, we are going to conduct the county's affairs as efficiently and economically as possible."[3] In reality and although he was the most important official in the county, Truman had difficulty trying to achieve efficiency. He had to share power with thirteen other executive heads over whom he had little financial control. There was no budget system, and accounting practices were antiquated. Even authority for construction and maintenance was divided between the county court and the highway engineer, an elective official.[4] The operation of the disjointed organization was made even more difficult by the patronage demands of the Goat organization and the stigma that could be attached to being a Goat.

Walter Matscheck of the Kansas City Civic Research Institute observed Judge Truman in action during these days, recalling:

I was so convinced that he was an honest, earnest, sincere man that I was very strongly impressed by him. He attended meetings and he sat forward in his chair; he looked sincere—earnest—listened to every word and knew what was going on. He kept himself thoroughly informed. He knew all about the county, as he later did about other things. He always was informed. Here was a man you could talk to that knew what was going on, and knew what ought to be done about it. And we just took advantage of everything we could with him to try to get what we thought, and he thought, generally, should be done.[5]

Road building became the field in which Judge Truman was to make an outstanding reputation. His previous experience as an officer of the court, as a farmer who had to get to market, as a solicitor of auto club member-ships, as an early owner of an automobile, and as president of the National Old Trails Highway Association had made him realize the importance of good roads. In January 1927, the court appointed Colonel E. Stayton and N. T. Veach, Jr., civil engineers, to make a survey of roads in the county, to plan for the future, and to work with the county highway engineer.[6] The two-man commission was bipartisan; Colonel Stayton was a prominent Democrat who had begun such a survey earlier, and Veach was a Repub-lican.

Some five months later this commission made a report outlining a plan for hard roads.[7] It pointed out the unsatisfactory character of the existing water-bound macadam and dirt roads, listing such defects as inadequate drainage, unsafe hill grades and curvatures, poor location, and prohibitive maintenance costs. The report presented a plan for 224 miles of concrete roads to furnish the basis for a modern road system and recommended proposing a $6.5 million bond issue to pay for building it. Judge Truman began at once to make plans for a bond issue. In addition to the $6.5 million for new roads, he included $5 million for a new courthouse and county jail, $500,000 for a county hospital, and $200,000 for a house for retarded children.[8] Because Kansas City was planning some $28 million in bond issues and competition for funds would be great, Judge Truman felt that he had to discuss his plan with Tom Pendergast. Truman later explained the meeting in this way: "I suggested to Tom Pendergast a county bond issue for a new courthouse and 250 miles of roads. Tom said, 'You can't do it. Bulger tried it and every other presiding judge for 20 years.' I told him I could and that I would tell them what I meant to do and the people would vote the bonds. Tom said, 'Go tell the voters anything you want to.' So I got authority from him."[9]

This was an interesting recognition of Pendergast's power. A man who had no official position in the county government apparently had granted authority to proceed with a bond proposal. Truman went ahead with his plans, setting the referendum on the bond issues for May 1928. Judge Tru-man started an intensive speaking tour on behalf of the bond issues. He secured the cooperation of the Kansas City Chamber of Commerce headed by Conrad Mann, his two fellow members of the county court, members of the special highway commission, the Farm Bureau, and various civic organ-izations. He promised that the road contracts would be awarded on the basis of competitive bidding and that the work would be done under the supervision of the bipartisan road commission. Each voter received a folder containing a map on which was marked every road that would be benefited. In addition, each voter knew that the proposed program would cost him annually seven cents for every hundred dollars of assessed valuation on his property.

Truman concentrated his efforts on the bond issues for roads and the hospital, both of which carried. But the issue for the new courthouse and practically all of the Kansas City issues lost. The voters were not quite sure of McElroy's business methods and his Pendergast connections. But Truman scored an important victory, demonstrating his leadership and persuasiveness in a vital area. The result indicated that voters had confidence in his honesty and integrity.[10]

The bond issue election also marked a change in the Kansas City Democratic organization that was to cause Pendergast and McElroy trouble later on. In the north side "Little Italy" district, John Lazia, an enterprising young Italian-American with underworld connections and a jail record, used strong-arm methods to displace Mike Ross, Pendergast's lieutenant in the area. Pendergast did not welcome Lazia at first, but later he accepted him. Lazia's activities soon helped give Kansas City a reputation as a crime center; increasing corruption of the ballot box was also introduced by Lazia.

As soon as the bond issue funds were available, the county court opened competitive bidding for the contracts to build the roads. The first contract was awarded to an out-of-state firm, the American Road Building Company of South Dakota. Shortly after, Tom Pendergast summoned Truman. He had heard about the awards from some local contractors—William D. Boyle, John Pryor, and Bill Ross. Jonathan Daniels records Truman's recollections:

I went and there were all the crooked contractors that caused the scandals under Bulger, Boyle and Pryor and Ross. Tom said, "These boys tell me that you won't give them contracts." "They can get them," I said, "if they are low bidders, but they won't get paid for them unless they come up to specifications." Truman smiles when he remembers Pendergast's reply. "Didn't I tell you boys," he said, "he's the contrariest cuss in Missouri?" After they left, Pendergast told me to go ahead.[11]

Pendergast thus did not insist on favored treatment in the county, as well as in the city, for contracting firms aligned with his organization. His mania for gambling made his greed for ready cash insatiable; perhaps it was easier to make money in the city than in the county. And he might have thought that Truman's reputation for honesty might be useful later on in getting electoral support for city bond issues, whose administration he could control.

Although Truman did not have to stand for reelection in 1928, his two colleagues did. The local papers praised the court and favored continuance of the two judges. One of the papers, the *Independence Examiner*, commented:

The tax payers of the county should recognize the fact that the present county court has done something no other county court has done recently and which is not done in Kansas City and which I understand is not usually done in large counties and cities. It let a quarter of a million dollars in road contracts to the low bidder, regardless of the fact that the home contractors were not the low bidders. It took courage to do that in this county.[12]

Judge Truman showed his continued interest in national politics by attending (as a spectator) the Democratic National Convention, which met in Houston, Texas, nominating Al Smith for president. Truman wrote that he did everything he could to carry the county for Smith. But Herbert Hoover carried it by a 12 percent plurality. Judge Barr, Truman's colleague on the county court, was reelected by a comfortable margin. The *Independence Examiner* commented: "A fine vote of confidence was given Judge Robert E. Barr as precinct after precinct reversed majorities when it came to voting for the candidate for county judge."[13] The work on county roads proceeded as announced under the careful supervision of the consultant engineers, who were asked to make recommendations for a ten-year road program, which they did in July 1930.[14]

When Judge Truman came up for reelection in 1930, a number of events affected his candidacy favorably. First, there was a national trend toward the Democratic party following the stock market crash of 1929. Second, the Republican President and the Republican governor of Missouri were blamed for not taking more vigorous action for the relief of economic suffering. Locally, Tom Pendergast had tightened his control over the government of Kansas City by his stunning victory in the 1930 city council elections. His candidates swept all nine seats by a twenty-five-thousand-vote margin, thus marking the beginning of a series of electoral successes. Walter Matscheck continued his criticism of city financial and personnel administration, but McElroy brushed these criticisms aside and managed to retain considerable support in the business community.[15] During the campaign, the Republicans charged the city manager with favoring the Pendergast business interests; a grand jury took a quick look at the charges and dropped the matter on the grounds of lack of evidence.

Truman brought many positive assets to the contest. Following the death of Mike Pendergast in 1929, Truman had become the leader of the Goat faction in the Eastern District and could count on eleven thousand votes won by legitimate organizational methods and persuasion. More important, he had established an excellent reputation for honesty and accomplishments, which had proved most useful in winning popular support for bond issues. The anti-Pendergast *Kansas City Times* stated that "his important achievements deserve the reward of renomination."[16] There was no contest in the 1930 primary for the presiding judgeship of Jackson County; Joe

Shannon had made his peace with Tom Pendergast in order to win support for his congressional candidacy. When Shannon appealed to Truman for support, Truman forgot his earlier grievance against the Rabbits and worked wholeheartedly for Shannon's nomination—another example of Truman's refusal to hold grudges. He realized that he might need Shannon's help in the future.

Judge Truman campaigned on the impressive record he had made. In his opening speech, he "reviewed the work of the present county court and suggested that it was on this record he asked for reelection and let it go at that."[17] Toward the end of the campaign, the *Star* wrote:

For presiding judge of the county court—Harry S. Truman, Democrat. Judge Truman has been extraordinarily efficient in supervising the expenditure of the 6½ million dollar bond fund on county roads; not a suspicion of graft has developed. He has been an earnest advocate of simplified county government and regional planning. His opponent, Herman K. Ritterhoff, is a high class man, but Judge Truman deserves re-election on his own record.[18]

During the campaign, Truman used radio for the first time, broadcasting at least two speeches toward the end of October.[19]

In the election he received 108,509 votes; the Republican candidate, Ritterhoff, a retired Bell Telephone Company executive, won 50,650.[20] The sizable majority of 58,000 was the product of both national developments in the economic and political fields and local developments in party efficiency.

So impressive was his victory that a few days later the *Odessa Democrat* suggested Truman for governor.[21] (Odessa is a small town in Lafayette County, immediately east of Jackson County.) A few months later the *Kansas City Star* mentioned the fact that some of Truman's friends had been promoting him for the governorship.[22] Truman revealed his political ambitions by getting James F. Ruffin, a lawyer, to open a Truman-for-Governor Club in Springfield. Representatives from fifteen counties cooperated, but this was not enough rural support, and the Pendergast endorsement went to Francis M. Wilson, who had already demonstrated in 1928 that he had a large rural following.

When Truman began his second term as presiding judge, he was vitally concerned with relieving economic hardships caused by the Depression. Unemployment was increasing, bread lines were forming, and Truman, anxious to take positive steps to provide jobs, pushed ahead with the plans to complete the road system, to provide for a new county courthouse in Kansas City, to remodel the existing courthouse in Independence, and to construct a detention home. The county court proposed bond issues totaling some $8 million for these purposes to be voted on in May 1931. City Manager McElroy had an even more ambitious program for Kansas City, which included a new city hall, an auditorium, a new police building, city road work, parks, playgrounds, and a new waterworks system. The proposed Kansas City bond issues totaled $32 million. This time Pendergast was anxious to link the county and city proposals since the voters had shown such confidence in the county road program in 1928.

Truman cooperated fully with the Kansas City Chamber of Commerce, the Ten Year Plan Committee of Kansas City, and other organizations in addressing rallies and making radio talks on behalf of the $40 million bond issues. He was part of a team of fourteen speakers who waged a strenuous campaign, arguing that the building program would furnish many jobs in depression-ridden Kansas City and Jackson County.

All proposals carried by a four-to-one margin. The need for jobs, the well-organized promotional campaign, and the growing efficiency of the Pendergast organization as a vote-producing mechanism were factors in this victory. The vote on the bond issues was the largest ever cast in a special election. Pendergast's support of Truman's policy of honest administration in the county had helped win over the voters of Kansas City to supporting bond issues. The Jackson County and Kansas City public works construction program attracted wide attention. William Allen White, renowned editor of the *Emporia Gazette*, praised it highly for furnishing "jobs and useful and beautiful public improvements" instead of soup kitchens.[23]

In planning the new courthouse, Truman made a twenty-four-thousand-mile automobile tour at his own expense to study the architecture of public buildings, stopping at Shreveport, Houston, Denver, Racine, Milwaukee, Buffalo, Brooklyn, and Lincoln. He was most impressed with the work of the architect of the courthouse at Shreveport, Edward Neild, and he hired him as consulting engineer. The Jackson County construction program proceeded without any scandals. Truman adhered to his practice of competitive bidding on contracts and careful supervision by the bipartisan commission. He was personally interested in every detail, including the dress uniform to be depicted in the equestrian statue of Andrew Jackson in front of the building. He hired Charles Keck, famous for his statute of Stonewall Jackson in Charlottesville, Virginia, as the sculptor.

Although 1932 was a year of great triumphs for the Goats, it was also a year of ominous warnings. Tom Pendergast reached the height of his power as a political leader, but at the same time he experienced some deterioration in his health, his wealth, and his reputation as a political seer.

Tom Pendergast's loyalty to former Senator Jim Reed led to the latter's presentation as a favorite son at the Democratic National Convention. Reed had no chance for the presidential nomination, but his candidacy as a favorite son enabled Tom to do some bargaining with the Roosevelt forces. Pendergast agreed with Jim Farley to release a few delegates to Roosevelt on each roll call so that Roosevelt might seem to be gaining. This happened according to schedule, and Farley felt indebted to Pendergast.[24]

Truman was not a member of the Missouri delegation to the convention, and he said later that he did not like Reed because of the way Reed had treated Woodrow Wilson. At the time, however, Truman, as a spectator, participated in the cheering for Reed. It was part of the game.

The governorship came up in 1932 as did the election of congressmen. The circumstances in this election were unusual: the 1930 census had reduced the Missouri delegation from sixteen to thirteen. Republican Governor Henry S. Caulfield had vetoed the reapportionment bill on the ground that the Democratic legislature had gerrymandered the districts, necessitating the election of all thirteen congressmen at large from the entire state. Pendergast was to reap considerable advantage from this development.

The election of the congressmen at large meant that the endorsement of the Kansas City organization would go a long way toward ensuring victory in the primary. Although Jackson County had only 10 percent of the state's population, it had over 22 percent of the Democratic primary vote. If a candidate had other strength, a Goat endorsement would supply the winning margin. In spring 1932, many candidates for the Democratic nomination for Congress trekked to Tom Pendergast's office. Of the ten candidates who received the endorsement of the boss, nine were elected, and the tenth came close.[25]

The matter of the governorship also developed favorably for Tom Pendergast. When Francis Wilson died after winning the gubernatorial nomination with Goat endorsement, the state committee met in Jefferson City and selected, at Pendergast's instigation, a relatively unknown circuit judge, Guy B. Park of Platte County.[26] Park was swept into office in the 1932 landslide, giving Tom Pendergast a governor who was anxious to listen to his advice on appointments and other matters of interest to the organization. In fact, the Missouri statehouse was soon called "Uncle Tom's Cabin."[27]

But roses have thorns. Especially prickly to Tom in 1932 was the defeat of his candidate for the Democratic nomination for U.S. senator, William Howell of Kansas City, a law partner of former Senator Jim Reed. Howell was defeated by Bennett C. Clark of St. Louis, a son of Champ Clark, former Speaker of the U.S. House. Clark, campaigning on an anti-Pendergast platform, blasted the corruption of Kansas City politics. With strong support from St. Louis and the outstate counties, Clark overcame the tremendous advantage Pendergast's candidate had in Jackson County.[28] In this year, Pendergast still lacked control of the election machinery.

Clark's defeat of Howell was serious but not as ominous as the rumblings in Tom's own bailiwick of Kansas City. Since John Lazia replaced Mike Ross, Tom had faced new problems. Lazia's theory had been that he would control the local underworld activities and keep violent and dangerous out-of-town characters away from the respectable citizens of Kansas City. When City Manager McElroy, by court order, won the home rule of the police in 1932, Lazia took over the recruitment of the police force from among his friends, some of them ex-convicts.[29]

Lazia's connections with the underworld were in part responsible for the scandalous episode of June 17, 1933, the so-called Union Station massacre. Frank Nash, an escaped convict, was captured in Hot Springs, Arkansas, by federal agents and local officers and was being returned to the federal prison at Leavenworth, Kansas. Lazia and others developed a plan to free Nash when he was taken from the train at Kansas City. Three out-of-town gunmen were selected for the job. The lawmen refused to cooperate, and the gangsters opened fire, killing four officers and Nash and wounding two other officers. Apparently the police were unable to apprehend the killers, although one of them was wounded and got medical attention in Kansas City. Lazia then arranged for the killers to leave the city unnoticed. The FBI investigation of the case showed Lazia's involvement.[30]

Lazia was already in difficulty with the federal tax authorities. On his behalf, Boss Pendergast sent the following letter to Postmaster General James Farley:

May 12, 1933

Jerome Walsh and John Lazia will be in Washington to see you about the same matter that I had Mr. Kemper talk to you about. Now, Jim, Lazia is one of my chief lieutenants and I am more sincerely interested in his welfare than anything you might be able to do for me now or in the future. He has been in trouble with the Income Tax Department for some time. I know it was simply a case of being jobbed because of his Democratic activities. I think Frank Walsh spoke to the proper authorities about this. In any event, I wish you would use your utmost endeavor to bring about a settlement of this matter. I cannot make it any stronger, except to say that my interest in him is greater than anything that might come up in the future. Thanking you for any and everything you can do. . . .[31]

This appeal did not stop the prosecution, which ended in a conviction. Lazia, however, was murdered in true gangster style a year later as he stepped from his car.

Criticisms of the Pendergast rule were also coming from other sources. Matscheck was sniping as usual, but he was no crusader. Samuel Mayerberg, a young rabbi, was. In spite of personal danger and harassment, he levied grave charges in 1932 against Pendergast, McElroy, Lazia, and others for harboring crime and vice, for manipulating city finances, for perpetuating fraud and terror in elections, for shaking down business by misusing licensing and taxing powers, for manipulating the administration of justice, and for using pressure to patronize companies run by leaders and the machine.[32] His charges presented Judge Truman with problems. Truman's two colleagues on the county court who were up for reelection in 1932 did not have any trouble winning at the polls, but it was serious to have such accusations levied against the organization that controlled Jackson County as well as Kansas City. Judge Truman had been harshly criticized for making alleged illegal patronage appointments of justices of the peace in Kaw township,[33] for buying oil for road purposes from favored Goat companies,[34] for not preventing county road machines from being used for bootleg distilleries, and for not taking a stand against election crooks.[35]

To make matters worse, when Guy Park became governor of Missouri in 1933, the control of elections in Kansas City was turned over to the Pendergast machine. By law, the board of election commissioners had to be half Democrat and half Republican. Boss Pendergast prevailed upon Governor Park to appoint to the board Republicans who would cooperate with the Democrats. These Republicans permitted the Democrats to run the elections in a fashion that allowed widespread election frauds, and they also aided the Pendergast candidates in city elections by putting up Republican candidates to weaken fusion or reform movements. The 1934 city elections were the culmination of the machine efforts to enhance its power by police intimidation and fraudulent manipulation of the electoral process. During the elections, four persons were killed and eleven were wounded. Gangsters hired by Lazia roamed the streets, with no interference from the police, intimidating workers for anti-Pendergast citizens' organizations. Many appeals were made to Governor Park to interfere on behalf of law and order, but he refused to act. The press clamored loudly at the high-handed methods that the machine used to get a record vote. Truman was concerned about the machine's increasingly bad image but kept silent. In answer to the criticisms made of him, Judge Truman redoubled his efforts to do a good job as presiding officer of the county court. He also extended his efforts as a public servant beyond the county lines.

In dealing with county affairs Truman came to realize the antiquated and inefficient character of county government and worked boldly for its reorganization, discussing the subject with various groups and backing reform bills before the state legislature that drastically reduced the number of counties in the state and simplified their organizational structure. The bill providing for a county budget system passed, but it did not go into effect until Truman had left the court. He brought about what improvements he could in county finances under the existing system. When he took office, the interest rate on county bank loans charged by Kansas City banks was 6 percent; he refinanced these through St. Louis and Chicago bankers first at 4 percent and later at 2.5 percent.

Heated discussion of deficits marked every election campaign for choosing county judges. Those in control were accused of deficit financing. On county financing, Judge Truman said in 1934:

Since 1932 the assessed valuation of Jackson County has been steadily on the decline and has not yet reached anywhere the level at which it will finally stabilize itself. As you know, more than 90 per cent of the county's revenues comes from a direct levy on real estate, and personal property, and the personal assessment always has been a joke and will continue to be a joke until we can assess and tax intangibles and tax-free securities.[36]

In meeting the problems of the Depression, Judge Truman was given an important role in 1934 when he was appointed federal reemployment director for Missouri by Secretary of Labor Frances Perkins. The post was without federal compensation because he wished to continue his road building job as county judge. The position, however, took him all over the state and brought him in touch with New Dealers Perkins and Harry Hopkins, to whom he indicated his great admiration for President Roosevelt.

Judge Truman gradually became better known nationally, and he made a solid contribution in the field of government planning. In recognition of his distinguished services in the development of county planning, he had been elected in 1929 to membership in the American Civic Association, an organization headed by Frederic A. Delano, uncle of Franklin Delano Roosevelt. Delano was to become chairman of the National Resources Committee, a national planning board set up during the Roosevelt years in the White House. Judge Truman also continued to be active in the National Old Trails Association, which was interested in national road planning. He was one of the leading spirits in establishing the Greater Kansas City Plan Association, concerned with planning in that metropolitan area. When the National Resources Committee began to stimulate the establishment of state planning boards, Governor Park appointed Truman chairman of the Missouri State Planning Board.

Truman's new contacts at the national, state, and local level were all gratifying, but he still faced the moral question of what to do about his connection with an organization that was acquiring an unsavory reputation. A Kansas City reporter who asked him about it got this reply:

I owe my political life to the Pendergast organization. I never would have had an opportunity to have a career in politics without their support. They have been loyal friends. I know that the organization has countenanced some things which I believe are wrong. But I do believe this, and that is that you can get further cleaning up a political organization from inside than you can from the out. At least, I can in the position I am in. If I came out against the organization and tried to wreck it, people would say I was a yellow dog, and they'd be right.[37]

Of the occupations in which he had been engaged, Truman found politics the most satisfying. He knew that he was not a great orator, but he liked political meetings, and he came to enjoy presenting his case to the voters. He got along well with people. He made friends with Matscheck, the efficiency expert and reformer, as well as with the organization leaders. Truman looked at the positive side of Pendergast's record and refused, naively perhaps, to believe the worst accusations made against Pendergast personally. He greatly overestimated his own power to clean up graft within the organization. A memorandum Truman wrote in the early 1930s noted:

I am obligated to the Big Boss. . . . I am only a small duck in a very large puddle, but I am interested very deeply in local or municipal government. Who is to blame for present conditions but sniveling church members who weep on Sunday, play with whores on Monday, drink on Tuesday, sell out to the Boss on Wednesday, repent about Friday, and start over on Sunday. I think maybe the Boss is nearer Heaven than the snivelers.[38]

According to Truman, the corrupters were the hypocritical businessmen who bribed the boss to obtain favors. He was desperately hunting for some justification for his loyalty to the boss.

chapter 11 | CANDIDATE FOR U.S. SENATE, 1934

Under our political system, an obscure man can be made the nominee of a major political party for the high office of the United States Senator by virtue of the support given him by a city boss.
—*St. Louis Post-Dispatch*, August 9, 1934

The year 1934 was clearly a turning point in Truman's career.[1] His selection in that year as the Goat faction candidate for the Democratic nomination for U.S. senator from Missouri was a product of the changing times and fortunes of that faction. In a three-cornered primary race, Truman had a good chance for nomination, especially with the aid of the huge vote that the Pendergast machine could muster now that it had gained control of the police and election machinery in Kansas City.[2]

Missouri's politics are typical of those of other border states. It was a well-developed two-party system with an even balance between the parties. Settlers from the North and their descendants have been largely Republican, while migrants from the South have been mainly Democratic. Severe factionalism has characterized the Democratic party, which contains such diverse elements as the Bourbons in the northeastern section of the state (called "Little Dixie" since it was originally settled by slave owners from Virginia and Kentucky), independent farmers in the eastern Ozark region who originally came from Tennessee, and urban workers. To bridge the gap between these different elements, strong political organizations were established in the two largest urban centers. In the 1930s, the most powerful Democratic machine was in Kansas City.

Tom Pendergast's political position had generally improved in the early 1930s. The tide began to turn nationally against Republicanism in 1930, following the onset of the Depression. Pendergast was bound to profit from this nationwide trend even though he was not especially sympathetic toward the new leadership in Washington. As a practical political boss, he knew that it was futile for him to fight an administration which was creating many jobs. If there was to be all that spending, then it was up to the state of

Missouri to see that it got its share of the federal largesse; the Civil Works Administration was ideally fitted to Pendergast's purposes because it turned over federal funds directly to the local authorities. City Manager McElroy claimed that this system was his idea and that it grew out of his success in spreading work for the unemployed by using city funds. Just before Harry Hopkins suggested the plan to Roosevelt in October 1933, he conferred with Reemployment Director Harry S. Truman. By February 1934, the *Missouri Democrat* reported that a hundred thousand men and ten thousand women were employed under CWA in Missouri. Boss Pendergast controlled at least the Kansas City end of this program.

At the state level, the elections had gone well, even though William Howell had been defeated by Bennett Clark for the senatorial nomination. The Goat machine had had a determining voice in the selection of nine of Missouri's thirteen congressmen and in the selection of the governor.

Boss Pendergast, who did not feel in 1934 that his organization was in serious trouble, did realize that he had problems, particularly with the press and radio and with the rival Democratic organization in St. Louis. Unfavorable publicity had complicated the job of running his organization and achieving his goal of greater power. The *Kansas City Times* and *Star* gave full coverage to the recent municipal election scandals, to Walter Matscheck's many revelations of irregularities in the city's budget, accounting, and personnel administration, and to Rabbi Mayerberg's grave charges of mismanagement, favoritism, and corruption in municipal affairs.[3] If Pendergast was to consolidate his power, he had to have candidates who could stand up to criticism and whose personal reputations were beyond reproach.

Pendergast still smarted under the sting of the defeat of his candidate in the 1932 senatorial primary by his critic Bennett Clark. To round out his ticket in 1934, Boss Pendergast needed a candidate for the U.S. Senate who could make a successful bid against Senator Clark's candidate, who would most likely run on an anti-Pendergast platform. The term of the Republican Senator Roscoe Patterson was coming to a close and the chances of the Democrats' capturing the second seat in the Senate looked excellent in view of the Roosevelt tide, which reached a peak in Missouri in 1932. Pendergast's requirements for the position were vote-getting abilities, particularly in the outstate counties, an understanding of the problems of the organization, and a willingness and the ability to defend the organization at the national level. With Governor Park in his corner in state affairs, Tom had the prospect of potential support from the state administration for his selection.

Senator Bennett Clark came forward first with his candidate for the nomination, Congressman J. L. "Tuck" Milligan, who in the 1932 statewide primary had won a nomination with Goat endorsement. Milligan had served seven terms in the House and had made a good record. Since he came from Richmond, in western Missouri, he could claim that he balanced the ticket geographically and that he would do well among the small town and rural voters.

Dorsett cites G. H. Foree, a St. Louis politician, to the effect that Congressman John C. Cochran of St. Louis entered the senatorial race at the instigation of Pendergast, who shrewdly believed that his candidate would have a better chance in a three-cornered contest. As Foree put it in a letter to E. Y. Mitchell, long prominent in Missouri politics and at the time assistant secretary of commerce: "Pendergast never did hunt ducks with a brass band. It has always been hard to tell what he is doing, but easy to tell what he has done the day after the election."[4] Foree contended that Cochran entered the race in order to take votes away from Milligan. In his own congressional district, Cochran had a dummy candidate who was ready to withdraw in Cochran's favor if necessary. Joe Shannon made a trip to St. Louis to talk with factional leader William L. Igoe, boss of the Democratic machine in the city, who was opposed to Senator Clark's getting a stranglehold on federal patronage, and Cochran himself went to Kansas City to talk with Pendergast. Directly after these meetings, Cochran announced his candidacy.

Cochran was a strong candidate in his own right, and he had close ties with the Igoe faction in St. Louis since he had been Igoe's secretary when the St. Louis leader was in Congress. In the statewide primary of 1932, Congressman Cochran had run second with the help of the Goat organization. It was thought that he would not lose too many votes in Jackson County and that he would pick up strength outstate. He had served continuously in the House since 1926, where he had built up a distinguished record. Marquis Childs, the Washington correspondent for the *St. Louis Post-Dispatch*, stated unhesitatingly that Cochran was the best candidate in the senatorial race. A group of five Washington correspondents placed Cochran among the five or six most useful members in Congress. Wiliam Hirth, head of the Missouri Farmers' Association, came out for Cochran. The opposition to a Goat candidate was formidable indeed.[5]

Pendergast asked Howell if he wanted to make the race again, but Howell declined; the opposition seemed too strong. Events since 1932 had added to the burdens that a Goat candidate had to carry.

Pendergast also considered former Senator James A. Reed, who had helped the Goat faction as mayor of Kansas City and who still fulfilled Tom's image of what a senator should be like. In Chicago, Reed even announced in May 1934 that he would go after the office he had vacated in 1928, but when he returned to Missouri he was silent.[6] He was seventy-two years old and opposed to the New Deal.

Pendergast then urged James P. Aylward, long-time chairman of the

Jackson County Democratic Committee and in 1934 chairman of the Missouri Democratic Committee, to make the run. Aylward was a successful Kansas City lawyer who had played along with both factions in Jackson County politics, had friendly relations with the St. Louis Democratic organization, and might have been able to capture that support.[7] He preferred not to seek office himself and declined to run.[8]

The boss next turned to his old rival, Congressman Joseph B. Shannon, who had made his peace with the Goats when he ran for Congress in 1930. Shannon, however, preferred the security of his seat in the House of Representatives to the uncertainty of a statewide Missouri primary. In addition, he was not too sympathetic toward the New Deal and wanted to concentrate on his hobby of reading and orating about Thomas Jefferson.[9]

There were, of course, others who were willing and ready to make the race, but they did not quite fit into Pendergast's scheme. One was Congressman Ralph A. Lozier, who had been backed by the Kansas City organization in the 1932 congressional primary and had ranked fourth from the top. He felt that if Howell did not run, he would get the Pendergast endorsement. After declining, Howell supported him and so did Congressman Clarence Cannon. Lozier waited for a call, which did not come.[10] His expected support from Hirth of the Missouri Farmers' Association went to Cochran.

On the urging of Jim Aylward and his nephew, Jim Pendergast, Tom Pendergast turned to Judge Truman.[11] One wonders why. The judge had no experience in Washington and had been elected only to local office. He had, however, cultivated statewide contacts for ten years. As a member of the state organization of county judges, he had become acquainted with county officials throughout the state. Later he was made a member of the State Planning Board. Early in the Roosevelt administration he became federal reemployment director for Missouri under Secretary Perkins, a task that took him all over the state, making friends everywhere. At the time he was asked to run, he was starting an intensive speaking campaign in favor of the proposed $10 million state bond issue for state eleemosynary institutions. His reputation for honesty was valuable in getting favorable votes on bond issues and, while careful of his own personal record, Judge Truman was loyal to the organization and could be counted upon to defend it within the limits of his powers.

Surprise was expressed, particularly in rival St. Louis, that such a relatively unknown county official should be given the Kansas City organization backing for such an important post as U.S. senator. By disparaging Truman's selection, the St. Louis press was undoubtedly firing the first gun in the campaign against him. We should recall, however, that as early as 1930, Judge Truman had been mentioned as a possible candidate for governor. When the organization supported Guy Park, Judge Truman loyally campaigned for this choice.

Cartoon by S. J. Ray, 1934. Reprinted, courtesy of *The Kansas City Star*.

Truman had certain assets that made his choice a reasonable one. In spite of the increasingly unfavorable publicity that the Goat organization was receiving, he had managed to keep his own record clean and to maintain a reputation for honesty and public service, which was widely recognized. He had many friends among the Baptists, the Masons, the Reserve Officers Association, and the American Legion. His ten years' experience as a farmer, including his active role in the Farm Bureau, helped him understand the farmers' problems, and his unsuccessful ventures into small business, including the failure of the haberdashery shop, made him a sympathetic figure as far as small businessmen were concerned.

Judge Truman now faced the question as to whether he should accept the offer of Pendergast support for such a difficult race. The presiding judge of the county court was limited to two terms of four years each. If he was going to stay in politics, he had to find another slot. Since he was still burdened by a heavy personal debt, he preferred such a position as county collector, which was very lucrative and would help him get on his feet financially, but Pendergast had promised this job to someone else.

Judge Truman had also considered a seat in Congress:

In 1934, when I had been presiding judge of Jackson County for eight years, I expected to run for Congress. Two years earlier new congressional districts had been set up for the state of Missouri, with the Fourth District in eastern Jackson County, with two of three eastern wards of Kansas City added. This was the district I hoped to represent in Congress, and if I had been permitted to run, I feel confident that I could have been its representative. I was maneuvered out of this and finally ended up by running for the U. S. Senate.[12]

It took some persuasion to get Truman to consent to run, but Jim Aylward and Jim Pendergast made an able team and finally met with success. Judge Truman would be the Kansas City organization candidate for the senatorial post. He did not minimize the task before him, and he braced himself for a mud-slinging type of campaign. In every way possible, his opponents, Milligan and Cochran, and their supporters tried to belittle his candidacy and to label him as the tool of the Kansas City machine.

The Goat forces turned their attention first to questions of organization. The Kansas City Democratic organization was always in a state of readiness in those days. Although federal relief activities might have been used to reduce the role of the party as a relief agency, in Missouri they were actually used to strengthen the Pendergast machine. A. R. Hendrix, the district director for the WPA and Truman's campaign manager in St. Joe, used his powers to help the organization. Still, the purely party charitable activities continued to be popular since they were administered with no questions and no red tape. Kansas City employees, selected on a patronage basis, were expected to contribute money and time to the campaign. Under Governor Park, state employees were also expected to help. Richard L. Harkness, a wire services correspondent, estimated that from five thousand to six thousand state employees from every section of the state would work for Truman.[13] Although he did not want to run himself, Jim Aylward assumed the duties of campaign manager for Truman. He helped organize clubs and sent letters to all county committeemen asking for support for Truman, and he saw to the distribution of some thirty-five thousand Truman-for-senator window placards.[14]

A campaign fund of substantial proportions was not as important in state politics in the early 1930s as it is today, but a small fund was essential. Truman chose as his campaign finance chairman his old friend and fellow artilleryman, Mayor Roger Sermon of Independence. The mayor reported expenses of $12,280 in the primary. Among the largest contributors were the Pendergast family (up to $1,400), William T. Kemper, banker friend of Truman ($1,000), and Joseph J. McGee ($1,000). Other contributors were the Aylwards, Mayor Bryce B. Smith and City Manager McElroy of Kansas City, and Colonel E. M. Stayton. There was a deficit of $3,335, but this was not regarded as serious.[15]

Governor Park indicated that while he would vote for Truman, he would not make speeches for him. Truman made it clear, however, that this was not all he expected from the governor:

Dear Governor:—In talking to some of my young Democratic friends down here, they tell me that some of the State employees are saying that I am a *nice* fellow and that they are for me but they think Cochran will win.

I'd rather be called any sort of a _____ than to be damned with faint praise.

Though perhaps you might be able to get them to say they think I can win and that I'll do the job when I do.[16]

Judge Truman was determined to wage a strenuous campaign, meeting as many voters as possible. Although he did not open his campaign officially until July 6, he began in May to cover northwest Missouri, stopping at St. Joseph, Maryville, and smaller cities and towns. He then toured the river counties and, in late June, the southeastern counties.[17]

For the opening of his campaign, he staged a big rally in Columbia, the Boone County seat, site of the University of Missouri, and a Democratic stronghold. According to the *Missourian*, "Columbia took on the appearance of homecoming week, with a large delegation of Kansas City, St. Louis and Independence supporters, as well as a bloc of about 400 Jefferson City supporters led by prominent state officials."[18] As an innovation in campaigning, Truman used a sound truck to carry his voice to the some twenty-five hundred to three thousand people gathered on the courthouse lawn, including his eighty-two-year-old mother. He was introduced by a state official from the community, Lieutenant Governor Frank Harris. In his speech he endorsed President Roosevelt and the New Deal program of social legislation. On his own initiative he declared that he favored payment of the soldier bonus as soon as the nation's finances permitted as an aid in the country's recovery from the Depression. In answer to the charges made against him that he was Pendergast's handpicked candidate, he said that both of his opponents had solicited and received the support of the Jackson County organization as candidates at large for Congress in 1932.[19]

Truman began an extensive tour of the state, which he continued for the next thirty days, even though at the beginning he suffered two broken ribs and a head bruise in an automobile accident. The *Examiner* stated that in his six weeks' campaign, the judge covered every county in the state.[20] Later Truman recalled that he went into 60 of Missouri's 114 counties, making from six to sixteen speeches a day.[21] His strategy was to show that he would be a more loyal supporter of the Roosevelt administration than had been his two main opponents, both of whom he criticized for failing to support the Roosevelt farm program. He promised full support if elected. William Hirth, of the Missouri Farmers' Association, had difficulty trying to explain Cochran's record on this issue. Truman also criticized his rivals' record on the bill granting powers to the President to reorganize executive departments. Here, Cochran responded scornfully that his negative vote was cast while Hoover was still president.[22]

In answering the charge that he would, if elected, be the senator from Pendergast, Truman had more difficulty. He used the familiar campaign tactic of accusing his opponents of being controlled candidates. Thus, Milligan was the tool of Senator Clark, who was trying to control both seats in the Senate so that he could build a machine of his own, based on federal patronage. Cochran was the tool of the St. Louis organization, which was just as much a machine as the Goat organization.

During the campaign Truman showed his interest in the common man, farmers, small businessmen, minority groups, and consumers who had been victimized by banks, stock swindlers, monopolists, and others. As he put it during the campaign:

For more than a year, the President has battered away at old untrue assertions, refusing to believe lies because they are old lies. He has shown the financial exploitation of the people by bankers, by security firms, by other sellers of worthless stocks and bonds, by tariff laws, by subsidies serving no good purpose, by monopolies in trade and finance, by stockrigging, by outrageous public contracts, by every trick and device through which unscrupulous and designing plunderers might pillage the public.[23]

Truman also promised to look after the interests of every section of the state, arguing that "both my opponents have been in Washington so long they have lost the Missouri point of view. Mr. Cochran, for instance, has been busy getting things for St. Louis, often to the detriment of the rest of the state."[24]

In his first statewide campaign, Truman's efforts to attract the labor vote were not so explicit as they became later. He stated that his experience as unemployment director had given him an understanding of the sufferings of labor while the Republican tariff was denounced as benefiting business, not labor. In one speech he asserted, "We are now going about the job of redistributing wealth that has amassed in the robust years. . . . In the past the profits of the machine have been going to the machine owner. It seems to me that now the profits must be divided more equally with labor."[25]

During the campaign Truman suffered considerable vilification principally because of his connection with the Pendergast organization but also because of his inexperience in national affairs. Senator Clark charged, "Mr. Truman has been conducting a campaign of mendacity and imbecility unparalleled in the history of Missouri."[26] Hirth referred to Truman as a "bellhop." The *St. Louis Post-Dispatch* had labeled Truman as "Pendergast's office boy" and "puppet."[27]

Truman could not count upon newspaper support to boost his candidacy. Practically the entire city press was hostile to the Pendergast machine and expressed shock at the criminal activities of some of its followers. Many rural newspapers were noncommittal for fear of endangering party unity in the general election.[28]

The preelection forecasts made in the neighborhood of Kansas City were all to the effect that in spite of the bitter campaign against him, Judge Truman had the edge. Tom Pendergast was quoted as saying: "I'm mum on how much of the state Truman will carry outside of Kansas City and Jackson County, but I will guarantee him a larger majority in the primaries than Cochran will get in St. Louis."[29] The results proved that Pendergast knew the strength of his organization. A record vote piled up in the city elections revealing what the new control of election machinery meant. Before the election, the betting odds favored Truman.

In a surprise move toward the end of the campaign, Truman's cousin, Colonel Ralph E. Truman, who was backing Milligan, alleged that Truman had a $500,000 slush fund. Truman's campaign manager, James Aylward, promptly denied this charge, and Colonel Truman could produce no evidence.[30]

The primary election itself took place peacefully. Because of padded rolls, the Kansas City vote was unusually high. Jackson County returns were late in being reported so it looked for a time that Truman might be defeated, but when these returns came in, it was clear that he was the winner. The final vote was 276,850 for Truman, 236,105 for Cochran, and 147,614 for Milligan. In percentage terms, the figures gave 41.9 percent for Truman, 35.8 percent for Cochran, and 22.3 percent for Milligan. Truman had only a margin of 6 percentage points over Cochran.

The charge was soon made that Truman's margin of victory was made up of "ghost" votes from the Pendergast wards where election irregularities were notorious. A closer look at the returns, however, shows that excluding Jackson County, St. Louis County, and the city of St. Louis, the results were 134,707 for Truman, 113,532 for Cochran, and 128,401 for Milligan. Truman thus had won a plurality of the votes from what Harkness called the "creek forks" and "grass roots." In Jackson County, the vote was 137,529 for Truman, 1,525 for Cochran, and 8,406 for Milligan. Considering the fact that 82,972 votes were cast for Cochran for Congress in Kansas City in 1932, this was a fantastic switch of opinion regarding Cochran's merits in a two-year period. He lost practically all of his 1932 vote. This massive swing was the product of the old-style organization methods. The Goat sample ballots were all marked for Truman in 1934 and the precinct workers backed up these ballots with oral instructions. Many WPA workers had their ballots marked for them.

Truman, who did not secure a majority of all the votes cast, was obviously helped by the division of the opposition votes between Cochran and Milligan. The Pendergast strategy of bringing in Cochran had worked. If Cochran had not run, some felt that Milligan might have received the St. Louis vote and won. Governor Park, however, had appointed William Igoe of the St. Louis organization as chairman of the St. Louis Board of Police Commissioners and hoped that Mayor Bernard F. Dickmann of St. Louis would support Truman. Cochran was a native of St. Louis and Milligan was not. The governor's views might have prevailed with Igoe and Dickmann if Milligan had been the only candidate. In other words, with Cochran out, Truman might have done well in St. Louis, as he did six years later. On the other hand, it would have been a much harder strategy to follow than the one adopted, which concealed Boss Pendergast's subtle control. It is interesting to note that the *St. Louis Star-Times* urged Milligan to withdraw so that Cochran might defeat Truman.[31]

Cochran attributed his defeat to the colossal vote that the Pendergast machine had piled up for Truman in Kansas City, a city half the size of St. Louis, ruefully reflecting that his own prediction of 125,000 votes in St. Louis might have spurred the Pendergast machine to even greater efforts. He also thought that Milligan fell down in the rural areas, allowing Truman to win in the outstate counties.[32] As for Cochran's own political fortunes, he ran again for Congress as planned and was reelected.

The press generally hailed the victory as one for Pendergast rather than for Truman. The *St. Louis Post-Dispatch* commented on the propensity of the Pendergast organization to "vote the tombstones or to ghost vote." By

MISSOURI

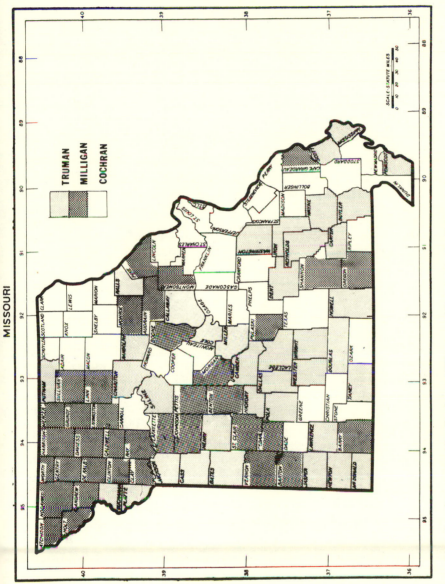

Map 1. Counties carried by Cochran, Milligan, and Truman in the Democratic senatorial primary August 7, 1934

downgrading Truman, the *Post-Dispatch* could indicate its disgust at the defeat of Congressman Cochran. Truman's title to the nomination was under a cloud. While in later years he did much to overcome this stigma, his enemies continued to use it against him throughout his public life. A few newspapers gave Truman credit for his efforts. The *Kansas City Journal-Post* made a favorable comment about his energetic campaign.[33] The *Independence Examiner* was more laudatory:

> We are particularly pleased that the Democrats outstate, the men and women in the small county districts, gave Judge Truman such fine support. Without this support he could not have been nominated. He is from birth and training and experience a country man as contrasted with those who have never left the sidewalks and the shadow of tall buildings.
>
> The nomination of Judge Truman is remarkable in several ways. Unknown in the outstate districts and known not at all in St. Louis, his campaign was entirely in the country and wherever he went he made friends and supporters. The campaign demonstrated another thing. The Democrats of Missouri did not like the idea of a man they had honored highly and whom they had nominated and elected to the United States Senate coming back at the next election and trying to dictate the selection of his colleague.[34]

Map 1 shows that in the Democratic primary, Truman carried some counties on the western border, some in the southwestern Ozark region that went Republican in general elections, a few in the eastern Ozarks that were traditionally Democratic in general elections, some in the cotton-growing lowlands of the southeastern Delta region, and a few in the so-called Little Dixie area in central Missouri. He did not do so well in the corn belt in northern and northwestern Missouri. This was Milligan territory, and Cochran was aided by the Missouri Farmers' Association. Cochran also did better in the German belt, the counties along the southern reaches of the Missouri River to the St. Louis area and continuing south along the Mississippi to the cotton counties, while showing some strength in Little Dixie and in the Ozarks. Truman's vote showed the influence of state patronage: he carried Cole County where the state capital is located. He also had the support of organized labor, doing well in cities such as St. Joseph and Joplin. Of course, he was popular among farmers in such areas as the delta, where he received help from the Missouri Farm Bureau members who liked the New Deal farm policies, which he strongly defended.

After a few weeks respite from campaigning, which he spent supervising the completion of the twenty-eight-story courthouse in Kansas City, Truman began an intensive campaign to defeat Senator Roscoe C. Patterson, the Republican candidate up for reelection. In accordance with national Democratic party strategy of playing down traditional party ties, Missouri Democrats presented the battle as one between New Dealers and conservatives. The aim was to hold progressive Republicans who had voted for Roosevelt in 1932.

Senator Patterson, conservative, played right into the hands of the Democrats. He attacked the Roosevelt administration on the ground that it was made up of radical New Dealers, and he pointed out that many former leading Democrats had deserted the Roosevelt ticket. Unfortunately for Patterson's chances of returning to the Senate, the defecting Democrats represented only a tiny minority, whereas the Republican progressives switching to Roosevelt were numerous. The tide in the midterm congressional elections was running strongly in favor of the President's party for the first time in American history. Usually, a president had to count on losing some of his party's congressmen and senators as a result of the midterm elections, but this was not the case in 1934. Patterson's victory in 1928 had been in another era. The days when Protestant America was almost unchallenged by the rising tide of Catholic voters, when Prohibition was still regarded as a noble experiment, when Americans were willing to accept the automatic controls of the free enterprise system that called for more bankruptcies as the cure for a depression, and when welfare activities were strictly local and private matters were gone.

Patterson's senatorial record was vulnerable on grounds of inadequate accomplishment. He had served on six committees—Military Affairs, Commerce, Immigration, Appropriations, Mines, and Civil Service—but had little legislation to his credit. Only one of his proposals, the Federal Kidnaping Act (the Lindbergh act), had become law. He had been one of seven senators opposing the Twentieth Amendment to the Constitution.[35]

His ideology was derived from that of former President Herbert Hoover, and his speeches were full of warnings about the danger of federal dictatorship, the loss of the free enterprise system, and the peril of communism. He hammered away at the issues of burdensome taxation, stifling government regulation, and government inroads on personal freedom. Federal bureaucrats, he charged, were telling farmers what to plant and what to harvest, and they were dictating to retailers what prices to charge. Patterson kept reminding his listeners that Roosevelt had failed to answer the challenge of the U.S. Chamber of Commerce to announce publicly if and when he intended to balance the budget, stabilize the currency, and encourage business initiative.[36]

Senator Patterson clung to the traditional Republican policies of the pre-Depression period, defending the Smoot-Hawley tariff act and pointing with pride to his part in bringing about the zinc tariff increase and maintaining the tariff on shoes. In accordance with Hoover's philosophy, he condemned excessive federal spending for relief. He picked up the allegations made by Senator Clark that Truman, as director of reemployment in Missouri, had used that position to obtain political workers.

Truman, however, pointed out that he had resigned his federal position in May in order to avoid such charges.[37] Admittedly, Patterson did not make as much use of the charges that Truman was tied to a corrupt organization as he might have.

Truman defended the New Deal vigorously. He contended that the Roosevelt relief policies represented a humane type of individualism in contrast to Patterson's rugged individualism. Far from being dictated from on high, the National Recovery Administration codes and the Agricultural Adjustment Act policies were hammered out by the businessmen and farmers themselves.[38] Further, he defended the constitutionality of the New Deal legislation, pointing out that the Supreme Court had supported widespread delegation of power in the case of the Federal Reserve System and the Federal Trade Commission. In fact, he held, the New Deal was not really new at all.[39] In contrast to his factual presentations in county elections, Truman spoke in general terms. Whereas he used to condemn deficit spending, now human suffering convinced him that efficiency and balanced budgets were not everything.

In this and later campaigns, Truman directed appeals to special interest groups. He did not find it difficult to court the support of organized labor, since Patterson had an antilabor record. On Truman's behalf, the Combined Building Trades Council declared: "He has been loyal to labor in its entirety in all respects, and has gone out of his way to help organized labor. Anything that can be done on his behalf will be greatly appreciated by 45,000 union people in Kansas City."[40] Truman also found it easy to appeal to the black voters since Patterson had alienated many of them by his vote for the confirmation of Judge John J. Parker, a notorious lily-white Republican who had scorned the black vote. The Pendergast organization, on the other hand, had welcomed black voters. As Roy Wilkins, then a resident of Kansas City, later put it:

I knew Truman back in Missouri, before he got to be a Senator. . . . Truman is and was a practical, down-to-earth politician. . . . But he was . . . politically astute on the race question before he ever came to Washington, because the Pendergast machine was politically astute on the race question. They weren't the fair-haired boys and they didn't believe in good government and they didn't necessarily love the Negro, but they believed in machine control and in marshalling whatever votes it took to keep the machine in power.[41]

Along with many other New Deal candidates, Truman was swept into office by an unprecedentedly large majority. He received 787,110 votes to Patterson's 524,954, almost three-fifths of the vote. He carried 75 of Missouri's 114 counties, much to Patterson's amazement.

Map 2 shows that Truman carried all of the counties that went tradition-

MISSOURI

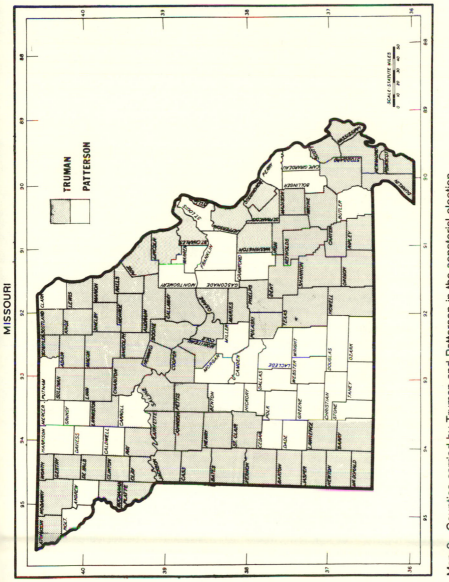

TRUMAN

PATTERSON

SCALE-STATUTE MILES
0 10 20 30 40 50

Map 2. Counties carried by Truman and Patterson in the senatorial election
November 6, 1934

ally Democratic during the period 1872-1952.[42] These were the counties around Kansas City, in Little Dixie, in central Missouri north of the Missouri River, the eastern Ozarks, and the cotton-belt delta. The politics of Little Dixie go back to pre-Civil War days when many southern slave owners moved into this prosperous farm area. After the Civil War, they remained conservative Democrats and continued to exert influence on the Democratic party in Missouri. The cotton-belt delta counties also contained many former southerners who, in contrast with Bourbons farther north, were less conservative and more willing to embrace New Deal policies. In addition to the traditionally Democratic counties, Truman also carried those on the western border, a share of those in the northern corn belt, and made inroads in the German belt, all sections that usually went Republican. Truman did better in the outstate counties than he was to do there six years later.

Although the party that controls the presidency is likely to lose seats in the congressional elections held in nonpresidential years, this did not happen in 1934. Instead the Democrats gained seats in both the House and the Senate. The voters were paying their first tribute to the new President who met the crisis of 1933 with so much coolness and willingness to act. On Truman's side, the election was a vindication and the first step in the removal of the stigma that he was put in office by a corrupt machine. As in the primary, Truman could point with pride to his energetic campaign.

Patterson had not been a strong opponent. The usually Republican *Maryville Daily Forum* put it brutally if somewhat colloquially: "Missouri is well rid of Senator Patterson and he can return to private life for a long time as probably the Republican party won't be calling upon him to run for office again for some little time about a lifetime we would say."[43]

Boss Pendergast could view the results with great satisfaction. He had thwarted Senator Clark's attempt to obtain exclusive control of federal patronage by his clever strategy of dividing the opposition and coming up with a record vote of his own. But he failed to see the danger in election deception, which was later on to pave the way for his downfall. In the Senate Truman might not be able to do everything that the organization might want him to do, but on patronage appointments, he had always been reliable. The 1934 demonstration of the strength of the Goat machine would bring Senator Clark around too if he wished to be reelected in 1938. The Goat organization had the federal situation well in hand.

Student of American history that he was, Truman must have realized that his route to the Senate was hardly a well-traveled one. Research has shown that over half of the senators at the time of their election were professional politicians—a designation Truman could not qualify for; he entered politics late and had been neither a congressman nor a governor. Nor was Truman an amateur politician. To qualify for such a designation he would need a distinguished record in business, law, or university teaching—something to indicate that his political ambitions lay outside his life's chosen work. Not a patrician, like Senator Henry Cabot Lodge of Massachusetts, whose family background was one of distinguished public service, nor an agitator, like Senator Joseph R. McCarthy of Wisconsin, who exploited the issue of anti-communism, Harry Truman was just a plain citizen of Missouri with only ten years in local-level politics. He was, for all of this, an exception among border Democrats.[44]

Truman understandably was both pleased and awed by his election. He felt that he was on his way, and he looked forward with great eagerness to the new challenge. Yet he was determined to proceed cautiously and to play the game according to the rules.

chapter 12 | THE "SENATOR FROM PENDERGAST," 1935–1940

"I don't follow [Tom Pendergast's] advice on legislation. I vote the way I believe Missourians as a whole would want me to vote."[1] Thus did the new senator announce himself to the press after indicating that the boss often sent him telegrams urging him to vote one way or another on certain measures. Truman's relationship to the Missouri Democratic organization was delicate; he could not repudiate Goat support without appearing to be an ingrate. Although he had always recognized and defended the patronage appointment rights of the organization, he could not afford to appear to be subservient to it. He had, in fact, to struggle to achieve an image of independence as a legislator. He had to show that he was not a mere creature of Boss Tom and also not just a cog in the Roosevelt juggernaut. Two questions arise: What did Truman, as senator, regard as his obligations to the Pendergast machine for patronage, special favors, and legislation? What were his obligations to the citizens of Missouri as their representative?

Victor Messall, Truman's first chief secretary, said long after he had left the senator's staff: "In the six years I never saw a letter from Tom Pendergast to Senator Truman or knew of a telephone call."[2] (This statement needs to be taken with reservations; Truman in his *Memoirs* admits of a telephone call.) As the image of the Pendergast machine worsened, Truman and those anxious to protect his reputation realized the need to divorce him from any connection with the questionable activities of the organization. Senator Truman viewed himself as a Burkean type of legislator, holding that he was independent of all of his constituents, not merely Pendergast. When a letter-to-the-editor appeared in the *St. Louis Post-Dispatch* criticizing him for voting his own convictions and not paying attention to his constituents, he wrote: "I voted for what I thought was the welfare of the country and was not governed by threats, pleas or political considerations."[3]

On patronage matters, however, as in the case of his county judgeship, Senator Truman regarded himself as part of the Missouri Democratic organization. When a Kansas City man sought Senator Truman's support for a job, the senator replied: "If you will, send us endorsements from the Kansas City Democratic Organization. I shall be glad to do what I can for you."[4] One of the chief interests of the Pendergast machine in a federal senatorship was the patronage involved. This not only included such traditional jobs as federal judges, district attorneys, internal revenue collectors, postmasters, and other federal posts but also a flood of new emergency agency jobs, which were precious indeed in times of depression. A machine such as the one in Kansas City, with its vulnerable parts, needed protection against unfriendly prosecution, and it also needed plenty of jobs. For a while, Truman's election brought both. Senator Bennett Clark had been anti-Pendergast but, looking ahead to his reelection in 1938, he felt he had to change his stance, so he cooperated with Senator Truman in urging the appointment of Matthew S. Murray as director of public works for Missouri.[5] Senator Truman, as former director for reemployment for Missouri, had maintained friendly relations with Harry Hopkins, so he convinced Hopkins to accept Murray for this post even though a former Democratic national committeewoman from Missouri, Emily Newell Blair, opposed the nomination. Murray had been director of public works in Kansas City under City Manager McElroy, so he understood the job needs of the Democratic organization. His appointment was the most important contribution that the Roosevelt administration made to the Missouri Democratic organization in the mid-1930s. All requests for federal relief jobs were routed through Murray, and in the 1936 election some WPA employees voted for Pendergast candidates under threat of losing their jobs.[6] In some large urban areas, as in New York City, WPA jobs were used in such a way that they undercut existing Democratic organizations, but in Kansas City before Pendergast's prosecution and conviction for income tax evasion, they were used to strengthen his machine.

Another example of the patronage power wielded for a while by the new senator was the ouster of Ewing V. Mitchell of Springfield, Missouri, as assistant secretary of commerce under Secretary of Commerce Daniel Roper. Mitchell, an independent Democrat who supported Roosevelt before the 1932 convention, was rewarded for his efforts by the position in the President's little cabinet. But Mitchell had bitterly denounced the Pendergast machine as un-Democratic in that it protected racketeers and plundered the taxpayers.[7] All of his charges against the Pendergast machine were amply proved in the next four years, but they were not established in 1935. Besides, Mitchell had severely criticized the administration of the Department of Commerce, and he was thus not popular among some of his fellow administrators. While national chairman James A. Farley helped Mitchell get his post in 1933, he did not protect him in 1935 when the two Missouri senators combined against him. Farley had a great admiration for the vote-getting capacity of the Pendergast machine, which at that time looked to be invincible.

In 1938 the situation had changed, and Senator Truman had a problem in securing a patronage appointment to which he thought he was entitled. He had recommended Fred Canfil, who had been active in his 1934 campaign, for U.S. marshal in the Western District, but President Roosevelt refused to make the appointment until he had consulted with Governor Stark. Farley protested that this was a federal appointment and the governor should not be consulted. Roosevelt countered by saying that the governor and Pendergast were having a battle for control and the governor might win.[8]

On legislative matters, Senator Truman was determined to assert his independence. A severe test of this stand came in 1935 in connection with the passage of the Public Utility Holding Company Act. Senator Burton K. Wheeler, who had befriended Truman in the Senate, and Congressman Sam Rayburn sponsored the bill; it aimed to complement the laws regulating the stock exchange and to prevent such disastrous holding company pyramids as the one Samuel Insull had constructed in the electric power field in the 1920s. The debate over this bill was bitter and explosive. Lobbyists for the utilities, including Wendell Willkie, concentrated on the so-called death sentence clause and spent at least $1.5 million to defeat it.[9] Senator Truman supported the proposed regulation in spite of the tremendous pressure brought to bear upon him by Kansas City business interests close to Pendergast and by the *Kansas City Journal-Post*, the only metropolitan newspaper supporting the Goats. As Truman put it in his *Memoirs:*

I was swamped with letters and telegrams urging me to vote against the bill. I did not let these messages alter my own convictions because I knew that the "wrecking crew" of Wall Street was at work behind the scenes and that it was responsible for the thirty thousand requests which eventually piled up on my desk. I burned them all, and an investigation of this uncalled-for propaganda barrage, which was aimed at many besides myself, was later undertaken by Senators Hugo Black, Sherman Minton, and Lew Schwellenbach.[10]

In 1936, a presidential election year, Senator Truman found that he had a much more important part to play in Missouri politics than he had ever played before, but it was still less than he thought he deserved. He was one of the delegates at large to the Democratic National Convention, which met in Philadelphia, but he was not selected to serve on any of the important committees.[11] He would have liked an appointment to the Resolutions Committee, but the best he could get was the honorary position of vice-president of the convention along with forty-seven other honorary vice-presidents, one for each state. Since Roosevelt's nomination was a foregone conclusion, the convention had little real work to do. Both President Roosevelt and Vice-President Garner were renominated by acclamation. At the convention, Truman's colleague, Senator Clark, played an important part in securing the repeal of the two-thirds majority rule for nominations, which had blocked his father's nomination in 1912. The change was to help Truman later on.

A number of events occurred outside the convention that had a profound effect on Truman's fortunes. One was the illness of Tom Pendergast, which marked the sapping of his energies and probably the warping of his judgment. Senator Truman aided Pendergast in his return from Philadelphia back to his elaborate hotel suite in the Waldorf-Astoria Hotel in New York. (In 1936 Pendergast had become an absentee boss, managing his Missouri affairs at a distance, always a difficult thing to do.) His illness was diagnosed as cancer of the rectum, and he underwent several major abdominal operations, from which he recovered. Truman later said that if he had died in 1936, he would have gone down in history as the greatest political organizer the country had ever seen.[12]

The Missouri Democratic organization had an important choice to make in 1936. It had to select a candidate for governor because the state constitution forbade a governor to succeed himself. William Hirth of the Missouri Farmers Association was an avowed candidate, but he had always been rabidly anti-Pendergast. On the other hand, Lloyd Stark had wanted the nomination in 1932 and was still seeking Goat support. Truman was impressed at the time with Stark's qualifications, and so was Senator Clark. A successful businessman, the largest grower of apples in the United States, Stark had acquired considerable support throughout the state, especially in the rural areas. The two senators brought Stark to New York to meet Pendergast, but Tom was not favorably impressed, and he said to Truman: "He won't do, Harry. I don't like the son of a bitch. He's a no good son of a bitch."[13] The Democratic national committeeman for Missouri, James P. Aylward, also had an unfavorable opinion of Stark.

Senator Truman, nevertheless, went to work to change Pendergast's mind on the question of Stark. He was later to regret his own success in this. Stark, with the machine's backing, was nominated by an overwhelming vote over Hirth in the August Democratic primary; his margin was 361,781 votes. A landslide plurality of an impressive 264,199 votes swept Stark into the governor's office over Republican candidate Jesse W. Barrett.[14] But there was a hitch; the huge Stark majorities in both elections were made up in part of ghost votes stolen by highly loyal machine workers in Kansas City. Ironically, Stark had earned a margin large enough to ensure election without illegal padding; the extraordinary efforts of the Pendergast machine were not only unnecessary, they were embarrassing, and eventually

Cartoon by Beidtinius, April 1937. Reprinted, courtesy of *The Kansas City Star*.

they proved disastrous to Pendergast. Truman, guilty of marked under-statement, called such practices "silly."[15] Arthur Krock visited Kansas City and made the following comment: "Any observer of city politics knows the real answer. Each party worker of the professional type is an office seeker. From him results are demanded in exchange for jobs. The better showing he makes, the higher his standing over rival precinct, ward or district workers. This competition has led 'the boys' to be what the boss calls 'overzealous.'"[16]

Following his sweeping election victory in 1936 in which he carried the state of Missouri by a plurality of 413,152 over Governor Landon, Presi-dent Roosevelt split the Democratic party by his proposal to enlarge and reorganize the U.S. Supreme Court. This plan divided the Missouri delega-tion to the Senate. Senator Clark fought the President's court reforms while Senator Truman supported them. On the other hand, when Senator Joseph Robinson died in the midst of the battle for these reforms, Truman did not agree with the President's preference for successor as majority leader in the Senate. There was a closely contested battle between the President and the vice-president for the control of the Senate leadership. President Roosevelt thought that Senator Alben Barkley of Kentucky would be a more sympathetic leader of New Deal proposals; Vice-President Garner thought that the Senate should control the choice of its own leadership and that Senator Pat Harrison of Mississippi was the logical choice under Senate customs.

In the developing dispute over the majority leadership, Senator Truman had a chance to show his independence of both Pendergast and President Roosevelt. On the advice of Vice-President Garner, Truman had already promised to support Senator Harrison. When, at the request of Jim Farley, Tom Pendergast asked Truman to support Barkley as the administration candidate for the position, Truman indicated that he had already pledged his vote to Harrison. Tom Pendergast understood and did not question the senator's right to stand by his commitments. Truman, however, was furious that President Roosevelt had asked Tom Pendergast to apply pressure. The President was acting as though the stereotype of Truman as a boss-controlled senator were true. Truman told a friendly newspaperman at the time, "I'm tired of being pushed around, tired of having the President treat me like an office boy."[17] He then phoned the White House to express his vexation. The President was not available, but Truman talked to Steve Early, his press secretary, who said that he would inform the President about the Senator's displeasure.

It was soon clear that the misgivings Pendergast and Aylward had about Stark were well founded—from their point of view at any rate. Once elected governor, Stark turned on the organization that had supported him and tried to seize the leadership of the party for himself. Politically ambitious, he realized that he could not succeed himself as governor, so logically he set his sights for the senatorship. While the Pendergast machine had helped elevate him to the governorship in 1936, the machine in 1940 would probably be for Senator Truman, who had proved more loyal. The governor calculated that if he could smash the machine, he would have a better chance for the nomination for senator, and he could then capitalize on the anti-Pendergast sentiment that seemed to be growing in the state.

The election frauds that had been committed in his own election were used by Governor Stark in his battle against the Pendergast machine. Congressman Joe Shannon, the old Rabbit leader, disappointed at the outcome of the judicial elections, was the first to cry fraud after the 1936 elections. When the *Kansas City Star* began an investigation of the vote frauds, the governor backed them up in the drive against the Pendergast machine by withholding patronage from the Goats and by enlisting the cooperation of the federal authorities. In December, the federal grand jury returned 278 indictments for election frauds. Federal District Attorney Maurice Milligan, sponsored by Senator Clark, with the aid of the Federal Bureau of Investigation, began prosecution of those involved in election irregularities. The situation was probably no worse than it had been in earlier elections, but the governor's backing and the interest of the federal government pushed the investigations along. The governor refused in 1937 to appoint officials to the Kansas City Election Board who were favorable to Pendergast. The new board that he selected cleaned up the election lists. Registration of voters in Kansas City dropped from nearly 270,000 in 1936 to 216,000 for the city campaign of 1938. A new registration law and a new board thus made a difference of over 50,000 votes. The names of nonexistent voters, "ghosts" as they were called, had been removed from the lists.[18]

District Attorney Milligan was very successful in his prosecution of the election cases. Of the 278 indicated, 259 were convicted in trials held in 1938 and sent to jail. The trials attracted national attention, and Pendergast could not silence the clamor against him.

Milligan's term as district attorney came to an end in 1938 while some of the election cases were still pending. Originally appointed on the recommendation of Senator Clark, Milligan's reappointment was backed again by the senior senator. To the members of the Pendergast organization, the name of Milligan was anathema. What was Senator Truman to do about this nomination? It was possible for him to block the reappointment by saying that Milligan was personally obnoxious to him. This was his right of senatorial courtesy. But President Roosevelt persuaded Truman not to object on the ground that the people of Missouri were demanding a continuation of the trials. Truman could have kept silent, but he preferred to strike back. He was angry at the infringement of his patronage rights as a senator, and he felt sorry for those caught in the meshes of the law. In a speech before the Senate, he accused Milligan of behavior involving conflict of interest:

Mr. Milligan has accepted emoluments in the form of fees in bankruptcy proceedings in the Federal Court of Western Missouri. In fact, he has received more money in fees in one case than his salary has been from the Federal Treasury for a whole year. The Federal Court at Kansas City is presided over by two as violently partisan judges as have ever sat on a Federal bench since the Federalist judges of Jefferson's Administration. They are Merrill E. Otis and Albert I. Reeves. Mr. Reeves was appointed by that great advocate of clean nonpartisan government, Warren G. Harding, and Mr. Otis was appointed by that other progressive nonpartisan, Calvin Coolidge.

I say, Mr. President, that a Jackson County, Missouri, Democrat has as much chance of a fair trial in the Federal District Court of Western Missouri as a Jew would have in a Hitler Court or a Trotsky follower before Stalin.[19]

While Senator Truman said that he did not condone election frauds, his case was weak, and it was torn to pieces by the opposition. Judge Reeves declared it was the "speech of a man nominated by ghost votes, elected with ghost votes, and whose speeches are probably written by ghost writers."[20] In the Senate, Republican Senator Styles Bridges presented proofs of malfeasance in Missouri politics, including the reported conviction of A. R. Hendricks, one of Truman's campaign managers in 1934. For Senator Truman, who had been striving to achieve an image of independence, his speech was a setback. It was the only open defense he made of the Pendergast machine in his Senate career, but the opposition press seized upon it. It played up the censure of Truman by the Lawyers' Association in Kansas City and a skit put on before the St. Louis Advertising Club that pictured Truman as Tom Pendergast's puppet.[21]

The Truman speech emphasized his loyalty to the party organization, his belief in party politics as a means of accomplishing given ends, and his mistaken faith in Pendergast, whose personal guilt in the wrongdoing of the organization had not yet been exposed. The victims of the vote fraud investigation were minor organization members, under orders in some cases and even unwitting in others, not the higher officials who could have prevented such corruption. After all, the original Boss Pendergast, Tom's older brother James, did not countenance election corruption. The practices that Tom Pendergast allowed to flourish were indefensible, as he himself was soon to learn.

The election fraud cases should have been a warning to Pendergast, but it was too late for him to change his course. Governor Stark had cleaned up the administration of elections in Kansas City and was hoping to defeat the machine in the city council elections to be held in March. The governor was disappointed when the machine won the city elections, but Pendergast's elation was premature and very short-lived. The organization plurality was large, for the voters were not yet aware of the rottenness of the city government, but the total vote was down, indicating that the days when the pluralities were inflated by fraudulent votes were gone. Governor Stark continued his challenge in the August primary by backing the election of Judge James M. Douglas of the Missouri Supreme Court. Pendergast accepted the challenge and put up a candidate of his own, Judge James V. Billings, an obscure circuit court judge from southwestern Missouri. The battle was a rousing one in which Governor Stark stumped the state, stirred the conscience of the voters, and brought victory for his candidate. Douglas's majority of 120,000 was produced largely by voters in the small towns and rural areas. The astounding Kansas City majorities of former days were cut in half. Governor Stark, proving himself a better vote getter in the state than Pendergast, caught President Roosevelt's attention, who advised Governor Stark on contacting the federal treasury officials, and told Farley that the governor was the future power in Missouri politics.[22]

A series of events now hastened the collapse of Tom Pendergast's control over the political affairs of the state. The downfall was the result of a combination of factors. For one thing, Pendergast's failing health and increasing absenteeism had loosened his grip upon party organization affairs. For another, his gambling losses and extravagant living expenses had led to insatiable demands for more and more ready cash. The favorable image that he was once able to maintain among businessmen and middle-class voters was becoming tarnished. Finally, a net of state and federal officials was closing fast upon his highly questionable activities.

In 1935, as Tom Pendergast and his family were about to start a luxury tour of Europe, a story by Marquis Childs appeared in the *St. Louis Post-Dispatch* commenting on the proposed settlement of the insurance rate case.[23] The courts had impounded the funds of some $9 million derived from increased fire insurance rates until an equitable settlement could be reached. The way in which this settlement was brought about did not come out in the open until three years later, in 1938, when Governor Stark refused to reappoint Emmett O'Malley as insurance commissioner. The governor then cooperated with federal officials in pressing the investigation of the transactions of the insurance companies in connection with the settlement. A tip led the investigation to Tom Pendergast. Milligan obtained a confession from a key insurance official to the effect that a $750,000 bribe had been offered to Pendergast for the settlement. Part of this had been paid in cash, and on none of it had Pendergast paid income taxes. The amount received had been lost gambling.

Pendergast's insurance deal was revealing; it clearly showed how the boss operated and how he served a variety of interests. Large-scale broker that he was, he tried to see that as many people as possible got something out of his deals. Nor did he take all of the bribe money himself; he divided it between O'Malley and the representative of the insurance companies. But he and his lawyers were getting careless; he should have paid the income tax. As for the settlement itself, it was praised and defended by the insurance companies, by prominent Kansas City real estate promoters, and by property owners.

When Pendergast was indicted for income tax evasion, Senator Truman did not believe that he was guilty, declaring that the indictment was "political."[24] But, in May 1939, Pendergast pled guilty to the insurance fund tax charge and to other extensive charges of income tax evasion. He threw himself on the mercy of the court, which sentenced him to fifteen months in jail, fined him $10,000, agreed to a settlement of his tax obligations for $434,000, placed him on probation, and forbade him to engage in political activities while on probation.[25] Here was a chance for Truman to repudiate Pendergast, but he preferred to tell the press that he would not.[26] Pendergast died in 1945 before his probation was over.

The investigations revealed that a majority of Kansas City area citizens were indifferent or had been badly misled regarding the true nature of the Pendergast machine.[27] City Manager McElroy's vaunted surpluses turned out to be huge deficits. An audit revealed a deficit in claims and accounts amounting to nearly $20 million. Almost $11 million had been unlawfully diverted from waterworks bonds and over three thousand employees were doing nothing but picking up their paychecks.[28] Walter Matscheck, former director of the Kansas City Civic Research Institute, had never been fooled regarding the nature of the system and when asked about it later said: "We pointed this out all through the years, and nearly everything the Institute said regarding the finances of the city and in fact other things was corroborated when we had the audits of half dozen different phases of city government in 1939 and 1940. In fact, some of the things we had said all through the years looked rather tame compared to what the auditors found."[29] While Matscheck found Truman honest and knowledgeable regarding county government, Truman had not heeded Matscheck's warnings regarding the Kansas City government.

City Manager McElroy resigned. He was indicted for income tax evasion but died before the investigation of his fiscal policies was completed. His unique system of bookkeeping was actually nothing more than a system of juggling the books to conceal a vast system of stealing from the public treasury. As county judge, he had not been in a position to use a trick system of bookkeeping for these purposes.

Other officials were caught in the web of the investigators. Former Insurance Commissioner Emmett O'Malley received a sentence for income tax evasion on the money he had received from the insurance companies' bribe. WPA Director Matt Murray was convicted on income tax evasion on funds he had received from Boss Pendergast, and so was Otto Higgins, director of the police department. The leader of the gambling syndicate, Charley Carollo, was sentenced to eight years in jail for using the mails to defraud and for income tax evasion.[30] Throughout 1939, new cases were prosecuted and additional members of the organization were sent to jail. The rout of the Pendergast Kansas City organization as led by Boss Tom was complete.

Senator Truman viewed the situation with concern, even consulting Senator Burton Wheeler about resigning from the Senate because he owed his election to Pendergast. Wheeler responded: "I asked if he was involved in way in the scandal. Truman said that he was not. I said there was no reason for him to resign and advised him to go about his business as if nothing had happened."[31]

After Tom Pendergast was sentenced to jail, the effectiveness of the party machine declined rapidly. There was no one at hand to furnish the strong leadership that Tom had provided. In the Kansas City council elections of 1940, the reform candidates won, and a new era in Kansas City politics and government was initiated. The new city manager was a professional who was anxious and willing to abide by the spirit of the city manager plan.

For Senator Truman, these events were most upsetting. The fact that the Pendergast organization was no longer the smooth-running machine that it once was would not prevent the opposition from exploiting his former connections and his failure to join the crusade for cleaning up the scandals. The chances of his securing a renomination and a reelection looked dim, regardless of his own reputation for honesty and the good record he had made as senator.

In retrospect, Truman's behavior in the Pendergast affair was certainly less than desirable. The press demanded that he should denounce Pendergast, but he refused to do so. Personal loyalty kept him from deserting an old friend in trouble.

The code that Truman followed did not interfere with his legislative functions as senator; there were limits to what he would do for the Goat machine. Patronage, to Truman's lights, was one of the honored prerogatives of the system, and in matters of this sort he was consistently loyal to the machine. This was something he felt he owed the organization for what it had done for him. Risks, of course, were part of the game: some of the appointees might turn out badly. When it came to the legislative needs of the people of Missouri, however, his vote was not for sale. He would vote for the best interests of the state or nation.

A gloomy political future loomed on the horizon for Truman as the fortunes of the Pendergast machine declined. Still, he found it impossible to accept, let alone condone, the actions of Governor Stark, whom he regarded as an ingrate. Stark followed another code of conduct, one that Truman found wanting. The governor had accepted the Pendergast support and then, following his election, had turned on the machine, assuming the role of a reformer. Most people justified such actions against those who had betrayed the public trust. As for the corruption revealed in his state, Truman did not regard himself as responsible. He had not voted in Kansas City nor had he run its election machinery. The other forms of graft never touched him. Indeed until Pendergast's plea of guilty, Truman thought him innocent, persecuted because he wielded so much power. When the evidence was in, he blamed Pendergast's downfall on his ill health and his mania for gambling. Truman reasoned, sympathetically. though perhaps not accurately, that there was a relation between the increasing problems Pendergast was caught in and the decline of his mental acuity, caused, Truman felt, by his physical suffering.

Senatorial prerogatives were guarded jealously by Truman. These were, he felt, his personal responsibility. Neither a Pendergast at one extreme nor a Roosevelt at the other should dictate how a senator should vote or how the Senate should be organized. Moreover, a president should know better than to try to exert pressure on a senator through the state's political organization. And, above all, he should not, in distributing patronage, recognize a governor when he has two senators, both of his own party, to work through. As a senator, Truman was becoming a staunch supporter of the traditions, the rules, and the privileges of the Senate.

chapter 13   LEGISLATIVE ROLE

*I found out very soon after I had settled down to a study of my duties
that the business of a good legislator is not to get things done quickly
and efficiently, as a good administrator has to do, but to prevent,
if possible, the enactment into the law of the land many crazy and
crackpot measures. I have found that much deliberation and study
on all proposed legislation is a great deal better for the public welfare
than too much hurry and immediate action.*
—Harry S. Truman, address, March 21, 1939

When Truman became the junior senator from Missouri, he felt very
humble. He had had no experience in the House of Representatives as had
many other freshmen senators.[1] As a newcomer to Washington, he had
everything to learn about the Senate's procedures and customs. Following
in the footsteps of such distinguished Missouri senators as Thomas Hart
Benton, Carl Schurz, and James Reed would be difficult indeed. As he put
it to the Washington correspondent for the friendly *Kansas City Journal-
Post*, William P. Helm, he was "only a humble member of the next Senate,
green as grass and ignorant as a fool about practically everything worth
knowing."[2]

We get a rather interesting picture of the "green as grass" senator from
Helm, who, during Truman's Senate career, received more or less favored
treatment in the form of exclusives from time to time. A Republican by
personal preference, Helm was won over by Truman's humility, naturalness,
and friendliness. In his *Harry Truman: A Political Biography*, Helm later
reconstructed Truman's view of the Senate on the day he was sworn in
this way:

It is a high honor, but a still higher responsibility to become a senator of the
United States and to be given a voice and a vote in the country's chief law-making
body. I realize this today in its full measure, more than I have ever realized it before.

I shall try to perform my duties to the best of my ability. In this I shall need the
help and the prayers of those who have given me the privilege of serving them. For
myself, I seek nothing from this service. My steadfast hope is that I may be given
wisdom to perform my duties acceptably to those whom I want to serve.[3]

Judge Truman's reception in the national capital was hardly royal. The senator from Missouri, Bennett Clark, his old World War I fellow officer in the artillery who had played jokes on him during the war and who had been bitterly anti-Pendergast in the primary campaign, took him by the arm to be sworn in. Some of the senators seemed to be cool to the newcomer, whose connections with the Tom Pendergast machine had been well advertised. This was especially true of Senator Bronson Cutting of New Mexico and Senator George Norris of Nebraska. Senator Cutting never had a chance to warm up to Senator Truman (he was killed shortly afterward in an airplane crash), but Senator Norris changed his view later.[4] On the other hand, Senator J. Ham Lewis from the neighboring state of Illinois greeted Truman cordially and said, "Mr. Truman, don't start out with an inferiority complex. For the first six months, you'll wonder how you got here. After that you'll wonder how the rest of us got here."[5]

Senator Carl Hayden of Arizona was also friendly to the new senator, advising him on Senate procedure. Following Hayden's advice, Truman tried to become a "work-horse" rather than a "show-horse." As he put it in his *Memoirs:* "I soon found that . . . the real business of the Senate was carried on by unassuming and conscientious men, not by those who managed to get the most publicity."[6]

A senator newly arrived in Washington needs immediate staff assistance for a wide variety of purposes—the customs of the legislative body and the techniques for getting things done are to be learned and followed, and advice is needed on living in the nation's capital. For this position national committeeman James Aylward proposed Victor Messall, formerly administrative assistant to Congressman Frank Lee from Joplin, Missouri, who had retired voluntarily from the House after the new districts had been drawn. Messall at first was not enthusiastic about working for "the senator from Pendergast" but agreed to help him get settled. One of the first things he tended to was housing; Messall helped him find a moderately priced apartment in Tilden Gardens, on upper Connecticut Avenue which, though small, met the minimum requirements of the family of four—Bess, her mother, Margaret, and Harry.

Messall was another of those who found his initial reaction to Truman subject to change: "By now I realized that my original impression of him was all wet. This was a man of real integrity and brains and no Pendergast or anyone else was going to push him around. Once you got to know him you knew he had something special. So I agreed to go to work for him."[7] In the early days of Truman's apprenticeship as a senator, Messall was invaluable because of his knowledge of the Congress, but as Truman caught on and made many friends he became less essential. In 1940, following the election, he left Truman's service to become a lobbyist, something about which Truman had reservations. In general Truman did not like to have former employees of his capitalize on their relations with him for their own benefit. He did not have this feeling, however, about his comrades-in-arms from the war. Messall recalled that one of Truman's first acts was to give him a list of Battery D veterans, all of whom were to get special considera- tion if they asked for anything.[8] In addition to Messall, Truman, in the early days of his senatorship, had on his staff two stenographers who had been with Congressman Lee and a third, Reathel Odum, who had been one of John Snyder's secretaries when he was a bank examiner.[9]

As a freshman senator, Truman followed the long-established tradition in the Senate of being seen but not heard for the first year or so. He stuck to his committee responsibilities and did his homework, taking a stack of books and papers back to his apartment every night in order to prepare for his next day's work. For a freshman senator, his committee appointments were good ones: Appropriations, Interstate Commerce, Printing, and Public Buildings and Grounds. He had wished to be on the Committee on Military Affairs, a predictable desire, which was satisfied later.

Regarding his experience on the Appropriations Committee, he wrote in his *Memoirs:*

The Appropriations Committee, composed of 24 members, was the largest of all the Senate Committees and was under the chairmanship of Carter Glass of Virginia. I never missed a meeting, for this committee examined in detail every federal expendi- ture and worked out the budget. By way of these meetings, I became thoroughly acquainted with the fiscal aspects of the national administration and gained an insight into the workings of federal finance that was of inestimable value to me in later years.[10]

Among Truman's mentors in the Senate, Burton K. Wheeler of Montana must be ranked among the most important. Wheeler was a Democrat who had deserted his party's ticket in 1924 to run for vice-president on the La Follette Progressive ticket. Truman could not have had a better teacher in the entire Senate. "Wheeler was a great legislator—there was none better," said Thomas G. Corcoran, who was President Roosevelt's liaison with Congress. He added that the keys to Wheeler's greatness were "a first class mind" and an intuitive understanding of his colleagues.[11] Wheeler was chairman of the Committee on Interstate Commerce and as one of the Senate's foremost interrogators, he taught Truman a great deal about Senate investigating committees. As a freshman senator, Wheeler had fear- lessly pursued the wrongdoers in the Harding administration and brought them to justice. Senator Truman acknowledged his debt to Wheeler, and although the two were to differ on some major issues later, they remained friends. Truman was not one to forget a friend who had helped him over some rough places. He wrote: "My committee experience was an education. On the Interstate Commerce Committee, I learned the history of railroad finance, civil aeronautics, communications, federal trade and became acquainted with several able and distinguished Senators."[12] Perhaps the most distinguished was Wheeler, regarding whom Joseph Alsop wrote:

His great forte was legislative fighting. His suspicions gave him a peculiar prevision of the enemy's next moves. He was energetic and tireless. He knew every twist and turn of the legislative game, and he was not above using its brutal expedients if they promised to be helpful. Although he had his own good share of vanity, he knew how to soothe the vanities of others, and he worked well with his team.[13]

Senator Truman was assigned at first to a subcommittee of the Interstate Commerce Committee, which held hearings on a bill that eventually became the Civil Aeronautics Act of 1938. The chairman of this subcommittee was Senator Pat McCarran of Nevada, and in the House the battle for new legislation to regulate the aviation industry was led by Congressman Clarence Lea of California. The industry was growing rapidly and needed uniform rules. Financial failures of new airlines were common due to unbridled competition, while the many crashes of army airplanes in their attempts to carry mail showed the lack of proper training and safety measures and a need for the development of military aviation along with civil aviation.

On June 7, 1935, President Roosevelt recommended to Congress that the Interstate Commerce Commission be designated to regulate all air carriers.[14] This proposal was not in accord with the report of the Federal Aviation Commission appointed to investigate the subject, but Senators McCarran and Truman went along with the President. The commission had recommended a new and independent regulatory commission to do the job.[15] The President's proposal met the bitter opposition of Senator Kenneth McKeller of Tennessee, a champion of the role of the post office in civil aviation. When McCarran became ill in 1937, Truman took over the defense of the bill, displaying knowledge of the subject, but he was no match for the obstructionist tactics of McKeller, and the bill did not pass in that session.

President Roosevelt then appointed a special interdepartmental committee, which also recommended a separate commission to regulate all phases of aviation. The President then asked Congress to formulate such legislation. A draft bill set up the Civil Aeronautics Authority to perform quasi-legislative and quasi-judicial functions, the administrator to perform executive functions, and the Air Safety Board to investigate accidents. A controversy arose between McCarran and Truman as to the powers of the President to remove the administrator, with Truman favoring presidential dismissal powers.[16] The administration turned to Truman as its spokesman for its favored version of the bill, and he performed so ably in defending presidential power that he won praise from Arthur Krock of the *New York Times*.[17]

The bill as passed stressed the military potential of aviation, brought about the establishment of the Air Safety Board with flyer representation, required compliance with hours and wages decisions of the National Labor Relations Board, and as far as possible used the terminology of the Interstate Commerce Act, which had been elaborately interpreted by the Supreme Court.[18] Arthur Krock again singled out the importance of Truman's efforts, his conscientious attendance at hearings, and his defense of presidential powers.[19] The act was also praised highly by transportation experts.[20] Senator Truman had learned well from his master teacher, Senator Wheeler.

RAILROAD HEARINGS AND TRANSPORTATION ACT OF 1940

Truman said that he spent more time on the investigation of railroad finance than on any other subject during his first term.[21] Even before the Great Depression, the railroads were in financial difficulties. Suffering severe losses in passenger and freight traffic to motor vehicles and beginning to lose traffic to airlines, they were no longer an expanding industry. The railroads, however, were still the backbone of the American transportation system and continued to handle the bulk of the heavy traffic for a complicated industrial system. Consequently the huge sums of money invested in the railroads needed to be safeguarded for the good of the free enterprise system. The Senate investigating committee was principally concerned with the mishandling of the railroads by holding companies controlled by Wall Street banks.

On February 4, 1935, Senator Wheeler introduced a resolution calling for an investigation into the financial problems that were crippling the railroads. At first Truman was not on the subcommittee selected to do the work, but he asked Wheeler if he could attend the meetings. Wheeler consented, and Truman became a faithful attendant at the long and complicated sessions. When a vacancy occurred on the subcommittee, Truman was made a member. This committee brought him in touch with Max Lowenthal, a labor attorney, who had been named counsel for the committee because of a book he had written on railroad finance.[22] This meeting was to prove crucial in Truman's career, because it was Lowenthal who convinced Sidney Hillman (later to form the Political Action Committee of the Congress of Industrial Organizations) that Senator Harry S. Truman would be a vice-presidential candidate acceptable to organized labor.

Lowenthal was important to Truman in other ways. A friend of Supreme Court Justice Louis Brandeis, he one day asked Truman if he would like to meet the justice. Truman said he was not accustomed to meeting persons of such status, but he consented to go and he was greatly impressed with Brandeis's philosophy of free enterprise and the need for strict regulation of large combinations. The justice took a liking to Truman and would corner him for a discussion of railroad finance.[23] Speeches Truman delivered in the

Senate on railroad high finance revealed clear signs of the Brandeis influence and perhaps Lowenthal's handiwork.[24] Tenets of this economic philosophy included distrust of Wall Street, protection of small business, defense of labor, opposition to government ownership, and belief in government regulation of economic activities.

In 1937, when Wheeler became absorbed in the Supreme Court reform battle, he left the railroad investigation largely to Truman. When the investigation turned to the exploitation of the Missouri Pacific by the Allegheny Corporation, a holding company, Lowenthal was concerned about Truman's ability to resist pressures. Truman told the staff, however, to treat this investigation like any other.[25] Lowenthal was impressed at the way Truman stood up under fire. He felt that Truman sensed the spirit of the American political system:

That has something to do with the way he ran his big investigations—it is an innate part of his personality to be fair and to know what is fair, and to exercise restraint when he possesses great power, particularly the power to investigate and detect, and the power to police. . . . He followed the instincts and policies of a good administrator—relied on his staff to get the data together and to conduct the questioning. He gave witnesses all the time they wanted.[26]

Investigation of the Missouri Pacific system presented a severe test for Senator Truman's independence and adherence to the Burkean concept of the role of the legislator. The eighty-company Missouri Pacific system had been acquired in 1930 by the Allegheny Corporation, a Cleveland holding company formed by the Van Sweringens with the aid of the investment bankers of J. P. Morgan and Company. The committee found that under Allegheny control, unjustified dividends were declared, no surplus for emergencies or expansion was established, accounts were juggled, payrolls were cut, maintenance was neglected, and the accounting regulations of the Interstate Commerce Commission were ignored. In the spirited argument over accounting procedures, the representative of the Price, Waterhouse firm hired by Morgan and Company admitted that misleading entries had been made.[27] The holding company also exerted undue pressure on the Missouri Public Service Commission, and the bankers overpowered the representatives of the insurance companies who were supposed to protect the interests of the investors. The business and political interests in Missouri were alarmed at the course of the investigation and flooded Senator Truman's office with protests. Lowenthal later told a reporter, "There were not two other senators who would have withstood such political pressure as Senator Truman did."[28]

The railroad investigation gave Senator Truman an opportunity to make two major speeches on the subject of railway finance and the American economic system. Jonathan Daniels was of the opinion that he was assisted by Max Lowenthal in writing these speeches.[29] Certainly the Brandeis influence was manifest. The first, delivered in the Senate on June 3, 1937, charged:

Some of the country's greatest railroads have been deliberately looted by their financial agents. Speaking of the Rock Island reminds me that the first railroad robbery was committed on the Rock Island back in 1873 just east of Council Bluffs, Iowa. . . . The same Jesse James held up the Missouri Pacific in 1876 and took the paltry sum of $17,000 from the express car. About thirty years after the Council Bluffs holdup, the Rock Island went through a looting by some gentlemen known as the "Tin Plate Millionaires." They used no guns, but they ruined the railroad and got away with $70,000,000 or more. They did it by means of holding companies. Senators can see what "pikers" Mr. James and his crowd were alongside of some real artists.[30]

In his December 10 speech, Senator Truman continued his denunciation of the railroad holding companies:

It is a pity that Wall Street with its ability to control all the wealth of the Nation and to hire the best brains in the country has not produced some financial statesmen, some men who could see the danger of bigness and of the concentration of the control of wealth. Instead of working to meet the situation, they are still employing the best law brains to serve greed and selfish interests. . . .[31]

One of the difficulties as I see it, is that we worship money instead of honor. A billionaire, in our estimate, is much greater in these days in the eyes of the people than the public servant who works for the public interest. It makes no difference if the billionaire rode to wealth on the sweat of little children and the blood of underpaid labor. No one ever considered Carnegie libraries steeped in the blood of the Homestead steel workers, but they are. We do not remember that the Rockefeller Foundation is founded on the dead miners of the Colorado Fuel and Iron Company and a dozen other similar performances.[32]

In this diatribe Truman failed to recognize the changed policies of the Rockefellers and the Carnegies. He would have been fairer to stick to the theme of bigness as he did in later passages.

This is Jeffersonian philosophy applied to the twentieth century. In practice, Truman did not follow it since he did not, as senator, neglect the interests of the two big metropolitan areas in his state. Truman's speeches and conduct of the investigations aroused the ire of the defenders of the legal and banking professions. Robert T. Swaine, in particular, denounced the "cynical New Deal inconoclasts . . . requiring the pound of flesh," and the epidemic of investigations.[33]

During the investigation, Truman also became a defender of railroad labor interests. When the railroad companies proposed in 1938 to meet their financial problems by cutting wages, he appeared before the President's fact-finding board and opposed the move on the ground that labor should not be made to suffer for losses due to fraud, wrong dividend policies, and mistakes by investment bankers. Wages were not reduced, and Truman won friends among the ranks and leadership of organized labor.

In 1939, Roosevelt asked Senators Wheeler and Truman to prepare a transportation bill that would combine the reports of several fact-finding commissions into one unified recommendation. With the exception of the pipelines, which prospered even during the Depression, other modes of transportation—railways, airlines, and motor and water transport—suffered from severe competition and loss of traffic. The bill that was drafted attempted to coordinate the necessary regulation of such modes in a just manner, but there was considerable opposition to the proposed consolidation.[34] Some senators as well as farm groups objected to the inclusion of water carriers. Secretary of Agriculture Henry Wallace denounced the bill as favoring the railroads, which had oppressed the farmers. Secretary of War H. A. Woodring thought the bill was an attack on his rivers and harbors program, while Maritime Commission Chairman Emery S. Land did not want to lose his authority over inland water carriers. Senator Clark, senior senator from Missouri, also opposed the bill as a threat to water carriers.

In replying to these objections, Senator Truman emphasized the fact that the railroads were still the major traffic movers, handling two-thirds of the nation's tonnage, and their welfare was essential to the national prosperity. There was, he argued, an overabundance of transportation facilities, and each mode should concentrate on what it could do best. Further, he pointed out, as a senator from a state with two great water systems, he was opposed to any bill that would put water carriers at a disadvantage. Since the waterways were public property maintained at public expense, they should be subjected to regulation. He noted that motor carriers had accepted such regulation and now were thankful for it.[35]

The act as it finally passed did not provide for a consolidation of all transportation; it omitted the airlines and made many exemptions for water carriers. Nor did it contain a provision for correlating government promotional and regulatory policies. Thus, it was still possible for one department to extend water and motor transportation while another might wish to curtail such modes. But the act was an important step toward such consolidation. It provided some protection for the railroads as the mainstay of American transport and gave some protection to labor. Truman's work in support of the act was praised editorially by the *New York Times* and the *Christian Science Monitor*.[36]

GENERAL LEGISLATIVE RECORD

Proud of his record in the field of transportation, Senator Truman knew that he could not hope to be an expert during his first term on the vast array of other subjects of concern to the legislature. In general he followed the leadership of the chief of his party, President Roosevelt, as he had promised during his campaign. But his voting did invite criticism from both sides. When he deviated from the President's recommendations, he was accused of breaking his promises; when he followed the party line more closely, he was labeled an unthinking puppet who could then be blamed for not trying to prevent some of the New Deal mistakes. Such strict observance of the Roosevelt line, of course, could endanger the image of independence he was trying to develop following the outstanding example of his mentor, Senator Wheeler.

On several occasions during his first term, he displayed just such independence of the Roosevelt leadership. For fiscal reasons, the President opposed the immediate payment of the soldiers' bonus. Senator Truman, however, had announced his position in favor of immediate payment during his campaign. True to this promise, he voted in 1935 and 1936 in favor of the adjusted Compensation Act and for overriding President Roosevelt's vetoes of these acts. On this question, his loyalty to his fellow veterans was greater than his loyalty to the President. When in March 1935 Truman voted against the McCarran amendment, providing for the payment of the prevailing wage scale in the President's work relief bill, the *St. Louis Post-Dispatch* called attention in an editorial to "Senator Truman's Flop."[37] As we have seen, he did not support Roosevelt's choice for majority leader of the Senate in 1937 because he was loyal to the Senate's prerogatives to choose its own leaders. Nor did he join the President's attempted purge of recalcitrant senators in 1938; rather he supported the renomination and reelection of his colleague, Senator Clark, whom the President had opposed as being antiadministration in the Court fight and on preparedness issues. In 1939, Truman voted against an administration proposal to allow the Tennessee Valley Authority to issue bonds to buy up private power facilities, a vote based on his economic belief that public projects should not compete with private enterprises.[38] Generally Senator Truman's voting record during his first term was almost solidly New Deal. He did not join the debate except when he had made a special study of the subject, as in the field of transportation.

In legislative matters, Truman tried to serve the interests of the varied groups in Missouri as well as he could within his idea of what was the national interest. Many times different groups had conflicting aims, and it was not possible to satisfy all parties concerned. Since the balance between the two major parties in the state was close, he could not afford to antagonize the traditional Democrats on too many issues and expect to get reelected. On the other hand, it was hopeless for him to try to please some of the conservative Republicans.

While Missouri businessmen normally voted with the Republican party, there were some Bourbon Democrats whose conservatism was that of the solid South.[39] Truman did not neglect the business interests. His aim in the railroad investigation was to help the operating companies and the investors holding their securities in their fight against the manipulations of Wall Street bankers and holding companies. He carefully cultivated businessmen throughout the state and could count among his friends bankers, airline and railroad executives, publishers, chamber of commerce officials, and real estate developers.[40] Department store executives praised his work on the freight forwarding bill. Businessmen in southwest Missouri appreciated his efforts on behalf of the Table Rock power project. He tried to convince the chambers of commerce in his various public addresses before them that President Roosevelt was trying to invigorate the business community.

As a representative from a state in which over three hundred thousand persons were engaged in agriculture, Senator Truman had a natural interest in the New Deal farm programs and claimed that he studied them carefully. After the Supreme Court declared the original Agricultural Adjustment Act unconstitutional early in 1936, it was necessary for the New Deal agricultural experts to devise a new formula, which they did in the Soil Conservation Act of 1936. The new law was based on the general welfare clause of the Constitution and contemplated eventual federal grants to the states for soil conservation and for the maintenance of farm income at fair levels.[41] Truman voted for this act, and in a radio address shortly after its passage he commented:

The Administration is making an honest effort to create a definite policy for agriculture, one which will place the farmer on a level with other industries.

For the first time in our history, we are discovering that the producer of food and fiber is a vital and essential part of our population, and that his interests and welfare are as important as the banker's, the manufacturer's and the building contractor's.

The welfare of the country demands that this policy should be carried to a successful conclusion and I am sure that the country as a whole will see that it is.[42]

Truman supported a number of other agricultural measures during his first term, including the Farm Mortgage and Farm Credit Acts of 1935, the Commodity Exchange and Rural Electrification Acts of 1936, the Farm Tenancy Act of 1937, and various farm subsidy acts. The Commodity Exchange Authority regulated commodity exchanges for the purpose of insuring fair practice and controlling those forms of speculation that often demoralized the markets. Truman undoubtedly remembered his father's

unfortunate experience on the grain exchange. His vote for the Farm Security Administration showed his concern for poor tenant farmers.

In 1938, Congress passed the comprehensive Agricultural Adjustment
Act, which Secretary Wallace called a new charter of economic freedom for
farmers and economic protection against scarcity for consumers. Marketing
control was substituted for direct production control in order to avoid constitutional challenges. The new legislation was based on the commerce
clause and attempted to assist farmers in obtaining parity prices and parity
income. The base period used in determining parity prices was the 1909-14
period during which the demand for agricultural goods kept up with
general production advances. Wallace, calling the plan the ever-normal
granary plan of balanced abundance, stressed the importance of systematic
storage as a basic part of this plan.[43] Truman had been a farmer during the
base period and the plan and storage facilities needed to implement it were
to become important issues in the 1948 presidential race.

On March 2, 1939, Senator Truman addressed the Senate on the agricultural progress and expressed some of his doubts:

> The farm program in the Middle West and the South is becoming more difficult. I
> am very much interested and anxious to find a solution.
> There is no desire on my part to be critical or to question the motives of Secretary
> Wallace and his various farm remedies. The farm bill as passed by the last Congress
> apparently is not working successfully.
> Whether that is due to the legislation itself or the administration, I do not know.
> But the fact remains that income to the farmer has not been materially increased.
> The farmer is not getting his fair share of the national income, and unless he can get
> his fair share there is no settlement of the problem.[44]

It was not until World War II brought tremendous demands for agricultural goods that the farm problem was to be solved, at least for the
duration. In the postwar period, President Truman continued to struggle
with some of these same problems.

Since over half of the Missourians lived in cities, Truman was also interested in labor problems. As his colleague, Senator Robert F. Wagner of
New York, put it, "Truman's . . . devotion . . . to the common people on the
farm and in the factory . . . stamped him . . . most useful member of the
United States Senate."[45] When the Wagner labor relations bill came before
the Senate in 1935, Senator Truman supported it but did not join the stormy
debate. In 1936 and 1937, he supported Wagner's housing bills, but in the
latter year he was disturbed by labor violence in Detroit and other areas and
voted for the Byrnes resolution declaring sitdown strikes illegal. Nonetheless, when the fair labor standards bill came before the Senate in 1937,
Truman supported it strongly, although he did not indicate this verbally at

the time. In later years, he worked consistently for increasing the minimum wage levels.

While President Roosevelt rarely supported or endorsed civil rights legislation, Senator Truman could not avoid involvement.[46] There were 130,000 black voters back in Missouri, strategically located in Kansas City and St. Louis.[47] In the 1934 senatorial campaign, Truman carried the wards inhabited largely by black voters, and he wished to retain this support. When compelled to go on record, he voted in favor of civil rights. In 1938 he explained to a southern senator when the Senate was debating an anti-lynching measure: "You know I am against this bill, but if it comes to a vote I'll have to be for it. All my sympathies are with you but the Negro vote in Kansas City and St. Louis is too important."[48] Though apparently lacking firm convictions on civil rights, in the Seventy-fifth Congress he signed cloture petitions and endorsed motions to close debate on the anti-lynching bill against which some of the senators were waging a filibuster; in 1940 he supported an amendment to the Selective Service Act to prevent discrimination against members of minority groups who wished to volunteer for military service. To these voters he supplied his strong support of the New Deal economic legislation, which helped underprivileged groups, and his outspoken civil-rights pronouncements in which he stressed the principle of equality.

The suffering caused by the Depression, which Truman had seen firsthand when he was reemployment director for Missouri, led him to support the social security bill when it was introduced in 1935. In the succeeding years, he supported amendments designed to improve the act and its administration. In 1939 before the Missouri legislature he said: "Our social security legislation may not be perfect, but it is a step in the right direction. No one wants to repeal it. It is an effort to give the everyday citizen who works for a living some hope and security that he won't be a burden in his declining years."[49] As president, Truman was to recommend improvements in the program, including Medicare.

A controversial issue that brought considerable division among the Democratic members of Congress during President Roosevelt's second term was the administrative reorganization bill, designed to carry out some of the recommendations of the President's Committee on Administrative Management.[50] Senator Clark opposed the measure vigorously while Senator Truman supported it. As Truman summarized the measure, it "called for the delegation of power to the president to reorganize federal agencies, to terminate or create them as changing needs require, to establish a new Department of Welfare, and to exercise greater freedom in emergencies to allocate appropriations without recourse to the Congress, but subject to review by an auditor general."[51] This bill was denounced as an attempt to deprive Congress of its constitutional powers and to set up a dictatorship, but Truman saw it as a measure designed to increase efficiency and economy and to provide for emergencies arising so quickly there was no time for Congress to act. The bill was defeated in 1938, but it passed the following year.

Toward the end of Senator Truman's first term, the gathering war clouds turned the attention of members of Congress to foreign policy, national security, internationalism, and America's position in a world where isolationism was becoming more difficult to maintain. Missouri was in the belt where isolationism was a strong tradition. Senator Clark was an isolationist, in part due to the large number of German-Americans in his section of the state. While Truman admitted that he was misled by the Nye investigation of the munitions industries into supporting the embargo on arms shipments under the Neutrality Acts of 1935 and 1937, the invasion of Poland, the fall of France, and the siege of Great Britain convinced him that the United States was in danger, and he supported President Roosevelt's requests for huge defense appropriations, for a peacetime draft, and for modification of the Neutrality Act. As his first term came to a close, he became more interested in military affairs than in transportation.

During the three Congresses of Truman's first term as a senator, he compiled a voting record as a loyal New Dealer. The *Congressional Quarterly*, by way of illustating party loyalty through voting, selected seventeen key votes for the period.[52] Twelve of these were considered party votes in that a majority of the Democrats opposed a majority of the Republicans. On all of these Truman was with the Democratic majority except the Public Utility Holding Act, on which he was recorded as not voting.[53] On the remaining five roll calls, both parties were on the same side. Truman was with the majority except on the reform of the Supreme Court when he sided with the President and not with a majority of his colleagues. About half of the time, he and Senator Clark voted on opposite sides of these roll calls, a most unusual situation for two senators from the same state and party.[54] Clark voted against the majority of the Democratic party on the Guffey-Snyder Coal Act, the Public Utility Holding Act, naval expansion, spending-lending, and compulsory military service, thus placing himself among the conservatives and the isolationists. It appears that Clark was responding to family tradition, to the sentiments of German-Americans in Missouri, and to his own conservative leanings. This behavior cost him his renomination in 1944.

Truman apparently learned his legislative lessons well although he began slowly. While he did not introduce many bills and, at first, did not make any speeches, this was in accord with the customs of the Senate for freshmen senators in the 1930s. Under the skillful tutelage of Senator Wheeler, however, he began his specialization early, and he became an effective legislator in formulating, guiding, and defending two important pieces of transportation legislation: the Civil Aeronautics Act of 1938 and the Transportation Act of 1940. He also acquired skill as a legislative investigator, demonstrating diplomacy, coolness, friendliness, courage in standing up to pressure, and an ability to concentrate on the main purpose of a hearing. He began to develop effective debating skills and, in the railroad finance hearings, gained invaluable training for the chairmanship of his own Special Committee to Investigate the Defense Program, which came to him in his next term. Truman was not a flashy senator, but he researched all issues and, as he had earlier in Jackson County, let the facts supply the rhetoric. In his first term, he established himself as an expert in transportation and, to a considerable extent, found himself increasingly attracted to the political philosophy of Justice Brandeis. At the close of his first term, he could consider himself well grounded, practically, politically, and philosophically, in Washington life.

chapter 14 | RETURNED TO THE SENATE IN 1940

Politics are almost as exciting as war, and quite as dangerous. In war you can only be killed once, but in politics many times.
—Sir Winston Churchill, 1920

If you pick up a starving dog and make him prosperous, he will not bite you. That is the principal difference between a dog and a man.
—Mark Twain, *Pudd'nhead Wilson's Calendar*

Truman faced an uphill struggle for his Senate seat in the election of 1940. It was, in a sense, a primer for his even more rigorous campaign eight years later. Starting in 1940 at a point of low ebb, he managed to work out a successful strategy. His forces first divided the opposition and then won the support of organized labor. Working under difficult circumstances, they raised a modest campaign fund, dodged the worrisome war and peace issues, and finally put together the organizational support so necessary in a primary. The Senate had proved a happy home for Truman, and he was determined to continue there if possible.[1]

As the senator approached the end of his first six-year term, the prospects of his securing a renomination and a reelection did not look promising.[2] Nationally, the Democratic tide was receding, indicated by the reverses that the party suffered in the 1938 congressional elections in which the aggregate vote for Democratic candidates was down 3 percentage points. War had broken out in Europe, and a wrong foreign policy decision could be disastrous in the deeply divided country. President Roosevelt's second term was up when Truman's term expired, and it was not clear whether the President would try to smash the tradition of no third term. If Roosevelt did not run again, the party would be without its most successful vote getter since the Civil War. Assuming he was nominated, Senator Truman might have had difficulty being reelected if President Roosevelt decided not to run. The future of the Democratic party in the nation and in the state was uncertain.

Even chances of securing a renomination looked dim for Truman. When political boss Tom Pendergast went to jail, the powerful machine that he had put together deteriorated. When the boss was paroled in 1940, he was forbidden to engage in politics. Truman could not count on the big margin that the machine had delivered for him in 1934, a vote based upon control of the election machinery, control of city, county, state, and federal patronage, and expectations of many favors to come. To make matters worse, Truman's refusal to repudiate Pendergast meant that he had to carry the burden of unfavorable publicity heaped upon the criminal activities of the Kansas City politicians. Truman knew that he would be pictured as the product of what was called the most corrupt political machine in the country even though he had not been directly involved in its activities.

What alternatives were open to a senator who did not try for reelection? Truman knew that his work on the Transportation Act of 1940 had earned a reputation for him in that field, and, in his *Memoirs*, he noted that Roosevelt had offered him in a "roundabout way" an appointment on the Interstate Commerce Commission. The term *roundabout* was not explained, however.[3] William Helm, Kansas City newspaperman, wrote that when Truman was asked if he would like to come back to Washington as a member of the ICC, he replied that if he could not come back as a senator he did not want to come back at all.[4] A Truman friend reports that Senator Bennett Clark was rather busy promoting Truman for the ICC,[5] and Victor Messall, Truman's staff assistant, told writer Alfred Steinberg that Roosevelt tried to get Truman to accept an appointment to that commission.[6] The picture is actually quite fuzzy and details are lacking. It is impossible to determine with any accuracy who, on behalf of the President, said what to whom. All one can state, lacking additional evidence, is that the possibility of such an appointment was being considered by several different parties.

At any rate, Truman announced on May 12, 1939, his intention to run again: "I am a candidate for re-election and nothing can stop me. My strength is in the country and anyone who opposes me will know he had been through a fight when the primary is over."[7] He was not quite so resolute ten days later when Tom Pendergast pled guilty to income tax evasion charges. But Messall urged him to file, and he did.

His difficulties came as no surprise to Truman. He had known as early as September 1939 that he would have some serious opposition to his efforts to secure renomination. At that time Governor Stark had announced that he would be a candidate for the Senate seat.[8] Truman reacted bitterly to the announcement and sent a blistering letter to the governor, in which according to Messall, "he called him everything in the goddamned book."[9]

Successful businessman and manager of the nursery that produced the famous Stark delicious apples, the governor for a while appeared to be in the good favor of President Roosevelt. He was invited on the presidential yacht and, much to the dismay of Senator Truman, was consulted on some federal appointments in Missouri, a procedure against which Democratic National Chairman James Farley protested.[19] Senator James Byrnes reported a revealing meeting he had with President Roosevelt: "Truman of Missouri,

like Gillette, had voted with the president on most of his controversial legislation, but this was not enough. Mr. Roosevelt entered the Missouri contest
and tried to nominate Governor Stark. At the request of Senator Truman, I
went to the president and urged that he remain neutral. The president told
me that while he did not know much about Mr. Truman, Governor Stark
was an intimate friend, was very progressive, and would make a great
senator."[11]

In the primary, Senator Truman's second opponent was Maurice M.
Milligan, former U.S. attorney for the Western District of Missouri, who
had gained widespread fame for his successful prosecution of the Kansas
City election frauds and the income tax evasion cases against Tom Pendergast and others. Milligan felt that he deserved to capitalize on smashing the
Pendergast machine more than did Governor Stark, and he hoped that he
would get the support of Senator Clark, who had backed his brother, Jacob
Milligan, in the 1934 senatorial primary race. He announced his candidacy
on March 27, 1940.[12]

One of the puzzles of the senatorial primary race of 1940 was why Milligan
entered the contest and thus divided the opposition to Truman's renomination. Milligan explained:

Harry Truman's closest friends were dubious about his chances of being re-elected.
Truman shared this belief himself. The opinion most widely held at that time was
that Senator Truman would decline to run and that President Roosevelt would
reward him with some appointive office. That was the understanding I had when
some of my friends proposed that I enter the Democratic senatorial primary race
myself. When some of Truman's own friends asked me to run, I took that as positive
assurance of the then senator's desire to stay out of the race. How could a Pendergast man get anywhere without a Pendergast?[13]

The trouble with this view is that Truman filed his nomination papers early
in February, and Milligan did not file until April. In January Truman told a
Kansas City Star reporter that his chances for reelection were "very fine,"
and if Maurice M. Milligan filed for senator, his nomination and election
would be assured.[14] In other words, the strategy was the same as it was in
1934: divide the opposition and win a three-way race.

A possible explanation of Milligan's desire to enter the race is based upon
his resentment at Governor Stark's sweeping claims for the greatest credit in
smashing the Pendergast machine. His personal account, published eight
years later, shows that he regarded his own role as crucial.[15] In addition to
the hoped-for Clark support, it appeared that Congressman Joe Shannon
might give him some help in Kansas City.[16] Truman's friends were probably
very flattering in their praises of Milligan and his importance.

Senator Truman faced some formidable press opposition too.[17] Only one
of the metropolitan newspapers supported him—the *Kansas City Journal*—

and that paper was shortly to cease publication. In an effort to improve the image of the state, the larger newspaper proprietors were taking on the role of crusaders in behalf of righteousness. The state, they argued, should be purged of all who had been associated with Pendergast. Truman, who was included in this group of those guilty by association, felt that he was being treated unjustly. He had repeatedly tried to show that he had not personally been guilty of any wrongdoing. His efforts were futile, however, and the St. Louis press, prompted by jealousy of the rise of Kansas City and its press to prominence under Pendergast, took out after Truman with especial relish. One example follows:

Harry S. Truman—Stooge of Boss Pendergast—Truman was one of the toasts of the Springfield dinner. He is the stooge of Boss Pendergast lifted from obscurity and placed in the U. S. Senate. He is the stooge who paid off his debt to Pendergast in the most abject way. He is the stooge who tried to prevent the reappointment of the fearless prosecutor, U. S. District Attorney Milligan, because Milligan was sending Truman's pals to the penitentiary. Well, Truman is through in Missouri. He may as well fold up and accept a nice lucrative federal post if he can get it—and if he does get it, it's a travesty on democracy.[18]

Truman's problem was to create the organization, so necessary to win a primary campaign. A candidate cannot rely upon voters' predispositions as in a general election; each vote must be won. The Pendergast machine was in disarray, and no one had picked up the pieces. By 1938 Governor Stark had gained control of the Kansas City election board and had seen that the lists were purged. The reformers gained control of the city hall in April 1940 and thus deprived the Democratic party of Kansas City of patronage, campaign contributions from officeholders, police powers to protect friends and harass enemies, taxing powers, privileged rackets, ready cash from the mayor's emergency fund, underworld tributes, and other spoils of office.[19]

The problems Truman faced in 1940 were baffling and complex. Governor Stark, now in control of the state patronage system, was building an organization of his own; Truman would have to rally other elements to his standard. Senator Clark probably was not a major force, having alienated himself from the Roosevelt administration, but he still had many friends about the state, and some of them had grievances against Stark. In January 1940, Truman was ready to consider campaign strategy and scheduled a conference in St. Louis. Only half of those invited came to the meeting, and those who did appear were gloomy about his chances. Some excused themselves, for one reason or another, from actively participating in the campaign.[20] Three of his close friends from Jackson County urged him not to run.[21] Vic Messall, however, was encouraging and agreed to act as campaign manager.

A plan to win the nomination was agreed upon.[22] First, Truman would clearly establish his own record for honesty and useful public service in the

Senate, and then he would firmly identify himself as the most faithful follower of President Roosevelt and the New Deal policies. He also had to show beyond dispute that he was the ablest representative of such special groups as farmers, organized workers, blacks, veterans, underprivileged economic groups, rank and file of the party faithful all over the state, and Missouri businessmen, especially the small businessmen. With the exception of registered Republicans, this list accounted for about all groups in the state of Missouri. Truman decided on a positive campaign and avoided attacks both on his opponents and on the hostile press. Rather, he emphasized the achievements of the Roosevelt administration, which he had supported. There was, in Missouri as nationally, concern about the fall of France, but the voters felt that the best way to stay out of war was to be prepared for it. Truman supported preparedness.

Senator Truman launched his campaign formally by a carefully planned rally on June 15, 1940, at Sedalia in the center of the state. His secretary, Vic Messall, acted as the head advance man for this occasion. Persons from all over the state attended, and his old friend, T. H. Van Sant, a banker from Fulton, presided. As the large crowd collected on the courthouse lawn, Senator Truman stayed on the ground level and shook as many hands as possible. When he spoke, he said, "I am going to announce and make the best campaign I can. As you know I will have no money but I hope I will find some friends who will work for me because they like me. I am going to make an active campaign at every point in the state that I can possibly reach, large or small."[23] The principal address was delivered by Senator Lewis B. Schwellenbach of Washington, who praised Truman as a senator:

There has been no more loyal supporter or better friend of President Roosevelt in the United States Senate than Harry Truman. I need not tell you that Harry Truman is not an orator. He can demonstrate that for himself. However, he has so gained the confidence and respect of the members of the Senate that when he speaks his words are listened to and respected even though he speaks quietly.

It seems to me it should be of particular interest to the people of Missouri to know of the peculiar way in which Harry Truman will fit into the solution of the very serious problems of the next few years (particularly the defense program). . . . No man in the Senate today has the experience which will better fit him for the handling of those problems than does Harry Truman. [24]

Conscientious about his Senate duties, Truman did not have time to campaign as vigorously as he would have liked to, but Senate recesses on several weekends gave him a few days before the August primary. He made the best of these, traveling continuously and covering some seventy-five counties, speaking day and night and shaking hands with thousands of voters.

The financing of the 1940 primary campaign was worrisome for Senator Truman. The impression that his cause was a lost one dried up campaign sources. No one wanted to accept the responsibility for raising a primary campaign fund, and appeals for help were largely ignored. Finally, as a compromise, Harry Vaughan, a book salesman, agreed to serve as treasurer. He was not a prominent Missourian—in fact, he did not live in the state. Truly the Truman forces were desperate to select such an unpromising campaign fund raiser.[25] Vaughan himself commented ruefully on the situation sometime later:

I said, "Of course, I'll do it, but you certainly could find somebody that would be of more financial authority than I, because I don't have any weight. . . ." You have to have something on some of these people to get them to contribute. They contribute to something that you want in hopes that when they're around collecting funds for something they can put the bite on you. That's been my experience. And I didn't have that kind of a lever on any of these people. . . . But it was certainly a Woolworth campaign and I suppose, the cheapest senatorial campaign that was ever put on in the United States, I feel sure. It was audited by a CPA—turned in, so I happen to know that everything was entirely legal.[26]

Victor Messall, however, had a list of those who had received favors from Senator Truman's office, and this list was vigorously canvassed. In addition, Bernard Baruch, the wealthy investment banker and adviser of presidents, considered President Roosevelt's half-concealed support of Governor Stark a continuation of the 1938 purge attempt. Baruch was opposed to presidential pressures on the voters in connection with senatorial campaigns. He therefore contributed $4,000 to the Truman campaign.[27]

In his *Memoirs*, Truman stated that the campaign cost a little more than $21,000, of which he put up some $3,685 himself, and that there were 1,026 contributors in all, by which he probably meant those who contributed substantial funds. Vaughan carried on an extensive mail campaign for contributions of a dollar and received over fifteen hundred replies in the first mailing. The railroad unions cooperated in this drive.

The expenditures for the Truman campaign, as filed with the clerk of the Senate under the Corrupt Practices Act, showed that over one-third went for headquarters expenses such as clerk hire, telegrams, telephone calls, rent, stationery, and periodicals, somewhat less than a third for printed materials and postage, and less than a third for such meeting expenses as travel, hire of sound truck, and entertainment. Only $284, or 1.5 percent of expenditures, were for radio, revealing how rudimentary was the use of radio and how modest were the outlays.[28]

Toward the end of the campaign, Governor Stark asserted that the Truman campaign was being financed by a slush fund furnished by Tom Pendergast. The charge was ridiculous—Pendergast was in deep financial trouble of his own and under a court order not to engage in politics. Harry Vaughan, treasurer of the Truman campaign, said that they did not even have enough money to buy radio time to refute the charges. As it turned out, the false accusation backfired against Stark; Truman pointed out that the governor was the one guilty of questionable campaign fund-raising devices. The governor had pressured state employees to contribute to his campaign fund. The Senate Committee Investigating Campaign Expenditures exonerated Senator Truman of any improper fund-raising activities and admonished Governor Stark for his indirect coercion of government employees.[29]

As far as his opponents were concerned, Truman mostly ignored them and waited for them to make mistakes. Governor Stark proved to be obliging. At a January Jackson Day dinner, Senator Clark's followers resented Governor Stark's ambitions and showed it by booing him.[30] Three months later at a party harmony banquet, Governor Stark made a slashing attack on the Pendergast organization. Truman threw aside his prepared speech and castigated the governor.[31]

One of the best weapons to use in a political campaign is ridicule. Prior to the Democratic National Convention of 1940, Governor Stark had difficulty deciding what office he wanted to run for. Before President Roosevelt made it clear that he might run again, Stark considered himself a possible presidential candidate. When the President's silence indicated that he probably would run, the governor went after the vice-presidency. Roosevelt did consider him for the post at one time but decided that he was too serious.[32] Governor Stark's name was also proposed in connection with a cabinet post: a change in the secretaryship of war was imminent in view of the increasing importance of the office after war broke out in Europe and the growing differences between Secretary of War Woodring and President Roosevelt on foreign policy. Senator Clark summed up Lloyd Stark's dilemma with sarcastic wit:

It is hard to estimate the political situation in Missouri just now since Lloyd's ambition seems to be like the gentle dew that falls from heaven and covers everything high and low. He is the first man in the history of the U. S. who has ever tried to run for president, vice president, secretary of the Navy, secretary of War, governor-general of the Philippines, ambassador to England, and U. S. senator all at one and the same time. At the same time that he is running for these offices, Lloyd is apparently trying to control the Missouri delegation and name the whole state ticket. It is rumored that he is an accepted candidate for both the college of Heralds and the archbishopric of Canterbury.[33]

Governor Stark's failure to concentrate on the senatorship undoubtedly hurt his candidacy.[34] While the governor asserted that Senator Clark "mistakenly assumed" that he controlled the Missouri delegation to the Democratic National Convention, it is equally clear that the governor did not control it either.[35] When President Roosevelt gave the nod to Secretary of Agriculture Henry Wallace for the vice-presidential nomination, Governor Stark was among the first to drop out.[36] Senator Clark's gibe was, "A man cannot get out of a race he never was in."[37]

GROUP APPEALS

In his appeals to different groups, Senator Truman was most successful in the response of organized labor. In Missouri the railroad unions were especially strong, numbering some fifty thousand, and they were grateful for Senator Truman's stand against a wage cut. One union official wrote:

I have never found the operating railroad brotherhoods as well organized in any campaign of which I have knowledge. The brotherhoods were active both in their individual interest and in small contributions of one dollar each from each member toward his election, and as a result of their activity Truman was nominated by a plurality of something over eight thousand votes. I think that labor can safely say that without their support Truman could not have been nominated; however, in view of the closeness of the final vote there are numerous other groups who could make the same assertion equally well.[38]

Truman also received the support of many other labor unions in the state.

Edward Keating, the editor of *Labor*, the organ of the railroad brotherhoods, published a special election edition for Missouri on July 30, 1940. The headlines in this publication, of which over half a million copies were distributed, featured Truman: "Harry Truman's Magnificent Record Entitles Him to Another Term"; "Consistent Friend of Farmer, Labor and Honest Business"; "Truman Fights to Free Railroads from Banker Rule"; and "Former Buddies Have Loyal Friend in Harry Truman."[39]

When the labor unions held a reception for Senator Truman, they sent a telegram to President Roosevelt asking him to send greetings to the meeting. Secretary Stephen Early replied for the President, indicating that he could not take part in any one primary contest and back his "old trusted friend" until after the primary.[40]

The farm vote was also of great importance in Missouri. Truman wrote about it: "The rural papers showed less bias against me and more appreciation for the facts of my political record, and I went after the farm vote. My record of support for every New Deal measure offering relief to the oppressed farm population assured me of voting strength in Missouri's rural areas."[41] Although he faced the determined opposition of William Hirth, head of the Missouri Farmers Association, who supported Governor Stark and wrote stinging editorials against Truman in the *Missouri Farmer*, Truman had many friends among members of other farm organizations, and he had his own record as a farmer and a member of the Farm Bureau.

Senator Truman made a special effort to attract the some 240,000 black

voters in the state. In his Sedalia speech, he said: "I believe in the brotherhood of man; not merely the brotherhood of white men, but the brotherhood of all men before law. . . . In giving to the Negroes the rights that are
theirs, we are only acting in accord with our ideals of a true democracy."[42]
A month later, he addressed the National Colored Democratic Association
in Chicago:

> That the administration has already done much for the Negro is clearly evidenced
> by the results of recent elections in such cities as Kansas City, St. Louis, and
> Chicago. In these and other large cities, the Negro wards showed a much larger
> proportion of the Democratic vote than the white wards. . . . Some say that the
> Negro is not capable of assimilating cultural study. I have always denied this and
> have studied the problem sufficiently to know that given an equal opportunity with
> white students, the Negro can more than hold his own.[43]

Senator Truman received the support of newspapers published largely for
black readers. Over the years he had cultivated the support of the editors of
these papers, among whom was C. A. Franklin of the *Kansas City Call.*

There were a number of other groups to which Truman made special
appeals. His military experience enabled him to attract the veteran vote. It
also gave him some popularity among Catholic voters because the troops
who served with him in World War I and remembered his fairness were
largely Catholic. His record as a leading Mason in the state brought him to
the attention of this group. As for the Jews, his former business partner was
a Jew and his eastern Missouri campaign manager, Dave Berenstein, was an
active Zionist. Senator Truman had business friends in all parts of the state,
some of whom were active in the campaign.

ORGANIZATION SUPPORT

Success in a Missouri statewide Democratic primary depended upon
winning a fair share of the vote in the two metropolitan regions, Kansas
City and St. Louis, and in the outstate. The support of the remnants of the
Goat organization assured Truman a plurality in his own bailiwick of
Jackson County and gave him some bargaining power with the other parts
of the state. He had at least to split even in the St. Louis metropolitan area
and outstate.

With the strong hand of Tom Pendergast no longer at the wheel of the
Goat machine, not much could be expected from this quarter. Tom's
nephew, Jim, however, was an able lawyer and a shrewd and informed
politician in his own right, and Truman was assured of his support. By
August 1940 the tabulation of registered voters in Kansas City showed a
decline from the 1936 registration of 67,632.[44] On the other hand, the Goat
machine still commanded the loyalty of the underprivileged, the minority

groups, the workers, and those with strong Democratic identifications.

A major problem of the Truman campaign was to obtain at least an even break in the St. Louis metropolitan area, which had a candidate of its own for the governorship, Lawrence McDaniel, who was opposed by Allen McReynolds with support in rural areas and some backing in Kansas City. In exchange for Goat support for McDaniel in Jackson County, Truman was to receive organization support in St. Louis from the Dickmann-Hannegan combination. Bernard Dickmann was the mayor of St. Louis, and Robert Hannegan was a successful lawyer and chairman of the St. Louis County and City Democratic Committee. In the early part of the campaign, Hannegan had not taken any firm stand on the senatorship, but Mayor Dickmann was supporting Governor Stark.

The Truman strategists had also made direct contacts with some of the local leaders in St. Louis. Jean Galdoni, a ward leader in an Italian-American district, was one of these, and Jordan Chambers, a black political leader, was another.[45] Chambers raised his own campaign funds and got Truman more than twenty-five hundred votes in the Nineteenth Ward of St. Louis, to which should be added eighty-five hundred votes from other wards inhabited largely by blacks.[46]

Governor Stark naturally brought pressure on the St. Louis organization to support him in the race for the nomination. The poor showing of only about three hundred persons in the Truman rally in St. Louis addressed by Senator Barkley further cooled the ardor of the Dickmann-Hannegan organization.[47] Galdoni told Mayor Roger Sermon of Independence that the McDaniel forces were responding to the governor's demands for support and were about to desert the arrangement with the Truman forces. Mayor Sermon threatened to cut the vote for McDaniel in the Kansas City area if the St. Louis agreement did not hold firm.[48] James V. Conran did the same for the Delta area in southeast Missouri.

The threat made by Senator Truman's friends had its effect. On the eve of the primary, Bob Hannegan directed his workers to support Senator Truman. Sample ballots marked for Truman were distributed in key wards, and the party workers verbally passed the instruction on to their voters.[49] The result was that Truman carried St. Louis by some eight thousand votes, approximately his margin in the state at large. Bob Hannegan, while not seeking public office, was to find himself thrust into a series of influential political and governmental posts.

Important also was the political backing of Senator Bennett Clark, who, although he had broken with the Roosevelt administration on the reform of the Supreme Court and on foreign policy and no longer had first claim to federal patronage, still had many friends throughout the state who wielded considerable influence. President Roosevelt had not dismissed many Clark-sponsored federal employees appointed prior to the Court fight. Senator Clark had been aloof during the first part of the primary campaign, and

Messall thought that he should come out for Truman in view of the support Truman had given him in his race for reelection in 1938. Messall's first attempt to persuade Senator Clark to join the Truman forces was unsuccessful. Senator Carl Hatch of New Mexico found Messall in a despondent mood and offered to intercede on Truman's behalf with Clark. Hatch succeeded in getting him to come out vigorously for his junior colleague.[50]

PRIMARY ELECTION RESULTS

On primary election night it was not clear who had won the nomination, but the next day the count gave a plurality to Truman. The final official count was 268,557 for Truman, 260,581 for Stark, and 127,313 for Milligan.[51] In a three-cornered race, the statewide margin for Truman was not large, only 7,966 votes, but it was sufficient to make Truman the Democratic nominee and pave the way for his second term in the Senate, which proved to be the base for his elevation to the White House.

Truman carried those counties in the north-central corn belt, which had largely gone for Milligan's brother in the 1934 primary, some of those in Little Dixie, where there were many conservative Democrats, some in the Ozarks of southwest Missouri, which were traditionally Republican in general elections but where Truman's friend Sam Wear was active, and some in the cotton-belt delta region, where a friend, James Conran, had a good organization. (See map 3.) Prosecutor Milligan did not fare nearly as well as his brother had in 1934, carrying only five counties. He lacked his brother's experience in Congress, and he was not as good a speaker as his brother. In addition, he did not have the support of Senator Clark. Governor Stark did better than Cochran had in 1934. He carried more eastern counties and more in the west, but he was still edged by Truman, who had a plurality in the two big cities.

For the state as a whole and for the various main regions the primary vote was as follows:

DEMOCRATIC VOTE IN MISSOURI SENATORIAL PRIMARY, 1940

		CANDIDATES	
REGION	Truman	Stark	Milligan
Jackson County	49,974	26,067	29,446
St. Louis City	70,132	61,741	17,744
St. Louis County	6,379	10,566	2,752
Outstate	142,072	162,207	77,421
Total	268,557	260,581	127,363

MISSOURI

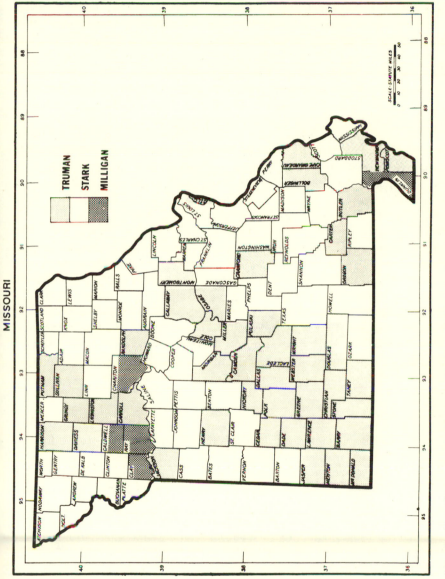

Map 3. Counties carried by Truman, Stark, and Milligan in Democratic senatorial primary August 6, 1940

Senator Truman fell behind in St. Louis County and the outstate, but he ran ahead in Jackson County and St. Louis City. In Jackson County the Truman total was much smaller than it was in 1934 when the Pendergast machine was operating. It was, however, almost fifty thousand votes—sufficient to overcome the outstate deficit.

Senator Truman felt that he had been vindicated. The Democratic voters had declared that his record deserved a second term. The stigma of his connection with the Kansas City machine had not been fatal, and he could no longer be justly categorized as the senator from Pendergast. What had looked like certain defeat had been turned into victory.

Truman's general strategy was sound in first making a great effort to establish his own integrity. As one friend phrased it, "His frankness, his tough fighting spirit, his plain approach gained him numerous votes."[52] Another friend agreed: "By the end of the 1940 campaign he had become a formidable speaker, capable of putting across to his listeners his great sincerity and deep conviction about whatever stand he might take."[53] In a letter to the loyal party workers, David Berenstein wrote: "It was our policy not to hurt or injure anyone; to ignore nasty and unjust attacks, and to devote our entire effort to presenting the real Senator Truman to the people as the best answer to undeserved attacks."[54] In a letter to President Roosevelt, Berenstein gave the following explanations for the victory: Truman's labor support won by his opposition to the proposed wage reduction for railway workers; Truman's excellent voting record in behalf of the New Deal; and Truman's promised support for the Roosevelt future programs.[55] As the Nazis advanced in Europe, Truman's vigorous support for military preparations was welcomed by the administration and by the voters.

ELECTION

In the 1930s a Democratic nomination in Missouri was equivalent to election, but this was not true in the early 1940s. Although Senator Truman was greatly pleased with his renomination, he did not take his reelection for granted. His Republican opponent, Manvel Davis, a Kansas City lawyer, had had legislative experience in the Missouri Senate, where he opposed the Pendergast organization. He won easily in the Republican primary.

Since the Senate remained in session because of the international crisis, Senator Truman could not make as strenuous a campaign as his Republican opponent did. He did, however, take advantage of every recess and of the fact that there were no roll calls in the Senate for most of October, and covered the main sections of the state. Because of the stirring foreign news and the primacy of the presidential race, reporting of Truman's campaign activities was spotty.[56]

Davis based his campaign on three main appeals. The first was that he was opposed to President Roosevelt and the New Deal. "Business and labor . . . should stand shoulder to shoulder in driving the new dealers out of Washington," he proclaimed in one of his speeches. In another he attacked Truman as "the ideal rubber stamp of Roosevelt" and "the new deal with all of its follies and its costly, foolish and inane experiments." His second appeal was based on the bossism issue. On the eve of the election he said: "Truman is my opponent and the symbol of the thing I hate with all my being—dirty, crooked machine politics."[57] In his third appeal he promised stable national government, stable currency, and the elimination of communists from Washington.

Senator Truman ignored the charges made against him personally and avoided mentioning his opponent, concentrating instead on showing that the New Deal programs would help Missourians more than the Republican programs. He also emphasized that "Willkie demonstrated no knowledge of public affairs, and could not be trusted to head the government in a crisis."[58]

Two events occurred during the campaign that concerned Truman's personal integrity. Although Truman insisted that he had nothing to do with the 1938 loan on his mother's farm made out of school funds, the foreclosure on the farm in 1940 by the sheriff was used against him. More helpfully, his selection as Grand Master of the Grand Lodge of the Masons of Missouri counteracted some of the charges made against him. When the Republican candidate for governor, Forrest C. Donnell, a fellow Mason, was asked, "Is Harry Truman a man of character worthy to be Grand Master of the Grand Lodge of Missouri?" he answered that he was.

Senator Truman was reelected, receiving 930,775 votes; Davis got 886,376. His statewide plurality of 44,399 was markedly below Roosevelt's 87,467, but the Democratic candidate for governor, Lawrence McDaniel, ran consistently behind Truman throughout the state and lost the election to his Republican opponent by 3,613 votes. (See map 4.) Truman carried the Democratic counties in the northeastern and southeastern parts of the state and those near Kansas City. As in the Democratic primary, he felt that now the voters of the state as a whole had vindicated his record and at least cleared him of the contamination of his former connection with the Pendergast organization.

Typical of a national trend, Truman did not do as well outstate as he had in the 1934 election. He still carried the traditionally Democratic Little Dixie counties of northeastern Missouri and the cotton-belt delta area of the southeastern part of the state, where his friend Conran had successfully rallied both white and black voters. His strength in the western Missouri Osage region was greatly reduced, while many voters in the northwestern

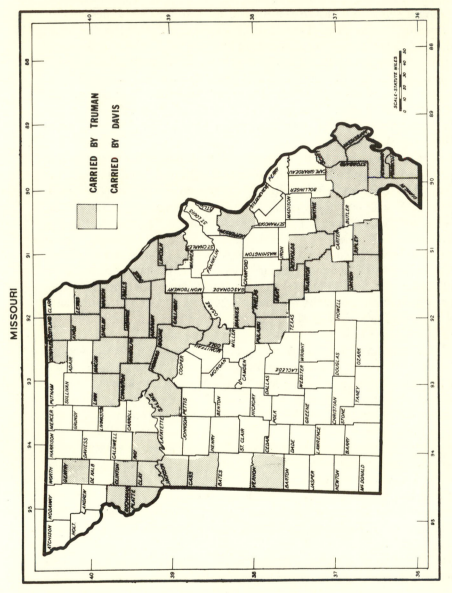

Map 4. Counties carried by Truman and Davis in senatorial elections November 5, 1940

corn belt and in the Ozark area returned to a traditional Republicanism traceable to Civil War and Reconstruction days. This marked a trend that persisted for several decades; as eastern Missouri became more Democratic, the western part of the state reverted to Republicanism.[59]

Against sizable odds, Truman had won reelection and had acquired a reputation as a fighter who refused to think negatively when those around him were filled with gloom. His victory demonstrated his optimism, his resourcefulness, his skill in selecting issues that appealed to the voters, and his ability to put together a team of key politicians who knew how to win primary elections and how to get out the loyal vote in general elections. He had formed a winning coalition made up of businessmen, professional men, labor union leaders and members, farmers, white and black underprivileged citizens, and middle-income groups. In presenting his case, he was improving in effectiveness, his sincerity was being recognized, and he made good use of his own record and that of President Roosevelt.

As in 1916 the position of the President on issues of war and peace was not yet clear. In 1916 the Democrats used the slogan, "He Kept Us Out of War" with great effectiveness. President Roosevelt was accused of warmongering but vehemently denied these charges. American citizens were sympathetic toward the British in the battle of Britain, but they were not yet ready to take sides. In Missouri, Truman did not at the moment have to choose between the two camps, but straddled the fence, welcoming the support of Senator Clark, the isolationist, while standing firm on all aspects of preparedness.

chapter 15 | TREASURY WATCHDOG, 1941–1944

> *Early in 1941, [Truman] sponsored and became the first chairman of what was to become famous as the Defense, and later the Truman War Investigating Committee. It was a master stroke. . . . The Senate War Investigating Committee made him famous and made him President.*
> —Robert S. Allen and William V. Shannon, *The Truman Merry-Go-Round*

There were, of course, a variety of causes that brought Truman to the White House, but certainly his rise to the level of national prominence as chairman of the Special Committee to Investigate the Defense Program was a major factor. The committee assignment developed into Truman's most significant responsibility during his second term, when he established his reputation as an effective legislator.

When the Seventy-seventh Congress opened in January 1941, the members were still deeply divided on issues of preparedness for national defense, but events in Europe and Asia soon tipped the balance against the isolationists. The fall of Holland, Belgium, and France in May and June 1940 and the battle of Britain had overcome much of the opposition to American industrial mobilization for defense. Congress passed the Selective Service Act and enacted appropriations and authorizations for more than $25 billion for defense purposes.[1]

Because there was still no clear mandate for national mobilization, President Roosevelt had used for the most part existing legislation to set up emergency agencies by executive order. His personal style as an administrator called for vague and overlapping authorities, which enabled him to hold the ultimate power to make decisions in his own hands, and he had set up a profusion of agencies to direct defense planning, allocate scarce goods and manpower, increase stockpiling of essential war materials, convert civilian factories to defense production, and control inflation.[2] Unfortunately, there was no central authority under the President to aid him in the mammoth task of coordinating these activities toward the goal of maximum defense production. For example, in January 1941, President Roosevelt created by executive order the Office of Production Management, which had two heads: a director, William B. Knudsen, from industry, and an associate director, Sidney Hillman, from organized labor. This office had a number of weaknesses and was highly vulnerable to criticism from industry, labor, the general public, the mass media, and Congress.

As a member of the Appropriations Committee, Senator Truman received many letters from constituents criticizing defense spending in Missouri. These letters charged that the construction, near Rolla, of the new army camp Fort Leonard Wood, named for the distinguished World War I general, was inefficient and wasteful. To satisfy himself that the charges were true, Truman set out in the middle of winter to inspect the situation at Fort Wood. From his experience in road and building construction, it did not take him long to detect waste, extravagance, looting, and stupidity in the work on this camp. This discovery led him to look at other camps and defense plants in an investigative trip that took him from Maryland to Florida, across to Texas, north to Oklahoma and Nebraska, and back east by way of Wisconsin and Michigan. Everywhere he found the same problem. The defense program was being bled by greed, ignorance, carelessness, and outright embezzlement. He was outraged. His indignation was heightened by the clear evidences he found at every hand that Missourians were being discriminated against in receiving federal defense contracts.

Truman's newspaper friend, William Helm, suggested that the senator propose an investigating committee to look into the waste, graft and favoritism in defense spending.[3] On February 10, 1941, the junior senator from Missouri made a speech on the floor of the Senate expressing concern about graft and concentration of governmental defense operations in certain small areas. He argued that greater use should be made of small business enterprises in the defense mobilization program:

> The little manufacturer, the little contractor, and the little machine shop have been left entirely out in the cold. The policy seems to be to make the big man bigger and to put the little man completely out of business.
>
> I am reliably informed that from 70 to 90 percent of the contracts let have been concentrated in an area smaller than England.[4]

Three days later Truman introduced a resolution (S. Res. 71), which was referred to the Committee on Military Affairs, of which he was a member; Senator Robert R. McReynolds of North Carolina, a sympathetic listener, was the chairman. The committee reported out the resolution favorably, and on February 22, it was referred to the Committee to Audit and Control the Contingent Expenses of the Senate. Its chairman was Senator James F. Byrnes of South Carolina, who was close to the President and cautious in handling a matter that might prove embarrasing to the administration.[5]

In the meantime, Congressman E. Eugene Cox of Georgia, an anti-

Roosevelt legislator, proposed a joint resolution "to investigate and keep currently informed on all activities of the federal government in connection with the national defense."[6] He also introduced another resolution to create a House investigating committee. He was particularly interested in strikes and labor disputes. To ward off a possible Cox committee, of which the administration was highly apprehensive, Byrnes approved a modest budget of $15,000 for the implementation of the Truman resolution before the House could act. Truman had requested only $25,000, a sum hardly adequate for any far-reaching investigation. Byrnes defended the initial meager budget later by saying that he thought Truman was going to investigate only army camps in Missouri.[7]

The wording of the resolution, however, was broad enough to cover the entire defense mobilization program. It proposed to investigate the types and terms of contracts awarded, the methods by which such contracts were awarded and contractors selected, the utilization of the facilities of small business concerns, the geographic distribution of contracts and location of plants and facilities, the effect of the defense program on labor relations, the performance of contracts and the accountings required of contractors, benefits accruing to contractors with respect to amortization for the purpose of taxation or otherwise, practices of management, and such other matters as were deemed appropriate.[8]

The resolution was reported out on March 1, 1941, and adopted without objection from any of the sixteen senators on the floor. This was a shaky start for the committee, which became the most important legislative investigating body during President Roosevelt's third term. Byrnes had assured the President that the committee would not cause him any trouble, and its small budget seemed to be a guarantee of this. Samuel Lubell reports Truman as saying just before he got approval: "I know there isn't a chance in the world of your reporting it out. But if you did I wouldn't conduct the investigation in a way that would hurt defense. You could count on me for that."[9]

A special investigating committee can be a trap that can ensnare the chairman, or it can be a bonanza and heap benefits upon the originator.[10] The committee had to win the support of the Senate, key defense officials, the business community, labor leaders, the mass media, and the general public. It had to show that there was no security risk, obstructionism, or headline hunting, and it had to demonstrate that it could make a positive contribution to defense mobilization.

Senator Truman's experiences as an investigator of transportation problems during his first term under the tutelage of Senator Burton K. Wheeler of Montana and his reading of the history of various war-investigating committees led him to seek the proper role for a defense investigating committee.[11] The Civil War Committee on the Conduct of the War had interfered with Lincoln's prerogatives as commander in chief of the armed forces and had tried to second guess him on military strategy. Truman, who liked to point out that General Robert E. Lee had said that the committee was worth two divisions to him, read the Civil War files in order to see for himself how bad a committee could be.[12] He recalled that after World War I, there were over one hundred committees looking into graft and profiteering, which could do little but stir up bitterness when the war was over. As he put it: "It doesn't do any good to go around digging up dead horses after the war is over. The thing to do is dig this stuff up *now* and correct it."[13]

If an investigating committee is to operate successfully, its members must work together toward a common end. Senator Truman had a share with Vice-President Wallace, Majority Leader Barkley, and Minority Leader Charles McNary in the selection of the members of the committee. The original seven, five Democrats (Truman as chairman, Tom Connally of Texas, Carl Hatch of New Mexico, James Mead of New York, Mon Wallgren of Washington) and two Republicans (Joseph Ball of Minnesota and Owen Brewster of Maine) were all, with the exception of Connally, younger senators who found the work a means for getting a good start in the Senate. Connally was put on the committee to watch the others, but he was so busy with his regular assignments, including the chairmanship of the Foreign Relations Committee, that he was not very active on this one. As the work load of investigation increased, three additional members were added: one Democrat, Harley M. Kilgore of West Virginia, and two Republicans, Harold H. Burton of Ohio and Homer Ferguson of Michigan.[14] Truman refused to accept the names of certain other senators who were suggested for the committee.

According to one account, "The distinguishing mark of the longest serving members—six Democrats and five Republicans—was a sort of unspectacular competence." Several members proved to be skilled interrogators. Brewster, Burton, Kilgore, and Ferguson were lawyers with extensive experience in cross-examining witnesses. All of the members showed themselves to be men of courage. They did not hesitate to challenge high government officials, powerful industrialists, and prominent labor leaders. In tangling with labor leaders, Mead and Kilgore were risking their own political careers because they both had been elected with labor support. The Democratic members of the committee challenged the leadership of their own party. President Roosevelt's conduct of the war production did not escape careful scrutiny of the committee and its staff, nor was the committee overawed by big business. In fact, Truman's distrust of great concentrations of economic power was shared by other members of the committee.[15]

During the time Truman served as chairman, all of the reports were unanimous, an achievement requiring not only compromises but also skillful diplomacy. Truman was generous in allowing each member to take credit for his subcommittee work by having him present his findings to the Senate. Thus, Mead as chairman of the Subcommittee on Steel, Labor and Transportation presented reports on aluminum, barges, steel, shipbuilding, and transportation; Wallgren as chairman of the Subcommittee on Aircraft and Light Metals submitted reports on lumber, aircraft, and magnesium; and Kilgore as chairman of the Subcommittee on Manpower submitted a report on that subject. Later events showed that some members were not easy to get along with, but Truman kept their disruptive tendencies under control. Brewster wanted to investigate military strategy, but he was restrained by Truman. The chief counsel of the committee discussed Truman's qualities as chairman:

It is not necessarily intelligence nor the ability to analyze facts which makes a good chairman, for others—subordinates—can do that. Rather, it is political ability, that is, the ability to get along with people, to head off opposition and to prevent clashes. . . .

I think everyone would agree that Senator Brewster was very intelligent and had had much more college training than Senator Truman. But Brewster lacked this political ability, while Truman possessed it in a remarkable degree.

Senator Truman had the knack of foreseeing an obstacle or clash before it occurred, and he had the ability and tact necessary to head it off. He foresaw things which I would never have thought of.[16]

STAFF

In selecting the chief counsel, Truman had asked Attorney General Robert Jackson for the best investigator he had. Jackson recommended his special assistant, thirty-five-year-old Hugh Fulton, who had directed work leading to conviction of two federal judges for fraud and who had brilliantly handled other important cases. Truman's first impressions of Fulton were not favorable: "He came in wearing a derby hat, a big fat fellow with a squeaky voice. I said to myself, 'Oh shucks!'"[17] But the chief counsel rendered diligent service. As two other observers of Fulton later wrote, "Fear is not in his make-up and his energy is nearly boundless. Coupled with his driving power is an acute understanding of diverse problems, a talent for grasping the essential points, and a lack of patience for conclusions not grounded solidly on facts."[18]

Truman reassured Fulton that, as committee chairman, his interests were not public status but accurate data on the problems that fell within the purview of the committee. No favoritism would be shown, and Fulton would be backed to the limit if he got the facts.

Beginning with a few suggestions from Truman as to the makeup of the staff, Fulton put together a force of lawyers and investigators on the basis of demonstrated merit. At the start, funds were so meager that reliance had to be placed upon the cooperation of various governmental agencies in placing staff members on their payrolls, a practice later forbidden. Fulton himself worked doggedly, making thorough preparations for the hearings, collecting masses of materials from existing records, and producing excellent drafts of reports.[19] Truman and Fulton worked closely and well together. Both were early risers, and they conferred on the agenda and drafts of reports in the morning before other members of the staff arrived.

Fulton felt that Truman, by concentrating on main problems, kept the committee on the right track. A huge variety of topics were brought before the committee in one way or another, but only the significant ones were investigated. Moreover, Truman refused to let personal or political considerations influence his decisions regarding methods or policies to be pursued.

The investigative process included field investigations, executive hearings, public hearings, and informal conferences. Truman explained the role of each under varying conditions:

> From the outset the committee has sought to obtain information from those who should know the facts. It has attempted to deal with witnesses in the manner best calculated to obtain results. As in the work of all other committees, the public hearings have been important sources of information. But they are only one source of information, and not even the most important one. In many cases, it is not possible to obtain all of the necessary facts through a public hearing, no matter how long or extended, or how carefully prepared it may have been. Frequently, high officials of both industry and labor, as well as government, hesitate to speak frankly in public hearings because of their fear that they may be misunderstood, or that their working relations with others may be hampered. In such cases, it is much better to proceed through private hearings, or even through private informal discussions of which no record whatever is made.[20]

ACTIVITIES

Truman first held a general session with top defense officials and then started an investigation of camp construction since he regarded this as less controversial than many other phases of defense mobilization. There was overwhelming evidence that the army had not properly planned the location and construction of cantonment facilities needed for the rapidly expanding military forces. In addition to trips already made, the members of the committee investigated Camp Meade in nearby Maryland, where they found a lack of planning that had greatly increased costs and delayed completion. The committee presented suggestions for improving the handling of contracts. They found that the average cost per man was almost twice as high on a cost-plus-fixed-fee basis than on a lump-sum basis, and they recommended that the camp construction function be transferred from the

Quartermaster Corps to the Corps of Engineers.[21] These changes were made, and the savings were estimated at $250 million.[22] Truman wrote to a friend regarding the selection of camp contracts for early investigation: "In other words, we have justified the existence of the committee and I don't believe that there will be any serious difficulty for us to get the necessary funds from now on. . . . I had to justify the existence of the committee in the preliminary stage and that is the reason I stayed shy of the real controversial issues."[23]

Favorable reaction in the Senate and in the press regarding the camp construction investigation insured that the committee would not lack funds. An additional sum of $50,000 was authorized in August, and from then on the committee had the funds to broaden its work. During the time that Truman was chairman, from March 1941 to August 1944, the committee had a total budget of $400,000.[24]

Truman was very careful to follow the most approved procedures for a legislative investigating committee. Although not adhering to the strict rules of evidence found in the courts, he insisted that the witnesses had the right to have counsel, that they should not be badgered, that they could see the transcript of the hearings, and that they could make corrections of fact.

Within the Senate itself, Truman obtained excellent cooperation by welcoming the assistance of interested senators, by maintaining close liaison with other Senate committees involved in defense programs, by prompt reporting, and by investigating subjects brought up by other senators. Members of the committee were also on such standing committees as military affairs, appropriations, small business, naval affairs, foreign affairs, education and labor, and judiciary.[25]

The committee established amicable relationships with the key defense officials by calling upon them to explain their problems and by maintaining close liaison through specially appointed officers. With Donald Nelson, whose appointment as chairman of the newly created War Production Board in January 1942 was in accord with the recommendations of the committee, the relations were especially close. Nelson appeared frequently before the committee, and his liaison officer with Congress, Edwin A. Locke, Jr., kept the committee fully informed regarding WPB developments. In differences with the armed services, the committee frequently supported Nelson's position and kept prodding him to exercise his authority more vigorously.

When Nelson wanted a subject investigated in order to promote his policy, he would refer the matter to the committee. The resignation of Robert R. Guthrie, head of the textile, leather, and clothing branch, on March 14, 1942, was a case in point. Upon his resignation Guthrie charged Philip D. Reed, chief of WPB Bureau of Industry Branches, with delaying conversion of private business firms to war production. The committee held hearings on the charges, and although it refused to uphold Guthrie's interpretation of motives, it did hold that conversion had been delayed. Nelson took strong exception to the report privately, but he made no public statements indicating his displeasure.[26]

When the renewal of the committee authority came up in 1943, Nelson expressed appreciation of its efforts:

First, your work has been broad in scope and has provided a needed incentive for the fullest coordination of our war effort. Such coordination has been most helpful, because of the fact that all war agencies are inescapably affected by the plans and operations of any one agency. . . .

Second, the quality of your analysis has been kept at a high level, noticeably avoiding personalities, minor issues, and biased or incomplete collection of evidence.

Third, the clear and unequivocal character of your conclusions has stimulated plans for improvements and has been especially helpful because of the care and thoroughness with which your supporting reasons and data have been marshaled.

Finally, perhaps the most conspicuous single characteristic of your work from the viewpoint of an administrative agency has been the constant emphasis you have placed upon the need for foresight—upon anticipating coming events and upon making adequate plans and taking appropriate action to meet them.

In short, I believe the committee has made a substantial contribution to the war effort and with it to the work of the War Production Board.[27]

Truman and his committee had a difficult time winning the cooperation of Under Secretary of War Robert Patterson and General Brehon Somervell of the Army Service Forces. After Pearl Harbor, Patterson wrote to President Roosevelt: "It is in the public interest that the committee should suspend for the time being. It will impair our activity if we have to take time out to supply the Truman Committee all the information it desires."[28] But, when the renewal of the authority of the committee came up, Patterson had changed his opinion about the committee:

I would like to express the appreciation of the War Department for the very constructive assistance that this committee has rendered. . . . The work done by the committee has been of the utmost aid in the prosecution of the war program. A great many of the measures that the committee has recommended have been put into operation. . . . Some of the very best features of our war program have their origin from the investigations made by this committee.[29]

General Somervell was somewhat harder to convince—he placed the needs of the army first and resisted efforts of the committee to keep the civilian economy in sound condition. The general was a hard-driving, aggressive administrator who was not tolerant of obstructions or delays. In contrast to Nelson, he was a veritable demon for administrative details. He took a most critical view of the Truman committee, alleging that it was "formed in iniquity for political purposes" in an effort to punish him for refusing to do a favor for Truman.[30] Yet, even the general modified this view in a number of specific situations.[31]

It was Under Secretary of the Navy James V. Forrestal, later elevated to the highest defense post by Truman, who, during the war years, showed great appreciation for considering military needs in relation to the soundness of the whole economy. In 1943, Forrestal wrote to Truman:

> The Truman Committee has served a useful purpose in proving a medium for the exploration of criticisms of the war effort. Its work has been as objective as I think it possible for such investigations to be, and both committee and counsel have endeavored to conserve the time of witnesses. . . . It [the navy] welcomes the kind of additional outside scrutiny which your committee has given.[32]

In its first annual report, the Truman committee indicated that it wanted to see that the defense billions were "efficiently and economically expended so as to obtain a maximum of production with a minimum of dislocation to the civilian economy."[33] It endeavored to expose carelessness, inefficiency, needless delays, excessive profits and fees, waste, fraud, defective products, and graft. It pointed out the inadequacy of overall planning within the government agencies, confusion, and delay because of conflicting authority, and it recommended greater concentration of authority within the civilian branch of the government. A wide range of subjects was covered, including administrative organization, strategic materials, manpower needs, and finished military hardware.

The Truman committee investigation of the aluminum and magnesium situation revealed a lack of advance planning on the part of the armed services and the Office of Production Management. It was not until early 1941 that OPM realized the need for greatly increased production of aluminum for manufacturing military aircraft. The principal American producer of aluminum, the Aluminum Corporation of America (Alcoa), in order to maintain high prices and its monopolistic position, had deliberately limited production and had persuaded OPM to discourage others from entering the field. When the shortage was realized, Alcoa negotiated a contract with the Defense Plants Corporation, run by Jesse Jones, that Truman regarded as most unfavorable to the public interest.[34] He criticized the contract so severely that a supplementary agreement was negotiated in December 1941 to correct the defects.

Truman also found the relationship between Alcoa and the German firm I. G. Farben highly adverse to American interests. In order to safeguard its own position, Alcoa had agreed to limit American production of magnesium, a metal similar to aluminum and widely used in German military aircraft production. The German firm was permitted to buy magnesium produced in the United States at prices below those charged to American consumers.

When the Truman committee investigated the rubber shortage in the spring of 1942, it discovered that the military had greatly underestimated their needs for rubber, that the defense agencies had not cut back civilian uses soon enough, that Jesse Jones had been too conservative in his stockpiling of crude rubber and in the financing of synthetic rubber plants, and that the cartel agreement between Standard Oil of New Jersey and I. G. Farben had greatly delayed the construction of synthetic rubber plants. Truman was particularly impressed with the testimony of Thurman Arnold of the Department of Justice on the cartel arrangements, which reminded him of the Justice Brandeis antitrust, antimonopoly, pro-individual philosophy. The committee reports on rubber issued in May concluded that there was a serious shortage, thus contradicting the overly optimistic view expressed by the Office of Facts and Figures a few days earlier.[35] It expressed the opinion, though did not recommend, that nationwide gasoline rationing might be necessary in order to conserve rubber. Regarding the conflicting responsibilities in the field, it recommended "that some one person should exercise full responsibility, and accordingly, full power to take all necessary action to provide such rubber as is necessary to the war program, subject only to responsibility to Mr. Nelson."[36]

The report on rubber failed to exert the immediate impact on the President and Congress that it should have had. Nelson persuaded the President in June to hold a White House meeting on the rubber situation. At this meeting, which Senator Truman did not attend, Nelson and Leon Henderson were unable to convince President Roosevelt of the serious shortage, and Secretary Ickes suggested a scrap rubber collection. The failure of the scrap rubber campaign and the President's veto of a bill passed by Congress to set up a separate rubber authority led Nelson to ask the President to request Bernard Baruch to head a committee to assess the rubber crisis and make recommendations. This was the first of many occasions in which Baruch outmaneuvered Truman and gained more credit than he deserved. Baruch's report relied heavily upon the Truman committee materials but came to more positive conclusions. Baruch's self-promoted prestige carried great weight with the President. Baruch recommended nationwide gasoline rationing at once and the establishment of a single rubber authority under WPB. These recommendations were acted upon, and William Jeffers, president of the Union Pacific Railroad, became rubber director.

Jeffers's zeal in implementing the Baruch report subsequently created other problems, which were duly investigated by the Truman committee. Construction of synthetic rubber plants required the use of scarce materials, which were also needed for producing high octane gasoline for airplanes

and for the building of ships. The committee brought together the conflicting parties and had them work out compromise solutions. In May 1943,
these coordinating activities were taken over by the Office of War Mobilization under James Byrnes.

In the summer of 1943, the Truman committee began the investigation of
the Canol project, a War Department scheme for moving oil from Canadian
oil wells in Norman by pipeline to Whitehorse to supply Alaskan military
bases.[37] Investigation revealed a poorly planned project. It was started in
1942 by General Somervell without proper consultation with army engineers,
army oil experts, the WPB, or the Office of Petroleum Coordinator for
War, headed by Secretary of the Interior Ickes. The original plan set the
completion date at October 1, 1942, which ignored difficulties of terrain,
climate, transportation, and manpower and thus was unrealistic. Actually it
was nearly two years before the project produced anything, and then it was
just a trickle.

When the folly of the project was pointed out to War Department
officials, they refused to admit to any mistakes. The staffs of Petroleum
Coordinator Ickes and the Bureau of the Budget made on-the-spot investigations and recommended the discontinuance of the project as nonproductive
and wasteful of materials and manpower. Other much more efficient,
inexpensive, and expeditious methods were available for getting oil to
Alaska. The Truman committee held thorough hearings on the project and
came to the same conclusions. It reported to the Senate: "There may be
some slight excuse for General Somervell's original hasty decision in view of
the tremendous pressure on him at the time, but his continued insistence on
the project in the face of these repeated warnings is inexcusable."[38]

On the basis of a misleading memorandum prepared in the Department
of the Army, the Joint Chiefs of Staff decided the completion of the project
was necessary for the war effort, an example of the military's using a label
to cover up a mistake and to avoid civilian interference. In the postwar
period, the committee succeeded in having the file of the Joint Chiefs on the
Canol project declassified. The file failed to reveal the military necessity,
vindicating the Truman committee.[19] The committee might have forced
some action if it had attacked Patterson and Somerwell personally, but it
refused to do this on the ground that it was contrary to committee policy to
make such attacks or to interfere in strategic decisions. Somervell was a
bold general and did a marvelous job as chief supply officer, but like
General MacArthur had a tendency to regard himself as infallible and above
criticism.

The Truman committee's positive contribution to the improvement of
American military equipment saved many lives. For example, it saw more
clearly than the Navy Bureau of Ships the advantages of the Higgins design
for landing craft, which successfully passed the tests for the amphibious

operations so crucial in the war. Navy bureaucrats tried to force the adoption of a design that had not met required tests. Under the prodding of the Truman committee, the bureau of ships was reorganized, its design for landing ships was abandoned, and Higgins-type ships were ordered and built.[40] The committee also made constructive suggestions regarding helicopters, emergency ship construction, Martin bombers, and the inspection of aircraft engines.

Congressional responsibility for seeing that small business enterprises made their maximum contribution to the defense program was divided among several committees. Senator James E. Murray headed the Special Committee to Study and Survey the Problems of Small Business Enterprises. The Truman committee, however, in its hearings and reports kept pointing out the plight of small businessmen; they were ignored in the awarding of defense contracts, their existing facilities were not utilized, they were unable to obtain the necessary materials to continue in business because of priority restrictions, and big business was squeezing them while charging the government monopolistic prices.

In 1942, the Murray committee introduced a bill to mobilize the facilities of small business and, during the debate on the bill, favorable mention was made of the Truman committee report on aircraft plants, especially the part supporting the work of small plants. The bill passed, and Lou Holland, a close friend of Truman who had been organizing small-business enterprises in Kansas City in order to spread defense work, was appointed by Nelson to head the Smaller War Plants Division, created in accord with the Murray Act. Truman did not want it said that he had applied any pressure on the WPB in favor of Holland, but later, when Holland was replaced for a lack of aggressiveness, Truman came to his defense.[41] Truman's relationship to Holland notwithstanding, the evidence remains clear; he actively supported the concerns of American small business, both within and without the boundaries of his own committee work. During the rest of the time he was with the committee, Truman, acquiring a reputation as a champion of small business, kept trying to convince Nelson and the procurement agencies that the proper use of small companies would speed up war production.

The Truman committee was concerned with many different problems of labor relations. Strikes, threatened strikes, labor shortages, maldistribution of labor, training needs, jurisdictional disputes between labor unions, excessive union fees, balancing of civilian and military manpower requirements, and emerging postwar labor problems were investigated. The committee had hardly begun to operate when the country was faced with a threatened coal strike. John L. Lewis, the rugged, flamboyant, and cantankerous head of the United Mine Workers, and the representatives of the coal operators were called before the committee. Testimony showed that the southern operators were blocking a settlement. Truman informed them that unless a settlement was reached within twenty-four hours, the northern owners of the mines would be called upon to testify. This threat helped break the deadlock, settle the strike, and bring the men back to work.

Later in 1941, the committee tangled with Sidney Hillman, co-head of OPM, regarding the awarding of a housing contract in the Detroit area. The Currier Company had submitted the low bid, but Hillman opposed the awarding of the contract to this company, since its workers belonged to the CIO rather than the AFL unions. Hillman had worked out special arrangements with the AFL unions, an action Truman vigorously denounced.

In the middle of the war, the Truman committee, investigating the problems connected with reconversion of war industries back to civilian production, took the view that the army and navy should not be allowed to determine conditions under which peacetime business was to be restored. It held that this was not a military function.[42] The peak of wartime production was reached in 1943, and some war contracts were terminated in that year. The committee recommended that one organization be placed in charge of disposition of surplus materials, that funds be provided for an orderly return to civilian production, and that steps be taken to stabilize working conditions. Nelson supported these recommendations, but the War Department, influenced by the military-industrial complex, opposed them. The armed forces won the backing of President Roosevelt, and Nelson was eased out of the picture in 1944, much to Truman's disappointment.

INFORMATION ACTIVITIES

Since it was not authorized to introduce legislation, disclosure of facts was the chief weapon wielded by the Truman committee. It used information activities positively to keep constant pressure on war agencies to release as much information as possible on the conduct of the war. Its exposure of inefficiency, war profiteering, lack of planning, and lack of good judgment helped reduce malfunctions.

Truman's image as an outstanding legislative investigator, the watchdog of war production, grew during the war. At the start, the committee attracted little attention, and some newspapers were skeptical about its possible usefulness, but the sound reports on the aluminum shortage and the ills of camp construction brought a more favorable reaction from the press. Marquis Childs of the *St. Louis Post-Dispatch*, who had been critical of Truman, wrote on November 8, 1942, that Truman had become "one of the most useful and at the same time one of the most forthright and fearless of the ninety-six." Regarding the Truman committee, he wrote, "There is no doubt that it has saved billions—yes, billions of dollars." Truman later estimated the savings at $15 billion.[43]

A sign of the growing recognition of the work of the committee was the

March 8, 1943, issue of *Time*, which carried a portrait of Truman on its cover and ran a feature article headed, "Billion Dollar Watchdog, spotlight, conscience, and sparkplug to the economic war-behind-the-lines . . . The closest thing yet to a domestic high command was the Truman Committee. Its members had no power to act or order. But using Congress's old prerogative to look, criticize, and recommend, they had focused the strength of public opinion on the men who had the power."

Chairman Truman explained the work of the committee in reports to Congress and in speeches around the country. He was becoming better known throughout the nation, and in 1942, he had an opportunity to employ another medium, the weekly magazine. This venture into journalism had somewhat mixed results. An article entitled, "We Can Lose the War in Washington," by Truman, appeared in the *American Magazine* for November 1942. It brought considerable publicity but also strained relations with the White House. Two of Truman's colleagues on the committee said that the article had been ghostwritten and that Truman had approved it without reading it carefully.[44] Ghosted or not, it was so critical that Roosevelt was incensed, but Senator Kilgore explained to the President that when Truman realized the nature of the article, he tried unsuccessfully to stop it. The President was somewhat mollified. Truman was beginning to learn slowly and painfully that a man in a prominent position has to consider most carefully the impact of words attributed to him.

The work of the Truman committee had a wide appeal to many different groups, winning over many conservatives, Republicans and Democrats alike, who welcomed the exposure of the shortcomings of the Roosevelt administration. It appealed to the liberals because it was critical of the military and the big business leaders, while some elements of the military were thankful for its wisdom in revealing shortcomings and mistakes in weaponry selection and production. Some labor leaders and their followers were appreciative of the committee's efforts to safeguard their interests. While small businessmen looked upon Truman as their champion, there were also larger firms that had benefited from the committee's efforts. One of the best-known American aircraft manufacturers sent a letter to Truman expressing great appreciation for the work of the committee. Farmers were thankful for the efforts of Truman and his committee on behalf of the farm machinery industry, which had been endangered by munitions manufacturers who thought that only guns won battles, forgetting the old saying that an army moves on its stomach. Finally, there were the mass media, the press, the radio, and expanding television, that liked Truman for his battle for freedom of information, for more news about ship losses, war production successes and failures, and for his splendid record as a source of news.

The Truman committee was the means by which Truman's image was so improved that he became a possibility for the Democratic vice-presidential nomination. The mass media forgot almost completely about the senator from Pendergast and extolled the virtues of the new Truman as the watchdog of the treasury. A well-known weekly magazine listed him as one of the ten men who had contributed most to the war effort and praised his patriotism, tact, persistence, skill in detecting fraud and sham, and devotion to duty. The work of the committee also brought him in contact with high government officials and advisers who were to figure in his administration as president later on.

chapter 16 | POLITICS AS USUAL, 1941–1944

I don't say Congress can't have a good thing once in awhile. The trouble is, Congress has a good thing all the time!
—Jimmy Lyons, *The Mirth of a Nation*

Political activity takes place on two levels. On the higher level there is the glory and grandeur of public service—accomplishments in the legislature, victories in diplomacy, public acclaim for stirring speeches, parades, adulation. But there is also the sheer, plodding work of getting elected. The elective official who wishes to be reelected must tend to his fences. War or peace, good times or bad, the American election system must go on in accord with the provisions of the Constitution, and the alert candidate who wants to stay in office must look to his patronage, his favors, his constituents, and their needs and expectations, as well as to the official matters of his office.

While the Washington Truman was becoming a figure of national reputation and esteem, the Missouri Truman was still involved in the everyday world of political survival. He lived in an area where political corruption abounded but so far he had remained relatively unscathed. The opposition press had accused him of being the tool of a corrupt boss, the beneficiary of election corruption, and the product of a machine operating in one of the worst eras of American politics. It was claimed that he personally had benefited from the loan made by the Jackson County School Board without proper security on land owned by his mother. But the charges had failed to stick. His Senate record clearly revealed that he was no tool of Tom Pendergast. It was true that Tom's workers were overly enthusiastic about getting out the vote, engaging in such practices as padded registration lists, fraudulent counting, ballot box stealing, and strong-arm intimidation of the opposition, but these were the acts of misguided zealots, responsible to Pendergast, not to Truman.[1]

The charge that Truman benefited financially from the school board loan was not supported by the facts. First, he knew nothing about it. His brother, Vivian, and his friend and political factotum, Fred Canfil, had signed the mortgage, although neither was legally qualified under Missouri law to do so. The fault also lay with the local board, and, at that time, Truman had been out of local politics for a decade.

Harry Truman never denied that he was a politician—or that politics was a dirty business. Seldom did he display a thin-skinned attitude about what the opposition said in a political contest. To succeed in politics, one has to have the skin of a rhinocerous, the waterproof feathers of a mallard, and the imperviousness to heat of an Indian fakir. Or, as Truman often remarked, "If you can't stand the heat, stay out of the kitchen."[2] The heat did not bother Truman. He had survived a number of grueling primary and election campaigns and had many of the skills requisite to succeeding in politics. His fellow senators well recognized this when they cheered him as he took his seat in the Seventy-seventh Congress.

PATRONAGE

One of the rules of the game of American politics as Truman played it was that the faithful must be rewarded. Robert Hannegan, whose last-minute support in the 1940 primary was important to Truman's narrow victory, is an illustration. A handsome Irish politician from St. Louis, a successful lawyer in his own right, a shrewd analyst of character, Bob Hannegan had a comfortable income from his private law practice and did not need a low-paying political job.[3] On the other hand, he did not come out of the 1940 political battle as unscathed as Truman. His candidate for governor on the Democratic ticket, Lawrence McDaniel of St. Louis, won in the primary but lost in the general election by a narrow margin to the Republican candidate, Forrest Donnell.[4] When an election is extremely close, it is natural for the losing side to demand an investigation. The Missouri General Assembly, which was controlled by the Democrats, passed on January 10, 1941, a joint resolution of both houses providing funds for a "general and sweeping investigation" of the election. Governor Stark vetoed the resolution and sought a writ of mandamus in the Missouri Supreme Court, which would require the Speaker of the House of Representatives to declare Donnell elected. The Supreme Court declared the resolution unconstitutional and directed the Speaker to declare Donnell elected.[5] McDaniel then filed a legal petition for a recount but soon saw his cause was hopeless and notified the contest committee that he accepted the original election returns. Hannegan was in the middle of this scheme, which backfired. The plotters were accused of trying to defeat the will of the

Cartoon by Fitzpatrick, March 29, 1940. Reprinted, courtesy of the *St. Louis Post-Dispatch*.

people. The press, particularly the *St. Louis Post-Dispatch*, howled in rage at the plotters, who showed themselves to be poor losers and bad sports.

By now, Hannegan was furious. He had been accused of trying to steal the gubernatorial election for McDaniel and wanted personal vindication. It came about in this way. Truman asked Hannegan if he wanted to be named collector of internal revenue for the St. Louis District, an important position in Missouri politics. After some hesitation, the reluctant Hannegan finally agreed. Truman recommended the appointment, and President Roosevelt sent the name to the Senate. As expected, the St. Louis newspapers were loud in their denunciation of the appointment. For Hannegan it became a question of vindication. He would show the citizens of Missouri that the press vilifications of him were wrong and that he could be an efficient, dedicated public servant. The question was, could Senator Truman secure confirmation of the appointment? Truman succeeded, and Hannegan, as district collector of internal revenue, made what appeared to be a good record. The efficiency rating of the district rose from last to first in the country. Such excellence on the job deserved another reward. Through Truman's influence, President Roosevelt and Treasury Secretary Morgenthau named Hannegan as commissioner of internal revenue for the entire country, and he was confirmed by the Senate. But later the Internal Revenue Service was involved in tax scandals, and Hannegan was remiss in not detecting and punishing fraudulent practices that were exposed.

Somewhat later, President Roosevelt needed a new chairman of the Democratic National Committee because chairman Frank Walker was stepping down. In his *Memoirs*, Truman states that the President wanted him to be chairman.[6] Roosevelt evidently recognized Truman's political abilities and felt that, as chairman of the Truman committee, he had acquired a splendid national image. Truman, however, did not want the job and suggested Hannegan for the position. But Hannegan did not want it either. General Harry Vaughan recalled:

Hannegan really didn't want to become chairman. Early in 1944 . . . when he heard that he was being considered for the chairmanship, he said he wasn't interested. "Hell, I don't want it," he said to Mr. Truman. He asked Truman what he should do if he was offered the job and I recall Truman saying "tell them you won't take it unless the President asks you directly." Neither Hannegan nor Truman expected the President to call directly, but he did. Hannegan called Truman back and asked sarcastically: "What do I do now, Coach?" Truman laughed. "You take it," he said.[7]

The Hannegan case was only one illustration of the fact that in his second term the junior senator from Missouri had acquired considerable influence in patronage matters. Federal judgeships had always been regarded as particularly valuable political positions. There were two vacancies in the federal district courts of Missouri to be filled. Senators Clark and Truman sent two names to the White House. Clark was uncertain about one of the names but went along with Truman on the recommendation. Attorney General Francis Biddle was also uncertain about the individual as shown by the following memorandum for the President:

You recently sent me a letter from Congressman _____, recommending _____ for the preparation of a reply. This I enclose.

My judgment is based on an FBI investigation. This shows that almost all of the lawyers who knew _____ consider him an inexperienced and mediocre lawyer. His local Bar Association refused to endorse him by a vote of 23 to 1. The one was a former law partner. This former law partner, _____ was indicated under the National Stolen Property Act, but was not tried as the principal witness died. . . .

Before _____ came to _____ he was constantly in debt, and caused severe losses to persons who had loaned him money. At one time he was a heavy drinker.

The keeper of a house where rooms were rented for prostitution says that he constantly took a girl to her place. _____ was married at the time and the girl admits the relationship.

The St. Louis Dispatch, and other newspapers, have vigorously opposed _____ ever since his name was suggested. This is unusual. In my opinion the appointment and ensuing publicity would hurt you in Missouri.

Under the circumstances, I strongly advise against the appointment of _____. An emphatic "no" from you to Truman would settle this.

> *Respectfully yours,*
> Francis Biddle
> Attorney General[8]

To this memorandum, President Roosevelt replied with a Memorandum for the Attorney General:

I have your memorandum about _____. This is one—I think the first—occasion where I cannot agree. I have done a good deal of checking and, in spite of what you say about his legal ability, I have a hunch that he has as much legal ability as at least half of the people we put on the District bench! What you need on the District bench is old-fashioned common sense. This is more important than being able to teach at the Harvard Law School!

Also, I cannot turn him down:

(a) Because a former partner of his was, once upon a time, indicted and not tried.

(b) Because it is alleged that he "kept" a lady years and years ago.

(c) Because before he came to _____ he was in debt (I hope this is not an allegation that he made money as a _____.)

The above are just a few of the WHEREAS clauses. Now, comes the WHEREFORE. Please tell Truman that if Clark will go along with it I will send _____ name up and I think Truman will be perfectly willing to let the other Judgeship go to the Southeastern part of the State.

> F.D.R.[9]

Even with Roosevelt's blessing, the appointment was still in danger. Could Truman avoid its going before the Judiciary Committee? If it got there, it would surely be turned down because the attorney general's memorandum would be shown to members. Could Truman outwit the Senate purists? On the last day of the session when everyone was pressing for adjournment, Truman brought the name up, praised the man, and without going before the committee and with no objections forthcoming, the nomination was confirmed.[10]

THE POLITICS OF THE TRUMAN COMMITTEE

Although the public image that Truman was constructing as chairman of the Special Committee Investigating the Defense Program was that of a great public servant with a single-minded devotion to the public interest, the work of the committee had its political uses and restraints despite the loud claims of strict nonpartisanship. Donald H. Riddle, in his capable study of the committee, pointed out that the "investigations involving members of Congress were among the poorest conducted by the committee because it 'ducked' the issues except in the case of Senator Bilbo (and he was in Senatorial disfavor for other reasons)."[11] Albert B. ("Happy") Chandler and his swimming pool also got off lightly. In July 1942, Senator Chandler had requested the Truman committee to investigate the charges made by a political opponent alleging that he had received a swimming pool from a war contractor for his services in obtaining contracts. There was no evidence that Chandler had intervened in the case as far as the committee could discover, but the questions regarding the propriety of a senator's accepting a pool from a government contractor were not raised. Truman was still a member of the club, and one did not make friends by disgracing one's colleagues.

The Truman committee gave its chairman a chance to bluster about alleged abuses, but he did not have to do anything about them. He railed against the dollar-a-year men loaned by big business on the ground they were still serving business, but when Nelson insisted that he needed them to win the war, Truman let the matter rest. The committee had no powers to do anything but issue reports and make recommendations.

The Truman committee talked loudly about labor abuses, but it was not about to make enemies among the ranks of organized labor. Truman was against strikes in defense industries and was opposed to labor unions' exploiting their position in a tight labor market by demanding higher wages and excessive initiation fees. On the other hand, he did not want to lose any of his labor friends, so he appeared as the champion of the rights of labor in the war and postwar periods.

Although the committee came down heavily on certain industries that were caught engaging in malpractices, it came to the rescue of what Truman regarded as deserving business enterprises. Small business firms in general and certain specialized industries came in for high praise.

VOTING RECORD

In his second term, Senator Truman's voting record continued to be that of a strong New Dealer. As the war overshadowed the domestic scene, there were far fewer controversial social measures introduced. On civil rights questions, he voted on two occasions for cloture when southern senators were filibustering against the antipoll-tax bill. On labor issues, he voted for the pay raise for rail workers and for eliminating the requirement for financial statements by unions. On social and economic questions, he joined other liberal senators in voting against bills ending the National Youth Administration, the National Resources Planning Board, Farm Security Administration, and the amendment to curtail Tennessee Valley Authority.

Senator Truman supported the Roosevelt administration wholeheartedly on defense issues. He voted for compulsory military service, for the Lend-Lease Act, for repealing the Neutrality Act, for the ship seizure bill, for the extension of selective service, for aid to China, for renegotiation of war contracts, and for military appropriations.

Truman's interest in an international organization that would have some sanctions to enforce the peace was indicated by his active support of Senate Resolution 114 introduced on March 20, 1943, by Senators Joseph Ball of Minnesota, Harold Burton of Ohio, Carl A. Hatch of New Mexico, and Lister Hill of Alabama. Since Ball and Burton were Republicans and Hatch and Hill were Democrats, the resolution anticipated the bipartisan foreign policy set-up of the Truman administration. The resolution stated that "the Senate advises that the United States take the initiative in calling meetings of representatives of the United Nations for the purpose of forming an organization. . . . We believe that it is wise that the firm position of the United States be established now so that all . . . will know that we intend to assume our full responsibility toward the building of a postwar world in which each nation will have all its rights." Although the Senate did not pass the bill, it adopted a milder resolution proposed by Senator Tom Connally of Texas, which had been improved some by a stiffening amendment backed by Truman. At this stage it appeared that Truman was more interested in international organization than was President Roosevelt. He thought that the best guaranty of the postwar security of the United States would be such an organization bolstered by American military preparedness.

The *Congresional Quarterly Almanac for 1945* selected some twenty-six key Senate votes for the period 1935-1944.[12] Of these votes, fourteen were party votes in that a majority of Democratic senators opposed a majority of Republican senators voting on the measure. No clash with President Roosevelt was involved in these roll calls. On all of them, Truman voted with the Democratic majority, receiving a high party unity score.[13] On nine votes, a majority of both parties were on the same side. On four of these, there was no difference with the President, but on five the Senate opposed Roosevelt. On these five, Truman sided with the President against a majority of his colleagues on three—the reform of the Supreme Court, the Smith-Connally Anti-strike Act, and the retention of the National Resources Planning Board. He opposed the President on the bonus bill and on the veto of the 1944 tax bill. President Roosevelt's veto message called it "not a tax bill, but a tax relief bill providing relief not for the needy, but for the greedy." This language was so intemperate that Congress passed the bill over the President's veto. With what he regarded as the honor of the Senate at stake, Truman sided with a majority of his colleagues against the President, although some of his friends supported the President.

A study of agreement and disagreement between Truman and Clark on the twenty-six votes shows that on measures where a majority of the two parties were on opposite sides, Clark differed from Truman two-thirds of the time. Clark had become increasingly anti-Roosevelt and isolationist. Truman and Clark became friends in the Senate, and the differences between them on policy matters did not seem to bother Truman, who supported Clark for renomination in the Democratic primary of 1944. Clark's stands did make a difference with the voters, however, who turned him down for renomination in favor of Roy McKittrick. In the general election, McKittrick was defeated in a very close race by the Republican candidate, Governor Forrest Donnell. Thus, policy differences between the two senators were part of a sequence of events that led to the replacement of a Democratic senator by a Republican one. In the election of presidential electors and members of the House of Representatives, however, the state was still Democratic.

On the basis of the *New Republic* charts for the twenty-three selected votes in the Seventy-eighth Congress, it is possible to present liberal-conservative scores for Truman and Clark.[14] Truman's score was 98 percent liberal; Clark's was 35 percent liberal. (Such scaling was found by two psychologists to be a valid method for determining the location of a senator along a liberal-conservative scale.)[15] Truman's two conservative votes in this Congress were that to override the President's veto of the 1944 tax bill and that confirming the nomination of Will Clayton as an aide to Secretary of Commerce Jesse Jones. Clayton was a cotton trader and, since Missouri contains some cotton farmers, Truman could not be expected to vote against Clayton. On the other sixteen measures on which he voted, Truman was on the liberal side.

PROSPECTS

Was Senator Truman politically ambitious? What did he want to achieve in American politics? Did he want to be president? Early in 1934, when he was looking for another political post, his highest ambition was to go to the House of Representatives. As a senator, it was his ambition to make a good record by diligent application and to be reelected. He fought tenaciously for his renomination and reelection. His success under adverse conditions gave him greater prestige in the august body that he once had approached with such humility. The investigating committee added many new laurels to his crown. At last he was where he thought he really belonged.

Beginning in 1943, there was talk about the Democrats' running Truman for vice-president. Was he attracted by this prospect? On January 31, 1945, in a letter to H. B. Deal of St. Louis, he wrote, "I don't want to be President."[16] He most certainly would not run against President Roosevelt if Roosevelt sought a fourth term. As for the vice-presidency, he liked his own job well enough.

There are times in American politics when a reluctant candidate does better than the obviously ambitious one. The boldest suitor does not always win. It takes a certain amount of coyness to attract the delegates to national nominating conventions. In the spring of 1944, Senator Truman was coy about the vice-presidency; it was nice to be considered.

chapter 17 | COMPROMISE CANDIDATE FOR VICE-PRESIDENT

For strictly personal reasons, I am interested in the straight story of how Henry A. Wallace didn't become President of the United States. I like to tell it to myself periodically to convince myself anew that democracy, with all its faults, is a system that works; that democracy's politicians can be as strong and pure as Knights of the Round Table; and that a benign Providence, for all its absent-mindedness about the muddled doings of us mortals, does see us through tight places.

—George E. Allen, *Presidents Who Have Known Me*

In 1944 as World War II was drawing to its final stages, Senator Harry S. Truman was selected as the Democratic candidate for vice-president of the United States. Henry A. Wallace, vice-president during Roosevelt's third term, had made it quite clear that he was very much out of accord with the growing American distrust of Soviet postwar policies.[1] Had he been renominated for the vice-presidency, postwar American foreign policy clearly would have been markedly different.

Before the nomination of Truman could be brought about, a number of decisions had to be made by the Democratic political leaders, by President Roosevelt, and by the convention delegates. First, the leaders had to agree upon a fourth term for the aging and ailing Roosevelt, and then they had to convince him that he should accept the nomination. Next they had to persuade him not to press for Wallace as a running mate as hard as he had in 1940. If a Wallace renomination could be prevented, a substitute would have to be found who was acceptable to the leaders and to Roosevelt, and, of course, who would agree to run. Finally, a majority of the delegates had to be persuaded to vote for this substitute.

As the Democratic leaders began preparations for their 1944 national convention, they were deeply concerned about problems of leadership succession in wartime. Roosevelt was not well and might not last another strenuous four years in the White House. The strain of eleven hectic years had taken its toll. On March 7, 1944, he wrote to Congressman Patrick A.

Drewry: "You who view things calmly will understand when I say that I would give a great deal personally to return to Hyde Park and Georgia just as soon as the Lord will let me."[2] His personal secretary noted a forgetfulness that alarmed her.[3]

In spite of his poor physical condition and the advice of many friends that he should not run again, President Roosevelt decided that it was his duty to continue in office if the voters wished him to do so. He was weary, but his personal physician, Vice-Admiral Ross T. McIntire, concealed the real state of his health. Medical reports made available later showed clearly that he had a heart condition. Roosevelt himself was confident he could bound back as he had in the past.[4] Political leaders were anxious to have him as their candidate since he was the party's best vote getter, and his position as commander in chief of American armed forces during a period of military victories would make it difficult for the voters to turn him down. In order to preserve the bipartisan foreign policy, he did not announce openly his willingness to accept a renomination until July 11, 1944.[5] Much earlier than this, however, the politicians took it for granted that he would run.

The main problem facing the Democratic party leaders was the selection of a candidate for vice-president. It now seems astounding that President Roosevelt did not pay more serious attention to this problem. The winning of the war, the making of the peace, and the future of his programs might devolve upon the vice-president. But in 1944 his attention was fully occupied with the crushing burdens of the war and world diplomacy. He was ill and tired and could not bring himself to face a bitter internal party struggle over the vice-presidential nomination.

In the twentieth century, it had been customary for an incumbent president who secured a renomination to go along with the renomination of an incumbent vice-president who was willing to run. Vice-President Wallace was willing to seek a renomination in 1944 but various forces, including President Roosevelt's indifference, were working against him. In 1940 Wallace had not been popular with many in the party, and his nomination for vice-president had been forced upon unwilling delegates by the threat that Roosevelt would not run unless Wallace was his running mate. During the 1940 campaign, Wallace's interest in mysticism threatened to embarrass the Democratic high command. A series of letters, allegedly written by Wallace to the guru, or teacher, of a mystic cult, fell into the possession of the Republican National Committee. Although their existence was widely known and caused a flurry in the Democratic headquarters, they were not published until eight years later.[6] In 1943 President Roosevelt was greatly provoked by Wallace's bitter feud with Jesse Jones, director of the Reconstruction Finance Corporation, over the funds for the activities of the Board of Economic Warfare, of which Wallace had been made the head. This dispute broke out shortly after the President had issued a strong warning that top officials should not quarrel in public. Vice-President Wallace had also been a disappointment in his congressional relations. As presiding officer of the Senate, he had made few friends in that body, and he failed to play the important role that Garner had during Roosevelt's first term. Although Wallace was a most successful farmer and businessman, he had acquired a reputation of being a wild-eyed liberal who, if he succeeded to the presidency, would be a menace to business.

Wallace had many enemies, but he also had friends among labor leaders, minority groups, farm leaders, brain trusters, such liberals as Governor Ellis Arnall of Georgia, Senator Claude Pepper of Florida, and Senator Joseph F. Guffey of Pennsylvania, and many officials in the administration. There was no question that Wallace was a loyal Roosevelt supporter and that in his field of agriculture, his reputation had been outstanding. President Roosevelt liked Henry Wallace personally and refused to take a definite stand on Wallace's acceptability.

By 1944, the movement to drop Wallace was acquiring support from many quarters. On the White House staff, General Edwin "Pa" Watson (a military aide), Chief of Staff Admiral William D. Leahy, and Judge Samuel Rosenman, one of Roosevelt's speech writers, were members of the anti-Wallace group. Among the cabinet members, Secretary of the Navy Forrestal and Secretary of the Interior Ickes were opposed to Wallace's renomination. Forrestal was opposed in part because he thought Wallace was "soft on communism." Ickes thought at first that Wallace would cost the ticket as many as 3 million votes. Ickes' preferred candidate early in the year was Justice William O. Douglas. By July Ickes supported Wallace on the ground that the Republicans would exploit Truman's Pendergast background and the role of the city bosses in his nomination. A third group opposing Wallace's renomination was made up of persons active in the Democratic party organization at the national and local level. Former national chairman Edward Flynn of New York, political boss of the Bronx; former national chairman Frank Walker of Pennsylvania, postmaster general; party treasurer Edwin Pauley of California, prominent oil man; party secretary George Allen of Washington, D.C., public relations specialist; Mayor Edward Kelly of Chicago, political boss of Cook County; and Mayor Frank Hague, boss of Jersey City, banded together early in 1944 to block the renaming of Wallace as Roosevelt's running mate. A fourth group was composed of conservative southern political leaders, including Senator Harry Byrd of Virginia, Senator William B. Bankhead of Alabama, Senator Kenneth McKeller of Tennessee, and Senator James D. Eastland of Mississippi, who vigorously opposed Wallace's liberalism on civil rights and economic issues and threatened to bolt the party if Wallace was renominated.

National chairman Hannegan proved to be a key figure in the convention struggle over the vice-presidential nomination. Although closely tied to Truman, he was reluctant to promote openly the candidacy of a fellow Missourian because his position required him to serve all of the states. He was active, however, in reporting to President Roosevelt evidences of the growing opposition to Wallace's renomination.[7]

Among the most persistent opponents of Wallace's renomination were Democratic treasurer Ed Pauley and former chairman Ed Flynn. Cooperating with "Pa" Watson in the White House, Pauley directed to Roosevelt's office a stream of visitors who opposed the renomination of Wallace, and he also tried to limit those favoring Wallace. As Democratic treasurer, he arranged many speaking engagements for Senator Truman at fundraising dinners, avoiding Vice-President Wallace for such occasions. He also made it clear that it would be difficult to raise campaign funds for the party if Wallace was renominated. Flynn, on his part, was commissioned by President Roosevelt to sound out the organization leaders on their views regarding Wallace. He reported that an attempt to force the renomination of Wallace would disrupt the party.[8]

The problem was deciding who was available; who would satisfy the various diverse elements in the Democratic party. Who would fit the criteria of availability? Who had the confidence of President Roosevelt and at the same time had proven vote-getting abilities, sufficient tact to handle the Senate and relations with the House of Representatives, the proper age, sound health, experience in administrative matters, a spotless personal life, an agreeable wife to grace the social functions, and a record of party loyalty? Who would be acceptable to the southerners, the labor leaders, the farm organizations, the center city dwellers, the minority groups, the organization leaders, the money raisers, and the more conservative elements found in the Democratic party? Who came from the right section of the country?

Several persons high in the Democratic party or the national administration hoped that the convention would turn to them after Wallace had been eliminated. From the standpoint of experience in high executive affairs, James F. Byrnes was considered a strong possibility. He had seen service as U.S. senator from South Carolina, as Supreme Court justice, and as director of the Office of War Mobilization. Speaker Sam Rayburn of Texas was a favorite candidate among party leaders early in the year. Senator Alben Barkley of Kentucky considered himself in line by reason of his services as party leader in the Senate. Because of his fine record as chairman of the Senate Special Committee to Investigate the Defense Program, Senator Truman was regarded by many to be a logical candidate. Among the favorite sons were Governor J. Melville Broughton of North Carolina, former Governor Paul V. McNutt of Indiana, and Governor Robert S. Kerr of Oklahoma. Among Roosevelt's cabinet members, Secretary of the Interior Harold Ickes hoped that the convention would turn to him.[9] Justice William O. Douglas was not a candidate for the nomination but stood high in President Roosevelt's esteem.[10]

As early as 1942 some of Senator Truman's friends urged him to go for the vice-presidential nomination in view of the favorable publicity that the Truman committee was receiving.[11] He always answered that he liked it where he was in the Senate and that he did not want to be vice-president. On January 25, 1944, the *St. Louis Post-Dispatch* commented that the election of Robert Hannegan as chairman of the Democratic National Committee boosted Truman's stock for the vice-presidential nomination, but Truman was reluctant to commit himself. In April, Truman told reporters: "I am not a candidate, never have been and don't want it. . . . I have spent nine years trying to be of use as a United States Senator. I do not think I should throw that away. I enjoy the active life of a senator, and not that of the presiding officer of the Senate."[12]

George Allen, secretary of the Democratic National Committee, wrote that an informal meeting was held at the White House in January 1944 at which Hannegan, Pauley, Walker, Flynn, and other party leaders told President Roosevelt that the renomination of Wallace would split the party. Senators Sherman Minton, Barkley, and Truman, Justice Douglas, Speaker Rayburn, and war mobilizer Byrnes were mentioned as possible substitutes. It was the consensus of the group that Senator Truman would be the best choice. President Roosevelt, however, made no firm decision and was reported as saying, "Let it cook."[13]

Jesse Jones claimed that in February 1944, after a luncheon in Secretary of the Senate Leslie Biffle's office with several senators, including Senator Truman, he prophesied that Truman would be the Democratic candidate for vice-president that year, but Senator Truman did not agree. Jones felt that the convention would not accept Wallace and would turn to the chairman of the Truman committee, who came from the Midwest.[14]

About the same time, Flynn and Pauley decided it was time that they concentrated on a candidate who might be able to defeat Wallace and went through a list of possible Democratic candidates then in the public eye whom they felt should be considered. Flynn objected to Byrnes and Barkley on the grounds that they were from states too far south; moreover Barkley, as majority leader in the Senate, had defied Roosevelt on the tax bill. After eliminating others for various reasons, the two men limited the field to Speaker Rayburn and Senator Truman. Pauley suggested to Flynn that they get in touch with the Speaker, the third-ranking official in the United States.[15]

At a private luncheon in Rayburn's office, Pauley, Flynn, and Rayburn agreed that they would be able to keep Wallace from being renominated.

Speaker Rayburn did not urge himself as a candidate, but he indicated that he would be willing to be considered. Pauley then stepped up his activity on behalf of Rayburn, arranging for him to speak at Jackson Day dinners in Los Angeles and San Francisco in late March.[16]

Pauley arranged for Senator Truman, who was then on a West Coast investigating tour for his committee, to attend a San Francisco dinner on March 30, 1944. At a cocktail party in Truman's suite at the Mark Hopkins Hotel, attended by Pauley, Rayburn, and Senators Wallgren and Kilgore, the last two mentioned that Harry Truman was a possible candidate for vice-president. Pauley agreed but said that he was already committed to Rayburn. Truman then proposed a toast to Rayburn as the next vice-president of the United States. In an impromptu speech at the dinner, he repeated his toast, getting tremendous applause.[17]

During April 1944, Truman and Rayburn kept mentioning each other for the vice-presidency.[18] At a dinner in St. Louis toward the end of the month, Rayburn's speech proposing Truman for the nomination received thunderous applause.[19] Pauley regarded the dinners as a great success—they received widespread press coverage and gave Truman a chance to meet prominent political leaders who would later become delegates to the national convention. When the convention met, Pauley claimed that more delegates knew Truman than knew Wallace.

In May, Vice-President Wallace's chances for renomination were given a setback by President Roosevelt's request that he go on a special mission to China and Siberia. He would be out of the country during the crucial time that the opposing forces would be struggling for delegates. Nor could he put together a preconvention organization before leaving. The trip was an exhausting one, and in Siberia Wallace was to reveal his naivete in evaluating the Soviet system.[20] As a loyal supporter of the President, Wallace could not get out of this wartime mission. While the vice-president was away, the anti-Wallace forces redoubled their efforts, all reflected in the press, which increasingly mentioned Senator Truman as a possible successor to Wallace.[21]

In June, Hannegan and Flynn increased their pressure on President Roosevelt not to back the renomination of Wallace strongly. Since the Normandy landings took place during June, it was very hard to get the President's mind off military matters. The campaign against Wallace, however, was beginning to have its effects. As Jonathan Daniels reported in his diary on June 17, 1944: "He [President Roosevelt] had thought the feeling against Wallace had been largely that of politicians but he was beginning to believe that it went down below. Some people told him that it meant forty per cent of the vote in their precincts. He said that if you cut that in half and then half again, it still might mean the loss of a million or two votes."[22]

Flynn claimed that in conversation with President Roosevelt, he had narrowed the field down to Senator Truman. Flynn admitted that while Byrnes was the strongest candidate from the standpoint of experience, he would be a poor choice because he had been raised a Catholic and had left the church when he married; the Catholics would oppose him for that. In addition, organized labor would be against him because of his hold-the-line policies on wages, and, coming from South Carolina, black voters in the North would oppose him.[23] President Roosevelt admitted the cogency of these reasons to Jonathan Daniels.[24] Flynn contended that Rayburn was a good choice, but he also was a southerner and the split in the Texas delegation made it difficult for him to run. Flynn continued his report to the President:

We went over every man in the Senate to see who would be available, and Truman was the only one who fitted. His record as head of the Senate Committee to Investigate the National Defense Program was excellent, his labor votes in the Senate were good; on the other hand, he seemed to represent to some degree the conservatives of the party, he came from a border state, and he had never made any "racial" remarks. He just dropped into the slot. It was agreed that Truman was the man who would hurt him least.[25]

Flynn claimed that President Roosevelt then asked him to "inject Truman into the picture." This he did by assembling the famous group for the White House dinner and caucus of July 11, 1944. Flynn listed in the cabal: Hannegan, Walker, Mayor Kelly, George Allen, and himself.[26] Why, in his account, Flynn omitted the name of Ed Pauley is hard to understand since Pauley's memorandum regarding the conference is one of the fullest accounts in existence.[27] Perhaps it was a case of "Freudian forgetting"— Flynn and Pauley were rivals for the claim of ditching Wallace and putting over Truman. At any rate, before the conference, Flynn told the unbelieving Hannegan that "Truman was the man." Hannegan then persuaded Kelly and Allen to support Truman.

The vice-presidency was not discussed at dinner, but the President was greatly interested in the progress that had been made in the preparations for the convention to be held in Chicago eight days hence. Pauley was director of the convention and had charge of physical facilities, tickets, hotel reservations, and other arrangements. These were powers that he admitted could be used to influence the convention's choice for vice-president.

After dinner, they adjourned to the President's study, where they discussed the various candidates for vice-president. Rayburn was eliminated because of the split in the Texas delegation; Byrnes because he was an apostate Catholic and came from the Deep South, whose racist views he shared; Barkley because of his age and apparent lack of loyalty to President Roosevelt. To Pauley's amazement, Roosevelt then injected Ambassador John Winant and Justice William O. Douglas into the picture. With sardonic glee, Pauley listed the totally irrelevant reasons that Roosevelt gave for favoring Douglas. Pauley claimed that Roosevelt said that Douglas had the same kind of following Wallace had; that he had practical experience from the backwoods as a logger; that he looked and acted on occasions like a boy scout; and he played an interesting game of poker. "When President Roosevelt had finished this, there was a dead silence on the part of everyone. No one wanted Douglas any more than Wallace. The President sensed this."[28]

Senator Truman's availability was discussed next. Roosevelt recalled having approved the naming of Truman as head of the Special Committee to Investigate the Defense Program and felt that Truman had done a good job. He said that he did not know him too well, but his work on the committee had demonstrated his ability and loyalty, and he had been trained in politics. Flynn said that Truman's connection with Pendergast organization was thoroughly discussed, and it apparently was not regarded as a disqualification. The President was also willing to overlook differences that he had had with Truman over the defense program, but he was concerned about Truman's age. Bill Douglas was a younger man. The group managed to change the subject, and Truman's age (he was only two years younger than Roosevelt) did not become an obstacle. The Allen, Pauley, and Flynn accounts agree that the President told them they should get behind Truman for the vice-presidency.[29]

Judge Samuel Rosenman's account of this famous caucus at which Roosevelt's successor was agreed upon was apparently based upon interviews with Hannegan and Walker very shortly after the meeting. His account is essentially the same, but with one difference. After the conference broke up, Hannegan told Walker that he was going to stay behind in order to get a letter confirming what was decided at the meeting in case he should need such proof at the convention. He told Walker to wait for him. In the meantime, the President called Walker over and told him to tell Jimmy Byrnes the following day, "It's Truman." Walker agreed and went downstairs to wait for Hannegan. When Hannegan came down he told Walker but not the others, "I got it." "It," according to Rosenman, was the famous Truman-Douglas letter he used later in the convention.[30]

President Roosevelt was convinced that to renominate Wallace would take a disrupting fight, which might split the Democratic party. Tired and heavily burdened with military responsibilities, he did not want to undertake such a battle. The problem was how to convince Wallace that he would be a liability on the ticket. The President liked Wallace personally, and he could not bring himself to do the task directly.

Even before Wallace returned from China on July 9, some journalists surmised that Roosevelt might not press the Democratic convention to renominate Wallace, writing that political advisers had persuaded Roosevelt not to fight for Wallace's renomination.[31] Roosevelt commissioned Rosenman to meet Wallace's plane on the West Coast and inform him that he could not risk creating a permanent split in the party by making the same kind of fight for him that he did at the convention four years earlier. Rosenman thought that the mission would be a hopeless one and so it proved. Wallace managed to avoid Rosenman until he got back to Washington; then President Roosevelt asked Secretary Ickes to join Rosenman in talking to Wallace, making the task all the more difficult because Wallace and Ickes were not friends. Wallace refused to talk politics until he had seen the President.

Vice-President Wallace had lunch with Roosevelt on July 13 and presented the case for his renomination. He indicated that about three hundred delegates were already pledged to him. He also showed a forthcoming Gallup Poll, which estimated that 63 percent of Democratic voters were for Wallace, 17 percent for Alben Barkley, 5 percent for Sam Rayburn, 4 percent for Senator Harry Byrd of Virginia, 3 percent for James Byrnes, 2 percent for Justice Douglas, 2 percent for Harry Truman, and 2 percent for Under Secretary of State Edward R. Stettinius. Roosevelt was impressed —he had not expected Wallace to show such strength. Wallace persuaded Roosevelt to write a letter that would permit Wallace to fight for the nomination on his own:

Hyde Park, N.Y.
July 14, 1944

My dear Senator Jackson:

In the light of the probability that you will be chosen as permanent chairman of the convention, and because I know that many rumors accompany all conventions, I am wholly willing to give you my own personal thought in regard to the selection of a candidate for Vice President. I do this at this time because I expect to be away from Washington for the next few days.

The easiest way of putting it is this: I have been associated with Henry Wallace during his past four years as Vice President, for eight years earlier while he was Secretary of Agriculture, and well before that. I like him and I respect him and he is my personal friend. For these reasons I personally would vote for his renomination if I were a delegate to the convention.

At the same time I do not wish to appear in any way as dictating to the convention. Obviously the convention must do the deciding. And it should—and I am sure it will—give great consideration to the pros and cons of its choice.[32]

This was apparently the kind of letter that Wallace wanted. In spite of its lukewarm character, it might help if no other communication from President Roosevelt was forthcoming.

In the meantime, Byrnes was pressing his case. As commissioned by President Roosevelt, Walker told Byrnes that there was considerable opposition to his candidacy for the position and that the political leaders favored Truman. Byrnes, though, was not convinced that he had been ruled out. He claimed that he had the support of Roosevelt, and he continued in the race, asserting that Hopkins had originally urged him to go out for the nomination. When he heard that the President was favoring Truman, he called Roosevelt and came away with the impression that the President would not indicate any preference and would leave the convention open.[33]

Knowing of the Truman support in certain quarters and of Truman's reluctance to declare himself a candidate, Byrnes shrewdly called Truman on Friday, July 14, and asked him to place Byrnes's name in nomination. Truman agreed, and he indicated that he would try to swing the Missouri delegation to Byrnes.

Byrnes's and Pauley's accounts of the meeting with Roosevelt and two party leaders on the train siding in Chicago on Saturday, July 15 (Roosevelt was on his secret journey to the West Coast) conflict. Pauley said that only he and Hannegan saw the President and the President still agreed to the pushing of Truman's nomination. Byrnes's version is that Hannegan and Mayor Kelly saw Roosevelt and convinced him that Byrnes was the man to push. Judge Rosenman, who was with Roosevelt on the train, said that only Hannegan talked with Roosevelt.[34] Mayor Kelly's letter to Jonathan Daniels seems to confirm the Rosenman version.[35]

The Byrnes forces informed the press that on Monday, July 17, Hannegan had told the labor leaders at a dinner that it was Byrnes. Sidney Hillman, head of the Political Action Committee of the Congress of Industrial Organizations, the most active arm of organized labor in the campaign, disputed this.[36] Apparently at the meeting the preceding Saturday, President Roosevelt had discussed with Hannegan the desirability of securing the support of organized labor for any vice-presidential candidate whom they were going to push. Byrnes was told that he had to get the backing of organized labor. Hillman was proving to be difficult.

Flynn arrived on Tuesday, July 18, and was told by Hannegan: "It's all over. It's Byrnes." Flynn disagreed—the President wanted Truman. Flynn insisted on a select committee meeting of a few political leaders to settle the matter. At the meeting, he told Mayor Kelly that if there was only one vote for Truman in the convention, it would be his. He added, "I had pledged my vote and I never went back on a pledge. I browbeat the committee. I talked. I argued. I swore, and finally they said if the President would tell them again he was for Truman they would agree."[37]

The news services reported that late that afternoon the President personally approved of Truman in a telephone conversation with party leaders.[38] Flynn had won his point. Byrnes had no letter from Roosevelt mentioning his name as a candidate, and he had failed to receive the support of organized labor, so he withdrew from the race, dating his withdrawal for the following day, July 19, in a letter to Senator Maybank. Byrnes was bitter at his defeat and struck out at those whom he regarded as responsible. He was especially provoked at Sidney Hillman. He informed the *New York Times* that President Roosevelt had told Hannegan "to clear everything with Sidney."[39] Chairman Hannegan later denied that he had quoted Roosevelt as saying this.[40] The hostile press and the Republican opposition pounced on this phrase and used it extensively to attract anti-Semitic, anti-Russian, antilabor, and antiliberal voters.

Let us now retrace our steps and see what was happening to Truman, the reluctant candidate, during these hectic days. While increasing attention was given to him in the press before the convention, he steadily insisted that he was not a candidate. His friend and former staff assistant, Max Lowenthal, told him that he ought to be the nominee for vice-president. Truman replied that he had talked with his wife and had decided not to be a candidate. He said that he was too poor. He also commented that he had a daughter, and the White House was no place for children.[41] Secretary Forrestal also told Truman that it was his duty to take the nomination for vice-president since the alternative would be Wallace, and that would have a disastrous effect upon American foreign policy. Truman admitted that he regarded Wallace with misgivings, but he thought his own place was in the Senate.[42]

Truman arrived in Chicago, Saturday, July 15, pledged to support Byrnes but was unsuccessful in getting the Missouri delegates to back Byrnes. Instead they caucused and pledged their support to Truman. At breakfast with Sidney Hillman, where he tried to win labor support for Byrnes, Hillman told him that he was for Wallace first but if Wallace did not win, he would support Truman; he was opposed to Byrnes. Hillman was willing to overlook the differences he had had with the Truman committee; Max Lowenthal had convinced him that Truman was sympathetic toward organized labor. Truman also saw several other labor leaders, including Philip Murray of the CIO, Al Whitney of the Brotherhood of Railway Trainmen, and William Green of the American Federation of Labor. All objected to Byrnes but would accept Truman. When Truman told the Maryland delegation that he was not a candidate, Governor Herbert R. O'Conor of that state shouted, "You're crazy as hell!"[43]

As the pressure mounted for Truman to declare himself in the battle to block Wallace, he turned to some of his friends to ward off the Truman boom. Although Roy Roberts of the *Kansas City Star* was a Republican and had always been a foe of Tom Pendergast, he was friendly to Senator Truman. The senator tried to get Roberts to issue a statement for him that would clearly remove him from the running. Roberts instead reported increasing demands that Truman become an active candidate. Truman also turned to his lifelong friend, Tom Evans of Kansas City, to come to his rescue, but Evans promoted Truman. The same thing happened in the case of John Snyder, a friend who had left government service to become vice-president of the First National Bank of St. Louis. Snyder ended by supporting Truman for the nomination.

When the Democratic convention opened on Wednesday, July 19, pressures were building up for Truman to make a decision. The Roosevelt letter on Wallace had been revealed the day before, and the general reaction was that its halfhearted character diminished Wallace's chances for getting the nomination.[44] The vice-president's backers, however, did not give up the battle. Wallace himself came to the convention to marshal his forces and received a rousing ovation. Hannegan, who had hinted about the Truman-Douglas letter written by Roosevelt, was now forced to reveal it. It read:

Dear Bob:
You have written to me about Harry Truman and Bill Douglas. I should, of course, be very glad to run with either of them and believe that either one of them would bring real strength to the ticket.[45]

It should be noted that this letter did not say that President Roosevelt preferred either of these candidates but merely that he would be willing to run with either of them. Candidates who did not have such a letter were practically ruled out. Byrnes was eliminated and left in a huff. When Barkley learned that he also had been vetoed, he nearly tore up his speech nominating Roosevelt, but he was prevailed upon by his friends to reconsider and delivered the address as though nothing had happened. Pauley pointed out that it was too late for the Douglas forces to start a boom, although it was suspected that some leaflets on Truman and Pendergast were distributed by friends of the justice.

Truman reported that the final decision was made as follows:

Hannegan called me from the Blackstone and asked me to come over for a conference. He said they were going to phone the President. I went over there. There were Ed Kelley, Frank Walker, Hannegan, Ed Flynn, Hague. They commenced raising hell with me to be vice president. Walker said the President wants you to be vice president. I said, "I don't believe you."
Telephone rang, and I could hear all Bob said and most of what the President said. Bob said, "No, he hasn't agreed yet."
President, "Well, tell him if he wants to break up the Democratic party in the middle of the war, that's his responsibility."
Bob: "Now what do you say?"[46]

Truman expressed great astonishment and surprise that he had not been informed of the President's wishes before, but he agreed to run. The stories that appeared in the newspapers for Thursday, July 20, indicated that Truman had at last become an avowed candidate. He was quoted as telling his friends: "I will win. I wouldn't be in the race if President Roosevelt didn't approve."[47]

The Wallace forces, however, were not yet beaten. With the aid of organized labor, they were making the best they could of the Roosevelt letter on Wallace. The vice-president said: "I told the President that in justice to himself, there should be no suggestion of dictation to the convention."[48] Wallace supporters were alarmed at the Truman-Douglas letter and called an emergency meeting at which Wallace, Hillman, Phillip Murray, Francis Biddle, C. B. Baldwin, James Carey, and Harold Ickes were present. Ickes, who had changed his mind about Wallace, decried the conspiracy of the Democratic bosses to nominate Truman and warned Roosevelt by telegram that such an outcome would be his "greatest political mistake in twelve years."[49]

The Thursday session of the convention was charged with excitement and suspense. In general, the delegates had no inkling of how Senator Barkley felt when he delivered his eloquent nominating address. But the highlight of the session was the stirring speech by Henry Wallace, seconding Roosevelt's nomination. Labor's Political Action Committee had packed the galleries. Pauley claimed that the Wallace supporters had counterfeited tickets, crashed the gate, pushed down a guard, and usurped the seats of many delegates.[50] There was a loud demonstration for twenty minutes, and the organist kept playing "Iowa—That's Where the Tall Corn Grows" until Pauley threatened to have the cable from the organ to the loudspeaker cut. Although the plans called for the vice-presidential nomination that evening, Pauley was afraid of a stampede for Wallace, and he got Hannegan's permission to call off the vote and adjourn.

The conspirators now went to work in earnest. It was reasoned that the more favorite sons nominated, the smaller would be Wallace's vote on the first ballot. On the other hand, if Wallace made a respectable showing on the first ballot, his strength might be used to frighten some of the favorite sons into switching to Truman on the second ballot; this would be especially true in the case of southerners who feared a Wallace nomination. Farley pointed out how this worked in the case of Illinois. He stated that there were twenty to twenty-five votes for Wallace in the Illinois delegation of fifty-eight but that Mayor Kelly put up Senator Scott Lucas as a favorite son. Lucas received all the first-choice votes and Wallace none.[51] Altogether there were ten favorite sons, but the organization leaders made sure that there were not too many. It was vital that Truman should make a good showing on the first ballot also.

Hannegan and his associates worked through the night trying to convince a majority of the delegates that Truman was the running mate that the President wanted. James C. Hagerty of the *New York Times* reported, "It took a good deal of talking and a good deal of pressure to get a majority of the party leaders and delegates to that opinion."[52] Drew Pearson reported that Postmaster General Frank Walker telephoned every chairman of every state delegation. White House assistant Gene Casey of Maryland persuaded the Maryland delegates to agree to switch to Truman on the second ballot.[53] By daybreak the leaders thought that they had the necessary support for Truman.

On Friday, July 21, the roll of states was called for nominations for vice-president. When the state of Missouri was reached, Senator Bennett Clark put his colleague, Senator Harry S. Truman, in nomination, saying that Truman "met the requirements of possessing all the qualifications necessary and desirable for the presidency."[54] Altogether twelve names were officially placed in nomination.

Wallace did better on the first ballot than was expected. He won 429½ votes to Truman's 319½ votes out of a total of 1,176 votes (589 were required for nomination). Wallace's main strength was in the Midwest, the Far West, and the Northeast, where he divided honors with Truman, falling behind in New York but forging ahead in Pennsylvania and Ohio. In the South, Wallace had the support of the Georgia delegation under Governor Arnall and half of the Florida delegates led by Senator Pepper. In general, he had the backing of the liberals. Truman's main strength on the first ballot was in New York, where Flynn proved to be persuasive, the border states, and some southern states. He won all of the votes in Arkansas, Louisiana, Missouri, New Mexico, and Rhode Island and some votes in half of the states.

As the roll was being called for the second ballot, Maryland shifted from its favorite son to Truman. Other states that shifted from minor candidates to Truman before the roll call was finished were Mississippi, Oklahoma, South Carolina, and Virginia, showing that Truman was regarded as acceptable in the South. The Texas delegation that had supported Bankhead on the first ballot was split between Wallace and Truman on the second, showing the liberal-conservative division in the state. When the last delegation was reached, the count was Truman, 477½, Wallace, 473, others, 225½. Then the state of Alabama was recognized for the purpose of shifting its votes to Truman, and the stampede was on. When the second ballot was tallied after the shifts, the count stood: Truman, 1,031; Wallace, 105; McNutt, 1; Barkley, 6; Cooper, 26; Douglas, 4; not voting, 3.[55] Some of the sting of Wallace's defeat was taken out by his fine showing.

Senator Truman accepted the nomination at once in one of the shortest acceptance speeches on record:

You don't know how very much I appreciate the very great honor which has come to the state of Missouri. It is also a great responsibility which I am perfectly willing to assume.

Cartoon by Berryman, 1944. Reprinted, courtesy of *The Washington Star*.

Nine years and five months ago I came to the Senate. I expect to continue the efforts I have made there to help shorten the war and to win the peace under the great leader, Franklin D. Roosevelt.

I don't know what else I can say except that I accept this great honor with all humility.

I thank you.[56]

This speech received a fine reception in some quarters. The *Sioux City Journal* wrote, "Nominee Harry Truman made an early and effective bid for popularity in the brevity, the informality, the spontaneousness, the modesty and the downright humaneness of his 60-second acceptance speech, which might well stand as an all-time beacon light for makers of political speeches."[57]

Bess Truman and Margaret were not so happy. They were nearly crushed by the crowd. When Bess finally reached Harry, she said: "Are we going to have to go through this all the rest of our lives?[58]

Robert Hannegan was accused of using his position as chairman of the Democratic National Committee to promote the candidacy of his fellow Missourian. He was described as a Machiavellian plotter who though supposedly neutral among the candidates had sabotaged Truman's opponents. It was said that he misused the Truman-Douglas letter by implying that it was stronger than it was and by holding up its publication until it was too late for the Douglas forces to get into action.[59] James Byrnes, who was the most prominent candidate eliminated after Wallace, blamed not Hannegan for his defeat, but rather Flynn and Hillman and President Roosevelt's change of mind about leaving the convention open. Byrnes excused Hannegan's actions after Roosevelt had clearly indicated a preference for Truman.[60]

The ambiguity of President Roosevelt's position on the vice-presidency was deeply resented by some of his liberal friends. After the convention, Mark Ethridge of the *Courier-Journal and Louisville Times* wrote to him:

Surely one who has followed you as devotedly as I have for so long does not need to apologize for saying to you that I think you have made the greatest moral and political mistake of your career in the way in which you brought about the nomination of Senator Truman. . . .

If you had said frankly that you did not want Wallace as a running mate again, that would have been understood and no doubt accepted—with disappointment, of course. If you had said publicly that you wanted Truman, that would have been understood and regretted by Wallace supporters. But, you were left in the position at Chicago of having said that if you were a delegate you would support Wallace and at the same time directing the fight against him. . . . Senator Jackson read your letter to the convention Wednesday morning, but Mr. Hannegan left the impression that he had his instructions on the previous Saturday and the report was that the instructions had been renewed with vulgar emphasis on Tuesday in a telephone call from Harry

Hopkins . . . it was absolutely evident that the big city bosses were moving heaven and earth to name Truman.[61]

But Ethridge was mistaken about the course of events. President Roosevelt chose the easiest way to let Wallace down. The vice-president found it difficult to reconcile Roosevelt's contradictory behavior, but he felt that he had gone down to defeat gracefully. President Roosevelt congratulated him on his fight and offered him any cabinet post except that of secretary of state (indicating that Roosevelt himself did not trust Wallace on foreign policy questions). As for the conservatives, they were sometimes disappointed in Truman later. In a letter to Wallace on July 31, 1944, George W. Norris wrote: "I think I ought to add that I am not classifying Truman as one of the enemies. I think his nomination was a very good one . . . he has done some very good work."[62]

Senator Truman owed his nomination for vice-president in part to President Roosevelt's indifference to the problems of succession due to wartime preoccupations and fatigue. The President was not thinking of someone to take his place but rather of a candidate who would be easy to nominate, who would offend the least number of voters, and who, if elected, would help him in putting over his programs in the Senate. His refusal to fight for Wallace's renomination was based on his own reservations about Wallace's possible helpfulness on the ticket and in the Senate and on the arguments of his personal and political advisers that any attempt to force Wallace's renomination would split the party. Opposed to Wallace were the southerners who did not like his racial and welfare policies, the conservatives who objected to his economic and foreign policies, and the professional Democratic politicians who distrusted his mysticism and doubted his loyalty to the party organization.

Wallace's defeat did leave a number of elements in the Democratic party disgruntled. Liberals in the South and the North, those friendly to the Soviet Union, organized labor, and minority groups, including blacks, felt that they had been let down by the convention. The seeds of revolt for the 1948 Progressive uprising had been sown.

In the sifting process that came up with Truman as a substitute for Wallace, the press played a key role since it projected a new image of the senator from Missouri. He was no longer the senator from Pendergast but rather the watchdog of the treasury during the war. The press reports regarding the Truman committee had erased for the time being the stigma of his political origins in Kansas City during the time that Tom Pendergast was the organization leader. As the *Kansas City Star* expressed it:

But as United States Senator he had shown unusual capacity for development. Modest, unassuming, industrious, Truman had gradually won the respect and friendship of his colleagues. . . . He was nominated for vice president with the approval of party leaders familiar with the handicaps of his earlier political record, who believed that his later achievements and development in the national field had eclipsed what had gone before. It is a measure of his growth that his party should have united behind him for second place on the ticket.[63]

In the actual nomination process, organized labor played an important part. The Political Action Committee had become a force to be reckoned with in the convention and in the election process. President Roosevelt directed the political leaders to consult with labor leaders regarding possible vice-presidential candidates, since he felt that the election would be close and labor support would be needed to win. Sidney Hillman, a trusted friend and head of PAC, indicated that Wallace was labor's first choice, and when it appeared that Wallace could not win, Hillman helped convince the other labor leaders that Truman would be a satisfactory alternative. Other candidates, including Byrnes, were opposed by organized labor.

Another group that helped put over Truman's nomination for vice-president was made up of the city bosses of New York, Chicago, Jersey City, and Memphis. President Roosevelt wanted the cooperation of the professional politicians in the convention and in the campaign. The organization leaders reassured him that Truman was acceptable to southerners, conservatives, minority groups, including blacks, farmers, and the party faithful. Ed Flynn, the shrewd boss of the Bronx, Robert Hannegan, the energetic national chairman, and Ed Pauley, treasurer of the party, all had important roles in persuading Roosevelt and the delegates to substitute Truman for Wallace.

The nomination of Truman as the Democratic candidate appears to have been a genuine draft. Until the last minute, he declared that he was not a candidate and that he preferred to stay in the Senate. Pressure from his friends, the city bosses, and President Roosevelt became so great that he was finally convinced that it was his duty to run. He clearly was not chosen because he was thought to be the best qualified man to be president but rather because his nomination presented no great difficulties, and his presence on the ticket would not disturb many voters.

chapter 18 | THE 1944 CAMPAIGN

Th' prisidincy is th' highest office in th' gift iv th' people.
Th' vice-prisidincy is th' next highest an' th' lowest. It isn't a crime
exactly. Ye can't be sint to jail f'r it, but it's a kind iv a disgrace. It's
like writin' anonymous letters.
  —*Dissertations by Mr. Dooley, The Vice-President*
  (Finley Peter Dunne)

Accepting the Democratic National Convention's nomination for a fourth term as president of the United States, Roosevelt said, "I shall not campaign in the usual sense, for the office. In these days of tragic sorrow, I do not consider it fitting. And besides, in these days of global warfare, I shall not be able to find the time."[1] It was hardly a customary beginning for a presidential campaign and made the job of the vice-presidential candidate, never an easy one, all the more difficult.

Even in the best of circumstances, the candidate for the office of vice-president has a difficult task to perform. He must, above all, avoid saying anything that would injure his running mate's chances of being elected. The least he can do is carry his own state, even if the ticket, nationally, goes down to defeat. Such was the case with Charles Fairbanks, Republican nominee for vice-president in 1904 and 1916. Fairbanks managed to carry his home state of Indiana although the Democrats carried the electoral college in the 1916 election.

Campaign activity on the part of vice-presidential nominees in the twentieth century has varied considerably. Theodore Roosevelt as Republican vice-presidential nominee in 1900 tried to rival William Jennings Bryan in his campaign efforts. Twenty years later, his distant cousin, Franklin D. Roosevelt, as Democratic candidate for vice-president, tried to emulate this example while his Republican rival, Calvin Coolidge, did very little. In 1932 and 1936, John Nance Garner, a Democrat, stayed mostly at home, while the Republican candidates, Charles Curtis in 1932 and Frank Knox in 1936, were more active.[2]

Truman would be an active candidate, but he would campaign with a handicap. To begin with, Senator Truman and President Roosevelt did not have many conferences regarding campaign strategy. The President was so busy working out the grand strategy of the war and running the military machine that he had little time or energy for even planning the campaign. He took a fatalistic view toward the election; if the people wanted him to finish the war job, he was willing to make the sacrifice and to give up thoughts of retiring. On the other hand, if the people wished to dismiss him, he was ready to step down. He felt that he had done his best, and if it was time for someone else to take over the awesome burdens of the presidency, so be it. Robert Sherwood, in referring to Roosevelt's indifferent attitude toward the campaign, said: "He seemed to feel that he had done his duty by allowing his name to be placed before the American people, and if they did not want to re-elect him, that would be perfectly all right with him. As Watson put it, 'He just doesn't seem to give a damn.'"[3] Under the circumstances, Senator Truman was not given much guidance on how to contribute to Democratic success in November.

In the early days of the campaign, the strategy of the Republican party and its candidate, Governor Thomas E. Dewey of New York, became clear. The issues would be the records of the candidates and the war—its beginnings, its conduct, and its aftermath. According to the Republican charges, President Roosevelt was the "Dictator"; World War II was a "Roosevelt war"; the Democratic administration was disjointed, extravagant, inefficient, and wasteful; high taxes and the crushing national debt would ruin the country economically; the government mismanaged war production, rationing, and price controls; it coddled labor, regimented agriculture, and crippled business; and it was made up of tired old men with New Deal pipe dreams. It was "time for a change."

Arthur Krock of the *New York Times* thought there was another issue: "the background, capacity and other qualities of Senator Harry S. Truman . . . the contention being that he may succeed Mr. Roosevelt because of the long strain on the president."[4] When Senator Truman was making his fine record as chairman of the Special Committee to Investigate the Defense Program, people tended to overlook or forget his political past, but as a candidate for vice-president, his vulnerabilities were exploited on a national scale by the opposition.

Within a week after Truman's nomination, the opposition press began to attack him and his record. He was accused of nepotism for hiring his wife as a secretary, though it was a not-uncommon practice on the Hill. He readily admitted that she had been on his payroll most of the time since July 1941 and added that she earned every cent of the $4,500 a year she received.[5] Among the foremost critics of Truman were the *Chicago Tribune* and the *New York Daily News*. The *Chicago Tribune* blasted:

If they confess that there is the slightest chance that Mr. Roosevelt may die or become incapacitated in the next four years, they are faced with the grinning skeleton of Truman the bankrupt, Truman the pliant tool of Boss Pendergast in looting Kansas City's county government, Truman the yes-man and apologist in the Senate for political gangsters.[6]

Democratic National Chairman Robert E. Hannegan, as a friend and protege of Senator Truman, was ready to support the Truman campaign efforts. How extensive should these efforts be? Krock claimed that the Democratic leaders considered whether "Truman's candidacy should be featured, or whether he should lie low, as John N. Garner did in compliance with the campaign policy of 1932."[7] While Truman's positive qualities and excellent Senate work were conceded, "Those who would have had him stay in the background sought thereby to make it more difficult for the Republicans to project the senator as a major issue, which they fully expect them to try to do."[8]

The indifference of President Roosevelt to the outcome of the election and his poor performance in the radio address from the Bremerton Navy Yard on August 12 alarmed Democratic leaders. Because of adverse conditions on the deck of a destroyer, general fatigue, and illness Roosevelt's delivery in Bremerton was halting and uncertain.

On August 18 the President had lunch with Senator Truman on the White House lawn, and they discussed plans for the campaign. Truman recalled: "He told me that because he was so busy in the war effort I would have to do the campaigning for both of us."[9] Roosevelt asked Truman to use trains rather than planes since, as he put it, "one of us has to stay alive." The President agreed to Truman's plan to hold the notification proceedings for the vice-presidential nomination on August 31 in the tiny town of Lamar, Missouri, where Truman was born. Truman's birthplace was not a log cabin but it was, as we have seen, a politically suitable simple frame house without plumbing or adequate lighting.

The acceptance speech was based on suggestions from President Roosevelt, other senators, and the staff of the Democratic National Committee. Truman claimed that he did the writing. As he told reporters, he proposed "telling the way I see things, as all my speeches do; wrote it mostly last night, at home, and my wife has gone over it and criticized it, not telling me what I wanted to hear about it as friends are apt to do."[10]

Truman's acceptance speech was devoted primarily to extolling the qualities of President Roosevelt's leadership. He pointed out that the President had unique knowledge and experience for the war and postwar tasks facing the nation. Although he did not mention or criticize Dewey personally, he said: "It takes a new president at least a year to learn the fundamentals of his job."[11] At the time he did not realize how prophetic that statement would be as applied to his own case. The immediate reaction to the speech was favorable, many praising it for its lofty tone.[12]

Senator Truman resigned from the Special Committee to Investigate the

Defense Program. The committee members wished him to continue, but he wanted to avoid getting the committee work involved in politics, and he was anxious to engage more heavily in campaign activities.[13]

Truman faced a vigorous Republican vice-presidential candidate, John W. Bricker of Ohio, who had served as governor of his state from 1939 to 1945. Governor Bricker's campaign efforts were just as strenuous as Senator Truman's, and they were better financed.

Truman's first regularly scheduled campaign speeches were in Detroit on Labor Day. Because of the intense rivalry between the American Federation of Labor and the Congress of Industrial Organizations, Democratic chairman Hannegan was concerned about avoiding conflict between the two organizations. He enlisted the aid of George E. Allen, a companion to several presidents and a shrewd public relations adviser, as advance man for the occasion. Allen got in touch with local politicians and with both wings of the labor movement and worked out a compromise solution. Truman would address each organization separately, one in the afternoon and the other in the evening. Truman made essentially the same speech in both places, criticizing the Republican economic policies after World War I, promising determined efforts to avoid postwar unemployment, and reminding labor of its responsibilities:

> Today American labor wants a government that can do something. If need be, a government that will do much.
>
> But now a word of warning from a friend. Labor has duties as well as rights. . . . You must elect and follow wise leaders of proved integrity. Your contracts must be sacred. Above all else you must turn in an honest day's work every day you are on the job. . . . You do your job, and the Democratic administration under Franklin D. Roosevelt will do its job. Your job is to produce; government's job is to see to it that you get a fair, square deal and the right to enjoy the product of your toil.[14]

In accordance with Roosevelt's wishes, the National Committee planned an extensive campaign tour for Truman, beginning October 12. Because of a shortage of campaign funds and Truman's modest tastes, the arrangements were simple. Truman and his staff, composed of Hugh Fulton, former counsel for the Truman committee, Matthew Connelly, Truman's secretary, Edward McKim, a personal friend, and George Allen, a representative of the Democratic National Committee, traveled in one Pullman, the *Henry Stanley*, which had a loudspeaker system, some typewriters, and a recording device; representatives of the press were in a second Pullman. This "bobtail special," as it was called, was attached to regularly scheduled trains, which meant that its own schedule was irregular. It was a small, informal group that went on this tour, and Truman liked to fraternize with the press and play poker between stops. Fulton and Connelly worked on the preparation of speeches. Such a small staff had a problem meeting deadlines. *Newsweek* claimed, "Fulton did most of the work on the campaign train while Truman merely edited."[15]

For the financing of the Truman campaign tour, a group of the senator's friends organized a small committee. His Kansas City friend, Tom Evans, owner of a chain of drugstores and a radio station, was elected chairman of the committee, and L. T. Barringer of Memphis, Tennessee, was elected treasurer. Examination of a partial list of contributors who gave a modest total of around $28,000 indicates that 60 percent of them came from Missouri.[16] Truman asked Evans to clear all contributions with him because he might want to refuse money from certain sources. His former business associate, Eddie Jacobson, was also active in raising funds, especially when money was needed for such emergencies as paying the railroads for moving the bobtail special to the next stop.

The tour, a dress rehearsal for Truman's famous whistle-stop campaign tour four years later, had some four major addresses planned in the beginning, but Truman ended up making about fifty-four speeches before large and small crowds. The number of important addresses was tripled, and to them were added some forty or more informal platform appearances at station stops. A newspaperman who covered these stops wrote:

> There was little of excitement during the campaign tour, Harry Truman, the likeable, sincere candidate was out making votes largely by pounding away at the major issues. It was not a colorful campaign—far from it. But there were pleasant experiences in poker games, stories, straight-from-the-shoulder, honest chats and in the farmer-neighborliness that early sold the skeptical and agnostic reporters on the genuineness of the man whose campaign they covered.[17]

Truman was given shrewd advice on how to conduct the campaign by Price Wickersham, a Kansas City lawyer:

> 1. Don't explain why you were chosen at Chicago or that you did not desire to be a candidate.
> 2. There is no need to commend Wallace, the ticket will get the votes from his followers anyway, and you will not get Republican votes by such unnecessary commendation.
> 3. Avoid having your picture taken with negroes and alleged city bosses.
> 4. Make your speeches, especially those on the radio, short. Speak slowly and give the impression to your hearers that you have a lot of common sense, that you are no radical or a visionary.
> 5. There are thousands of people who believe, rightly in a way, that the President may not serve out his full term and that the Vice President may become President, so pitch your public utterances on a high plane.
> 6. Avoid story telling. Make your hearers believe you are a solid, practical, clear-thinking American, capable of being President in the event of an emergency.

7. Emphasize and reemphasize our duty to our fighting men and women after the war. That's what the mothers and fathers want to hear.

8. I repeat, don't explain that you really didn't want the nomination. That will not make a single vote; on the other hand, it will permit the opposition to charge that the Bosses forced you to accept, etc. Get votes, don't lose them.

9. On your radio speeches have a competent assistant carefully check grammar, and for doubtful words mark pronunciation. Mark in margin in big figures each minute the reading takes, so you will know whether you are "on time."

10. As to the housewife, tell her that of course rationing is annoying perhaps, but this is an all-out war; better for all to get some meat and vegetables than to let the rich get the most of it. No better plan is suggested by the Republicans. That rent control is the best plan ever devised to prevent high rents, etc., etc.

11. Don't try to convince our people that a big public debt is all right because the Government owes that money to our people and not to foreigners. The public are not economists and can't differentiate between public and private debts.

. . . You will note I speak of "Progressive Legislation" rather than "New Deal." The people have been deluged with criticism of "New Deal," so circumvent that criticism by speaking of "Progressive Legislation."

Ignore sectional controversies, such as poll-tax, avoid attacks on the press, don't permit attacks on Dewey personally. Do not assume that the American voter is apathetic to the war; on the contrary, he is vitally and very personally interested and involved in it. He is interested in this election only as it concerns the war and the peace to follow.[18]

This memorandum, written by an acute lawyer and containing much sound advice, is not the sort of document that would have been prepared for a political candidate by a sociologist, a social psychologist, or a student of race relations. The failure to capitalize the word *Negro* would, at that time, have been offensive to some black citizens. Wickersham took a cynical view of the intelligence of the average voter and of his ability to understand economics. Nor did he have a very high opinion of Truman himself, whom he warned to watch his grammar, his pronunciation, and his tendency to appear too humble. Public relations advice in political campaigns was in its infancy at this time, and this document is clearly a beginning effort. How much influence it had on Truman is not known.[19]

The first stop of Truman's campaign tour was at New Orleans, where he made a nonpolitical speech on flood control and soil conservation before the Flood Control Congress he had addressed on several occasions before. As a long-time member of the Mississippi Valley Flood Control Association, he refused to change the subject to a more purely political one.

On the way to California, the train stopped at Uvalde, Texas, so that Truman could greet his old friend the former Vice-President John Nance Garner. Of the vice-presidents Truman had known, Garner was the most admired and respected. As a freshman senator, Truman had been invited frequently by Garner to "strike a blow for liberty" (take a drink of whisky) in the vice-president's office. It was part of Truman's code of loyalty that he would pay no attention to the fact that Garner had fallen from grace among the New Dealers. Since 1935, relations between Roosevelt and Garner had been cooling. The two men had disagreed on labor legislation, court reform, presidential interference in congressional primaries and elections, leadership contests, and spending.[20] As far as Truman was concerned, these differences should not interfere with cordial greetings for a man whose career he regarded as a model of what a vice-president could do and who had once helped him in his struggle for recognition in the Senate. No speeches were made, but the crusty old man in his soiled farm clothes and stained hands was invited aboard the train to "strike a blow for liberty."[21]

In Los Angeles on October 16, Truman made a major speech on reconversion and on national defense against the Japanese. In this speech, he drew heavily upon his experiences as chairman of the Senate Special Investigating Committee. He criticized Dewey for grossly miscalculating America's war potential, for shillyshallying on foreign policy with one policy for isolationists in Wisconsin and another for interventionists in New York, and for misquoting the reports of the Truman committee. Regarding this meeting, he was quoted as saying, "The toughest audience I had to deal with was in Los Angeles. It was completely hostile and must have thrown more than a hundred pointed questions at me."[22]

The tour continued up the coast to Seattle, where Truman delivered an address on light metals and power development, topics on which his committee had been well briefed. In the same speech, he criticized Dewey for not taking a firmer stand on the need for international collaboration for maintenance of peace in the postwar world. He said: "Can you afford to take a chance on a fence-straddler with a record on foreign affairs like that of the Republican candidate, when your future and that of your children is at stake?"[23]

The National Committee pressed Truman to make a speech in Montana, but he hesitated to do this; his friend Senator Burton K. Wheeler was opposed to the Roosevelt foreign policy. George Allen, on the other hand, was concerned that Truman might make some friendly gesture toward Wheeler that would be embarrassing to the administration.[24] Truman avoided these potential problems by not letting Wheeler know he was going to speak in the state. His speech was mostly concerned with the postwar reconversion of the copper industry and with the extension of government water power, irrigation, and rural electrification. He did not mention isolationism.[25] Wheeler resented the speech, but Truman mollified him later by pointing out that he was under great pressure to do something he did not want to do and he still sought and needed Wheeler's advice.[26]

The next major speech was in Peoria, Illinois, on October 26. Here Truman anticipated the strong appeal he was to make four years later to the farmers:

Every American deserves a fair break, and he will get it under the Democratic Administration. . . . How their [the Republicans'] tune has changed since the Republican Convention of 1944. You may remember when one of the key speakers of that convention solemnly pronounced that under the Democratic Administration the farmer works all day and keeps books all night. He did not choose to remind the American farmer that under the administration of Hoover a farmer worked all day, worked all night and had no books to keep.

The government under the three Republican administrations was so busy helping big business to spare any time for the farmers. . . . We Democrats will not say it is unAmerican to help the farmer and the workingman in hard times.[27]

Shortly before this speech was made, the Hearst papers broke a story alleging that Truman had once been a member of the Ku Klux Klan. This accusation was based on affidavits made by persons who were personally hostile to Truman. In his Peoria speech, Truman categorically denied the charges: "The isolationists are desperate to win this election. The Hearst papers even go so far as to call me a member of the Ku Klux Klan. That charge is a falsehood. I never have been a member of the Klan or attended one of its meetings in my life."[28]

Truman was originally scheduled for a speech in Boston, but this was cancelled and President Roosevelt spoke there instead. On October 30, however, he addressed a Democratic rally in Providence, Rhode Island. At a press conference in this city, he made a reference to Senator David I. Walsh of Massachusetts as an "isolationist," adding that Walsh had two more years on his present term in which "we have a chance to reform him."[29] Walsh deeply resented this comment, which caused some alarm in the White House; the high command was not sure of winning the state. Roosevelt tried to smooth over the situation by inviting Walsh to board his train and ride with him to Boston. Walsh accepted and rode from Worcester to Boston but did not attend the Boston rally.[30] It is difficult to evaluate the importance of this incident. Truman's brutally frank off-the-cuff remark was delivered in a bantering manner, and some thought that it helped bring out the nonisolationist vote.[31] Roosevelt and Truman carried the state by about the same margin as the national ticket had in 1940 so no loss could be attributed to Truman's remark. The incident was, nonetheless, one of Truman's early lessons in the need for a national figure to weigh in advance the possible consequences of informal remarks.

The opposition continued to hammer away at Truman's weak points with the Walsh incident pictured as a great blunder. Governor Bricker and others kept repeating the "clear everything with Sidney" slogan with its anti-foreigner, anticommunist, anti-Russian, and anti-Jewish overtones. A rumor was circulated that Truman was Jewish.[32] He was criticized about the school board loan foreclosed on his mother's farm. He was accused of being anti-Negro. The Republicans kept repeating that Roosevelt was dying, and his passing would elevate a bumbling, boss-controlled, New Deal, rubber-stamp vice-presidential candidate if the people voted for the Democrats.

Seven days before the election, the Liberal party of New York arranged a mammoth meeting in Madison Square Garden, New York, at which both Truman and Henry A. Wallace were to appear. Since this was a Wallace group, it was imperative that Wallace should not seem to overshadow Truman. George Allen and Senator Robert F. Wagner took great care to see that Truman and Wallace entered together so that both would share in the applause. The event went off as planned, although there was a wait for Wallace. Truman, who had had reservations about Wallace as vice-president, praised him as a great secretary of agriculture, but Wallace failed to return the Truman praise. For the first time in a major address, Truman touched on civil rights and accused the Republicans of appealing to racial and religious prejudice.[33]

Truman wound up his campaign by speeches in West Virginia and St. Louis and Independence, Missouri. In his election eve speech in his home town, he said:

I have found three things to be uppermost in the minds of all Americans.

First, is the winning of the war, quickly and completely.

Second, the winning of the peace so that our children and our children's children will never again be called upon to lay down their lives on the field of battle.

Third, the reconversion of our vast production facilities now developed for the destruction of our enemies to production for peace. Production that will afford freedom and opportunity to not only this generation but to the generations to come.[34]

Only on the final lap of the tour did Bess and Margaret Truman ride on the bobtail special. Margaret Truman was very enthusiastic about the trip.[35]

On election night, Truman watched the returns in the Muehlebach Hotel in Kansas City. After Dewey conceded at 3:45 A.M., Roosevelt and Truman exchanged telegrams. Roosevelt wired: "I am very happy that things have gone so well. My thanks and congratulations for your splendid cooperation." Truman replied: "I am very happy over the overwhelming endorsement which you received. Isolationism is dead. Hope to see you soon."[36]

The Roosevelt and Truman ticket won the election with 53.8 percent of the major party vote, carrying thirty-six states with 432 electoral votes;

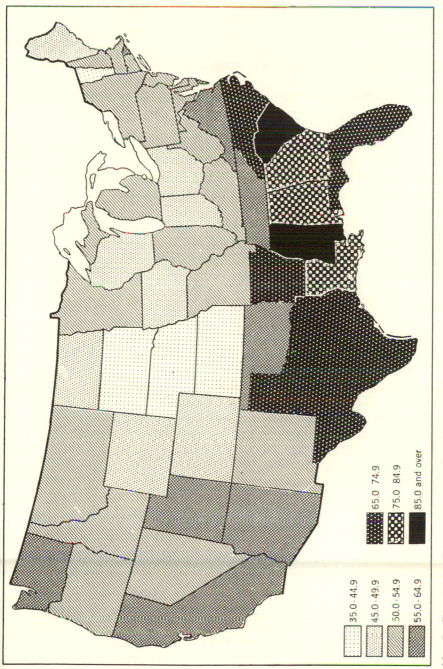

Map 5. Percentage Democratic vote of total vote, 1944

35.0 - 44.9	65.0 - 74.9
45.0 - 49.9	75.0 - 84.9
50.0 - 54.9	85.0 and over
55.0 - 64.9	

Dewey and Bricker carried twelve states with 99 electoral votes. The Dewey-Bricker ticket carried the New England states of Maine and Vermont, the midwestern states of Indiana, Ohio, Wisconsin, Iowa, Kansas, Nebraska, South Dakota, and North Dakota, and the mountain states of Wyoming and Colorado. A shift of 3 percentage points would have changed the results. Map 5 shows the relative strength of the Roosevelt-Truman vote in the various states. The South, which looked so safe in this election, was to be upset by party dissension over civil rights in the next presidential election. On his own in 1948, President Truman was to do better in the farm belt but not quite as well in the Northeast because of the Wallace dissension (he was to lose four southern states to the Dixiecrats).[37] Truman spoke in eighteen states, two of which Dewey carried, Wisconsin and Ohio. The Republicans carried Bricker's home state of Ohio, and the Democrats carried Truman's home state of Missouri.

In his *Memoirs*, Truman stated that the campaign was the easiest in which he had ever participated.[38] Shortly after the election, however, he seemed to hold a different view. On November 10, 1944, Hopkins had written to him: "I think the dignified way you handled the bitter personal attacks on yourself was one of the high spots of the campaign and you deserve a tremendous lot of credit for the answer on Election Day." To this he replied on November 16, 1944: "It was a very bitter and one of the dirtiest I have ever had a hand in, but I think their mud and slush backfired on them."[39]

It is difficult to estimate how effective Truman's campaigning was in 1944. He was clearly not the top Democratic performer even though he was the hardest-working one. President Roosevelt, in just four masterful speeches, made a great impact on the electorate. He had opened his campaign on September 23 with a hard-hitting address at the banquet of the Teamsters Union, which will be long remembered for its famous passage on his dog, Fala: "These Republican leaders have not been content with attacks on me, or my wife, or on my sons. No, not content with that, they now include my little dog Fala. Well, of course, I don't resent attacks . . . but Fala does resent them."[40] In Philadelphia, New York, Chicago, and Boston, President Roosevelt made vigorous speeches before mammoth audiences, which responded with enthusiasm. In a rainy New York City, he toured in an open car in order to show that he was as fit as ever.

Truman's performance in the campaign was sharply criticized by some newspapermen who downgraded his campaigning and noted a sharp contrast between his style and that of the President. Clearly Truman had not yet established his reputation and identity as "give 'em Hell, Harry." In fact, on many occasions he appeared to be a mild-mannered man with a midwestern twang, who paraded facts but failed to arouse emotions.

Some observers did come to his defense as a campaigner. One wrote: "While Truman was not a great orator in any sense he was a man that when the people went to hear him speak, whether they were for him or not, they always came away from a meeting with an admiration for his fighting ability, his absolute honesty and fairness in what he thought was right in a situation and a friendly feeling for him.''[41]

As far as the Wickersham advice was concerned, we do not know whether Truman paid any attention to it. An examination of his speeches shows that some were in accord with the suggestions made, and some were not. Since Truman mentioned his own record only in connection with the Truman committee and his voting in the Senate, it appears that he agreed with Wickersham that it was better not to explain how he was chosen as the Democratic candidate for vice-president. His speeches were dignified and lofty in tone as though he were running for the top post himself. On many occasions, Truman emphasized postwar responsibilities and plans to avoid unemployment.[42] He did not discuss rationing, price control, or the public debt. Since his provocation was great, he can hardly be blamed for not following Wickersham's advice in his attacks on the Hearst papers and the *Chicago Tribune*.[43] He attacked Dewey for his support of isolationist congressmen while still pretending to hold an internationalist position, for his misuse of Truman committee findings to criticize President Roosevelt, for his lack of experience in national and international affairs, for his poor record on civil rights, for his unfair use of the communist label, and for his belated acceptance of Democratic policies after opposing them in the first place. Truman could hardly avoid mentioning Wallace at the Madison Square Garden meeting in New York where he called attention to his own liberal record in supporting an antilynching bill, a bill to outlaw the poll tax, and a bill to establish a fair employment practices committee.

Truman's attacks on Republican congressmen were more pointed and persistent than were his attacks on Dewey. He castigated the Republican record of opposition to preparedness in the 1930s and early 1940s, to the Selective Service Act, to the Lend-Lease Act, to the prewar progressive programs to aid workers and farmers, to the Tennessee Valley Authority with its multiple-purpose program of flood control, irrigation, water transportation, water power, fertilizer plants, and farm improvement, to rural electrification, and to social security for unemployed and the elderly. He accused the Republican party of favoring big business, Wall Street, speculators, reactionaries, and bankers. He reminded his listeners that the Democratic party had helped workers, farmers, and consumers, had brought the country to prosperity from the depths of the Depression, and had prepared the country for its part in World War II and that the leader of that party was President Franklin D. Roosevelt, who was qualified by experience to finish winning the war, to make the peace, and to bring postwar prosperity.

On the duties of a president and the qualifications required for the holder of that office, Truman's words uttered during the campaign may have haunted him later. In a radio address on October 3, 1944, he referred to the presidency as the biggest job in the world. It involved "leading us through the final stages of victory in this war," "helping to make and to secure a world-wide and lasting peace," and "getting us back on the march of progress we began in 1932." The job required experience, wisdom, foresight, determination, and the ability to choose the right people for the right jobs. "Reconversion and jobs and security are matters for a man who has *already* looked and thought and planned ahead. I submit that that means a *big* man, . . . a mighty big man . . . a Franklin Delano Roosevelt."[44]

Senator Truman was carried into the vice-presidency by the success of President Roosevelt in winning his fourth election to the White House. The Republican attempt to make the contest one between Truman and Dewey on the ground that Roosevelt would not last four years was a failure. A majority of the voters were convinced that the health issue was not a sound one; traditional Democrats in particular held this view. The Democrats took the position that this issue had been used before, and events had shown it to be false. Roosevelt himself, his doctors, and his associates managed to conceal the precarious state of his health from the party faithful who wanted to believe that he was strong enough for another term.

On the basis of the public opinion sample surveys taken before the election, Hadley Cantril concluded that few people who classified themselves as liberals would vote for Dewey rather than Roosevelt just because Wallace was not on the ticket.[45] The election returns bore out the soundness of this observation—the Roosevelt-Truman ticket did not suffer in the minority areas. On the other hand, Truman's presence on the ticket was a real contribution since the South, which had threatened to bolt if Wallace had been renominated, stayed within the fold. The election was the last one since Reconstruction days in which the South was to remain solid. The southerners thought that Truman would be on their side on civil rights matters. Later, when Truman had to take a stand on race relations issues, he lost part of the South.

During the campaign, Truman obtained valuable experience, which was to help him four years later when he was on his own. Although he had not yet developed his political style so that it was generally recognized, he made some important steps in that direction. He had to face some of the mechanical problems of organizing a campaign tour, conserving his strength and voice, meeting the deadlines of the mass media, and adjusting his appeals to the wishes and reactions of the electorate.

chapter 19 | EIGHTY-TWO DAYS AS VICE-PRESIDENT, 1945

Once there were two brothers. One ran away to sea, the other was elected Vice-President, and nothing was ever heard of either of them again.

—Thomas R. Marshall, *Recollections*

On January 20, 1945, Harry Truman was sworn in as vice-president by outgoing Vice-President Wallace. President Roosevelt had downgraded the inaugural ceremonies in part because of the war and in part because of his poor health. Instead of elaborate celebrations in front of the Capitol, the swearing in was on the White House grounds, and there was no parade. President Roosevelt, who was obviously not well, spoke for five minutes and then departed, leaving his wife, Eleanor, and the Trumans to carry on the ceremonial greetings to the selected group of guests.

In the twentieth century the vice-presidency has become an office of increasing importance. Vice-President Truman aspired to follow in the footsteps of Vice-President Garner, who in the early days of the New Deal was a real link between the legislative and executive branches of the government.[1] Truman clearly wanted to avoid antagonizing the senators in the manner that Vice-President Charles Dawes had done in his challenges to Senate procedures. And compared with Vice-President Wallace, Truman believed that he had a great advantage in his ten years of experience in the Senate where he had made many friends.

Vice-President Truman's success as a liaison between the White House and the Hill depended on close relations with the President. Here he was at a disadvantage when compared with Garner. During the first hundred days of Roosevelt's first term, Garner was part of the inner circle. But in 1945, President Roosevelt's preoccupation with the war and international conferences and his failing health ruled out a close working arrangement with the new vice-president. During the eighty-two days that Truman was vice-president, he saw Roosevelt only twice for official appointments, twice at cabinet meetings, and at a few informal socials such as the White House showing of the film *Woodrow Wilson*, where Truman was aghast at how emaciated Roosevelt looked. Moreover, Roosevelt refused to face the problem of succession, failing to brief the vice-president on the broad outlines of his foreign policy. He was either too tired to care, or he had confidence in his ability to last out his fourth term since his doctors had been much less than frank with him.

Before Roosevelt left for Yalta, he asked the new vice-president to assist in the solution of a rather delicate problem: the replacement of Jesse Jones as secretary of commerce by Henry Wallace. Roosevelt had promised Wallace any cabinet post other than secretary of state as a reward for his loyalty. Wallace chose the commerce post, which would accomplish two goals for him: the ouster of his archenemy, Jones, and the improvement of his image in the business community, something close to the heart of a man who still had visions of the presidency when Roosevelt stepped down. In talking to Jonathan Daniels in 1949, Truman said: "When Roosevelt told me he was going to make Henry Wallace Secretary of Commerce, I said, 'Jesus Christ!' FDR called me to help and I told him I'd see every Senator I could."[2] It was a tough assignment for Truman. Generally the President was softhearted when it came to dismissing old hands, but with Jones he was harsh and direct. In his letter to Jones, Roosevelt put his request for resignation in frankly political terms: Wallace deserved the reward for his loyal services in the campaign. Jones, a southern conservative, had used his vast powers, which included lending as well as regulating, to build a small empire of his own. He had many friends in Congress who were indebted to him in one way or another, and his dismissal and the nomination of Wallace brought protests from Congressman John Robison who asked, "Why did he [Roosevelt] write that awful letter to Mr. Jones in which he stated that he was appointing Mr. Wallace to this very, very important office in order to pay off a political debt?"[3] Vice-President Truman, in fact, was convinced that getting the nomination through the Senate would be a considerable undertaking; the publicity made his job all the more difficult. Conservative senators did not want Wallace to dole out the RFC billions, and, if the union of the two jobs—secretary of commerce and federal loan administrator—was continued as under Jones, there was a strong chance that Wallace would not be confirmed.

Truman pleaded with his friends in the Senate to support the appointment. They told him bluntly that Wallace could not be confirmed for the two jobs, and legislation was introduced by Senator Walter F. George separating the two posts. A dramatic scene occurred in the Senate when the confirmation and the George bill were being considered. If the appointment came up first, confirmation might fail. If the George bill was passed, confirmation might be tolerated. Senator Robert Taft jumped to his feet to call up the nomination. Majority Leader Barkley was supposed to call up the George bill first, but he was asleep at the switch, and Truman was supposed to recognize the senator who rose first. He pretended not to see Taft, and someone nudged Barkley, who then rose to his feet. Truman recognized Barkley, and the Wallace appointment was saved.[4]

After partial success in the Wallace battle, Vice-President Truman continued his attempt to bring the legislative and executive branches together. The next split came over the confirmation of Audrey Williams as head of the Rural Electrification Administration. Truman fought valiantly, but the conservative coalition was too strong. Williams's identification with the underprivileged groups was too close to bring the groups together, and Williams was rejected.

President Roosevelt did invite Vice-President Truman to attend cabinet meetings. In his talks with Daniels, Truman downgraded the importance of Roosevelt's cabinet meetings: "Roosevelt never discussed anything at his cabinet meetings. Cabinet members if they had anything to discuss tried to see him privately after the meetings."[5] The Forrestal diaries, however, seem to contradict Truman's pessimistic view regarding the importance of those meetings. On March 9, in addition to six other topics, the method and theory of United Nations trusteeships were discussed, and on March 16 the President reported on the "considerable difficulty with British relations. He stated that the British were perfectly willing for the United States to have a war with Russia anytime."[6] These were hardly unimportant questions.

Because of the war and his failing health, President Roosevelt neglected the social functions attached to the office, a situation that made the Trumans the social lions of the capital. They were invited to every important social function and became one of the main attractions of the social set. They were deluged with invitations to teas, cocktail parties, and dinners. Truman drank but did so moderately, and on a day when there was a heavy round of parties, he had to be careful of the amount of alcohol he imbibed. He did this by drinking at a very slow pace, sometimes holding the same drink in his hand for the whole evening.[7]

At first the round of socials was exciting and enjoyable—the Trumans met a lot of important people, native as well as foreign. But after a while, Truman found the social obligations a boring burden that left him little time for serious reading. Cutting down on the number of socials he could attend, he longed for his old position as chairman of the Truman committee in which he spent more time on important national problems.

Since President Roosevelt was away at Yalta during February and then went on vacation to Warm Springs, Truman was called upon to make speeches at formal occasions. One of these was a Washington's Birthday celebration speech he made at Jefferson City, Missouri, which was broadcast nationally. He used the occasion to plead for the support of a world organization for peace.

Truman had been vice-president for six days when the news broke that Tom Pendergast had died. The question facing Truman was whether he should pay attention to this event, which to him was a sad one. He could ignore the event completely; he could send sympathy to the immediate family; or he could go to the funeral in Kansas City and face the howls of righteous indignation from those aghast at their vice-president's honoring the memory of an ex-convict. Harry hesitated not a moment. Tom had done wrong and had paid a penalty. He had lost his worldly goods, his wife, and his health, and his public image had been blackened. Truman, who attributed Pendergast's downfall to deteriorating health and a gambling mania, remembered him as a strong, wise, and shrewd organizer who had picked many winning candidates and who had visions of a greater Kansas City, a greater Jackson County, and a greater Missouri. Truman had worked hard to wipe out the canard that he was the senator from Pendergast. He might invite a revival of the old charges if he went to the funeral, but there was only one thing for him to do: go. No one could say that Harry Truman let down a friend.

The country was still at war, and transportation was in short supply. Truman ordered an army bomber to take him to Kansas City. The opposition press had a field day. It was bad enough for the vice-president to go to the last rites of such a man as Pendergast, but to commandeer a bomber seemed all the worse. Truman justified this use by indicating that he wanted to be back on duty as soon as possible. The incident highlighted a quality that Truman was to exemplify many times in days to come: loyalty to friends.

In the Senate, the vice-president has no vote except in case of a tie, and Truman missed being part of the roll calls. On only one occasion did he break a tie, and this was when his negative vote defeated a Taft amendment to the Lend-Lease Act which would have prevented postwar delivery of lend-lease goods contracted for during the war.[8] This question was one of great importance and sensitivity in the postwar relations between the United States and the Soviet Union.

As senator, Truman was used to handling mail and requests from Missouri. Now mail and callers came from all over the United States. To assist him in these duties, he was given a military aide. He appointed Colonel Harry H. Vaughan, his old wartime friend. Many requests came from women endeavoring to get their men released from military service. Rather than bringing pressure to obtain such a release, Truman turned such letters over to Vaughan with instructions to advise the family to proceed through channels by making affidavits of hardship, which the soldier would present to his commanding officer. Truman refused to interfere with the military.

Truman, who had always had good relations with the members of the press corps, still had a few things to learn about them. He was invited to the

Press Club where, in response to a friendly request to "play us a tune," he sat down at an upright piano. Actress Lauren Bacall was waiting in the wings, and, as soon as the pianist was seated at the instrument, she was perched atop it by a few sly members of the corps: "Harry, that was great! Give us another!" Harry swung around with a grin. Flashbulbs popped, and the next day the picture hit the pages of the nation's papers.[9] The photo was held to be in poor taste. Bess Truman neatly understated the incident; she told her husband to stop playing the piano in public.

Actually Truman was genuinely interested in increasing the dignity and importance of the office, and when he had a chance, he did just that. He was proud of his role in getting President Roosevelt to report in person before Congress on the results of the Yalta conference, feeling that such an appearance would help quiet rumors about Roosevelt's health and about secret deals made at Yalta. He also thought that it would be a friendly gesture and might help as the time for making peace treaties approached.

Although Truman did not see the President personally about this proposal, he talked at length with James F. Byrnes, who had been at Yalta, and with the White House secretariat.[10] The President agreed and delivered his famous address sitting in his wheelchair. It was not Roosevelt's best performance, but it had its reassuring aspects. One could see that Roosevelt, though wan and fragile, was still on the job. The bargain at Yalta that gave three votes to the Soviet Union in the proposed United Nations Assembly was a bad one, and it had been a mistake to conceal it, as Roosevelt had done.

Truman's great ambition to become an outstanding vice-president was being thwarted by Roosevelt's inaccessibility. A successful liaison between the White House and the Capitol depended upon close contact with the President. But Truman saw less and less of Roosevelt.

William D. Hassett, White House confidential secretary, wrote in his diary, *Off the Record*, on March 30: "Tonight had another talk with [Dr.] Howard Bruenn about the president's health. I said: 'He is slipping away from us and no earthly power can keep him here.'"[11] President Roosevelt was so tired that he could not face the problem of succession. A few more days in Warm Springs, he felt, and his health would bounce back as it had before. He hoped, too, that he would soon recover his old zest for life in the White House.

Truman should have been Roosevelt's closest companion if the President wanted his policies carried on after he was gone. Truman should have been briefed on all aspects of foreign and domestic policy, on the awesome atom bomb, on the postwar aims of the Soviet Union, on the real nature of dictator Stalin, on the postwar ambitions of the British to regain some of their lost imperial glory, on the character of General Charles de Gaulle, on the postwar liquidation of colonialism, on the dangers of postwar inflation and runaway labor disputes, on the revival of domestic reforms after the war, and on a thousand other pressing problems. But Roosevelt was not available.

Truman was on his way to Sam Rayburn's hideaway in the Capitol on April 12, 1945, when an urgent call came from Steve Early in the White House. "Please come right over," said Early in a strained voice, "and come in through the main Pennsylvania Avenue entrance."

Truman dashed out in such a hurry that he eluded his secret service man, something he would soon learn was not the proper procedure under the circumstances. Upon arriving at the White House, he was ushered into Eleanor Roosevelt's study. In his *Memoirs* he described what came next:

"Harry," she said quietly, "the President is dead." For the moment I could not bring myself to speak. The last news we had had from Warm Springs was that Mr. Roosevelt was recuperating nicely. In fact, he was apparently doing so well that no member of his immediate family, and not even his personal physician, was with him. All this flashed through my mind before I found my voice.

"Is there anything I can do for you?" I asked at last.

I shall never forget her deeply understanding reply, "Is there anything *we* can do for *you?*" she asked, "For you are the one in trouble now."[12]

Arrangements were made at once for the swearing-in ceremony. Chief Justice Harlan F. Stone was summoned immediately to the White House to administer the oath. A hurried call was put through to the Truman home. Margaret Truman relates the conversation:

"Hi, Dad," I greeted him jovially.

"Let me speak to your mother," he said. His voice sounded tight and funny.

"Are you coming home to dinner?" I inquired. "I'm going out!"

"Let me speak to your mother," Dad repeated, not rising to my bait.

"I only asked a civil question!" I pouted into the phone.

"Margaret," my father said, "Will you let me speak to your mother?"[13]

The group that witnessed the swearing-in ceremony at the White House was small and select. It included Bess and Margaret Truman, the members of the cabinet, some key officials from Capitol Hill, some close personal friends, and representatives of the press. Harry S. Truman was president of the United States.

PART II | ACCIDENTAL PRESIDENT

chapter 20 | THE ROOSEVELT-TRUMAN TRANSITION, 1945

Tragic fate has thrust upon us grave responsibilities. We must carry on. Our departed leader never looked backward. He looked forward and moved forward. That is what he would want us to do. This is what America will do.

With great humility I call upon all Americans to help me keep our nation united in defense of those ideals which have been so eloquently proclaimed by Franklin Roosevelt.

—Harry S. Truman, address before Congress, April 16, 1945

When on April 12, 1945, Vice-President Truman was suddenly catapulted into the presidency, he promised to carry out the Roosevelt policies as he understood them. As he explained to Henry Wallace, his main complaint was, "They didn't tell me anything about what was going on."[1] As long as the war lasted, Truman concentrated on military matters with a minimum interference with existing arrangements, but the war was fast nearing an end, and demobilization and reconversion would loose a hundred conflicting forces that had been constrained by the overriding goal of winning the war. Roosevelt's postwar plans had been nebulous. Current economic forecasts varied. Some thought there would be a postwar depression; others thought that inflation would be the chief problem. Assumptions based on a wrong forecast might bring great dislocations. Truman's stand on reconversion as chairman of the Truman committee showed that he did not want big business to tighten its grip on the economy during the postwar period. Although he had been selected as a compromise candidate for vice-president because he seemed acceptable to business, labor, agriculture, minority groups, and the South, his record as a senator had been that of a New Dealer. He was also an internationalist and firmly behind the Roosevelt plans for an international organization.

The office that Truman inherited had acquired many new functions of vast proportions. It had control over the largest American armed forces in U.S. history; it had built up a complicated wartime system of regulations affecting business, labor, agriculture, consumers, and foreign trade under which many elements were chafing; it had more obligations in foreign countries than ever before; it had both the biggest budget and the biggest deficit and the largest number of civilian employees; and with the development of new mass media, it was subject to closer scrutiny than ever before. Even Roosevelt had been crushed by these overwhelming burdens.

It was not only the task itself but people's thinking about it which made the transition difficult. Franklin Roosevelt had been in the office longer than any other president, and many people could picture no one else in that office. The public could not adjust itself to the fact that a plain midwesterner with a flat voice and thick spectacles was sitting at a desk so recently occupied by one of the most charismatic and glamorous leaders in modern times. President Roosevelt had operated in a highly personal style, and he had not bothered to institutionalize many of the functions that were passed on to his successor, except in a few areas such as the Executive Office of the President, which included a small White House staff primarily drawn from several of the old departments.[2]

The transition from Roosevelt to Truman was particularly difficult because it was so sudden and had to be accomplished without any advance preparations. In addition, Roosevelt's planning for the peace and for solving reconversion problems was woefully inadequate. The 1943 Congress had abolished the National Resources Planning Board, which had been engaged in postwar planning. Roosevelt's death caught Truman unprepared, unbriefed, inexperienced, and dismayed.

The war was not over yet. Truman had not been told about the Allied military strategy, the atom bomb, the postwar aims of the Allies (particularly those of the Soviet Union), the results of previous Allied conferences, and the postwar plans for demobilization, reconversion, and reemployment.

Without experience in a high federal administrative post, without first-hand knowledge about many of the key officials running the government and those in high positions in the Allied governments, Harry Truman found himself suddenly thrust into a seat of great responsibility with many crucial decisions to make. He felt overwhelmed. As he remarked to a group of reporters outside Secretary of the Senate Leslie Biffle's office: "Did you ever have a bull or a load of hay fall on you? If you have, you know how I felt last night. I felt as if two planets and the whole constellation had fallen on me. I don't know if you boys pray, but if you do, please pray God to help me carry this load."[3]

Although Truman prided himself on his ability to judge the character of those with whom he dealt, he had had few dealings with many of the top Roosevelt appointees, and there was so little time to learn. In selecting his staff, Truman appeared to be using the following criteria: Could he count on the person's loyalty to the New Deal program? Had he direct proof of the individual's capacity to do the job? If the position was one of close personal contact, would the individual be companionable? Would he be loyal to the new president?

These criteria involved reviewing old acquaintanceships and earlier impressions of Washington officials.[4] For one appointment, he went back to his high school days. For several others, he went back to his former military companions of World War I and his buddies of the veterans' organizations and the Reserve Officers' corps. These appointees were labeled the "Missouri gang." His ten years in the Senate had given him a chance to evaluate his Senate colleagues and their staffs and had brought him in touch with many officials of the Roosevelt days. In the case of some of them, he had many chances to observe their performance in connection with the hearings before the Interstate Commerce Committee, the Appropriations Committee, the Military Affairs Committee, the Public Buildings and Grounds Committee, and his own Special Committee to Investigate the Defense Program.

Roosevelt's team was loyal to him and his memory. His secretary, Grace Tully, told Wallace, "I just can't call that man President."[5] Roosevelt's appointees had been selected to fit his style of leadership, which was clearly not Truman's. The late President had been a virtuoso who did not mind a little competition among his appointees; jurisdictional conflicts meant that ultimate decisions came back to the White House.[6] Truman wanted a more orderly procedure. He preferred to delegate powers and to hold his appointee responsible for the proper exercise of those powers. He could not see himself trying to hold too many reins in his own hands.[7] Nonetheless, he needed Roosevelt supporters to carry out Roosevelt policies.

Over the years the presidency has acquired traditions and momentum that keep the office going after a fashion even though the president may be temporarily out of the picture. The last eighteen months of the Wilson administration, for example, were a severe test of how the office could function with an incapacitated occupant.[8] The presidency went on during Warren G. Harding's administration even though Harding admitted his own incompetence and ignorance as to where to turn for information and advice.[9] In both instances, the results were bad, but they might have been worse. During President Roosevelt's three terms and three months, there were extended periods when Roosevelt was out of the White House for conferences abroad or for rest and recuperation. The routine of the presidency went on during these absences.

Although President Roosevelt had not institutionalized the presidency to the extent needed, he had taken some steps in that direction. The Reorganization Act of 1939, which Truman supported in the Senate, enabled Roosevelt to establish the Executive Office of the President, to which were transferred the White House staff and the Bureau of the Budget.[10] These were two tools that President Truman found immediately available for use. The Executive Office also furnished the Office for Emergency Management, a mechanism for the creation of the many defense agencies necessary for war production, war manpower needs, war food production, inflation controls, war information activities, and civil defense. As chairman of his investigating committee, Senator Truman had followed closely the development and operation of these emergency agencies. He had been alarmed at the extent to which big business had had its way during the war.

WHITE HOUSE STAFF

President Truman inherited a White House staff that he had to rely on temporarily to bridge the gap between the two administrations. In his first press conference on April 17, 1945, he stated: "Now, I have asked Mr. Early and Mr. Hassett, Mr. Daniels and Judge Rosenman, and they have offered to stay and help me get things organized, for which I am very grateful. And my staff will stand the training with those gentlemen."[11]

Judge Samuel Rosenman had been a speech writer for Roosevelt for sixteen years, and his services were invaluable in helping Truman prepare his early speeches. He could furnish a link between the New and the Fair Deal because he had participated in the Roosevelt policy making. Judge Rosenman's position was counsel to the President, and he stayed on until February 1, 1946, when he finally persuaded President Truman to accept his resignation. During this period, he helped with three major messages that Roosevelt had planned to deliver.[12] Judge Rosenman did not spend full time in Washington during this period but commuted between Washington and New York City, where he had a law office.[13]

One of the most important presidential aides is the press secretary. The way in which he handles the press and other media has a good deal to do with the image the public forms of the president and with the effectiveness of the president in molding public opinion. He should be able to protect the president against publicity errors, to advise him regarding the possible public reaction to certain policy decisions, and to help him with his news releases and public speeches. He has to be well informed regarding presidential thinking and actions, and he has to maintain friendly relations with those representing the media. Under constant pressure from the White House correspondents to reveal everything, he must at the same time guard against betraying presidential secrets and against slips that will put the president in an unfavorable light.[14]

President Roosevelt's press secretary, Steve Early, was a star performer in the position. He had Roosevelt's confidence and the cooperation of the press corps, and he betrayed neither. He had an uncanny ability to forecast the consequences of certain deeds or language, and he was not afraid to tell the President what he was up against.[15] President Truman had great need for such a press secretary and asked Early to stay on. Early had other plans and could stay only a few weeks, but he helped Truman in his first press conference. He also warned Truman against calling his former high school English teacher in Independence, Missouri, to inform her that he planned to appoint Charlie Ross, his school chum, as his regular press secretary. Early said this would create problems with the press. Unheeding, Truman called his former teacher. Early proved right, and the President had to apologize to the press at his next press conference for giving an exclusive to a small town newspaper, the *Independence Examiner*, to which the teacher had leaked the news of the appointment.[16]

Prior to announcing that Charlie Ross would be his press secretary, Truman tried out a three-day experiment with J. Leonard Reinsch, who had been connected with a radio station run by James M. Cox, the Democratic presidential candidate in 1920. On April 17, Truman announced that Reinsch would help him with press and radio affairs. He had met Reinsch during the 1944 campaign when Reinsch was connected with the Democratic National Committee.[17] Protests from the press corps greeted the announcement because Reinsch had no newspaper experience. President Truman hastily withdrew the appointment on April 20, reading as an excuse a telegram from Cox requesting that the President let Reinsch return to the broadcasting station.[18] Cox generously gave Truman a convenient excuse for the cancellation of Reinsch's appointment.

After Early's departure, Jonathan Daniels of the *Raleigh News and Observer*, one of Roosevelt's administrative assistants who had also served as press secretary, filled in as Truman's press secretary until Ross had finished his reporting of the Conference on the United Nations at San Francisco for his paper, the *St. Louis Post-Dispatch*. Although Daniels had difficulty at first adjusting himself to Truman as Roosevelt's replacement, he grew to appreciate Truman's good qualities, reporting that he thought the early press conferences of the new President were a great success.[19] Unlike his predecessor, Truman did not enjoy press conferences, but he won approval of the correspondents by his willingness to answer questions and by the directness of his replies.[20]

From the first, President Truman had Charlie Ross in mind as his press secretary, but he could not immediately pry him loose from his ties with the *St. Louis Post-Dispatch*.[21] After graduating from the University of Missouri School of Journalism, Ross had a distinguished career as a professor and journalist, winning the Pulitzer Prize during the 1930s for a series, "The Country's Plight—What Can Be Done About It?" published in the

St. Louis Post-Dispatch. President of the Gridiron Club in 1933, Ross was well liked by his fellow practitioners, but he lacked the foresight, the quick wit, the willingness to correct his chief in a press conference when he made a slip, the literary ability, the personal magnetism, and the contagious enthusiasm that the job required. His timing of news stories was inept, and he failed to give Truman the guidance in his press conferences and public relations that he needed.[22] He tried hard in a job that was too much for him while still managing to save Truman from making some mistakes in his press relations.

The fourth Roosevelt holdover whom President Truman mentioned in his first press conference was William D. Hassett, correspondence secretary. Hasset had not met the new president, but when he went to the White House after Roosevelt's funeral, President Truman sent for him. In his diary for April 16, 1945, Hassett wrote: "He very gracious; invited me to remain on the job; frank and forthright in manner. Said that unexpectedly he had been called upon to shoulder the greatest responsibilities, in the discharge of which he would need all of the help and cooperation he could get, and added, 'I need you, too.' His attitude toward his duties and obligations magnificent."[23] Two journalists wrote that Hassett was indispensable to the White House staff. On returning to his desk, he went to work handling the thousands of messages of confidence and goodwill that were arriving. He knew about presidential papers, was discreet, and during the war had accompanied Roosevelt on trips as his confidential secretary. Hassett was to serve Truman well. He could have served him even better if Truman had let him. Hassett could have spared him the bad publicity he received for his handwritten letters of outrage he wrote to critics of his daughter's singing. Hassett could thus have helped him preserve the dignity of the presidential office. He was not, however, a policy man.

When Truman became president, he took along with him his appointments secretary, Matthew J. Connelly, who had served as investigator for the Truman committee and later as secretary to Truman in his capacities as senator and vice-president. Connelly, the son of a school janitor, was born in the small town of Clinton, Massachusetts, and came to Washington, D.C., during the Depression.[24] He finally located a job as investigator for the Works Progress Administration. Later, he worked for a Senate investigating committee and met Senator Truman. The two got along well, and Truman asked Connelly to join the staff of his committee. Connelly became part of the inner circle of Truman's friends who enjoyed poker, storytelling, and moderate drinking. The position of appointments secretary controls who will see the president and thus has important powers. If an official or citizen cannot present his case to the president, opposing views may prevail. Connelly relished his importance and in some cases tried to influence policy decisions.[25] During the Truman days, he managed to remain inconspicuous, but the Department of Justice during the Eisenhower administration found records that got him into trouble.[26] Because he was the chief dispenser of the President's time, he was sought after by congressmen and party officials who wanted jobs, patronage, or favors. He had an assistant who performed liaison chores on the Hill, and he kept in touch with the national chairman and state party officials.

A more conspicuous member of President Truman's White House staff from the start was military aide Harry H. Vaughan.[27] He had been a personal friend of Truman since 1917 when they were military associates in World War I. Subsequently they served together in the Field Artillery Officers Reserve Corps. In 1940 Vaughan served as treasurer for Senator Truman's 1940 reelection campaign committee.[28] Before going on active duty in World War II, he was secretary to Senator Truman. After being honorably discharged for injuries suffered in a plane crash, he became a liaison officer for the Truman committee in 1944. In his new post with the President, Vaughan became a brigadier general, much to the resentment of some regular army officers. General Vaughan was a natural extrovert, and from the beginning his remarks and back-slapping behavior attracted attention. As two commentators put it, "The crowd around Truman, the public felt, was funnier than it was dangerous. They were not putting their hands in the till; they were too busy putting their feet in their mouths."[29] It was not until a year later that General Vaughan had a confrontation with the columnist Drew Pearson and began his feud with the press, which he claimed was a deliberate plot worked out by Republicans and certain journalists to discredit President Truman by smearing those close to him.[30] As military aide, General Vaughan was a gladhander, a companion on trips, and a liaison man with veterans' organizations, the FBI, and the Pentagon. He was not regarded as important in making policy decisions.[31]

In seeking a naval aide, President Truman went to St. Louis for James K. (Jake) Vardaman, a business friend and fellow artilleryman in World War I. In the 1930s, he had joined the naval reserve and during World War II was called to active duty in the navy, where he served with distinction in the African, European, and Far Eastern theaters. He had been president of a bank in St. Louis before he joined the service. After eight months in the White House, Commodore Vardaman was promoted to the Federal Reserve Board. His chief contribution to the Truman staff was his appointment of a young St. Louis lawyer, Clark Clifford, as his aide. Clifford went on to become what one author called "the Golden Boy of Truman's administration."[32]

It was in the field of foreign affairs that President Truman felt that he needed immediate staff assistance. From his work as senator, he recognized the importance of the role that President Roosevelt's chief of staff, Admiral William D. Leahy, had played in national defense and foreign policy matters.[33] Admiral Leahy was familiar with all of the facilities in the Map Room, and he was on the list to receive all top-secret dispatches. Secretary of State Edward Stettinius provided factual material collected by the Department of State staff, but this was not always sufficient for policy-making purposes. To fill the gaps in his information, President Truman turned to Admiral Leahy, who had been present at many of the top international conferences. In his *Memoirs*, Truman recollected that when he asked the admiral to stay on, the admiral replied, "Are you sure you want me, Mr. President. I always say what's on my mind." Truman answered: "I want the truth and I want the facts at all times. I want you to stay with me and always tell me what's on your mind. You may not always agree with my decisions, but I know you will carry them out faithfully."[34]

President Truman liked the admiral's blunt manner, directness in expression, and independence of judgment. The admiral, on the other hand, was pleased with Truman's firm stand on commitments that President Roosevelt had made and the strong stand he took in his meeting with Molotov on April 23 to show his displeasure at Soviet actions in Poland.[35] The two men got along well. Some liberals thought that the admiral had too much influence.

President Roosevelt used one of his administrative assistants, William H. McReynolds, as his staff man for personnel matters—liaison with the Civil Service Commission, the Bureau of the Budget, the different agencies, and Congress on matters relating to personnel management in federal service. He was a talent scout and an expediter of appointments. McReynolds stayed for only a few weeks. His place was filled by R. R. Zimmerman, who regarded the post as one designed to strengthen personnel administration in the federal government.[36] He tried to build up the personnel offices of the various departments. He regarded Executive Order 9830, providing for federal personnel administration and amending the civil service rules, as one of the accomplishments of his term of service. He went to the meeting of department heads at which President Truman held that it was up to agency heads to effectuate the new executive order. He admired the way that Truman did not mince words.[37] Two years later, he was replaced by Donald Dawson.

Another of President Truman's administrative assistants who was a Roosevelt holdover was David K. Niles, formerly an aide to Harry Hopkins, who continued to handle relationships with minority groups in a highly individualized fashion.[38] His assignment put him in the middle of the civil rights controversy and the struggle over the recognition of Israel.

It took time for Truman to find the people he needed for his White House staff and to work out their assignments. He was unable to persuade some of the Roosevelt holdovers he liked to stay on and was constantly searching for able people.

THE BUREAU OF THE BUDGET

On fiscal and budgetary matters, the director of the Bureau of the Budget, Harold Smith, continued to perform the valuable services he had rendered Roosevelt.[39] He and his staff kept the President informed about the budget needs of the various agencies, their capacity to spend funds requested in an efficient manner, the organization and management problems of the government, the probable impact of the proposed programs on the economy, the estimated tax revenues needed to finance the programs projected, and possible sources of tax revenues. He was also an adviser on legislative matters, keeping the President informed on legislation proposed by various agencies, seeing that the administration bills were cleared with the various agencies concerned, and recommending upon consultation with agencies involved presidential action on legislation passed by Congress.

As a member of the Appropriations Committee of the Senate, Truman had had an opportunity to observe Smith in action. He was favorably impressed so he greeted Smith cordially when Smith came to his office six days after his swearing in as president. Before the director started to present his problems, the President interrupted: "I know what's on your mind and I am going to beat you to it. I want you to stay. You have done a good job as Director of the Budget and we always thought well of you on the Hill. I have a tremendous responsibility and I want you to help me."[40]

When Smith mentioned that the director of the budget was always bringing up problems, President Truman said that he liked problems so Smith need not worry on that score.

Smith went on to indicate that there were several points to discuss. With respect to the last budget, President Roosevelt had delegated the complete responsibility to him. He added:

I would now suggest that it be understood between us that the delegation be completely withdrawn. I said that the consequence of this would be that the President would have to devote considerable time in conference with the Director of the Budget over issues as they arise. This would give me a chance to see the turn of his mind with respect to all sorts of problems, and it would give him a chance to see how we proposed to deal with them in the Bureau of the Budget and to get as much historical background as he desired. I pointed out that this would be rather burdensome and would probably require at least two sessions a week between the President and the Director of the Budget. President Truman responded by saying that he would like this arrangement, adding that he was used to dealing with facts and figures so I need not hesitate about presenting situations to him in some detail. He indicated that he was heartily in accord with my suggestion. His whole attitude pleased me because it showed that he was anxious to plunge deeply into the business of the Government.[41]

In the second meeting with the President, Smith discussed cutting back wartime authorizations and expenditures of the emergency agencies in view of the imminent victory over Germany.[42] He also proposed the liquidation of some war agencies at once, such as the Office of Civilian Defense. In addition to revisions downward of the budget, the two men discussed many other questions. On governmental organization, President Truman requested a proposal for the consolidation of the scattered labor functions, a solution for the conflicts between the Bureau of Reclamation and the Army Engineers on valley authorities, and the memorandum on the organization of intelligence in the government, which the bureau had been working on with the idea of introducing new concepts and better-trained personnel. On policy issues, the President asked for a proposal for increased unemployment and old age assistance and a draft message on education. They discussed the questions as to whether lend-lease should be used for rehabilitation and agreed that it should not because of the isolationist sentiment that would break loose. In his notes on the conference, Smith concluded, "The whole conference was highly satisfactory from my point of view. It revealed to me that the President is actually accepting me as Director of the Budget and that much of my worry about the possibility that I would stand in the way of the development of the Bureau of the Budget as an institution was allayed. The President's reactions were positive and highly intelligent."[43]

Smith continued to hold frequent conferences with President Truman throughout 1945 on such questions as budget cuts in war appropriations as victory came nearer, the many reconversion issues involving liquidation of emergency agencies and redeployment of personnel, the use of the president's fund (part of which was unvouchered for FBI men in South America), reorganization questions that involved the defense services, State, Commerce, Agriculture, and Labor Departments, the wording and content of presidential addresses, and congressional relations, including the clearance of proposed bills and presidential action on enrolled bills. Many different agencies came up repeatedly in these conferences.[44]

The day after Truman took office as president, the staff of the Bureau of the Budget began an analysis of Truman's actions as senator.[45] The director called the resultant volume to the attention of the President on August 18, 1945. Truman seemed not only amused but interested, saying that no one should take too seriously what he did as senator. Now as president of the United States, he wanted the opportunity to change his mind. He was no longer a legislative representative from one state; he represented all of the states, and he had to give each one the same treatment as he gave the others.[46]

In another August conference, Director Smith pointed out that he thought the bureau should have no authority except the delegated and reflected authority of a president.[47] He mentioned two pieces of major legislation passed that gave the director independent authority. One gave him the power to set personnel ceilings, a power that could almost close down a government agency. He could be stopped only if a president fired him, or Congress repealed the act. Another law gave the director power to set up reserves and thus alter congressional appropriations. The President was unaware of the latter authority. The director was concerned because he thought that these powers might put him in the impossible position of serving two masters. He said that Congress passed these laws so it could call the director to account before congressional committees since it could not call the president. Smith mentioned his concern over these powers since the director of war mobilization and reconversion was not clearing everything with the Bureau of the Budget. The President said that he would speak to the director.

Apparently the strain of trying to solve the many difficulties that characterized the reconversion period, the dislocations caused by the liquidation of agencies, the ineffectiveness of the government in preventing or stopping the many strikes, consumer shortages and inflated prices, job insecurities, and the declining morale of federal employees took a great deal out of the director of the budget. On October 16, 1945 he told the President that the government was having a difficult time in the transition from war, that morale was low, and that people were tired. He added: "Then went on to say that I sometimes gauged how well bureaucracy was working by the number of hours I stayed awake at night worrying about it. I pointed out that recently I had been staying awake quite frequently. The President said that up to now he had not been staying awake."[48] This was an illustration of the ability of the President to make decisions and dismiss the subject from his mind. He was not a person to worry and have regrets.

The Bureau of the Budget helped greatly to smooth the transition from Roosevelt to Truman. Since its methods tended to emphasize restraint, efficiency and economy, budget cuts, work simplification, reorganization, and personnel ceilings, it could not be expected to furnish the initiative in bringing forth new programs and coordinating the activities of existing agencies.[49] These were the functions of the cabinet officers, the heads of the independent agencies, and such policy planning agencies as the president and Congress might devise. President Truman early turned his attention to policy planning.

Although it appeared at first that Truman might rely upon the Bureau of the Budget as Roosevelt had, in the troubled times after V-E Day he turned more to the directors of OWMR—Vinson from April to July 23, 1945, Snyder from then until June 25, 1946, and Steelman for most of the rest of the year—for guidance on domestic legislative and policy matters. Richard Neustadt, formerly with the bureau and then with the White House staff, states: "By mid-summer 1946 the Budget Bureau's status in the Presidential orbit had reached its lowest point. OWMR seemed superficially to be assured a strong, perhaps a permanent position." Actually, of course, OWMR's end was near.

CABINET CHANGES

When he learned of President Roosevelt's death, Vice-President Truman called the cabinet together: "I shall only say that I will try to carry on as I know he would have wanted me and all of us to do. I should like all of you to remain in your Cabinet posts and I shall count on you for all the help I can get. In this action I am sure I am following out what the President would have wished."[50] Nevertheless he was planning drastic changes in the Roosevelt cabinet, which was not suited for the new administration. It contained some personal friends of the late President who would naturally have difficulty in transferring their loyalty to the new President, who had such a different background. It also contained others who had adjusted their roles to the Roosevelt competitive style of conducting the presidency, which involved giving duplicate assignments and holding many decisions in abeyance until one seemed the best. This meant that power gravitated to the president, but the process was not an orderly one, and it was not the way that Truman wanted to operate.[51] Within two and a half months, over half of the Roosevelt cabinet holdovers were gone.

President Truman was determined to delegate responsibilities in an orderly fashion. He wanted cabinet officers who would carry out presidential decisions faithfully. He also wanted to be kept informed about important developments, but he did not want to try to decide the details of administration.[52] He also wanted to keep his decision making at the presidential level. If a cabinet officer could not carry out his responsibilities in a satisfactory manner, then he should be replaced. President Truman did not want to operate as President Roosevelt had, with power gravitating to the inner White House favorites rather than to the cabinet officers whose duties were defined by law. Truman's White House staff served him personally. It was also involved, however, in some major decisions.[53] The principal decision-making powers rested with the cabinet officers in consultation with the President. Truman was ready to back up his cabinet officers to the limit when they were carrying out presidential policies. Criticism from Congress and the mass media would not move him to desert a cabinet officer if he was convinced that no error had been made. Yet from the beginning he was jealous of his executive powers, and he would not tolerate a cabinet officer's making decisions that he thought a president should make. As he took over the office of president, Truman realized that he had much to learn about how to operate it, and he turned eagerly to those whom he thought could help him most.

Among the cabinet officers ill fitted to the needs of the new President was Secretary of State Edward Stettinius, who never pretended to be a formulator of foreign policies. He had been selected by Roosevelt as a man who would carry out foreign policy decisions made by the President.[54] While Roosevelt tried to be his own secretary of state, President Truman needed someone who would help him formulate foreign policy and who could protect him against making the wrong decisions. Secretary Stettinius was kept on until after the United Nations Conference in San Francisco; he had been designated the head of the American delegation by President Roosevelt, and Truman did not want to disturb this arrangement.[55] In July 1945 he was named U.S. ambassador to the United Nations. In his *Memoirs*, Truman admitted that Stettinius had been most useful in preparing briefing materials to fill in the gaps in his information. But his lack of political and electoral experience bothered the new president since in the absence of a vice-president, the secretary of state is next in line for the presidency.[56] Senator Vandenberg of Michigan was indignant at Stettinius's dismissal on June 27: "Stettinius deserved better treatment after his rare performance at Frisco. . . . Just as we have, at long last, got Russia to understand that we occasionally mean what we say, Stettinius gets the axe."[57]

Two days after he became president, Truman offered the post of Secretary of State to his former Senate colleague and rival for the 1944 vice-presidential nomination, James F. Byrnes. In making the offer, he stated that he was influenced by the question of succession to the presidency. Byrnes had been elected to the House of Representatives and also to the Senate, and he had served as director of the Office of War Mobilization. He had likewise been at Yalta and had taken elaborate notes of the conference. Truman had greatly admired the genial Byrnes as a senator and had thought that Byrnes was better qualified for vice-president than himself. He thought that the appointment might help balance things up after Byrnes's disappointment at not being nominated by the convention.[58] In *Newsweek*, Ernest K. Lindley wrote, "If Truman had chosen anyone else for Secretary of State, it would have been astonishing." In experience, Byrnes was "unquestionably the No. 2 Democrat of today," and he was "a man of steady judgment."[59] Byrnes's skill as a parliamentarian and compromiser was beyond question, but his ability to handle the difficult diplomatic tasks that lay ahead and his loyalty to Truman were other matters. Byrnes had to learn that the U.N. Security Council was not like the U.S. Senate and that even though he thought that he deserved to be president rather than Truman, Truman was still president.

There were four holdover members of the Roosevelt cabinet that Truman wanted to keep on as long as possible. Two of them were in defense posts— Secretary of War Henry L. Stimson and Secretary of the Navy James V. Forrestal—and two were in key domestic posts and had important political followings—Secretary of the Interior Harold L. Ickes and Secretary of Commerce Henry A. Wallace.

As head of the Truman committee, the President had had agreeable relations with Secretary Stimson, and he thought the elderly statesman liked him. When Stimson submitted his resignation to the new President, Truman, according to Stimson, "promptly and earnestly assured his Secretary of War that he was wanted not just temporarily but as long as he could stay, and Stimson and the War Department continued to receive from the White House the firm and understanding support to which they had become accustomed in the previous five years."[60] President Truman was not interested in handling the details of administration that went on in the Pentagon, and he did not want to disturb the team that was clearly winning the war. Stimson was nearly seventy-eight, and he agreed to stay on until the victory was won.

Secretary of the Navy Forrestal, who came to Washington in 1940 from a most successful career on Wall Street and soon demonstrated his superior administrative abilities as under secretary of the navy, was elevated to the office of secretary when Frank Knox died in April 1944.[61] As in the case of Stimson, Senator Truman had observed Forrestal in action before his Senate investigating committee. He had found Forrestal a fine champion of the needs of the navy and at the same time an administrator who appreciated the needs of the other services and the civilian economy.[62] Forrestal, who was a conservative and no admirer of Truman, was to stay longer in Truman's service than any of the other Roosevelt cabinet holdovers. (His final severance from the service in 1949 was marked by the personal tragedy of a nervous breakdown and subsequent suicide.)[63] For four years, however, Forrestal, in opposition to Henry Wallace and other liberals, was to battle for national security in the face of communist threats.

President Truman recognized that Secretary of the Interior Ickes had become an institution in American political life.[64] When first appointed in 1933, he was a stranger to President Roosevelt, but over the years he acquired a reputation for honesty, for legal safeguards for public spending, for bluntness, for using hard-hitting language in political campaigns, for upholding valiantly the New Deal, for defending fiercely the cause of conservation, for planning the proper use of natural resources, and for protecting fearlessly the rights of minorities. The "old curmudgeon," as he called himself, was a useful political ally and had a following of his own among liberals.[65] His presence would continue to give a moral tone to the cabinet. President Truman decided to leave him alone and that is what happened, until 1946 when political exigencies found the President in a position where he had to choose between Ickes and Pauley.

The new secretary of commerce, Henry A. Wallace, could also be a political asset.[66] He had a large New Deal following and was popular with farmers, organized labor, and intellectuals. Although deeply disappointed in not winning a renomination in 1944, he had campaigned vigorously for Roosevelt. Truman had just been through a fight in the Senate to get Wallace confirmed. From the standpoint of good politics, Wallace should remain and that is what he did until he could not restrain his desires to influence U.S. foreign policies, particularly those concerning American relations with the Soviet Union.

The first Roosevelt cabinet holdover to leave was Postmaster General Frank C. Walker, who had informed President Roosevelt before he died that he wished to retire.[67] In view of political custom, his logical replacement was Robert E. Hannegan, who in January 1944 had already replaced him as Democratic national chairman. James Farley from 1933 to 1940 and Walker himself from 1940 to 1944 had held both of these posts. Hannegan had demonstrated political abilities and as a cabinet officer was one who would keep his eye on the next election.[68] President Truman counted on him to support policies that he thought would help the party win votes. As an administrator, Hannegan had won the praise of Secretary of the Treasury Henry Morgenthau, and at this time he had a good record for his service as commissioner of internal revenue.

Secretary of Labor Frances Perkins was the only woman in the holdover cabinet. Although she was a long-time personal friend of President Roosevelt and Eleanor Roosevelt, she never had been too popular with organized labor because the labor leaders wanted their own person in the post. Roosevelt, however, had stood by her firmly in spite of all efforts to replace her.[69] When Roosevelt died, she was ready to step down. She had seen many of her functions whittled away by the emergency agencies. President Truman said that he asked her to stay on, but she said she needed a rest. In his staff meeting, he said that he did not want a woman in his cabinet. Later on he was to use Perkins as U.S. civil service commissioner and in other capacities.

For secretary of labor, President Truman nominated his former Senate colleague, Judge Lewis Schwellenbach. He defended his appointee as an able lawyer, a good senator, and a "real, honest-to-goodness liberal," hardly sufficient qualifications for handling mounting postwar strikes and labor unrest.[70] Schwellenbach was not well, and he knew little about labor problems so President Truman had to turn elsewhere for advice on labor matters. John Steelman became his White House counsellor on labor problems.

In 1945 there were serious food shortages, for which Secretary of Agriculture Claude Wickard was blamed, although the war food administrator had been made responsible for production and distribution of food supplies after 1943.[71] The shortages arose from the mistaken assumption of postwar surpluses. Congressman Clinton Anderson was appointed chairman of the Special Committee to Investigate Food Shortages. The committee found substantial evidence of widespread violation of meat price and rationing regulations and of black market operations, and it criticized the war food program for not providing the increased storage facilities needed.[72] When Secretary Wickard resigned, Anderson was appointed in his place. The President was surprised when Wickard told him that he was interested in becoming head of the Rural Electrification Administration, but he had no hesitation in making the appointment.[73]

Attorney General Francis Biddle came from an aristocratic family in Philadelphia and was a personal friend of the late President.[74] Truman as senator had his difficulties with the office. A politically minded president such as President Truman would be expected to want his own appointee as attorney general. In his *Memoirs*, Truman wrote that Biddle was a good attorney general and that he did not ask Biddle to leave, but Biddle resigned voluntarily.[75] This account does not agree with Biddle's own account or with Dean Acheson's note of a conversation he had with Biddle at the time: "Steve Early called him [Biddle] up last Monday and said that the President wanted his resignation. Francis replied that a Cabinet Officer might expect to hear that from the President himself. Whereupon the President sent for him and told him the same."[76]

Some Washington correspondents had prophesied that Hugh Fulton, who had done such a fine job for the Truman committee and who had worked so hard on the 1944 campaign train, would be the new attorney general. Fulton had gone into private law practice, and the fact that he sent out announcements advertising himself as the former counsel of the Truman committee displeased the President.[77] Matt Connelly, John Snyder, and Harry Vaughan also opposed an appointment for Fulton. The result was that Fulton was not appointed to this or any other post in the Truman administration.

During the war, a Department of Justice lawyer from Texas, Tom Clark, was made chief of the war frauds unit, which brought him in touch with the Truman committee. He took advantage of the situation to cultivate Senator Truman. Later Clark became assistant attorney general. Although some expressed doubt about his performance in this post, he was strongly backed by Speaker Rayburn and Senator Connally of Texas for attorney general.[78] President Truman appointed him to the post on June 15, and two weeks later Clark became attorney general. Clark was not destined to make as good a record as Biddle had made. Some of his assistants had difficulties, which necessitated their being fired by Truman later on. Within a year, when the President was in trouble with bad publicity regarding Kansas City election frauds allegedly perpetrated in the Democratic primary defeat of Congressman Slaughter, a conservative whom Truman was opposing, the Department of Justice helped quiet the affair.

The last Roosevelt holdover was Secretary of the Treasury Henry Morgenthau, another close friend of the late President and the author of the controversial Morgenthau plan for the ruralization of postwar Germany. The treatment of postwar Germany was clearly a function of the State and War Departments, but under President Roosevelt such confusion regarding departmental responsibilities was tolerated. Although Truman had always been suspicious of the aristocratic and distant Morgenthau, he tried to warm up to him.

Truman's account in his *Memoirs* of Morgenthau's resignation does not agree with the *Morgenthau Diaries* or with the official announcements. Truman claimed that he accepted Morgenthau's resignation promptly when the latter threatened to resign if he was not taken to Potsdam.[79] Actually it appeared that Truman wanted Morgenthau to remain at his post until after the Potsdam conference but was persuaded to accept his resignation while at sea in order to give greater freedom to his new appointee, Fred M. Vinson of Kentucky.[80]

Vinson's appointment as secretary of the treasury was a natural one for Truman to make. After ten years in the House of Representatives, where he acquired a fine reputation as a legislator and troubleshooter, Vinson was appointed to the federal bench. President Roosevelt asked him to leave this quiet post to become director of economic stabilization during the war. After the abrupt dismissal of Jesse Jones as secretary of commerce and loan administrator to make way for Henry Wallace, Congress separated the two posts, and Roosevelt appointed Vinson as federal loan administrator. Vinson proved to be a skillful administrator and won the support and admiration of those under him and those with whom he had dealings.[81] He was regarded as one of the best minds in the new cabinet. His views tended to be moderately conservative.

Until the end of the war, this was the Truman cabinet—four Roosevelt holdovers and six new secretaries. Except for Byrnes and Vinson, both of whom held high posts under Roosevelt, the new cabinet members were not from the top echelon of government. Hannegan had been commissioner of internal revenue, and Clark had been assistant attorney general, but Anderson and Schwellenbach had had no administrative experience. As a whole, the competence of the Truman cabinet was less than that of the Roosevelt cabinet that had been inherited. It reflected, however, the background and experiences of the President. Instead of four cabinet officers from New York, only two New York holdovers were left, both in defense positions. The new cabinet members were from the South, from Midwestern border states, and from the West. Whereas President Roosevelt had had two cabinet members from Pennsylvania, Truman had none. Four northeasterners were replaced by three new members from west of the Mississippi and a member from a state bordering the Mississippi. A Catholic replaced a Catholic, a Protestant replaced a Jew, and a man replaced a woman. Four of the new members had had service in either the House of Representatives or the Senate. All of them had worked with Truman in some capacity—as fellow legislators, as witnesses before the Truman committee, or as fellow Democratic politicians. Some were potential threats to the Truman administration when the press and the Republicans began to look for weak links in the Truman armor. The new President had come to the top through the aid of a tough political organization, and he was not as fully aware of the slips that the politically minded can make as was the late President.

Truman felt comfortable with his former congressional colleagues, his southern and border state friends, and his party associates. Next to Wallace and Ickes, the most liberal man on the cabinet was Hannegan, who was aware of the factors that had kept the Roosevelt coalition together.[82] The others were moderates or slightly conservative. Stimson, Forrestal, and Byrnes were conservatives. The initiative for the preliminaries to the Fair Deal program were not to come primarily from the cabinet as it was constituted in the summer of 1945. On his belief in surrounding himself with those representing various viewpoints, Truman stated: "Early in my administration I set out to achieve a balance between conservative and liberal points of view among the members of my cabinet and other advisers. I wanted to be exposed to opposite poles of opinion in forming my own conclusions and making my own decisions on basic policy matters."[83]

PRESIDENTIAL AGENCIES

The Truman committee discovered that during the war there was need for better coordination between agencies at the presidential level. President Roosevelt found that he had to coordinate the activities of the emergency agencies that were fighting the battle against inflation. He therefore created by executive order in October 1942 the Office of Economic Stabilization, which had jurisdiction over the Office of Price Administration, the National War Labor Board, the Reconstruction Finance Corporation, the Department of Agriculture, and other agencies concerned with price and wage controls, monetary restraints, government loans, and other measures designed to check inflation.[84] Roosevelt persuaded Justice James Byrnes to step down from the Supreme Court bench to become director of economic stabilization, a position that some referred to as assistant president. Because Roosevelt was preoccupied with international and military affairs, this appointment of a well-known and respected troubleshooter was a great help, but it was not sufficient to meet the administrative crisis in the domestic field. In May 1943 the President established at an even higher level the Office of War Mobilization, which was put in charge of harmonizing the operations of the War Production Board, the War Department, the Navy Department, the Maritime Commission, the Office of Defense Transportation, the War Food Administration, and other war agencies. Byrnes was promoted to director of this new office and, in 1944, following legislative authorization, of the Office of War Mobilization and Reconversion (OWMR). After returning from Yalta, Byrnes resigned, and President Roosevelt, just before he died, appointed Judge Fred Vinson as director of OWMR.

President Truman was familiar with these presidential agencies. Their directors and officers had appeared before the Truman committee, which had recommended their creation. He was an admirer and friend of Judge Vinson, who had a distinguished record in Congress, on the bench, and as a top-level administrator, and he was glad to continue him in the post. Judge Vinson performed creditably in this difficult office, building up an able planning staff, standing firm against the military leaders who were resisting reconversion, and setting some postwar policies. As a close observer put it, "Despite aggressive and affirmative actions on many fronts, Vinson ended his stay without substantial attacks from any quarter. He left OWMR with his reputation for wisdom, balance, and forthrightness unsullied."[85]

Until the end of the war in September 1945, the new administration functioned with reasonable smoothness. Business interests, working persons, and consumers were willing to make sacrifices in order to win the war. The difficult problems of reconversion were emerging gradually, but they had not challenged Truman and his advisers with their full force. Truman viewed the presidency as a place where decisions had to be made, and with his top administrators he was acquiring the reputation of making decisions on the basis of facts presented to him. Criticism in Congress and in the press was muted; there was the general feeling that Truman should be given a chance to show what he could do.

chapter 21 | LEARNING DIPLOMACY, 1945

Nearly every international agreement has in it the element of compromise. The agreement on Poland is no exception. No one nation can expect to get everything it wants. It is a question of give and take—of being willing to meet your neighbor half-way.
—Harry S. Truman, radio report on the Potsdam Conference, August 9, 1945

As long as the war lasted, President Truman tried to follow Roosevelt's foreign policies as he came to understand them. In the foreign more than in the domestic field, the President had to rely on advice from holdovers from the Roosevelt administration since he had never specialized in foreign affairs. Considering the crucial questions that soon had to be answered, it was extremely urgent for him to fill in his scanty background. He had not been on the Senate Committee on Foreign Relations, and his only travel abroad had been to France as an American artillery officer in World War I.

As the war came to an end, the international situation changed radically, and it was necessary to make new assumptions on which to base American foreign policy.[1] The collapse of Germany created a power vacuum in Europe. Two world wars had brought financial ruin to the British empire, which was too weak to stem the rising tide of nationalism in its colonies even though Churchill was a confirmed imperialist. General de Gaulle was valiantly trying to rebuild French pride and national power, but it was not easy to wipe out the stigma of surrender to the Nazis in 1940. The Soviet Union had suffered terrible losses during the war—20 million casualties, cities and factories destroyed, and lands laid waste—but when hostilities ceased, it had the largest land forces that were in physical occupation of Eastern Europe, including the eastern part of Germany. Stalin had appeared to be cooperative at Teheran and Yalta, but he was deeply suspicious of the British and Americans because of their alleged broken promises regarding a second front and needed supplies.[2] What assumptions should be made about Soviet postwar intentions? Had the Communist party of the Soviet

Union lessened its push toward world revolution? Were Russian intentions peaceful? Was their military posture purely defensive? Would they block the recovery of the world under the free enterprise system? Before he died, Roosevelt was becoming concerned about Soviet foreign policies, which appeared to be aggressive in Eastern Europe. He had several sharp exchanges with Stalin regarding Poland and the British-American peace overtures to the Nazi generals in Italy.

Harry Truman, upon becoming president, immediately found himself deeply immersed in foreign affairs. One of his first decisions was to continue exactly as scheduled the San Francisco conference to frame the U.N. Charter.[3] He expressed high hopes for this organization as a guardian and preserver of the peace. Along with others from the Wilsonian school of diplomacy, he made the optimistic assumption that world organization for peace and freedom was possible.

Roosevelt, Cordell Hull, Harry Hopkins, Sumner Welles, John Foster Dulles, and others held the universalist view: all nations shared a common interest in each other, and a world organization would be a much better guarantee of postwar peace than the old discredited sphere-of-influence view, by which each great power would be left to dominate its own area of special interest.[4] The universalist view, based on Wilsonian idealism and the concept of free international trade, found expression in the Atlantic Charter, the Moscow Declaration, the U.N. Charter, and the Declaration on Liberated Europe. Very few top American officials questioned this approach. Among the balance-of-power through spheres of influence advocates, however, were Secretary of War Stimson, George Kennan, a Russian expert in the American embassy in Moscow, and Henry Wallace, who later gave public expression to his views. Stimson thought that acceptance of spheres of influence would avoid a direct confrontation with the Soviet Union. President Truman, an old Wilsonian, accepted the universalist approach. Roosevelt had sometimes qualified his universalist approach.

With reference to the Soviet Union, contradictory views were held by different advisers. President Roosevelt had hoped that he could charm Stalin, who would listen to reason and would make concessions in order to get American aid. At Yalta, however, American economic aid was not mentioned in the main meetings. Harry Hopkins, close to the late President, had operated on the Roosevelt theory and had won the confidence of Stalin, who thought of him as a friend of the Soviet Union. Joseph E. Davies, former ambassador to the Soviet Union, was also friendly to the Russians. Henry Wallace in particular felt that the Russians' security aims should be respected and that American economic aid should be granted to them. Other advisers believed the opposite. A number held that Stalin was a paranoid who could not be charmed or persuaded by promises of aid and other concessions to give up what he regarded as essential to the security of the

Soviet Union—friendly nations on his western borders—or to give up his ideological hostility to capitalism as embodied in its leading exponent, the United States. To Stalin the word *friendly* meant subservient, and the United States was the quintessence of capitalism and therefore always hostile. Secretary Stettinius was scheduled to be replaced by James Byrnes, but he had put together fact-gathering machinery, under the leadership of Under Secretary Joseph Grew, which was critical of the Soviet union.[5] Chief of Staff Admiral Leahy, also critical of Soviet policies, was kept on by Truman in part because of his wide experience in foreign and military affairs, his attendance at the Yalta conference, and his knowledge of the secrets of the White House map room. Also unfriendly to the Soviet Union was Secretary Forrestal, who, relying upon dispatches from Ambassador Harriman in Moscow, held that no economic aid should be given to the Soviet Union, that Stalin regarded American generosity as a sign of weakness, and that any attempt to interfere with Soviet control of Eastern Europe was a hostile act. Forrestal believed that the Soviet Union would actively pursue its worldwide revolutionary aims.[6] As a senator, Truman had expressed a view that was not friendly toward the Soviet Union. When the Nazis attacked the Soviet Union in 1941, he was quoted as saying, "If we see that Germany is winning we ought to help Russia and if Russia is winning we ought to help Germany and that way let them kill as many as possible, although I don't want to see Hitler victorious under any circumstances."[7] Truman modified this view later and accepted the Soviet Union as an ally.

Particularly as far as China was concerned, a number of wrong assumptions were made. It was claimed that a "democratic compromise" could be worked out between the Nationalists under Chiang Kai-shek and the Communists under Mao Tse-tung. In the meantime, Chiang Kai-shek was regarded as the man to support in a limited fashion. Events were to prove that democracy was not a form of government feasible in China under existing conditions and compromise was not what either side was willing to accept. The Communists were not just agrarian reformers but hard-core revolutionaries with an army well trained for both guerrilla and regular warfare. Chiang Kai-shek was difficult to deal with; he refused to take advice, was unable to check inflation or to win the support of the population, and was unwilling to fight. The Atlantic first policy of Roosevelt had reduced aid to China to a trickle, and Chiang had not been pressured hard enough to adopt sound economic and military policies.

President Truman inherited these assumptions regarding China and its leaders and the mission of Ambassador Patrick Hurley, who was instructed by Roosevelt to bring the Nationalists and Communists together to fight the Japanese, an impossible task. At first he was naive in praising Chiang, but he was soon corrected.

Regarding the nature of the postwar world, some American political leaders assumed that one of the aims of the war was the same as in World War I: to make the world safe for democracy and free trade. At Yalta, American negotiators talked about free elections in the liberated states of Eastern Europe and said that as a sign of its good faith, the Soviet Union should accept the results of such free elections. Stimson pointed out to Truman that this was an unrealistic view: "We have to understand that outside the United States, with the exception of Great Britain, there are few countries that understand free elections; that the party in power always runs the elections."[8] Stalin bluntly told Truman at Potsdam in talking about the Eastern European states, "Any freely elected government in these countries will be an anti-Soviet government, and we cannot allow that."[9]

President Roosevelt believed that the days of colonialism as practiced by the Western European powers were waning and that the United States should encourage the development of nationalism. He failed to implement this policy as far as Great Britain was concerned, and he neglected to communicate this way of thinking to Vice-President Truman, who relied upon advice from the State Department on attempted reestablishment of old colonial empires.[10] In the case of French Indochina, this meant the beginning of a long series of events that involved the United States in a most unpopular limited war. The Dutch also were misled by American permissiveness regarding restoration of old colonial empires, and they wasted men, materials, and goodwill in attempting to reestablish themselves in the East Indies.[11]

From the standpoint of the need to negotiate from strength, a most disastrous contention was that with the war over, peace was automatic and American armed forces in Europe could be safely demobilized at once. A corollary of this view was that American military might was invincible. It is true that the United States soon had a monopoly on the atom bomb and that the air force and the navy were not demobilized as rapidly as the ground forces were. Secretary Forrestal battled vigorously for a navy adequate to fulfill America's postwar obligations.[12] But for European duty and for limited warfare in remote areas, in view of the character of all-out atomic warfare, ground forces were necessary, and the United States was soon at a disadvantage in dealing with the Soviet Union, which had large ground forces of its own in physical occupation of Eastern Europe and indigenous communist guerrilla forces in countries that it was trying to subvert as in Iran.

In the postwar period, President Truman soon found out that revolutionary insurrections aided by the communists could cause trouble all over the world; the communist bloc would not hesitate to keep insurrectionists well supplied with ideological weapons and with modern military hardware and logistic help. In the postwar period of limited wars, ground forces trained in guerrilla tactics and in countering subversive propaganda were deemed necessary to meet communist aggression. Truman gradually came to agree with this view. Forrestal was greatly distressed at the rapid demobilization,[13] but Americans were eager to get back to normal. After all, the Allies had won the war, and most Americans idealistically thought that the United Nations would preserve the peace. But within a short time, the Soviet Union had annexed large slices of foreign territory and extracted huge reparations from the defeated Germans and also from Eastern European nations they were soon to subjugate. Ambassador Harriman's dispatches from Moscow clearly forecast these events,[14] but it took time for President Truman and his new secretary of state, James Byrnes, to realize the nature of the postwar world.[15]

The Truman mistakes in conducting American foreign relations during 1945 were based on faulty intelligence and wrong assumptions. It is still disputed whether the use of the atom bomb to defeat Japan was necessary because some believed the Japanese were on the verge of a military collapse. It is also questionable whether Soviet military help was needed to end the war in the Far East. Intelligence officers should have warned Truman that rapid American demobilization in Europe would hand over Eastern Europe to the Soviet Union. Churchill was aware of these dangers, but American advisers, including Joseph E. Davies, had warned President Truman against Churchill and his imperialistic policies.[16] The United States might have used the atom bomb or atomic blackmail to save Eastern Europe but opinion toward such a recent ally could not be changed fast enough to do that, particularly when Truman and Byrnes continued to believe that Stalin could be brought around to cooperate in time of peace as he did in time of war.

From his first day in the White House, President Truman had to make important foreign policy decisions and meet top foreign dignitaries. He was not the glamorous charmer that Franklin Roosevelt was, but his family, especially his mother, had trained him to hold the ideal of a Christian gentleman. In his personal contacts, he was naturally friendly. He did not mind getting into formal clothes (his experience as a Mason had given him a liking for pomp and circumstance). On state occasions he was dignified, and his life as a senator and vice-president had prepared him for official Washington. Bess Truman would never try to emulate Eleanor Roosevelt, but she was a genteel hostess and performed her official duties faithfully and in good grace.

In tackling the job of foreign policy determination, President Truman brought another solid asset to the task: he was not afraid of work. He took a stack of documents, reports, and dispatches to his living quarters each evening. Whereas President Roosevelt was too ill to go over a mass of papers on his way to Yalta, Truman went through mountains of reports and drafts and held daily conferences with his staff on his way to Potsdam.[17] As one commentator put it, there was not a lazy bone in his body.[18] He lost no time in trying to fill in the gaps in his knowledge of world affairs. (One writer, however, remarked that he did not work as hard as Secretary Byrnes did in preparing for the Potsdam conference.)[19]

Highly conscious of his inexperience and lack of knowledge of foreign affairs, President Truman strove to appear to be decisive. To him the presidency was a place where decisions had to be made. "The buck stops here" was the motto on his desk. In making decisions, he had to rely upon the advice of others. Sometimes he had to choose between conflicting alternatives. He did not always make the right choice.

RELATIONS BETWEEN THE PRESIDENT AND THE SECRETARY OF STATE

In the conduct of foreign policy, a president must have a secretary of state who will give him sound guidance, who will keep him informed, who will usurp no presidential prerogatives, who is on good terms with Congress, and whom he finds compatible. Regarding Secretary Stettinius, whom he inherited from President Roosevelt, Truman had doubts on the first and last categories. Stettinius was a good manager and expediter, but he was not a policy formulator. His smooth public relations techniques did not appeal to Truman any more than they did to Dean Acheson, who was to become an important foreign policy adviser even before he became secretary of state.[20] President Roosevelt, however, had appointed Secretary Stettinius to head the delegation to the San Francisco United Nations conference, and Truman did not want to disturb this arrangement. Although he had spoken to Byrnes about making him secretary of state, he postponed the appointment until after the San Francisco conference.

In the meantime, for foreign policy advice he had to rely upon Under Secretary Joseph Grew, who became acting secretary while Secretary Stettinius was in San Francisco for two months and while Byrnes was in Potsdam for one month. Grew was a career officer who was close to the foreign service corps. He was noted for his long service as ambassador to Japan during which he recorded on January 27, 1941, that the Japanese would probably attack Pearl Harbor. His conversations with Truman were highly varied. For instance, during May 1945, he had at least twenty-four conversations with the President, who was seeking background information and guidance regarding American foreign policy.[21] While Stettinius was at San Francisco, Grew, as acting secretary of state, gave Truman many details regarding the status of American foreign relations. Included in the topics discussed were the crisis with Yugoslavia regarding the control of the Italian port of Trieste, which involved Tito and his armed forces who were threatening the Allies; plans for dealing with postwar Germany, which as far as the State Department was concerned meant abandoning the drastic Morgenthau plan for the ruralization of Germany; the German surrender plans; arrangements for VE Day, the future of Poland, Austria, and other liberated countries; policy toward Palestine, which involved de Gaulle's armed forced in Beirut; military bases in the Philippines; relations between China and the Soviet Union concerning the concessions promised the Soviet Union at Yalta for declaring war on Japan; French and Dutch participation in the war against Japan; the Japanese surrender terms, including the abandonment of the unconditional surrender formula and the guaranteeing of the status of the emperor; the agenda of the proposed Big Three meeting; relations between the United States and France concerning the confrontation between American and French troops in Stuttgart in Germany and Val d'Aosta in Italy; progress of the United Nations conference at San Francisco; legislation of interest to the department pending in Congress; assistance to Belgium, Brazil, and other members of the United Nations; and plans for modernizing and expanding the foreign service. Grew was torn between those in the department who urged a tough policy with the Soviet Union and those who advocated caution and patience. In May he agreed with the British that American troops should advance into Austria and Czechoslovakia in order to be in a better bargaining position.[22] Later in a conference at the White House on Tito's advances in Venezia Giulia, Grew took a cautious position regarding challenging the Yugoslav forces.[23] He was secretly anti-Soviet and was limited by the traditional values and points of view of the professional diplomats. Such a bold program as the Marshall Plan was needed right after the end of the war in view of widespread economic dislocation, but the Department of State was not then set up to produce such a plan.

The problems that Grew discussed with Truman were frequently closely related to the military situation. The army was still in control of occupation problems, and it was moving as fast as feasible away from the Morgenthau plan. De Gaulle's military adventures in Stuttgart and Val d'Aosta were squelched by the threats of Truman to withhold American supplies from the French troops. In the process Truman formed a very low opinion of de Gaulle. The decisions regarding how to conclude the war with Japan were based on military considerations until the last moment. Truman would have done much better if he had followed Grew's advice regarding the emperor sooner.

Within less than two weeks after becoming president, the inexperienced Truman was faced with the serious problem of how to deal with the deteriorating relations with the Soviet Union. Ambassador Harriman's dispatches from Moscow warned that the Soviet Union was disregarding the Yalta accords regarding a reconstructed Polish government. The Soviet-backed provisional Polish government in Warsaw was excluding elements from the

Polish government in exile in London. Returning to Washington, Harriman, in a long talk with Truman, explained that the Russians respected strength, and a firm policy would be safe because they would be anxious to get American aid. General John R. Deane, head of the Moscow military mission, and Secretary Forrestal supported Harriman's position. Truman was impressed and told Harriman that he was not afraid of the Russians and would make no concessions.

After Roosevelt's death, Stalin agreed to send Foreign Secretary Molotov to the San Francisco conference on the establishment of the United Nations. On his way, Molotov stopped in Washington to see President Truman. Before the April 23, 1945, meeting of the two, Truman had a session with his top advisers. Stettinius, Harriman, and Forrestal urged the President to take a strong position on behalf of the American point of view, which backed an independent and democratic Poland. Stimson and Marshall recommended caution. Truman, anxious to appear decisive, accepted the hard line, handed Molotov a strong message to Stalin, and bluntly expressed American displeasure at events in Poland.[24] The two men clashed over the interpretation of the Yalta accords. According to Truman's account in his *Memoirs* Molotov complained: "I have never been talked to like that in my life."[25] Truman claimed he replied: "Carry out your agreements and you won't get talked to like that." The official records do not show any such exchange. Harriman was wrong on the effect of this encounter. Instead of softening the Russians, it hardened their position. At the time, Truman and his advisers were willing to use only rhetoric to advance their stand. They had no inclination to use force or threats of force and were seeking a peaceful solution of their differences with the Soviet Union.

Alarmed by what he learned about the blunt encounter between Truman and Molotov, Joseph Davies, who wished to preserve friendly relations with the Soviet Union, sought an interview with the President. On April 30, he tried to explain the Russian point of view and to impress upon Truman the seriousness of the situation. At the end Truman asked: "Did I do wrong?" Davies urged Truman to seek a meeting with Stalin at which he would try to win the confidence of the Russians.[26]

The end of the war in Europe on May 8 brought not joy to the Allies but a continuing falling apart of the alliance and growing feelings of distrust regarding each other's intentions. Even the deciding of when to declare the victory proved to be a source of dissension. The Soviet Union was not sure all Nazi resistance had ceased on its front and suspected until the end that Western powers might make separate agreements with the defeated Germans. President Truman and General Eisenhower found this episode trying.[27]

The precipitous ending of lend-lease for European operations without warning on the same day that the German surrender was announced had most unfortunate repercussions on American foreign relations. Although the economic damage was much more serious in the case of Great Britain, the psychological reaction of the Russians was more vehement. Stalin later told Harry Hopkins that he regarded this abrupt cutting off of aid to which he thought his country was entitled as unfortunate, even brutal, scornful, a sign of distrust, and a form of pressure.[28]

The order ending lend-lease in Europe was prepared by Leo Crowley, the foreign economic administrator who had taken over the lend-lease program in 1943 along with other international economic programs. A former Wisconsin utility executive, he was characterized by Truman as being "as anti-Russian as Wallace was pro-Russian."[29] Under Secretary of State Grew was with him when Truman hastily signed the order without reading it or reflecting upon it. This was one of the few incidents mentioned in his *Memoirs* where Truman admitted he had made a mistake.[30] Actually the ground for this action was laid by President Roosevelt, who insisted on unconditional lend-lease to the Russians and failed to warn them about limitations imposed by Congress. Crowley's staff interpreted the order too literally and cut off lend-lease goods already in transit. The uproar that followed led Truman to cancel the order for the turnaround of ships within twenty-four hours. He confessed that he should have read the original order carefully and pondered its consequences. He failed to see at this time the postwar economic needs of Europe. Harriman and Secretary Stettinius, who were familiar with lend-lease problems, were upset. In his Moscow conversations with Stalin, Hopkins had to explain carefully that there was no attempt or desire on the part of the United States to use lend-lease as a pressure weapon, and the incident had no policy significance.[31] But the damage had been done; central economic planning in the Soviet Union had been dislocated without warning, and Hopkins could only partially repair the breach.

President Truman was concerned about the worsening of American relations with the Soviet Union, and he turned to a device that President Roosevelt had often employed: a special mission outside the regular channels of the Department of State. The status of Poland was causing increasing friction and was endangering the San Francisco conference. Contrary to the Yalta agreements, which called for free elections, Stalin was stubbornly standing by a puppet regime in Poland. President Truman was impressed by what Hopkins had told him about his previous missions to the Soviet Union, and he persuaded the ailing roving ambassador of the Roosevelt days to undertake a final mission to Moscow in late May along with Ambassador Harriman. Acting Secretary Grew was not enthusiastic about the mission, but he was not strong enough in Truman's councils to block it.[32] The British were kept informed regarding this mission but were not asked to participate in it, a decision that Hopkins later regretted.[33]

The mission was at first hailed as a success. A compromise solution on Poland was reached, which eventually provided the London Poles with minority representation in the cabinet. Stalin selected Potsdam for a July summit meeting. He agreed not to press for the veto in the U.N. Council on procedural matters, a rock on which the San Francisco conference was foundering. Some said that this decision saved the conference. Stalin also confirmed his promise to declare war against Japan at a later date and he appeared to be willing to support Chiang Kai-shek. Hopkins seemed to have Stalin's confidence, and he won what looked like major concessions. Subsequent events, however, showed that Hopkins was too trusting. He and Stalin read the opposite meanings into the word *friendly*. A friendly Poland to Stalin meant a Poland under his thumb; to Hopkins it meant a free and independent Poland that was not hostile to the Soviet Union. To George F. Kennan, however, Hopkins admitted he had doubts.[34]

Another sign that Truman had not given up on trying to negotiate with the Russians was shown by his sending Joseph E. Davies to London at the same time he sent Hopkins to Moscow. The object of the Davies mission was to inform Churchill that the Americans were trying to preserve Allied unity. On May 21 Davies had suggested to Truman that "if he could talk with Churchill, he could make him see the light." Steve Early, the press secretary, had also suggested such a mission. Churchill had been urging that for bargaining purposes American troops not be withdrawn immediately from their advance positions in the Russian zone of occupation. He had also been proclaiming the dangers of Soviet aggressive behavior. At the time, Truman did not perceive the unsuitability of Davies for such a delicate mission. Churchill was furious at being lectured to and in effect reprimanded by a man whose favorable views on Soviet policies were regarded as naive. When Davies told Churchill that Truman wanted to meet Stalin alone before the Big Three meeting, Churchill sent a stiff message to Truman: "I should not be prepared to attend a meeting which was a continuation of a conference between you and Marshal Stalin. I consider that at this victory meeting, at which subjects of greatest consequence are to be discussed, we three should meet simultaneously and on equal terms."[35] In his *Memoirs* Truman denied that he had proposed a separate meeting with Stalin. His next message to Churchill stated that all three would meet at the same time at the forthcoming conference at Potsdam. As for the holding of American troops in the Russian zone, Truman turned down Churchill's request and agreed with his military advisers that they should be withdrawn. The Davies mission irritated Churchill, and it may have added some suspicion regarding Churchill's aims among Truman's top advisers.

When the conference on the United Nations began in San Francisco on April 25 the Soviet Union proposed the admittance of the Polish provisional government. Truman agreed with Churchill in rejecting the proposal until the Polish government was reorganized in keeping with the Yalta agreement.[36] In a cable to Truman on May 12, 1945, Churchill had expressed his profound concern over the European situation and the movement of American military power out of Europe. He contended that an "iron curtain" had come down on Poland and the Balkan states.[37]

Molotov, temporarily frustrated in his demands for the recognition of the Soviet-dominated Polish government, made trouble in other areas. He protested vigorously the admission of Argentina to the United Nations on the ground that during the war it had aided the Axis powers and had only recently switched to the Allied side when it appeared that the Axis powers were losing. The Latin American states wanted Argentina admitted in exchange for agreeing to give the Soviet Union three votes in the U.N. Assembly as proposed at Yalta. President Truman supported the admission of Argentina in order to promote Western Hemisphere solidarity.[38]

Like many other Americans who were optimistic about the possibilities of a world organization for peace, the new President was enthusiastic about the work of the U.N. conference. Although he and Senator Vandenberg had been skeptical about the abilities of Secretary Stettinius, both agreed that he had run the conference well.[39] Truman and many others looked upon the new international organization as the mainstay of the universalist hopes for a peaceful world.

After the San Francisco conference was over on June 26, Byrnes was appointed secretary of state, and Stettinius was made chief delegate to the U.N. Preparatory Commission and ultimately ambassador to the United Nations. For a while, there was a struggle in Congress to elevate this position to a level equal to that of the secretary of state, but this proposal lost and the secretary remained the chief foreign policy adviser.[40]

Secretary Byrnes had been at the Yalta conference, but the conduct of foreign relations was not his specialty. Senators Tom Connally and Arthur Vandenberg, who had concentrated on this field, were not pleased with the appointment.[41] Byrnes brought to his job, however, a mastery of compromise and a quick intelligence. He was to learn soon that compromise was not the technique favored by the Russians who understood and respected only raw power and fought fiercely to protect their own interests, which included extending their borders and advancing their plans for expansion elsewhere in accordance with the communist philosophy.[42] A peace in terms of the Atlantic Charter, which expressed the hope that "all the men in all the lands may live out their lives in freedom from fear and want," was out as far as Stalin and the Soviet Union were concerned. Soviet troops were in Eastern Europe, and there they would stay.

Secretary Byrnes was appointed just a few days before it was necessary for him to depart for the Potsdam conference. There was no time for him to reorganize the department before he left, so Under Secretary Grew continued as acting secretary during the conference.

In his *Memoirs* Truman implied that he owed Byrnes the appointment as secretary of state since in his own view the vice-presidential nomination in 1944 should have gone to Byrnes rather than to himself. As he expressed it:

Byrnes felt that by virtue of his record of service to the Party and the country, he had been the logical choice to be the running mate of Franklin Roosevelt in the 1944 election. In fact, he had asked me to nominate him and give him my support before that convention.

As it turned out, Roosevelt and the convention willed otherwise, and Byrnes, undoubtedly, was deeply disappointed and hurt. I thought that my calling on him at this time might help balance things up.[43]

Byrnes was willing to serve under a man whom he regarded as his inferior. This situation was not conducive to the best relations between the White House and the Department of State, but differences did not develop until later.

POTSDAM CONFERENCE

The first big task facing the new secretary of state was the Potsdam conference. Although Byrnes had not concentrated on foreign relations, he had served as Truman's representative on the interim committee on the atom bomb, and he had vast experience in public affairs. Some historians of the period have praised Byrnes for his diligence and skill as a negotiator under trying circumstances.[44]

The call for the Big Three summit conference at Potsdam, the only such conference that President Truman attended, grew out of the general feeling that at the time of his death, Roosevelt had left many unsolved problems. Churchill and Truman believed that a new meeting of the Big Three was necessary to consider some of these problems. It was now necessary to disarm Germany, set up the zones of occupation, and decide on reparations. Stalin told Hopkins that he would be willing to hold such a conference in July in Potsdam, a suburb of Berlin in the Russian zone. Secretary Byrnes was in charge of the American delegation, and the supervision of the completion of the position papers started under Acting Secretary Grew. General Eisenhower was asked to see that the physical arrangements for the meeting were satisfactory, a job that required tact and diplomacy in dealing with the Russian generals. At this time, President Truman had great admiration for the leader of American armed forces in Europe.

The new President was not particularly anxious to attend this conference. He was keenly aware that he personally could not fill the great void left by the death of Roosevelt, a man who knew all of the principals and the details of recent negotiations. Yet he felt it was his duty to try to settle a number of pressing matters, which could be decided only at the top level. Just before landing, he wrote to his mother and sister: "I wish this trip was over. I hate it. But it has to be done."[45]

On the trip to Europe on board the U.S.S. *Augusta*, President Truman displayed some of the traits that characterized his presidency. He worked regularly on the preparation of position papers and on acquiring background information. The special communications equipment on board enabled him to keep in touch with his domestic duties, which he did not neglect. At meal times and in the evenings, he relaxed and became his old informal self. He stood in line with the sailors for mess and enjoyed looking at movies in Secretary Byrnes's cabin. Some thought he could have spent more time on the preparations for the conference.[46] On the other hand, Truman's ability to relax and to throw off the cares of state at times contributed to his vigor.

At Potsdam Truman wanted to meet Stalin before he met Churchill in order to reassure the Russian dictator that the English-speaking powers were not ganging up on him. Perhaps he felt guilty about the statement he had made in 1941. Stalin, however, was late because he had suffered a slight heart attack, and Churchill called before Stalin arrived. Roosevelt's death had been a devastating blow to Churchill, who later wrote:

In this melancholy void one President could not act and the other could not know. Neither the military chiefs nor the State Department received the guidance they required. The former confined themselves to their professional sphere; the latter did not comprehend the issues involved. The indispensable political direction was lacking at the moment when it was most needed. The United States stood on the scene of victory, master of world fortunes, but without a true and coherent design.[47]

While Churchill had his reservations about Truman at first, he later recalled that he "was impressed with his gay, precise, sparkling manner and obvious power of decision . . . he invited personal friendship and comradeship, and used many expressions at intervals in our discussion which I could not easily hear unmoved. I felt here was a man of exceptional character and ability, with simple and direct methods of speech, and a great deal of self-confidence and resolution."[48]

During the conference Churchill confided to his physician that Truman was much firmer in dealing with the Russians than Roosevelt had been. He added: "If only this had happened at Yalta."[49]

Regarding his first meeting with Churchill, Truman wrote:

I did not feel that I was meeting a stranger. I had seen him on several occasions when he had been in Washington for conferences with Roosevelt, although I had not talked to him then. We had had a number of telephone conversations since I had been President, and in that way a personal contact had already been made.

I had an instant liking for this man who had done so much for his own country and for the Allied cause. There was something very open and genuine about the way he greeted me.[50]

At the time, Truman was a little more wary of Churchill than this indicates since he had been warned by Joseph Davies and others that Churchill was an eloquent defender of British interests, which were not always the same as those of the United States.

At Potsdam, President Truman met Stalin for the first time. He was pleasantly surprised at the courteous manners and relaxed behavior of the man who had a reputation for ruthlessness.[51] In his country Stalin was known for his organizing and executive ability, his plebeian conduct, and his foresight. He was noted for his patience, skill at intrigue, cold-bloodedness, and energy. He was sparing of words and unscrupulous in pursuing his objectives. His personal appearance and quiet ways at Potsdam seemed to belie his reputation. Truman later said that Stalin reminded him of Boss Tom Pendergast.[52] Apparently he thought of the two men as strong leaders who expressed their views plainly and fearlessly, who held to the main issues, who could not be sidetracked, and who were good judges of people.

Truman had read Ambassador Harriman's dispatches from Moscow, but he seemed unaware of the purge trials and summary executions of Soviet leaders in the 1930s that Stalin had ordered. (Khrushchev's famous speech describing the crimes Stalin committed against his colleagues was delivered eleven years later.) Here was another failure in intelligence. Truman and Byrnes did not know the true nature of Stalin. Ambassador Harriman, Charles Bohlen, and George Kennan were aware of the situation, but they were not close enough to Truman at this time. Stalin was not as courteous to Churchill and Churchill's successor at the conference, Labor Prime Minister Clement Attlee, as he was to Truman. It is likely that Churchill felt at the time that Truman was inept in his handling of Stalin.[53]

At the conference, Truman displayed impatience at delays and long harangues (particularly Churchill's) and an eagerness to arrive at decisions quickly. As he put it, "I said I did not want to discuss. I wanted to decide. Churchill asked if I wanted something in the bag each day. He was as right as he could be. I was there to get something accomplished, and if we could not do that, I meant to go home."[54]

Among the subjects discussed at the Potsdam conference were the establishment of the Council of Foreign Ministers of the United Kingdom, the Soviet Union, China, France, and the United States in London to draw up the treaties of peace; the proposal of territorial settlements and the consideration of other matters related to it; the laying down of political and economic principles to govern the treatment of Germany in the initial control period; an agreement on how reparations claims were to be met and statements on the annexation of Konigsberg by the Soviet Union; the trial of war criminals; the status of Austria, Poland, Italy, Bulgaria, Finland, Hungary, Rumania, and former Italian colonies; the orderly transfer of German populations from the newly defined Poland, Czechoslovakia, and Hungary; and military talks regarding the war against Japan.[55]

At Stalin's shrewd suggestion, Truman was made chairman of the conference. In carrying out this task, he relied heavily upon Byrnes and top holdover Roosevelt advisers. In the early sessions, he presented the American proposal for a Council of Foreign Ministers to draw up peace treaties. Stalin objected to the inclusion of France and China in this council. A compromise solution was reached excluding China from the council sessions preparing peace treaties with European countries and France from sessions dealing with Hungary, Rumania, and Bulgaria. With these changes, the Council of Foreign Ministers was set up. Feis contends that this procedural step, which Truman hailed as unifying, accomplished little on substantive matters because grave differences developed regarding the treatment of Italy and the former satellites of Germany.[56]

At the suggestion of his diplomatic and military advisers, Truman proposed the international control of inland waterways, including as an initial step the opening of the Rhine and the Danube to the trade of all countries. The Soviet delegates postponed consideration of this proposal, which did not fit their ideas of a closed economic system in Eastern Europe. Stalin was unwilling to have the subject even mentioned in the final report, much to Truman's disappointment.

While Truman and Byrnes were pleasantly surprised at Stalin's outwardly polite manner, they soon discovered that Stalin and Molotov were stubborn and greedy bargainers. Truman was set back when Stalin called the Soviet seizure in Rumania of oil equipment that belonged to Americans and Britons a "trifling matter."[57] He was also greatly disappointed in the failure of Stalin to fulfill the Yalta pledges regarding free elections in Eastern European countries. Churchill and Truman disputed sharply Stalin's claim that the British and American charges that an iron fence had come down on their missions in Rumania and Bulgaria were "all fairy tales."[58] Truman insisted that the United States would not extend recognition to the satellites until their governments were reformed in accordance with the Yalta pledges. Stalin insisted that the satellites should have the same liberal treatment that Truman was advocating for Italy. The impasse was referred to the Council of Foreign Ministers, which also floundered on this issue. Both Truman and Churchill were alarmed at Stalin's request for a trusteeship in North Africa.

In the discussion of the Polish frontiers, Truman protested strongly against the Soviet Union's assigning to the Polish provisional government, without consultation with the British and Americans, a zone of occupation of Germany extending to the Oder and the western Neisse. He indicated that this action would reduce the capacity of Germany to pay reparations and would increase the burdens of the British and Americans in their respective zones of occupation. Western Germany would be deprived of foodstuffs and coal, and refugees from the disputed area would flee to the west.[59] Churchill argued even more vigorously against the Soviet action and favored fixing the frontier farther east, but Truman did not want to fix a frontier at this conference. Byrnes's compromise left the question unsettled, with the Poles in physical possession of an area that had been German. Thus, the Russians who had committed many wrongs against the Poles, including the invasion of 1939, the failure to come to the defense of the Poles fighting Germans in 1945, and (according to some) the massacre of Polish officers at Katyn, sought to appease them at the expense of the Germans.

A major issue at the Potsdam conference was the treatment of Germany. At the Quebec conference of 1944, Germany had been divided into occupational zones. Prime Minister Churchill was present at the conference and agreed to the zone lines.[60] Later in 1945, he wanted to go back on his word and use English and American troops in the Soviet zone to bring pressure on the Russians to fulfill their obligations regarding Poland and the former Axis satellites. President Truman and his military and diplomatic advisers did not want to disregard American promises. Certainly it was a grave mistake to set these zones so early and in a manner so favorable to the Soviet Union. During the war, President Roosevelt had concentrated on winning the war, and he failed to produce a plan for winning the peace. He had worked on a plan for the zones of occupation that would have safeguarded American interests much better than the plan adopted, but he was so busy with other things that he failed to follow through with the promotion of that plan.

The political and economic principles to govern the treatment of Germany in the initial control period emphasized disarmament, demilitarization, destruction of Nazi institutions, education for democracy, a judicial system that protected human rights, local self-government, freedom of assembly, freedom of speech, and an economic system that eliminated cartels and trusts and maximized transport services, coal, agriculture, housing, and utilities. The Russians and the other Allies interpreted these principles in vastly different ways. Already in the Soviet Zone, vast quantities of nonmilitary goods had been seized as war booty, communist state trusts were not cartels, education was for communism, a Sovietized judiciary ignored human rights, freedom of speech was limited to communist propaganda agencies, and freedom of trade and movement was barred.

The decisions at Potsdam seemed reasonable compromises at the time, but they laid the basis for dividing Germany in two parts. Although it was specified that Germany should be treated as an economic unit, the Soviet Union was given a veto on the Control Council, which was charged with achieving this unity. The Soviet Union thwarted all plans for achieving unity. In addition, as part of the Byrnes deal worked out at the end, it was decided to let the Soviet Union take reparations from its own zone and to receive a percentage of an indeterminate amount of German equipment from the other zones. This brought an immediate division. Stalin wanted to set German reparations to the Soviet Union at $10 billion, but Truman and the British objected. Truman did not want any reparations plan that depended indirectly upon American financing.[61] Curiously, the American delegation, including General Eisenhower, did not see the importance of specifying in writing clear access land routes to Berlin.

Revisionist historians have criticized the reparations provisions of the Potsdam conference on the ground that they were unfavorable to the Soviet Union.[62] Kennan was of the view that no collaboration with the Soviet Union on reparations should even have been attempted.[63] Truman's misgivings that Soviet reparations from the Western zones of Germany would ultimately be paid by American taxpayers proved to be true, as General Lucius Clay, who tried valiantly to get along with the Russians, discovered.

The conferees, Clement Attlee replacing Churchill at the end, maintained the shaky alliance for the time being. The principles to govern the treatment of Germany did not propose the partition of Germany, but that is what happened. The Soviet Union soon disregarded its promises regarding free elections in Poland and the other Eastern European countries. W. W. Rostow contends that the agreements were not poor in themselves, but there was a lack of determination to enforce them and a failure to appreciate what needed to be done by the Americans to carry them out.[64]

President Truman did not realize then the need for maintaining American armed might in Europe, and Secretary Byrnes looked upon his task as one of negotiation. Byrnes did not want to appeal to Truman to launch the strenuous campaign at home that would be needed to slow down the rapid American demobilization in Europe.

At the end of the Potsdam conference, the relations between Truman and Byrnes were friendly. Truman, in his radio address of August 9 on the conference, praised his secretary of state, whose services were also commended by the leaders of the other two powers.[65] A few days later, the President read a laudatory citation accompanying the presentation of the Distinguished Service Medal to Byrnes. At this time Truman was hopeful that the cooperation of the Big Three would continue in the making of the peace. There was no call to arms to contain Soviet power or to roll back communist advances.

THE ATOM BOMB

While Truman was at Potsdam, the first atom bomb was exploded at Alamogordo, New Mexico. Some historians allege that the conference was delayed deliberately in order to have the bomb as a diplomatic weapon.[66] Truman told Stalin informally about the successful explosion of a new weapon, but the Russian dictator did not seem greatly impressed or alarmed. As subsequent revelations of Soviet espionage showed, Stalin probably knew a great deal about the project except, perhaps, the exact moment when it was to be tested. Truman was not told about the awesome secret of the bomb and the terrible responsibilities that it would impose upon him and his country until after he had been sworn in as president. Before that he was only vaguely aware of the enterprise. The Truman committee had started in 1943 to look into highly secret military complexes in Tennessee and the state of Washington's spending millions of dollars, but Stimson had requested him to stop investigating them, which he did. At that time, Stimson told Truman that the project was the greatest in world history. After Truman became president, Stimson filled in the details of the destructive power of the new weapon. Later Byrnes added that it was powerful enough to destroy the whole world.

At a White House meeting on April 25, 1945, Secretary Stimson proposed the appointment of the Interim Committee to make recommendations regarding nuclear policy. Truman named his prospective secretary of state, James Byrnes, as his personal representative on the committee. Other members besides Secretary Stimson were the head of a science organization, two university presidents, and two top Navy and State Department officials. J. Robert Oppenheimer, director of the Los Alamos Scientific Laboratory, was the head of the advisory scientific panel. This committee reported to Truman on June 1 that the bomb should be used against Japan as soon as ready, that it should be used to demonstrate its power against war plants and houses, and that it should be used without prior warning. Truman indicated no disappoval of these recommendations. Stimson thought the bomb might be useful in negotiating with the Russians, but he had no plan as to how that influence might be exercised.

What was President Truman's role in the decision to drop the atom bomb on Japanese cities without warning the populations? Knebel and Bailey contend that there is no indication in the Manhattan papers (*Manhattan* was the code name for the project) that Truman ever made an affirmative decision to drop the bomb.[67] George Elsey claims that Truman did send a message authorizing the dropping of the bomb.[68] Truman certainly assumed it would be used when ready. Churchill recalled that at Potsdam the decision whether to use the bomb was not even an issue.[69] General Leslie Groves, in charge of the administration of the project, stated that Truman "was like a little boy on a toboggan who never had an opportunity to say yes. All he could have said was no." Truman never exercised a veto. Feis contended that at this stage it would have required a most resolute and courageous act of will—rarely found in history—to have stopped the plans.[70]

In his *Memoirs* Truman wrote that he made the decision to drop the bomb on Japanese cities of military importance.[71] A draft of the directive of July 24 to General Carl Spaatz, commanding general of the Army Strategic Air Force, from the Joint Chiefs of Staff instructing him on the use of the bomb was sent to Stimson and Marshall at Potsdam for approval, no doubt with the knowledge that they would consult the President.[72] In his announcement of the use of the bomb at Hiroshima, Truman indicated that he agreed with the decision and did not think that a full justification was necessary. He was proud of a scientific project that harnessed the basic power of the universe, loosed the force from which the sun draws its power, had more than two thousand times the blast of the largest British bomb, ushered in a new era in man's understanding of nature's forces, and brought with it the danger of world destruction.

Of the main contestants for and against the use of the bomb for military purposes without warning, Truman did not hear the full case of those who were opposed. Secretary Stimson and Major General Leslie Groves had access to the President, and they explained and defended the military use of the bomb without a preliminary demonstration of its power. Admiral Leahy let Truman know he was opposed to the use of the bomb, and Under Secretary of the Navy Ralph A. Bard objected to its use without adequate warning. General Eisenhower was opposed to the first use of the bomb in war by the United States, but he was not consulted.[73] The scientist, Leo Szilard, who had gravest misgivings about the bomb as a military weapon never had direct access to the President. While the Interim Committee heard some of his arguments, his last-minute plea, supported by many other scientists, was never presented to the President, who asked Secretary Byrnes to listen to him. Byrnes was unfavorably impressed. On the moral issus involved, Truman relied upon the physicist Arthur Compton, whom he consulted a week before the bomb was dropped. He asked Compton to be his conscience. Compton, a deeply religious man, consulted with Stimson and others and came to the conclusion that the bomb would save lives.[74] Truman, thus, came to believe that the bomb did save lives.

Closely linked with the decision to use the bomb was the question whether Japan could be induced to surrender without any such great shock. In his May 8, 1945, statement to the Japanese people urging them to surrender, Truman did not go as far as Under Secretary Grew wished him to go in reassuring the Japanese that their emperor would be allowed to remain as head of state. Grew argued that unless the revered imperial institution was protected, the Japanese would continue to fight. The emperor might, on the other hand, be a strong force for peace.[75] Truman clung to the disputed Roosevelt formula of unconditional surrender.

Grew continued to press for a clarification of Allied surrender terms, which might induce Japanese surrender. The ultimatum of July 26 issued during the Potsdam conference and signed by the United States, the United Kingdom, and China did not contain any reference to the emperor, any indications of the Soviet intentions to enter the war against Japan, or any clear warning of the power of the atom bomb. Subsequent events proved that Grew's advice about the emperor should have been followed in this and the earlier ultimatum. Byrnes was among those who opposed any concessions on the emperor. The Japanese rejected the Potsdam ultimatum, and the first bomb was dropped on Hiroshima. The second bomb was dropped on Nagasaki three days later. This was hardly time for the Japanese to come to a decision on surrender.

The decision to use the bomb against Japanese cities was based on certain assumptions that have been shown since to be wrong. It was estimated that without such severe treatment, the Japanese would have continued to fight for many months to come. It was also calculated that it would be necessary to invade the Japanese home islands at the cost of a million American casualties.[76] Naval officers questioned this view at the time, and later the Strategic Bombing Survey came to the conclusion that both of these calculations were wrong and that the Japanese would have surrendered in any case by early fall.[77]

A striking characteristic of Truman's behavior is that he had no regrets. His role in the decision to drop the bomb without prior explicit warning on a target containing thousands of civilians was based on the best advice available to him at the time. Secretary Stimson, a chief adviser on this issue, had long contemplated the awesome consequences of using the new weapon in the manner indicated. In later years, Truman stuck by the decision made at the time and defended the use on the ground that it shortened the war and saved many lives.

President Truman and his advisers were not ready to use the new weapon as an arm of diplomacy against an opponent in the manner that the Soviet Union was to use it against France and Great Britain in the Suez crisis of 1956. While some writers have since alleged that the dropping of the bomb was aimed more at the Soviet Union than at Japan, the record does not show that President Truman argued more persuasively or aggressively at Potsdam after he knew of the success at Alamogordo.[78] It is one thing to express the hope privately, as Truman and Byrnes did, that possible rivals would respect the power of the bomb and listen to American proposals and quite another to say to these rivals to do as told. It seems that the Americans at Potsdam either did not know how to use their command of the new weapon effectively as a threat or chose not to use it in that way.[79] In the case of Japan, Truman could remind the American public of Pearl Harbor, Bataan, the forced march, and other atrocities suffered at the hands of the Japanese. On the other hand, the Soviet Union had not attacked American forces, it had born the brunt of the Nazi assaults, its cooperation was essential for the success of the United Nations, and its ground forces could not be overcome merely by bombing. At the time, American diplomacy relied upon peaceful negotiations and faith in international conciliation.

During his first four months in the White House, Truman was a war president with full war powers granted by the Constitution and by Congress. He commanded the largest armed forces that the United States had ever assembled, and he supervised the greatest war production program that the world had ever seen. Truman had not asked for these powers. He had been catapulted into this position of world leadership without warning by the death of Roosevelt, whose lifelong ambition had been to have a large share in shaping the world's destiny. Without being briefed, he found himself responsible for executing Roosevelt's postwar plans. After doing his best to learn all he could about those plans, he consulted his predecessor's advisers regarding policies to follow in new emergencies.

During these days, Truman showed his leadership qualities in standing up to Stalin and Molotov on the reparations issue, in forcing de Gaulle to withdraw his troops confronting Allied forces in Stuttgart, Val d'Aosta, and Beirut by threatening to withhold American military supplies from the French, in turning down Churchill's pleas for retention of American troops in the Soviet Zone of occupation as a means of exerting pressure on the Russians in other fields, and in facing Tito in Trieste. He did not see through Stalin's dissembling ways, he had a low regard of de Gaulle, he admired Churchill but was unwilling to follow his lead in confronting the Soviet Union so soon after V-E Day, and he was no admirer of Tito. While a striking contrast to Roosevelt, Truman was picking up the reins of American leadership in international affairs.

A world leader must have a stable domestic situation behind him. During his first four months, Truman had ample war powers to maintain domestic peace, and the people were generally united in accepting hardships in order to win the war. American foreign and military policies, the ratification of the United Nations Charter, the extension of reciprocal trade agreements, the way in which lend-lease was handled, the victory over Germany, the dropping of the atom bomb and the surrender of Japan, and the Potsdam agreements were all received favorably. This was Truman's honeymoon period in the conduct of American foreign relations. He and the American people did not yet see clearly the problems of the postwar world, how to solve them, and how to win American support for the sacrifices involved.

chapter 22 | DEMOBILIZATION AND RECONVERSION, 1945–1946

> *I have been thinking every week that perhaps the next week will not be quite so hectic as the week just passed, but the coming week is always just a little more hectic. This is one place where you never lack for action, and where there is always a crisis just around the corner and I have to do something about it.*
>
> —Harry S. Truman to fellow workers, *New York Times*, April 12, 1946

For the Allies, victory had been in the air since the successful landings on Omaha Beach in northern France on June 6, 1944. About that time, Senator Truman was concerned with the problems of reconversion since war production had reached its peak, and the need for war goods would be declining. The armed forces had resisted the Truman committee's reconversion plans. Top military officials were favorably inclined toward big business interests, which in turn wanted to hang on to war profits as long as possible. When reconversion came, they wanted to squeeze out small competitors.[1] Upon becoming president, Truman, realizing that the end of the war in Europe was very near, wanted to bring about the adoption of sound plans for American reconversion to civilian production.[2] At this early stage, he had the services of Judge Vinson, a moderate conservative, as head of the Office of Stabilization and Reconversion. Vinson had taken over the office from James Byrnes just before Roosevelt died, and he had recruited an efficient staff to assist him in the reconversion functions. Immediately after the May 8, V-E Day, some of the plans were put into effect.[3] It was the estimate of the military that victory over Japan might be a year to eighteen months away, so reconversion could be worked out gradually.

As in the foreign field, a number of wrong assumptions were made about the nature of domestic problems facing the postwar nation. Most economists assumed that there would be a serious recession and high levels of unemployment as war industries closed down and the troops were mustered out of the service. They thought that in the postwar period, deflation might be more serious than inflation. Some domestic consumers, with the war over, thought that shortages would come to an end soon.[4] They failed to realize that the shortages were worldwide and that it would take years for the restoration of agricultural and industrial production in the war-torn areas. The devastation of farm areas in Europe and the Far East, the shortage of farm workers because of the draft, war casualties, and the attraction of war production jobs meant that there would be tremendous food shortages in the postwar world. George F. Kennan, a foreign service officer, traveled over what was formerly East Prussia and saw nothing but a desert in place of the most productive farm area of prewar Europe.[5] If Americans wanted to keep less fortunate individuals from starving, it would be necessary for them to expand farm production and reduce domestic consumption. All restraints on American food production should have been removed at once and emphasis placed upon maximum production possible to stave off starvation in liberated areas and occupied countries.[6] President Truman received warnings of a world famine crisis from the State Department, from Herbert Lehman, director of United Nations Relief and Rehabilitation Administration,[7] from Judge Samuel Rosenman, who had undertaken a food survey mission for President Roosevelt just before the latter died,[8] and from former President Herbert Hoover, who had been commissioned by Truman to survey the world food situation.[9]

As subsequent events soon showed, there was little danger of a postwar depression. High wartime wages and a scarcity of consumer goods meant that there were considerable wartime savings. This in turn created a demand, which would call for full production of consumer goods as soon as factories could be converted to civilian use. There was relatively little unemployment because of the manpower shortages in consumer industries.[10]

With a huge unsatisfied demand for postwar goods, inflation was the postwar threat. Without allocation, wage, price, and ration controls, the fierce competition for scarce goods would force up prices. Workers would demand higher wages, and employers would seek higher prices to offset higher costs.

As long as the war lasted, the controls were left intact.[11] Since the price level had risen only 30 percent during World War II as compared with 100 percent in World War I, the retention of controls until consumer demands were met was a reasonable course.[12] Allocating and rationing provided a generally fair distribution of available goods. There was some black market cheating, but this was not too disruptive. Although the Office of Price Administration was condemned by business and disliked by consumers, it performed in a generally effective fashion.

In addition to price controls and rationing, President Truman inherited production controls involving the allocation of scarce resources among various claimants, fiscal and budgetary controls over all government service including the military, wage controls, and antistrike legislation applying to the emergency. These controls appeared to be adequate to meet those domestic crises that arose during the first four and a half months of the Truman administration. Wartime patriotism kept dissidents from making serious trouble. Organized labor was dissatisfied with the emergency controls, but take-home pay, due to high wage rates and overtime, was considerable and complaints gave rise to strike action only occasionally.[13] Businesses with government contracts were in a particularly favorable position because their work was usually done on a cost-plus basis.

Harry Truman had gotten ahead in American politics partly because he appeared to be successful in acting as a broker for various social and economic groups. He wanted to be thought of as a representative who looked after the interests of as many of his constituents as possible. He tried to keep down the number that he displeased by listening to the pleas of as many different groups as he could.[14] Above all was his idea of the public interest. When group interests clashed with what he regarded as the general interest, he opposed the special interests.[15] While as a senator he had been harsh about certain trusts, he was not antibusiness. When he became president, Roy Roberts, proprietor of the *Kansas City Star*, wrote: "Harry Truman is no man to rock the boat. He's not as cautious as Calvin Coolidge. . . . But he has the innate, instinctive conservatism in action of the Missouri bred countrymen. They want to know where they are going before they leap. And they are not fond of leaping just for the pleasure of headlines."[16]

For twelve years, conservative business leaders had fretted under the New Deal policies, which they thought favored labor, liberal welfare policies, and restrictions on business. While shipping interests, the aviation industry, the oil industry, and government war production contractors were willing to accept what amounted to government subsidies, industry in general resented the protection of trade unions, the regulation of business, and government intervention in the marketplace, in particular some of the wartime restrictions. When Frederick von Hayek gave expression to these views in *The Road to Freedom* in 1944, the response of the business community was tremendous.[17]

President Truman always had around him men who shared the views of conservative businessmen. Of the Roosevelt holdovers that he kept during the war period, Stimson, Forrestal, Robert Patterson, Kenneth Royall, and Stettinius were conservatives. One of the first of his new appointments was that of John W. Snyder, a Missouri bank president, as federal loan administrator. Throughout the entire Truman administration, Snyder, a personal friend, furnished conservative counsel in various capacities. As loan administrator, he was in a good position to do favors for business, as he had under him the Reconstruction Finance Corporation, which was established in the Hoover administration to help ailing businesses. During the Roosevelt administration, Jesse Jones did just that.[18]

As soon as Truman entered the White House, reconversion problems were upon him because the war in Europe was winding down rapidly. He had extensive administrative powers to meet these pressing crises, but he also needed legislation to take the place of wartime regulations and to pave the way for a smooth transition to a prosperous peacetime economy.

As President, Truman, a natural conciliator, hoped to improve relations between the executive and legislative branches of the government. Unlike Roosevelt, he had had no overpowering ambition to be president and to exercise the great powers of the office. After seven years in the White House, he said: "There are a great many people, I expect a million in the country, who could have done the job better than I could, but I had the job and I had to do it."[19] To represent his state in the Senate had been his goal in 1944. While he felt that as president he was obligated to do what he could to carry out the Roosevelt program, he did not want to use Roosevelt's methods, which glorified personal power at the expense of others and involved caustic criticism of Congress. Truman wanted to keep his friends in the Senate and in the House, both Republicans and Democrats. Although he respected the role of Congress, now that he was president he would do his best to live up to the responsibilities of that office. At first, this meant trying to get congressional action on as many parts of the Roosevelt program as he could. He would talk to the congressional leaders, send messages to Congress, veto bills he thought were contrary to the program, and, if necessary, remind Congress of its duties in his public statements. He would maintain a friendly and respectful manner.

Especially in the field of foreign and military affairs, Truman believed it important to cultivate congressional leaders of both parties in order to ensure that the bipartisan foreign policy inaugurated by Roosevelt and certain Republicans in Congress would furnish the basis for building a world organization and a sound peace. As a senator, Truman had become an admirer of Senator Arthur Vandenberg, Republican senator from Michigan and a former isolationist who loyally supported the war measures after Pearl Harbor and who made a dramatic speech on January 10, 1945, pledging cooperation on postwar peacemaking, if Roosevelt would deal with the Republicans in a spirit of "honest candor."[20] Without the support of Senator Vandenberg, the ranking Republican member of the Senate Committee on Foreign Relations, it would be impossible to get the necessary two-thirds vote in the Senate to ratify any peace treaty. Truman was conscious of Woodrow Wilson's failure to obtain Senate approval for the League of Nations treaty, and he was just as determined as Roosevelt had been not to repeat the mistakes Wilson had made.[21]

As long as the war lasted, the Truman policy of friendly relations with Congress presented no serious problems. Until the Japanese surrendered, Congress and the public seemed willing to put up with wartime controls and restraints, but after that, the pressures for relaxing unpopular wartime measures became tremendous, and there was a wild scramble among competing interests to preserve or increase special benefits enjoyed during the war.

The Democratic majorities in the House and the Senate of the Seventy-ninth Congress reflected the disparate elements that made up the coalition that Roosevelt had been building over twelve years. In the Senate there were 38 Republicans and 57 Democrats, of whom 20 were southerners. In the House there were 191 Republicans and 242 Democrats, of whom 95 were southerners. Thus it was possible in both houses for the southern Democrats and the Republicans to make up a majority. Their combined forces made up 58 in the Senate and 286 in the House. Southern Democrats were more likely to support a Democratic president on international than on domestic issues. Northern Democrats from urban areas and from strong labor districts could be counted on to support both presidential programs. Democrats from farm areas might be more isolationist. As president, Truman tried to keep the Democratic coalition together. This meant getting along with the representatives in Congress who depended on various elements for reelection. President Truman was well aware, however, that he represented the whole nation and that there were bound to be clashes with Congress.

From the very beginning, President Truman tried to conciliate Congress. He relied on his friend, Les Biffle, secretary of the Senate, to help him invite the congressional leaders of both parties to his swearing in. On his second day as president, he asked Biffle to arrange a luncheon in his office with the leaders of Congress of both parties so he could tell them of his earnest desire and need for the fullest cooperation between the legislative and executive branches. Biffle invited thirteen senators and four members of the House of Representatives, all of whom gave Truman a most cordial welcome. Truman told the group that he wanted to address a joint session of the Senate and House three days hence. Regarding this meeting, Senator Vandenberg wrote in his diary: "Truman came back to the Senate this noon for lunch with a few of us. It shattered all tradition. But it was both wise and smart. It means that the days of executive contempt for Congress are ended; that we are returning to a government in which Congress will take its rightful place."[22]

In preparing his speech to be delivered before Congress, Truman relied on Steve Early and Judge Rosenman. He also went over some of the points with legislative leaders on the train coming back from the Roosevelt funeral in Hyde Park. When he entered the House on April 16, he was greeted by a standing ovation. He was so excited that he did not wait for Speaker Sam Rayburn to introduce him, and the Speaker had to interrupt him. In his speech, he pledged himself to carry out the war and peace policies of President Roosevelt. He asked for support for a strong United Nations organization. The speech was mainly about the war and peace, but it contained a significant passage on domestic issues: "Let me assure the forward looking people of America that there will be no relaxation in our efforts to improve the lot of the common people."[23] Truman ended his address with King Solomon's prayer: "Give therefore Thy servant an understanding heart to judge Thy people, that I may discern between good and bad for who is able to judge this Thy so great a people? I ask only to be a good and faithful servant of my Lord and my people."[24]

This speech was well received, indicated the comment in the *New York Times:*

Truman's first address yesterday to Congress and the people was all that it should have been: simple and straightforward. Truman has risen to the occasion of the great moment in history with a straightforward statement which carries deep sincerity. His address deals with all the essentials of a fateful hour. . . . He promises nothing which is beyond achievement. He sounds a call to duty. We believe that the country will respond willingly and confidently to the appeal for support made by this man.[25]

President Truman continued the Roosevelt practice of weekly meetings with the so-called big four, a group composed of the vice-president, the speaker of the House, the majority leader of the House, and the Senate majority leader. Speaker Rayburn, House Majority Leader John McCormack, and Senate Majority Leader Barkley, as old friends, contributed to the cordiality of these meetings. Although he was not as congenial as the others, Senator Kenneth McKellar, as president pro tempore of the Senate, took the place that had been the vice-president's, including sitting in on cabinet meetings. The President gave the group the latest information on the war and diplomatic fronts and outlined the need for budget cuts.

Speaker Rayburn was one of the men whose counsel the new President sought three days after taking office. After warning him about incompetent staff assistants who might want to build a fence around him and about sycophantic special interests who might flatter him, Rayburn said: "Mr. President, I will want to see you about two or three little things once in a while. And I can't afford to walk through those newspapermen out there and say we didn't talk about anything." To this Truman replied, "Just any afternoon after five o'clock, come in the East entrance of the White House, over by the Treasury, and walk through there and come up to my study. I'll be in there."[26]

The legislative leaders responded favorably to the new President's friendly approach. The Democratic senators showed it by a resolution passed in a special conference expressing grief for the passing of Roosevelt. Of Truman they said:

Resolved further that this conference expresses its confidence in the new President, Harry S. Truman, who has assumed the great responsibilities of the office to which he has been called, and pledges to him its genuine and sympathetic cooperation in bringing the present war to a prompt and victorious conclusion, and establishing a just, honorable and permanent peace, and in so readjusting the economic processes incident to the postwar period as to bring our nation and to the world the greatest possible happiness and prosperity.[27]

Republican Senate leaders also responded approvingly to the new President's attitude toward Congress. Truman talked with a group of them headed by Senator Robert Taft of Ohio, the recognized Republican leader on domestic issues, about the conduct of the war. Taft asked to be briefed on later developments, and Truman consented. When Roosevelt was president, Taft had not been welcome in the White House. Senator Vandenberg, as the Republican leader on foreign policy issues, attended these meetings. Republican Senator Alexander Wiley of Wisconsin, along with Senator Vandenberg a member of the Committee on Foreign Relations, said on the floor of the Senate on April 16, "Truman is a born cooperator."[28]

In the field of domestic legislation, the Truman leadership did not fare as well as in the international field, but it was still heeded on many matters during the period before V-E Day. Truman did not try to present any new program of his own until later. The Democratic program had already been put forward by the national convention of 1944 and by Roosevelt's state of the union and budget messages of 1945. Truman did not face any major domestic crises during the period because the spirit of wartime patriotism restrained the selfish interests of organized labor, business, the farmers, and the consumers. In general, big business favored the wartime controls as long as the government was paying the cost plus a big profit for war production.[29] Victory over Germany in May followed by cutbacks in military spending began to shake the national consensus but not enough to alarm the great industrial magnates.

During the war, inflation had been regarded as the principal danger to the domestic economy. The experience of World War I and the lesson of Weimar Germany had bolstered support for rationing and price and wage controls. The new President regarded himself on firm ground when he made an earnest White House statement on May 1 for the extension of the Price Control Act, in which he praised highly the work of Price Administrator Chester Bowles.[30] At this time, Bowles was strongly suported by Fred M. Vinson, the director of the Office of War Mobilization and Reconversion (OWMR).

The debate in Congress on the extension of the Emergency Price Control Act of 1942 and the Stabilization Act of 1942 focused on criticisms of the Office of Price Administration and the endeavor of the farm bloc members to secure higher price ceilings on farm products. Combinations of Republicans and Democrats in both houses were successful in securing amendments for the benefit of the farmers. As amended, the resolution extending the acts for one year passed on June 30.[31]

In Director Vinson of OWMR, President Truman had an able adviser on problems of reconversion, which with the end of the European war and decline of Japan's military fortunes were becoming very pressing. Vinson had recruited an able staff on reconversion headed by Robert Nathan, who had distinguished himself as a program planner under the War Production Board. President Truman's special message to Congress on unemployment compensation of May 28, 1945, incorporated some of the thinking of these advisers. The plan called for extending the coverage to maritime workers and government employees, raising the weekly unemployment benefits, and extending the period of payment.[32] Two days later, by a letter that Vinson sent to the chairman of the Banking and Currency Committee, Senator Robert Wagner of New York, President Truman was committed to strong support of the full employment bill.[33] No action was taken by the Seventy-ninth Congress on these proposals during its first session.

In the field of manpower needs, President Truman had backed Roosevelt's request for renewal of the Selective Service Act of 1940 and for the passage of a universal military training act. When Congress tried to amend the Selective Service Act by exempting farmers as a group, the new President in a message to Congress on May 9 vetoed the resolution as being contrary to the spirit of the original act, which gave no privileged position to any group.[34] This action took courage because it aroused the ire of the farm bloc. An attempt to override the veto failed. The Republicans were almost solidly against the president, voting 154 to 12 to override.[35] As one journalist put it, "If he can get away with that he can veto anything."[36]

AFTER THE RECESS

When Congress reassembled after the recess on September 5, the situation was entirely new. The atomic age had begun, the United Nations was fast becoming a reality, and postwar reconstruction was piling up legislative problems here and abroad. The war was now over; the Japanese had surrendered on August 14. Demobilization and reconversion presented many difficult questions. The public, unaware of the worldwide problems of the postwar period, demanded that the troops be sent home at once. They failed to realize that peace negotiations could be conducted to American advantage only from strength. The Soviet Union, with its troops occupying all of Eastern Europe, was in no hurry to demobilize.[37] The emergency measures passed by Congress during the war automatically came to an end when the war was declared over. Reconversion was bound to bring some dislocations such as unemployment, maldistribution of materials, wage adjustments, squeezing of small business firms, housing shortages, food shortages, consumer goods shortages, heavy goods shortages, and other problems. Farmers wanted the market restraints removed so that they could get higher prices while the heavy demand for agricultural products continued. Trade unions wanted to conserve their wartime gains based on overtime and to secure new benefits. Big business wanted to see the end of price controls and was willing to accept some inflation if its profits remained high. Strikes, rising prices, black markets, scarce goods, outraged consumers—all of these conditions had begun to develop. To solve these problems would take a genius. Harry S. Truman, ex-farmer, ex-haberdashery owner, ex-county official, ex-senator, was no genius. He was the first to admit that. While he had great admiration for the presidency, he frankly did not have admiration for himself in that job. He had never developed the ambition that some had for the position. However, he had the job and he would do the best he could in it.[38]

Up to this point Truman had relied on Roosevelt's messages and the Democratic platform of 1944, which he had helped to formulate, as a guide to policies to be followed. His conservative advisers held that there was no need for a new message. They contended the course of wisdom was for him not to demand too much all at once. Some contemporary observers accused Truman of incompetency, straddling, indecisiveness, and stupidity.[39] He had tried to please all kinds of groups. His budget cuts and conservative appointments should please business. He had always stood by the farmers and organized workers. His strong support of OPA should please the consumers.

Apparently one of the events that rankled the new President was the charge of the Hearst papers that he was a conservative and that he had been taken into the conservative camp.[40] This aroused the ire of the President, who always had regarded himself as a New Dealer. He would show the critics where he really stood.[41] Another thought that rankled was the accusation that he had no policies of his own. He was characterized as a follower, not a leader.[42] He would show the world that he could step forward and proclaim his own program.

Truman did not have enough experience to anticipate who might be alienated by such a performance, and his press secretary, Charlie Ross, did not have the insight to warn him of the consequences. He had no adviser at this time whom he trusted on such matters and whose advice had proved sound. His impulse was to assert himself. Although he did not think highly of himself as president, he thought highly of the office. He had seen Roosevelt send such messages. He would act in the way he thought the incumbent should act. As he put it in his *Memoirs*, he was going to show them that he was president in his own right.[43]

Judge Rosenman was the chief architect of the message. While they were returning from Potsdam, the President asked him to prepare a draft as soon as they had finished the message on the Potsdam conference. Rosenman was elated by the assignment because to him it meant that Truman was not taken in by the conservatives and that there would be a continuation of the New Deal, on which he had worked for over twelve years. He attacked the task with great enthusiasm and came up with a draft incorporating the programs that Truman had told him to put in it.[44] President Truman read it but apparently he did not have the knack that President Roosevelt had of editing such drafts.

Director of OWMR John Snyder was opposed to the message. He thought that it was too liberal, that it promised too much, that it was unrealistic considering the conservative character of the Congress and the alliance between the Republicans and southern Democrats, that it would lead to frustration, that the President would be accused of asking for more than he knew he could get, that he would be accused of insincerity, that his legislative record would be called a failure, and that the presidential image would be harmed. Snyder did his best to dissuade the President from sending it. Truman thanked him for his advice.[45] He wanted all shades of opinion among those close to him. He believed Snyder was sincere. But he also believed in his own liberal philosophy and would take a chance on his reputation.

In his *Memoirs*, Truman states that he also called in Clark Clifford, John Steelman, Charlie Ross, and several other advisers.[46] There is no question that he called in Ross, who had come on duty as press secretary on May 15.[47] Clifford was assistant to naval aide Vardaman at the time, but he had not yet been called in to aid Rosenman in general speech writing. As to Steelman, Truman's memory slipped here also. Steelman did not come to the White House until the fall of 1945. The President never met him until then. Clifford and Steelman were part of Truman's speech writing crew later on but not for this message.

Truman wrote that he also sent the proofs of the message to the various agencies and the cabinet members for comments. From this it can be inferred that Anderson, Hannegan, Wallace, Vinson, Clark, Schwellenbach, and Ickes were favorably impressed. The published *Forrestal Diaries* do not comment on this subject, although there is a discussion of later messages that followed.[48] Secretary of State Byrnes was busy with the council of foreign ministers and did not comment on this message in his *All in One Lifetime*.[49] Stimson was in the process of resigning.

President Truman did get some sound criticism of the speech from Budget Director Smith, which apparently he did not follow closely. Smith recorded in his diary:

I told the President that I was concerned about the draft which I had seen. I felt that the message was too long, that it covered too many subjects, and that it had not been carefully digested. . . .

I then gave him some examples of what I had in mind. I pointed out that the message dealt with the request that he had already made to the Congress for reorganization legislation, and that this part was good as it stood. However, in other parts of the message there were indications of how the President would dispose of the Employment Service, the extent to which he would use the War Powers Act in connection with certain reorganization proposals, and so forth. I stated that I felt that these other parts were quite inconsistent with the request for general reorganization authority, and that if the President showed his hand with respect to some of these possible actions, he might very well jeopardize the passage of the reorganization bill. The President commented that he had not thought of the matter in this light and he felt that I had a good point.

Also, I mentioned the danger in connection with his proposed statements on public works, as well as some other subjects. I indicated that if we were not quite cautious, the Government would be launched prematurely on a public works program, although such a program probably would not be needed until a later time when many of the consumer wants had been satisfied.[50]

On September 6, President Truman sent his famous twenty-one-point message to Congress, and it was read by the reading clerks in both houses. He did not want to read it in person because it was so long, approximately sixteen thousand words. It was a mistake for Truman not to read it in person because the attendance in the two houses was small when it was read.[51] Of course, each member of Congress had a printed copy on his desk.

The message started by outlining eight reconversion policies for the reestablishment of expanded peacetime industry, trade, and agriculture: demobilize the armed forces rapidly, settle war contracts, convert war plants to peacetime production, hold the line on prices and rents, hold wages in line, remove all possible wartime controls, keep only those controls helpful to reconversion, and prevent rapid decrease of wage incomes.[52]

The famous twenty-one points in summary form were: (1) unemployment compensation supplementation, (2) Fair Labor Standards Act, (3) cautious removal of wartime controls, (4) authorization of executive agencies' reorganization, (5) full employment, (6) permanent Fair Employment Practices Committee, (7) labor dispute and wage stabilization, (8) temporary extension of U.S. Employment Service, (9) support of agriculture by crop insurance and development of exports, (10) Selective Service, (11) housing, (12) scientific research, (13) transition tax revision, (14) single administrator for surplus property disposal, (15) small business, (16) veterans' benefits, (17) public works and natural resources, (18) postwar reconstruction abroad, (19) increase in congressional, executive, and judicial salaries, (20) sale of surplus ships, and (21) stockpiling of strategic materials.[53]

The program received a mixed reception. Liberals and lower-income groups hailed it as a continuation of the New Deal. Minority and underprivileged groups were heartened by the emphasis on FEPC, higher minimum wages, extension of unemployment benefits, the promise of full employment, and low-rent housing. Farmers were assured of continued benefits, and small businessmen were told that they would not be forgotten during reconversion. Here was the beginning of Truman's Fair Deal. On the other hand, many points in the program alarmed the conservatives, especially those in the South. FEPC was particularly troubling to them. Speaker Sam Rayburn told his biographer that this proposal would be buried in committee.[54] The speech was Keynesian in tone. There was no mention of a balanced budget. Instead there would be spending to secure full employment, to subsidize farmers, to underwrite low-rental housing, to build more TVAs to compete with private utilities, to satisfy veterans' demands, and, worst of all as far as the isolationists were concerned, to prop up the shaky economies of other countries. Uncle Sam was about to become Santa Claus to the world. Southern Democrats and Republicans could easily unite in determined opposition to these points in the program.

Some conservative thinkers did not take the program seriously. *Nation's Business* commented: "A neat and scholarly catalogue of current pressures, group aims, ambitions, visions; but it was not offered as a legislative program, is not so accepted on the Hill."[55] This magazine took the point of view that Speaker Rayburn did on FEPC: the new president was letting Congress play its role in the American system. The twenty-one points were rhetoric, and Congress would do nothing, or at least not much, about them.

No language in the message could be regarded as a bitter attack on capitalism. Truman in his 1937 Senate speech had excoriated big business in harsh terms, but this message was conciliatory in tone.[56] Arthur Krock of the *New York Times* wrote:

No message from a Republican Chief Executive at the peak of the country's acceptance of capitalism ever contained more favorable words for the free enterprise system, or expressions of confidence in the wish and ability of American industry to create the full production and employment which he holds essential to successful reconversion and enduring national prosperity.[57]

To the Republicans the message was a clear indication that Truman's honeymoon period with Congress was over. They could now attack this partisan president. House Minority Leader Joseph Martin of Massachusetts said, "Not even President Roosevelt ever asked for as much at one sitting. The scenery is new and there is a little better decoration, and he [Truman] does dish it out a little easier. But it is just a plain case of out-New Dealing the New Deal."[58]

Minority Whip Charles Halleck of Indiana joined his colleague, remarking, "For the Democrats, it is just more billions and more bureaus."[59] Truman's speech was the Democrats' first volley in the 1946 congressional campaign. The Republicans confidently felt that opinion was on their side. The postwar reaction against executive power, big government spending, and economic restraints would sweep them in just as it had in 1918 and 1920 following World War I.

President Truman followed up his September 6 message with some six special messages on different subjects during the balance of the session. On October 3, he sent a message on peacetime uses of atomic energy and the need for civilian control of its uses and also one on the St. Lawrence-Great Lakes seaway.[60] On October 23, he personally urged Congress to adopt a program of universal military training.[61] The next month he presented his controversial national health program calling for federal aid to hospital construction, expansion of compulsory social insurance to cover medical expenses, and use of federal funds to help needy persons to get medical care. This proposal started a long and bitter struggle with the American Medical Association.[62] On December 3, he appealed to Congress to establish fact-finding boards to investigate labor disputes during a thirty-day cooling-off period, during which strikes would be outlawed.[63] Finally, he asked for legislation unifying the armed services into a single defense department.[64]

At first President Truman did not press Congress to act on his program, but in October he made his cabinet members and agency heads responsible for contacting Congress regarding proposals that fell within their jurisdiction. Curiously, John Snyder, who had opposed the program, was asked to coordinate these activities. He selected Secretary of the Treasury Vinson to head a cabinet committee on full employment legislation. Bailey in his history of the bill relates how Snyder faltered in his testimony before the House committee and did more harm than good.[65]

Congress was slow to act on Truman's recommendations, and he increased his pressure on that body. He became critical of delays and in a radio address urged the people to contact their congressmen on behalf of his program. He began to call in key members of committees bottling up his bills and give them stern lectures. In the case of the full employment bill, when the lecture did not work, he made certain concessions.[66] In a strongly worded veto message of a $51 billion appropriation rescission, he excoriated the rider providing that the U.S. Employment Service would be decentralized and returned to the states within one hundred days.[67] In a press conference he complained that reconversion had become a "political football in Congress." On the full employment bill he made the following identical plea to Senator Wagner and Congressman Carter Manasco: "No bill which provides substantially less than the Senate version can efficiently accomplish the purposes intended. I urge the conferees to support the essential characteristics of the Full Employment Bill as contained in the legislation adopted by the Senate."[68]

THE SECOND SESSION

President Truman decided to combine his first State of the Union and his first budget messages for the second session. The result was the longest message ever sent to Congress and it took over two hours for the clerks to read it on January 21, 1946.[69] In preparing this message, Truman had the help of his cabinet officers, the staff of the Bureau of the Budget, and his special counsel, Samuel Rosenman, who had helped him prepare his twenty-one point message the preceding September.[70] This was Rosenman's last task before he resigned and Clark Clifford took over in his place.

The message repeated the twenty-one points, which were based on the belief that the government should keep the economy competitive and help achieve full production and full employment. Truman especially stressed the need for a loan to Great Britain, extension of selective service, and a permanent national housing agency. And he requested the following new legislation: increased self-government for Puerto Rico and the Virgin Islands and statehood for Alaska and Hawaii, extension of the War Powers Act beyond June 30, 1946, improvement of the social security system, federal grants to state educational systems, extension of price controls, and continuation of subsidies to farmers in order to keep food prices down and farm income up. Complaints were made in and outside Congress that the message was too long and that it did not contain much that was new, but favorable comments were made regarding the appeal for a balanced budget.

For the control of the economy, the President used his budget message with its estimates for appropriations, its recommendations for taxes, and its forecast of a surplus or a deficit.[71] He also used the Treasury policies on debt funding and monetary affairs and the borrowing power of many executive agencies. As a senator, Truman had been interested in the budget. Upon becoming president, he recognized at once the importance of this instrument of administrative control. The budget for fiscal year 1946 was already in the mill. With the end of the war, the big job was the rescinding of unneeded appropriations.[72] In view of subsequent history, this was done too precipitously, as was the demobilization of the troops. The end of World War II did not bring an end to the need for military preparedness.[73]

Truman's first budget was the one for fiscal year 1947. It projected a cutback in federal expenditures from the $67.4 billion estimated for fiscal 1946 to $35.9 billion. He estimated that the 1945 tax reductions would produce a deficit of around $4.3 billion, which would be met out of the Treasury's cash balance. He assumed "generally favorable business conditions but not on an income reflecting full employment and the high productivity that we hope to achieve. . . . The still extraordinarily large expenditures in the coming year and continuing inflationary pressures" precluded his recommending any further tax reductions.[74]

In the postwar period, the size of the defense budget has been a continuous source of contention. Involved in determining this were a series of assumptions that events later challenged. It was assumed that demobilization could proceed rapidly without endangering American security, that with an American monopoly of the means of nuclear warfare outlays for other types of military hardware could be reduced, that the American people would not support a large armed force and greatly increased military expenditures in peacetime, and that the American economy could not sustain a huge military budget. Among Truman's advisers these assumptions were strongly held by his budget directors, his treasury chiefs, and his economic advisers during the first five years of his administration. Secretary of the Navy Forrestal was among the most outstanding advocates of a higher military budget. He reflected the demands of the military professionals and the armaments industries for ever more expensive weapons systems.[75] Secretary Byrnes would have liked a stronger military establishment to back up his bargaining in foreign policy negotiations, but he was unwilling to ask President Truman to launch the campaign that this would have required.[76] In this situation the conservative fiscal advisers won out with Truman; the military budget for fiscal year 1947 was only $11.8 billion out of a total budget of $39.2 billion.

In the fight against inflation, Truman failed to back up the liberals who were carrying the brunt of this battle—men such as Chester Bowles, price administrator and later economic stabilizer, and Robert Nathan, planner in the OWMR—and listened instead to the conservative counsel of John Snyder, who replaced Vinson as head of OWMR and later as secretary of the treasury.[77] With the removal of price controls and allocation powers, inflation ran rampant, and there was a severe shortage of consumer goods.

In early 1946, a clash occurred between Bowles and Snyder. Bowles wanted to hold down the price of steel, but Snyder, who was then director of OWMR, overruled Bowles in favor of the steel companies. Bowles wrote to Truman on January 24, 1946, outlining his concern, concluding:

> It is not yet too late to re-establish the integrity of our efforts, but it is rapidly becoming too late. . . . If you make it clear to the responsible officials of the government that a firm anti-inflation program must promptly be substituted for the present policy of retreat, I believe that the government can ride successfully through this crisis and emerge with its prestige enormously enhanced. Otherwise, the stabilization policy will, I believe, progressively disintegrate.[78]

Truman took no action to uphold Bowles, and the stabilization policy disintegrated as this letter forecast. Bowles was about to resign, and the President realized there was a crisis in the battle against inflation.[79] Truman used Bernard Baruch and James Byrnes as his representatives in trying to convince Bowles to stay on in the administration—this time as director of the Office of Economic Stabilization (OES), with Paul Porter as price administrator.[80] Bowles agreed to accept this widened responsibility, but when Congress emasculated the stabilization program, Bowles resigned from OES on June 28, 1946. In his letter of resignation, he wrote:

I have participated in the fight to keep down the cost of living for four and one-half years. The great majority of our people, who understand clearly the gigantic issues which are involved, have given me their wholehearted support. . . . However, a few bitter opponents of price and rent control have claimed that I am personally anxious to extend these essential controls indefinitely and unnecessarily. The announcement of my resignation at this time, effective July 10th, will eliminate any vestige of doubt as to my own position and further sharpen the grave issue which Congress must face in the next 72 hours, in the event of your veto.[81]

Truman wrote a laudatory letter in reply expressing his deep regret at Bowles's leaving the government in spite of the fact that he had not supported his champion in the battle against inflation.[82]

The price control bill that was finally passed in June so weakened the program recommended that Truman vetoed the measure, to the dismay of the congressional leaders who were unable to override the veto. This meant the lapse of all controls. The price increases were so steep and the outcries of consumers so loud that after twenty days, Congress passed a new compromise bill, which Truman reluctantly signed. The damage to the economy had been done, and it was very difficult to reassemble the machinery that had been dismantled. The new controls did not work well.

Labor-Management Relations

Throughout his political career, Truman had been cultivating organized labor. As a senator, Truman had voted for legislation backed by organized labor. During the months that the war was still on, there were no prolonged labor crises. The powers of the National War Labor Board, based as they were on a no-strike pledge on the part of organized labor and backed up by the power of the government to seize plants under the Smith-Connally Act, were sufficient to meet most wartime labor crises. Work stoppages were only intermittent and on a small scale. For all practical purposes, collective bargaining was suspended, and the NWLB acted as a compulsory arbitration board.[83] In April 1945 a strike of hard-coal miners belonging to John L. Lewis's United Mine Workers (UMW) disrupted coal production needed for the war effort.[84] After the strikers ignored the NWLB order requiring resumption of work, President Truman issued an executive order directing Secretary of the Interior Ickes to take over the mines.[85] Truman, in this first confrontation with Lewis, had the powers to solve the crisis.

The end of the war changed the economic situation and brought on the problem of labor-management relations. Labor unions were no longer willing to submit to voluntary restraints. Business wanted to keep wage controls but not price fixing. Consumers complained about rationing, a lack of goods, and high prices. Farmers wanted high price supports for agricultural production and lower prices for the things they had to buy. Truman tried to play the game of consensus politics by distributing the benefits as widely as possible and holding the shaky coalition together as much as possible. But the President had to preach continued sacrifices until reconversion began to supply the needed consumer goods. The various pressure groups were impatient, however, and Truman's popularity began to plummet.

On August 18, 1945, Truman modified wartime wage controls by an executive order permitting wage increases without government approval, provided such increases were not used to secure increases in price ceilings. The order also allowed the NWLB to approve wage increases, even if they meant price increases, provided they were needed to correct inequities. The President placed great hopes in a Labor-Management Conference that met in November, but it failed to reach agreement on the need for wage increases and upon machinery to prevent strikes after collective bargaining had failed.[86] At the end of the year, Truman issued an executive order abolishing NWLB and establishing the National Wage Stabilization Board (NWSB), which had far fewer powers and was greatly weakened by the lapse of price controls.[87]

Truman's actions in the labor field were ineffective in preventing labor strife. The loss of man-days due to strikes was four times higher in 1945 than in 1944, and most of these strikes occurred after V-E Day. Serious work stoppages occurred in electrical, packinghouse, steel, automobile, soft coal, hard coal, and maritime industries.[88] While the power of the government to seize plants lasted, some of these strikes were settled by the government's taking over the companies and negotiating wage increases, which usually resulted in price increases.[89] For instance, in the case of the strike against the petroleum refineries, the President issued an executive order authorizing the secretary of the navy to take possession of and operate the refineries until a wage settlement was reached.[90] The oil companies accepted the government's proposal, and the strike was settled.[91] The public was becoming more and more incensed at organized labor, which was holding up reconversion for its own hopes for benefits. Actually the wage earners were the greatest sufferers, since they lost their income during the strikes. Management made up its losses by increased sales when production was resumed. In settling labor disputes, Truman relied upon John R. Steelman, the assistant to the President. His secretary of labor was too closely identified with labor interests to play this role. During his many years as a labor-management mediator, Steelman had tried to conciliate both labor and management. He was a listening post for labor, management, and the fraternity of private arbitrators and labor relations experts. He was also the President's chief adviser on appointments in the labor field and was active in the actual negotiation of disputes that reached the White House.[92]

In 1946 labor strife reached new high levels, with a total of 103 million man-days lost. Truman's plan for fact-finding boards did not meet the approval of either labor or management. Labor thought the boards were too close to being compulsory arbitration boards, and management did not want to reveal its profit and loss figures. In the settlement of disputes, Truman took a firm stand against labor's view that it could strike any industry regardless of how disastrous a stoppage might be for the country as a whole. The most serious clash came in the railroad strike of May 1946.[93]

One of the most controversial special messages Truman delivered before Congress was the one of May 25, 1946, urging legislation for industrial peace in connection with the railroad strike, which was in its second day in defiance of the government seizure of the lines.[94] He was alarmed at the thought of the damage to the country and to the people dependent upon American food supplies that a prolonged rail strike might inflict. His first draft of a speech requesting strikebreaking authority was so strident that his press secretary, Charlie Ross, refused to have it typed and persuaded the President to have Clark Clifford rewrite it.[95] Clifford did an excellent job in toning it down and at the same time keeping it tough.[96] As in the radio address to the public given night before, the special message to Congress singled out Alvanley Johnston, president of the Brotherhood of Locomotive Engineers, and A. F. Whitney, president of the Brotherhood of Railway Trainmen, as responsible by their obstinate arrogance for the crisis.[97] Truman asked for power to draft railwaymen into the army if the strike continued. In the meantime, John Steelman was negotiating to end the strike. In the middle of the speech, Leslie Biffle, secretary of the Senate, handed Truman a note that the strike had been settled.[98] The President so informed Congress and continued his speech.

The Republicans and private business managers in general applauded the message, but organized labor denounced it. In addition, some congressmen thought that it was staged for dramatic effect; they believed that Truman knew in advance that the strike was settled. Labor leader Whitney, who had supported Truman in his 1940 bid for renomination and reelection as senator, was so incensed that he pledged his union's funds of $47 million to defeat Truman in 1948. William Green and Philip Murray, other heads of organized labor, were also bitter in their denunciation of the proposal. Truman insisted that he was a friend of labor and not opposed to strikes against private industry, but he could not tolerate a strike against the government that would paralyze the country.[99] While the House passed the drastic bill for ending the railway strike in May by an overwhelming majority, the Senate, following the leadership of Senator Taft, refused to endorse the House version. Taft argued that the House bill was unconstitutional and that it gave the President too much power.[100] The two houses then passed the antistrike Case bill, which Truman vetoed on the ground that it was too antilabor.[101] The House failed to override the veto by the narrow margin of five votes. Truman's labor record thus was mixed.

Demobilization of Nonwhites

Before President Roosevelt died, it was clear that the postwar position of blacks and other nonwhites in America would not be the same as in the prewar era. Race relations were changing drastically during the war.

Upon becoming president, Truman tried to follow in Roosevelt's footsteps as far as civil rights measures were concerned. The black vote had been won over to the Democratic party largely by the New Deal welfare programs designed to help the poor. While Roosevelt benefited greatly from the black vote in his last three presidential elections, he refused to take steps on behalf of blacks that he thought would alienate southern whites. He issued the Fair Employment Practices Committee executive order in 1941 only to avoid a threatened march on Washington by black workers. He never advocated the passage of civil rights or voting rights legislation. Some executive departments—the War Department and the Department of the Interior were two—had black advisers to help avoid racial friction. During the Roosevelt administration, the delicate balance was maintained between the growing demands and expectations of black people and the stubborn southern resistance to changes in the dogma and practice of white supremacy and segregation. Truman did not want to disturb this balance, but circumstances of demobilization and reconversion were to compel him to do so if he wished to retain political power. During his first four months, the demands for change were not pressing.[102]

Truman soon began to realize that the balance between whites and blacks in the northern cities that held in Roosevelt's time was changing and that the returning black veterans were not going to be satisfied with conditions as they left them. Like Roosevelt, Truman wanted to win the black vote without losing the support of southern whites, who were of importance in Congress and in the electoral college. His formula was a simple one: make a strong verbal appeal for civil rights legislation, such as a permanent FEPC, but do little to antagonize the bill's opponents. The hope was that blacks would be appeased by rhetoric and welfare programs.

On civil rights legislation, President Truman was cautious at first and went no further than Roosevelt had gone.[103] A bill to establish a permanent Fair Employment Practice Commission, to take the place of a committee set up in 1941 by executive order, had been reported out by the House Labor Committee on February 20 but was blocked by the Rules Committee, which was dominated by southern Democrats. On June 5, 1945, Truman sent a letter to Congressman Adolph J. Sabath (Ill.) of the House Rules Committee concerning the bottling up of this bill and urging the Rules Committee to adopt a rule permitting a vote so that the principle and policy of fair employment practice regardless of race, creed, or color could be upheld.[104]

The opposition of the southern Democrats to such legislation was adamant. The Rules Committee chairman was favorable, but his southern colleagues blocked every move. The principle of FEPC was also challenged by the southern Democrats when the funds for the temporary committee came up for consideration. In the House the southern Bourbons eliminated the funds for this purpose. The Senate, however, restored less than half of the funds, and the House agreed to this reduced appropriation, which expired in a year. It was hardly a great victory in the fight against discrimination on account of race.[105] During the second session of the Seventy-ninth Congress, the President was no more successful in getting Congress to act on civil rights legislation.

During 1946 a number of racial murders in the South upset Truman's attempt to please both sides of the civil rights question. In September 1946, a group of nationally prominent liberals organized as the National Emergency Council Against Mob Violence pressed upon the President the need for action.[106] At the suggestion of his administrative assistant on minority groups, David K. Niles, Truman appointed a committee to investigate federal, state, and local law enforcement procedures and to recommend ways of strengthening "current law enforcement measures . . . to safeguard the civil rights of the people." By executive order, he established on December 5, 1946, the Civil Rights Committee, headed by Charles Wilson, then president of General Electric, with Professor Robert Carr as executive secretary. Educators, unionists, blacks, and liberals were represented on this committee, which soon issued an epoch-making report.[107]

Agricultural Reconversion

The fears of the farmers that with the end of the war the demand for agricultural products would fall off and they would be faced with surpluses and declining prices were unfounded. The end of the war soon brought the realization that there was a world food crisis, and the United States was in the best position of any other country to help ease this crisis. The farmers who should have been encouraged to engage in maximum production were not pressed to do so by Secretary of Agriculture Anderson, who failed to realize that there was no world surplus of food and that inflation of food prices, not deflation, was the danger.[108] Price administrator Bowles, on the other hand, correctly pointed out the nature of the problem. This brought him in conflict with Anderson, who was more concerned with the demands of the commercial farmers than he was with the needs of consumers at home and abroad. The first battle came over the retention of food rationing. Bowles advised Truman that it was needed until increased production brought down food prices, but Anderson won this fight, and food rationing was abandoned.[109] He was to regret this later when there were meat shortages.

In early 1946 Anderson was finally made aware of the worldwide food crisis and the inadequacy of American food production to meet it. He urged increased food prices as a means of stimulating farm production. At first, Bowles was able to halt this move and urged subsidies to keep prices down. It was found that these subsidies would not work without rationing, and in view of the public climate, it was extremely difficult to reestablish rationing. When President Truman vetoed the weakened price control bill, a period of no controls followed. Food prices soared and meat production reached new highs as farmers rushed their animals to market to take advantage of the high prices.[110] Congress then passed a modified bill, weak but better than nothing, and the President signed it. An attempt to restore meat controls resulted in greatly diminished supplies of meat as farmers withheld animals from the market in a move to abolish price controls. The meat shortage turned the public against OPA, which had been popular with housewives and labor. Truman held conferences on the crisis and tried to hold the line, but pressures were too great and he abandoned controls. Anderson won the battle against the stabilization program, thus helping to stimulate inflation. Again Truman had been wrong, and the public suffered.

Full Employment Legislation

Before Congress convened, President Truman in a radio talk on January 3, 1946, urged the conference committee of the two houses considering two versions of a full employment bill to agree upon the Senate version, which was more liberal.[111] The bill passed by the House had eliminated the word *full* from the title, had weakened the government's role in providing employment, and had established in place of the cabinet an independent Council of Economic Advisers composed of three members, appointed by the President by and with the consent of the Senate, who would formulate and recommend national economic policy. Upon the urging of Secretary of the Treasury Vinson, Truman had agreed to a compromise with the House leaders in the hope that the conference committee would turn to the Senate version. In his message to Congress of January 21, he repeated his preference for the Senate version.[112] He failed, however, to follow up this recommendation with concrete proposals. Vinson prepared a draft for the conference committee, which Truman referred to John Snyder, chief of the Office of War Mobilization and Reconversion, who in turn pigeonholed it although Truman had given him responsibility for pushing it through. The committee and its staff worked out a compromise by which the federal government undertook to promote maximum employment by means of all of its functions and resources.[113] The compromise measure passed as the Employment Act of 1946, and the President signed it on February 20, 1946. Both liberals and conservatives claimed victory, interpreting the language in different ways. The law did provide for a new mechanism, the Council of Economic Advisers, which has become an important part of the executive establishment. Truman obtained less than he had hoped for, but he felt that the law still retained the essentials of his original proposal.[114]

Atomic Energy

Another bill carried over from the previous session that Truman was anxious to see passed was the Senate bill on atomic energy. As far back as his statement of August 6, 1945, announcing the use of the atom bomb at Hiroshima, President Truman said he would recommend that Congress establish a commission to control the production and use of atomic power within the United States. He did so in a special message on October 3, 1945.[115] He proposed that total control of "the use and development of atomic energy" be vested in an Atomic Energy Commission, which would take over all existing facilities from the military, acquire minerals, conduct research for peaceful as well as military uses, license others to perform research, and establish security regulations.

In the House, Congressman Andrew May of Kentucky, chairman of the House Military Affairs Committee, introduced a bill drafted by the War Department that called for a nine-member, part-time commission, with powers to select a full-time administrator, whom the military officers hoped would be one of them. Hearings on the bill raised the issue of civilian versus military control of the commission, scientists arguing for civilian control in opposition to the military.

Senator Edwin C. Johnson of the Senate Military Affairs Committee introduced a companion to the May bill, but the Senate decided to set up its own special committee on the subject under Senator Brien McMahon of Connecticut who introduced a bill placing the control in civilian hands, a proposal more to the liking of President Truman.[116] Senator McMahon pointed out that "military control of atomic energy, though necessary and useful during war, is a form of direction to which scientists in peacetime will not willingly submit."[117] Truman strongly supported the McMahon bill in a letter of February 1, 1946, to Senator McMahon. A heated debate in the House on the civilian-military issue followed the consideration of the Senate bill. The Republicans, alarmed by the Canadian disclosure of Soviet spying on nuclear activities, objected to government monopoly and patent provisions and the lack of adequate security safeguards. Many amendments to the Senate bill were passed in the House. As finally coming out of the conference committee and passing both houses, the Atomic Energy Act of 1946 gave full control over all materials, facilities, production, and research to the Atomic Energy Commission, composed of five civilians named by the president and confirmed by the Senate.[118] Also created by the act were the

Military Liaison Committee, a compromise insisted on by the House, the General Advisory Committee on Scientific Matters, and the Joint Committee on Atomic Energy of the House and Senate to act as a congressional watchdog on all developments in the field. The new law ensured civilian control of atomic energy activities in the United States, but it did not facilitate international control of nuclear fission, which was encountering trouble in the United Nations.[119]

Housing

The subject of housing was one of the special legislative interests of the White House. Truman stated in his *Memoirs* that he regarded housing as one of the most pressing postwar problems confronting him because of a prewar housing deficit, the suspension of construction of dwelling units during the war, the greatly increased number of marriages, and the desire of returning veterans for decent housing.[120] To carry out his emergency housing program, Truman had created the position of housing expediter in the Office of War Mobilization and Reconversion and had appointed Wilson Wyatt, the dynamic mayor of Louisville, Kentucky, to the job. Congress already had before it a comprehensive national housing bill sponsored by Senators Wagner, Taft, and Allen J. Ellender, which had passed the Senate but which was blocked in the House by Jesse P. Wolcott of Michigan, the senior Republican on the House Banking and Currency Committee and a bitter foe of all public-housing legislation. Wilson Wyatt said that the bill was killed by "very potent private lobby groups" that were strongly opposed to the resumption of public housing. The Veterans' Emergency Housing Act, however, was passed during this session, providing for price ceilings on new homes for veterans and aids to producers of building materials for veterans' housing.

DEMOBILIZATION AND RECONVERSION: A SUMMARY

What went wrong? President Truman wanted to hold the line against inflation, but he failed to do so. Food prices soared, and so did the prices of other consumer goods. Truman listened to the wrong advisers. Secretary Snyder's counsel was almost always poor as far as Truman's avowed stabilization aims were concerned. Chester Bowles gave good advice, but it was overruled. Truman should have hung on to price and rationing controls until the consumer industries were in full production. The stabilization machinery was complicated, and once it was dismantled, it was difficult to reassemble it in order to hold down spiraling prices. When Truman tried to reimpose controls, he was confronted with a recalcitrant Congress. The combined strength of the southern Democrats and the Republicans was sufficient to block efforts at liberal legislation. After 1937, even President Roosevelt had been unable to move this stubborn bloc of conservatives. Truman tried at first to conciliate Congress, but his efforts failed. He was soon the target of bitter attacks by opposition legislators.

On the food crisis, Truman was mistaken in relying upon Secretary Anderson, who reflected the point of view of prosperous farmers and was slow to recognize the worldwide food shortage. Chester Bowles furnished sound advice, but it was not heeded and Congress was not cooperative.

On labor-management relations, Truman acted too hastily in removing wartime controls, and he failed to press soon enough for labor legislation that would help ease discord in the labor field. Moreover Congress was not receptive to his ideas on labor matters.

In the United States, except in times of emergency and under skillful presidential leadership, the legislative processes are slow and cumbersome. In this century, there are only three occasions when a president has secured swift legislative action. These were Woodrow Wilson's experience with the first session of the Sixty-third Congress, Franklin Roosevelt's with the first session of the Seventy-third Congress, and Lyndon B. Johnson's with the first session of the Eighty-ninth Congress. In the first two cases, a new and charismatic leader brought in a fresh program when he and his party came to power, displacing the opposition. In the third case, an outstanding legislative leader came to the presidency with a huge party majority behind him.

President Truman's situation was quite different from these three. He did not have a huge party majority in both houses of Congress. There was no recognized crisis that seemed to demand emergency powers. (Actually, there was an inflation crisis, but it was not yet evident to Congress and the public.) Finally, Truman did not have the outstanding qualities of legislative leadership possessed by Wilson, Roosevelt, or Johnson. He had not been a Senate leader as had Johnson. He lacked the eloquence and flaming idealism of Wilson. His plebeian manner was in sharp contrast to that of the glamorous Roosevelt of the golden voice and sparkling wit.

How can a president's legislative leadership be measured? How much time should be allowed for Congress to act on his recommendations? How closely should the final legislation resemble the original proposal? A tough measure would be how many proposals became law during the session in substantially the form presented by the executive.

Did Truman make a mistake in asking for too much too soon? Some contemporary observers thought so. Neustadt commented that "everything was put on the record fast, in a sort of laundry-listing of postwar requirements with little indication of priorities or emphasis," in an effort to rekindle the social outlook of the New Deal and to remind all of the "continuity between the new national leadership and the old."[121] It was Truman's way of reaffirming his own economic and political philosophy, of showing that he had a mind of his own, and of finding out who his real supporters were. Whereas the New Deal was breaking new ground, the Fair Deal was attempting to find ways to satisfy the demand for its consolidation and development.

That the accomplishments of the Truman leadership were not greater during the Seventy-ninth Congress was the product of the peculiar ways of Congress, the seniority rule for committee chairmanships (which put conservative Democrats in key posts), the reactionary character of the Rules Committee, the lack of a national viewpoint among congressmen chosen from local districts, the lobbying strength of organized business, the conservative character of the two largest farm organizations, such powerful professional groups as the American Medical Association, the lobbying weakness of consumers and of minority and underprivileged groups, and the determined opposition of a combination of conservative Democrats, mostly from the South, and the Republicans.

Revisionist historians contend that during this period, President Truman displayed indecisiveness, inconsistent behavior, poor judgment, and a lack of leadership. Measured by such criteria as the relative number of strikes, the inflation spiral, the supply of needed products such as agricultural goods, and the acceptance of his domestic policies by the public, they regard his administration as a failure in these years. For how much of this record was Truman responsible? Some political scientists contend that Americans expect too much of their presidents. A president's powers are limited, and he should not be expected to work miracles. It is a mistake to say that Truman was indecisive. His top counselors all testified that he had the capacity to make decisions. To be sure, he sometimes made wrong decisions, often resulting from an overreliance on inadequate advisers. He also made some decisions too quickly. He inherited from Roosevelt a combination of conservative and liberal advisers. He recruited on his own both types and many in between. In trying to maintain a balance between the various forces, he made mistakes.

On the positive side, Congress, in addition to passing notable bills in the foreign field including the Bretton Woods Monetary Agreements, the Reciprocal Trade Agreements, the United Nations Charter, representation in the United Nations organization, the British loan, and additional aid to UNRRA, enacted the price control and stabilization extension, reorganizations of executive agencies, repeal of daylight saving time, the Armed Forces Voluntary Recruitment Act, tax reduction, appropriations rescission, amendments to veterans' legislation, a measure providing for national elections in the Philippines, atomic energy controls, surplus ship sales, a federal airport construction program, organization of surplus property disposal under a single administrator, to say nothing of passing appropriation bills amounting to more than $39 billion for the fiscal year 1946-1947.

President Truman achieved partial success in his requests for extension of the draft, price control, stockpiling of strategic materials, full employment, delay in returning the U.S. Employment Service to the states, a veterans' housing program, and funds for reclamation and power projects. The Senate adopted a resolution declaring that the United States would accept compulsory jurisdiction by the Court of International Justice and agreed to ratification of the convention of the International Civil Aviation Organization.

The administration backed some thirty-six measures, of which Congress passed eighteen in the original or modified form. Those regarded as most important were the Employment Act, the Atomic Energy Act, the Veterans' Emergency Housing Act, and, of course, the budget, which is paramount every year.

An analysis of the roll calls shows that the bipartisan alliance between the Republicans and the southern Democrats was largely responsible for the defeat or blocking of many presidential measures. In the House, forty-six southern rural congressmen consistently voted contrary to their party leader on domestic issues. On the other hand, only ten liberal Republicans could be counted upon by the northern Democrats. In both of the houses, the Democrats showed less party unity than the Republicans did. Two-thirds of the Republican senators voted with the majority of their party at least three-fourths of the time, while fewer than three-fifths of the Democratic senators did so. In the House, the ratios were five-sixths for the Republicans and less than three-sixths for the Democrats. Only on voting on foreign policy questions did the southern Democrats support the administration.

While Truman was more explicit in 1946 than in 1945 in urging Congress to pass legislation to carry out his program, he did not introduce specific bills, and he was willing to have Congress draft its own measures to solve the problems he outlined. He tried to maintain friendly relations with individual congressmen regardless of their opposition to his recommendations. Les Biffle, secretary of the Senate, continued to keep him informed regarding the course of legislation. The President held regular weekly meetings with the leaders of the two houses, and he paid high tribute to Senator Barkley at the dinner honoring the majority leader, even though he did not agree with Barkley's views on the Case and the price control bills. At a press conference on the day Congress adjourned, he showed irritation with Congress, but he denied that he blamed Congress for failing to follow his leadership, saying, "I blame conditions over which nobody really has any control."

chapter 23 | TEAM CHANGES, 1946–1948

The president is still one man, but he is also, like any man with a thousand helpers, an institution. Most of the wheels go round steadily whether he watches them or not. . . . One must be especially careful today in reading newspapers to distinguish among what he says for himself, what his aides say for him, and what his aides say for themselves.

—Clinton Rossiter, *The American Presidency*

CABINET LEVEL CHANGES

President Truman's hectic experiences during 1945 strengthened his conviction first formed from his experiences as chairman of the Senate Special Committee to Investigate the Defense Program that the U.S. diplomatic and military services needed reorganization and consolidation. He felt that lack of coordination among the Army, Navy, and State Departments was one of the conditions that had contributed to the disaster at Pearl Harbor.[1] When he was a candidate for vice-president, he had published an article in *Colliers*, "Our Armed Forces Must Be United."[2] In that year the War Department had presented a merger plan to Congress that proposed a unified department of defense. Bitter opposition to this plan by the navy had secured postponement of its consideration during the war.[3] Secretary of the Navy Forrestal realized when Truman became president that the Navy Department would have to present a substitute plan of its own if it wished to influence Truman's thinking on the subject. On June 19, 1945, Forrestal directed Ferdinand Eberstadt, former chairman of the Army-Navy Munitions Board, to make a study of the unification of the War and Navy Departments and of postwar relationships of military services and other government departments concerned with national security.[4] In September 1945 Eberstadt came up with a report recommending coordination rather than unification of the armed services, the establishment of a council of common defense, which included the State Department as well as the military departments, and provisions for improving intelligence and defense resources planning.[5] About the same time, the Senate Military Affairs Committee held heated hearings on a unification plan drafted by Lieutenant General J. Lawton Collins that was denounced by the navy spokesmen who were fearful that the navy would be eclipsed by the scheme.[6]

In spite of a warning from Postmaster General Hannegan that the army plan would invite an unnecessary fight in Congress, which might be lost, Truman said that he felt it was his duty to send a message on unification because it represented his strengthening conviction as he faced the conflicting demands of the services. Such a message was sent to Congress on December 19, 1945, calling for a single department of defense with a civilian head of cabinet status, who would coordinate the army, navy, and air forces.[7] The President wanted a secretary who would relieve him of the burden of integrating the policy-making and budgeting activities of these three branches of the military services. Under the secretary of defense would be a single chief of staff and commanders for each service, who would constitute an advisory council for the president and the secretary. The message also reflected the Eberstadt recommendations regarding cooperation between the military and diplomatic agencies in defense planning and in intelligence activities.[8]

This message did not bring an immediate solution. As a matter of fact, the navy spokesmen deeply resented it and felt that they were muzzled.[9] Before congressional committees, they still opposed it vigorously. On May 13, 1946, Truman asked the two sides "to identify their points of agreement and disagreement." Secretaries Patterson and Forrestal agreed to abandon the single chief of staff concept, but they still disagreed on the idea of a single department, the status of the three branches, the scope of naval aviation, and the future of the marine corps. In a letter of June 15 to the two secretaries and the congressional leaders concerned, Truman upheld the view of the War Department. With his assistant, Clark Clifford, the President held a White House conference in September at which negotiations were continued. No bill was passed before adjournment.[10]

On January 16, 1947, Secretaries Patterson and Forrestal advised the President that they had agreed on a compromise solution. Rear Admiral Forrest Sherman and Major General Lauris Norstad drafted a bill that, after some alterations suggested by Clifford and others in the White House, was submitted to the Republican Eightieth Congress. It was passed in July and became the National Security Act of 1947 upon being signed by the President.[11] As amended in 1949, the act established both the Department of Defense and the National Security Council, whose mission was to advise the president with respect to the integration of domestic, foreign, and military policies relating to national security. Richard Neustadt, onetime member of Truman's White House staff and later university professor, wrote: "It is no more than mild exaggeration to call NSC 'Forrestal's Revenge.'"[12] The secretary of defense was a cabinet officer, but the secretaries of the army, the navy, and the air force were not. Only a limited staff and limited powers were given to the new secretary. The act also placed the Central Intelligence Agency under the NSC and legalized the then informally organized Joint Chiefs of Staff. Truman had not secured the kind of unification he sought originally, but he had moved in the direction of his goal, the admirals were reconciled to this step, and he had demonstrated his ability as a compromiser.

The Central Intelligence Agency grew out of the experiences of the Office of Strategic Services under General William Donovan in World War II. It had engaged in clandestine intelligence operations in order to supplement the intelligence activities of the Department of State and the armed services. It also coordinated and analyzed incoming data from all sources and cooperated with the resistance forces behind enemy lines. One of President Truman's first problems in dealing with the Russians grew out of Allen Dulles's secret exchanges with the Nazi generals regarding the surrender of German forces in Italy.[13]

With the end of the war, the question arose as to what to do with the activities of the OSS. It was clear that the coordination and analysis of intelligence materials must be continued in view of the great postwar expansion of American international responsibilities. President Truman discussed this situation a number of times with budget director Smith.[14] Should these functions be lodged in the Department of State or the armed forces? It was decided to establish a separate civilian agency, the Central Intelligence Group, by executive order on January 20, 1946.[15] This group, renamed the Central Intelligence Agency, was transferred to NSC under the National Security Act of 1947. The chairman of NSC was the president, and thus Truman was closely in touch with the activities of the CIA, which included countering communist intelligence and espionage, coordinating all American intelligence activities, and planning worldwide activities for the protection of American security abroad. The CIA was to become one of the principal means the United States used in waging the cold war. Truman first appointed a navy man, Rear Admiral Roscoe Hillenkoetter, as CIA director. Relying on the provision of the National Security Act stating that the CIA could be empowered to perform "such other functions and duties related to intelligence affecting national security," the NSC on December 17, 1947, issued NSC-4-A authorizing Rear Admiral Hillenkoeter to conduct covert psychological operations in cooperation with the State and Defense Departments.[16] The first covert operations included clandestine radio and leaflet operations aimed at Soviet bloc nations. Later operations included secret aid to friendly elements seeking to counter communist subversive activities. The cover for such operations, which were closely linked with intelligence gathering, included labor, student, political, and other groups. The authorization came from the White House. One of Truman's "proudest accomplishments as President was the creation of CIA," wrote Margaret Truman.

He joked about it with Admiral Leahy and Rear Admiral Sidney W. Souers, the first CIA chief:

To My Brethren and Fellow Doghouse Denizens:
   By virtue of the authority vested in me as Top Dog I require and charge that Front Admiral William D. Leahy and Rear Admiral Sidney W. Souers, receive and accept the vestments and appurtenances of their respective positions, namely as personal snooper and as director of centralized snooping.[17]

The appointment of the first secretary of defense was a crucial matter in the implementation of the unification act. Somehow, the admirals had to be won over to the purpose of the act. Truman first tried to get Patterson to accept the post, but the last secretary of war was determined to retire to private life. Next, Truman turned to Forrestal, who had worked so diligently to get an act that the admirals could accept. Although Forrestal did not like Truman and thought him weak, his great sense of duty urged him to accept.[18] In his new position, however, he found that he lacked sufficient powers. From the standpoint of the admirals, his appointment eased the transition to the new order. The roles of the Department of Defense, the NSC, and the CIA were to evolve gradually. Forrestal was not anxious to centralize too rapidly and too drastically. Circumstances, frustrations, and the intensifying of the cold war compelled him to modify his earlier views on unification.[19]

Although the President presided over the NSC, he frequently did not appear so that the members would feel freer to express their views and so that he would not be committed to any recommendation that they might make. He wanted to reserve his right to make any final decisions. He welcomed advice but was determined to make his own decisions.[20]

No drastic reorganization of other cabinet and high level posts was undertaken during this period, although there was a turnover in every cabinet post except that of attorney general. Some of these cabinet changes were brought about in a manner that was damaging to the administration.

The resignation of Secretary of the Interior Harold L. Ickes took place under most unfortunate circumstances for the image of the President. Ickes was the last survivor of the original Roosevelt cabinet appointed in 1933 that had had continuous service since that time. He had threatened to resign during the Roosevelt years, but FDR had always talked him out of it. He was valuable because of his reputation for integrity and his power as an invective campaigner. Truman could have avoided losing this valuable cabinet officer if he had been more careful with his language. In the contest over the confirmation of Edwin Pauley, an oil magnate, for the position of under secretary of the navy, Truman was loyal to the wrong man. The way in which the departure of Ickes was brought about injured the Democratic party and soiled Truman's reputation.

Secretary Ickes was a most difficult person to get along with. He was highly sensitive, petty, cantankerous, proud of his record as "Honest Harold," and jealous of any infringement on his prerogatives. Truman obviously did not know how to handle him.

According to Truman's code, Ed Pauley was clearly entitled to political preferment. A key figure in the Truman nomination for vice-president in 1944, an energetic campaign fund raiser, a tireless organization leader in the crucial state of California surely deserved recognition for his faithful party services. The late President Roosevelt had discussed with Secretary Forrestal the possibility of Pauley's appointment as assistant secretary of the navy. Truman sent Pauley's name to the Senate for the position of under secretary of the navy.[21] Pauley was an aggressive defender of oil interests, and some eyebrows were raised when he was named to this post since the navy uses huge quantities of oil and had jurisdiction over vast oil reserves. The Teapot Dome oil scandals of the Harding administration showed the danger of appointing the wrong person to such a post. Yet Truman seemed to be aware of this aspect when he cautioned Ickes to go easy on Ed at the hearings. This was hardly the thing to say to Ickes.

Ickes had been petroleum administrator for war, and Pauley had served under him. At the Senate confirmation hearings in February 1946, Ickes was blunt. In testifying that Pauley had approached him in 1940 with "the rawest proposition ever made to me," he claimed that Pauley had exerted pressure on him to drop a suit to claim federal control of offshore tidelands oil fields. Pauley denied the accusation so the question came up as a direct clash. At his press conference of February 7, 1946, President Truman was questioned regarding the Pauley case. He insisted that Pauley was honest, was a capable administrator as shown by his performance as reparations director, and he, Truman, was backing Pauley. He added, "Mr. Ickes can very well be mistaken the same as the rest of us." Ickes responded by writing a lengthy letter of resignation to the President, who regarded it as discourteous. In this letter he stated that Truman's remark was, in effect, a declaration of no confidence. He expressed a willingness to stay on for six weeks to wind up his affairs, but Truman accepted his resignation effective the following day. Ickes went on the air to defend his conduct, and his farewell press conference was dramatic.[22]

In his *Memoirs* Truman defended his handling of the Pauley-Ickes affair on the ground that he had to maintain the power and dignity of the presidency. The net effect of the episode, however, was harmful to the office and his conduct of it. Pauley asked that his name be withdrawn because the senators were unfavorable. Truman's loyalty to Pauley accomplished nothing as far as Pauley was concerned. The President, however, lost the services of Ickes, a man whose devotion to the defense of the public interest he freely admitted was beyond question and whose standing with the liberals was high. At this time the Truman administration was losing status with the liberals. With a little more tact and less self-righteousness, Truman could have kept Ickes in the cabinet. Later developments, including the record of the man Truman named to replace Ickes, were to show that he needed men of curmudgeon caliber. If the President had had more men of Ickes's stature around him, the so-called Truman scandals might not have occurred.[23]

To replace Ickes, Truman chose Julius Albert Krug of Wisconsin, an engineer protégé of Bernard Baruch who had extensive government experience, three years with the Tennessee Valley Authority, and two years as chairman of the War Production Board. Krug lacked political experience, however, and he failed to live up to the standards set by his predecessor. He liked to make speeches, so he left the running of the department largely to Oscar Chapman, the under secretary, who had been with Ickes since 1933 and thus was thoroughly familiar with the programs run by the agency.[24]

The next change in the cabinet was in the Treasury Department. When the President in June 1946 appointed Secretary of the Treasury Fred Vinson to be chief justice of the United States Supreme Court, he lost one of his wisest cabinet advisers on domestic affairs.[25] In his place as secretary of the treasury, he appointed an old friend from Missouri, John W. Snyder, who unfortunately lacked the ability of his predecessor and was strongly oriented toward the protection of business. Snyder, like most other secretaries of the treasury, was a conservative restraining influence on the Truman administration. The President appeared to want to have all points of view represented on his cabinet. Snyder's sabotaging of the efforts to promote Truman's Fair Deal program did not bother the President, but it did agitate the liberals who were in favor of seeing the programs move forward.[26]

Like the Ickes case, the resignation of Secretary of Commerce Henry A. Wallace took place under circumstances that added little glory to the Truman administration. In this episode, Wallace lost his job, but he felt vindicated as he left the government.[27] He had previously written a long letter to the President explaining his views and his opposition to the direction that American foreign policy was taking. He had been asked by the Progressive Citizens of America to make a speech at the Madison Square Garden. The speech that he prepared called for a reversal of the "get tough with Russia" policy, for a repudiation of foreign reactionaries who were trying to provoke a war between the United States and the Soviet Union, for complete abandonment of the peoples of Eastern Europe, and for strengthening the United Nations rather than building regional alliances that might lead to war. The pro-Soviet bias of the Wallace speech is clear throughout. At points it repeats communist charges about British imperialism, totally ignoring the Soviet imperialism of this period that far exceeded British imperialism, which was receding rather than advancing. Wallace was accused of adopting the communist stance that the Soviet Union could not commit imperialist acts since its military aggressions on weaker nations were called liberation movements, which freed the farmers and workers from the clutches of economic fascists and exploiters. [28]

Wallace's adviser, C. B. Baldwin, told him that the only way he could get permission to make the speech would be to clear it personally with Truman himself since it dealt with foreign policy, which was outside the jurisdiction of the Department of Commerce. If the Department of State learned of it, they would surely veto it. Wallace set up the appointment with Truman for September 10, and the two discussed the Wallace speech. In his *Memoirs*, Truman states that he did not have time to read the speech. At his press conference of September 12, he did not repudiate a reporter who quoted Wallace's statement that he had read it. [29] Wallace's comment was that Truman did not understand it. He knew that the speech would precipitate an interdepartmental row, but that did not bother him. He was so convinced that he was right that he took the risk of damaging the Truman administration. Wallace was loyal to his convictions, not to the chief executive. He hoped that he might influence American foreign policy. If all he produced was confusion, he would not worry. Under any circumstances, Wallace felt compelled to speak out. Arthur Krock blames Wallace for not being frank about his objectives and for not resigning before he made the speech. Krock commented that Wallace did not have that kind of integrity. [30]

One thing seems clear: for political purposes, Truman wanted to keep Wallace in the cabinet. The secretary of commerce had a large following among liberals, trade unionists, farmers, and those friendly toward the Soviet Union. National chairman Hannegan had been urging Truman to appease Wallace. Why did Truman fall into a trap that was to defeat his political objectives? Contemporaries blamed him for ineptness, bumbling, prevarication, and stupidity. Presidents must protect themselves against such charges by surrounding themselves with competent assistants who will warn them of impending dangers. Ross failed to do this at the press conference of September 12. On the day the speech was to be delivered, Ross was warned of the unfortunate consequences, but he contended that it was too late to get Wallace to alter his speech. [31]

It appears that Truman had to learn from his mistakes. When Secretary Byrnes, in the midst of difficult negotiations with the Russians in Paris regarding the draft treaties with Italy and the Balkan states, learned of the Wallace speech and Truman's endorsement of it, he was stunned. [32] So were Senator Vandenberg and Republican adviser John Foster Dulles. [33] Soon the wires were busy and the air waves were saturated with hot exchanges. Was American foreign policy being changed? Byrnes's lengthy and scorching dispatch made Truman face the harsh reality of choosing between Byrnes and Wallace. From the political standpoint, he did not want to do this. He would have preferred to have them both stay on, and if one or the other had to go, it would be far better for the departure to be without such adverse publicity.

Another explanation of this episode is that Truman realized that the speech would not be popular with the anti-Russian elements. At a dinner at Clark Clifford's, he was reported as saying the speech might bring about a little trouble between Henry and Jimmy but that it could be straightened out.[34] For domestic reasons Truman felt it was necessary to let Wallace speak. It was a politician's straddle. He thought he could balance on top of the fence without falling off on either side. It was a gross miscalculation.

.In the speech, Wallace said, "I want one thing clearly understood. I am neither anti-British nor pro-British—neither anti-Russian or pro-Russian. And just two days ago, when President Truman read these words he said they represented the policy of his administration." Did Truman's approval apply only to this sentence? He could have saved himself some trouble if he had taken this stand, but at his press conference before the speech was delivered on September 12, he said specifically that he approved the entire speech.[35] After the furor, he acquired a reputation for distorting the truth when he denied that he had approved of Wallace's speech but merely had agreed to Wallace's expressing his own views. This explanation was not accepted by the press. Senator Vandenberg, who was advising Byrnes in Paris, said that he could not serve under two secretaries of state.

Wallace had promised after a long conference with Truman and Ross not to discuss foreign policy publicly, but on his way out of the White House, he talked to reporters about his views. Truman immediately asked for Wallace's resignation, which was granted. To his mother and sister, he wrote: "Well I had to fire Henry today, and of course I hated to do it. Henry Wallace is the best Secretary of Agriculture this country ever had unless Clint Anderson turns out as I think he will. If Henry had stayed Sec. of Agri. in 1940 as he should have, there'd never have been all this controversy, and I would not be here, and wouldn't that be nice? Charlie Ross said I'd shown I'd rather be right than President, and I told him I'd rather be anything than President."[36] At the urgent insistence of Clark Clifford, the White House clearance procedures were tightened.[37]

In Wallace's place, Truman brought in William Averell Harriman, a prominent businessman introduced to government service by Roosevelt during the National Recovery Administration days. Under Truman, Harriman had served as ambassador to the Soviet Union and as ambassador to Great Britain. He had been acquainted with the work of the Department of Commerce since 1933 when he began serving on the business advisory council for the department. He added strength to the cabinet since he was much better qualified to run the department than Wallace had been, and he had the respect of the business community. The one drawback to the appointment was that over the years he had become more interested in foreign than in domestic affairs. In less than two years he was glad to be released from the post to become roving ambassador for the Economic Cooperation Administration (ECA).[38]

On May 6, 1948, Truman appointed as secretary of commerce a wealthy businessman from Cincinnati, Ohio, Charles Sawyer, who had dabbled in Ohio politics. After being elected to the Cincinnati City Council, he ran unsuccessfully for mayor and then made an unsuccessful bid for Congress. Persisting, he was elected lieutenant governor in 1932. His attempts to win the governorship were failures. A modest campaign contributor, President Roosevelt appointed Sawyer ambassador to Belgium where Truman met him on his way to Potsdam in 1945. As secretary of commerce, Sawyer proved to be the most conservative and reactionary member of the cabinet.[39]

Robert Hannegan was finding his dual role as national democratic chairman and postmaster general too demanding for his failing health. Although he had done a good job in managing the 1944 presidential campaign, the adverse conditions facing the Democratic party in the congressional and state elections of 1946 were too much for him. He failed to discover how to stem the unfavorable tide running against his party.[40] Hannegan resigned as national chairman on October 29, 1947, and Senator J. Howard McGrath of Rhode Island was elected to the post.[41] When he also resigned as postmaster general, Truman appointed Jesse M. Donaldson, a career executive who had come up through the ranks, in his place. Donaldson had started in the post office as a letter carrier in 1908 and had risen to be the first assistant postmaster general. Truman thus departed from the practice of putting a politician in this office.[42]

When Clinton Anderson resigned as secretary of agriculture in June 1948 in order to run for the U.S. Senate from New Mexico, Truman elevated to the secretaryship Charles Brannan, who had been with the department since 1935 and who was serving at the time as assistant secretary. A Colorado lawyer, Brannan worked closely with Oscar Chapman in connection with the local Young Democrats. He entered government service in 1935 when he became the regional attorney for the Resettlement Administration, an agency sponsored by Rexford Tugwell to help submarginal farmers. He was brought to Washington as assistant secretary in 1944. During his service, he was to prove to be very useful in politics and in working out new programs.[43]

After Secretary of Labor Schwellenbach died on June 10, 1948, Truman named Maurice Joseph Tobin of Massachusetts to be his successor. Tobin had been mayor of Boston and governor of Massachusetts. As governor he had made a good record as far as organized labor in his state was concerned.

He was an enthusiastic backer of Truman's labor policies. When he came to Washington, he discovered that John Steelman, not the secretary of labor, was the real power in the administration on labor-management relations and at his swearing-in ceremony, he said: "I hope that I shall be able to fill the shoes of my late distinguished predecessor, John R. Steelman."[44]

At the end of Truman's first term as president, the cabinet contained only one Roosevelt holdover, Defense Secretary Forrestal, and only one of his original replacements, Attorney General Clark. Truman had lost the two liberal Roosevelt holdovers, Ickes and Wallace, and had replaced them with two experienced executives, who were not liberals. Career men had taken over in the Post Office and Agriculture Departments, and this marked an improvement in the administration of these departments. Two businessmen had been appointed secretaries of the Treasury and Commerce Departments, a move decidedly to the right. As Truman filled out the remainder of Roosevelt's term, only Brannan and Tobin could be clearly marked as liberals in his cabinet. Truman regarded his cabinet officers as administrators, and he held them responsible for the conduct of their departments.[45] In his campaign for reelection, he received relatively little help from cabinet officers, except in the case of Brannan, Clark, and Tobin, all of whom campaigned vigorously.

EXECUTIVE OFFICE OF THE PRESIDENT

It was not his cabinet but the National Security Council and the executive office of the president that Truman used to formulate policies. The latter office he inherited from the Reorganization Act of 1939, which he had supported as senator. It included the White House office, the Bureau of the Budget, and the emergency agencies, which he had been liquidating. To these offices was added the Council of Economic Advisers by the Employment Act of 1946. As the burdens placed upon the President increased, it was necessary for him to enlarge the staffs in these offices. This encountered some jealousy on the part of Congress so it also enlarged its staff.

White House Office

President Truman maintained friendly, informal relations with the members of his staff, and he tried to keep the some top twenty advisers friendly with each other. The staff meetings did not decide major policy questions, but they enabled the President to make assignments, settle disputed questions, and check on the progress that various staff members were making in their work.[46]

The functions of the appointments secretary, the press secretary, the correspondence secretary, the executive secretary, and the military aide continued unchanged. Moreover there were no changes in the personnel occupying these positions from 1946 to 1948.

The office of the special counsel to the President, however, increased enormously in importance due to the advent of a new personality of outstanding abilities. Truman greatly prized his first special counsel, Judge Samuel Rosenman, who had served under Roosevelt, but the judge was weary of government service and insisted on resigning in January 1946. At first, Truman thought of not filling the position, but he soon saw the need to do so. He chose a Missourian highly recommended by Rosenman, with whom he had worked for nearly half a year. The personable Clark Clifford was originally brought into the White House by naval aide Vardaman on July 4, 1945, to work on a message dealing with universal military training and the postwar army and navy. Handsome, articulate, and highly intelligent, Clifford performed brilliantly as Truman's special counsel, skillfully outlining the strategy to be followed and implementing it with shrewd advice on speeches and legislation. He and his assistants prepared a memorandum on relations with the Soviet Union in September 1946 which anticipated the Truman Doctrine and the Marshall Plan, and in 1947-1948 he was one of the architects of Truman's upset election victory. He became the leader of the liberal forces on the White House staff, and he led the battle for Truman's support on many issues against the assistant to the president, John Steelman, who took a more conservative position.[47]

The chief function of the special counsel was the preparation of the speeches, messages to Congress, executive orders, and other presidential papers. Truman sought advice not only on how these documents should be worded but what policies should be advocated. According to Richard Neustadt, "The special counsel held the acknowledged staff lead on preparation of all the formal documents which expressed, explained, defended, the President's major policies and programs, foreign and domestic, executive and legislative, governmental and 'political' alike."[48]

Clifford recruited and developed a fine staff, which acted as a team in helping him perform these functions. He attracted men with excellent government experience and bright ideas. Chief among these was Charles Murphy, an able lawyer who was an excellent draftsman. He had spent thirteen years in the legislative counsel's office of the Senate before, early in 1947, he became one of the administrative assistants to the President, working chiefly with Clifford, whom he was to replace in 1950. Also working closely with the special counsel were George M. Elsey, a military aide who proved to be efficient as a researcher and writer, David D. Lloyd, lawyer and lobbyist for the Americans for Democratic Action, James L. Sundquist, a Bureau of the Budget administrative analyst who had been a newspaper reporter, and David E. Bell, author Bureau of the Budget administrative specialist.[49]

Special Counsel Clifford was involved in policy decisions on many different questions coming before the Truman administration from 1945 until he resigned in 1950, especially when the decision involved a message to Congress or a speech. Although his role in influencing foreign policy, military, and budget matters was somewhat less than in domestic matters, nevertheless his memorandum of September 1946 on relations with the Soviet Union was of considerable importance.[50]

In the fall of 1945 at the suggestion of Secretary of Labor Schwellenbach, who realized his desperate need for help in the labor field that was upset by many strikes, Truman had appointed John Roy Steelman of Arkansas to be the assistant to the president in charge of labor relations and liaison with domestic agencies. Educated in economics at Vanderbilt, Harvard, and the University of North Carolina, Steelman had impressed Secretary of Labor Frances Perkins with his genial personality and his knowledge of labor problems. She hired him to work on mediation problems and in a few years made him director of conciliation service. While lacking the brilliance of Clifford, he worked hard and became known for his skill in bringing opposing parties together. As the White House became more directly involved in labor disputes, Steelman's importance increased. In June 1946, he was appointed director of the Office of War Mobilization and Reconversion (OWMR), which had statutory powers over cabinet officers. Holding this job for six months until OWMR was abolished, Steelman was able to establish contacts with cabinet officers who kept coming to him on problems within his jurisdiction. His back-slapping techniques were offensive to some, but Truman did not mind his manner and tolerated his conservative leanings. Steelman got along with both labor and management, and he was able to bring top officials together.[51]

It was inevitable that Steelman and Clifford would clash over certain questions. Since Truman did not like quarrels among the members of his staff, these differences had to be kept under cover. Clifford was adroit in his personal relations and Steelman did not like to start a fight in the open, so friction between the two did not often rise to the surface. Steelman did most of his business on the telephone or in conferences. Undoubtedly when Clifford left in 1950, Steelman's importance increased because the new special counsel, Charles Murphy, was not as aggressive as Clifford had been.[52]

On July 6, 1947, Truman appointed Donald S. Dawson as administrative assistant in charge of personnel matters for the White House. Dawson came to Washington in 1933 and rose to a top personnel position in the Reconstruction Finance Corporation before he was transferred to the White House. There he discovered that personnel recruitment was a function shared by Democratic National Chairman Hannegan, Appointments Secretary Connelly, cabinet officers, the Civil Service Commission, top administrative officials, and members of Congress. An example will illustrate how the system operated under Dawson during the Truman administration.[53]

A friend of Truman's brother, Vivian, was a candidate for a Kansas City post in the Department of Commerce. Dawson told the executive assistant to the secretary to assure a rating for this man that would place him among the top three on the list of eligibles compiled for the Civil Service Commission. The executive assistant, a top career administrator who believed in the merit system, refused to manipulate the ratings and rated the man fourth. Secretary Sawyer, under pressure from Dawson, told the executive assistant to find a way to appoint this favorite candidate, which he did by obtaining waivers from the first two persons on the register. This practice was legal, but the executive assistant was not happy about it and said that it would not have happened under Secretary Wallace or Harriman, who would have resisted such pressure from the White House, nor would it have happened under President Roosevelt, who upheld the merit system. Truman was trained in the Pendergast school of politics, and patronage appointments were to be expected. Dawson got in trouble later in connection with the RFC investigation by Senator J. William Fulbright.[54]

Bureau of the Budget

Budget director Harold Smith started out by being one of Truman's closest advisers. They worked together well in liquidating the war agencies and in scaling down the federal budget from its all-time highs during the war, but in the winter of 1945-1946 when the public clamor arose because of the woes of reconversion and the food shortages at home and abroad, Smith seemed to lose his cool assurance and became somewhat distressed and alarmist. He wrote in his diary on February 8, 1946:

I said, "Mr. President, there are some serious administrative difficulties today which are accumulative. While you, yourself, are an orderly person, there is disorder all around you and it is becoming worse. There are a couple of points—and not many more—at center of these difficulties. For one thing, you need good, continuous, organized staff work and you are not getting it." The President said, "I know it, and the situation is pretty serious."

I continued by saying, "I will give you just one example, but I could give you many others. Not more than three or four weeks ago top people in Agriculture were making speeches which indicated their worry about a possible food surplus in this country. Now you are issuing a statement about black bread [reference to world food shortage]. Of course the international picture was not taken into consideration, but I doubt that a food surplus would have existed even for this country alone.[55]

These administrative deficiencies were primarily the fault of Secretary of Agriculture Anderson who was determined to protect the interests of the

American farmers first and did not give sufficient consideration to the needs of consumers at home and abroad.[56] Smith was not well, and the frustrations of the exacting job were obviously wearing him down. Moreover, he had lost out in influence with Truman to Director Snyder of OWMR, whose advice, apparently, added to the confusion. Smith resigned in July 1946.

James E. Webb, an industrialist and government official, was brought from the Treasury Department to become budget director in place of Smith on July 28, 1946. He worked out a satisfactory relationship with President Truman, encouraged greater use of the budget staff, and persuaded some of his staff to transfer to the White House office. Officers who worked under Webb regarded him as an outstanding director.

When OWMR was abolished and Steelman was transferred to the White House as the assistant to the president, he hoped to move the core of the liquidated organization with him, but he was frustrated in this maneuver by cabinet members and congressmen. This left the Bureau of the Budget as the organization that could furnish the President with the legislative liaison service he needed. Webb promptly came forward with the offer of his agency's help. He reorganized the bureau's legislative reference service so that it not only cleared legislative proposals and reports but helped create new programs in cooperation with Clark Clifford and Charles Murphy in the White House. Webb tried to make the service sensitive to congressional schedules, he encouraged House and Senate committees to ask the bureau for its views on pending bills, and he backed up staff evaluations of measures passed by Congress, staff alternatives to measures vetoed, and suggested additions to bills signed with reservations.[57] After his first conference with Truman, Webb wrote:

This morning I had my first real private talk with the President. He was most cordial and handled every item discussed with complete frankness and a matter-of-fact approach which utilized every minute of the time so none was wasted.

The President then started off by telling me that I had a hard job, but, next to members of the Cabinet and the President, the most important in the Government; that he was counting on me to give him the facts as I saw them, regardless of pressures; that he would make any decisions to deviate from facts but did not expect me to try to anticipate him or color facts to suit him.

I told him that this was the policy we had been following and would continue to follow. I also told him that both the State Department and the Navy Department were unhappy over recent recommendations made to him, but that in answer to their protests I had told them the only way I could do this job was to call the shots as I saw them. He said, "You just keep on doing that and we'll get along all right." I told him he would probably have complaints due to this policy, and he said that if he did he would have me in with the complainer so that we could both talk it out in his presence. He said, "I will not make decisions about you behind your back—you can count on that."[58]

The struggle over military budgets continued until the Korean war broke out in 1950. Truman and Webb upheld the side for economy during these years, and when Forrestal was appointed secretary of defense, he was brought into the picture of trying to adjust the conflicting demands of the services for the limited funds declared available by the President.[59]

Council of Economic Advisers

It is ironic that the presidential institution created by the Employment Act of 1946, the Council of Economic Advisers, was initiated by congressional opposition to a full employment policy. It was hoped that such a council would bring presidential advisers out in the open where they could be watched by Congress. The council was made responsible for preparing the economic report. Truman accepted the institution and came to rely upon it. There were two theories about the function of the council. One, held by the first chairman, Edwin G. Nourse, an orthodox economist from the Brookings Institution, was that the council should be above politics and furnish impartial expert advice. The second view, held by the vice-chairman, Leon Keyserling, a lawyer and economist, former administrative assistant to Senator Robert Wagner, and general counsel to the housing administration, was that the council should take an activist role, help to formulate sound economic policy, and assist the President in carrying out that policy by testifying before congressional committees and making public speeches. During its first four years, the council was deeply divided by the fundamental cleavages between Nourse and Keyserling. Nourse came to be ignored, and Keyserling was listened to more and more.[60]

The establishment of the council was a delicate matter since the functions assigned to it overlapped to some extent the functions of the Treasury Department and the Bureau of the Budget, both of which had been considered by the legislators for the duties involved. The Bureau of the Budget helped the council get organized, but the practice was established that the council hired its own professional economists.

GENERAL OBSERVATIONS

During this period, when the rivalry between Clifford and Steelman was keen, jurisdictional lines were sharply drawn, and operations were at their most effective stage. Each staff member knew what he had to do and to whom he was responsible.

Truman kept in touch with his staff by means of his daily staff meetings, by calls upon him by senior staff members, who were always welcome, and by visits to their offices. Access to the President was never denied within a reasonable length of time, and the morale of the team was high.

Truman had lost two valuable cabinet officers. His replacement of Ickes by Krug as secretary of interior did not turn out well. His appointment of Harriman in place of Wallace was a wise move, but when Harriman left, he made an inferior choice, Sawyer. Except for Harriman, who performed well in many roles, Truman could ill afford these changes.

Finally, the period brought the establishment of the Department of Defense, the National Security Council, the CIA, and the Council of Economic Advisers. President Truman used each of these new agencies to formulate and carry out policies.

chapter 24 | RELATIONS WITH SECRETARY OF STATE BYRNES, 1945–1947

At Potsdam, President Truman had found the Russians to be intractable negotiators, and he never tried another summit conference. He preferred to rely upon his secretary of state and other foreign policy advisers. His relations with Secretary Byrnes were not ideal, but they lasted for eighteen months.[1] When the secretary was in Washington, he had a standing appointment with the President each Monday and Thursday for foreign policy discussions. After the Potsdam conference, Under Secretary of State Grew retired, and Truman and Byrnes persuaded Dean Acheson to take the post. When Byrnes was out of the country attending international conferences, which occurred quite frequently, Acheson was acting secretary of state.[2] Acheson, son of an Episcopalian bishop, a graduate of Yale and of the Harvard Law School, a law clerk for two years to Justice Louis D. Brandeis, and a member of the outstanding Washington law firm of Covington and Burling, became assistant secretary of state for economic affairs under Secretary of State Cordell Hull in 1941 and assistant secretary for congressional relations under Secretary of State Stettinius in 1944. The Stettinius appointment was supposed to be a demotion, but Acheson made such an outstanding success of it that he was marked for greater responsibilities by both Truman and Byrnes.[3] Tall, handsome, elegant, quick witted, extremely articulate, and loyal, Acheson was, as Alistair Cooke put it in the *Manchester Guardian*, one of the most creative political minds of the time.[4] He was a firm believer in the free enterprise system and a vigorous opponent of Soviet expansionism.

The first meeting of the Council of Foreign Ministers was held in London during September 1945. At the suggestion of Senator Vandenberg and in accordance with the bipartisan foreign policy, Secretary Byrnes included in his delegation a prominent Republican foreign policy adviser, John Foster Dulles. Son of an upstate New York Presbyterian minister, grandson of John Watson Foster (secretary of state under President Benjamin Harrison), nephew of Robert Lansing (secretary of state under President Woodrow Wilson), and outstanding international Wall Street lawyer with financial interests around the world, Dulles had been deeply immersed in American foreign relations since his early thirties, starting under his uncle, serving as reparations adviser to President Wilson, and becoming Governor Thomas Dewey's adviser on foreign affairs in the 1940s when Dewey was running for president. His ideas on diplomacy and peace were deeply influenced by his religious background and by his experience in international economic affairs. He was an implacable foe of the Soviet Union. While consultant to Byrnes, Dulles furnished the Truman administration strong support in its foreign policies.[5]

At the start of the London conference, it was agreed by the American, British, and Soviet delegates that France and China could participate in the discussions of peace treaties with Eastern European countries but could not vote on these treaties. In the middle of the conference, Molotov announced that this procedure was a mistake and that France and China should be excluded from the discussions. Byrnes telegraphed President Truman to appeal to Stalin to overrule Molotov on this issue. Truman could not be reached, but Admiral Leahy sent the message on Truman's behalf. Later the President approved the message.[6] Stalin, however, would not budge, and the conference broke up without even a protocol. The Russians were holding out for full recognition of their satellite governments in Eastern Europe. In his radio address of October 6, however, Byrnes refused to accept as yet the idea of a divided world.[7]

On October 16, Byrnes, Forrestal, and General Marshall agreed that "it was most inadvisable for this country to continue the demobilization of our Armed Forces at the present rate." Forrestal wanted the President to go before the American people and make clear the breach between the Soviets and the Western powers, but Byrnes opposed this step, and Truman did not override his secretary of state.[8]

At the Moscow conference in December, arranged by Byrnes without consulting Truman, without Republican advisers, and contrary to the judgment of veteran diplomats, the secretary of state accepted the existing Rumanian and Bulgarian governments after Stalin had made some slight concessions, which he later ignored. Byrnes did not keep Truman well informed as to the changes he was making in the American recognition policy, and he kept Harriman from making the customary reports of progress to the President. On the question of the control of atomic energy, Truman kept Byrnes informed of unfavorable reactions of Senators Vandenberg and Connally to proposals made.[9] Byrnes's actions in Moscow were severely criticized by a number of commentators, including Sumner Welles, who denounced the settlements as a betrayal of the Balkan peoples and of Roosevelt's ideals.

Just what happened between Byrnes and Truman when the secretary returned to the United States from Moscow is disputed. In William Hillman's *Mr. President* and in Truman's *Memoirs*, Truman wrote that he was dissatisfied with the way Byrnes kept him informed about what happened in Moscow. He insisted that his presidential prerogatives to decide foreign policy had been infringed upon. He claimed that on January 5, 1946, he read a letter to Byrnes that set forth these views in no uncertain terms.[10]

Byrnes's account of his relations with Truman during these days is radically different. In his *All in One Lifetime*, he denies that Truman read or showed him the letter and claimed that he would have resigned if Truman had written or talked to him in those terms.[11] The fact that Byrnes was kept on for a year after this shows that there was no serious break between the two men at this time. Truman did not like face-to-face confrontations.

Senator Vandenberg and John Foster Dulles kept urging Byrnes to take a firmer stand against the Soviet Union, and their strong position had an effect on Truman's thinking. Under Secretary Dean Acheson later wrote that there were some differences between the President and the secretary of state, but they did not come to an open disagreement. In the showdown on American policy toward the Soviet Union that came to a head the following summer, Truman backed Byrnes and dismissed Secretary of Commerce Wallace from the cabinet.

During the time that Byrnes was secretary of state, the failure of the Soviet Union to remove its troops from Iran by March 2, 1946, in accordance with the Tripartite Treaty of Alliance among Iran, the Soviet Union, and Great Britain of January 29, 1942, led to a series of crises that involved Truman.[12] Under the treaty the Soviet Union had stationed troops in the northern part of Iran, and Great Britain had troops in the southern part in order to safeguard the transshipment of war goods to the Soviet Union. Both countries had promised to withdraw their forces from Iranian territory not later than six months after the war ended. Under the auspices of the British, the United States had stationed noncombatant troops in Iran to facilitate transport. The Russians had used their position to subvert the northern provinces by supporting the Tudeh (communist) elements in rebellion against the central government.

President Truman was aware in 1945 of the danger that the Soviet troops presented to Iranian independence. At Potsdam he supported the British proposal for the immediate evacuation of all foreign troops from Iran and indicated that he expected to have all American troops out in two months. Stalin wanted his troops to remain much longer but promised to take no action against Iran.

In his *Memoirs*, Truman indicated that he kept in touch with the situation in Iran during the fall of 1945. He was alarmed by the reports that, contrary to Stalin's promise, Russian army units were interfering in Iranian affairs and encouraging a revolt in the northern province of Azerbaijan, which adjoined the Soviet Union.[13]

Truman endorsed Byrnes's speech of February 28, 1946, before the Overseas Press Club in which Byrnes said: "We will not and we cannot stand aloof if force or threat of force is used contrary to the purposes and principles of the Charter." In a speech two weeks later, Byrnes said: "Should the occasion arise, our military strength will be used to support the principles and purposes of the Charter." It was clear from the charges made by Iran and from news reports that Byrnes was referring to the Iranian situation.[14]

It is difficult to determine the exact role that Truman played in the Iranian crisis. In the spring of 1946, greatly concerned with the situation, he told Ambassador W. Averell Harriman: "We may be at war with the Soviet Union over Iran."[15] Truman's later accounts of what took place in 1946 have raised a number of questions. At a press conference in 1952, he claimed: "I had to send an ultimatum to the head of the Soviet Union to get out of Persia. They got out because we were in a position to meet a situation of that kind."[16] In compiling the record for the *Foreign Relations* volumes, the historical office of the Department of State found no document on the sending of an ultimatum to the Soviet Union in the files of the State or Defense department. A White House spokesman explained at the time that "the President was using the term ultimatum in a non-technical layman sense. He said that the President was referring to the United States leadership in the United Nations, particularly in the Security Council and through diplomatic channels, in the spring of 1946, which was a major factor in bringing about the Soviet withdrawal from Iran."[17]

The records show that on March 5, 1946, Byrnes sent a note to the Soviet Union expressing "the earnest hope that the Government of the Soviet Union will do its part, by withdrawing immediately all Soviet forces from the territory of Iran." This was followed by notes to the Iranian government urging it to file an appeal to the Security Council and promising American support if such an appeal was filed.[18] This note was hardly an ultimatum. The appeal was made on March 18, and the Soviet Union requested a postponement of the hearings. In a press conference, Truman backed Byrnes in refusing the Soviet request for postponement.[19] The Soviet Union, embarrassed by these developments in the new Security Council and concerned about the implications of Churchill's speech and the naval presence of the United States in the eastern Mediterranean, withdrew from the council and began pulling its troops from Iran.

While ostensibly living up to its promises to withdraw its forces from Iran in early 1946, the Soviet Union continued to back the rebellion in Azerbaijan and to stir up trouble by initiating strikes throughout the country and by demands for oil concessions. The British moved troops in Iraq near the oil fields, and the Iranian government, with encouragement from the United States, put down the rebellious elements in the north. The Soviet Union failed to send combat elements to support its side in Azerbaijan, in part because of fear of the U.N. Security Council and world opinion.[20] This experience convinced Truman that strong support of victims of attempted Soviet subversion would thwart Russian designs because the Soviet Union did not want to risk war for the time being. The result of the Iranian crisis was that the Soviet Union got no oil concessions from Iran, and American oil companies did.[21]

Turning to another international problem of overwhelming proportions, Truman and Byrnes pondered the impact of the development of nuclear weapons on American security. As Truman put it in his October 3, 1945, speech: "Civilization demands that we shall reach at the earliest possible date a satisfactory arrangement for the control of this discovery in order that it may become a powerful and forceful influence towards the maintenance of world peace instead of an instrument of destruction."[22] He realized that the American monopoly of the atom bomb could not last many years and that the security of the United States, long protected by two oceans, would soon be threatened by the Soviet Union when it developed the bomb and could deliver it on a global basis. Along with others upon whose advice Truman relied, Byrnes had an image of the Russians as expansionist and a threat to the free world.

In framing a policy regarding the international control of nuclear energy, President Truman had to consider the advice of American civilian and military leaders, the thinking of congressional leaders, the counsel of the British and the Canadians who had collaborated in nuclear research, and the reactions of the Russians, whose cooperation was essential for the success of any plan of control. Because of losses in men and materiel during the war, the Russians felt insecure and were extremely suspicious of the other Allies, whom they saw as brandishing about military power and who seemed to be unsympathetic toward Russian security needs.

There were wide differences of opinion among Truman's advisers regarding nuclear policies. Secretary of War Stimson had done systematic thinking on the subject. Culminating his various briefings of the President was his performance at a cabinet meeting on September 21, 1945, when he proposed a direct approach to the Soviet Union even though the Russian postwar behavior had been far from reassuring. On the theory that to win trust, one has to be trusting, he argued that to present a plan without consulting with the Russians first would lead to bitterness on their part. The scientific theories of nuclear fission were well known, and the United States could not keep the Russians from developing their own atomic weapons; furthermore, a nuclear arms race was to be avoided at all costs. He wrote in a memo-randum:

My idea of an approach to the Soviets would be a direct proposal after discussion with the British that we would be prepared in effect to enter an arrangement with the Russians, the general purpose of which would be to control and limit the use of the atomic bomb as an instrument of war and so far as possible to direct and encourage the development of atomic power for peaceful and humanitarian purpose. Such an approach might more specifically lead to the proposal that we would stop work on the further improvement in, or manufacture of, the bomb as a military weapon, provided the Russians and the British would agree to do likewise.

The Stimson proposal did not make clear what sort of protection in the form of inspection and control the United States should insist upon in return for sharing its nuclear knowledge and limiting its own atomic bomb capabilities.[23]

The cabinet meeting was a historic occasion. Stimson's view on the direct approach to the Russians was supported by Robert Patterson, who was to be his successor. A Wall Street lawyer, Patterson was a conservative and could be expected to be anti-Stalinist, but he had been convinced by Stimson that the risk had to be taken to avoid an atom bomb race. Acting Secretary of State Acheson also supported Stimson in spite of his distrust of the Soviet Union. He was a realist in international politics and felt that the United States should do everything possible to reach an agreement to outlaw atomic weaponry. Postmaster General Robert Hannegan, a liberal who wanted to keep leftist elements within the Democratic party, backed Stimson. Secretary of Commerce Henry Wallace, the most sympathetic of all cabinet members to the Soviet point of view, could be expected to agree with Stimson. In his *Diaries*, Secretary of the Navy Forrestal greatly exaggerated the role of Wallace at the meeting, stating that Wallace was "completely, everlastingly, and wholeheartedly in favor of giving it [the secret of the atomic bomb] to the Russians," implying that this should be done without concern for inspection and control. Among the leaders of the opposition to the Stimson plan was Forrestal, whose record of anticommunism, anti-Stalinism, and anti-Soviet system was notorious.[24] Backing Forrestal was Secretary of the Treasury Fred M. Vinson, whose knowledge of the subject was limited but whose lack of confidence in Stalin and his cohorts was profound. Secretary of Agriculture Clinton Anderson, far from sharing the views of Roosevelt's first secretary of agriculture, disliked what he knew about the Soviet Union. Finally, Attorney General Thomas C. Clark, undoubtedly influenced by the Federal Bureau of Investigation and its crusade against communist subversion in the United States, particularly the stealing of bomb secrets, opposed any sharing of knowledge about atomic energy with the Soviet Union. Truman seemed pleased with the cabinet discussion, but Acheson wrote that he found it unworthy of the subject. Historians have agreed with this verdict. Later events indicated that Stimson had not won over the President to his point of view or that the President had not understood it.[25]

A story leaked to the *New York Times* stated that at the cabinet meeting, Wallace had sponsored a proposal to reveal the secret of the atom bomb to the Soviet Union, but two days later Truman denied that Wallace had made such a recommendation.[26] Members of Congress were agitated by these stories, and Truman reassured Senator Connally that American atomic energy policy would be determined by Congress.

Stimson's advice that the Soviets should be approached directly on the question of international control of atomic energy was not followed. Byrnes, in contrast to Acheson, was opposed to this approach and expressed great distrust of the Russians in a meeting of the secretaries of state, war, and navy. Truman himself dealt a blow to the Stimson plan when he made it clear that he was not planning to share knowledge regarding the details of making atom bombs with any foreign government, including Great Britain and Canada, whose leaders thought they had an agreement to share such knowledge. Truman's press secretary urged the President to declare the remarks off the record, but Truman, not realizing the worldwide significance of his statements, put them on the record, thus causing a global news explosion.[27] British Prime Minister Clement Attlee immediately sought a meeting with the Canadian Prime Minister Mackenzie King and President Truman in Washington on atomic energy questions. At this conference Byrnes and Truman agreed to seek the establishment of a U.N. commission on atomic energy, the very procedure that Stimson had warned the President against.[28] The Joint Declaration on Atomic Energy of the three nations was very displeasing to the U.S. senators who regarded themselves as leaders in the formulation of the nation's foreign policy: Vandenberg and Connally.[29] They also objected strongly to the instructions that Secretary Byrnes carried to the Moscow Conference of Foreign Ministers in December on the steps to be taken in gaining Soviet cooperation for a U.N. atomic energy commission. They thought that the establishment of a system of inspection should precede any disclosure of information regarding atomic energy.[30] Truman directed Acting Secretary Acheson to send a telegram to Byrnes in Moscow informing him of the views of the senators. Acheson did, and Truman endorsed the telegram.[31] At the Moscow conference the Soviet Union agreed to the establishment of the U.N. Atomic Energy Commission. Senator Vandenberg was dissatisfied, however, with the communique of the foreign ministers; he still thought it did not safeguard American atomic weapons secrets.[32]

Byrnes appointed Acheson as chairman of a committee to devise a plan for the international control of atomic energy that could be presented to the

U.N. Commission on Atomic Energy established by the U.N. Assembly in January 1946. Achson reluctantly accepted the assignment and suggested a board of consultants headed by David Lilienthal, chairman of the Tennessee Valley Authority, to work out detailed plans. The consultants came up with the proposal that an international Atomic Development Authority should take over all activities essential to atomic energy production, including materials, plants, and research. Acheson presented the Acheson-Lilienthal plan to Byrnes for transmittal to the president, and he also sent it to the Senate Special Committee on Atomic Energy. It appeared that members of this committee leaked it to the press.[33]

Secretary Byrnes next proposed to Truman that Bernard Baruch present the plan to the U.N. commission. Acheson protested this selection, calling Baruch's reputation "without foundation in fact and entirely self-propagated," but he was overruled, and Baruch was appointed, partly on the ground that he was well liked in the Senate.[34] Baruch's strong distrust of Stalin did not augur well for an accommodation with the Russians. It soon developed that Baruch was concerned about the publicity that had been given the Acheson-Lilienthal plan prior to his appointment. If this was the policy, he wondered why he was needed? Apparently Baruch had grandiose ideas about the importance of his role as adviser. Both Byrnes and Truman had to remind him that the President made policy.[35]

Acheson's premonitions about Baruch turned out to be well founded. To the Acheson-Lilienthal plan Baruch and his advisers added punitive sanctions for violations, which made the plan all the more unacceptable to the Russians. Truman agreed to these changes, although his enthusiasm for Baruch had lessened somewhat after the encounter with the elder statesman's challenge to presidential prerogatives.[36] In the commission, the Russians criticized the plan as being an invasion of state sovereignty, and after abstaining from voting on its adoption by the commission, they presented their own scheme for the immediate destruction of all atomic weapons and a later discussion of controls. The Russian plan, however, was unacceptable to the American delegation. During the debate before the commission, Henry Wallace sent his letter to Truman in which he criticized the Baruch plan on the ground that it gave the Russians reasons for being distrustful. He implied that the American plan was designed to discover what raw materials and objectives the Russians had in the atomic energy field. The United States would retain its monopoly and would decide when to submit to controls. There was a bitter clash between Wallace and Baruch, which did not end when Wallace was asked to resign from the cabinet. As an independent writer and speaker, Wallace continued to denounce the Baruch plan.[37] The American plan was adopted by the commission for presentation to the U.N. Security Council, where the Soviet Union vetoed it. Truman had failed to avoid an atomic weapons race.

Another important question facing Truman and Byrnes during this period was the implementation of the Potsdam agreements regarding the defeated and impoverished Germany. The Americans soon discovered that Soviet actions in their zone of occupation were rapidly making cooperation between the East and the West impossible. The Soviet Union wanted to root out all bourgeois elements and establish in its zone a communist dictatorship by forcibly suppressing all opposition and nationalizing all production and trade. The Potsdam objective of economic unity for all Germany was effectively blocked by Soviet trade restrictions and suppression of all freedoms, including freedom of movement in the Soviet zone.

Truman had agreed to the appointment of General Lucius Clay as military governor of the American zone of occupation in Germany, which made him a member of the Control Council for Germany. Clay was close to such former Wall Street lawyers as Assistant Secretary of War John J. McCloy, and he believed that German revival should be based on free enterprise and political freedom. The Germans, particularly the Christian Social Democrats, could take over their own government when a stable economic system was established. Because the harsh provisions of the general directive to the U.S. commander in chief regarding the military government of Germany proved to be unworkable in view of the severe need of the German population for food, shelter, clothing, and other necessities, Clay began to work toward the economic rehabilitation of the western zones of Germany by bringing them together in one trade area and by stimulating economic growth through revival of private enterprise.[38] The French as well as the Soviets proved to be a serious obstacle to Clay's plan, however. President Truman sent Byron Price, a journalist, on a special mission to survey conditions in Germany, and his report strongly supported Clay's position.[39]

In May 1946 Clay stopped all reparations payments from the American zone to the Soviet Union and to France on the grounds that these countries were blocking all efforts to treat Germany as an economic unit and their actions were forcing the United States to subsidize Germany. The British soon followed suit in their zone. The Soviet Union interpreted these moves as an attempt on the part of Western capitalists, who were strongly represented in the American military government in Germany, to protect their investments in Germany and to use a revived Nazi state as a bulwark against the Soviet Union.[40]

In September 1946, with the French still refusing to cooperate, Clay persuaded the British to consider bizonal agreements, which merged the zonal administrations for food and agriculture, transport, finances, and communications. Economic aid was poured into these new units, established in January 1947, and trade and industry began to revive.[41]

Secretary Byrnes and Senators Vandenberg and Connally favored the bizonal arrangements. In order to counter Soviet attempts to attract the

Germans to their side, Byrnes made his famous address in Stuttgart on September 6 in which he promised economic aid and an early return of self-government to the Germans in Bizonia. He tried in vain to get clearance from Truman for the sentence "as long as there is an occupation army in Germany, American armed forces will be part of that occupation army," but Truman could not be reached. Clay reassured Byrnes that Truman would agree to this view.[42]

Byrnes was so preoccupied with European conferences that he did not have time to devote to Far Eastern affairs. The occupation of Japan was proceeding in an orderly fashion under General Douglas MacArthur, who was placed in sole command of occupied Japan in spite of protests from the Soviet Union. Chinese affairs, however, were becoming confused and unstable. Ambassador Patrick Hurley, a flamboyant ex-soldier, suddenly resigned on November 27, 1945, denouncing the government's policy and some of the Department of State officials who advised that the Chinese Communists were closer to the people than the Nationalists. Hurley's actions were a great surprise to both Byrnes and Truman.[43] As for the officials critized by Hurley, they were fully vindicated by later events.[44] On the suggestion of Secretary of Agriculture Anderson, Truman handled this crisis by replacing Hurley with General George Marshall, whom he greatly admired. Marshall spent a year trying to bring the Chinese Nationalists and Communists together, but he found the task impossible. Chiang Kai-shek and Mao Tse-tung were implacable foes, and Marshall could not bring about any lasting fusion. Both Byrnes and Truman left decisions on China largely to Marshall, who held the view that the United States was unready to make the sacrifices in men and money needed to influence the course of events in China.[45]

The famous iron curtain speech that former Prime Minister Winston Churchill made at Westminster College, Fulton, Missouri, on March 5, 1946, had an impact on the development of the cold war.[46] It is ironic that a speech by a former British prime minister at a little-known American college in which he used words that he had employed before should create such a worldwide sensation and appear to have official American sanction. The origin of this occasion is even more curious. Truman's controversial military aide, Harry Vaughan, had graduated from Westminster College and upon learning that the president of the college was looking for a prominent speaker thought Churchill might be a possibility. Truman cooperated and extended the invitation, stating that he would introduce the speaker.[47] Churchill was looking for a forum and accepted. Truman rode on the train with Churchill to Fulton, Missouri. It was assumed by newspapermen that the two men discussed the content of the speech, the most famous passage of which was: "From Stettin in the Baltic to Trieste in the Adriatic, an iron curtain has descended across the continent." But Truman stated that he was in no way responsible for what Churchill said.[48]

The reactions at home and abroad were instantaneous. Stalin denounced Churchill as a firebrand of war. Anti-Russians hailed it as a clear call for the defense of the free world against the aggressive communists bent on world domination. Those alarmed at the growing tension between the Soviet bloc and the free world called Churchill a warmonger and asked Truman to repudiate any notion that this was the American policy.[49] On the domestic scene, sharp criticisms of Churchill's speech and Truman's involvement were made by former Governor Harold E. Stassen, who had been a delegate to the U.N. San Francisco conference, Henry Wallace, who asserted that the American air base in Iceland was a threat to the Soviet Union, former Secretary of Interior Harold L. Ickes, who demanded a return to Roosevelt's policies, and Senator Claude Pepper of Florida, who denounced the new anti-Sovietism.[50] Byrnes complained that he was being "shot in the back" by friends and colleagues.

In the middle of April 1946, Byrnes feared that he had developed heart trouble, and he told Truman that he wanted to resign after finishing the minor peace treaties. He thought they could be completed by July, but this timetable was unrealistic. Truman had already decided to name General George Marshall as secretary of state when Byrnes resigned. In the meantime, further medical examination showed that Byrnes had stomach rather than heart trouble. He continued the negotiations in Paris regarding the peace treaties with Italy, Bulgaria, Rumania, and Hungary. Some concessions were wrested from the Russians on Trieste and on former Italian colonies, which were put under British control. With the completion of these treaties, Byrnes resigned on January 21, 1947.[51]

Byrnes and Truman were both under great pressures during the year and a half that Byrnes was secretary of state. Byrnes was frustrated in trying to secure what he regarded as the main objective of American foreign policy at the close of the war: the preservation of Allied unity. Trained as a legislative and administrative negotiator on the American scene, he had much to learn about Soviet objectives and diplomatic methods. Unwilling to urge Truman to warn Americans that rearmament was necessary to meet the Soviet threat, he had to fall back upon rhetoric and appeal to moral principles. He was pressed to do this by his Republican foreign policy advisers, Senator Vandenberg and John Foster Dulles. The result of this stand was a widening of the gap between the East and the West. Truman followed Byrnes's lead. When he deviated from this position, as in his attempt to appease Henry Wallace, who opposed a tough Soviet policy, he found himself in trouble.

Until February 1946, Byrnes tried to conciliate the Russians. After this he followed a tougher line. He had been accused of practicing appeasement after the London and Moscow conferences, but in the Iranian crisis he had been firm. In the Balkan states, the United States was faced with two alternatives: give in to the Russians or back them off by war. Byrnes and

Truman were unwilling to accept either of these choices. The unity they sought was shattered, and the cold war began.

Truman was sensitive about certain criticisms levied at his conduct of the presidency. Byrnes was extremely self-confident and was actually somewhat condescending in his attitude toward Truman, who, although modest, was jealous of the prestige of the presidency and insisted that respect be paid to the office, if not to him personally. In a letter dated January 5, 1946, Truman may have been giving vent to his frustrations. The president determines foreign policy, and to perform this function he must be kept informed. The open break between Truman and Byrnes did not come until 1949 when Byrnes attacked Truman's domestic policies.

During the little more than eighteen months that Byrnes was secretary of state, there was a pronounced change in American foreign policy as far as relations with the Soviet Union were concerned. At the beginning, Byrnes strove to work out compromises with the Russians on the status of their satellites, on the international control of nuclear energy, on a unified treatment of all of Germany, on the position of Chang Kai-shek in China, and on other questions. While irritated at Byrnes's independence and lack of communication, Truman supported his secretary of state. Toward the end of 1945, the Byrnes-Truman policies came under severe attack from Senators Vandenberg and Connally, from Republican isolationists, from some of the press, and from such conservative Truman advisers as Admiral Leahy, Secretaries Forrestal, Vinson, Anderson, and Clark, Ambassador Hurley, and others. Events played into the hands of those advocating a tougher policy toward the Soviet Union. The critics denounced the failure of the London conference as due to Soviet stubbornness, the Moscow communique as appeasement, Stalin's speech of February 9, 1946, as a veiled threat of war, the exposure of a Soviet atomic spy ring as alarming, Churchill's iron curtain speech as a rousing call to action, the refusal of the communists to withdraw their troops from Iran as alarming, the Soviet failure to accept the U.N. proposal on the control of atomic energy as damaging to future world peace, and the collapse of the reparations plans as inevitable in view of Soviet actions regarding Germany. Byrnes and Truman felt pressed to take firmer stands against Soviet demands. The Truman administration offered a loan to Great Britain, but loan negotiations with the Soviet Union broke down. Defenders of Russian policies, such as Henry Wallace, argued in vain that Soviet intentions were defensive, not aggressive. The Byrnes-Truman resolute policy on Iran, resistance to Soviet pressure on Turkey, and cutting off of reparations to the Soviet Union from Western Germany were among the early developments in what came to be called the cold war. Truman, however, did not personally attack the Soviet Union and communism during this period but continued negotiations even though his hopes of Allied postwar unity were fading.

chapter 25 | CHANGING POPULARITY AND THE 1946 ELECTIONS

We Americans need hard-fought elections to remind us we are a democracy, as a dog should have fleas to remind him he is a dog.
—*Independent* (Corona, California)

When Truman became president, his popularity was high for some of the same reasons that made him available as a candidate for vice-president in 1944. Some of the Roosevelt haters were glad to see him gone from the White House. Truman had been acceptable as a vice-presidential candidate to labor, farmers, conservative southerners, northern liberals, and minority groups. At first, businessmen thought he would at least stop the trend toward greater governmental activity. His votes on labor issues in the Senate had been satisfactory to trade union leaders, and his votes on farm issues had generally pleased the leaders of the farm groups. He was a moderate and thus did not alarm those in the center. The Gallup Poll released in April 1945 gave him a rating of 87 percent favorable on the conduct of the presidency, higher than any rating that Roosevelt had received.[1]

One of Truman's first announcements was that he would carry out the Roosevelt policies. His problem was that in many cases he had to find out what those policies were. FDR had said many things to many people that were not recorded, and he had left many problems unsolved. Events were moving rapidly, and new problems arose every day. Who could say what Roosevelt's solution would have been for these problems? Among the ranks of the former Roosevelt advisers there were many differences of opinion. Who could say whose advice Roosevelt might have followed in one of these new situations?[2]

In the field of public relations, it was clear that Roosevelt believed in trying to win popular support for his policies by whatever means were available. His most effective means had been his fireside chats broadcast over the radio and his two news conferences each week. Truman continued the use of these two media, but he lacked FDR's virtuosity as a radio artist. It was inevitable that there would be changes and that Truman would have to search for a style of his own. He was on good terms with the White House correspondents since he had met many of them when he was chairman of the Special Senate Committee to Investigate the National Defense Program, when he was the vice-presidential candidate, and during his short term as vice-president.[3] In contrast to Roosevelt, he was direct, and homespun. He might revert to the language of the barnyard, the barracks, or a Jackson County Democratic ward meeting.[4] He followed the Roosevelt rules that there should be no direct quotation unless this was indicated and that background information given to the press for its guidance and use could not be attributed to the President. He reduced the number of news conferences to somewhat less than one a week on the ground that he needed to devote more time to the heavy load of business he had to handle. His press secretary, Charlie Ross, held a press conference every day and kept his office open all day. In addition to the regular news conferences and fireside chats, Truman continued limited live radio broadcasts on special occasions and limited transcribed radio broadcasts urging special action, and he began increased use of television as that medium developed. He also used formal messages to Congress, general proclamations, announcements, official memos to executive offices, talks and correspondence with congressional leaders, public addresses, executive orders, release of letters and telegrams, and statements issued by his press secretary. Truman gradually built up a staff in which he had confidence that could help him perform these various functions effectively. Some of these staff aides were holdovers from the previous administration, and others were his own appointees.[5]

At his first news conference held on April 17, 1945, five days after he became president, he was taut; he knew that the 350 correspondents who crowded into his office would compare him with FDR. He met the questions head on and did not make any blunders.[6] Jonathan Daniels, who had been press secretary to Roosevelt, thought that he did well. In his *Memoirs*, Truman relates proudly some of the answers he gave to questions asked, commenting, "Other questions followed, usually unrelated questions that forced my mind to leap in many directions."[7]

For the first six months or so, the press was favorably disposed toward Truman. There was no personal feuding such as marked the Roosevelt period. In 1945 the journalists found him friendly and cooperative. They were invited to go along with him on his trips and to join him in bull sessions and in poker games.

Gradually the general friendly atmosphere changed to a more critical one, however. Some journalists objected to the favorable treatment that certain correspondents received from Truman. For example, Ernest Vaccaro, whom Truman had known during the vice-presidential campaign, was given a ride to his office in the official presidential limousine the week Truman was sworn in, thus establishing a special relationship. The turning point, however, in his popularity was the end of the war and his comprehensive message to Congress of September 6, 1945, presenting a twenty-one point program for the reconversion period, which clearly indicated that he would work for the completion of the Roosevelt New Deal. Those who opposed Roosevelt's domestic policies were disappointed; they had hoped that Truman would be found in the conservative camp.[8]

It took Truman a while to realize that a statement he made in an offhand manner might have worldwide repercussions. A good example is a press conference that he held on October 8, 1945.[9] Truman made what he thought was an innocent routine remark, but the newsmen rushed to the telephones and the item was flashed around the world: "Truman Says U.S. to Keep Atom Bomb Secret."[10] He had not discussed this position with the British and the Canadians, who were partners in the project.

In his press conferences Truman sometimes showed an impetuosity, which got him into trouble from time to time. In discussing the budget on August 3, 1946, Truman said that he sent for the Republican who predicted the Republicans could effect a 20 percent reduction in taxes and asked him how he would do it. He said the man, whom he identified as Congressman Harold Knutson of Minnesota, could not tell him how. But the President had mixed up his identities. He corrected his mistake at a later press conference, admitting that the president made mistakes as well as anybody else.[11]

The honeymoon was clearly over by 1946, and the media began to find fault with Truman's performance—and he with theirs. Strikes were not prevented, and it took too long to settle them. The seizing of the coal mines and the granting of substantial increases to the miners in wages and to the owners in price increases were resented by the public. The press accused him of ineptitude in handling the meat crisis. Truman's foreign policies seemed to be vacillating. To some his handling of the "communist menace" seemed ill boding. They characterized his efforts to reach agreements with the Soviet Union as appeasement. On the domestic scene, his efforts to thwart communist subversive activities were held to be insufficiently vigorous. He did not appear to be greatly alarmed by the *Amerasia* case, which involved some foreign service officers, or by the Ottawa spy ring, or by the charges made against Harry Dexter White, a high Treasury official. Congressman Edward H. Rees of Kansas called for "an immediate and thorough house cleaning of all those of doubtful loyalty."[12]

The decline in his popularity is shown by the Elmo Roper study, which surveyed changes in attitudes toward Truman as president from 1945 to 1946:[13]

	NOVEMBER 1945	APRIL 1946
Truman is doing such an excellent job that he is likely to be considered one of our greatest Presidents.	20%	6%
While Truman has made some mistakes, on most things he is doing a good job.	62	46
While Truman has done some things well he is not really capable of handling the job.	9	34
It is an extremely bad thing for the country to have a man like Truman as President.	4	6
Express no opinion.	5	8

Truman gave his press secretary, Charlie Ross, many hard times. Ross was vitally concerned with getting the President to avoid words or actions that might damage the presidential image. Truman's informal comments on the difficulties of the presidency left the impression with some that he felt unequal to the job. Ross tried to offset these remarks. To one old friend, Truman said in 1946 that he would not run again in 1948. Ross had to deny this vehemently for political reasons—otherwise the powers of the presidency would have been weakened. He also had to downgrade the importance of Truman's pardoning members of the Pendergast organization convicted of vote frauds, claiming they were merely routine matters. Complaints Truman made about the hard bargaining practices of the Soviet Union got back to Moscow, where they were regarded as unfriendly. Ross tried to counter such impressions.[14]

One of the biggest problems that Truman created for himself in 1946 was his purge of Congressman Roger C. Slaughter from his home district in Missouri. Slaughter was originally nominated and elected with Truman's blessing in 1942, and he was reelected in 1944. In the House, Slaughter was appointed to the important Rules Committee, where he proved to be a stumbling block. Truman was especially incensed at Slaughter's holding up the bill for a permanent Fair Employment Practices Committee. Since Slaughter was from his own district, the President justified his opposition and felt that it was not a general purge, such as Roosevelt tried in 1938. At his press conference on July 18, Truman announced, "I am against Slaughter. If Mr. Slaughter is right, I am wrong."[15] If he had left his participation at that, he could have avoided later repercussions, but his anger was such that he called Jim Pendergast to the White House and asked him to do what he could to defeat Slaughter. Apparently he did not try to conceal this White House visit. The Pendergast machine was not as effective as it used to be, but this was an invitation to them to go all out against Slaughter.[16] The organization selected Enos Axtell to run against him.[17] Some of Jim Pendergast's men reverted to their former practices. Because Truman had pardoned those convicted of election frauds in the past, they regarded a return to election manipulation as safe. But their course of action was disastrous. Slaughter was defeated in the primary, but the cost of this purge was much too high. Friendly Roy Roberts of the *Kansas City Star* looked at the lopsided returns in the four strongest Pendergast wards and sent two reporters to investigate. Although Hannegan announced that Axtell's primary victory was a "strong vote of confidence in President Truman," it turned out to be anything but that. The reporters soon discovered many election irregularities, and the *Kansas City Star* turned over the evidence to U.S. Attorney Sam Wear, who forwarded it to Attorney General Clark, who was naturally embarrassed by the situation. Clark wiggled out of the mess by having the FBI make a halfhearted review of the *Star* evidence. Three federal judges found only minor violations. The *Star*, however, kept up the crusade against the election frauds, and Truman was charged by the opposition press with complicity in them. The accusations damaged the party image in the November elections, and in his district Axtell was defeated by a Republican. This case was to plague Truman for years to come because of its unsavory aspects, and the Republican senator elected from Missouri in 1946, James P. Kem, made the most of them.[18]

When the 1946 general congressional elections came along in November, the magic name of Roosevelt was available only as a memory although the Democrats vainly attempted to cling to it by broadcasting records of his old speeches. President Truman stood helplessly by, his aid not being sought by congressional, state, or local candidates. Why was he shunned? A year before, his popularity was running high and the universal view was that he was trying very hard and most people hoped that he would be successful. According to a Gallup poll taken in July 1946, approval of the way he was handling his job as president dipped to 43 percent.[19] It seemed that the harder he tried to please the divergent groups, the more they seemed displeased. He was not antilabor. Why wouldn't the railroad workers realize that he was trying to save the country from disaster when he proposed the drastic step of drafting striking railroad men? He was not opposed to the farmers. Why were they feeding grain needed for humans here and abroad to animals, and why were they withholding their cattle from the market, thus creating a shortage of meat? As for the consumers and their complaints about shortages, rationing, and higher prices, he had asked Congress for adequate controls and had been turned down. As for the minority groups, he had not yet announced his committee on civil rights, but the black leaders knew that he was organizing such a committee.[20]

Truman's popular image had been damaged by the events of the past year. It was all too evident that he lacked the finesse of his predecessor. Otherwise, why had he lost the services of those two liberals, Ickes and

Wallace? The latter had been campaigning for certain liberal congressmen, but the returns were to show that Wallace's support was a negative factor because of his close association with the communists, who were becoming more and more unpopular both at home and abroad. Postmaster General Hannegan at a cabinet meeting in September urged cabinet members to hold themselves free to make speeches, but he excused Forrestal and Patterson, much to their hearty agreement. Defense posts should be kept out of politics.[21]

The impression was widespread that Truman had failed to give strong support to those who were vigorously fighting inflation, and at the same time he had not won over business leaders since his rhetoric was still strongly tinged with New Deal words, and the farmers were not satisfied because they wanted higher prices for their produce. Minority groups of foreign stock were dissatisfied because the American government had not saved Poland, Hungary, Rumania, Bulgaria, and the Baltic states of Lithuania, Estonia, and Latvia from the Soviet Union. At the same time, those friendly toward the Soviet Union thought that Truman was too tough on the Russians, who had made great sacrifices to win the war and felt that they were entitled to reparations and protection against future attacks from Central Europe. There were too many different elements to please, and they could not all be satisfied at the same time.

The Republican national chairman, Congressman B. Carroll Reece of Tennessee, was adroitly leading the attack against the faltering Democrats. Following the meat crises and Truman's order ending all meat controls, he charged that the President was taking action "after the horse has gone to the butcher shop." The Republican slogans, "Had enough?" and "It's time for a change," took hold. Reece promised "orderly, capable and honest government in Washington" and the replacement of "controls, confusion, corruption and communism" if the Republicans took over Congress. The purge of Congressman Slaughter by Pendergast methods was proof of Democratic corruption, which went right up to the White House.[22]

The 1946 election results were a disaster for the Democrats, and a sweet victory for the Republicans who had passed through sixteen lean years. The Republicans increased their Senate membership from 38 to 51, their House delegation from 190 to 246, and they captured enough additional governorships to bring their total to 25 out of 48. The elections gave the Republicans a majority in both houses of Congress and a majority of the governorships. The Democrats had lost 12 seats in the Senate, 55 seats in the House, and 3 governorships. It was their lowest point since 1928.[23]

On November 7, 1946, Senator J. William Fulbright of Arkansas suggested that President Truman appoint Senator Arthur Vandenberg as secretary of state and then resign, making Vandenberg president.[24] Truman

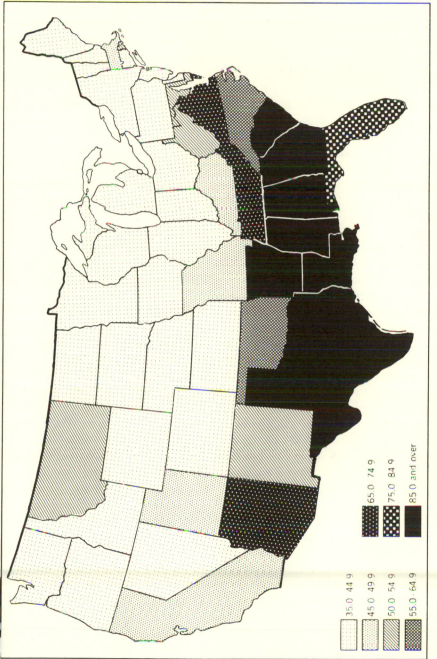

Map 6. Percentage Democratic vote of major party vote for the House of Representatives, 1946

35.0 - 44.9
45.0 - 49.9
50.0 - 54.9
55.0 - 64.9
65.0 - 74.9
75.0 - 84.9
85.0 and over

exploded at this suggestion and remarked, "A little more United States land grant college education on the United States Constitution and what it meant would do Fulbright a lot of good." His daughter, Margaret, termed the idea a "bit of idiocy," reflecting her father's point of view.[25] Harold Ickes backed Fulbright.[26]

The 1946 elections were in part the result of the swing of the pendulum that is typical of American politics. From its low point in 1924, the Democratic party climbed steadily until its peak in 1936, after which it began to decline as measured by its percentage of the major party vote. The full cycle ran from 1924 until a new low point in 1946. In each congressional election that followed the 1936 peak, the Democratic percentage of the aggregate vote for congressmen declined until 1948, when a new cycle made a faltering beginning. In presidential elections, the low point for the Democrats was reached in 1952 and 1956.

Map 6 of the 1946 elections based upon the percentage Democratic vote of the major party vote for the House of Representatives by aggregate vote for each state shows that of the states north of the Mason-Dixon line, only Montana in the West and West Virginia, Maryland, and Rhode Island in the East were carried by the Democrats. The Old South was still for the Democrats, but the Republicans carried the border states of Missouri and Kentucky. In Truman's home state of Missouri, the Democrats lost three seats, the delegation dropping from 7 to only 4 of the 13 seats assigned to the state.

The elections were clearly a disaster for the President and his party. How great a downfall he would find out later when some of the notorious members of the Senate "class of 1946" got into action: John W. Bricker of Ohio, William E. Jenner of Indiana, Joseph R. McCarthy of Wisconsin, and John J. Williams of Delaware. As the Republican candidate for vice-president in 1948, Bricker was to excoriate Truman in devastating terms. As leaders of the so-called McCarthy era, Senators Jenner and McCarthy were to blast the Truman administration unmercifully. Senator Williams was to lambast the Truman budgets.

In the House of Representatives, there were some significant newcomers. Included were two future presidents, John F. Kennedy and Richard M. Nixon, both of whom became senators on their way to the White House. Nixon was to become a scourge of Truman and of the Democrats on the anticommunist issue.

When Truman and his party hit this low point, they calculated that the only way they could go was up. Under the skillful guidance of Clark Clifford and his associates, that is exactly what Truman did. He began to climb back into the confidence of the electorate after the 1946 elections by making the Eightieth Congress his prime target.

chapter 26 | BATTLING REPUBLICAN OPPOSITION, 1947–1948

> *The Republicans always waited politely for Mr. Truman's proposals on labor, taxes, inflation, civil rights and education however scant the regard they intended to pay them.*
> —Clinton Rossiter, *The American Presidency*

THE FIRST SESSION OF THE EIGHTIETH CONGRESS

The Eightieth Congress presented President Truman with an entirely new situation. Both houses were controlled by the Republicans, and under the Legislative Reorganization Act of 1946, the number of committees had been drastically reduced.[1] The new Speaker of the House was Congressman Joseph Martin of Massachusetts, who, in looking back at the years 1947-1948, recalled, "I led the Republicans in what looks in retrospect like the last stand against heavy federal spending, high taxes, centralization, and extravagances."[2] Although the president pro tempore of the Senate was Arthur Vandenberg, who had been working closely with the President in foreign affairs, the leader in domestic affairs was conservative Senator Robert A. Taft of Ohio, chairman of the Republican Policy Committee and of the Labor and Welfare Committee. The chairman of the House Appropriations Committee was John Taber of New York, who promised to apply a "meat-axe to government frills."[3]

On the eve of the first session, Senator Taft stated in a radio address: "The main issue of the election was the restoration of freedom and the elimination or reduction of constantly increasing interference with family life and with business by autocratic government bureaus and autocratic labor leaders."[4]

The new chairman of the House Ways and Means Committee, Harold Knutson of Minnesota, proposed a 20 percent tax reduction in order to "stop the New Deal practice of using tax laws to punish its enemies." President Truman opposed this cut; his economic advisers told him it would be inflationary, he wanted to balance the budget, and he wanted to reduce the national debt during an upward swing of the business cycle without cutting back on government services. The Republicans wanted to balance the budget, but they preferred to do it by slashing expenditures.

On Truman's return trip from Independence, Missouri, after the election, Clifford found him "terribly downcast" about his legislative program. A strategy for the President's relationship with an opposition Congress was worked out by James H. Rowe, Jr., a former administrative assistant to Roosevelt, who had lobbied with Tom Corcoran for New Deal measures and who was at the time consultant to the Bureau of the Budget. In a memorandum in December 1946, he advised Truman to submit general proposals, avoiding specific recommendations or draft bills, which might be rejected or drastically altered by the Republicans. In order to make a record, he might send special messages on a few topics of great public concern. He suggested that the veto be used sparingly in cases where the "public interest" was involved "and on which public opinion has been clearly solidified." He also urged bipartisan cooperation and regular, scheduled meetings with minority leaders Rayburn and Biffle, who could serve as liaison men with the opposition. Former Speaker Rayburn was reluctant at first to accept House minority leadership, but Truman and the southern congressmen persuaded him to take the job.[5]

Truman started out publicly in a way that indicated he was following Rowe's advice. Privately, he told Secretary Forrestal, who urged the same nonpartisan approach, that he felt "not much will come of such an attempt, that political maneuvering is inevitable, politics and our government being what they are."[6]

Truman showed the influence of the Rowe advice in his first press conference following the elections. He urged conciliation and cooperation between the executive and legislative branches and denounced narrow political actions for partisan gain. Accepting the verdict of the election, he said, "I do not claim for myself and my associates greater devotion to the welfare of our Nation than I ascribe to others of another party."[7]

Anticipating Republican attacks on remaining wartime controls, Truman terminated by executive action most of the remaining wage and price controls. He placed the blame for inflation on Congress—"The real basis of our difficulty is the unworkable law which the Congress gave us to administer" —glossing over the fact that this law had Democratic as well as Republican support in Congress.[8] While he decried bitterly partisan appeals, he was to make a few of his own during the next two years, and the Eightieth Congress was to be one of his targets.

The Republicans, with control of both houses of Congress for the first time in eighteen years, had an opportunity to make a record and build a new coalition, but they failed. In accordance with the seniority system, the conservatives—Taft, Martin, Halleck, Knutson, and Taber—came into key positions, and they thought they could abolish the New Deal programs, balance the budget by drastic cuts in expenditures, reduce taxes, curb the labor unions, and restore the free enterprise system by abolishing the restricting regulations on business. These aims failed to take into consideration the vested interests of farmers, workers, investors, and the unfortunates in the legislation on the books that was designed to protect them.[9]

President Truman made a formal presentation of his program in the form of three instead of the usual two presidential messages: the state of the union message, the budget message, and the economic report of the president, the first report made under the provision of the Employment Act of 1946. All three messages were moderate in character.

On January 6, Truman delivered in person his mildly worded seven-thousand-word state of the union message to a critical Congress, which regarded him as an ineffective holdover. He wanted to pacify his Republican opponents and gave lip-service to the free enterprise system: "Private enterprise must be given the greatest possible freedom to continue to expand the economy. . . . Now that nearly all wartime controls have been removed, the operation of our industrial system depends to a greater extent on the decisions of businessmen, farmers, and workers." He advocated five major economic policies "to provide for the long-range welfare of our free-enterprise system": (1) the promotion of greater harmony between labor and management, (2) the restriction of monopoly and unfair business practices, (3) the continuation of an aggressive program of home construction by enacting comprehensive housing legislation similar to the Taft-Ellender-Wagner "nonpartisan bill passed by the Senate last year," (4) a balancing of the budget and achievement of a surplus to reduce the debt, and (5) the protection of a fair level of return to farmers in postwar agriculture. In the balance of the message, he reiterated his plea for a national health program and the establishment of a Department of Welfare, he announced his creation of the Commission on Civil Rights, and he requested action on the development of the great river systems.[10]

The first economic report of the President described the prosperous state of the economy but cautioned about the forces threatening to undermine the growing economy, particularly the imbalance of the price-wage relationship; prices were going up faster than wages, thus depressing the workers' position. To guard against this danger, Truman repeated items in his "long-range programs," including higher social security, a higher minimum wage, a housing program, and plans for health insurance, public welfare, and federal aid to education.

The budget message called for estimated expenditures of $37.5 billion for fiscal 1948, which was $1.4 billion less than the actual expenditures for fiscal 1947. President Truman was opposed to tax reduction because he was anxious to lower the national debt, which then stood at $260 billion. His economic advisers were conservative about the rate of economic recovery and had underestimated the surplus, which at the end of the fiscal year was $8 billion. The budget estimates included justifications of his programs. He asserted that the figures were at rock bottom, but some conservative Republicans found them "shockingly disappointing" and predicted deep cuts.[11]

The struggle over the budget came in connection with the defense estimates. Some of the national security planners contended that the air force should be the first line of defense because its bombers were capable of carrying atomic weapons against an enemy anywhere in the world. The 70-group air force which would provide for 700 heavy bombers instead of 580 was the aim of these planners, who were naturally popular with the aircraft industries. The admirals were clamoring for a large aircraft carrier, which they claimed would be capable of carrying the battle to all hemispheres. With Republican backing—Senator Henry Cabot Lodge of Massachusetts was most insistent—the air force won most of its demands, and the aircraft carrier was abandoned.

Until the middle of May, Truman managed to stay on friendly terms with Congress, partly because the Republicans were bitterly divided and could not put through their bills on labor reform and tax reduction until June. He had also made some conservative appointments, which were pleasing to the Republicans. In addition to the selection of Marshall as secretary of state, there was the appointment of A. L. M. Wiggins, a banker who had critized New Deal programs as under secretary of the treasury, and Lewis W. Douglas, a Republican, as ambassador to Great Britain.[12] Truman also undercut the opposition by his special message of February 19, which recommended repeal of war and emergency statutes.

On the constitutional amendment limiting presidential tenure, the Republicans were united and were joined by thirteen Democratic senators and forty-seven Democratic congressmen, most of them southerners. The Republicans urged limitation as a means of preventing any tendency toward dictatorship. Democrats charged it was an attack on the memory of Roosevelt and "a limitation upon the people." Truman later defended Roosevelt's bid for his third and fourth terms as a response to pressing national emergencies and stated that the precedent should be continued by custom, not by a constitutional amendment.[13]

Regarding the confirmation of David E. Lilienthal as head of the newly created Atomic Energy Commission, there was a lively debate, which was won in the end by the President, because of the support of some Republicans, such as Senator Vandenberg, who favored civilian control of atomic energy and was not moved by wild charges made against Lilienthal about alleged "softness on communism." Senator Kenneth D. McKellar of Tennessee had been carrying on a vendetta against Lilienthal for six years because the latter, while TVA head, had insisted on merit rather than patronage appointments.[14] Even Senator Taft joined the group of senators making highly questionable accusations against Lilienthal. The President stood firmly behind his nominee and in press conferences refuted the objections and upbraided Senator McKellar. The *New Republic* termed Vandenberg's defense summary "his highest hour in nineteen years as senator."[15]

There were indecisive skirmishes over the budget. Truman left the details of the justification of the estimates to subordinates. He met with the Republican members of the Senate Appropriations Committee in the hope that they would be more open to reason than the House was. At his February 13 press conference, he mildly opposed cuts in the estimates. In his Jefferson Day speech of April 5, he followed Secretary of Commerce Harriman's advice, emphasizing national responsibility and counseling against damaging reductions in the areas of reclamation, soil conservation, water resources, and the functions of the Labor Department.[16]

In handling legislation designed to reverse a Supreme Court decision upholding labor claims for portal-to-portal wages (pay for time spent on job location in changing clothes, assembling tools, and traveling within the plant), Truman followed a new tactic. He took no stand at first when the Republicans introduced legislation aiming to curtail such claims. A White House aide, aiming to preserve the substance of the Fair Labor Standards Act, suggested legislation providing for a statute of limitation on claims and giving the wage and hour administration authority to issue decisions on what constituted a workday. Although this suggestion had support within the administration, Truman failed to endorse it. Both parties were divided on the issue. Truman met with cabinet officials and his White House staff to discuss the Republican-proposed legislation. Clifford, Secretary of Labor Schwellenbach, and Leon Keyserling of the Council of Economic Advisers were opposed, while Attorney General Clark, Secretary of Commerce Harriman, and Secretary of the Navy Forrestal approved the bill. Truman compromised the issue by signing the bill and adding his interpretation as to how it should be carried out. Justice William O. Douglas had assured Truman that the courts would consider presidential comments in determining the intent of the law. The President did not want to antagonize Congress while his crucial request for Greek-Turkish aid was still pending. This was the end, however, of his appeasement strategy.[17]

After the middle of May, friction between Truman and Congress developed. A group of liberal advisers, including Clifford, Federal Security Agency Administrator Oscar Ewing, Leon Keyserling, Assistant Secretary of Labor David A. Morse, and Charles S. Murphy, Clifford's assistant, met weekly to establish liberal positions and to urge Truman to act in a way that would hold New Deal support.[18] In a special message to Congress on health and disability insurance on May 19, 1947, he took the offensive against a Republican measure that provided federal assistance in medical care only to the poor and backed a bill that was much broader in its coverage.[19]

On the advice of his Council of Economic Advisers, who regarded an income tax cut as inflationary, Truman had consistently opposed such action. The Republicans, however, were adamant. Harold Knutson, chairman of the House Ways and Means Committee, favored a 20 percent cut. The Senate Finance Committee revised this proposal down somewhat. The legislation passed was practically unanimously opposed by high officials of the Truman administration. Federal Works Director Fleming was the only top official recommending approval. In a vigorous veto message sent to Congress on June 16, the President denounced the bill as the "wrong kind of tax reduction at the wrong time" because it was "likely to induce the very recession we seek to avoid." He added, "It is not the proper way to remedy the current price situation," and it was "neither fair nor equitable." The House failed to override the veto by two votes.[20]

The next famous veto was of the Taft-Hartley labor bill on June 20, 1947. In his January messages, Truman had admitted the need for a mild reform of labor legislation. Unpopular strikes, jurisdictional disputes, violations of labor contracts, arbitrary trade union leadership, and denial of apprenticeships to minorities had aroused a public demand for legislation to curb labor abuses. The Republicans grasped this opportunity with zeal. The majority report of the House Labor Committee on the Hartley bill claimed that the legislation was necessary to decrease industrial strife, to equalize labor-management relations, and to rescue the worker who, as result of the Wagner Act, had "been deprived of his dignity as an individual." In the Senate, Taft, who had his own version of a labor bill, met considerable opposition within his own party, but by adroit maneuvering he obtained most of what he wanted. In the conference committee, Taft worked to tone down the harshest features of the Hartley bill. When the Taft-Hartley bill came to the White House, there was division among the councils. A number of Truman's advisers, including Fleming, Snyder, Harriman, Forrestal, and Anderson, opposed a veto. On the other hand, the Clifford-Ewing-Keyserling group urged a veto as a necessary step to win the support of labor, which bitterly denounced the legislation as a slave labor bill. Three-fifths of the Democratic national committeemen favored a veto. Truman held no formal cabinet meeting on the measure but announced June 20 that he was sending a veto message to Congress. The message was well researched by John Steelman, who conferred with top officials on every aspect of the bill. In rhetoric it was stern; it contained such phrases as "unworkable," "drastic," "dangerous," "arbitrary," and "unwarranted." On the radio, Truman denounced the bill as a shocking measure.[21] In a radio reply, Taft accused the President of misrepresenting the bill. Although the veto was overridden, the battle left Truman solidly on the side of labor and wiped out resentments that had lingered after his speech on the railway strike. Even the *New York Times* commented that the veto showed the President had administrative talent in creating an organization that prepared the information needed for arriving at a decision.[22]

Another controversial veto was delivered on June 26 when the President sent a message rejecting the wool price support bill on the ground that its import fee would have a disastrous effect on pending international trade negotiations. It was a regulation that would invite retaliation. In his message, the President indicated what measures he would accept, and Congress passed such a law.[23]

In July Congress again passed an income tax cut bill, which Truman vetoed as he had warned he would. This time the Senate failed to override the veto by the narrow margin of five votes. The Democrats, even the southerners, held together on this issue, and three liberal Republicans joined them.[24]

The end of the first session of the Eightieth Congress was not the end of the vetoes or of the recriminations. Senate Republicans sought to obtain unanimous consent to vote on a resolution to investigate the Justice Department, which, they claimed, had whitewashed the charges of election fraud in the Kansas City Democratic primary of 1946 in Truman's congressional district, but the Democrats blocked the vote, much to the anger of the Republicans. Truman pocket vetoed the National Science Foundation bill because Congress had placed the foundation outside presidential control.[25] Budget Director Webb wrote that the "enactment of this legislation would be injurious to the whole tradition of presidential responsibility for the administration of the Executive branch and would also serve as a bad precedent for future enactments." Truman also vetoed a bill excluding newspaper vendors from social security coverage. The Treasury Department and Federal Security Agency recommended a pocket veto, claiming it was justified on the ground this was a piecemeal attack on the social security system, which should be expanded, not contracted.[26] The President signed a bill concerning consumer credit controls but added the comment that permanent controls were necessary, and this was not the way to control inflation.

The session ended with a widening chasm between the President and Congress. On domestic legislation, the President's program was thwarted by the coalition of southern Democrats and Republicans except in the case of the income tax cut, which practically all Democrats opposed. On foreign policy issues, the Democratic ranks held together better, and they were aided by Republican internationalists led by Senator Vandenberg. Truman came out of the battle with the legislators with an enhanced reputation as a friend of labor and the common man. He was building the image that he needed to win the election of 1948.

THE SPECIAL SESSION OF 1947

Because European conditions worsened, in October Truman called a special session to deal with interim aid for Europe, and he used the same occasion to put forth his anti-inflation program in a message drafted by Keyserling, Bell, Elsey, and Stauffacher.

In a radio address explaining his decision to call a special session, Truman emphasized the need to control inflation, even though this brought in a domestic issue that might endanger the bipartisan foreign policy. He thought that the need was "too pressing—the results of delay too grave" to wait until the next regular session. The seriousness of the situation had been brought to his attention by former Price Administrator Chester Bowles and by his Council of Economic Advisers. Truman brought forth a ten-point program, which included:

1. To restore consumer credit controls and to restrain the creation of inflationary bank credit.

2. To authorize the regulation or speculative trading on the commodity exchanges.

3. To extend and strengthen export controls.

4. To extend authority to allocate transportation facilities and equipment.

5. To authorize measures that would induce the marketing of livestock and poultry at weights and grades that represent the most efficient utilization of grain.

6. To enable the Department of Agriculture to expand its program of encouraging conservation practices in the United States and to authorize measures designed to increase the production of foods in foreign countries.

7. To authorize allocation and inventory control of scarce commodities that affect the cost of living or industrial production.

8. To extend and strengthen rent control.

9. To authorize consumer rationing on products in short supply that affect the cost of living.

10. To authorize price ceilings on products in short supply that affect the cost of living or industrial production and to authorize such wage ceilings as are essential to maintain the necessary price ceilings.[27]

Truman's program was comprehensive, but he could not—or chose not to—rally the full support of his top administrators behind his proposals. In their testimony before Congress, Secretary of Commerce Harriman, Secretary of Agriculture Anderson, and Secretary of the Treasury Snyder failed to back the full program. Snyder in particular opposed the special reserve requirement for member banks, which the chairman of the Federal Reserve Board, Marriner S. Eccles, suggested for implementing point 1. Although the Council of Economic Advisers urged Truman to press for the special reserve clause, he refused to act although in his public remarks he still supported the whole program.[28] In a press conference of October 16, Truman had made the serious mistake of calling price controls and rationing "police state methods."[29]

Under the circumstances, it was not to be expected that the Republican-controlled Congress would give the President his whole program. The

House considered some mild measures but failed to act. The Senate bill reinstated consumer credit controls, extended export and rail transportation controls, gave authority for food conservation at home and food production abroad, and called for voluntary agreements concerning regulation of commodity speculation and allocation and inventory controls. When the Senate bill came to the House, it was passed and sent to the President, who signed it reluctantly, characterizing it as "pitifully inadequate" and "feeble."[30]

The special session accomplished two major objectives for Truman. He got the interim aid he regarded as essential for pulling Europe through the winter, and his anti-inflation program put him on the side of the consumers. The failure of Congress to adopt the most important features enabled him to put the blame for further inflation on that body.[31]

THE SECOND SESSION OF THE EIGHTIETH CONGRESS

In their memorandum of November 19, 1947, Clifford and Rowe outlined a legislative strategy for the Truman administration to follow in a presidential year during which Congress was controlled by the opposition. "Its tactics must . . . be entirely different than if there were any real point to bargaining and compromise. Its recommendations tailored for the voters, not Congressmen; they must display a label which reads 'no compromise.'" Thinking the Marshall Plan was safe, Clifford urged positions on high prices, housing, tax revision, and natural resources that would provoke political controversy.[32] As his assistant Elsey put it, the state of the union speech "must be controversial as hell, must state the issues of the election, must draw the line sharply between Republicans and Democrats. The Democratic platform will stem from it, and the election will be fought on the issues it presents."[33]

An early step taken by the White House staff in carrying out the strategy for winning the 1948 election was the preparation of the annual reports to Congress. The general messages and the special messages were designed to implement the memorandum of 1947. On the state of the union message, which had the broadest scope, Truman had help from Clark Clifford, Charles Murphy, George Elsey, Charles Stauffacher, Dave Bell, Leon Keyserling, John Steelman, and John Snyder. Materials were furnished by the Departments of Defense, State, and Justice. A short message was prepared so that Truman could deliver it in person. Relying on facts rather than eloquence, he read it in his flat voice.[34]

The first goal mentioned was to secure the essential human rights of American citizens. A specific item was the safeguarding of civil rights. Clifford had called for emphasis on this point if the Democrats hoped to hold the black vote, which was being assiduously cultivated by the Republicans, especially by Governor Dewey. A message on following up the report of the President's Committee on Civil Rights was promised.[35]

The second goal was to protect and develop American human resources, including extension of old age and unemployment benefits and introduction of medical care. The President also recommended greatly increased aid to education and the establishment of a cabinet office devoted to health, education, and welfare affairs. A long-range housing program, which would outbid the Republicans who, under Senator Taft's leadership, were concerned with the problem, was another item, along with veterans' housing, low-cost housing, and rent control.

The third goal was to conserve and use American natural resources. An appeal to the West was made by outlining water resources planning, extension of reclamation, development of waterpower, and land-use planning.

The fourth goal was to lift the standard of living for all Americans by strengthening the economic system and sharing more broadly the goods produced. The loyalty of the farmers was sought by asking for continuation of farm price supports, crop insurance, extension of rural electrification, and improvement of farm marketing practices. On the labor front, the message indicated continued opposition to the Taft-Hartley Act but pledged that as long as the law was on the books, the President would carry out his constitutional duty and administer it. The speech also called for increasing the minimum wage, improving collective bargaining, and strengthening the economic system so as to raise the standard of living.

Truman warned that these goals were unattainable if inflation was not contained and taxes were not maintained. He contended that his ten-point anti-inflation program presented to Congress in November was still essential, including the power to impose rationing and price controls if necessary. He charged Congress with enacting this plan or taking the blame for inflation. His tax plan called for a $40 credit for everyone as an offset for higher living costs. The loss in revenue was to be made up by increasing the tax on corporation profits.

The fifth goal, in the field of foreign affairs, was to achieve a world peace based on principles of freedom and justice and the equality of all nations. The message emphasized the President's role in the formulation and execution of the Marshall Plan and in aid to Greece and Turkey. Clifford had pointed out that the President should not be overshadowed by Secretary of State Marshall and by Senator Vandenberg. On the problems of foreign relations the message stated:

We have learned that the loss of freedom in any area of the world means a loss of freedom to ourselves—that the loss of independence by any nation adds directly to the insecurity of the United States and all free nations.

We have learned that a healthy world economy is essential to world peace—that economic distress is a disease whose evil effects spread far beyond the boundaries of the afflicted nation.[36]

When the speech was given, the Republicans applauded only the passage pledging enforcement of the Taft-Hartley Act and the part urging military strength.[37] After the address, they pounced upon it. Congressman Knutson exclaimed, "My God, I didn't know inflation had gone that far! Tom Pendergast paid two dollars a vote and now Truman proposes to pay forty dollars." Senator Taft denounced the message in a radio speech characterizing it as New Dealish, economically unsound, unnecessary, and tending toward totalitarianism. As he put it, "The Federal Government comes forward again as Santa Claus himself." Taft was caught in a dilemma. He was not wholly conservative and had welfare programs of his own, but his rhetoric enabled Truman to denounce the Eightieth Congress as reactionary. The *New York Times* viewed the speech as a "sort of economic manifesto"; Truman called it a "blue print for American programs for the next ten years." The Republicans, referring to the coming elections, called the speech a plan for the next ten months.[38]

Five days later, the budget message followed, a formidable document that requested appropriations of some $39.7 billion for fiscal year 1949, of which four-fifths was war related and one-fifth was for domestic programs. Truman announced an expected surplus of some $7.5 billion for fiscal year 1948, most of which would be used to retire part of the national debt. This surplus undoubtedly encouraged the Republicans in their endeavors to cut taxes. Secretary Forrestal was greatly concerned that more money was not requested for defense purposes.[39]

President Truman was convinced by Budget Director Webb, Treasury Secretary Snyder, and the Council of Economic Advisers to follow a conservative fiscal policy. In times of prosperity, he favored a budget surplus, which could be used to reduce the national debt. In 1948 the greatest pressure to increase federal expenditures came from the military. National security had to be balanced against possible dangers to the domestic economy. Following the warnings of possible war from General Clay and the Czechoslovakian coup, President Truman on March 17, 1948, requested from Congress a supplemental military budget. The Council of Economic Advisers was alarmed and wrote to Truman about the danger of inflation and the need for controls. Secretary Forrestal submitted an estimate of $9 billion furnished to him by the services. Truman told Forrestal that he could support a supplemental request to Congress of only $3 billion. Webb proposed that this be reduced to $2.5 billion in view of the fact that Congress had overridden the President's veto of the tax reduction bill. He was concerned about possible deficits, inflation, and the obvious difficulties of trying to secure controls and higher taxes. Forrestal argued that the world situation did not warrant such a reduction, and he asked for a conference with the President. On May 7, Forrestal, Webb, Marshall, Snyder, Steelman, and Sidney Souers (Truman's assistant for national security affairs) met with the President to discuss the supplement and the estimate of a $15 billion ceiling for fiscal 1950. Marshall, on being asked by the President to comment on the question, did not give Forrestal much help. He assumed that there would be no war, and he thought war preparations would be provocative. He also was concerned about the public reaction to a mounting defense budget. Truman agreed with Marshall's reasoning and supported Webb's ceiling for defense spending.[40]

On May 13 the President announced his decision to adhere to the $15 billion ceiling for fiscal 1950 at a meeting with the Joint Chiefs and the service secretaries, Webb and Forrestal. He said he would stick with this "unless world conditions deteriorate much further." He expected "these orders to be carried out wholeheartedly, in good spirit, and without mental reservation." The original services' estimate had been $30 billion, twice the ceiling. Forrestal appointed a board, which reduced it to $23.6 billion. He insisted that the Chiefs had to make allocations to the respective services within the Webb ceiling. Two of the services finally agreed to a proportional reduction of the agreed-upon $23.6 billion. The differences among the services were deep and involved vested interests in weapons systems. Forrestal sent two budgets to the White House, an intermediate one of $16.9 billion and one within the prescribed ceiling, which was now $14.4 billion. On December 9, the President met with Forrestal, Webb, the chiefs, the service secretaries, Gruenther, and Souers. After the presentation, Truman announced that the ceiling stood. Although the Berlin blockade and the possible requirement of American troops to help the United Nations enforce peace in Palestine supported Forrestal's plea for a higher budget, the President, in the absence of a strong plea from Marshall and in view of the accusations that he was the prisoner of the industrial-military complex, stood firm with his economic team, Webb, and the Council of Economic Advisers.[41]

The President's economic report prepared by the Council of Economic Advisers cautioned that the country's prosperity was fragile because it was based in part on inflation. In addition to the anti-inflation and other recommendations contained in the other two messages, this one proposed an expanded and improved system of higher education.

The Republicans in Congress tackled the income tax reduction as a first item of business. Truman had weakened his position by his own proposal for a tax abatement, which had not been cleared with Democratic leaders in Congress.

The Republicans were willing to make certain compromises in order to win enough Democratic support to override a veto. The new bill provided greater relief for low-income groups, extended the income-splitting provision, and reduced the revenue loss. Truman cleared his tax-cut veto with the Democratic leaders in Congress, and this left them in a better mood. A combination of Republicans and Democrats overrode the veto, and the Republicans scored a victory on one of their main proposals.[42]

The President waged a losing struggle with Congress regarding social security coverage. He vetoed two bills that excluded certain groups from coverage; one group was composed of newspaper and magazine vendors and the other of door-to-door salesmen, home workers, and taxi and truck drivers. The courts had attempted to include them, but some congressmen thought that Congress, not the courts, should make such a determination. Truman took the position that social security coverage should be expanded, not contracted, and held that those involved had the right to immediate coverage. Congress overrode his veto in both cases. This made him a defender of social security and Congress a hostile foe.[43]

Congress frustrated Truman's efforts to reorganize and strengthen the Labor Department. He submitted a reorganization plan that placed the U.S. Employment Service (USES) and Bureau of Employment Security in the Labor Department. Republicans denounced the plan. They had no confidence in the Labor Department, having already shown this by reducing its powers in the Taft-Hartley Act. Both houses rejected the plan. Congress then tried to achieve immediate transfer of USES back to the federal security agency by a rider to a supplemental appropriations bill. Truman vetoed the bill, saying that such legislation did not belong in an appropriation bill, but Congress overrode his veto.

Truman faced defeat in his attempt to augment public power facilities. Here he ran up against conservative Republicans, who were opposed to any competition between government and private business and against those economy-minded states that did not benefit from public power projects. The Tennessee Valley Authority urgently needed a supplementary steam plant and additional federal transmission facilities. Congress turned down the requests, thus giving private companies a bonanza in the transmission and sale of government-produced electricity. Truman called the decision bad, foolish, reckless, irresponsible, and a "capitulation to special interest groups."[44]

Congress also limited the antitrust program of the administration by passing a measure making it possible for railway carriers, operating within associations, to exercise an initial veto over rates proposed by individual carriers and thus hinder the filing of proposed rates that might be in the public interest. Following the advice of the Justice Department and his Council of Economic Advisers, Truman vetoed the bill because it represented "a departure from the present transportation policy of regulated competition and it was contrary to the administration's stand against monopolies." Congress overrode the veto.[45]

In the second session of the Eightieth Congress, Truman vetoed forty-three measures, eleven more than he had in the first session. On five major bills, his vetoes were overridden, marking a sharpening of the clash between these two branches of government. Truman used these actions to castigate Congress as the worst one in history.[46]

Truman launched an offensive against Congress by a deluge of special messages covering many vital topics. His rhetoric increased in shrillness as the session progressed. He was accused of playing politics, but this was a presidential year and he had to pose as a tribune of the people and run against the record of Congress if he hoped to gain votes.

Civil Rights

As he had promised in his state of the union message, Truman sent a special message on civil rights. Drafts of this message were worked on by Elsey, Phileo Nash, Robert Carr, Milton D. Stewart, David E. Bell, Murphy, Spingarn, George Washington, J. Donald Kingsley, Oscar Ewing, Clifford, Ross, and Steelman. The President looked at the eighth draft and refused to recommend representation in Congress for the District of Columbia. On February 2, 1948, he sent to Congress his ten-point program on civil rights:

1. Establishing a permanent Commission on Civil Rights, a Joint Congressional Committee on Civil Rights, and a Civil Rights Division in the Department of Justice.
2. Strengthening existing civil rights statutes.
3. Providing federal protection against lynching.
4. Protecting more adequately the right to vote.
5. Establishing a Fair Employment Practice Commission to prevent unfair discrimination in employment.
6. Prohibiting discrimination in interstate transportation facilities.
7. Providing home-rule and suffrage in Presidential elections for the residents of the District of Columbia.
8. Providing statehood for Hawaii and Alaska and a greater measure of self-government for U.S. island possessions.
9. Equalizing the opportunities for residents of the United States to become naturalized citizens.
10. Settling the evacuation claims of Japanese-Americans.[47]

In addition Truman promised an executive order restating government policy against discrimination in federal employment and a military order

Cartoon by C. K. Berryman, March 18, 1948. Reprinted, courtesy of *The Washington Star*.

ending segregation in the armed services. His program did not go as far as his Civil Rights Commission had recommended and, from our current vantage, does not seem very advanced because it did not mention desegregation of schools. Nevertheless at the time it was regarded as revolutionary by southerners. An angry delegation of southern governors asked national chairman McGrath to repudiate the proposals, but he refused. Governor Strom Thurmund of South Carolina, who had been a Truman supporter as recently as October 2, 1947, asked, "Will you now, at a time when national unity is so vital to the solution of the problem of peace in the world, use your influence as chairman of the Democratic National Committee to have the highly controversial civil-rights legislation, which tends to divide our people, withdrawn from consideration by the Congress?" To this McGrath answered "No." He tried to convince the southerners that the federal government would stay within its constitutional limits, but the delegation was unsatisfied.[48]

President Truman was unable to get Senator Barkley to sponsor the administration omnibus civil rights bill, which was then shelved. A bill for a permanent FEPC was introduced by the Republicans, but it never reached the floor. The same fate met an antilynching bill introduced by the Republicans. Truman risked losing parts of the South by his civil rights efforts, but he gained support among liberals and blacks in northern cities.

Without the civil rights acts he urged upon Congress following the report of his Commission on Civil Rights, Truman's administrative powers to advance the interests of minority groups were limited. Congress failed to include antisegregation amendments in the Selective Service Act of 1948, and some civil rights groups threatened civil disobedience. President Truman met this situation by issuing an executive order that provided for a progressive removal of segregation barriers in the armed services, to be completed by June 30, 1954. The order met with considerable resistance in the services and was only slowly implemented. Truman also issued an executive order barring discrimination in the hiring or treatment of federal employees. The order established the Fair Employment Practice Board to review complaints.[49]

Agricultural Policies

President Truman sent a number of requests to Congress for agricultural legislation. He recommended sustaining farm prices temporarily at 90 percent of parity, but the Department of Agriculture wanted to revise the parity formula. It wanted to introduce flexible price supports and to use production controls selectively to reduce chronic surpluses of certain crops. It also favored expanded consumption of farm products. Cotton and wheat farmers held out for high, fixed supports.[50] The House stuck with the existing system, and the Senate adopted a flexible formula. A compromise post-poned action on the Senate proposals. Although the Democrats were largely responsible for Truman's defeat in his long-range program, Truman denounced Congress, when signing the bill, for prohibiting the Commodity Credit Corporation from acquiring more storage space (this was to become a campaign issue), for failing to adopt measures to expand production to push ahead on soil conservation, and to improve rural housing, health, and education.[51]

As secretary of agriculture, Clinton Anderson continued to struggle for what he regarded as the interests of the farmers. This brought him into conflict with some of the international economic policies pursued by the Department of State and with the anti-inflation policies advocated by liberals in the Truman administration. Under Secretary of State Will Clayton was the most persistent advocate of freer international trade, which to him meant an end to high tariffs, import quotas, export subsidies, preferential customs arrangements, currency manipulation, bartering, and cartels. The growing productivity of American agriculture brought ever-increasing surpluses in grain and other foods, which Anderson wished to sell abroad by means of export subsidies. On the other hand, increasing competition abroad in the production of wool, sugar, cotton, and other agricultural commodities brought a demand for tariff protection and import quotas. The agricultural programs inherited from Roosevelt's New Deal enabled the secretary of agriculture to impose import quotas in order to maintain domestic prices of farm products threatened by foreign competition. A clash between Anderson and Clayton took place over the role of the Food and Agriculture Organization (FAO) of the United Nations. Sir John Boyd Orr, director general of FAO, proposed a world food board, which would set maximum and minimum world food prices for storable commodities and maintain these prices through management of buffer stocks. This proposal was supported by Norris E. Dodd, under secretary of agriculture, but not by the State Department. Truman did not interfere in the struggle, and the Clayton supporters had their way.[52] On this the *Nation* commented: "The State Department's objections to the world food board seem to be wholly doctrinaire, with no recognition of the significant difference between restrictive nationalistic controls and international controls which have as their aim stimulation of production and trade."[53]

The battle between the two departments continued in the conferences held in 1946, 1947, and 1948 to create the International Trade Organization. Anderson's support of American wool growers presented the first debated point. Clayton claimed that the wool bill laid the Americans open to charges of insincerity in trying to lower trade barriers. Truman's veto on June 26, 1947, of the wool bill helped save the conference on ITO for a period, but it bogged down later on the demands of American agriculture to retain its export subsidies. The British were unwilling to give up their empire preference system, and American business groups denounced the proposed charter as a betrayal of free enterprise. No congressional committee reported out the charter, and Truman let it die.[54]

In March 1948, a wheat agreement involving thirty-three importing countries and three major exporters (Canada, Australia, and the United States) was worked out for the sale of about half of the amount entering world trade at prices within a predetermined range. It was supported by the new secretary of agriculture, Charles F. Brannan, and the Farm Bureau but was opposed by the grain dealers. Congress failed to act and in the presidential campaign was accused of favoring grain traders over wheat farmers.[55]

Farmers' concern about possible future surpluses of farm products and declining prices for those products laid the basis for various proposals for agricultural legislation. The conservatives clung to the restrictionist view based on parity prices and reduced acreage. On the other hand, liberals urged expansion of agricultural production. Increased consumption should take care of surpluses, free market prices should replace artificial parity prices, and income payments rather than price supports should be used in a depression. For the transition period, farm policy was fixed by the Steagal amendment to the Emergency Price Control Act of 1943, which stipulated that the commodities for which the secretary of agriculture requested production increases must be supported at 90 percent of parity for two years after the official termination of the war.

Truman declared that World War II officially ended December 31, 1946, so the Steagal amendment applied through 1948. Only famine in Europe saved the U.S. government from the possible disastrous consequences of this amendment. As it was, potato production under this amendment illustrated how calamitous the operation of this amendment might have been. The surplus of potatoes, a perishable commodity, was such in 1946 that 22 million bushels had to be destroyed while people were starving in Europe. In 1947, thirty thousand bushels had to be burned. The losses cost the government $223 million in 1948. From the beginning of the potato program in 1943 to its termination in 1950, the government spent nearly a half billion dollars.[56]

Secretary Anderson saw the need for long-range planning, and he followed the suggestions of the Bureau of Agricultural Economics in urging southern cotton growers to make their product competitive by increased efficiency. The southern conservatives were bitter in their criticisms. They wanted the old high support prices maintained. On December 30, 1946, Anderson appointed Brannan as chairman of the Program and Policy Committee, which shaped a program based on the doctrine of abundance rather than restriction. Consumption was to be subsidized by school lunch and industrial feeding programs. Food allotments would be made to low-income families. Although there was a shift in the leadership of farm organizations, with the midwestern elements replacing conservative southerners, it was some years before elements of this program were accepted by Congress and the public.

In the meantime, the problem of farm surpluses was temporarily solved by the food crisis in Europe, which called for more grain than the Americans could readily supply. Anderson still dallied in pushing measures to meet the crisis, such as increased production and reduced domestic consumption. In June 1947 Truman, alarmed by shortages, appointed the Citizens' Food Committee to put on a voluntary food conservation drive. This program proved to be a failure. As Assistant Secretary Brannan put it, "Our efforts to induce distillers, brewers, bakers, and others to eliminate voluntarily the non-essential consumption of grain has not been a success, largely because these industries are unwilling to cooperate with the government and the public." Truman recommended price controls in his message to Congress of November 17, 1947, but failed to get support for this step from Anderson.[57]

The world food crisis was gradually met in 1948 by aid to European farmers through the Marshall Plan and by increased production of exports by Argentina and Australia. Reports were also coming in that the American grain crop would be good. Republicans decried the subsequent decline in grain prices and blamed the Department of Agriculture. Anderson defended the department and in May resigned to run for the U.S. Senate. Truman had supported him in spite of his quarrels with Bowles, Marshall, Clayton, and his liberal advisers. The new secretary, Charles Brannan, was much closer to the Clifford-Ewing-Keyserling group and played an important part in the 1948 campaign.

Labor Policies

Following the passage of the Taft-Hartley Act over his veto, Truman faced problems in its enforcement. His attempts to secure the repeal of the act in the second session of the Eightieth Congress were a failure. He had criticized the act severely and had prophesied more strikes and a breakdown of collective bargaining. He had to decide how to administer the act. In the case of the printers' strike against Chicago's five major dailies, the National Labor Relations Board brought the International Typographical Union into court, and a federal district judge issued a temporary injunction restraining the union from continuing its strike for a closed shop, which had been forbidden by the act.[58]

Truman soon found that it was wise for him to use the national emergency provisions of the Taft-Hartley Act in seven labor disputes in September 1948. In four of these, eighty-day injunctions were invoked. In all but one of these cases, the dispute was settled, and no strike was called after the waiting period. The threat of an injunction may have aided other settlements.

There was no increase in the number and extent of strikes following the Taft-Hartley Act, although Truman claimed this in his 1948 campaign. As a matter of fact, the act did not affect the unions as adversely as the labor leaders thought it would. These leaders, nevertheless, continued to denounce the act and to agitate for its repeal since it curtailed their powers and made it harder for them to retain their grip on the unions. Truman capitalized on labor's reactions in his campaign for reelection. He had stood against labor when he thought paramount national interests were at stake, but in the struggle between labor and management, he wanted to appear to support labor's legitimate demands.

TURNIP DAY SESSION, 1948

The question whether to call a special session of Congress to deal with unfinished business was debated seriously within the Truman administration. At first the arguments against it seemed strong: the session might do something to embarrass the President, it might act on his recommendations, and it would be condemned as purely political. But then the counterarguments put forward by Murphy and Rosenman began to prevail.[59] In their nominating convention, the Republicans had adopted a platform that advanced the record of the Eightieth Congress. Why not call the Republican legislators back to make good on their party's platform? If Congress did not act, it could be condemned as a "do-nothing Congress." If it passed some good legislation, it could claim credit for it. The strategy was to drive a wedge between the Congress and the Republican presidential nominee, Thomas E. Dewey.

Truman's use of his acceptance speech at the Democratic National Convention to make the announcement of his coming call for a special session was hardly the proper procedure; it clearly branded the whole move as narrowly partisan. But apparently Truman did not care. He was in a battle for his political life. The use of the term *Turnip Day* showed Truman's rural Missouri background. July 26 was considered the proper day to sow turnips in that state.

The special session proposal was denounced by the Republicans and some journalists as sheer demagoguery. In an election year summer special session, who could expect much to be done? Members of Congress were concerned about their own reelection. There would be no time and no inclination in such a session to try the impossible. Republican National Chairman Hugh D. Scott charged, "It is the act of a desperate man who is willing to destroy the unity and dignity of his country and his government for partisan advantage after he himself has lost the confidence of the people."[60]

Walter Lippmann was even more drastic in his denunciation of the proposal for the special session. He wrote that it was

a deliberate effort to make voters believe that they must choose not between a Truman administration and a Dewey administration, but between Truman's legislative proposals and the legislative record of the 80th Congress, that because Harry S. Truman cannot lead the Congress, Mr. Dewey will not want to lead and will not be able to lead the next Congress. . . . [The plan] subordinates public interest to strategy and tactics of his campaign. . . . [a] reckless and frantic effort to exploit domestic issues, [a] danger to bipartisan foreign policy.

In preparation for the special session, Truman took greater care than he had the previous year. He called upon his Council of Economic Advisers to produce an anti-inflation program. Although not the chairman, Leon Keyserling took the lead in this. In order to prevent dissents from the program such as had happened in 1947, he read his message at a cabinet meeting, and no one dissented. William L. Batt of the Democratic National Committee mobilized private interest groups behind the program. During the seven days preceding the special session, Press Secretary Ross released the details piecemeal, thus making the front page every day.[61]

In the formal address before Congress on July 27, 1948, Truman concentrated on inflation, housing, aid to education, minimum wage, social security, displaced persons, a loan for the United Nations, the wheat agreement, public power, federal pay raise, and civil rights. This was a long list for a two-week session. In addition, he added, if time permitted, Congress should consider health insurance, replacement of the Taft-Hartley Act, a long-range farm plan, a better reciprocal trade act, universal military training, a natural science foundation, stronger antimonopoly legislation, and the St. Lawrence Seaway Treaty. He did not leave anything out. Considering the slow pace of legislative behavior, it is clear that Truman did not expect much action. He was trying to put the Republican-controlled Congress on the spot.[62]

Republican leaders in Congress responded to Truman's message by pointing out that the middle of an election campaign was not the time to consider and enact legislation. They could see no emergencies, and the Democrats had failed to act on the problems raised when they controlled Congress.[63] In order to divide the Democrats, Republicans introduced an antipoll-tax bill. Some Democratic senators started a filibuster, and the measure was shelved.

On inflation controls, certain limited steps were taken on consumer credits and on reserve requirements. Truman pointed out that the Republican leaders were unwilling to allow Congress an opportunity to vote on direct price control and authority to allocate. Both houses passed the weak bill.

Another weak bill was passed in the field of housing. It merely attempted to stimulate private construction of low-rent housing. In view of opposition in the House, Senator Taft did not attempt to push his comprehensive housing bill. Democrats halfheartedly supported the bill as better than nothing.

On the positive side, only the loan of $65 million for the United Nations headquarters was passed. Other proposals were postponed, bottled up in committee, or ignored.

Truman was pleased with the results. He could continue his denunciation of the "do-nothing Congress." He pointed out the failures of the Republican legislators to carry out their party's platform promises. The meager accomplishments of the special session forced Dewey to continue his lofty rhetoric, which avoided concrete issues.[64]

Truman's record as a leader in legislation in 1948 was not as negative as it appeared at the end of the special session. The *Congressional Quarterly* reported favorable action on thirty-seven of the eighty-one proposals he made during the year. Some of the measures approved were highly important in the field of foreign affairs.

chapter 27 | THE TRUMAN DOCTRINE, 1947

Soviet activities throughout the world, with respect both to individual states and to international organizations, are in support of this policy of increasing the relative power of the Soviet Union at the expense of her potential enemies. . . .

Until Soviet leaders abandon their aggressive policies . . . the United States must assume that the U.S.S.R. may at any time embark on a course of expansion effected by open warfare and therefore must maintain sufficient military strength to restrain the Soviet Union.

—*American Relations with the Soviet Union*, A Report to the President by the Special Counsel to the President, September 1946

Historians generally agree that the year 1947 marked a turning point in the trend of American foreign relations. The policy of isolationism, which had dominated the thinking of American political leaders since 1776, was being replaced by a willingness to assume greater responsibilities in world affairs. What role did President Truman have in bringing about this fundamental change? To place praise or blame for the changing policies is risky since events are likely to be more important than the actions or words of a single man, even the president of the United States.[1]

Soviet actions and propaganda and the interpretation of them by Truman's advisers were inextricably woven into the pattern of the foreign policies he pursued. The case of Poland is an example. The postwar government of Poland was handpicked by the Soviet leaders, which in practice meant by Stalin. How should this act be interpreted? The Russians held that it was a defensive act. Within the century, the Germans had invaded Russia twice by this route. Soviet sacrifices in men, materials, and human suffering had been great. They were determined to defend themselves against the recurrence of such a disaster again. There must be a friendly government in Poland, one that the Soviet Union could control.

The day following Truman's swearing-in ceremony as president of the United States, Secretary Stettinius handed him disturbing information about Poland.[2] And ten days later Truman had his famous encounter with

Molotov, who was on his way to the San Francisco conference. Revisionist historians argue that if Roosevelt had lived, he would never have damaged relations with a top Soviet official the way Truman did. We will never know whether they are correct. Truman relied upon Roosevelt's advisers, and they told him to be firm in dealing with the Soviet Union.

It was almost a year later when another incident pushed American thinking toward a policy of containment of the Soviet Union. Curiously enough, the thrust came not from Wall Street financiers but from a scholarly retiring foreign service officer in Moscow who was asked to reflect on Soviet intentions and did so in his classic dispatch from Moscow of February 22, 1946. George Kennan became famous in government circles overnight, and his reputation soon became global. Secretary of the Navy James Forrestal was especially impressed and circulated the document widely. Parts of it were incorporated in a report to the President by his special counsel. The Kennan dispatch held:

At the bottom of the Kremlin's neurotic view of world affairs is a traditional and instinctive Russian sense of insecurity. . . . They have always feared foreign penetration, feared direct contact between the western world and their own, feared what would happen if Russians learned the truth about the world without or if foreigners learned truth about the world within. And they have learned to seek security only in patient but deadly struggle for total destruction of rival power, never in compacts and compromises with it.

It was no coincidence that Marxism, which had smouldered ineffectively for half a century in Western Europe, caught hold and blazed for the first time in Russia. Only in this land which had never known a friendly neighbor or indeed any tolerant equilibrium of separate powers, either internal or international, could a doctrine thrive which viewed economic conflicts of society as insoluble by peaceful means. After establishment of the Bolshevist regime, Marxist dogma, rendered even more truculent and intolerant by Lenin's interpretation, became a perfect vehicle for the sense of insecurity with which Bolsheviks, even more than previous Russian rulers, were afflicted. In this dogma, with its basic altruism of purpose, they found justification for their instinctive fear of the outside world, for the dictatorship without which they did not know how to rule, for cruelties they did not dare not to inflict, for sacrifices they felt bound to demand. In the name of Marxism they sacrificed every single ethical value in their methods and tactics. . . . Thus, Soviet leaders are driven by necessities of their own past and present position to put forward a dogma which regards the outside world as evil, hostile and menacing. . . . Basically this is only the steady advance of uneasy Russian nationalism, a centuries-old movement in which conceptions of offense and defense are inextricably confused. But in a new guise of international Marxism, with its honeyed promises to a desperate and war torn outside world, it is more dangerous and insidious than ever before.[3]

Kennan, regarded as one of the leading theorists on the cold war, failed to agree with some of the policies adopted by Truman in his attempts to contain the Soviet Union. Kennan soon denounced the Truman doctrine, which he himself had done so much to create.[4]

Secretary Byrnes was never given major credit for starting the cold war, but his Stuttgart speech of September 6, 1946, had a part in increasing the tensions and disagreements between the Soviet bloc and the Western nations that resisted the growth of communism. Under pressure from Senator Vandenberg and others, Byrnes had adopted a tougher stance toward the Soviet Union, but he still hoped for a negotiated peace. In the Stuttgart speech, which Truman cleared, he stated, "I want no misunderstanding. We will not shirk our duty. We are not withdrawing. As long as an occupation force is required in Germany the army of the United States will be a part of that occupation force." President Roosevelt had indicated that he thought American troops would be out of Europe in two years after the end of the war. Now an American secretary of state was indicating that the United States would stay and assume postwar responsibilities.[5]

In addition to Kennan, Harriman, Stettinius, Forrestal, Grew, Byrnes, and others, Special Counsel Clark Clifford played an important role in convincing Truman to formulate the containment doctrine. Assisted by George Elsey, in September 1946 he brought the many currents of policy together in a compelling document, "American Relations with the Soviet Union." The report was based on careful estimates of current and future Soviet policies, extensive reports on recent Soviet activities affecting the security of the United States, and recommendations concerning American policy with respect to the Soviet Union submitted by Secretaries Byrnes, Patterson, Clark, and Forrestal, Admiral Leahy, Ambassador Pauley, Director of Central Intelligence Rear Admiral Hillenkoetter, and others with special knowledge in the field. Clearly forecasting the Truman doctrine, the report warned, "The Soviet Union is interested in obtaining the withdrawal of British troops from Greece and the establishment of a 'friendly' government there. It hopes to make Turkey a puppet state which could serve as a spring board for the domination of the eastern Mediterranean." Regarding general policy, it stated:

The key to an understanding of current Soviet foreign policy, in summary, is the realization that Soviet leaders adhere to the Marxian theory of ultimate destruction of capitalist states by communist states, while at the same time they strive to postpone the inevitable conflict in order to strengthen and prepare the Soviet Union for its clash with the western democracies.[6]

The appointment of General George C. Marshall as secretary of state on January 8, 1947, was a major factor that contributed to the change in American foreign policy. Truman, the former captain of artillery in World War I and a colonel in the reserve, had a great admiration for the five-star general.[7] Even while Roosevelt was alive, Truman acclaimed the general as "the greatest living American." Although a professional soldier had never before been appointed as secretary of state, Truman had such confidence in Marshall's judgment that he broke the precedent. As he put it in his *Memoirs*, "General Marshall is one of the most astute and profound men I have ever known. Whenever any problem was brought before him, he seemed to be able to put his finger at once on the very basic approach that later would usually be proposed by the staff as the best solution."[8] In addition, the general had the confidence of Congress, and he had clearly indicated that he had no presidential ambitions. On the day he was appointed, he said, "I will never become involved in political matters and therefore I never can be considered a candidate for political office. . . . I'm assuming that the office of Secretary of State, at least under present conditions, is nonpolitical, and I will govern myself accordingly."[9] There was no problem with Marshall's confirmation as secretary of state. Senator Vandenberg arranged it so that it was done immediately without reference to the Committee on Foreign Relations for hearings. The appointment received favorable press comments except from left-wing publications that questioned the idea of a military man's serving as secretary of state.[10]

As a successful military leader, General Marshall knew how to use staff. He immediately discarded some of the Byrnes administrative practices, which had resulted in a loose and uncoordinated organization.[11] Marshall concentrated operating and administrative functions in his chief of staff, Under Secretary of State Dean Acheson, whom he persuaded to stay on for six months. Acheson insisted that at the end of that period he had to get back to his private law practice.[12] Marshall also set up an executive secretariat to control and centralize routing of communications and the Policy Planning Staff. All orders would go out under Acheson's signature. Marshall wanted only the main policy questions to come to him, and they had to be in the form of completed staff work, usually on a page or two with suggested solutions. The morale of the department was greatly improved by the Marshall innovations. George Kennan, the foreign service officer who was made chairman of the Policy Planning Staff, described his feelings toward Marshall:

Like everyone else, I admired him, and in a sense loved him, for the qualities I saw in him, some of them well known, some less so: for his unshakable integrity; his consistent courtesy and gentlemanliness of conduct; his ironclad sense of duty; his imperturbability—the imperturbability of a good conscience—in the face of harassments, pressures, and criticisms; his deliberateness and conscientiousness of decision; his serene readiness—once a decision had been made—to abide by its consequences, whatever they might be; his lack of petty vanity or ambition; his indifference to the whims and moods of public opinion, particularly as manifested in the mass media; and his impeccable fairness and avoidance of favoritism in the treatment of subordinates.[13]

One of the first problems that Truman and his new secretary of state faced was the question of aid to Greece and Turkey. The British had been the traditional protectors of Greece and Turkey because both were vital to communications with the British empire. It was only their desperate financial situation and the success of the Labour party at the polls in 1945 that led them to give up this role. In October 1944 Churchill and Stalin had reached an informal agreement that Hungary, Rumania, and Bulgaria would be in the Russian sphere of influence and Greece would be in the British sphere. President Roosevelt was opposed to postwar spheres of influence but in the case of Greece was persuaded by Churchill to accept a temporary wartime arrangement, which in fact developed into a postwar position.[14] After the retreat of the Germans from Greece, British troops moved into the ravaged country to help restore order. Their efforts to bolster up a reactionary monarchy were resisted by communist-led guerrillas who received support from neighboring communist-dominated countries.[15]

On February 21, 1947, the British ambassador to the United States handed Under Secretary of State Acheson a note to the effect that the British would have to pull out of Greece and Turkey by March 31, withdrawing both troops and financial aid.[16] This note raised a number of fundamental questions that had to be answered in about six weeks. Did the British really need to cut off this aid and to do it so precipitously? What would happen to Greece and Turkey if the United States did not step in and furnish aid? Who was threatening the Greek regime—internal or external groups? Was the Soviet Union backing the uprisings? Had Stalin taken any hand in this crisis? If Greece went communist, what would happen to its neighbors and to Turkey, Palestine, Egypt, Italy, and France? The British government was having financial troubles and was trying to relieve the strain on its budget in any way possible. With the empire crumbling, Greek aid had a low priority. The U.N. Balkan Investigating Commission found that Greece's northern neighbors—Albania, Yugoslavia, and Bulgaria, all communist controlled —were aiding the Greek communist guerillas and furnishing them with supplies, training, and sanctuaries. Were the Soviet satellites being directed by Moscow? Although the international communist movement was regarded as being monolithic at this time, being rigidly controlled by Stalin, available evidence indicates that Stalin was not enthusiastic about the Greek rebellion. He had made an agreement with Churchill, and he appeared to be following a hands-off policy.[17] An emissary from the Greek communist movement was told to follow a policy of collaboration with other elements in Greece, but he refused to accept this advice. The Russians had criticized British military actions in Greece that were employed to put down rebellion, but they had done this with tongue in cheek because they were using similar methods in the Balkans and calling them actions of liberation. What was the evidence available to American officers at the time? The American ambassador to Greece, Lincoln MacVeagh, sent cables to the effect that the Soviet

Union was directing the rebellion and wanted complete control of Greece. That was the evidence that Truman had to go on at the time.[18] If the rebels had won, Greece might have set up a Tito-like regime because the split between Moscow and Belgrade was about to shake up the communist world and destroy the myth of Stalin's control.

How close was Greece to falling into the communist camp? Its foreign exchange was exhausted, its food supplies were running low, the communist guerrillas seemed to be making headway in view of the widespread discontent. In 1946 the Greek government had asked for a huge loan, and Truman had sent Paul Porter, former head of the Office of Price Administration, on an economic mission to Greece. Mark Ethridge, the editor-journalist, was already in the area as head of the U.S. Investigating Commission in the Balkans. These two special envoys and Ambassador MacVeagh all reported that Greece was on the verge of collapse. Truman, Marshall, and Acheson relied upon these reports.[19]

Within the State Department, there was general agreement that the President should request Congress for funds to replace the aid that Great Britain was soon to cut off. Marshall and Acheson together and singly kept Truman informed regarding what the department was doing to prepare recommendations and to clear them with the War and Navy Departments. The President, convinced that it was vital to the security of the United States to bolster the national independence of Greece and Turkey, approved the steps proposed by the Department of State and endorsed by the War and Navy Departments. Since Congress was controlled by the Republicans, Truman knew he must rely on bipartisan support to pass such a measure. On February 27, 1947, Truman held a meeting in the White House with the leaders of Congress. Marshall presented the economic needs of the Greeks. Acheson, feeling that this argument was not strong, emphasized the critical strategic situation and the danger of a Soviet breakthrough in the Middle East if the United States did not take vigorous action. He described the crisis in global terms as part of a power struggle between aggressive communism led by the Soviet Union and free peoples, who must now look to the United States for leadership.[20] Actually, he was enunciating the domino theory, which became popular with Secretary of State John Foster Dulles, who succeeded him in 1953. Senator Vandenberg was impressed and urged the President to make an equally strong statement before Congress, which would "scare the hell out of the country."[21] Since Marshall was leaving for Moscow on March 4, he asked Acheson to take charge of implementing the proposals to meet the crisis. In his *Memoirs*, Truman failed to mention Acheson's key role in creating a crisis atmosphere and he exaggerated his own role, saying, "I told the group I had decided to extend aid to Greece and Turkey." Most certainly, Truman knew better than this. The most he could do was to request Congress to provide such aid.[22]

President Truman held a cabinet meeting on March 7 at which the situation was thoroughly discussed and unanimous agreement was reached to go ahead with a request to Congress for aid to Greece and Turkey. Regarding this meeting, Admiral Leahy wrote: "This was the first cabinet meeting that I have attended where a definite decision was reached and clearly announced. The President's stand will require courage of a high order. He will be sustained by a sense of righteousness, and he has plenty of courage."[23]

A draft of the President's message to Congress on Greek and Turkish aid based on Acheson's presentations, the request of the Greek government for aid, which had been solicited by the Department, and the estimates of the interdepartmental committee on the amount of aid needed, the form it should take, and how it should be administered was prepared by Joseph Jones of the State Department staff, a young man with great enthusiasm for America's assuming a larger role in world affairs. The draft was sent to the White House where Clifford made suggestions for strengthening it along the lines of his September 1946 report to the President. In his *Memoirs*, Truman stated that he returned the draft to Acheson with a note asking for more emphasis on a declaration of general policy. This was to be "America's answer to the surge of communist tyranny." He wanted no hedging. Acheson states that Marshall approved the message, but Charles Bohlen claimed that Marshall expressed to Truman his view that the President was "overstating his case a bit." Kennan also objected to the sweeping character of the language and the inclusion of military aid to Turkey, which he thought would be provocative. He considered political aid to Turkey and economic aid to Greece as sufficient. His objections came too late to effect any changes in the message. Thus, the more sober opinion within the department was that there was no "surge of communist tyranny" that warranted so tough a speech.[24]

The March 12 message to Congress, delivered in person by the President, was global in scope and alarmist in character because Senator Vandenberg and Acting Secretary Acheson thought that kind of rhetoric was needed to move an economy-minded Republican Congress to action.[25] There was no specific mention of the Soviet Union, but references to American protests against coercion and intimidation, in violation of the Yalta agreements regarding Poland, Rumania, and Bulgaria, left no doubt as to the identity of the foe. The primary emphasis in this message was on economic and financial aid. A key passage in the speech was: "I believe that it must be the policy of the United States to support free peoples who are resisting attempted subjugation by armed minorities or by outside pressures." The words *free peoples, armed minorities*, and *outside pressures* were subject to varying interpretations. The underlying assumptions of this document seemed to be that the Soviet Union was expansionist and would move into a power vacuum, that Russian imperialism would endanger the free enterprise system in international trade, that the subjection of Greece and Turkey was among Soviet goals, that the protection of these two countries against Soviet encroachment was vital to American economic and military security, that American political, economic, and military aid could bolster the Greek and Turkish governments in spite of their imperfections, that the Soviet Union would not risk a direct confrontation with the United States in this area and therefore Soviet-attempted advances could be contained, and that a failure of the United States to act might endanger all of Europe and ultimately the rest of the noncommunist world. The President requested $400 million for assistance to Greece and Turkey, authority to detail American civilian and military personnel to assist in supervising this aid, and authority to provide the goods and equipment needed.

This message was to be called the Truman doctrine, and it has been sharply debated ever since its enunciation. It has been regarded as a landmark in the cold war, a term used by Bernard Baruch in April 1947 and picked up by Walter Lippmann. A former American ambassador to the Soviet Union states that in his view, the cold war was initiated not in Truman's message but in Stalin's speech on February 6, 1946, in which he rejected the postwar policy that Litvinov had hoped would be followed, a policy based on cooperation with the United Nations. Some commentators place the origin of friction between Russia and the Allies earlier than this, at the failure to start a second front in 1942 and to a slowness in furnishing more aid when the Soviet Union's needs were greatest.[26]

The Truman doctrine failed to answer the crucial question as to where the line against communist aggression would be drawn. Should the United States support Chiang Kai-shek's Nationalists against Mao's Communists and if so, to what extent? Should South Korea be supported against North Korea? Should the Philippine government be helped in its fight against the Huks? Should the French in Indochina be backed in their struggle against Ho Chi Minh's Communists? Could the United States afford to support non-Communists anywhere in the world they might be threatened by insurrectionists? Must the United States support a status quo noncommunist regime regardless of how corrupt, reactionary, or inefficient it might be? Was the United States opposed to all revolutionary movements?

Although the first reaction of the American press was generally favorable and the public opinion polls showed that a majority of the public interviewed supported the Truman doctrine, there was vigorous opposition on the extremes, Left and Right. On the Left, Henry Wallace and Senators Claude Pepper and Glen H. Taylor denounced the doctrine on the ground that it might bring war, that it divided the world into opposing camps, and that it did not promote freedom because the Greek and Turkish governments were reactionary. On the Right, conservatives stressed the financial burden and the potential increase in wartime controls and executive powers. They thought the confrontation was dangerous and was not necessary for the security of the United States.[27]

Some other democratic countries welcomed America's assumption of greater international responsibilities, and others criticized the interventionist character of the actions. Communist bloc countries were highly critical of the message. Ambassador Gromyko in the United Nations denounced the United States for interfering in Greek internal affairs before the U.N. Commission on the Balkans had made its report. The Soviet press indicted American policy as a threat to Russia's territorial integrity and as an example of capitalistic imperialism. However, in the Moscow conference of foreign ministers called to consider the German problem, there was no discussion of Greece and Turkey.[28]

Senator Vandenberg was a key figure in the defense of the request for aid to Greece and Turkey. At first he had criticized severely the bypassing of the United Nations. He then proposed a compromise amendment providing that the United Nations could terminate the program when it found that its actions made U.S. assistance unnecessary or undesirable. On such a question, the United States would waive its veto power. The State Department was pleased to back this compromise, which insured Vandenberg's strong support.[29]

In defending the policy before congressional committees, Acheson qualified the sweeping generalizations enunciated by Truman. The immediate problem was confined to Greece and Turkey. Other situations that might arise in the future would be dealt with in accordance with local conditions and strategic needs. The Greek government was far from perfect, but it was preferable to a communist-controlled regime. The possible application of the Truman doctrine to China was not handled very well by Acheson. Congressman Walter Judd and others pointed out that American policy was not strongly anticommunist in China because the Nationalists had been urged to work out an accommodation with the Communists. Judd contended that insufficient aid was being given to the Chinese Nationalists. Acheson explained that the circumstances in China and Greece were vastly different. He stated that the Nationalists were in no immediate danger and that American aid was adequate. Later events showed that both of these statements were wrong. The Nationalists were in great danger, and the aid being given them was far too little to save the situation. Acheson was following Marshall's position that the Nationalists could not be trusted to use additional aid in an effective manner, that the American public was not willing to make the sacrifices that a full-scale intervention would entail in so vast a country, and that support for the Communists was unthinkable in view of the climate of American domestic opinion at the time. Truman relied upon Marshall and Acheson for advice regarding American policy toward China, and in view of his own unpopularity at home he was not about to defy the advice of the two officials he trusted most and embark on a program that involved being soft on Mao.[30]

The American Congress did not meet the deadline set by the British for the granting of aid to Greece and Turkey, but it did pass the desired legislation on May 15. Truman signed the bill on May 22.[31] Thus the policy of containment of the Soviet Union was inaugurated. It was to lead logically to an increase in military and economic aid to Nationalist China, but such aid was never sufficient to shore up the crumbling Nationalists, to provide military support to South Korea in its struggle to defend itself against North Korea, to provide advice and aid to the Philippine government in its opposition to the communist Huks, and to provide political, economic, and military assistance to South Vietnam's attempts to resist a North Vietnamese takeover of the entire country. As we have seen, the Central Intelligence Agency under the National Security Council was one of the principal instruments for the conduct of clandestine cold war activities.

chapter 28 | THE MARSHALL PLAN, GERMANY, ISRAEL AND NATO, 1947-1948

The economic plight of the continent [in 1947] was rapidly revealing itself as far worse than anyone had dreamed, and was steadily deteriorating. . . . A pall of fear, of bewilderment, of discouragement, hung over the continent and paralyzed all constructive activity. . . . Compare that with today? [April, 1948]. . . . Recovery is progressing rapidly in the West. New hope exists. People see the possibility of a better future. The Communist position in France has been deeply shaken.

—George F. Kennan, *Memoirs, 1925–1950*

THE MARSHALL PLAN

The debate regarding the Truman doctrine raised many larger questions about the role of the United States in world affairs. The economic needs of many other European countries were just as pressing as those of Greece and Turkey. As a matter of fact, it was more important for the United States to think of their needs because they were more highly industrialized and could make better use of such aid.

European countries faced a disastrous winter in early 1947. The war had greatly depleted gold reserves and foreign exchange, the means by which they could start to rebuild. Moreover, an unusually severe winter had created coal shortages, food shortages, unemployment, and industrial stagnation. Efforts to repair war damages and restore economic well-being were frustrated by these man-made and natural disasters. Winston Churchill described Europe as "a rubble heap, a charnel house, a breeding ground of pestilence and hate." While the United States had the goods needed, the European countries lacked the dollars to pay for them. American journalists, led by Walter Lippmann, urged the U.S. government to take action regarding this situation by providing outright aid or loans on easy terms in order to move American goods and fill Europe's needs.[1]

In working out a foreign aid policy, President Truman had the assistance of Marshall, Acheson, Clayton, Anderson, Krug, Kennan, and many others inside and outside the government. Present throughout the initial stages of the plan was the persuasive under secretary of state, Dean Acheson, who on March 5, 1947, before Truman addressed Congress on Greek-Turkish aid, asked the State-War-Navy Coordinating Committee (SWNCC) to examine the problems of achieving economic recovery in Europe as a whole. Truman was aware of the work of this committee because Acheson, as acting secretary of state, had mentioned it in a cabinet meeting on April 8.[2]

On April 5, the under secretary of state for economic affairs, Will Clayton, had submitted a memorandum asserting that prompt aid was urgently needed for gravely threatened countries and suggested that Congress be requested to provide an emergency fund of $5 billion for the fiscal year. As a former successful merchant in the international cotton market, Clayton was committed to faith in the free enterprise system based upon multilateral trade of the freest sort. Brought into the State Department by Stettinius in 1944, he constantly advocated the use of American economic power to open up international trade. The British felt this in his attacks on the imperial preference system. Acheson stated that Truman was aware of Clayton's views.[3]

Secretary Marshall's participation in the plan that bears his name began after he returned from the Council of Ministers in Moscow where he had been disturbed by the conditions he saw and the stubbornness of the Russians in pushing their demands. He was convinced that the Soviet Union would not agree on German economic unity, demilitarization, and reparations. On April 29 he directed the chief of the newly established Policy Planning Staff, George Kennan, to prepare a report on the long-range problems of economic rehabilitation of Europe. Kennan quickly assembled a small staff in early May and began working intensively on the report, using the economic studies prepared by Clayton's office and those of the Special Committee of SWNCC.[4]

President Truman had shown his interest in American foreign economic policy in an address in which he expressed the belief that free world trade was an inseparable part of the peaceful world.[5] The economic war of the 1930s had strangled trade, had impoverished those trying to save, and had made farmers lose their lands. The President was scheduled to make another address on foreign economic policy May 8 at the modest but influential Delta Council of cotton farmers in Cleveland, Mississippi. Political turmoil in the state made it wiser for him to send a substitute. Acheson was chosen to make the speech, and this enabled him to prepare what Truman called the prologue to the Marshall Plan. Acheson called upon Francis Russell and Joseph Jones of his staff to make suggestions.[6] Jones, an enthusiastic younger officer, had been attending meetings of the Special Committee of SWNCC and urged that the speech contain a comprehensive statement of America's foreign reconstruction policy.[7] Acheson asked Truman if he could make a speech on the financial crisis in Europe, urging American aid to support the economic rehabilitation of Europe. The President agreed and asked that the draft be cleared with all departments concerned.[8] As delivered, the speech said in part: "Since world demand exceeds our ability to supply, we are going to have to concentrate our emergency assistance in areas where it will be most effective in building world political and economic stability, in promoting human freedom and democratic institutions, in fostering liberal trading policies, and in strengthening the authority of the United Nations." He also stressed the importance of pushing ahead with the reconstruction of Germany and Japan. A striking passage in the speech was: "The war will not be over until the people of the world can again feed and clothe themselves and face the future with some degree of confidence."[9] The speech received more attention in England than in the United States since Acheson had alerted three British correspondents regarding its importance. After it received wide attention abroad, it was picked up by key American newspapers.[10]

Kennan's Policy Planning Staff submitted to Secretary Marshall on May 23 a report on economic aid to Europe. It pointed out that although Europe was temporarily exhausted, it had great military-industrial potential. The emphasis was not on anticommunism but on positive economic aid to those Western European countries that were ready and willing to help themselves. Kennan thought that the Truman doctrine was too negative and too sweeping in its promise of military aid to any kind of anticommunist regime.[11] The plan concluded that massive aid to Nationalist China would be useless; under Chiang Kai-shek's corrupt regime and chaotic economic system, such aid would end up in Mao's communist camp. Marshall held a series of conferences on the plan with high-level officials. Kennan convinced the doubters who questioned whether the European countries should draw up their own needs and priorities. He urged that this procedure would lessen the charges of American domination and interference. The Soviet Union should also be invited to demonstrate that the plan was not merely anticommunist and that the United States wanted to avoid dividing Europe into two camps.

After six weeks in Europe, Clayton prepared a second memorandum, dated May 27, which estimated that the United States would have to undertake an aid program of at least $6 billion a year for three years to save Western Europe from economic collapse. He made a strong oral presentation of his views to Marshall and the top officials of the department.[12]

The deteriorating situation in Europe led Marshall to seek as soon as possible a forum at which he would put forth the main features of the plan. A request to make an address at the Harvard University commencement on June 5 presented a suitable opportunity. The secretary asked Bohlen to prepare a draft for the occasion.[13] Using memoranda produced by Clayton and Kennan, Bohlen completed a draft early in June. It had three key paragraphs:

The truth of the matter is that Europe's requirements for the next three or four years of foreign food and other essential products—principally from America—are so much greater than her present ability to pay that she must have substantial additional help or face economic, social, and political deterioration of a very grave character. The remedy lies in breaking the vicious circle and restoring the confidence of the European people in the economic future of their own countries and of Europe as a whole. The manufacturer and farmer throughout wide areas must be able and willing to exchange their products for currencies the continuing value of which is not open to question. . . .

It is logical that the United States should do whatever it is able to assist in the return of normal economic health in the world, without which there can be no political stability or assured peace. Our policy is directed not against any country or doctrine but against hunger, poverty, desperation, and chaos. Its purpose should be the revival of a working economy in the world so as to permit the emergence of political and social conditions in which free institutions can exist. Such assistance, I am convinced, must not be on a piecemeal basis as various crises develop. Any assistance that this government may render should provide a cure rather than a palliative. Any government that is willing to assist in the task of recovery will find full cooperation, I am sure, on the part of the United States government. Any government which maneuvers to block recovery of other countries cannot expect help from us. Furthermore, governments, political parties, or groups which seek to perpetuate human misery in order to profit therefrom politically will encounter the opposition of the United States.

It is already evident that, before the United States government can proceed much further in its efforts to alleviate the situation and help start the European world on its way to recovery, there must be some agreement among the countries of Europe as to the requirements of the situation and the part those countries themselves will take in order to give proper effect to whatever action might be undertaken by this government. It would be neither fitting nor efficacious for this government to undertake to draw up unilaterally a program designed to place Europe on its feet economically. This is the business of Europeans. The initiative, I think, must come from Europe. The role of this country should consist of friendly aid in the drafting of a European program and of later support of such a program so far as it may be practical for us to do so. The program should be a joint one, agreed to by a number, if not all, European nations.[14]

This speech became the basis of what came to be known as the Marshall Plan, although in itself it was not a plan but an invitation to make a plan. Its passage within ten months by a hostile Republican Congress was an outstanding example of executive-congressional cooperation, and it became one of the great achievements of the Truman presidency. Although Truman's firm backing of the plan was never in doubt, he preferred to keep in the background.[15] He subordinated his own role and emphasized that of the general. Because his domestic programs were unpopular and Marshall's prestige was high, this stance helped gain supporters for the plan. From references to the SWNCC in cabinet meetings, from Truman's endorsement of Acheson's Delta Council speech, and from his daily meetings with Marshall, it is clear that the President was aware of discussions that led to the Harvard speech and that he strongly backed the decisions made. Acheson wrote that he did not know whether the general discussed the speech with the President, but it was hard to believe that they did not discuss it.[16] Clark Clifford had to push Truman into claiming more credit for the Marshall Plan for his own political good.[17]

On June 11 in a speech before the Canadian Parliament in Ottawa, President Truman indicated in general terms that he fully supported the Marshall Plan. He specifically backed General Marshall's proposals for economic aid for Europe in his press conference of June 26.[18] In answer to Senator Vandenberg's request for more information, he appointed three special study groups. One, headed by Secretary of Commerce Harriman, included nineteen prominent leaders from labor, business, agriculture, education, and government service, and it undertook to advise coordination of domestic resources with foreign needs.[19] The second group, headed by Secretary of Interior Krug, was selected to study available raw materials and production capabilities within the nation and abroad. A third group was appointed under the Council of Economic Advisers to study the effect of the proposed foreign aid program upon American domestic economy. The reports of these groups helped win the support of Senator Vandenberg, whose role was crucial in winning acceptance of the Marshall Plan. He was the recognized leader of the Republicans in international affairs. Truman was willing to make concessions to secure his support.[20]

The success of the Marshall Plan also resulted from prompt and able assistance from abroad. British Foreign Minister Ernest Bevin, shortly after he had read the Harvard speech, got in touch with French Foreign Minister Georges Bidault, and the two held a preliminary conference in Paris.[21] The Harvard address was general in terms, and details were needed to produce a feasible plan. Bevin took the lead in getting other countries to agree on concrete terms. The preliminary estimate of the need for $29 billion astounded Clayton, the hardest American bargainer, and he urged a revised estimate with far more mutual aid.

The reaction of the Soviet Union to the Marshall Plan had next to be determined. An early propaganda blast from Moscow had been unfavorable, but Bevin and Bidault decided to invite Soviet Foreign Minister Molotov to Paris anyway. Accepting the invitation, Molotov seemed interested at first, but he soon balked at the plan for full disclosure of economic information and withdrew, later putting pressure on Poland, Czechoslovakia, and Hungary not to participate and denouncing the plan as an interference in the internal affairs of European nations. Molotov had advocated direct American aid to individual countries with no conditions attached. Revisionist historians claim that the conditions for aid made it extremely unlikely that the Soviets would accept the plan.[22] Soviet rejection eased the way for the ultimate passage of the plan by the U.S. Congress. The blame for dividing Europe would be placed upon the Communists. The financial burden to be placed upon the United States would be much less. In view of rising American anticommunism, it would be much easier to secure congressional consent. What the Soviets gained from this action is unclear. As participants in the plan, they would have been in a better position to sabotage it. Truman owed a debt of gratitude to Stalin for this colossal error on the part of the Russians.[23]

Some sixteen Western European countries, accepting the August invitation of British and French governments, met in Paris and created the Organization for European Economic Cooperation (OEEC), which on September 22 submitted a report indicating what use the countries could make of their own existing productive capacities and what was needed in the way of American aid. The organization reported:

One country after another is already being forced by lack of dollars to cut down vital imports of food and raw materials from the American continent. If nothing is done a catastrophe will develop as stocks become exhausted. If too little is done, and it is done too late, it will be impossible to provide the momentum needed to get the program under way. Life in Europe will become increasingly unstable and uncertain; industries will grind to a halt for lack of materials and fuel, and the food supply of Europe will diminish and begin to disappear.[24]

Truman made this report public on September 25, 1947, and at the same time called a meeting of congressional leaders to discuss foreign aid plans. He had to make it clear on October 23 that so desperate was the need that he had to ask for immediate interim aid of $580 million for France, Italy, and Austria in order to meet the winter needs.[25]

To carry the public and Congress with him, Truman supplemented the activities of government committees with those of business leaders, bankers, and foreign affairs experts and speeches of his own. Acheson, now in private life, served energetically on one of these citizen committees. His place as under secretary of state had been taken by Robert A. Lovett, a Wall Street banker who had been assistant secretary of war for air during the war and thus had Marshall's full confidence. Lovett was not as active in promoting the Marshall Plan as Acheson had been, so a greater burden was imposed upon the President, who made a strong plea for interim aid, and then on December 19, at a special session of Congress, presented the carefully worked-out European Recovery Plan (ERP) with a request for $17 billion over a four-year period. This message, worked on by Lovett, Kennan, Elsey, Murphy, Bell, and others, summarized the reports of all the committees and concluded: ''In providing aid to Europe, we must share more than goods and funds. . . . We must develop a feeling of teamwork in our common cause of combatting the suspicions, prejudices, and fabrications which undermine cooperative effort, both at home and abroad."[26]

The congressional battle for interim aid and for ERP was bitterly fought. Senator Taft argued that the proposals were financially dangerous, strained American resources for welfare and socialistic purposes abroad, and failed to meet the greater needs in China. On the other hand, Henry Wallace condemned the proposals for economic aid as provocative and divisive.[27]

It was the Soviet Union, however, that gave the Marshall Plan the boost that it needed to secure congressional support. Shortly after the opening of the second session of the Eightieth Congress, the Communists in Czechoslovakia, with Soviet troops on the border to back them up, staged a coup d'etat that threw opposition leaders in prison and brought into power a full-fledged communist regime, which soon demonstrated its complete mastery over internal affairs and its subservience to the Soviet Union. Of the Eastern European countries bordering the Soviet Union, only the Czechs had retained democratic institutions, and now these were gone. The Russian bear was still on the march. It was believed that if the remaining European countries did not unite, pool their resources with each other, and accept the generous offer of the United States, their future independence was in danger, and so was the security of the United States.[28]

Some diplomatic historians now claim that the Marshall program forced the Soviet Union to take action in Czechoslovakia.[29] The Czechs certainly wanted to join ERP, but they had obediently followed Soviet orders to stay out long before the coup. The Czech Communist party was facing serious losses in coming elections, and the actions of the opposition gave them their chance. President Benes was a sick and weak figure in this crisis, and death by violence eliminated Jan Masaryk. President Truman was shocked by these events and renewed his efforts to secure passage of the Marshall program. This was accomplished on April 2, 1948.

The passage of this legislation by a Republican Congress that was economy minded was a masterful accomplishment. Truman owed a great deal to Vandenberg, who was able to persuade most of his Republican colleagues to cooperate.[30] While Truman favored Acheson to head up the new program, Senator Vandenberg insisted on the appointment of a Republican industrialist, Paul Hoffman, who was reluctant to accept the appointment but was persuaded to do so.[31]

GERMANY

The provisions of the Potsdam protocol were contradictory regarding the treatment of conquered Germany. One provision called for the achievement of economic unity in Germany. Another declared that the Soviet Union could take reparations from its zone without reference to the other zones. The reparations provision for the Soviet Union could lead nowhere but to a divided Germany. On top of the extractions of reparations, the Soviet forces of occupation imposed a communist dictatorship, which eliminated capitalistic and other opposition elements and controlled all employment and trade.

General Lucius Clay, head of the American occupation forces, tried to work out an economic agreement with the Russians that would treat Germany as a whole.[32] The Russians, however, vetoed every proposal for joint control except on their own terms. So at first did the French, who could not forget the three invasions they had suffered at the hands of the Germans.

Soon after Marshall had been appointed and confirmed as secretary of state, he rushed to Moscow in March 1947 to attend a meeting of the Council of Foreign Ministers, which was to consider mainly the future of Germany. In accordance with the bipartisan foreign policy, which he strongly supported, he invited John Foster Dulles, the Republican spokesman on foreign affairs, to go with him as an adviser.[33] Although he knew the Truman speech on aid to Greece and Turkey was about to be delivered and that it might complicate affairs in Moscow, he did not hesitate to proceed with his plans. Although the Truman speech was not mentioned in Moscow, it set the tone for Soviet intransigence. Marshall was convinced that the Russians did not want a settlement except on their own harsh terms. Nothing was decided at the conference.[34]

In summer 1947, Secretary of Commerce Harriman sent Truman a summary of conditions in Germany:

We cannot attain our basic objective unless we are ready to move rapidly to reconstruct German life from its present pitiful and chaotic condition. The recovery of Germany in feeding and in industrial production has lagged far behind western Europe. We cannot revive a self-supporting western European economy without a healthy Germany playing its part as a producing and consuming unit.[35]

The second meeting of the Council of Foreign Ministers on the German question, held in London in December 1947, failed to reach any settlement, and it was clear to Marshall that the Soviet Union was determined to seek complete control of Germany.[36] The current economic and political chaos in Germany was an invitation to the Communists to attempt a takeover. To bolster up the defense of Europe against such a catastrophe, England, France, Italy, and the three Benelux countries met in London from February to June 1948 and agreed upon the establishment of a West German state, on plans for European economic integration, on an International Control Authority for the Ruhr, and on a Military Security Board. The Soviet Union denounced these moves as contrary to the Potsdam agreements and accused the Americans of trying to restore Nazi capitalists and of using economic pressures to establish trade advantages for American businessmen.

The Marshall Plan included West German needs. Ultimately, more aid was given for the reconstruction of West Germany than to any other country. The British and American zones, already joined in September 1946 to establish bizonal administration for economics, food, and agriculture, were ready to make good use of this aid. Later, the French also joined to form the trizonal administration.[37]

The Russians, alarmed by these developments, calculated that Berlin was a vulnerable spot that could be used to slow down the unification of western German zones and the establishment of an independent West Germany. On March 5, 1948, Clay sent this top-secret telegram: "I feel a subtle change in Soviet attitude which I cannot define but which gives me a feeling that it [war] may come with dramatic suddenness."[38] Soviet representatives walked out of the Allied Control Council on Berlin on March 20, 1948, and notified the American military government in Berlin that all U.S. personnel passing through the Russian zone to Berlin would be checked and that all freight shipments would be inspected. U.S. military authorities rejected these demands, insisting on the American right of free access to Berlin. The Soviet Union then sealed off all highway, rail, and river traffic into and out of Berlin, but there was a written agreement establishing the air lanes from West Germany to Berlin.[39]

The crisis deepened after the British, French, and Americans announced on June 18, 1948, that they would set up a new currency in their zones. The Russians had plates of the old currency and had used them to flood the western zones, thereby getting goods and services for nothing and adding to the inflation in West Germany. The Russians were using the blockade as a means of resecuring their favored currency position and as a means of thwarting the plans for uniting the zones and creating West Germany.[40]

Truman took the problem up at the June 25 cabinet meeting. He made it clear that he was determined to remain in Berlin. The question was how this could be accomplished without risking war, which General Clay feared might break out over this crisis.[41]

The blockade by land and by water forced Clay to begin the famous airlift. Truman backed him up and directed that every plane available be put under the European command.[42] At a meeting of the National Security Council on July 22, 1948, General Clay said: "The abandonment of Berlin would have a disastrous effect upon American plans for Western Germany. It would also slow down European recovery, the success of which depended upon more production, particularly from Western Germany."[43]

Truman and his advisers considered the relative risk of the airlift as opposed to attempting to supply Berlin by land convoy, which was urged by Ambassador Robert Murphy and General Clay, and came to the conclusion that the airlift was less dangerous even though Air Force Chief of Staff General Vandenberg pointed out that a concentration of air power in Europe would expose the United States. Truman faced a hard election, and if a convoy started a war, he would be blamed. Once the decision was made, General Vandenberg did everything he could to make the airlift a success, which historians generally agree it was from the physical point of view.[44]

In the meantime, in spite of Soviet protests, steps were taken to reestablish German self-government and to relinquish occupational controls in the western zones. The Parliamentary Council was established. It met on September 1, 1948, and elected Konrad Adenauer, who had a fine anti-Nazi record, as president.[45]

PALESTINE AND THE FORMATION OF ISRAEL

While Marshall was secretary of state, the American policy toward Palestine continued to be a divisive issue within the administration.[46] Upon becoming president, Truman was immediately subjected to pressures from the Zionists to support the idea of a Jewish state in Palestine. Rabbi Stephen S. Wise saw Truman on April 20, 1945, and after the interview declared that Truman supported Roosevelt's policy of unrestricted immigration to Palestine.[47] Right after the Potsdam conference, Truman wrote to Prime Minister Attlee bringing to his attention the report of Earl G. Harrison, the U.S. representative to the Intergovernmental Committee on Refugees, which suggested the granting of an additional one hundred thousand certificates for immigration to Palestine. Truman accepted this report, but Attlee suggested a joint Anglo-American Committee of Inquiry to find a solution to the problem. In its report of April 20, 1946, this distinguished committee recommended a national home for Jewish people in Palestine and the admission of a hundred thousand Jewish refugees, approximately the number in camps in Germany and Austria. Truman accepted this report also, but the British and Arabs did not.[48] British Foreign Secretary Ernest Bevin attacked Truman bitterly, saying that the President's October 4, 1946, statement that a hundred thousand Jews should be admitted to Palestine was made to counter Governor Dewey's more sweeping statement on the issue. Truman was angered because his position had been made clear to the British months before.[49]

When Marshall became secretary of state, the British had given up trying to solve the Palestine problem by negotiations with the Americans, Arabs, and Jews and had referred the question to the United Nations. The Department of State and the new Defense Department, led as they were by military men and ex-Wall Street bankers, were opposed to any action that would alienate the Arab states because of the importance of Mideast oil to European and American defense and industrial production.[50] Secretary of

Defense Forrestal was particularly anxious not to offend the Arabs.[51] Truman was aware of President Roosevelt's understanding with the Arab states that they would be consulted regarding any Palestine settlement. He soon found that to consult them was one thing, to satisfy them was another. As for the top State Department officials who opposed a Jewish homeland, he thought that they were anti-Semitic. In favor of the Zionist cause for the establishment of a new state of Israel were the President's political advisers, Clark Clifford, Judge Rosenman, David Niles, and his old crony and fellow haberdasher, Eddie Jacobson. The pressures brought to bear upon Truman from all sides were enormous. He resented the harsh criticisms from the Zionists when he thought that he was doing the best he could for them under the circumstances. Chaim Weizmann was one of the Zionists who impressed him favorably, particularly when he pointed out that the Jews had demonstrated that they could make the deserts bloom. Truman had long been interested in irrigation problems.[52]

Truman's decision to support Jewish immigration to Palestine was based on political, humanitarian, and sentimental reasons. He felt that the Jews had suffered greatly at the hands of the Nazis and that the world owed them a homeland where they could take care of the Jewish refugees who had serious problems of resettlement. His political advisers kept him aware of the importance of the Jewish vote in the northern cities and of the strenuous efforts of the Republicans to attract that vote. He had great respect for Marshall and Acheson, who urged him to go slow in offending the Arabs. With the British, Truman was exasperated. He realized that Mideast oil was Britain's lifeline, but he contended that the British were committed by the Balfour Resolution of 1917, by the Committee of Inquiry report of 1946, and by the British Labour party platform to admitting a hundred thousand Jews to Palestine. Secretary Bevin had been won over to the Arab point of view by the British Foreign Service, which, like its American counterpart, was not sympathetic to Zionism. The British officers in Palestine had to contend with the illegal smuggling of Jewish refugees and the terrorist activities of the fanatical Jewish extremists. The financial and military burden of maintaining the British mandate over Palestine was enormous, and the British felt that they had to find a way out.

The U.N. General Assembly set up the Special Committee on Palestine on which none of the so-called great powers were represented. This committee held hearings in Palestine, but the Arabs there refused to cooperate.[53] On August 31, 1947, it rendered its report; seven members recommended partition of Palestine into a Jewish state, an Arab state, and a separate internationalized city of Jerusalem. Three members recommended a single federal state. The Arabs rejected the majority report and the question was bitterly debated in the U.N. Assembly with the Zionists bringing pressure in favor of partition. President Truman criticized the extreme methods that

were used to get a favorable vote. On November 29, 1947, the General
Assembly voted in favor of partition by a vote of thirty-three to thirteen.
Terrorist activities increased in Palestine. Truman supported the U.N. plan
for partition, but important members of his administration did not. George
Kennan and his Policy Planning Staff opposed partition and recommended
a reversal of Truman's policy backing it. The view of the State Department
specialists was that American support for an independent Jewish state was
based not on sound foreign policy considerations but on domestic politics
and the need of the Democrats to corral the Jewish vote and financial
support in the coming presidential elections. Curiously enough, reversing a
former position, the Soviet Union supported partition. This stance concerned Truman because he did not want the Soviets to make inroads in this
area.

The British announced that they would end their mandate on May 15,
1948. What would happen then was far from settled. Armed hostilities had
already broken out between the Arabs and Jews in Palestine. The British
and Americans were considering a trusteeship under the United Nations to
take the place of the British mandate. With the withdrawal of the British
troops, the United Nations had no police force of its own to take their
place. The Zionists were opposed to a trusteeship, and great pressure was
brought to bear upon Truman who became so incensed that he refused to
see any representative of the Jewish point of view. It was at this juncture
that the Zionists prevailed upon Eddie Jacobson to see the President in
order to arrange an interview for Chaim Weizmann. Truman felt that he
could not refuse to see his old friend.[54] At first he would not discuss the
question of Israel but when Jacobson referred to Truman's admiration of
President Jackson as the kind of regard he had for Weizmann, Truman
agreed to a secret meeting with Weizmann. On the day following this meeting, March 19, 1948, Senator Austin, the American representative to the
U.N. Security Council, proposed that the plan to partition Palestine be
suspended and that pending a decision on its permanent status, Palestine be
placed under a U.N. trusteeship. Truman had been informed by the State
Department about the trusteeship plan, but he had not made clear to
Weizmann what the American position was. He was taken by surprise at the
uproar made by the Jews following Austin's speech. He proclaimed his own
position as still in favor of partition, but he did not repudiate Secretary
Marshall, who backed trusteeship. He called Clifford and Daniels to his
office and asked, "How could this happen? I assured Weizmann that we
were for partition and would stick to it. He must think I am a plain liar.
Find out how this could have happened." Clifford contacted Under Secretary of State Lovett, who explained that Marshall had approved an attempt
to try trusteeship if they could not get partition. Truman knew what was
going on, but he refused to blame himself for not making it clear to Weiz-

mann. He claimed that the State Department had pulled the rug from under him and that his reputation with the Jews was ruined.[55]

In the middle of May, the question came up again on the eve of the British termination of its mandate. The President, still favoring partition and recognition of an independent Jewish state, held a conference on the question. Marshall and Lovett were opposed to immediate recognition. Clifford and Niles were urging Truman to take immediate action. Clifford argued that Truman was on record as favoring an independent state, and it was unrealistic to pretend there was no such state. As Clifford later told Daniels, "Marshall's face flushed. 'Mr. President, this is not a matter to be determined on the basis of politics. Unless politics were involved, Mr. Clifford would not even be at this conference. This is a serious matter of foreign policy determination'. . . . He said it all in a righteous God-damned Baptist tone."

Marshall held firm, and Truman backed him, but the next day Lovett again opened the question and indicated that although Marshall had agreed to recognition, the department wanted to delay in order to consult with the British and the French. The U.N. General Assembly was in the middle of considering how to solve the Palestine crisis. Clifford persuaded the President to act at once, and the United States became the first nation to recognize Israel after it announced its independence on May 14, 1948 and the new regime requested American recognition.[56] This was done without informing all of the American representatives in the U.N. Assembly. The head of the delegation, Senator Austin, was so shocked that he left for home in disgust without telling his colleagues. The precipitous recognition left the American delegation and its U.N. friends in consternation. What was American policy in the Near East? To the Arabs the action meant war. The Zionists in the United States soon appealed for the lifting of the arms embargo and the granting of American financial aid to the new state. Truman insisted that no American soldiers would be used. One of the reasons he had failed to follow Marshall's advice was that he wished to assert his independence and to quiet critics who were saying that Marshall made all of the foreign policy decisions. A main factor was, of course, that he was in the middle of a fight for his political life and the Jewish vote was a key element in the populous eastern states, which exercised disproportionate weight in the presidential electoral college. Truman and his advisers were aware that the Republicans would try to outbid them for the Jewish vote as Dewey had done in the New York gubernatorial election of 1946.[57]

THE BEGINNINGS OF NATO

The Western European countries were alarmed at the communist assault on the Marshall plan, which took the form of riots and strikes in France and

Italy, at the failure of the London Conference of Foreign Ministers of November 1947 to reach an agreement on the future of Germany, and at the bitter Soviet propaganda attacks on them. In December 1947 Secretary Marshall had talked with Foreign Secretary Bevin about the defense of Europe. On January 13, 1948, Bevin informed Marshall that he was planning to discuss defense problems with France and the Benelux countries, and he wanted American views on the subject. Marshall consulted with Truman, who authorized him to inform Bevin that "we agreed with them on the urgent need for concerted measures by the nations of Western Europe."[58]

The February 1948 communist coup in Czechoslovakia deepened the fears of Western European governments and hastened the negotiations for a mutual defense pact. Kennan pointed out that Clay's war scare was based on Soviet plans to impose the Berlin blockade, not on any intentions to start a war. Truman, nevertheless, had the Central Intelligence Agency prepare a special estimate, which declared that war "was not probable within sixty days." Within that time, the Russians started the blockade of western Berlin.[59]

President Truman considered the situation so dangerous that he asked to address a joint session of Congress on March 17. A first draft of this alarmist speech was prepared by Elsey and Bell. The second draft was examined by Clifford, Bohlen, Murphy, Marshall, Harriman, Schwellenbach, Ross, and Hassett. Although this was an imposing array of talent, the absence of Kennan, who did not share the alarm, should be noted. In this speech Truman deplored the events in Czechoslovakia, specifically named the Soviet Union as the enemy of peace, and encouraged the five European nations—Great Britain, France, Holland, Belgium, and Luxembourg—which were signing the fifty-year Brussels Pact for economic cooperation and common defense against aggression. He indicated that the United States, by appropriate action, would "extend to the free nations the support which the situation requires." Included were requests for legislation establishing universal military service and a temporary revival of the draft.[60]

On the evening of the same day Truman said in his St. Patrick's Day address in New York City: "I do not want and I will not accept the political support of Henry Wallace and his Communists." He was particularly bitter because Wallace had said that the Czech Communists had seized power to protect themselves from a rightist coup in Czechoslovakia. Wallace had added that Ambassador Laurence Steinhardt had issued a statement that aided the rightists' cause and helped precipitate the crisis.

Following the President's speeches, Secretary Marshall and Under Secretary Lovett began conversations with Senators Vandenberg and Connally on ways of meeting the defense needs of Western Europe. At a meeting of the National Security Council on April 22, 1948, according to Forrestal,

[Lovett] outlined tentative proposals for as nearly concurrent action as possible by the Senate and the President, not in terms of a treaty, but a statement that we were willing to consider under Article 51 of the United Nations, steps looking to the construction of a regional agreement, if it proves to be in the interests of the security of the United States. The tactics would be to have this action initiated by the Republicans and to have the ball picked up immediately by the President, who would state his interest in the plan and make some further appropriate remarks.[61]

Under Secretary of State Lovett had established friendly relations with Senator Vandenberg, and the two men worked together on drafting a Senate resolution that would indicate the willingness of the United States, under proper constitutional safeguards, to cooperate with Western European nations in establishing regional collective security arrangements under article 51 of the U.N. Charter. They strove to bypass the Soviet veto on questions involving peaceful settlement of disputes. Late in April, with reservations, the resolution was discussed at Blair House, where Dulles praised it. Senator Vandenberg introduced the resolution in the Senate on May 11. Eight days later, the Senate Foreign Relations Committee approved the draft unanimously. The resolution was called up in the Senate on June 11 and passed by a vote of sixty-four to four.[62] A key passage stated: "Association of the United States by constitutional process, with such regional and other collective arrangements as are based on continuous and effective self-help and mutual aid, and as affect its national security."

President Truman approved on July 2 a policy statement calling for the implementation of the Vandenberg resolution, which, though vague, enabled him to push toward the goal of a defensive alliance with the North Atlantic nations. The Berlin blockade, made complete on June 28, increased the urgency of these negotiations.[63]

Under Marshall and Lovett, the progress toward the alliance moved slowly because of the uncertainty of the coming presidential election. But with Truman's reelection, the course was clear. A draft treaty was ready by the end of 1948, and it was mentioned in Truman's 1949 inaugural address.

Although Marshall had weaknesses as secretary of state, he was awarded the Nobel Peace Prize for his contribution to the economic recovery of Europe. During his term as secretary of state, Marshall maintained his position as nonpolitical, and he was not subjected to the bitter attacks that came later. He felt compelled to resign in early 1949 because of ill health.

chapter 29 | NOMINATION FOR A FULL TERM

We, of the Democratic Party, are proud of our great President.
We have reason to be proud. Regardless of the ridicule and false
propaganda spread daily by the organs of monopoly and special
privilege, the true qualities of our great leader are becoming more
and more apparent to the people.
—Mon Wallgren, Democratic National Convention, 1948

After two and a half rough years in the White House, Truman had to decide whether to try for a full term.[1] His chances of winning did not look bright since the congressional, state, and local elections of 1946 indicated that the tide was running against the Democrats. Truman's popularity as shown by the public opinion polls had declined considerably below the 50 percent mark by November 1946.[2] The metropolitan press was critical of him and his administration. Party morale had declined because of the dismal prospects of success in 1948. Inflation, labor disputes, consumer shortages, and unrest among minority groups, particularly Jews and blacks, had confused the domestic scene.[3] In foreign affairs, peace seemed to be a long way off, and the President appeared to vacillate between playing up to the Russians and getting tough with them. He was labeled by his detractors as inept, weak, bumbling, inconsistent, too easily swayed, without ideas of his own, and unfit for the presidency.[4]

In his political career, Truman had never run from an uphill battle. Beginning with his first election to local office and continuing with his two bitter contests for a seat in the U.S. Senate, he had fought strenuously against great odds. In view of the criticism of him as president, he felt that he had to run to vindicate himself.

It is hard to determine when Truman decided to run. Probably the day he was sworn in he had in mind the thought of winning the presidency in his own right. A delegation of Pennsylvania Democrats, including Mayor David L. Lawrence and Senator Joseph F. Guffey, had told the new President on April 25, 1945, that he would have their support in 1948. At the time Truman made no comment.[5] Two weeks later *Newsweek* asserted: ''President Truman is already running for re-election in 1948. There is no coyness about his intentions around the White House. He discusses political strategy with his intimates and they in turn, discuss his prospects with outsiders. In a general way, Truman's plans are set.''[6] In his *Memoirs*, Truman explained that he decided to run in 1948 in order to try to preserve the heritage of liberalism that had come down from Jefferson to Roosevelt, which the Republicans did not want and were trying to destroy: "There was still unfinished business confronting the most successful fifteen years of Democratic administration in the history of the country.''[7]

The results of the 1946 elections were discouraging, but Truman was an optimist. He would make the best of adversity. The Eightieth Congress would be a target for him to attack. He would blame it for failing to follow his recommendations regarding inflation, poverty, inadequate defense, poor housing, discrimination, and other problems. Commentators wrote before the election that the 1948 Democratic campaign was an improvised one put together at the last moment by an incompetent crew.[8] Material in the Truman papers shows that this view was badly mistaken. The strategy of the campaign was carefully laid out a year in advance, and it was adhered to closely.

On Truman's campaign strategy board were Sam Rosenman, Clark Clifford, Robert Hannegan, Charles Murphy, J. Howard McGrath, Oscar Chapman, Oscar Ewing, Jonathan Daniels, Charles Ross, and others. The leader of this group was Clark Clifford, special counsel and chief speech writer, who with the aid of James Rowe prepared for President Truman the now famous memorandum of November 19, 1947, outlining a course of action to be followed in order to win the election of 1948.[9] With extraordinary accuracy, the memorandum predicted coming events: the nomination of Governor Dewey by the Republicans, the minor party candidacy of Henry Wallace, the possible loss of some of the northeastern states, and the winning of the vote of laborers, farmers, nonwhites, the foreign born, westerners, moderates with liberal tendencies, and consumers concerned with high prices. Postelection analyses confirmed the accuracy of these prophesies. Only on one point did the memorandum fail to foresee coming events clearly. It was overoptimistic about holding the solid South, failing to anticipate the Dixiecrat movement, which cost Truman four southern states. Clifford and his helpers can hardly be blamed for this. It was impossible for them to know in the fall of 1947 that the civil rights issue could not be straddled in a manner that would hold the South just as Roosevelt had done in four elections. They could not anticipate that the young mayor of Minneapolis, Hubert Humphrey, would lead a successful fight in the convention to strengthen the civil rights plank. Yet a majority of the southern states stuck with Truman in the election, even though they opposed him in the convention.[10]

The memorandum set the target areas, and the Truman campaign was organized accordingly. From the time that Truman discussed the plan with

Clifford until election day, the course of action, the issues to be stressed, the regions to be visited, and the groups to be won were set. The plan called for a preconvention nonpolitical inspection tour to prepare the way for the more intensive postconvention campaign, thus anticipating the June 3-18, 1948, nonpolitical trip to make a commencement address at the University of California.

The plan suggested that the President cultivate key labor leaders, prominent liberals, well-known scientists, and intellectuals. It argued that the public image of the President was based in part on such contacts. Truman did not follow this advice literally, but he did make up with his old friend, A. F. Whitney of the Brotherhood of Railway Trainmen, who had been alienated during the railroad strike of 1946 by Truman's tough speech. Jack Redding of the Democratic National Committee cooperated in bringing the two men together.[11] The President renominated David E. Lilienthal, the well-known liberal, to head the Atomic Energy Commission.[12]

The Clifford-Rowe memorandum recommended a new national chairman for the Democratic party and a drastic overhauling of the machinery of the national committee. (This part must have been written before October 29 when Hannegan resigned.) Chairman Hannegan had performed many useful services, but his health was failing and he was not physically up to the job. Before he left, Hannegan stressed the importance of hitting Taft hard. He calculated that even if Dewey tried to run on a "me too" program, he could not repudiate Taft's record in Congress. On Truman's recommendation, the Democratic National Committee elected on October 29, 1947, Senator J. Howard McGrath of Rhode Island as the new chairman, a man who was thoroughly versed in the mechanics of politics and who acquired his political views from the patriarch of the Senate, Theodore Green, also of Rhode Island. McGrath retained the energetic executive director, Gael Sullivan, who worked with local groups, and the able publicity staff headed by Jack Redding, who skillfully exploited every Republican error and put on an effective publicity campaign even though strapped for funds.[13]

Clark Clifford persuaded chairman McGrath to set up a research division under the national committee to aid speech writers in the White House. William L. Batt, Jr., was placed in charge of this work. A Harvard graduate, a World War II veteran, and an unsuccessful candidate for Congress from a Philadelphia suburb, he had been recommended to Clifford by David Morse, under secretary of labor. He recruited David D. Lloyd, a promising young lawyer who was research director for Americans for Democratic Action (ADA). Lloyd made such a fine impression that he was later invited to join the White House staff. The research division made a splendid contribution to speech preparation and campaign tour arrangements even though its function was not always understood by other parts of the committee.[14]

Truman worked continuously to improve his speaking style. After his formal address before the American Society of Newspaper Editors on April 17, 1948, he made some impromptu remarks without a manuscript, discussing American relations with the Soviet Union in an informal manner, which enabled him to appear more natural.[15] The newsmen applauded these remarks more enthusiastically than they had his formal address. Truman and his advisers realized that he was on the right track and used this technique more often. The chances of a slip were greater, but they seemed worth taking. On May 6, Truman wrote: "I appeared before a family life conference at 12:30 and spoke over all four networks without a manuscript. The audience gave me a most cordial reception."[16]

Truman's efforts to improve his radio techniques were evident in his remarks at the Young Democrats dinner on May 14, 1948, which were carried on a national radio broadcast.[17] Two months earlier he had announced through a statement by national chairman McGrath that he was a candidate for the Democratic nomination for president, so a speech before such a group was avowedly political. In spite of this, the speech had general appeal. The *New York Times* referred to it as a "fighting" speech "in the new Truman manner."[18] It reflected the attempt of his advisers to project an image of Truman as a man of sincerity, forthrightness, and courage. The speech ridiculed the Republicans on domestic issues, praised the bipartisan foreign policy, and expressed clearly Truman's confidence in himself and the future of his party.

THE JUNE TOUR

The Clifford-Rowe plan called for a nonpartisan tour on the part of the President before the political conventions met. An invitation to deliver a commencement address on June 12 at the University of California at Berkeley furnished the excuse for such a trip, which was classified as not being political and therefore could be charged to the President's travel fund.[19] The trip was by train, so there were many demands for presidential appearances along the way. The train was routed in a big circle covering the central and northern route going and the southern route returning. On the train, helping write the speeches, were Clark Clifford, Charles Murphy, George Elsey, Matt Connelly, and Charles Ross. They set off June 4 in the eighteen-car presidential special and returned June 18. Elsey concentrated on the outlines for the rear platform whistle-stop impromptu remarks, relying on materials furnished by Batt's research division in Washington.[20]

During the first week, the tour suffered numerous problems. Bert Andrews, a friend of Charlie Ross and one of the *New York Herald-Tribune* reporters, telegraphed Ross on June 9:

News stories in east—whether from special correspondents or press associations and radio people—indicate a succession of boners is plaguing the president on his tour. Top incidents published in East include poor turnout in Omaha, snubbing of party officials in Nebraska and Montana, Pocatello speech in which president said, "They have never been able to prove it on me," and mixup over airport dedication at Carey, Idaho, in which the president condoled with parents over male war hero who turned out to be a civilian girl. All these add up to picture in eastern newspapers and all radio of ineptness and confusion as far as president and arrangements are concerned. Occurred to me you might like to present picture as you see it. . . . giving your views on mishaps, reasons therefore, and your assessment of trip, crowds, and results.[21]

Each of these incidents had a reasonable explanation, but they all showed that the mechanics of the tour needed many improvements. The small crowd at Omaha was the result of poor advance planning and confusion as to whether the general public was invited to what was described as a veteran's meeting. Oscar Chapman soon took hold of the advance planning, and future errors of this sort were avoided.[22] Party officials were not snubbed. It was the policy of this tour not to invite any local politicians to meet the President on the train. The remark at Pocatello was clearly a serious mistake. The words could easily be interpreted as meaning that Truman was in on some of the Kansas City grafting that took place under Pendergast, but he was never caught. It is probable that what Truman meant to say was that he had been accused of wrongdoing, but all of the accusations had proven false. The Carey incident was the result of an impulse on the part of Harry Vaughan who heard that an airport was to be dedicated and did not find out all the details. There was no press release, no official stenographer was present, and therefore there is no official record of what happened.[23] As a result of this procedural error, much more care was taken from then on to see that the advance work was thoroughly done.

Soon the fortunes of the tour began to turn. On June 5, Truman stopped at Boystown, Nebraska, where his friend, Edward D. McKim, had alerted advance man Oscar Chapman of the importance of this stop because Father Flanagan, the founder of Boystown, had recently died.[24] The President paid a glowing tribute to the late monsignor and related how he had used him to make a report on Austria.[25] At Spokane, Washington, a chance remark to a reporter on June 9 that the Eightieth Congress was "the worst since the first one met in Washington's day" brought a vigorous reaction from the Republicans, who called Truman the worst president. On June 11, Senator Taft told the Union League at Philadelphia that Truman was "blackguarding the Eightieth Congress at every whistle station." The party on the train and the Democratic National Committee picked up this remark and sent telegrams to all cities on their itinerary asking them if they considered themselves "whistle-stops." This slur upon the cities brought indignant replies.[26]

Truman's verbal blunders were not over. On June 11 at Eugene, Oregon, he made an off-the-cuff remark that his detractors seized upon. Recalling his experiences at Potsdam, he declared, "I got very well acquainted with Joe Stalin, and I like old Joe! He is a decent fellow. But Joe is a prisoner of Politburo. He can't do what he wants to. He makes agreements, and if he could he would keep them; but the people who run the government are very specific in saying he can't keep them."[27] Such a remark in a set speech would have been caught by Bohlen, Kennan, or Harriman, who could have told Truman about the true nature of Stalin. Truman was warned firmly not to repeat such a remark.[28] Dealings with the Russians gradually changed Truman's views, and he became more aware of the true character of the Soviet tyrant. In 1948, however, he did not have the benefit of Krushchev's denunciation of Stalin delivered at the Congress of Soviets in 1956. At Potsdam, Stalin had been polite and restrained.

At Berkeley before an audience of fifty-five thousand, Truman read a dignified address on foreign policy that emphasized the need of the Marshall Plan for the economic reconstruction of Europe in view of the Soviet threat of aggression against countries showing economic weaknesses.[29] A draft of this speech by Bohlen had been revised by Kennan, Elsey, Clifford, Phileo Nash (a minority group expert), Murphy, and Admiral Souers.[30] *Time*, usually a Truman critic, called the address "one of the best speeches of his career, delivered with dignity, poise and eloquence."

The reception at Los Angeles was warm in spite of the split in the Democratic party and the movement to support Dwight Eisenhower for president, led by the late President Roosevelt's son James. While some of the respect paid Truman was directed at the office he held, there was genuine admiration for the plucky man who was putting up a game fight. James Roosevelt was put on a spot because he had to lead the delegation to meet the President, who recalled later, "I got him [Roosevelt] in a corner and told him 'you're one hell of a fellow. Here I am trying to do everything I can to carry out your father's policies. You've got no business trying to pull the rug from under me.'"[31] Roosevelt sidestepped the issues as to how the California delegation would vote in Philadelphia.[32] The speech at the Los Angeles Press Club had been drafted with the aid of Charles Lawton, Charles Stauffacher, David Stowe, and Elmer Staats of the Bureau of the Budget, Edwin G. Nourse of the Council of Economic Advisers, Batt of the national committee, and Clifford, Murphy, Bell, Neustadt, and Steelman of the White House staff.[33] The speech was on economic issues and included discussion of measures to control inflation, aid to agriculture, and the provision of more social security, better housing, and federally funded medical care.[34]

The June tour, which covered ninety-five hundred miles and involved seventy-five speeches, started out with some fumbles, but as the team acquired experience, as advance preparations improved, and as Truman developed his own style, the crowds became larger and more enthusiastic.

Toward the end of his trip, he told an audience in Dodge City, Kansas: "I have seen, I imagine, about two and a half millions of people. I have talked to a great many people, and a great many people have talked to me, and I think I have found out what the country is thinking about. I think I have definitely fixed the issues which are before the country now. It is merely the fact: are the special privilege boys going to run the country or are the people going to run it?"[35] Barnet Nover, a journalist, expressed the view that Truman's efforts were winning support from the masses and altering the political equation. He warned that it would be a mistake for the Republicans "to take victory for granted before the ballots have been counted."[36]

RIVAL CANDIDATES

To win the 1948 election, Truman had to outdistance not only the Republican nominee, but he had to face three serious rivals within his own party—one who was being considered as his replacement and the other two who led minor party movements of more than usual strength. One attempt was made to deny him the nomination, and two attempts were made by splinter groups to deprive him of the required majority in the electoral college by dividing the electors three or more ways. The party offshoots were at the opposite ends of the political scale. One was a conservative based mainly on the South and the other was a radical based upon left-wing elements, including the communists.

In March 1948 after the precipitous decline in Truman's popularity following his civil rights speech, the Democratic coalition composed of conservative southerners, northern liberals, city bosses, and labor leaders began to fall apart. Truman was regarded as a sure loser, and the diverse elements in the party began to look around for a more promising candidate.

As early as 1945 the possibility of General Dwight D. Eisenhower's running for president appealed to widely different elements. At a press conference in Abilene, Kansas, on June 22, 1945, Eisenhower stated: "I'm a soldier, and I'm positive no one thinks of me as a politician. In the strongest language you can command, you can state that I have no political ambitions at all. I'd like to go even further than Sherman in expressing myself on the topic."[37]

General Eisenhower claimed that in a private conversation at Potsdam Truman offered to support him for the Democratic nomination for president in 1948. The general recalled Truman as saying: "General, there is nothing that you may want that I won't try to help you get. That definitely and specifically includes the presidency in 1948."[38] Eisenhower did not take this offer seriously at the time, and Truman never confirmed it.

The Clifford-Rowe memorandum of November 19, 1947, stated on the Eisenhower candidacy: "For example, one of the reasons privately circulated by the men promoting today's tentative boomlet for Eisenhower is that the general knows foreign policy much more than theoretically; that he is accustomed to dealing directly with British, Russians, French and Germans."[39] About this time, a story was circulating that the President used Secretary of War Kenneth C. Royall to sound out Eisenhower on the Democratic nomination, with Truman as vice-president. Truman denied this story categorically.[40]

In February 1948 when General Eisenhower announced that he would retire as chief of staff and become president of Columbia University in June, both political parties began to consider him a possible candidate for president. In the public opinion polls, he topped all other candidates, Republican and Democratic, in general popularity, and in a hypothetical race against Truman, he swamped the latter.[41] His name was proposed for the Republican presidential primary in New Hampshire in March. On January 22, 1948, he released a letter to Leonard V. Finder of the *Manchester Evening Leader*, refusing to permit his name to be entered in the primary:

It is my conviction that the necessary and wise subordination of the military to civil power will be best sustained, and our people will have greater confidence that it is so sustained, when lifelong professional soldiers, in the absence of some obvious and overriding reasons, abstain from seeking higher political office. . . .

. . . On the other hand, nothing in the international or domestic situation especially qualifies for the most importance office in the world a man whose adult years have been spent in the country's military forces. At least, this is true in my case. . . .

In any case, my decision to remove myself completely from the political scene is definite and positive.[42]

About the time of Truman's formal announcement of candidacy for the Democratic nomination in March, the Americans for Democratic Action was circulating a memorandum indicating that the staff of the Congress of Industrial Organizations-Political Action Committee (CIO-PAC) was concerned about finding a candidate who would have a better chance of winning than Truman.[43] Although the Finder letter ended the Republican boom for Eisenhower, it helped start a Democratic one. Some Democratic leaders interpreted the letter as meaning that Eisenhower would not accept a Republican nomination, and a curious combination of elements within the Democratic party came together to promote the general's candidacy. It included some leftist groups, which did not have the slightest evidence that the general thought as they did, some Democratic organization leaders, who felt that they could get along with the general, some labor leaders, who had no inkling of what Eisenhower thought of the Taft-Hartley Act, and a mixture of southern politicians of diverse views, who without any proof to support them held that the general was their man and understood their point of view on race relations.[44] Subsequent events were to show that all of these assumptions were wrong, but at the time the popularity of the general was extremely attractive to those who were looking for a winner. Even the liberals prized expediency above principles.

Active among the liberal draft-Eisenhower advocates were the late President Roosevelt's three politically minded sons—James of California, Franklin D., Jr., of New York, and Elliott of Texas—and others in the South and West.[45] James was engaged in a bitter struggle with the conservative wing of the party in California led by Ed Pauley, the oil magnate and Truman's friend. He had embarrassed national chairman McGrath at a Jackson Day dinner by organizing a crowd that booed Truman's name and cheered for Eisenhower. Franklin D., Jr., was a vice-president of ADA, and he issued a statement that after the communist coup in Czechoslovakia, the American people had the right to call the general back into active public service. Elliot issued a similar statement. Two former heads of the Office of Price Administration (OPA), Leon Henderson and Chester Bowles, both active in ADA, also joined the draft Eisenhower movement. On April 11, the ADA board declared regarding Truman, "But we cannot overlook the fact that poor appointments and faltering support of his aides have resulted in a failure to rally the people behind the policies which in large measure we wholeheartedly support." Eisenhower, they claimed, "would stir the popular enthusiasm which will sweep progressive candidates across the country into Congress."[46]

A curious combination of southerners was attracted by the possibility of an Eisenhower candidacy. It included moderates—Senators John Sparkman and Lister Hill of Alabama and Senator Claude Pepper of Florida—and conservatives—Governors J. Strom Thurmond of South Carolina, Ben Laney of Arkansas, and William J. Tuck of Virginia. They were brought together by the belief that Eisenhower would be in favor of states' rights and of letting the southerners handle race relations in their own way. Senator Pepper was the most persistent in pressing the draft. In spite of Eisenhower's protests that he was not available for and could not accept nomination to high political office, the senator said, "He may be pulling the door a little close to him, but I didn't hear the door click."[47]

Among the organization Democrats in the cities who were pressing for Eisenhower's nomination were Cook County chairman Jake Arvey of Chicago, Mayor Frank Hague of Jersey City, and Mayor William O'Dwyer of New York. In the state of Illinois, Arvey made two wise state selections, Adlai Stevenson for governor and Paul H. Douglas for senator, but on the national scene he had to backtrack to Truman. While Truman was to lose New Jersey in the fall, his loss margin was about one-fourth of what Hague said it would be.

The labor leaders were not all united behind the dump-Truman movement. President William Green of the American Federation of Labor expressed surprise at the Eisenhower boom: "Labor does not know the economic, social, or industrial views of General Eisenhower."[48] In contrast, Philip Murray, president of the Congress of Industrial Unions, and Jack Kroll, head of its Political Action Committee, tried to persuade Truman to withdraw in Eisenhower's favor.

On the initiative of James Roosevelt, nineteen well-known party leaders sent a telegram to all of the convention delegates inviting them to a meeting to be held just before the convention to select "the ablest and strongest man available" as the party nominee. Eisenhower again held off, declaring, "I will not, at this time, identify myself with any political party, and could not accept nomination for any office or participate in partisan political contest."[49] Even this strong statement did not end the draft movement. Senator Pepper proposed that the Democratic party deliver itself to the general, who would write his own platform and choose his own running mate. On July 9, Eisenhower replied, "No matter under what terms, conditions or premises a proposal might be couched, I would refuse to accept the nomination."[50] This statement at last convinced the Eisenhower admirers that he would not run, and they called off the preconvention meeting. Mayor Paul O'Dwyer of New York and Jake Arvey of Chicago tried to make amends for their activities by coming out for Truman and stating that the draft-Eisenhower movement was a reflection of popular will.[51]

A group of liberals led by Leon Henderson had turned to Justice William O. Douglas as an alternative to Eisenhower in the stop-Truman movement. But this action had little support among the organization leaders, among the voters at large, and among the southerners, who were well aware that Justice Douglas was in favor of enforcing civil rights. Henderson was unable to persuade Douglas to leave the bench, and the movement died.[52]

The final desperate effort in the stop-Truman drive was put on by Senator Pepper who modestly offered himself as the only man now available to carry on the tradition of Franklin D. Roosevelt. So few agreed with him (the leaders of the ADA and the CIO turned him down) that he withdrew his name before the convention called for nominations.[53]

The Eisenhower threat was over. If the general had agreed to run, there certainly would have been a rousing convention battle. James Hagerty of the *New York Times* surveyed the general's prospects while the movement was still alive and concluded, "President Truman is facing a hard and possibly losing fight for the nomination." The President, however, insisted in his *Memoirs* that he controlled the convention.[54]

BEFORE THE CONVENTION

Truman discounted the public opinion polls, but it is idle to deny that they had no effect on his destiny. At least it can be said that they alerted him to the precariousness of his position, and they had a soporific effect on the Republicans, reassuring them that they were bound to win and should not disturb the situation by slashing attacks on Truman and the Democratic program. Many Republicans bitterly accused Dewey of throwing away victory by his high and lofty stand and his lackluster campaigning, which failed to arouse the voters.

Throughout the first half of 1948, the polls based on the question of party affiliation indicated that as far as party preferences were concerned, a majority of the voters were still Democratic.[55] Other things being equal, they felt that the Democratic party would serve them better than the Republican party. But other things were not equal. Truman was not Roosevelt. The President had been under severe criticism, and many thought that the party should produce a more promising leader.

The polls on the President's performance gave an idea as to how the public was reacting to criticisms of his conduct in office. Here there were great fluctuations. In January Truman received a 52 percent vote of confidence in the polls. Four months later his popularity index had dropped to 36 percent, the greatest decline taking place in the South where there was rising indignation against his civil rights stands.[56]

The polls on the hypothetical choice between Truman and Republican hopefuls were important since they influenced the delegates to the Republican convention. A potential Republican candidate who outpolled Truman was in a good position to win the nomination. One who did not would have a hard time convincing the delegates that he was the one to get the nomination. For Truman to trail any Republican possible candidate was discouraging to the Democrats. At the beginning of the year, Truman was ahead of all Republican rivals, but with his declining popularity, he began to lose in a hypothetical race with Governor Dewey. He even trailed Harold Stassen at one point. Taft was the only prominent Republican in the running whom he led at every poll. According to the public opinion sample surveys, prospects looked grim for the Democrats as they assembled in Philadelphia with Truman far in the lead for the nomination.

THE DEMOCRATIC NATIONAL CONVENTION

The Democratic National Convention opened in Philadelphia on July 12, 1948, in an atmosphere of despondency. As Senator Alben Barkley expressed it, "When I arrived in Philadelphia the Saturday before the convention opened, I found the most discouraged and down-cast group I had ever seen. You could cut the gloom with a corn knife. The very air smelled of defeat. 'Listen!' I told the committee officials, 'Don't walk on your chins too soon.'"[57] It was clear that the delegates were stuck with Truman, whom they regarded as a loser. Speakers seeking to praise Truman referred to adverse criticisms. Said one, "We of the Democratic party are proud of our great president. . . . Regardless of the ridicule and false propaganda spread daily by the organs of monopoly and special privilege, the true qualities of our great leader are becoming more and more apparent to the people."[58]

The keynote address was given by Senator Barkley of Kentucky, who provided a temporary lift to the discouraged delegates with his flamboyant praise of the Democratic record and with his scorching condemnation of the Republican record, especially that of the Eightieth Congress. His speech was interspersed with biblical references in true revival style, and he did not forget a humorous touch. His answer to Dewey's proposal to clean the cobwebs from the government at Washington was: "Well, I am not an expert in cob-webs, but if my memory does not betray me, I recall that when the Democratic party took over on March 4, 1933, even the spiders were so weak from starvation they could not weave a web in Washington."[59]

A first draft of materials to be used by the Resolutions Committee in preparing the Democratic platform was made by Rosenman and revised by Clifford, Murphy, Bell, and Elsey.[60] The research division of the Democratic National Committee also furnished suggestions. The platform praised the Roosevelt and Truman administrations and denounced the Republican Eightieth Congress. It pledged support to the United Nations, aid for the state of Israel, a return to free collective bargaining, wider social security benefits, a continuation of farm security, and many other items in Truman's program as expressed in his messages to Congress and public addresses.

The real excitement in the convention came over the adoption of the civil rights plank in the platform. The southern delegates soon showed signs of discontent about the civil rights statements being formulated. Truman and his advisers had approved the same wording that had been used in the 1944 platform. They thought that it straddled the issue in a fashion acceptable to the southern states and was still not too objectionable to the blacks and liberals. The plank adopted by the Resolutions Committee read:

> The Democratic party is responsible for the great civil rights gains made in recent years in eliminating unfair and illegal discrimination based on race, creed or color.
>
> The Democratic Party commits itself to continuing its efforts to eradicate all racial, religious and economic discrimination.
>
> We again state our belief that racial and religious minorities must have the right to live, the right to work, the right to vote, the full and equal protection of the laws, on a basis of equality with all citizens as guaranteed by the Constitution.
>
> We again call upon the Congress to exert its full authority to the limit of its constitutional powers to assure and protect these rights.[61]

The committee soon discovered that the days of soft statements on this issue were gone. The southerners believed that the fourth paragraph canceled the first three since to them constitutional powers meant states' rights. They wanted, however, to weaken the plank some more, and to that end they proposed three much milder statements. Former Congressman Andrew J. Biemiller of Wisconsin and the brash young mayor of Minneapolis, Hubert H. Humphrey, both active in the ADA, led the battle for a more outspoken plank on civil rights. The Biemiller-Humphrey plank provided the following substitute for the fourth paragraph of the Resolutions Committee version:

> We highly commend President Harry Truman for his courageous stand on the issue of civil rights.
> We call upon the Congress to support our President in guaranteeing these basic and fundamental American principles: The right of full and equal political participation, the right to equal opportunity of employment, the right of security of persons, and the right of equal treatment in the service and defense of our Nation.

This plank does not look very advanced in view of later developments. It does not, for example, mention segregation.[62]

For a time there was concern whether the convention leadership would allow the minority pleas to be heard, but with three southerners seeking the floor, the permanent chairman, Speaker Sam Rayburn, could not deny all of them a hearing and a roll call. David K. Niles, administrative assistant to Truman for minority affairs, tried to persuade Humphrey not to speak on behalf of his substitute, but Humphrey would not be restrained. He pleaded eloquently, "To those who say that this civil rights program is an infringement on States' Rights, I say this, that the time has arrived in America for the Democratic party to get out of the shadow of States' Rights and to walk forthrightly into the bright sunshine of human rights."[63]

The first minority plank presented by a southerner, Governor Dan Moody of Texas, was voted on next. It was rejected on a roll call vote of 309 to 925. The other two southern amendments were rejected by similar votes. When the Biemiller-Humphrey amendment came to a roll call vote, it carried by 651½ votes for to 582½ against. The southern delegates were, of course, solidly against it, and so were the border states, including Truman's Missouri and Barkley's Kentucky, but the larger northern and the western states were all for the amendment. Some of the smaller northern states opposed it.[64] Curiously, Truman in his *Memoirs* claimed credit for the plank, stating that he insisted on plain language being used.[65] At the convention, his administrative assistant, Niles, Senator Scott Lucas, and national chairman McGrath all worked against the ADA amendment. The big bosses of the northern states wanted to attract the black vote for their state and local tickets, and they were not so concerned about the possible loss of some southern states because they did not think Truman's chances were very good under any circumstances.

The civil rights battle in the convention disturbed the delicate balance that held the southerners and the northern liberals and blacks within the Democratic party. The revolt of the southern extremists had been fomenting ever since the President had sent his civil rights message to Congress in February. Now the Mississippi and part of the Alabama delegations walked out of the convention hall, not even waiting to see who the candidate might be.

The convention then proceeded to the nomination of its presidential candidate. Alabama yielded to Georgia, and the vice-chairman of the Georgia delegation placed the name of Senator Richard B. Russell of Georgia in nomination in a speech that concentrated on states' rights as opposed to civil rights but that made no threats of a bolt. Arizona then yielded to Missouri, and Governor Phil M. Donnelly of Missouri presented the name of Harry S. Truman with the usual laudatory comments, praising the Democratic record during the preceding fifteen years and Truman's record as president, particularly in the field of foreign affairs. Congressman Will Rogers, Jr., son of the famous comedian, seconded Truman's nomination and also touched on this theme: "They say that Harry Truman is a man of small stature. He has given us one of our greatest conceptions. He has given us a program whereby the productivity of one continent could be used to help in the rehabilitation of another."[66] A delegate from Florida, who had been active in the attempt to draft Eisenhower and did not know where to turn, nominated former Governor Paul McNutt of Indiana, stating, "People who sent me here do not believe our party can win like it is . . . if we are to win we must have new leadership."[67]

Truman won on the first ballot—947½ votes against Russell's 263 votes. Except in North Carolina, Truman received no votes from eleven southern states. Russell's vote was only 21.6 percent of the total, so even under the two-thirds rule, Truman would have won. Contrary to the usual practice, there was no motion to make the nomination unanimous.

The nomination of the Democratic candidate for vice-president did not go according to Truman's plans. His first choice for the position was Justice William O. Douglas, whom he thought would be attractive to the liberals. Truman tried to get Douglas to agree to run, enlisting a plea from Eleanor Roosevelt, but it was to no avail.[68] The justice decided to stay on the bench, and Truman found himself without a candidate, a bad position for a presidential candidate who wanted to control the selection of his running mate.

In the meantime, Les Biffle, secretary to the Senate and sergeant at arms at the convention, was promoting the candidacy of the majority leader, Alben Barkley, his boss in the Senate, for the vice-presidential nomination. At one point Truman was concerned that Barkley was seeking the presidential nomination. In his role as keynoter, Barkley had been popular with the delegates, who gave him an enthusiastic ovation when he finished his address.

Truman, however, was not happy about Barkley with him on the Democratic ticket. The senator was too old, seventy at the time, he came from an adjoining state and therefore could not furnish a geographic balance to the ticket, and he was too closely identified with the legislative establishment. Biffle played a smarter game than Truman did. He practically sewed up the nomination before Truman realized what was going on. To veto Barkley at this stage would have caused a furor. Truman capitulated and accepted his old friend Alben as a running mate, saying that he would be a great help in getting legislation through Congress.[69] The nomination was made by acclamation.

The hour was late, the delegates were hot, tired, and dispirited; the prospects for the party did not look bright with the Republicans controlling Congress and their own ranks split by the defection of the states' rights advocates on the Right and the Henry Wallace supporters on the Left. President Truman had been advised to accept the nomination in person, and to that end he had been waiting for four hours in the wings. During these long, hot hours he said that he ruminated about the presidency and its incumbents over the span of American history. He was particularly interested in those presidents who had an uphill fight, who had been viciously attacked, and who never lost their courage. He identified with Andrew Jackson and Andrew Johnson.[70]

At 2 A.M. the time came at last for the dapper little man in a white suit to appear on the rostrum and accept the nomination. At least the party had vindicated his record. Using his newly found natural style, speaking from an outline worked out by Clifford, Rosenman, Murphy, Bell, and Elsey rather than from a set speech, he gave the most rousing speech of his career.[71] He tore into the opposition, which from his point of view was the Eightieth Congress controlled by the Republicans. It was a fighting speech aimed to bolster up the morale of the party workers and the party faithful: "The Republican party . . . favors the privileged few and not the common everyday man," the tax reduction measure passed was a "Republican rich-man's tax bill," and the "Taft-Hartley Act . . . will cause strife and bitterness . . . if not repealed." He castigated Congress for not passing legislation on housing, price controls, aid to education, civil rights, a national health program, an increase in the minimum wage, extension of social security, public power, and an adequate displaced persons bill without anti-Semitic and anti-Catholic biases. He concluded his remarks by saying that he was going to call Congress back in special session on Missouri's turnip day to give it a chance to act on the promises put forth in the Republican platform.[72] For the moment, he inspired the delegates with a hope of victory.[73] His critic, Clare Boothe Luce, wrote a warning, "The end of the Philadelphia story is not yet." Two days after the convention, a friend wrote to the

President, "That acceptance speech was a knockout, and what a resurgence of courage it gave all of us."[74]

The acceptance speech has become a classic in American political history. At the time, most journalists failed to detect its prophetic character. It was an important part of the strategy that was to confound the Republicans, the pollsters, and the pundits. Although it was Truman and his staff who produced it, Margaret Coit claimed that Sam Lubell suggested the idea of calling Congress back to Bernard Baruch, who in turn passed it on to the President in June.[75] Truman was in a battle for his political life. The speech was the first round in his campaign as the Democratic candidate for reelection.

chapter 30 | THE OPPOSITION: DEWEY, THURMOND, AND WALLACE

Jealousies and mismanagement delayed cooperation until it was too late. . . . And each candidate probably preferred Dewey to the other.
—Eugene H. Rosenboom, *A History of Presidential Elections*

Press Covers the Progressive Convention. Reporters were impressed by the eager enthusiasm of the delegates. . . . but they were virtually unanimous in declaring the convention to be Communist-controlled and manipulated.
—Curtis D. MacDougall, *Gideon's Army*

THE REPUBLICAN NOMINATION

In view of the Republican electoral victories in 1946 and the declining popularity of President Truman, the Republican presidential nomination in 1948 looked like a great prize. Consequently the competition was keen, and the hopeful candidates were numerous. By the beginning of 1948, there were four avowed candidates and an additional four who were under consideration by Republican party leaders.

Among the declared candidates, Governor Thomas E. Dewey was the frontrunner before the presidential primaries began in March. He was the most widely known candidate because he had been the party's nominee against Roosevelt in 1944, and he had won an impressive victory in 1946 in his campaign for reelection as governor of New York.[1] Clifford and Rowe in their November 1947 memorandum correctly estimated Dewey's strength.[2] The governor was internationalist in his foreign views and moderate in his domestic policies. The sailing for him during the ensuing months, however, was by no means smooth. Republican tradition held that a one-time loser did not deserve a second chance. In trying to overcome this obstacle, Dewey supporters could point to his excellent record as governor and his high standing in the polls. The presidential primaries, he thought, would furnish additional proof of his availability.

A second eager candidate was former Governor Harold E. Stassen of Minnesota, who had attracted attention by defeating the Farmer-Laborites in his home state in the 1930s. He had an notable war record and was named by Presidents Roosevelt and Truman as a delegate to the San Francisco conference on the U.N. Charter. While Stassen lacked Dewey's financial resources, efficient campaign staff, and widespread recognition, he was energetic, confident, and willing to campaign at an exhausting pace. He agreed with Dewey on international issues, but among his supporters was Senator Joseph McCarthy of Wisconsin, who was later to display his isolationism and his extreme views on the danger of alleged Communists in the government. In his preliminary appearances, Stassen was more outspoken than Dewey in criticizing Truman and denouncing the Democrats.[3]

Senator Robert A. Taft of Ohio had a consuming ambition to follow in the footsteps of his father, William Howard Taft, who was in the White House when Robert was in his twenties. In the Senate, Taft was known as "Mr. Republican" since he was the leader of the conservative Republicans, particularly on domestic issues. He was the favorite of the traditional elements and the organization leaders of his party, but he did not do as well in the polls as did Dewey or Stassen. His stern logic, forthright stands on issues, and lack of warmth in personal contacts hindered his candidacy. As Truman's popularity declined, Taft's chances of winning the nomination rose. In any case, Taft and the Eightieth Congress were targets for the Democrats. Taft did not want to enter any of the primaries except in Ohio, where he was a favorite son. He was, however, compelled to run in Nebraska since the law there did not permit him to withdraw unless he said he would not accept the nomination. Taft was critical of Truman, but the President respected his integrity.[4]

A fourth candidate was the flamboyant General Douglas MacArthur, who was strongly supported by the Hearst papers and the *Chicago Tribune*. The general was presented as the favorite son of Wisconsin because he had been appointed to West Point from that state. Although he did not leave Japan during the campaign, his supporters, who included former Wisconsin Governor Phil La Follette, son of the late Senator Robert M. La Follette, entered his name in the Wisconsin primary, and like Taft he could not escape the Nebraska primary.[5] The *Chicago Tribune* was one of Truman's harshest critics. In June, it declared Truman "devoid of diplomatic skill," "a catastrophic failure as director of foreign policy," and a pardoner of "vote thieves."[6]

Among the candidates who were willing to accept a draft but did not wish to contest the primaries, the most prominent was Governor Earl Warren of California, who won renomination for governor of his state in both major parties, which was then permissible under the California election laws. His record as an administrator was outstanding, attracting favorable mention by both conservatives and liberals. He was known for his moderate policies and his ingratiating manner.[7]

Senator Arthur H. Vandenberg of Michigan also refused to enter the presidential primaries, but if a deadlock developed in the convention, he stood ready to accept a draft. As the chief pillar on the Republican side of the bipartisan foreign policy, he was respected as a statesman. He was greatly irked by Truman's denunciation of the Eightieth Congress, which passed the legislation implementing the Truman doctrine and the Marshall Plan. The *Private Papers of Senator Vandenberg* reveal that although he did well in the polls, he did not go after the nomination because he wanted to stay in the Senate where he was the leader of the internationalists, at sixty-five he thought he was too old, he had some reservations about his own and his wife's health, and he thought that state governors were more logical candidates than were congressmen for the presidency.[8]

Speaker Joseph W. Martin of Massachusetts did not want to wage an active campaign for the presidential nomination, but he stood ready if the occasion called. He was a confirmed conservative and isolationist. Regarding his own ambition he later wrote, "I had come to the convention well advertised as a dark horse candidate for president, one to whom the delegates would be likely to turn in case of a deadlock. . . . I have never been bitten by the presidential bug, nor have I ever plotted for the nomination. In 1948 I was the Speaker of the House of Representatives. That office was the greatest ambition of my life."[9]

General Dwight D. Eisenhower was the most popular man in the public opinion polls, but he refused to accept a nomination from either of the major parties. The Republican leaders took him at his word.[10]

The first of the presidential primaries was held in New Hampshire on March 9, 1948. Governor Dewey had decided to enter key primaries in order to enhance his position as the leading candidate. For Stassen the primaries were a necessity because they constituted the principal means by which he had to prove his popularity among the voters. In New Hampshire, Dewey had an advantage; he was better known there, coming from a neighboring state, and he had the backing of Governor Charles M. Dale and his New Hampshire organization. Dewey did not appear in the state, but Stassen made two visits. Of the eight delegates, six were won by Dewey and two by Stassen. This was a good start for Dewey, and it did not eliminate Stassen.[11]

The next primary was held in Wisconsin on April 6. Four years earlier, Dewey's effortless victory here had eliminated Wendell Willkie, but in 1948 conditions were far different. Not only had Stassen put on the most intensive campaign of speaking and handshaking ever witnessed in a presidential primary, but the supporters of General MacArthur had staged an elaborate campaign for the absentee candidate using the mass media and local enthusiasts, including Taft Republicans and former Progressives. All the general did was issue a statement that he would not "shirk . . . accepting any duty to which I might be called by the American people." Dewey campaigned in the state only two days. The press proclaimed MacArthur the preelection favorite, which did not help him. The results were a surprise to all. Stassen's efforts paid off handsomely, winning nineteen delegates for him. MacArthur won only eight and Dewey none. The primary eliminated the general and put Dewey's candidacy in danger.[12]

Democratic National Chairman McGrath drew a moral from the Wisconsin results, which gave hope to Truman: "The results in Wisconsin proved the fallacy of the political judgments of the principal sources of information. This leads me to the conclusion that to insure the election of the Democratic ticket in November we need only have the commentators united in predicting defeat."[13]

The Nebraska primary came eight days later, featuring the seven main contenders: Dewey, Stassen, Taft, Warren, Vandenberg, MacArthur, and Martin. Stassen had cultivated this state assiduously, and the last-minute tours of Dewey and Taft were insufficient to turn the tide. Of the popular votes cast, Stassen won 43.5 percent, Dewey 34.4, Taft 11.6, Vandenberg 5.1, MacArthur 3.7, Warren 1.0, and Martin 0.5. This was a stunning victory for Stassen, and the polls taken following the primary placed him ahead of Dewey.[14]

Stassen continued to capture the headlines by forging slightly ahead of Dewey in a write-in campaign put on in Pennsylvania late in April. The results were not binding on the delegates, but they contributed to Dewey's decline in the polls. A Gallup poll in May indicated that those surveyed placed Stassen ahead of Truman in a hypothetical race between the two.[15]

The Ohio primary of May 4 marked a setback in Stassen's fortunes, and at the same time it was not helpful to Taft. Contrary to the accepted party rules, which frowned upon challenging a favorite son, Stassen entered the Ohio primary against Taft in selected districts. Of the twenty-three contested seats, Stassen won only nine. Thus he could not count it as a great victory. He had chosen the districts where he thought Taft was weakest. On the other hand, Taft was injured since he failed to demolish the invader. The bitterness engendered prevented the two men from getting together in a later stop-Dewey movement. James Reston wrote in the *New York Times:* "One more 'victory' like this one would be the undoing of both candidates."[16]

The crucial primary left was in Oregon on May 21. If Stassen won this decisively, he might well have stopped Dewey. Both candidates waged all-out campaigns using buses equipped with loudspeakers. Dewey had the advantage in financing his efforts, buying radio time and newspaper space and sending out literature. The campaign was climaxed by a radio debate on the issue of outlawing the Communist party. Dewey, with his skills as a prosecutor, came out best in the debate, opposing such a law, and he won all twelve delegates from the state, thus reestablishing himself as the front-runner and crushing Stassen's chances.[17]

The Republican convention began its sessions in Philadelphia on June 21. The delegates were buoyant, feeling sure that their candidate would be the next president of the United States. The internationalist wing represented by Dewey, Stassen, and Vandenberg felt it could hold off the conservative isolationist wing led by Taft and Martin. Both wings were united in denouncing the Democrats and the Truman administration. While the record of the Eightieth Congress, run by the Republicans, was praised by the convention orators, the platform of the party was less conservative than the Republican congressmen had been. It supported liberalized social security, aid to low-income housing projects, aid to education, civil rights, a bipartisan foreign policy, foreign aid to anticommunist countries (including Nationalist China), recognition of Israel, a fight against Communists inside and outside the government, and anti-inflation legislation.[18] Truman was to take advantage of the liberalism of the platform by challenging the Republican congressmen to enact their program.

The convention speakers did not spare Truman and the Democratic administration. From the standpoint of vituperation, the highlight of the convention was the speech of former Congresswoman Clare Boothe Luce, who referred to Truman as a "gone goose." The Democrats, she said, were divided into "a Jim Crow wing, led by lynch-loving Bourbons . . . a Moscow wing, masterminded by Stalin's Mortimer Snerd, Henry Wallace . . . and a Pendergast wing run by the wampum and boodle boys . . . who gave us Harry Truman in one of their more pixilated moments."[19]

As Clifford and Rowe had predicted eight months earlier, Governor Dewey was the Republican candidate. He was nominated on the third ballot with Taft as the runner-up on the first two ballots. The stop-Dewey forces could not get together because Stassen refused to withdraw in Taft's favor. After the campaign, some observers thought that Stassen would have run a better race. They contended that with the full backing of the party, he would have put on a more vigorous campaign than Dewey did.[20]

Dewey's remarks after receiving the nomination were pitched at a high level. He thanked his rivals for their gracious concessions and then, without denouncing the Democrats, turned to the theme of his campaign, unity:

The unity we seek is more than material. It is more than a matter of things and measures. It is most of all spiritual. Our problem is not outside ourselves. Our problem is within ourselves. We have found the means to blow our world, physically, apart. Spiritually, we have yet to find the means to put together the world's broken pieces, to bind up the wounds, to make a good society, a community of men of good will that fits our dreams.[21]

The nomination for vice-president left some scars, which may have alienated certain conservatives. The House majority leader, Charles A. Halleck of Indiana, a conservative with leanings toward Taft, claimed that Dewey's strategists offered him the vice-presidential nomination if he would swing his delegation to their side. Halleck did his part. After being nominated, Dewey repudiated any such deal made by his advisers and upon consultation with a group of Republican leaders selected Governor Warren as his running mate. (While Dewey carried Indiana, he failed to carry Ohio, Illinois, and Wisconsin where the liberalism of the two candidates was not welcomed by Old Guard Republicans. The Dewey-Warren ticket failed to win in California.)[22]

During the Republican nominating process, Dewey was not strengthened as a candidate by what he had to go through to win the nomination. His defeats in Wisconsin, Nebraska, and Pennsylvania showed that he could be beaten by vigorous campaigning. The desperate bargaining conducted in the convention did not help build the unity he talked about in his acceptance speech. Dewey was, however, a formidable candidate; he had experience in presidential campaigning, and he had an efficient staff and a good record as governor of New York. The Dewey-Warren ticket was well balanced, coming as it did from the two most populous and widely separated states.

J. STROM THURMOND, STATES' RIGHTS CANDIDATE

The revolt of the southern states against Truman and his civil rights program had been building since Truman's special message to Congress in February.[23] A delegation of four southern governors had tried to get national chairman McGrath to repudiate the stand, but he refused. A preliminary conference was held in Jackson, Mississippi, on May 10 at which it was decided to convene again if the Democratic convention either nominated Truman or adopted a strong civil rights program.

Two days after the Democratic convention adjourned, the Mississippi and Alabama delegates who had walked out of the hall summoned other dissatisfied elements for a rump convention in Birmingham, Alabama. South Carolina sent three who had been delegates to the Democratic convention, including their governor, but most of the other southern leaders stayed away. The hope of the movement was that a strong states' rights candidate might attract enough electoral votes to throw the election into the House of Representatives by depriving both major party candidates of the majority needed in the electoral college. The loosely organized convention composed of delegates from thirteen southern states chose the name States' Rights Democratic party and adopted a platform condemning the Democratic party's "infamous and iniquitous program of equal access to all places of public accommodation for persons of all races, colors, creeds and

national origin.''[24] (Actually, the Democratic platform did not mention
desegregation.) Attempts were made to draft Senator Russell of Georgia as
a candidate, but he did not want to desert the Democratic party. He had
been a candidate in the convention, and he was running for reelection to the
Senate on the Democratic ticket. The convention then nominated Governor
J. Strom Thurmond of South Carolina for president and Governor Fielding
L. Wright of Mississippi for vice-president. The new party, Dixiecrat as it
was called, captured the Democratic label in Alabama, Mississippi, Louisiana, and South Carolina. It tried to deny Truman the Democratic label in
other southern states but did not succeed. It managed to get on the ballot in
ten other states as a minor party.[25]

The southern leaders were wary of the new party. They did not want to
lose their seniority rights in Congress, and they did not want to see a Republican in the White House who would deprive them of federal patronage.
Any Truman civil rights measures, they believed, could be filibustered in the
Senate.

HENRY WALLACE AND THE PROGRESSIVES

In their November 1947 memorandum, Clifford and Rowe advised that
the only safe working hypothesis was to assume that Henry Wallace would
run on a third-party ticket. They urged that efforts should be made to dissuade him and at the same time to identify him and isolate him in the public
mind with the Communists.

Following his dismissal as secretary of commerce, Wallace became the
editor of the *New Republic*, and he undertook extensive lecture tours
abroad and in the United States criticizing American foreign policy. His
speaking was done under the auspices of his magazine and the Progressive
Citizens of America, although he did not join that organization. As early as
April 11, 1947, in a speech in London he stated that he would be campaigning in 1948, but he could not guarantee that he would be for the Democratic
ticket.[26] In a press conference the day before, President Truman had said he
had no desire to read him out of the party.[27] About the same time a number
of journalists had predicted that Wallace would lead a splinter party
movement.

The Progressive Citizens of America (PCA) was formed in December
1946 out of the National Citizens-Political Action Committee (NC-PAC)
and the Independent Citizens Committee of the Arts Sciences and Professions (ICC-ASP), both of which were formed in 1944 to aid in Roosevelt's
reelection. NC-PAC was sponsored by labor leader Sidney Hillman, who
became its first chairman, and ICC-ASP was led by such men as James
Roosevelt, Harold Ickes, and the artist Jo Davidson. Neither communist
nor anticommunist, Hillman refused to eject persons from NC-PAC for

ideological reasons. As a result, the organization was infiltrated by Communists. Hillman left the organization, and C. B. Baldwin, former associate of Wallace in the Department of Agriculture, became the operating head.[28] ICC-ASP also became infiltrated with Communists and its leadership changed, with Ickes and several others dropping out. PCA failed to establish a broad base because it was unable to enlist the main labor organizations. Those liberals who objected to working with communists founded in January 1947 the Americans for Democratic Action (ADA) with Wilson Wyatt and Leon Henderson as co-chairmen. The new organization refused to join with PCA in criticizing the Truman doctrine of aid to Greece and Turkey.[29] Most of the trade unions, except those controlled by Communists, avoided criticism of American foreign policy.

Henry Wallace undertook a strenuous speaking campaign in opposition to the Truman doctrine and the Marshall Plan. On December 2, 1947, he decided that an independent political party was needed to carry on his campaign against American foreign policy. The PCA executive committee proposed on December 15, 1947, that Wallace run for president on an independent ticket. It was not until December 29 that Wallace made a formal announcement in a radio broadcast in which he referred to those backing him as a "Gideon's army," small in number, powerful in conviction, and ready for action.[30]

The announcement was followed by some resignations from PCA of persons who did not agree with the plan for a third-party movement. When the American Labor party of New York endorsed Wallace's independent candidacy, the Amalgamated Clothing Workers of America withdrew from the ALP, leaving it with only the support of the communist-controlled unions.

In the early part of 1948, several events seemed to boost the morale of the Wallace supporters. One was the January Gallup poll, which showed him winning 7 percent of those interviewed.[31] A second event was the willingness of Senator Glen Taylor of Idaho to run for vice-president on the Wallace ticket. Taylor, an eccentric campaigner who used songs and a horse as publicity gadgets, had been very critical of Truman's foreign policy, but he went along with the Truman administration on domestic issues.[32] The third event was the election of Leo Isacson, the American Labor party candidate, to Congress in a by-election on February 17 from the Twenty-fourth Congressional District of New York over the Democratic candidate, Karl Propper, who was backed by Bronx boss Ed Flynn and by appearances on the part of Mayor William O'Dwyer and Eleanor Roosevelt. This victory alarmed the Democratic leaders. Former Democratic National Chairman James Farley predicted that Wallace might get from 6 million to 7 million votes.[33] National chairman McGrath used the occasion to denounce the communist backing of Wallace.

Wallace's attempt to alarm the American public about the dangers of an anti-Russian foreign policy was largely ignored because events were speaking louder than words. The communist coup in Czechoslovakia and the Berlin blockade were ample testimony of Stalin's aggressive policies. From a peak of 7 percent in the February polls, Wallace's popularity declined to 4 percent in the November polls.[34]

After the other party conventions, the Progressives held a convention in Philadelphia starting July 23, in which they ratified the choice of Wallace for president and Taylor for vice-president and adopted a platform. Although Rex Tugwell, a New Dealer under Roosevelt, was chairman of the resolutions committee, the substance of the platform was controlled by the communists. Proof of this was furnished by the convention's rejection of the Vermont resolution, which read, "Although we are critical of the present foreign policy of the United States, it is not our intention to give blanket endorsement to the foreign policy of any nation." The convention had a bad press, partly on this account, and also because of Wallace's news conference regarding his interest in mysticism.[35]

Henry Wallace, the candidate of the Progressive party, was a curious combination of idealism, mysticism, and naïveté. Regarding himself as the rightful heir of Roosevelt, he was deeply disappointed in not being renominated for vice-president in 1944. Naturally shy and retiring, he steeled himself to campaign strenuously for his liberal principles and longings for world peace. His meetings were like religious revivals and raised campaign funds. While recognizing the drawbacks of communist support, he refused to repudiate it even though Tugwell urged him to do so.

Clifford kept urging that Wallace be discredited for his communist connections. Former PCA leaders, trade union heads, and the press joined the Truman forces in pressing this argument. The close similarity between the communist and Wallace programs was emphasized. Wallace, by disclaiming knowledge of communist views, did not improve his position. Truman openly repudiated any help from Wallace and his Communists.[36]

The lineup of opposition candidates looked ominous to the Democratic party leaders. The Wallace vote might pull away enough Democratic voters to permit Dewey to win in some key northern states. The loss of support in the southern states might throw the election into the House of Representatives. The polls indicated that Dewey would be a formidable obstacle to Truman's chances to return to the White House. The lack of confidence some Democrats had shown in Truman did not auger well for the kind of effort needed to elect the doughty fighter from Missouri.

chapter 31 | UPSET ELECTION OF 1948

A straw vote only shows which way the hot air blows.
—O. Henry, *Rolling Stones*

CAMPAIGN STRATEGY

There is an old maxim of military and political strategy, which Adolph Hitler repeated in his *Mein Kampf:* "Strength lies not in defense but in attack." The Truman administration had a vulnerable record to defend. Reconversion from a war to a civilian economy had been fraught with many mishaps. While Truman had listened to the advice of conservatives in his administration, his rhetoric, his vetoes, and some of his actions had alarmed business interests. Labor strife and inflation had hurt the economy and alienated consumers. His stand on civil rights had frightened many southerners. At the same time, his slow and hesitant actions in the field of race relations had dismayed many blacks. He had not acted quickly and decisively enough in the troublesome dispute between the Arabs and Jews over the future of Palestine to please the American liberals and the Zionists. His determined policy to contain the aggressions of the Soviet Union had displeased the advocates of peace, those who were apprehensive about the danger of an atomic holocaust, and the left-wing elements. On the other hand, the rabid anti-Communists felt that he should have taken a much firmer stand against communism at home and abroad. At the same time, the staunch defenders of civil liberties felt that he had gone too far in purging alleged Communists.[1] Truman agreed with Clifford that the best strategy was to attack the Eightieth Congress and the Republican record of sixteen years of opposition to the New Deal.

The President's acceptance speech was in accord with the strategy. As Helen Fuller put it, he "had an accurate pulse count on the audience he was to address. Truman's remarks were cannily suited to the time, the place, and the crowd as any speech Franklin Roosevelt might have made. . . . It, and the confident, determined man Truman presented to the bedraggled convention, made a hit. For that night at least, Harry Truman was a real leader."[2]

The disastrous congressional elections of 1946 furnished the Democrats with a convenient scapegoat. The mishaps of 1947 and 1948 would be placed upon "the do-nothing Eightieth Congress." The hands of the administration had been tied by the failure of this Congress to act upon the recommendations made by the President. The Taft-Hartley Act was the cause of labor troubles. Inflation had resulted because of the failure of Congress to act on the President's program. Gains that the farmers had made since 1933 were threatened by the Republican majority in Congress, which was dismantling price supports, soil conservation, reclamation, and farm security programs. The development of river basins and public power projects were menaced by private-utility-minded Republicans, who were controlled by Wall Street.[3]

President Truman continued his strenuous attack on the Eightieth Congress. Governor Dewey could have defended the Republican Congress more vigorously than he did because the record of the Congress was good in many respects, especially in the field of foreign affairs.[4] But Truman ignored this accomplishment and concentrated his fire on the domestic record of Congress. Clark Clifford summed up the strategy: "We were on our own 20-yard line. We had to be bold. If we kept plugging away in moderate terms, the best we could have done would have been to reach midfield when the gun went off. So we had to throw long passes—anything to stir up labor and other mass votes."[5]

On the basis of the public opinion polls, which showed him well in the lead, Governor Dewey and his strategy board decided to wage a lofty campaign emphasizing national unity. Since there were more voters with Democratic identifications than there were with Republican, he had to attract new voters, independents, and dissident Democrats in order to win. A sharp attack on Democratic policies and candidates might alienate some potential supporters.[6] Dewey told Republican chairman Hugh Scott, "he . . . wasn't going to get into the gutter with Truman and he might not even mention Truman's name."[7] He had tried a slashing prosecuting attorney style of campaigning in 1944 against Roosevelt, and it had not worked. He did not think he needed to put on that type of campaign in 1948.

The Truman record was vulnerable, and a bitter attack on it by Governor Dewey might have aroused more interest in the campaign and brought Democratic defections. The Dewey strategy board, however, called for a different approach. The bungling Truman would make such attacks unnecessary. At the convention one Democratic delegate had displayed the sign, "I'm just mild about Harry." Republican attacks would create sympathy for him. Governor Dewey would soar in the clouds above the din of

Cartoon by Jim Berryman, 1948. Reprinted, courtesy of *The Washington Star.*

the battle and come down to earth when the shouting was over and march to victory with a united country behind him. He felt that it was unnecessary for him to discuss issues in detail or to make promises that might be difficult to fulfill.[8]

CAMPAIGN ORGANIZATION

At the beginning of the campaign, the press hailed the efficiency of the Republican campaign organization and downgraded Democratic National Chairman Howard McGrath and the staff of the Democratic National Committee. After November 2, it was necessary to take a new look at the organization. Dewey, with claims of efficiency, had a two-headed campaign headquarters, his own in Albany and another in Washington D.C. National chairman Scott was left off by himself, and the party state leaders felt isolated. McGrath headed a single organization, and he kept in touch with the state and local politicians. His campaign headquarters was in New York, and William Boyle ran the Washington end. The Alsops called it "the loneliest campaign," but Truman had good help from the party.[9]

The publicity activities of the Democratic National Committee were outstanding. These were directed by Jack Redding, who had an able assistant in John Brightman. The advertising account executive selected to help the committee, Sam Youngheart, of Warwick and Legler, did a fine job considering the lack of funds and the strong Republican bias of the press, two-thirds of which backed Dewey.[10] The staff arranged for radio broadcasts, news releases, and the production and distribution of party literature, made a documentary film that was shown in theaters, placed newspaper advertisements downgrading Dewey, and put out other campaign paraphernalia. Crucial work was also done in making special appeals to labor, farmers, women, young people, blacks, and other minority groups.[11]

The colored cartoon booklet on Truman's life was a popular item all over the United States. There was a demand for many more copies than the 3 million distributed. An analysis of the content of this pamphlet shows that it appealed in subtle ways to young people, farmers, workers, small businessmen, homemakers, minority groups, and all "patriotic" American citizens. It did not mention some of the problems that Truman encountered during his rocky rise to power.[12]

The documentary film on Harry Truman was also a triumph. It was compiled from news clips, and the headquarters staff managed to get it widely distributed at relatively little cost. It more than countered the efforts of the Republicans in this direction.[13]

Another publicity triumph scored by the Democrats was a radio broadcast that included Eleanor Roosevelt, Senator Barkley, and Governor Lehman. Eleanor Roosevelt—somewhat lukewarm on Truman—held off from the campaign at first, but Ed Flynn and Jack Redding talked her into doing the broadcast by indicating that her help was crucial.[14] Lash points out that her reluctance was real.

Following the Republican victory in the 1946 congressional elections, it became increasingly difficult for the Democrats to raise campaign funds. President Truman was faced with the problem of selecting a finance chairman for the party. Among those considered for the position was Bernard Baruch. Since Baruch had never served in such a capacity, he turned down the request. This made Predident Truman angry, and he sent a sharp letter to Baruch to the effect that politics was not a one-way street.[15] Also Considered was Jesse Jones of Houston, former secretary of commerce and federal loan administrator. In his autobiography, *Fifty Billion Dollars,* Jones wrote:

> The President said they wanted me to accept the chairmanship of the Finance Committee to raise funds for the campaign. I thanked the President, but told him I could not accept the appointment. I hated to decline because I liked Mr. Truman very much, but had about reached the conclusion that the Democrats had been in power long enough, and that a change would be helpful to the country.[16]

President Truman next turned to Louis Johnson, who had served as assistant secretary of war under Roosevelt. Johnson was ambitious to become secretary of defense, and after a talk with President Truman he accepted the responsibility for raising funds for the campaign.[17]

Considering the discouragement of the Democrats, Johnson did an outstanding job in raising funds and in tiding over financial crises. From time to time, he used his own funds as loans to the party to meet emergencies. The Democratic national-level political spending in 1948 was $2.3 million, about $1.4 million less than the Republican spending, but organized labor almost made up for the difference with its $1.3 million in expenditures. However, the Democratic National Committee was at a disadvantage in financing its own activities.[18]

At the precinct level the Democratic organization left much to be desired. Because of the election reverses in 1946 and the downward trend of Truman's popularity, local party workers were disheartened. The party seemed to lack funds and a salable candidate. Those urban party leaders who had taken part in the dump-Truman movement had to be won over and stimulated to action. Boss Arvey of the Chicago Cook County machine made a last-minute effort to help.[19] Democrats who were "mild about Harry" were, however, concerned about their state and local contests and made strenuous efforts to win those. The election returns in November showed that Truman ran behind some state tickets. It was organized labor, however, that furnished many of the workers needed at the local level. Union activists urged voters to register, canvassed precincts, and helped get out the vote. Labor had to match the ample funds the Republicans had to man the polls on election day.[20]

WHISTLE-STOP TOUR

Truman decided to employ the extended campaign tour by train as his principal campaign technique. Redding of the Democratic National Committee had urged this as fitting to Truman's style.[21] This technique broke all precedents in American history. From the beginning it had been regarded as undignified for a president seeking reelection to take to the hustings. President Jefferson stayed in the White House in 1804, and so did Andrew Jackson in 1832, Lincoln in 1864, Grant in 1872, Cleveland in 1888, McKinley in 1900, Theodore Roosevelt in 1904, Wilson in 1916, and only in 1912, when Taft was in political trouble, did a president make a few speeches. Truman was the first president to make an extensive tour.[22]

With the development of jet travel after 1948, train travel became increasingly obsolete. It was too slow, and too inflexible, and it required too much advance planning. In 1948, however, it fit the requirements of Truman's strategy. The President, a man of the people, was out to mingle with crowds and to show himself as he was—direct, informal, folksy, friendly, and a scrapper.

A tour by train had been inaugurated as a campaign device by William Jennings Bryan in 1896. About that time the railroads had reached their maximum development as the backbone of the American transportation system. Bryan, however, had no elaborate campaign train. He rode coach all over the country and slept sitting up. President Truman used as his campaign tour headquarters the special armor-plated car called the *Ferdinand Magellan*; it had been built for President Roosevelt and had sleeping quarters, a bath, a dining room, and a sitting room. It also had communication facilities, which enabled the President to keep in touch with the White House and his presidential duties.[23] Dewey's campaign train arrangaments were even more elaborate.

Careful advance preparations were made for each Truman whistle-stop, sometimes as many as sixteen a day. Background material was obtained on local events, personalities, and candidates. Special outline notes were prepared for the brief impromptu speeches. Active in these preparations were Elsey of Truman's train staff and William Batt of the Research Division of the Democratic National Committee. Longer speeches were drafted first in the White House by Murphy and then revised by Clifford, Elsey, Daniels, and others on the train. Advance agents went ahead of the President's train and made arrangements for stirring up a crowd and for making contacts with local candidates, party leaders, and other dignitaries. Oscar

Chapman was active in this capacity during the first part of the tour, and later Donald Dawson took over some of these functions.[24]

Accompanying the President in the unprecedented whistle-stop campaign tour whenever possible were his wife and daughter. They did not speak but were presented in the following manner: "Now, I usually take my greatest assets around the country with me. How would you like to meet my family? I will present Mrs. Truman first—she runs me and the White House. Now I have the privilege of presenting my baby, my daughter Margaret." He sometimes added, "the boss's boss." The crowd always loved this domestic scene.[25]

Truman made his first formal political speech of the campaign on Labor Day, September 6, in Cadillac Square, Detroit. He had made rear platform remarks from his train at seven other points in Michigan and Ohio that day before big crowds. At Grand Rapids, he announced, "It is a great day for me. It is a great day for you. I am just starting on a campaign tour that is going to be a record for the President of the United States, and when I get through you are going to know the facts."[26]

Everywhere he denounced the Taft-Hartley Act and promised to work for its repeal. He reviewed what the Democrats had done for organized labor since 1935 and forecast dire consequences to labor if the Republicans should win the presidency. In his main address, he warned:

Important Republican newspapers have already announced in plain language that Republicans in Congress are preparing further and stronger measures against labor. . . . If this Taft-Hartley law remains in effect, labor's position will be bad enough. But suppose, while the law is in effect, a reactionary Republican administration were to bring upon us another "boom and bust" cycle similar to that which struck us during the last Republican administration? . . . You can already see signs of it. The "boom" is on for them, and the "bust" has begun for you.[27]

The speech was carried on a nationwide radio broadcast, which was nearly canceled for lack of funds. Only desperate last-minute efforts on the part of Oscar Chapman and Governor Roy Turner of Oklahoma saved the broadcast.[28]

The President was pleased to see that both the AFL and the CIO sponsored the Cadillac Square meeting. Although some labor leaders had stayed away from the Democratic convention, they drifted back in September and pledged their support to Truman. Philip Murray, president of the CIO, paid a visit to the White House and announced that CIO's Political Action Committee (PAC), its political arm, would put its four hundred state and local groups behind him. The American Federation of Labor, following the passage of the Taft-Hartley Act, also established a political arm, Labor's League for Political Education, which became active on behalf of Democratic candidates in 1948.[29]

The first extended tour got under way on September 17. As Truman was leaving Union Station in Washington, Senator Barkley remarked, "Mow'em down, Harry!" Truman replied, "I'm going to fight hard. I'm going to give 'em hell!"[30] This set the tone for the tour, and the press began to picture Truman as a scrappy fighter.

In his first major speech of this tour at Dexter, Iowa, on September 18, Truman tore into the opposition. He denounced the Wall Street reactionaries as the "gluttons of privilege" who were out to beat the farmers and workers down so they could increase their profits and establish an "economic dictatorship." He exclaimed:

This Republican Congress has already stuck a pitchfork in the farmer's back. They have already done their best to keep the price supports from working. Many growers have sold wheat this summer at less than the support price, because they could not find proper storage. . . . These big-business lobbyists and speculators persuaded the Congress not to provide storage bins for the farmers. . . . They are preventing us from setting up storage bins that you will need in order to get the support price for your grain.[31]

The issue of price supports for farm products was a complicated one, and the Democrats were quick to take advantage of Republican mistakes in this field. Governor Dewey had delegated the job of discussing farm issues to Harold Stassen. On September 2, Stassen issued a statement in Albany criticizing the timing of government purchases of food for military and foreign aid purposes. Truman and his secretary of agriculture, Charles Brannan, seized upon this as a general attack on the farm price support system, and Dewey tried in vain to correct this impression. An Ohio newspaper owned by James M. Cox, the Democratic candidate for president in 1920, had brought to the attention of Secretary Brannan and Senator McGrath the hardships imposed on farmers because the Eightieth Congress had forbidden the Commodity Credit Corporation to build additional storage facilities. Truman and other Democratic candidates speaking in the farm belt exploited this issue to the full. After the election some Republicans questioned the validity of these charges. During the campaign, however, Dewey failed to quiet the fears of many farmers.[32]

Truman's campaign train moved west, and he made speeches on reclamation, conservation, and public power projects. At the Denver, Colorado, state capitol, he delivered a hard-hitting address, which was carried on a nationwide radio broadcast. He denounced the Republican party as the party of "Wall Street," the reactionaries, the big businesses, selfish big real-estate lobby interests, special interests that were squandering our natural resources for quick profits and undermining all measures for conservation, reclamation, public power, and flood control.[33]

As Truman continued on to the coast, he blasted away at the opposition "do-nothing" Eightieth Congress and the shilly-shallying Republican candidate for president. He praised the state and local Democratic candidates at each stop and castigated their Republican opponents. At Fresno, California, he became highly personal and direct: "You have a terrible Congressman here in this district. He is one of the worst. He is one of the worst obstructionists in the Congress. He has done everything he possibly could to cut the throats of the farmer and the laboring man. If you send him back, that will be your own fault if you get your throat cut."[34] The sitting congressman was a Republican with seven terms to his credit, and he went down to defeat in November.

Moving on to Los Angeles, Truman delivered an address in which he criticized Dewey for dodging the issues. He denounced "high-level" platitudes, the million-dollar real-estate lobby in Washington that blocked a comprehensive housing bill, the broken Republican promises on social security, the well organized medical lobby that persuaded the Republican Congress to kill a plan for national medical care, and the Republican failure to pass measures to control inflation. In speaking of the forces of progressive liberalism, he warned liberals attracted by the third party (he did not mention Wallace's name or that of Wallace's party) that the communists were using and guiding this party and a vote for it would play into the hands of the Republican forces of reaction.[35]

Truman then headed back east, crossing New Mexico, where he made strong statements backing his former secretary of agriculture, Clint Anderson, who was running for U.S. senator against General Patrick J. Hurley, who had caused Truman trouble over American policy toward China.[36] In Texas, which Democratic candidates for president had avoided in previous years, Truman made twenty-four stops in which he carefully evaded his civil rights program. He emphasized the differences between the Democrats and Republicans on public power, taxes, reclamation, farm price supports, irrigation, inflation, federal aid to education, and the rural electrification program. Practically all prominent Texas politicians accompanied him on his trip through the state, including Governor Beauford Jester (who had accused him of "stabbing the South in the back"), Senator Tom Connally, Attorney General Tom Clark, Congressman Lyndon Johnson (the Democratic candidate for senator), former Speaker Sam Rayburn, Congressman Wright Patman, and Democratic National Committeeman Wright Morrow. Truman stopped at Uvalde to pay his respects to John Nance Garner, Roosevelt's first vice-president. On hand there at daybreak was a crowd of four thousand and an angora goat in a gold blanket with the words "Dewey's Goat" in red letters. As usual on such occasions, Truman and Garner "struck a blow for liberty." Truman regarded the Texas tour as a success, and it was there that he was to receive his largest majority percentage.[37]

Traveling north through Oklahoma, he gave strong support to the Democratic candidate for senator, Robert S. Kerr, a former governor of the state. At Oklahoma City, he made a major speech, broadcast nationwide by radio, that mainly dealt with the relationship of communism to American national security. Truman criticized the attempts of the Republicans to exaggerate the internal danger of communist penetration of American government. He insisted that the FBI had this threat to American security well in hand. Republican congressmen were interfering with the FBI and making matters worse. His loyalty board investigations had revealed that less than two-tenths of 1 percent showed questionable loyalty. The main battle against communism was abroad in countries where misery and want made the dispossessed easy targets for communist propaganda. Here the Truman doctrine and the Marshall Plan were holding the Communists back. [38]

Leaving Oklahoma, Truman made hurried trips through Missouri, Illinois, Kentucky, and West Virginia. At these stops he kept hammering away upon familiar topics to those who had been following his campaign. A few new metaphors appeared. The Republicans "have begun to nail the American consumer to the wall with spikes of greed." In Lexington, he said, in a partial admission that he was behind, "It's the horse that comes out ahead at the finish that counts. I am trying to do in politics what Citation has done in horse races." Altogether, upon arriving back in Washington, he had traveled eighty-three hundred miles and had delivered 140 speeches. [39]

Governor Dewey also took a swing around the circle, following Truman. He did not get up as early as Truman did, and he did not make as many stops. His crowds were generally smaller, particularly in the early hours, and he was not waging as exciting a campaign as Truman was. He kept to generalities and did not bother to try to answer Truman's gibes. As a speaker, he was far superior to Truman, and his rich baritone could make the most of his favorite phrases, such as the "biggest unraveling, unsnarling, untangling operation" in Washington when he took over. The mechanics of his train tour were carefully worked out, and advance copies of his main speeches were always ready well in advance. To some, his cliches were boring. He refused to be specific about any problem or issue. Since he felt himself more liberal than some of the congressmen, he decided not to defend the record of the Eightieth Congress as vigorously as he might. He saw that the issue of internal security against the Communists was attracting attention, but he had no fears of communist threats in the United States, and he did not want to infringe upon freedom of speech. He refused to mention Truman's name and did not take advantage of Truman's mistakes. There were beginnings of what were later called the Truman scandals but Dewey, the prosecutor, ignored them. [40]

The Democrats were not as gentlemanly in their campaigning. Every mistake that Dewey or Taft made was pounced upon with glee. At Beaucoup,

Illinois, Dewey's train started to back into a crowd. Dewey was reported as saying, "Well, that's the first lunatic I've had for an engineer. He probably should be shot at sunrise, but we'll let him off this time since no one was hurt."[41] On this Truman quipped, "He objects to having engineers back up. He doesn't mention that under the great engineer, Hoover, we backed up into the worst depression in history."[42] The Democratic National Committee claimed that Governor Dewey told a Veterans of Foreign Wars legislative committee that all civil service employees were mediocre. He was quoted as saying, "You'd have me paying these sons of sea cooks for just breathing and it will not happen, not while I'm Governor. If I had my way I'd abolish civil service!" Later Dewey was accused of calling the movement for higher pay for teachers the biggest lie since Hitler and their lobby as "more vicious than the power or real estate or liquor lobbies." These accusations injured Dewey among labor groups, civil servants, and teachers. Denials never catch up with accusations.[43]

Truman hit hard in his campaign speeches, but he insisted on fair play and he had an honest respect for worthy opponents. During the 1948 campaign, the publicity bureau of the Democratic National Committee needled Senator Robert Taft. Their publication, *Capital Comment*, began to coin words of ridicule. A *Tafter* was a Republican who bowed to the real-estate lobby, *Tafting* described one who carried out a Taft policy, and *Taftivists* were those who agreed with the Ohio senator. The President told Redding that Taft had integrity. He found the puns distasteful and asked that they be discontinued. The Democratic headquarters, however, could not resist exploiting Senator Taft's remark that with the prices of meat so high, poor people should eat beans. Taft's "Let 'em eat beans" was compared with Marie Antoinette's "Let them eat cake."[44]

The proposed Vinson mission was a major campaign incident occurring between Truman's two main tours whose effects on the election are difficult to estimate. It was started by two eager campaign speech writers, Albert Z. Carr and David Noyes, who were hardly responsible for determining American policy. They believed that if Chief Justice Vinson could go to Moscow as the President's personal representative and talk with Stalin, he might find Stalin receptive to relieving tensions.[45] In his *Memoirs*, Truman wrote: "Vinson's mission as an off-channel approach to Stalin, might expose the Russian dictator to a better understanding of our attitude as a people and of our nation's peaceful aspirations for the whole world. I had a feeling that Stalin might get over some of his inhibitions if he were to talk with our own Chief Justice."[46] Truman referred to the precedent of Viscount Reading, the chief justice of England, who in World War I came to the United States to lessen friction. Truman was being attacked by Wallace for warmongering. The Republicans were claiming that Senator Vandenberg, John Foster Dulles, and the nonpolitical Secretary of State Marshall were really working out American foreign policy. If Truman, on his own, could make this peace gesture, it would help him in the campaign. It is surprising that Clifford did not veto this idea. Vinson was strongly anticommunist, he had little understanding of Russian psychology, he was unfamiliar with current negotiations, and unlike Hopkins he had no contacts in Moscow. Truman was persuaded to try this desperate expedient in spite of warnings from Senator Connally and Under Secretary of State Lovett. In talking to Justice Vinson on October 3, he had a hard time convincing him to make the trip. While Vinson correctly insisted that this was not the proper function for a chief justice, he finally consented to go. Press Secretary Ross was instructed to set up a radio broadcast for an important presidential announcement. When he asked for nonpolitical time, the networks insisted on finding out for what purpose. Ross told them and cautioned them to keep the information confidential. As a last precaution, the President decided to clear the trip with Marshall. When he approached him, Marshall was appalled, and Truman cancelled the whole affair, including the radio broadcast. Marshall was engaged in delicate negotiations at the U.N. Security Council on a resolution condemning the Berlin blockade. The Vinson trip was a unilateral adventure, which would greatly offend America's allies. Truman must be given credit for standing by his secretary of state, but he deserves no praise for letting the affair go as far as it did. In his *Memoirs*, he defends the cancellation on the ground that hostile newspapers had leaked the wrong interpretation. The only trouble with this view is that the cancellation came before the leak.[47]

Of course, the radio companies leaked the news. The Republicans could have seized upon this aborted mission, but that approach did not fit into Dewey's strategy. Dewey and his foreign policy advisers, Vandenberg and Dulles, regarded the error as too serious to exploit for political purposes.[48] Senator Taft criticized the President sharply by saying that Truman had weakened the case against the Soviet Union, just after we had submitted the Berlin dispute to the United Nations, thus discrediting Secretary Marshall and the United Nations itself. Most newspaper men called the affair a colossal blunder. Dewey attacked the Democratic party for its "daily shifts in policy" and for leaving "our friends, at the world council tables for peace" stunned and the "work for peace paralyzed," but he insisted in an earlier statement that "the nations of the world can rest assured that the American people are in fact united in their foreign policy."[49]

Opinions differed as to the net effect of the cancelled mission on the campaign. Although the Republicans did not exploit it to the full, they felt that it damaged Truman's chances for reelection. On the other hand, Truman felt that it indicated he was a man who was desperately interested in peace.[50] As he put it in his speech before the American Legion convention in Miami on October 18: "In recently considering sending a special emissary to Moscow, my purpose was to ask Premier Stalin's cooperation in dispelling the present poisonous atmosphere of distrust which now surrounds the negotiations between the Western Powers and the Soviet Union. My emissary was to convey the seriousness and sincerity of the people of the United States in their desire for peace.'' He added: "The proposal had no relation to existing negotiations within the scope of the United Nations or the Council of Foreign Ministers. Far from cutting across these negotiations, the purpose of this mission was to improve the atmosphere in which they must take place and so help in producing fruitful and peaceful results."[51] Truman may have hoped the mission could have accomplished these objectives, but he knew that his secretary of state, whom he trusted, did not agree with him.

The *New Republic* backed up Truman and pointed out that Vinson's main mission was to get Stalin to reinterpret the communist doctrine holding that war between communism and capitalism is inevitable. Truman was sure that Stalin could clear the atmosphere and thus put negotiations on a better basis.[52] Walter Lippmann also thought the incident helped Truman because it identified him with those seeking peace as against the hard-liners in the State and Defense Departments.[53]

Another campaign incident concerned the boundaries of the fledging state of Israel. The U.N. Assembly in November 1947 had awarded the Negev to the Jews although it was sparsely inhabited by Arabs. The U.N. mediator, Swedish Count Folke Bernadotte, in his June 1948 negotiations with both sides suggested the transfer of the Negev to the Arabs and the inclusion of western Galilee in Israel. Secretary Marshall agreed with the Bernadotte proposal and obtained Truman's approval of this position. This was another example of Truman's lack of understanding of what he was approving and the consequences of that action. Bernadotte was assassinated on September 17 by Israeli terrorists, but his completed report was submitted three days later. Marshall issued a statement on September 21 endorsing the Bernadotte report, a step he felt Truman had authorized him to take.[54]

The Marshall announcement outraged American Jews who thought that Israel should keep the Negev and that they had not been fully informed. Because of the Democratic platform and his own statements endorsing partition, Truman wanted to reverse Marshall, but Under Secretary Lovett persuaded him not to do it at that point, indicating the unfortunate international consequences of such an action. However, when Dewey brought the issue into the campaign on October 22, Truman reversed his earlier approval of the Bernadotte plan and undercut Marshall in a statement of October 24. Here, as in the trusteeship case, domestic politics outweighed foreign policy considerations.[55]

During October Truman made two shorter campaign tours. His first was a three-day trip through Delaware, Pennsylvania, New Jersey, and upstate New York. Everywhere he had good crowds and enthusiastic welcomes in spite of bad weather. In Philadelphia Convention Hall, he jeered at the Republicans for what he called their theme song, "Me, too, but I can do it better," and he gibed: "They [the Republicans] want to take the industrial workers and the white-collar workers, and the farmers, and all other plain people in this country, and roll them all together in one big company union, and run it for the benefit of the National Association of Manufacturers." Attacking the Dewey unity theme, he said,

> They have all their promises wrapped up in a package called "Unity!" which they guarantee to cure more ills than any patent medicine man ever saw. . . . I don't believe the American people will be taken in by that kind of quackery. . . . We don't believe in unity of slaves, or the unity of sheep being led to slaughter. We don't believe in unity under the rule of big business—we will fight it to the end.[56]

On this trip, Truman lambasted individual Republican congressmen. In Auburn, New York, he fired both barrels of his verbal shotgun at Congressman John Taber, chairman of the House Appropriations Committee:

> I'm sorry to say that your Congressman from this district has used a butcher knife and a sabre and a meat-axe on the appropriations that have been in the public interest both for the farmers, for rural electrification, and for every other forward-looking program that has come before the Congress. I saw a cartoon the other day called "The Sabre Dance," in which they showed a big man with a sabre cutting the heads off all the appropriation for the Interior Department and the Department of Agriculture. Well, I have a better name than that. I named it the "Taber Dance."[57]

The second tour, regarded as a success by Thomas W. Walsh, was through the Midwest, with stops in Ohio, Illinois, Minnesota, Wisconsin, and West Virginia.[58] In his *Memoirs* Truman recalls how impressed Frank Lausche, the Democratic candidate for governor of Ohio, was with the crowds and their zeal.[59] Truman was spurred on in his attacks. At Akron, on October 11, he said: "[The Republicans] have tasted blood and they are waiting eagerly for the time when they can go ahead with a Republican Congress and a Republican President to do a real hatchet job on the New Deal."[60] In Milwaukee, in a speech worked on by Daniels, Bell, and Elsey, he accused the Republicans of plotting to turn over atomic energy developments to private companies for their profit.[61]

In the last week of the campaign, Truman spoke in Pittsburgh, Chicago, Cleveland, Boston, New York, St. Louis, and Independence. At Pittsburgh he put on his famous doctor skit, poking fun at Dewey:

> Now, let's imagine that we, the American people, are going to see this doctor. It's just our usual routine checkup which we have every four years.
> And, "doctor," we say, "we're feeling fine."
> "Is that so?" says the doctor. "You been bothered much by issues lately?"

"Not bothered, exactly," we say, "Of course, we've had a few. We've had the issues of high prices, and housing, and education, and social security, and a few others."

"That's too bad," says the doctor. "You shouldn't think about issues. What you need is my brand of soothing syrup—I call it 'unity.'"

Then the doctor gets a little closer.

And he says, "Say, you don't look so good."

We say to him, "Well, that seems strange to me, Doc. I never had a brighter future. What is wrong with me?"

Well, the doctor looks blank and he says, "I never discuss issues with a patient. But what you need is a major operation."

"Will it be serious, Doc?" we say.

"Not so very serious," he says. "It will just mean taking out the complete works and putting in a Republican administration."[62]

In Chicago, Truman made a speech, written by Noyes and Carr, that tried to compare Dewey with Hitler, Mussolini, and Tojo: "In our own time, we've seen the tragedy of the Italian and German people, who lost their freedom to men who made promises of unity and efficiency and security. When a few men get control of the economy of a nation they find a 'front' man to run the country for them."[63]

In Boston Truman stressed the communist scare issue and linked it to a hero of the Boston Irish, Alfred E. Smith, who had been the Democratic candidate for president in 1928.

All this Republican talk about Communism is in the same pattern with their appeals to religious prejudice against Al Smith in 1928. . . . I resent the contemptible Republican slur that charges me with being "soft" where Communist tyranny is concerned. . . . The Communists would like to bring about my defeat and elect a Republican President. . . . Now the Republicans tell me that they stand for unity. In the old days, Al Smith would have said: "That's baloney." Today the Happy Warrior would say: "That's a lot of hooey." And if that rhymes with anything, it is not my fault.[64]

Finally, in New York, he made several appearances, appealing mostly to minority groups. For the benefit of the Jews he said, "It is my desire to help build in Palestine a strong, prosperous, free and independent democratic state. It must be large enough, free enough, and strong enough to make its people self-supporting and secure."[65] Before a black audience in Harlem, he described the report of his Civil Rights Committee, his message to Congress, the failure of Congress to act, and his issuance of two executive orders, one on equality of treatment and opportunity in the armed services and the other on fair employment practices within the federal establishment.[66]

In the final days of the campaign, Dewey did not change his strategy except in one or two cases. At Erie, Pennsylvania, he blasted Truman for his veto message of the Taft-Hartley bill, describing it as "the wrongest, most incompetent, most inaccurate document ever put out of the White House in 160 years." He pointed out that the results Truman predicted had not come to pass. There were fewer strikes, fewer jurisdictional disputes, and fewer discharges. While Dewey wanted to make a strong reply to Truman's invective of October 25 about the Republicans being potential fascists, his staff restrained him. Dewey merely said that the Democrats

have spread fantastic fears among our people. They are openly sneering at the ancient American ideal of a free and united people. They have attempted to promote antagonism and prejudice. They have scattered reckless abuse along the entire right of way from coast to coast and have now, I am sorry to say, reached a new low of mudslinging. . . . This is the kind of campaign that I refuse to wage.[67]

During his whistle-stop tours, Truman covered some 21,928 miles and delivered 275 speeches. He bore up well under this heavy schedule. Just as Franklin D. Roosevelt had learned how to conserve his energy during a national campaign while campaigning for vice-president in 1920, so Truman had learned the art in 1944. He returned to Independence in order to vote, well satisfied that he had done his best and outwardly confident of the results.

In this campaign the President had strong assistance from many Democratic leaders. Senator Barkley was a tireless campaigner who covered almost as much ground as did Truman.[68] Secretary of Labor Tobin, an effective speaker, hammered away at the Taft-Hartley law. Attorney General Clark spoke extensively on internal security. Secretary Brannan concentrated his activities in farm areas. The ADA endorsed the President and formed the National Independent Committee for Truman. Chapman persuaded former Secretary of the Interior Ickes to speak under the auspices of this committee.[69] Ickes attempted to "disabuse many who may still regard Wallace as spokesman for the Roosevelt tradition." An unusual number of attractive congressional, state, and local candidates were carrying the party burden in their respective constituencies. To mention a few, there were Adlai Stevenson and Paul Douglas in Illinois, Hubert Humphrey in Minnesota, and Estes Kefauver in Tennessee. In the South, where Truman was kept off the ballot in four states, the outstanding leaders rallied to the Democratic ticket. Among these were Congressman Sam Rayburn of Texas, Senator Walter George of Georgia, Senator Claude Pepper of Florida, and Governor Marion B. Folsom of Alabama.

ELECTION FORECASTS

During the campaign, journalists and pollsters indicated a clear Republican lead. Elmo Roper, in his last poll in August, gave Dewey 52.2 percent,

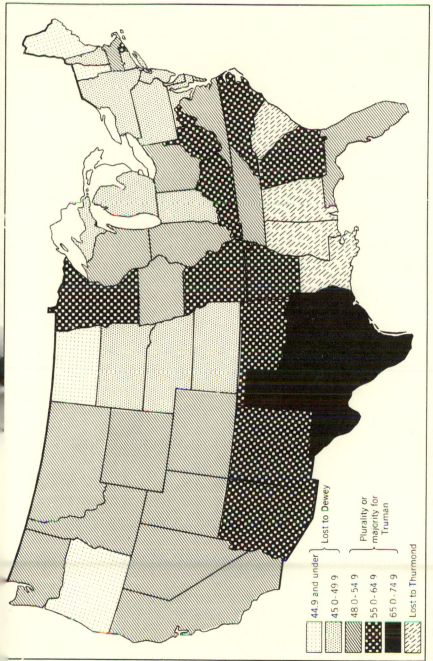

44.9 and under
45 0 - 49 9 } Lost to Dewey

48 0 - 54 9
55 0 - 64 9 } Plurality or majority for Truman
65 0 - 74 9

Lost to Thurmond

Map 7. Percentage Democratic vote of total vote, 1948 presidential election

Truman 37.1 percent, Wallace 4.3 percent, and Thurmond 5.2 percent. Roper's earlier reputation for accuracy was entirely undeserved because his sampling techniques were defective, but this was not publicly revealed until later. Gallup and Crossley conducted their last polls in the middle of October. Gallup's final survey gave Dewey 49.5 percent, Truman 44.5 percent, Thurmond 2.0 percent, and Wallace 4.0 percent. Crossley gave Dewey 49.9 percent, Truman 44.8 percent, Thurmond 1.6 percent, and Wallace 3.3 percent.[70]

All of these polls indicated that the two movements that splintered off the Democratic party would cut seriously into Truman's share of the vote. As the election returns were to show, they greatly exaggerated these trends. Either the polls were wrong, or many voters with Democratic identifications who had been leaning toward the extremes came back into the fold toward the end of the campaign. Wallace did not attract as many of the leftist elements as he hoped he would, and Thurmond was disappointed in his showing among the conservatives of the South. Truman's losses at the extremes were nowhere as great as the polls indicated they would be.[71]

In their predictions, journalists tended to agree with the polls. Arthur Krock of the *New York Times* stated that he looked at the party canvass reports and found that they agreed with the polls. The *Times*'s summary, based on reports of correspondents, gave Truman only eleven states. *Newsweek*'s summary from its correspondents showed that not one of them gave Truman any chance of winning the election. An election guess by James S. Mulloy of *Look* gave Truman only 123 electoral votes.[72]

President Truman made a sarcastic speech in Cleveland on October 26, 1948, belittling the polls:

These polls that the Republican candidate is putting out are like sleeping pills designed to lull the voters into sleeping on election day. You might call them sleeping polls. . . . Now these Republican polls are no accident. They are a part of a design to prevent a big vote, to keep you at home on November 2nd, by convincing you that it makes no difference whether you vote. . . . They know that a big vote means a Democratic victory.[73]

His own private estimate preserved by Elsey gave him 340 electoral votes.[74]

Senator McGrath presented an analysis of the polls based upon errors of previous polls and concluded that the election would be close. As chairman of the Democratic National Committee, he made the usual claim of victory for Truman. Homer S. Cummings, former national chairman and attorney general under President Roosevelt, also made an analysis of the polls and predicted that Truman would win. William M. Boyle, an assistant to McGrath, made an analysis based on previous election returns, which came out well for Truman.[75]

Dewey and his supporters claimed an overwhelming victory, but they did not look closely enough at the warnings of the coming disaster, and they did not know how to evaluate the polls. On September 9, the neglected Republican National Chairman, Scott, said "I never regard an election as over until election day. . . . Overconfidence can lose an election. . . . I wish to call upon all Republicans to increase their efforts to elect Republican candidates to every office at stake this year."[76] In October warnings came from several different sources. The *Baltimore Sun*, the *New York Times*, and *Time* magazine all noted that Dewey's campaign was sagging and that Truman was attracting larger crowds. Tom O'Neil of the *Sun* reported that "some of those around Dewey were concerned by confidential reports that the GOP campaign was sagging in parts of the country." Later he reported, "There is a trace of concern that high prices for agricultural products and abundant markets may influence Western farmers to vote for the status quo—the Democrats."[77] Roy Roberts of the *Kansas City Star* told Dewey on October 14 that the farmers of the Midwest were defecting. Harry Darby, a national committeeman from Kansas, also commented on disaffection among farmers.[78] But Dewey and his top staff paid no attention to these warnings.

ELECTION RETURNS

When the early returns began to come in, the radio commentators were astounded. President Truman was ahead from the beginning. H. V. Kaltenborn kept saying until early the next morning that the tide would turn when the rural returns came in. Later on President Truman derived great pleasure from mocking the Kaltenborn broadcasts. The *Chicago Tribune* came out with an early edition with the headline, "Dewey Defeats Truman." President Truman later held up this paper for the news photographers. The *Washington Post* invited Truman to a "Crow Banquet," but he declined saying, "I bear no malice or feel badly toward anyone."[79]

It was an occasion when the public opinion polls, the press, the radio, the politicians, and the political analysts miscalculated. The pollsters committed a number of technical errors, which threw them off the track. Their middle- and higher-income groups, which were stronger for Dewey than for Truman, were overweighted. They failed to poll near enough to the election to catch a last-minute trend to Truman and to take into account the impact of the voting participation patterns. Those classified as doubtful voters were more likely to support Truman when they came to the polls. There was much indifference to the election. The pollsters' survey methods of interpreting and analyzing the results did not clearly separate the voters from the nonvoters in advance. They did not know what kind of voters would come to the polls, and their interviewers failed to overcome the reluctance of many voters in 1948 to tell strangers how they intended to vote. Truman had been severely criticized, and interviewers did not like to tell interrogators they were going to vote Democratic. Finally, the polling organizations were not frank with the public as to the limitations of their methods. They failed to make clear their own reservations regarding their findings.[80]

The errors of the pollsters, in turn, misled the journalists and the commentators. In the past, journalists had done more of their own sampling and had made their own independent judgments. The size of the Republican victory in 1946 congressional and state elections was misleading. There was a breakdown in party intelligence, since many Democratic leaders were too pessimistic and Republican leaders were generally too confident.

Truman himself said that the labor vote was responsible for his victory. Sample surveys of voters indicated that over three-quarters of skilled and semiskilled workers voted Democratic in 1948.[81] Union members were more strongly Democratic then were nonunion members. While Truman failed to carry some of the larger states—New York, Pennsylvania, Michigan, and Indiana—each with its large urban centers, the loss resulted from the defection of voters to Wallace and to a dropping off of the Democratic vote in Philadelphia and Detroit. In other urban centers—Chicago, Cleveland, Saint Louis, Boston, Milwaukee, San Francisco, and Los Angeles—Democratic majorities were crucial to Truman's success.[82]

Analysis of the returns shows that Truman did unusually well among the farmers, who were alarmed by his warnings of a depression in agriculture. He captured Iowa, Wisconsin, and Ohio, the three states that Dewey had carried in 1944. Without a sizable switch in the vote of farmers, Truman could not have carried these three states. The Democrats also won six seats in Illinois, five in Indiana, eight in Ohio, three in Michigan, and one each in Utah and Nebraska. According to a sample survey, two-thirds of farm operators voted for Truman. Senator-elect Karl Mundt said: "The rural vote was decisive. If Dewey had gotten it he would have won in Ohio, California, and Illinois. Farmers failed to accept his support of farm support prices as enthusiastic, as genuine, and as vigorous as that of President Truman."[83] The 101 electoral votes of the Midwest were sufficient to carry the election for Truman.

Truman ran well among minority groups except among the Jews. Two-thirds of the Catholics—Irish, Italians, and Slavic groups—voted for him. The black vote was crucial in Ohio, Illinois, and California. Among the Jewish voters, however, the 1948 vote was down as compared with Roosevelt's vote in 1940 and 1944—only 75 percent as compared with Roosevelt's 90 percent. Two factors were important. Wallace took away 15 percent of the Jewish vote, and the Israeli boundaries dispute lost Truman some Jewish votes. Dewey carried New York with its large Jewish population.[84]

The 1948 election had certain characteristics that distinguished it from the other presidential elections. The turnout was low, the margin between the two major parties was close, the President ran behind local candidates in many states, and the general pattern was not too far from the four Roosevelt elections. As a percentage of the estimated enfranchised population, the vote was the lowest since 1924. On the low vote, Angus Campbell commented that it was "the prototype of the low-stimulus Presidential election."[85] Neither candidate aroused much enthusiasm. In the popular vote, there was a difference of only 4.4 percentage points, lower than in any of the Roosevelt elections. A shift of 2.5 percentage points would have changed the popular vote. In the states a swing of some thirty thousand votes properly distributed in the key states of California, Illinois, and Ohio would have given Dewey the victory in the electoral college. A swing in any two of these states would have put the election into the House of Representatives.

Truman won, but only by a small margin. In the country as a whole, he ran behind some state candidates. Of the 49,363,798 ballots cast, some 683,382 were not marked for the presidency.[86] The election as a whole had been called a maintaining election because the traditional voting patterns of the Roosevelt elections were maintained.

The results of the election may also be partially explained in terms of the personalities of the two candidates and how they were viewed by the voters. Elmo Roper's interviewers found that many people viewed Truman as a warm, direct, down-to-earth, sincere, hard-working, well-meaning man. Those who failed to vote for Dewey focused their dislike on the grounds he was too sure of himself, too expedient, too young, too little for the job, a one-time loser and too cold.[87]

The two minor party movements, the Wallace Progressives and the Thurmond Dixiecrats, actually helped to reelect the President. The Progressives with their communist cohorts nullified the charges that the Truman administration was soft on communism. Curiously enough, the special session of Congress that President Truman had called gave an impetus to the investigation by Congress of alleged communist infiltration into American government. In November 1948, Wallace, not Truman, personified the red menace in the United States. On the other hand, the Dixiecrats were not strong enough to throw the election into the House of Representatives. They did, however, help remove doubts among blacks in the North regarding President Truman's convictions on civil rights issues. The black vote was crucial in some of the northern urban states.[88]

The 1948 election meant that the voters were not yet ready to abandon the coalition that President Franklin Roosevelt had put together. Although four states in the Deep South defected to Dixiecrat J. Strom Thurmond and parts of the Northeast were split off by Wallace's Progressive party, in the main the lines of the Roosevelt coalition held firm. Truman carried the remaining southern states and the rest of the Northeast, and he divided the Midwest. The results showed that the 1932 election did not bring a realignment of the parties that depended on Roosevelt's personality alone. The changes transcended the ebullient Roosevelt. Truman's election meant that the balance between the two major parties had changed in the United States. The Democrats now occupied a dominant position based upon an alliance of the South, labor, agriculture, small business, underprivileged citizens, and urban dwellers.

During the campaign, President Truman caused some concern, particularly when he seemed to ignore Republican participation in the nonpartisan foreign policy, but after the election, Senator Vandenberg, the personification of that policy, said: "You've got to give the little man credit. There he was flat on his back. Everyone had counted him out but he came up fighting and won the battle. He did it all by himself. That's the kind of courage the American people admire."[89]

Enough time has elapsed to say that the election of 1948 is a classic on the necessity during an election campaign for every candidate to work hard and cling to a vision of victory. Harry S. Truman never would have been reelected if he had been defeatist regarding his own chances and had not campaigned strenuously.

PART III | PRESIDENT IN HIS OWN RIGHT

chapter 32 | THE FINAL TEAM, 1949–1952

The Cabinet is not merely a collection of executives administering different governmental functions. It is a body whose combined judgment the President uses to formulate the fundamental policies of the administration.
—Public Papers of the Presidents: Harry S. Truman, 1945

In drafting people for important jobs, the President often says:
"I'm going to put your feet to the fire!"
—New York Post, August 20, 1945

Following his reelection in 1948, President Truman acquired a new self-confidence. No longer did he need the pose of excessive humility. His native cockiness reasserted itself, and he took pride in his decision making.[1] During the next four years, he faced many crises: the Soviet Union exploded a nuclear device; the war in Korea broke out and the Chinese Communists entered it, leading to mobilization and inflation at home; General MacArthur was dismissed; and a major steel strike broke out. Truman had to make use of all the self-confidence he could command.[2]

The President was immediately faced with the necessity of making changes in his top personnel. Usually he tried to find the best people available for the big problems he faced. For the lesser jobs, he wanted persons around him who were congenial. This requirement was to lead him into difficulties during his closing years in the White House. Ill health caused some of his key officials to leave, and the conduct of others during the campaign led him to replace them. The President felt that he had to make changes in his cabinet, the White House staff, the Executive Office of the President, and the independent agencies. In making these changes, he emphasized experience and allegiance to the Truman policies.[3] Certain minor officials who were personally loyal did not always perceive that their conduct might be damaging to presidential prestige. Truman stuck by them regardless.

CABINET CHANGES

Truman greatly admired Secretary of State Marshall and the programs he had inaugurated, but he knew that Marshall was not well and was anxious to retire.[4] He turned to Dean Acheson who had been acting secretary of state many times since the fall of 1945. The President had great confidence in Acheson, who was recognized in most circles as being an outstanding diplomat.[5] It was remarkable that two such different men took such a strong liking for each other—Acheson, the product of Groton, Yale University, and the Harvard Law School, aristocratic in bearing and in language, and Truman, son of the soil, largely self-educated beyond high school, plebeian in manner, and often crude in his language. Acheson's name was submitted to the Senate, which, after debating his association with the Hiss brothers and his policy toward communist countries, confirmed him by a vote of eighty-three to six.[6] The two men seemed to complement each other. Truman was used to the rough and tumble of politics. When Acheson was viciously attacked, Truman defended him fearlessly. Acheson knew that he could get a decision from Truman when the facts were presented. He had not liked Roosevelt's patronizing attitude. The two men developed a fine working relationship—Acheson keeping the President fully informed and Truman granting access freely for consideration of foreign policy questions on a regular or emergency basis. They were both intensely loyal to each other.[7]

During his full term as President, Truman had a greater turnover in the office of the secretary of defense than in any other department. This was brought about by the illness of incumbents, by the fact that the unification of the armed forces was still incomplete and highly contentious, and by radical changes in defense policies and budgets, the latter resulting partly from the Korean war.

After the 1948 election, it soon became clear that Secretary of Defense Forrestal would be replaced. Like Marshall he had assumed that his position was above politics, and he had taken no part in the 1948 election. Actually he was shocked by Truman's reelection. There had been strong differences between him and the President on unification of the armed services, on military budgets, on Palestine, and on Mideast oil.[8] Truman was disappointed in Forrestal's failure to reconcile the services to unification and his inability to control the military budget; thus he felt no obligation to keep him on. Besides, he was receiving reports that Forrestal's health was failing and that he was becoming paranoid that Communists wanted to get him.[9]

The circumstances surrounding the appointment of Louis Johnson as the successor to Forrestal are controversial. Various accounts are contradictory. It appears that Truman had come to an understanding that if Johnson undertook the difficult job of finance chairman of the Democratic National Committee, he would be in line for the defense post. Johnson had served as assistant secretary of war under Secretary Woodring in 1939 and 1940 and had been vigorous in pushing Roosevelt's preparedness programs. He thought that the President would appoint him secretary of war in 1940, but the post went to Henry L. Stimson in a move to win bipartisan support. Now Johnson counted on Truman to fulfill his long-standing ambition.

In some circles, the selection of a man for such an important administrative post on political grounds was severely criticized.[10] Nevertheless, Johnson was a tough, capable administrator, who had had useful experience. In Truman's mind the fact that he had done an outstanding job under difficult circumstances in raising campaign funds should not disqualify him. After the election, Johnson claimed that he sought no reward, but Forrestal, wanting to retire, recommended him to the President to be his successor. Johnson also claimed that Generals Marshall and Eisenhower backed him for the position. Persons close to Forrestal, on the other hand, claimed that Forrestal did not regard Johnson as qualified and was not willing to resign voluntarily to make way for a political appointee.[11]

The need for replacing Forrestal was evident. Obviously suffering from great nervous strain, Forrestal was finding it increasingly difficult to carry on. In late January, he was informed that Johnson would succeed him, and he began briefing Johnson. On March 1, 1949, Truman asked for his immediate resignation. Forrestal was greatly disturbed when Johnson was sworn in later in the month. Overwhelmed by a sense of personal failure, despising the President under whom he had worked for four years, disagreeing with his governmental policies on many questions, despairing of the future of his country and of the world, he committed suicide on May 22.[12] In view of the tremendous powers of destruction he had controlled, this was an appalling situation that had worldwide repercussions.

Forrestal, a conservative businessman from Wall Street, with nine years' experience in top defense assignments and a reputation for dedication to the building of strong security forces, was replaced by a successful lawyer with three years' experience in a top defense post and a reputation for upholding strong civilian control of the military. The press, unaware of the imperative need for a change, was generally critical of the appointment. Liberals welcomed Forrestal's departure. He had been too close to Wall Street, the oil interests, and defense contractors, and he was too opposed to Israel. The Senate confirmed Johnson's appointment by a unanimous vote.[13]

When Johnson became secretary of defense, he was thoroughly committed to the Truman policy of unifying the armed forces and cutting back defense spending in order to spare the domestic economy. Living up to his reputation, he was tough and firm in carrying out both assignments. He did not hesitate to retire the admirals who had worked against unification.[14]

When the budget requests were submitted in 1949 for fiscal year 1950, Johnson backed Truman's limitation on defense spending to $15 billion. In January 1950, however, the National Security Council had begun work on a new defense plan, NSC 68, which called for vastly increased military expenditures. Johnson was inflexible in opposing this plan at first, but the Korean war furnished the impetus for putting the plan into operation, and it also highlighted the unpreparedness of the United States for limited warfare. The blame for the lack of combat readiness on the part of American troops fell on Secretary Johnson. Reports came to the President that Johnson was trying to undercut Acheson with certain Republicans and that he was ill.[15] In this emergency, Truman turned to his most admired military man, George C. Marshall, who reluctantly came out of retirement in September 1950 to accept the post of secretary of defense after Congress had changed the law so as to make him eligible for it. (The law had specified that the post should be held by a civilian; career officers were ineligible until ten years following their retirement.) There was debate in the Senate over Marshall's confirmation and the changing of the law. Republicans criticized his role in China. In the House debate, Congressman Frederic R. Coudert of New York argued that "no one man in 150 million Americans is indispensable, certainly not a 70-year old man with one kidney." Senator William E. Jenner of Indiana declared, "General Marshall is not only willing, but he is eager to play the role of a front man for traitors. The truth is this is no new role for him, for General George C. Marshall is a living lie."[16] Marshall's nomination was confirmed by a vote of fifty-seven to eleven.[17]

Marshall held the post for a year, but he was far from happy in the position. Secretary Acheson was now his superior in cabinet rank, and this situation required tact. He was not pleased with having to clash with General MacArthur, but he performed his duty and joined the others in urging the general's dismissal. Within a year, when the Korean war had settled into a troublesome but not threatening stalemate, he persuaded Truman to let him resign. Marshall recommended as his successor his under secretary, Robert A. Lovett, a banker, who had been serving in high Defense and State Department posts since 1940. There was no problem in securing Lovett's confirmation by the Senate as he was popular with the senators, and the press was also enthusiastic about him. Arthur Krock of the *New York Times* called the appointment "a triumph of both loyalty and merit." Lovett was noted for his success in settling disputes among the services as to their relative rates of expansion. With his many connections in the armed services and in defense industries, he was well fitted to implement the military buildup in Europe and the Far East.[18]

After his election, Truman had a variety of reasons for looking closely at the record of his secretary of the interior. Julius Krug had not distinguished himself as the successor to the redoubtable Harold Ickes. His administration was not noted for outstanding accomplishments in the conservation field. On the advice of Bernard Baruch, he did not take active part in the 1948 presidential campaign. During that time he was out West inspecting wildlife refuges. The jealous Ickes commented, "Where was Krug during the campaign? Oh, he was visiting wildlife reservations, was he? . . . And did he get a lot of votes from the ducks?"[19] In addition, Krug's style of living came in for some criticism. After the press reported that he was involved in a lawsuit over a $750,000 loan and his name was discovered on a lobbyist's expense account, Truman accepted his resignation on November 11, 1949.[20]

In Krug's place, the President appointed Oscar Chapman, under secretary of interior, who had been with the department for over sixteen years and was thoroughly familiar with its various programs. The *New York Times* referred to him as "a liberal who is spokesman for the whole West." This appointment was in accord with Truman's growing practice of recognizing the value of experience, loyalty, and devotion to an agency's objectives. Chapman had also been active in the 1948 campaign. Chapman went on to make many fine contributions to the conservation of natural resources in the fields of public power, reclamation, national parks, and minerals. He was also a tireless advocate for statehood for Alaska and Hawaii, for the St. Lawrence Seaway, and for justice to minorities. He was a skillful operator who restrained selfish interests that were seeking to exploit American natural resources.[21]

The Department of Justice under Truman failed to maintain the high standards that had been set under Roosevelt. The morale of the department declined while Tom Clark was attorney general, and a number of unfortunate practices began to develop during that time. Clark, originally sponsored by Speaker Rayburn, had not been a distinguished cabinet officer, but he had been politically useful to Truman, particularly in the embarrassing 1946 Kansas City primary election frauds cases. Clark was loyal politically, he had campaigned in 1948, and when a vacancy occurred on the Supreme Court in August 1949, President Truman appointed him associate justice at the urging of Chief Justice Vinson, who wanted a colleague who would support his point of view. Justice Clark proved to be such a colleague.[22]

Merle Miller's oral interview with former President Truman cites a statement attributed to Truman that the appointment of Tom Clark to these two positions was his biggest mistake.[23] This seems wrong because of the respect that President Truman had at the time for Speaker Rayburn and Justice Vinson, who recommended Clark. Truman's later antagonism toward Clark was undoubtedly the result of Justice Clark's decision in the steel case.

In Clark's place, Truman elevated J. Howard McGrath, Democratic national chairman, who had been U.S. district attorney, governor of Rhode Island, U.S. senator, and solicitor general. His political credentials were impeccable after the successful election of 1948, but his legal qualifications were questioned by some. While serving in various public offices at modest salaries, he had acquired great wealth through his connections with race-tracks.[24]

The Department of Justice was later involved in tax and other scandals that damaged the Truman administration.[25] McGrath and the President failed to agree on the methods that were needed to clean up charges of wrongdoing. McGrath was very ambitious, and he had hoped that he might be appointed to the Supreme Court, but this hope was dashed in April 1952 when the President suddenly demanded his resignation over differences as to how the Department of Justice scandals should be investigated.

For the balance of his administration Truman continued in office Secretary of the Treasury Snyder, Postmaster General Donaldson, Secretary of Agriculture Brannan, Secretary of Commerce Sawyer, and Secretary of Labor Tobin. Snyder and Sawyer tended to be conservative, but Truman said that he was glad to have their views even when they were contrary to the policies he was advocating.[26] Brannan and Tobin were classed as liberals, and they could be counted upon to support Truman's Fair Deal. Donaldson was mainly concerned with the efficient management of his department. With Steelman in the White House still functioning in the labor field and with the continuation of special labor boards and services outside the Department of Labor, Tobin concentrated on speaking and public relations.[27]

Although President Truman claimed that he used his cabinet to formulate decisions, in practice many important decisions were made by special groups containing cabinet officers and others. He did not want a cabinet secretariat or formalized meetings. He wanted an easy exchange of information, and he was always accessible to cabinet officers. The details of administration he left to his cabinet officers; he was proud of his ability to delegate authority and to hold those receiving it responsible for its proper exercise. He did not attempt to hold all the power in his own hands as President Roosevelt had done. Some claimed he did not hold the reins tightly enough.[28] Truman liked to think that he was weighing all of the alternatives and hearing all views when he was making important decisions.

The Korean war furnishes some examples of the malfunctioning of the decision-making process during the Truman years. The President's reliance on General MacArthur's assurance that the Chinese Communists would not enter the war proved to be disastrous. A number of the decisions Truman made have been criticized because they did not cover the full range of alternatives, and there was no advocate for an unpopular but sound opinion. Decisions were arrived at by ad hoc groups that included cabinet officers, service secretaries, Joint Chiefs of Staff, roving ambassadors, and special advisers, but not the men whose advice would have saved many lives and resources by presenting alternative courses of action, which would have lessened the likelihood of America's deep involvement. Notably these groups failed to include such men as George Kennan, whose advice proved to be the soundest on the Korean situation, both militarily and politically.[29]

EXECUTIVE OFFICE OF THE PRESIDENT

White House Staff

There were not many changes in the White House staff, but an important one was in the office of special counsel. After a brilliant record of nearly five years, Clark Clifford's exhilaration at rendering useful public service had begun to wane. He was also troubled by the lack of devotion to the public interest on the part of some Truman appointees, so he resigned in January 1950 to enter the private practice of law.[30] In his place, Truman elevated Charles Murphy, assistant special counsel, who continued to maintain high standards of draftsmanship, discretion, and restraint but who did not claim to be the operator that Clifford had been. Murphy was more judicial in temperament and was not inclined to continue the battle that his predecessor had waged against Steelman for power over domestic affairs. As special counsel, Murphy was concerned with plans and programs, with the preparation of the President's speeches and messages to Congress, with staff work on legislative proposals, with the final review of enrolled bills, and with the preparation of executive orders. These were important powers, which Murphy and his small staff used with discretion. They explained and defended the President's foreign and domestic policies before Congress and the public. They helped him choose the issues and put them into words in time to meet the deadlines set for the speech or message. The staff was composed of David Lloyd, an ADA lawyer, David Bell, an economist who later became director of the Bureau of the Budget, Richard Neustadt, a political scientist who later became a professor at Cornell, Columbia, and Harvard, Donald Hanson, who worked on loyalty and security matters, and Kenneth Hechler, a political scientist who later was elected to Congress from West Virginia. In addition, Marshall Shulman, Acheson's speech writer, helped on foreign policy speeches and messages. It was a team of able men, evidenced by their performance of later assignments.[31]

In certain fields, Murphy had to work closely with other officers. In budget matters, the main responsibility was with the budget director but Murphy was sometimes the link between the President and the director. In foreign and military affairs, Murphy sometimes tried to make his influence felt if a major speech was involved.[32]

Continued on the White House staff was the assistant to the President, John Steelman, who coordinated main domestic operations and who specialized in techniques of settling disputes within the government and among private parties, including labor and management. He attended cabinet meetings, although he did not speak up at them. He listened to cabinet officers and other officials and brought their problems to the President, offering suggestions but not telling the parties what to do. In the labor field, he listened to all sides and to the fraternity of private arbitrators, mediators, and labor relations experts. He made recommendations for appointments in the labor field, and he actually engaged in the mediation of labor disputes. Steelman was an effective channel for the settlement of interagency problems. He was discreet, did most of his business over the telephone, and usually was found on the conservative side of questions. At the President's request, he could evade or smother a problem. He would sit on it indefinitely or find someone who would shelve it in some other fashion.[33]

The job of press secretary continued to be a hard one during Truman's last four years in the White House. Torn between the demands of persistent and ever-present correspondents for more and faster news and the obligation to protect the President from mistakes and to further his programs, two press secretaries died in the position during the period. Charles G. Ross, the faithful counselor of the President, died at his desk on December 5, 1950, and his successor, Joseph H. Short, Jr., had a fatal heart attack on September 18, 1952. Roger W. Tubby, his assistant, finished out the term.

Ross was liked personally by White House correspondents, but some thought that he did not manage his office efficiently as an outlet for news. The President had absolute confidence in him but sometimes failed to inform him about important developments. Ross could have found out about these events if he had been more assertive. This lack of aggressiveness also kept him from informing the President that he was about to make a mistake. On the other hand, Charles Murphy called Ross "wise, wonderful, scholarly, [doing an] extremely effective job, so universally admired and respected."[34]

Press Secretary Joseph Short organized his office so that it could render prompt service to the correspondents. He also persuaded Truman to keep him informed about developments that would turn up in the news. He had a strong, tense personality and was able to make his advice felt in crises. He was also keenly aware of the possibility of error in his job. Some of the correspondents did not like his channeling all presidential news through his office; they preferred to pick up stories that might be available elsewhere. Short, however, thought that this process was necessary to protect the President.[35]

Roger Tubby, who had been an assistant to Leo Crowley, administrator of the Foreign Economic Administration, joined Short's staff in 1949 at the instigation of William Hillman, who edited Truman's *Mr. President*. Tubby was in the midst of the MacArthur dismissal in 1951 and expressed the opinion that Secretary Johnson should have disciplined MacArthur sooner. When he replaced Short in September 1952, he took part in Truman's campaign tour for Governor Adlai Stevenson and worked so hard that he was exhausted at the end of the campaign.[36]

Truman continued on his White House staff his appointments secretary, Matthew Connelly, who guarded Truman's time and screened visitors carefully but who failed to protect his own reputation against detractors; administrative assistant Donald Dawson, who was concerned with personnel matters, trying to achieve meritorious appointments as well as satisfying political considerations; correspondence secretary William Hassett, who was a true professional at handling correspondence; administrative assistant George Elsey, who had demonstrated his skills as a speech writer; military aide General Harry Vaughan, whose job it was to maintain liaison with the military and the veterans but whose propensity to do favors for people made him subject to criticism; naval aide Admiral Robert L. Dennison, who did an outstanding job in the field of maritime policy and shipping operations; and David Niles, who handled problems with minority groups until late in 1951 when his assistant, Phileo Nash, took over for him.[37]

President Truman had excellent working relations with his White House staff. He discouraged quarrels among his subordinates and fostered friendly feelings among them by his daily morning staff meetings at which any member could bring up a matter for discussion. He was a friendly man, and it was not difficult for a staff member to see him. Connelly sometimes caused delays but not for long. The President himself frequently dropped in on Murphy, Steelman, Short, and other staff members.[38]

Developments at the subcabinet and White House staff level were important during the Truman administration. Particularly significant was the ad hoc policy group organized by the special assistant to the attorney general, Oscar Ewing, in 1947 shortly before he was appointed federal security administrator. Invited to this group were Under Secretary of Agriculture Charles Brannan, Council of Economic Advisers member Leon Keyserling, Under Secretary of Labor Dave Morse, Under Secretary of Interior Jebbie Davidson, Chairman of the Federal Communications Commission Wayne Coy, Special Counsel Clark Clifford, and White House staffer Donald Kingsley, who was later made assistant federal security administrator. The group operated during the 1948 election campaign and continued until Adlai Stevenson was nominated for president in 1952. When Clifford left, Murphy replaced him in the group.

Clifford was quoted as telling *New York Times* writer Cabell Phillips that the policy group operated without Truman's knowledge and pitted its ideas against those of the cabinet officers.[39] Ewing, however, stated in his oral history that Truman was aware of what the group was doing. It met every Monday in Ewing's apartment. It kept no notes, no minutes, and no records. Among the positions it took on different issues, it advocated the veto of the Taft-Hartley bill, and supported national health insurance, fair employment legislation, unification of the armed forces, federal housing, the transfer of unemployment insurance to the Department of Labor, the extension of social security, aid to medical schools, and the establishment of a Jewish state in Palestine. Ewing stated that if the President found the advice good, he would take it. Truman was his own man. History records that he found much of the advice of the policy group good.[40]

Bureau of the Budget

When Budget Director James Webb was made under secretary of state in 1949 at Secretary Acheson's suggestion, Truman appointed Assistant Budget Director Frank Pace as his successor. Pace had graduated from Princeton University and Harvard Law School at an early age and made a remarkably rapid rise as a lawyer, a prosecuting attorney, a tax expert, and an efficiency expert to Postmaster Generals Hannegan and Donaldson. Webb brought him into the Bureau of the Budget as assistant director at the age of thirty-six. After a year's experience in this position, he was made director. In another year he was appointed secretary of the army, and Fred Lawton, a career budget officer, replaced him as director.[41] Pace indicated later that he preferred not to remain as director of the budget because of his differences with Leon Keyserling, whom he regarded as more liberal than himself.

Pace handled the budget for fiscal year 1950, and Lawton the budgets for the fiscal years 1951-1953. Truman wrote that he met with these two directors at least twice a week as he had with Smith and Webb. These were years of greatly expanded budgets, which called for many supplemental hearings because of the Korean war, the buildup of NATO forces, the construction of the hydrogen bomb, foreign aid, and increased domestic spending. The federal government was spending four times as much on national defense at the end of the Truman term as it was in 1949. Pace and Lawton introduced in 1950 the so-called performance budget, which was based on functions, activities, and projects as recommended by the Commission on Organization of the Executive Branch of the Government (the Hoover Commission). Lawton was called upon to defend the requests for higher taxes to meet the increased expenditures largely arising out of defense expenditures past and present.[42]

Council of Economic Advisers

The Council of Economic Advisers began to play a more important part in policy decisions when Leon Keyserling became the chairman in 1950, some months following the resignation of the first chairman, Edwin Nourse. The CEA was an attempt to make the President institutionalize his sources of advice on economic affairs in a way that would make them more visible. Truman had no objections to this idea because he liked formalized staff procedures. Keyserling was part of the liberal group, and he worked closely with such liberals as secretaries Chapman and Tobin. As an economist, Keyserling did not believe in the scarcity policies of the early New Deal but rather in the virtually unlimited opportunities for growth to be found in American capitalism. He thought that the emphasis should be on an ever-expanding economy. Economic policy should work for the optimum balance between consumer purchasing power and corporate income in order to maintain full employment and expansion. The way to meet inflation was to expand production capacity to meet demand.[43] Truman accepted Keyserling's reasoning in his speech to a Kansas City audience on September 29, 1949. During the Korean war Truman and Keyserling gambled on a quick ending of the war and the building of an economy that would provide both guns and butter. When the war lasted longer than expected, they reluctantly turned to controls. The expansion policy, however, was a success; the gross national product increased from about $250 billion in 1949 to $350 billion in 1953.[44]

In his second term Truman had a better team than he had in his first term, but in spite of this, he got more trouble both in the foreign and domestic fields. Some of the events that occurred after 1948 were clearly beyond the control of the administration, which had to take the blame for them. The fall of Nationalist China had been coming for some time; Roosevelt was partly responsible as far as American actions were concerned. In his policy meetings, Truman followed what one author calls the fusion technique, partly judicial and only slightly competitive. Truman rejected Roosevelt's heavy reliance upon competitive management. He preferred orderly delegation and clear lines of responsibility. Sometimes, as in the case of the Korean crisis, he did not have all the options before him. One of the causes of Truman's troubles was faulty intelligence. American military policy relied upon the monopoly of nuclear weapons and the intelligence community did not anticipate the early breaking of that monopoly by the Soviet Union. With proper intelligence the Korean war would not have escalated as it did. The new Central Intelligence Agency performed reasonably well, but its findings were not followed in the field. Truman was blamed for General MacArthur's failures in intelligence.

In the domestic field, the problems of reconversion continued to defy easy solutions. There was no moral equivalent of war to bring the conflicting interests together. There was a gross undercalculation of the seriousness of the Korean war. Secretaries Brannan and Chapman performed well, but they ran into the conservative coalition of Republicans and southern Democrats that had stymied Roosevelt. Secretaries Snyder and Sawyer did little to help solve problems of inflation and labor management. Truman's legal advisers let him down in the steel case of 1952. As for the red scare and McCarthyism, which made great inroads in Democratic popularity, Truman's staff stood up bravely against the hysteria, but their own excesses of cold war rhetoric and domestic red hunting played into the hands of the extremists.

chapter 33 | NATO, GERMANY, AND CHINA, 1949–1952

We live in dangerous times because of the decisions of another power which are beyond the control of any or all of us. There is no formula which will exorcise these dangers. The decisions which create them will be affected by the facts which we are helping to forge from the unfolding future. The task calls for steady nerves and determined purpose.

—Dean G. Acheson, September 30, 1948

The role of this Government in its relations with China has been subject to considerable misrepresentation, distortion, and misunderstanding. Some of these attitudes arose because this Government was reluctant to reveal certain facts, the publication of which might have served to hasten the events in China which have now occurred. In the present situation, however, the mutual interests of the United States and China require full and frank discussion of the facts. It is only in this way that the people of our country and their representatives in Congress can have the understanding necessary to the sound evolution of our foreign policy in the Far East.

—Harry S. Truman, August 4, 1949, *Public Papers of the Presidents: Harry S. Truman*

NATO

Upon becoming secretary of state, one of Dean Acheson's first duties was to pick up the threads of the negotiations for the North Atlantic Treaty. Curiously, until Acheson was confirmed as Secretary of State, Lovett did not feel free to discuss all of the details. This was in contrast to the Truman policy during the transition from the Truman to the Eisenhower administration, when the Eisenhower cabinet designees were fully briefed. Acheson had, however, kept in touch with the development of the Marshall Plan, and it did not take long for him to get up to date on the status of the draft treaty. He continued the practice he had followed earlier as acting secretary of state of keeping President Truman fully informed of each step.[1]

Differences of opinion among the nations involved developed as to what countries should be included. At first Acheson opposed the admission of Italy since it was not on the Atlantic. Kennan agreed, and so did Senators Connally and Vandenberg. The French, however, wanted Italy in, and they threatened to block the inclusion of Norway if Italy was not accepted. Acheson then told Truman that this was a decision to be made by Europeans. Truman concurred. Acheson also won over the senators. During the negotiations, Truman in his press conferences supported Acheson's positions and refused to make comments of his own.[2]

Secretary Acheson had some difficulties in getting the support of Senator Connally for the provisions of the proposed treaty referring to the military commitment involved, and he asked the President to straighten Connally out on a proposed revision of Article 5, which would have weakened it. Truman succeeded in securing Connally's cooperation. He also strongly backed Acheson's public statements on the treaty.[3] At the signing of the treaty on April 4, 1949, by the representatives of the twelve nations and in a special message of April 12 transmitting the treaty to the Senate, Truman praised the "efforts for collective defense and for the preservation of peace and security."[4]

During the Senate debate on the treaty, Truman and Acheson depended heavily upon the support of Senator Vandenberg, who was eloquent in his defense and anticipated some of the attacks of the isolationist senators. John Foster Dulles, appointed as senator from New York to fill a vacancy, also defended the treaty. One point that Vandenberg raised concerned the admission of new members. Acheson replied that he had Truman's agreement that the admission of new members would require a new treaty for each, which would be submitted to the Senate for advice and consent.[5] On Acheson's denial of plans for German rearmament, for the sending of larger numbers of American troops to Europe, for security pacts, and for the approval of the colonial policies of other pact members, Truman was noncommittal in his press conference, but the assumption was that he supported Acheson in these denials. Circumstances were later to compel these two men to reverse themselves on all of these positions.[6]

The Senate voted eighty-two to thirteen in favor of the treaty on July 21, 1949, thus reversing the fundamental American foreign policy of no entangling alliances, which had been firmly held since the founding of this country.[7] Four days later, President Truman sent a special message to Congress on the need for a military aid program. His message did not mention the Soviet Union or Germany, but both were in the background. It was assumed that the Soviet Union had aggressive intentions that endangered Western Europe. To meet this threat, it would be necessary for the United States to join a Western European defense system, which would eventually include West Germany.[8] George Kennan of the State Department Planning Staff contended that the Soviet intentions were not aggressive, that an alliance was not necessary, and that it was a mistake to emphasize military rather than economic measures. He thought that it was still possible to negotiate with the Russians for a neutralized Germany that would not be under Soviet domination.[9] Secretary Acheson held to the view that such negotiations were not possible and that the Western Europeans had to be reassured of their security or economic recovery would not go forward. Because of his experiences at Potsdam, President Truman agreed with Acheson that it was frustrating to try to bargain with the Soviet Union.[10]

During 1949 both Truman and Acheson denied that American policy contemplated the creation of a small army in West Germany.[11] Both, however, backed the establishment of a West German government and the end of military occupation and the limitations on German production.

GERMANY

An immediate German problem that Truman and Acheson faced in 1949 was the blockade of Berlin, a dangerous situation perilous to all parties concerned. From the Soviet point of view, it had failed to stop the establishment of a West German government, and the counter-blockade was causing economic damage to the Russians and their satellites. From the Allied point of view, the airlift was expensive, risky, and costly in lives of pilots. Soviet Premier Stalin's answers to an American correspondent's questions on January 30, 1949, indicated a willingness to lift the blockade if the formation of a West German government was postponed pending a meeting of the Council of Foreign Ministers.[12] Acheson coordinated his reply to this with Truman. Publicly they were opposed to a summit meeting on these matters between Stalin and Truman, but privately the Department of State explored the possibility of negotiating the end of the blockade. The Soviet Union withdrew its objections to the new German currency, the blockade and counter-blockade were ended May 12, and the Council of Foreign Ministers was convened on May 23. By this time the West Germans had already completed the Bonn constitution and the civilian-Allied High Commission had replaced the military occupation regime. Truman had supported the transfer of authority, and he appointed John J. McCloy as high commissioner for Germany on May 18.[13]

Truman and Acheson did not have much confidence in the Council of Foreign Ministers, which met in Paris in May to consider the making of treaties with Austria and Germany. They considered asking Senators Connally and Vandenberg to go with members of the delegation but decided the senators were needed at home to support pending defense legislation. To carry out the principle of bipartisanship in foreign affairs, they selected John Foster Dulles as a delegate, a role he had played under Secretary Marshall.[14] At the conference, Acheson was very careful to keep the President fully informed daily regarding all developments. The Western trio (Great Britain, France, and the United States) and the Russians rejected each other's plans for Germany. On June 21, 1949, the President issued a statement reporting on the Paris meeting. He praised the progress made toward the conclusion of a treaty with Austria but deplored the lack of progress toward a treaty with Germany.[15]

In the summer of 1949, both NATO and the independence of West Germany were advanced. President Truman asked Congress to pass a mutual defense assistance bill as a means of implementing the alliance. On August 24 the establishment of NATO was proclaimed by the President. The West German government with Konrad Adenauer as chancellor was established on September 21. Two days later Truman disclosed that a Soviet atom bomb had been exploded. He and his advisors were surprised and alarmed because their calculations were that the Soviet Union could not do this for several more years. Congress reacted by passing the Mutual Defense Assistance Act, the first step in the revision of American defense policies following the loss of a monopoly over nuclear weapons. The need for a stable German economy became more pressing. In November Acheson was able to secure the end of dismantling of German industrial plants except for a few war production facilities.[16]

The North Atlantic Council under the chairmanship of Secretary Acheson worked out an integrated defense plan, which President Truman approved in January 1950. After the North Korean attack in June, Acheson changed his ideas about German participation in European defense. In a memorandum to the President, he advocated incorporation of German units into a European army, the stationing of more American troops in Europe, and a unified command.[17] The French resented the rearming of the Germans, but they liked the idea of a supreme commander, and Eisenhower was their candidate. Truman, Acheson, and Marshall, now secretary of defense, agreed and in October, Truman obtained Eisenhower's consent. A formal request for Eisenhower from the NATO council was sent in December, and at the time Truman announced the sending of additional American troops to Europe, policies that were vigorously attacked by Republicans and isolationists.[18] Truman made a spirited defense of Acheson against such critics as Joseph P. Kennedy, former President Hoover, and Senator Taft, all of whom advocated a withdrawal from Europe:

How our position in the world would be improved by the retirement of Dean Acheson from public life is beyond me. Mr. Acheson has helped shape and carry out our policy of resistance to Communist imperialism. From the time of our sharing of arms with Greece and Turkey nearly 4 years ago, and coming down to the recent

moment when he advised me to resist Communist invasion of South Korea, no official in our Government has been more alive to communism's threat to freedom or
more forceful in resisting it.[19]

In his memorandum to the President on his briefing of General Eisenhower on January 4, 1951, Secretary Acheson expressed his belief that the
economy and governmental system of the Soviet Union had not been as
badly damaged as the political and economic structure of Western Europe
had, that the Europeans, in view of their own military weakness, were
paralyzed by fear of possible Soviet invasion or subversion, and that since
the intentions of the Soviet Union were unknown, preparations should be
made to deter further Soviet aggressions.[20] George Kennan and other Soviet
specialists questioned these assumptions, holding that the Soviet Union had
suffered great damage during the war, that its leaders were unwilling to
challenge American military might, and that they had no intentions of
invading Western Europe. Subsequent events have supported Kennan's
views.[21]

On February 21, 1951, General Eisenhower arrived in Paris to take up his
duties as supreme commander of the North Atlantic Treaty defense forces.
In April the Senate approved the plan to send four more American troop
divisions to Europe to be part of Eisenhower's command. In May, West
Germany became a full-fledged member of the Council of Europe, as Bonn
Chancellor and Foreign Minister Adenauer took his place on the Committee
of Foreign Ministers. Acheson and Adenauer got along well together; both
were anticommunist and pro-European community. In July the new North
Atlantic Treaty headquarters, known as SHAPE (Supreme Headquarters of
Allied Powers in Europe), was opened at Rocquencourt, France.[22]

During 1952, Admiral Lynde D. McCormick, commander of the U.S.
Atlantic fleet, was appointed supreme commander of NATO naval forces
and General Lord Ismay, secretary of commonwealth relations, was
appointed secretary general of NATO. In May President Truman replaced
General Eisenhower as supreme commander of Allied Forces in Europe
with General Matthew B. Ridgway, who had done such an outstanding job
in Korea. Eisenhower had given in to the entreaties of the Republican
politicians to enter the race for the Republican nomination for president.
This marked the beginning of a coolness that developed between Truman
and Eisenhower, whose relations up to that point had been cordial.[23]

West Germany was proving to be a worthy member of the Western European community. It was the first country to ratify the Schuman coal and
steel merger plan in February 1952. The Soviet Union made another bid for
the creation of a united Germany, but it was rejected by Acheson and British
Prime Minister Churchill. In May the big three western powers and West
Germany signed the Bonn agreement that gave restricted sovereignty to
West Germany, an instrument that was ratified by the U.S. Senate in July.

Acheson and Truman were anxious to have West Germany integrated into the NATO defense system, but this did not happen while they were in office.[24]

CHINA

The failure of America's China policy in 1949 had its origins at least as far back as 1927 when the Chinese Nationalists and Chinese Communists broke with each other and started a long struggle for the mastery of China. Then in the 1930s, the Japanese began their undeclared war on China. The drain on the economy of China caused by the war undermined the economic, social, and political stability of the country. No revenues were obtained from the conquered cities, and the maintenance of the Chinese armies, inefficient as they were, required vast outlays. Inflation was completely out of control.

In 1936, Chiang Kai-shek came to a wartime understanding with the Communists. The communist manifesto referred to the formation of a "united front" with the Kuomintang against the Japanese, but the details as to how this front was to operate were never worked out.[25] The Chinese Communist armies maintained their own independence and in their own controlled territories were able to harass the Japanese by guerrilla tactics. After America's entrance into World War II, the plan to have an American, General Joseph W. Stilwell, in command over both Nationalist and Communist armies was vetoed by Chiang Kai-shek and President Roosevelt on the ground that such a step infringed on China's sovereign rights.[26] The President sent Patrick J. Hurley as his personal representative to try to bring the Nationalists and Communists together to fight the Japanese, and he sent General Albert C. Wedemeyer to head American troops in China in the place of Stilwell who had been recalled upon Chiang's stubborn insistence. At first, Hurley thought that the goal was attainable, but later he turned against the Communists. His mission ended in failure, and its aftereffects were disastrous as far as America's China policy was concerned. Hurley contributed to the rejection of the advice and services of the State Department's best China experts, who clearly saw the collapse of Chiang and the rise of Mao.[27]

The Marshall mission followed at a very critical time in the civil war in 1945-1946. It also was doomed to failure because both the Nationalists and the Chinese Communists were unwilling to yield to each other. In August 1946 Marshall placed an embargo on aid to the Nationalists. The situation in China so deteriorated in 1947, particularly in Manchuria, that President Truman returned General Wedemeyer to China on a fact-finding mission. The Wedemeyer report, submitted to the President on September 19, 1947, noted the shortcomings of the Nationalist regime—corruption, nepotism, incompetence, oppression, reaction, inflation, and disintegration—and at the same time it pointed out the danger of a communist victory in China. It recommended immediate action by the United Nations to place Manchuria under the guardianship of the five powers, including the Soviet Union, or a U.N. trusteeship. Secretary Marshall and the President thought that this recommendation would be offensive to Chinese sensibilities as an infringement on Chinese sovereignty, and they therefore refused to make the report public. Among the recommendations were military and economic aid to China under a program of assistance over a period of at least five years on the condition that China make effective use of its own resources, implement urgently required political and military reforms, and accept American advisers to assist in utilizing aid in the manner for which it was intended. The suppression of the report by Marshall and Truman alienated Wedemeyer, who became a critic of American policy in China. On the advice of Marshall, who wanted to avoid heavy involvement in China, Truman did not act on the recommendations. Two years later, when the report was made public, some critics said that the American government's failure to implement it caused Chiang's downfall.[28]

During 1948, the Chinese Communists went on the offensive in Manchuria and took over the leading cities. As Marshall and Wedemeyer had warned Chiang Kai-shek, the Nationalist forces that had been moved to Manchurian cities were isolated, and, finding themselves unpopular with the local population and hard to defend, they defected or surrendered with little or no resistance.[29] The Communists had been greatly strengthened by the Japanese arms that they received with Soviet help, by American lend-lease equipment received from the Russians, and by American equipment abandoned or sold to them by the Nationalists. The morale of the Chinese Communist troops was high, while that of the Nationalists was sinking fast because of lack of food, lack of military supplies, poor leadership, and loss of faith in the Nationalist cause. Nationalist administrators were highly unpopular in the cities; the Communists, on the other hand, were careful to try to win over local leaders. Under Republican pressure, Congress passed a China aid bill in 1948, which the President signed, but it was a case of too little and too late.[30] Secretary Marshall recognized the difficulties. On February 20, 1948, he said:

> The conduct by the government of the civil war in progress, particularly in view of geographic disadvantages—exposed and lengthy communications, and the inherent difficulties in dealing with guerrilla warfare—demands a high order of aggressive leadership in all major echelons of command, which is lacking. The civil war imposes a binder on the national budget of 70 percent or more and the financing is now carried on by means of issuance of paper money. . . . The results are an extreme, really a fantastic, inflation of currency and an inevitable speculation in commodities as well as hoarding.[31]

Truman and Marshall proposed economic aid and opposed increased military aid at this time. But no Republicans were willing to advocate the kind of military aid that would have been needed at this point to save Nationalist China from defeat by the Communists.

When Acheson became secretary of state in January 1949, the fate of China had practically been decided. Acheson's main interests were in Europe, but he was compelled to spend time on American relations with China. In a letter to Senator Connally, he wrote on March 15:

> Despite . . . very substantial . . . aid extended by the United States to China . . . the economic and military position of the Chinese government has deteriorated to the point when the Chinese Communists hold almost all important areas of China from Manchuria to the Yangtze River and have the military capacity of expanding their control to the populous areas of the Yangtze Valley and of eventually dominating South China.[32]

The bipartisan foreign policy that had worked well in the formulation of American policy toward Europe did not extend to China. In early 1949 Senator Vandenberg, who had always been a firm supporter of bipartisanship on the Republican side, was sounded out by Les Biffle, secretary of the Senate, as to whether he would be interested in becoming secretary of state. He replied in the negative, indicating that he thought he would be more useful in the Senate. He congratulated Truman on his reelection and received a friendly letter in return, but he was disturbed that the minority representation on the Senate Foreign Relations Committee was cut from six to five and that he was not consulted regarding the selection of Acheson as secretary of state.[33] In the hearings on Acheson's confirmation, however, Senator Vandenberg defended the appointment.[34] The relations between the senator and the State Department were not as cordial as they had been when General Marshall was secretary and Lovett was under secretary. Vandenberg never regarded China as coming under the bipartisan policy because of a lack of consultation regarding Chinese issues. He had opposed the attempts to establish a coalition government, but after this was abandoned by Truman, he supported the China aid bill of 1948 strongly in the Senate even though he was not too optimistic about the course of events. In January 1949 he wrote:

> . . . the situation in China has disintegrated so rapidly that we . . . confront the grave question as to how any sort of American aid can be made effective and not be a waste of American resources. . . . It seems to be apparent that this progressive disintegration has cost the National Government the support and sympathy of a large portion of all the Chinese people. Indeed, it is now probable that the Nationalist Government will fall before we could ever sustain it with a new program of aid. . . . If we made ourselves responsible for the Army of the Nationalist Government, we

would be in the China war for keeps and the responsibility would be in ours instead of hers. I am very sure that this would jeopardize our own national security beyond any possibility of justification.[35]

This was Vandenberg's answer to Republican critics, such as former Governor Alfred Landon who had attacked Truman for his blunders in China and remarked that the bipartisan foreign policy had kept Republicans from talking freely. Vandenberg asserted that a bipartisan foreign policy had not been followed in China. The senator himself was soon involved in criticizing the administration's China policies. He opposed the nomination of R. Walter Butterworth to be assistant secretary of state for Far Eastern affairs on the ground that he was too closely identified with China policies that were turning out to be failures. Butterworth was not confirmed until September 27, 1949.[36]

A group of Republican senators was becoming increasingly critical of America's China policies. On February 4, 1949, at a cabinet meeting, Truman approved a National Security Council recommendation to suspend military aid to Chiang on the ground that it would be captured by the Communists. At a meeting with congressional leaders three days later, he and Acheson tried to explain the move, but they could not convince even Senator Vandenberg of the wisdom of the action, so Truman changed his mind and opted for no formal suspension. This step was not enough for a group of forty Republican congressmen who sent a letter to the President that, in effect, accused the administration of letting the Nationalists collapse. On February 24, Acheson met with the senators, but his explanations backfired when he commented: "We cannot tell what the next step is until some of the dust and smoke of disaster clears away and see where there's a foundation on which to build."[37] To the press and to the congressmen, this statement meant a do-nothing policy. At the same time, Senator McCarran, an old foe, introduced a bill to provide a loan of $1.5 billion to Nationalist China for military and economic purposes. Senators H. Styles Bridges, McCarran, and William F. Knowland called for an investigation of American China policy. Truman and Acheson were defended by Senators Connally and Fulbright. The McCarran bill was not voted on.[38]

With mounting congressional and press criticisms of America's China policies and with bitter denunciations of the United States by both the Nationalists and Chinese Communists, Truman and Acheson decided that the public needed information on the true situation in China. In March Truman authorized the preparation of a white paper that would explain the Chinese situation in all its aspects going back to 1844 but centering on the last five years. Ambassador at Large Philip C. Jessup was selected as editor in chief. The white paper, *United States Relations with China*, released in August 1949, did not calm the situation, however; it exacerbated it.[39] Even Senator Vandenberg wrote:

Speaking of China, I am . . . [on] the front pages today, with my brief statement on the White Paper. Nothing that I said about China warranted any such attention. I simply wanted to nail down the fact [among others] that the China "crime" goes back to Teheran and Yalta where F.D.R. sold Chiang Kai-shek down the river in order to get Joe Stalin into the Jap war (just four days before the Japs surrendered).[40]

In his letter of transmittal to the President, Acheson tried to clear his government of any blame for the collapse of China:

The unfortunate but inescapable fact is that the ominous result of the civil war in China was beyond the control of the government of the United States. Nothing that this country did or could have done within the reasonable limits of its capabilities could have changed that result; nothing that was left undone by this country has contributed to it. It was the product of internal Chinese forces, forces which this country tried to influence but could not. A decision was arrived at within China, if only a decision by default.[41]

Acheson also wrote in his introduction to the white paper, "Ultimately the profound civilization and the democratic individualism of China will reassert themselves and she will throw off the foreign yoke," and in another place, "The Communist leaders have forsworn their Chinese heritage and have publicly announced their subservience to a foreign power, Russia." Both of these statements were grossly mistaken. Acheson, before the Korean war broke out, was following a policy that counted on the Soviet Union's and Communist China's falling apart because of their conflicting interests.[42] After Stalin's death it was clear to all that Communist China was not just another Soviet satellite. As for "democratic individualism in China," few signs of it can be found today.

The white paper was meant largely for the domestic audience, but its effects abroad were most unfortunate. It enabled Mao to tell his people that the United States was a "paper tiger." Capitalist imperialism had failed in China. The Americans were "newly upstart and neurotic" for revealing publicly such sinister and childish machinations. The white paper convinced the Soviet Union that the United States would not interfere in the civil war in China.

Truman took a direct interest in the actual preparation of the white paper. He edited the part on Marshall's mission and had it revised. Jessup enlisted the President's support to overcome the opposition of the Joint Chiefs of Staff and Defense Secretary Johnson to releasing the paper. Truman read the text before it was issued on August 4, 1949.[43] It was composed of 409 pages of narrative and 645 pages of documents, many of which had to be declassified.

General Claire Chenault, hero of American air efforts in China, warned Jessup that the release of the white paper would make matters worse at a critical time in the civil war, but Jessup would not listen.[44] William C. Bullitt, former ambassador to the Soviet Union, protested strongly against the document after it had been released, saying it was

proof of the lengths to which our government officials will go to protect their vested interests in their own mistakes. To publish an inquest on a faithful ally—not yet dead but fighting in despair to preserve its National independence—is incompatible with any standard of decent conduct. And our Department of State has done this not to serve a national American interest but to serve domestic political expediency.[45]

Ambassador Stuart also criticized the document, saying, "There was a multitude of things that this counry did which contributed decisively to the loss of China."[46] Professor Kenneth Colegrove of Northwestern University was even more emphatic: "[Acheson's] letter of transmittal was thoroughly dishonest, especially the paragraph which says that . . . the United States left nothing undone that might have saved him . . . that obviously was a lie."[47]

Truman in his *Memoirs* did not try to defend the white paper, nor did Acheson in his *Present at the Creation* try to answer his critics.[48]

The white paper was prophetic. China was taken over by the Communists, and the People's Republic was declared on October 1, 1949. Chiang fled to Formosa on December 8 with something less than half a million of his troops and some $365 million in gold and silver reserves that belonged to the former Nationalist Treasury in Nanking. This laid the basis for America's two-China policy, which was obviously contrary to the facts and led to unrealistic actions on the part of the United States for twenty-three years.

Which China would the United States now choose as the China entitled to diplomatic recognition and a seat in the Security Council of the United Nations? The Soviet Union had recognized the People's Republic the day after it was proclaimed. Other communist countries followed shortly, and on December 30, 1949, India became the first noncommunist state to recognize Peking. Acheson tried to get the British to hold off their recognition, but he failed and the British followed India on January 5, 1950, in recognizing the new regime. Traditionally, the United States had followed two different recognition policies. One was to extend recognition to governments in de facto control of their people and territory regardless of the nature of the regime. The other policy, initiated by President Wilson, was to use recognition as a sign of approval or disapproval. This second policy had been applied to the Soviet Union for sixteen years. When President Truman was asked in a press conference on October 19, 1949, under what circumstances we would recognize Communist China, he replied, "I hope we will not have to recognize it." Truman's opposition to recognition was strengthened by the harsh treatment by the Peking government of Angus Ward, the American consul general in Mukden.[49]

Acheson and his advisers tried to persuade Truman early in 1950 to adopt a policy that would drive a wedge between Peking and Moscow and encourage the Communist Chinese to become more friendly toward the United States. The details of such a policy were not worked out. The existence of the Nationalist regime on Formosa and the strong support given Chiang by the Republicans, the China lobby, and some American military leaders made it difficult to find a way to carry out the Truman-Acheson policy. On December 29, 1949, the National Security Council considered a recommendation of the Joint Chiefs of Staff for more military equipment for Chiang on Formosa. Acheson was opposed, and Truman decided against the military.[50] The decision was leaked to the press, and there was a great outcry. The Republicans wanted to use the navy to protect Formosa. Acheson appealed to the ailing Senator Vandenberg, to no avail. Truman in his press conference of January 5, 1950, announced: "The United States Government will not pursue a course which will lead to involvement in the civil conflict in China."[51] Senator H. Alexander Smith of New Jersey and Senator William F. Knowland of California told Acheson that this was the end of bipartisan foreign policy.[52]

A number of basic assumptions contributed to American policy failures in China. President Roosevelt tried to treat Nationalist China as a great power, which it was not. He paid deference to Chiang's sovereignty, which certainly was not deserved. American public papers of Roosevelt and Truman referred to the democratization of China, which was clearly not a solution that either the Nationalists or Communists were willing to accept. To defeat Japan, it was thought necessary to buy Russian help at the expense of China. Russian control of Manchuria proved disastrous to Nationalist China. Truman and Acheson had an ambivalent view of Communist China, whose dynamic qualities they greatly underestimated. On one hand, they assumed that communism was monolithic and that the Chinese Communists had come under the influence of Stalin. On the other hand, Acheson hoped that Mao might have Titoist tendencies, but he failed to stand up to the Republicans who were blind to the significance of Titoism and stuck to the hopeless cause of Chiang in exile on Formosa. In pursuing the Truman doctrine, the President and Acheson were not consistent. The doctrine did not apply to the communist mainland, but it came to apply to Formosa. It was assumed that American aid would be omnipotent, which it was clearly not. It was the estimate of Truman and his advisers that the American people were not willing to make the sacrifices necessary for an attempt to save Nationalist China.

chapter 34 | LIBERAL LEANINGS THWARTED, 1949– 1950

> *As a practical proposition, the executive branch of the government*
> *can no more operate by itself than can the Congress. . . . But no*
> *President has ever attempted to govern alone. Every President knows*
> *and must know that the congressional control of the purse has to be*
> *reckoned with.*
> —Harry S. Truman, *Memoirs*

EIGHTY-FIRST CONGRESS, FIRST SESSION

The 1948 presidential and congressional elections restored Democratic control to the Senate by a 54 to 42 count and to the House of Representatives by a 263 to 171 count. The Republican factions were bitter toward each other because of the defeat, but they were united in opposing the Truman program, especially on internal security, labor, public power, economic controls, tax and appropriation cuts, and presidential appointments. Only on foreign affairs and housing could Truman expect some help from the Republicans. The illness of Senator Vandenberg, however, soon cut into the Republican support for a bipartisan foreign policy.[1]

The Democratic majorities appeared ample, but there was little likelihood that the southern bloc in the Senate and the House would follow presidential leadership on civil rights, internal security, labor questions, agriculture, taxation, and general appropriation cuts. On such questions the southerners, as in the past, would probably line up with the Republicans to produce the conservative majority that had frustrated Truman since he came to power. On certain crucial questions, there would be no Democratic majority. The conservative bloc was strengthened by the fact that many key leadership positions in the House and Senate were in the hands of conservatives whose power to block legislation was great.

At the beginning of 1949, President Truman still thought that inflation was the main problem, and he asked Congress for anti-inflationary controls. Actually, however, during the first six months of 1949, there was a drop in nonagricultural employment, in industrial production, and in consumer prices, especially those of farm products.[2] To meet this decline, President

Truman adhered to his easy money policy based on the federal reserve support of the government bond market. He wanted to keep down the cost of servicing the public debt. From his days as county judge, he had been concerned about low interest rates.

The success of Truman's legislative program depended in part on how well he could work with the leaders of Congress.[3] On the Democratic side, the leadership was little changed in the House. Sam Rayburn again became Speaker and Congressman John McCormack was reinstated as majority leader. Rayburn was an able leader, but he was a southerner and there were parts of the President's program that he would sabotage—civil rights, offshore oil rights, and the regulation of natural gas. Key committee chairmanships were held by southerners who enjoyed seniority, and they could bottle up bills they did not like. On the Senate side, when Barkley became vice-president, Senator J. Scott Lucas of Illinois became floor leader, and Senator Francis J. Myers of Pennsylvania was chosen as whip. Lucas was not as strong a leader as Barkley had been. As in the past, Truman held regular meetings with Lucas and Rayburn and with Republicans Senator Kenneth Wherry of Nebraska and former Speaker Joseph W. Martin of Massachusetts.[4]

During the Eighty-first Congress, the House loosened its rules a bit by the twenty-one day rule, which provided that the chairman of a committee that had reported a public bill that was held up by the Rules Committee for twenty-one days could get immediate consideration of the bill by the House. The Senate, on the other hand, tightened its cloture rules governing filibusters, making it more difficult to get action on a bill opposed by a determined minority.[5]

President Truman originally planned to send his message on the state of the union to Congress in writing because it would be long. He also planned to repeat the important points of his legislative program in his inaugural address, but Clifford and Elsey objected strongly to this plan. They urged the President to appear in person before Congress with a short general message because a long, detailed one would offer little hope for conciliation and compromise on minor points. They also urged that all foreign policy issues be reserved for the inaugural address, which would attract world attention. Truman took Clifford's and Elsey's advice in the final drafts and presentation.[6]

The state of the union message reflected Keyserling's economic philosophy of the expanding economy, and it contained the key label, the Fair Deal, which Truman used to describe his program. It recommended legislation on consumer credit, bank credit, regulation of commodity exchanges, export controls, priorities and allocation of transportation and materials, rent controls, standby authority for price controls, new taxes to raise $4 billion in revenue, repeal of the Taft-Hartley Act, farm price supports, national medical insurance, extension of social security, public power projects, resource planning, public housing, lower-priced private housing, an increase in the minimum wage, aid to education, civil rights, universal military training, and government power to build steel plants and other facilities, "if action by private industry fails to meet our needs."[7]

The economic report listed the indexes showing favorable economic growth and elaborated on the economic policies needed to carry out the program of maximum employment and maximum production, to combat inflation, and to guard against a depression. The budget message proposed no striking increases in expenditures. The proposed tax increases were designed to reduce the national debt. In July Truman acknowledged in his midyear economic report that rising unemployment and falling production lessened the need for the anti-inflationary measures that he had advocated in January.[8]

Truman's inaugural address concentrated on foreign policy. It began by pointing out the dangers of world communism. It outlined four major policies: (1) unfaltering support of the United Nations, (2) continuation of programs for world economic recovery, (3) strengthening freedom-loving nations by joint security agreements such as the North Atlantic Treaty, and (4) "a bold new program for making the benefits of our scientific advances and industrial progress available for the improvement and growth of under-developed areas." The last of these policies came to be called "Point Four."[9] It originated as an idea put forth by Benjamin Hardy, a State Department employee in the Office of Public Affairs. Finding no interest in it in his agency, he brought it to Clifford and Elsey, who had been searching for a significant and dramatic topic for the inaugural address. They approved of it and incorporated it in an early draft, which went to the State Department. There Acting Secretary Robert Lovett and Paul Nitze of the Planning Staff did not like it, but President Truman did and it remained in the speech.[10] It attracted favorable mention all over the world. It took time, however, to implement the policy because the details had not been worked out. Truman admitted this in his press conference of January 26, 1949.[11]

The Truman record in securing favorable action on his proposals was mixed. The House acted quickly in February on his request for authority to reorganize the executive departments along lines recommended by the Hoover commission (organized in 1947 under the chairmanship of former President Hoover), but the Senate did not concur until June. The House passed a three-year extension of the reciprocal trade program and export controls, and in March both the House and the Senate passed a rent control bill that met the approval of the President.

In April both houses debated and passed a renewal of the European

Recovery Program. The debates concerned special advantages to ship owners, marine insurance companies, producers of agricultural surpluses, food processors, and small business.

Agriculture

President Truman and many Democratic party leaders realized how important the farm vote was in the 1948 presidential election. Consequently, they were favorable to a generous farm program with high price supports. The Republicans had been pictured as opposed to the interests of the farmers. Truman's victory led his chief adherents in agriculture to urge 90 or even 100 percent of parity. Prominent among his most active supporters were the Farmers Union and the Production and Marketing Administration committees, both of which urged high-level price supports after the election.[12]

Truman and Secretary of Agriculture Charles Brannan had not worked out their legislative program for agriculture when Congress convened. The President's economic report was to repeat his earlier endorsement of flexible price supports, but Brannan and his top advisers were moving in another direction. By April 6, 1949, they had worked out what was later called the Brannan plan, which the Department of Agriculture historians summarized as follows: " (1) the use of an income standard, based on a 10-year moving average beginning with the years 1938-47, as a method of computing price-support levels for farm products; (2) support for major products at full income standard levels; (3) support of the incomes of growers of perishable commodities by direct payments by the Government of the difference between the price received in the market and the support price established; (4) restriction of supports to large-scale farmers to what an efficient family farm unit could produce; and (5) requirement of compliance with approved conservation practices and production or marketing controls in order to receive benefits."[13] If this plan brought unmanageable surpluses, then controls would be imposed. The plan was designed to be attractive to medium-size farm operators and to consumers generally. Brannan explained it to President Truman, who assured the secretary that he would support it. The secretary then presented the plan to a joint hearing of the House and Senate committees on agriculture on April 7, and a stormy debate ensued. Lined up behind the plan were the Democratic organization leaders, the Farmers Union, labor unions, Americans for Democratic Action, northern Democrats, and some small farmers in the South and West. Opposed to the plan were the American Farm Bureau Federation, the National Grange, chambers of commerce, the National Association of Manufacturers, livestock associations, grain dealers, cotton planters, milk producers, and Republicans. The big industrial farmers objected bitterly to the $25,700 limitation which left them out. The Republicans feared that the plan might cement a farmer-labor coalition that would prolong a Democratic ascendancy. The attack centered on the probable cost of the plan, the burden of the controls, the huge bureaucracy, and the regimentation of agriculture. In the House, one Republican critic said that the authors of the plan were Henry Wallace, Rexford Tugwell, and Alger Hiss. These tactics included branding the plan as "socialistic." The House killed the plan by voting for a substitute bill, which provided merely for high rigid supports benefiting largely the commercial farmers.[14]

In the Senate the Brannan plan was not even introduced following its defeat in the House. Senator Anderson, a former secretary of agriculture, had other ideas and failed to support the administration's plan. Truman, however, continued to advocate the plan, praising it in his Labor Day speech in Des Moines and in his state of the union message of 1950.[15] Senator Elmer Thomas of Oklahoma introduced a bill providing for production payments for potatoes, but it got nowhere. With the outbreak of the Korean war, there was a great demand for farm products, and the Brannan plan was dead. Truman had hoped to win votes with the scheme in the elections of 1950, but Democratic candidates stayed clear of the issue, and some who had supported it were defeated.[16]

Labor and Welfare

In May it was apparent that the House was not going to repeal the Taft-Hartley Act when the majority leader and the chairman of the labor committee voted to recommit the bill. Lucas proved to be a weak reed in this battle for organized labor. During 1949 there were strikes in the coal mines, the automobile industry, and the steel industry. President Truman appointed a fact-finding Steel Industry Board in July, which made a report in September recommending a company-supported pension plan. Labor and management accepted the arrangement. This solution did not invoke the Taft-Hartley Act. In the case of the coal miners, Truman took no action in 1949 because he did not think the situation had reached crisis proportions.[17]

In the Senate and the House, a bill for federal aid to education raised a hot religious issue in May. The House version confined support to public schools. Cardinal Spellman of New York denounced this provision and criticized Methodist Bishop G. Bromley Oxnam and Eleanor Roosevelt for supporting it. President Truman backed the latter against the cardinal on this matter.[18] The Senate also passed a bill strengthening the position of the defense secretary, and both chambers passed an amendment to the Commodity Credit Act, which provided for the government's acquisition of grain storage facilities, a hotly debated issue in the 1948 campaign.

In June, President Truman sent seven messages to Congress transmitting reorganization plans for a new Department of Welfare, a Bureau of Employment Security, Post Office Department, National Security Council and National Security Resources Board, Civil Service Commission, United States Maritime Commission, and Public Roads Administration. In this month the Senate Committee on Labor and Public Welfare had spectacular hearings on a compulsory health insurance bill, which incorporated provisions recommended by the President in his special message to Congress of April 22. The American Medical Association called the measure "socialized medicine" and ran a massive campaign against it.[19] The Senate itself followed the House in shelving any attempt to repeal the Taft-Hartley Act. The House, after a bitter debate (during which rules chairman Adolf J. Sabath and Eugene E. Cox of Georgia engaged in physical combat), passed the housing bill, and it went to the President, who signed it.

Civil Rights

Truman and the black leaders had hopes for civil rights legislation in the Eighty-first Congress, but they were soon disappointed; the coalition of Republicans and southern Democrats was as strong as ever. The Republicans ignored their platform and stood with the southerners in blocking all attempts to liberalize the Senate cloture rule. Without an easier rule, civil rights legislation would have no chance against a southern filibuster. In the battle to change the rules, Truman backed Majority Leader Lucas, but he did not help matters by an offhand remark in favor of a far more liberal cloture rule than the senators were considering. Senator Vandenberg, on a technicality, stood with the southerners. The result was a cloture rule far stiffer than the old rule.[20]

In his address to Congress, the President was just as forthright as he had been before in advocating civil rights legislation. Following a meeting with members of the National Citizens Council on Civil Rights on January 12, 1949, he announced that his office was already drafting bills to implement his recommendations to Congress.[21] Stephen Spingarn of the White House staff was largely responsible for this drafting. The President obtained congressmen to introduce his bills outlawing the poll tax, making lynching a federal crime, prohibiting segregation and discrimination in interstate commerce, establishing a permanent FEPC with enforcement powers, and protecting the right of suffrage. These bills got nowhere in the first session of the Congress except for the antipoll-tax bill, which passed the House. Senator Richard Russell offered some compromises, which Truman told him he could not accept.[22] Black leaders were already criticizing the Democrats in Congress for going back on their party platform, and the President did not want that criticism to extend to him. He would hold fast to his declared program. By October 1949, however, Truman acknowledged defeat in his civil rights legislative program during the first session and agreed to postpone the issue until 1950.[23]

In August the Senate, swayed by the "socialized medicine" charges, disapproved the plan for creating a new Department of Welfare. In both chambers the minimum wage proposals were considered. Agreement was reached on a minimum, but the coverage was reduced.

The first session of Congress adjourned on October 19 with considerable unfinished business. The House had acted on extension of social security, the basing-point bill which aimed to protect pricing systems by eliminating transportation differentials, and amendments to the Displaced Persons Act, but the Senate had not.

THE SECOND SESSION

In his state of the union message of 1950, President Truman praised Congress for its positive achievements during the preceding year, reviewed progress during the last half of the century, and outlined goals for the future. He pointed to the tremendous responsibilities that the nation faced abroad, and he asserted that it had the strength to meet them. He specifically endorsed the Brannan farm plan, the International Trade Organization, a National Science Foundation, the liberalization of the displaced persons law, a housing program for middle-income families, and aid to education, and he promised a series of proposals to aid small business.[24]

The President's economic report summarized the causes for the slight recession during the first half of 1949 and put forth a program for accelerating the recovery. He emphasized the necessity for growth, for extension of benefits to all groups, for a fiscal policy to contribute to growth, and for vigorous action on trouble spots in the economy. Among the specific recommendations he stressed were revising the tax structure, liberalizing the Reconstruction Finance Corporation policies, establishing a Columbia Valley administration, developing the St. Lawrence Seaway, providing technical assistance to underdeveloped countries, and giving additional authority to the federal reserve system.[25]

The annual budget message provided a slight reduction in total expenses of the government for fiscal year 1951 and outlined an ambitious management improvement program, including reorganizations, performance budgets, strengthened personnel management, and more modern accounting practices. A deficit of $5 billion was anticipated. This budget failed to take into consideration vast proposed increases in defense spending that were being formulated by the Departments of State and Defense under the leadership of Acheson and Paul Nitze and that would soon take the form of NSC 68.[26] Events were also to throw this budget out of kilter before the end of the fiscal year. Principal among these was the Korean war and the building up of the defenses of NATO.

Truman's first statement on congressional actions was his January 21 criticism of the rejection of the Korean aid bill by the House.[27] In view of the Republican charges made later in the year after the Korean war had started that the administration had neglected Korea, this action by the House was ironic. The House was partly responsible for Korean unpreparedness.

The President's first special message to Congress, sent on January 23, was on tax policy. He recommended a reduction of excise taxes, a reduction of depletion exemptions in oil and mining industries, the elimination of other tax loopholes, and the improvement of estate and gift tax and the corporation tax laws. The House took six months to produce a revenue bill that little resembled the President's recommendations, but in the meantime, the Korean war changed the situation. In response to a presidential letter of July 25 to the chairman of the Senate Committee on Finance, both houses increased taxes to meet war needs.[28]

Civil Rights

At the beginning of the second session, the President again urged Congress to enact the civil rights proposals he made in 1948. On January 17, 1950, he met with delegates of the National Civil Rights Mobilization and told them "that every effort is being made to get a vote on these measures in the Senate."[29] When Speaker Rayburn, however, refused to recognize Congressman John Lesinski from Michigan, who was trying to introduce an FEPC bill under the twenty-one-day rule, Truman refused to interfere. On this situation, Arthur Krock noted: "Very seldom do informed observers agree with Representative Marcantonio [New York], yet a good many did when he remarked: 'it is obvious that everybody wants civil rights as a campaign issue but not as a law and that goes for Harry Truman, the Democratic party and the Republican party.'"[30]

In spite of the Speaker's opposition, the House liberals continued to fight and made use of calendar Wednesday to introduce an FEPC bill in February, thus bypassing the Rules Committee. The Republicans introduced a substitute amendment for an FEPC without enforcement powers. A combination of Republicans and southern Democrats put this measure over, but it was not a bill that Truman could accept. The press, black and white, denounced the performance of the House.[31]

In the Senate, meanwhile, Senator Lucas went through the motions of supporting an FEPC bill. On April 11, after conferring with the President, the senator decided to postpone Senate action on a committee-cleared FEPC bill in order to obtain a quick vote on the Marshall Plan appropriations. In his April 13 press conference, Truman defended this action:

The reason for the postponement was due to the fact that the ECA appropriation should get into the omnibus appropriation bill in the House. Unless it is passed promptly, it will not get into that omnibus bill. The FEPC will be carried to the logical conclusion and every effort will be made to pass FEPC promptly without starting a filibuster against an international matter that is of vital importance to the whole world.[32]

As Truman had promised, on May 5 Lucas introduced a motion calling for the introduction of an FEPC bill. When a filibuster started, he next petitioned for cloture, which the Senate turned down by a vote of fifty-five for to thirty-two against. On the next attempt in July to get a cloture vote, the President, spurred on by Murphy and Spingarn, commissioned Democratic National Chairman Boyle to send telegrams to party officials asking for their support. The Senate vote still fell short, ending the civil rights battle in the Eighty-first Congress.[33]

While Congress was stalemated in the field of civil rights, the executive branch had other means of action. Stephen Spingarn and Philleo Nash of the White House staff contacted the executive departments and agencies, the courts, and minority group organizations on civil rights matters. President Truman kept in touch with their activities by means of his daily morning staff conferences. Their work was channeled through the presidential counsel, Charles Murphy.[34]

The Department of Justice was in a good position to carry on the battle for civil rights by use of the device of amicus curiae in certain cases. Stephen Spingarn in a brief memorandum to Clark Clifford recommended that the Justice Department request additional lawyers and clerical staff for its civil rights section so that full use could be made of amicus curiae briefs. Clifford's assistant, Charles Murphy, contacted Attorney General McGrath, who is in turn enlarged his budget request for the civil rights section.[35]

Following the Supreme Court decision in the 1948 *Shelly* v. *Kramer* case that racially restrictive covenants were not enforceable, Solicitor General Philip Perlman pressed the Federal Housing Authority to amend its rules so as to bar mortgages on homes whose deeds contained restrictive covenants.[36] The court decision followed an amicus curiae brief prepared under Attorney General Tom Clark. The FHA changed its rules on February 15, 1950.[37]

With additional backing for civil rights cases, the Justice Department filed briefs in the *McLaurin* v. *Oklahoma* and the *Sweat* v. *Painter* cases in support of black students who challenged southern state universities' right to discriminate against them in their graduate and professional schools. The argument at this stage was that this discrimination was contrary to the separate but equal doctrine of the *Plessy* v. *Fergusson* case. There were no segregated black graduate or law schools that were equal to the white schools. The Supreme Court decided in favor of the plaintiffs.[38]

An amicus curiae brief was also filed in *Henderson* v. *United States*, which challenged discrimination in interstate transportation. Perlman requested the court to repudiate the segregation doctrine set forth in *Plessy* v. *Fergusson*. The Vinson Court decided in favor of Henderson. This case and the higher educational cases set the stage for further erosion of the legal philosophy of segregation embodied in *Plessy*.[39]

While the Department of Interior worked to desegregate its facilities, it was the Defense Department that had the biggest job in this field and the greatest obstacles. President Truman continued his program of desegregation in the armed forces begun in 1948, but his committee on the subject made slow progress. There were a few blacks in the navy, but the department agreed to seek more. The Marine Corps stopped segregated basic training but kept some all-black units. While retaining quotas, the air force agreed to start desegregation. The army moved even more slowly. Truman promised Secretary Gray secretly that he could restore quotas if he thought it necessary.[40]

Labor

In February the coal miners went on strike, and Truman requested an injunction under the Taft-Hartley emergency provisions, which was granted by a federal court. When this did not settle the strike, he asked Congress for power to seize the mines. The strike was settled two days later, and Truman rescinded his request for seizure of the mines.

In 1950 there were strikes by automobile workers, railway workers, carpenters, and electrical workers. In August after the Korean war had started, President Truman issued an executive order taking control of the nation's railroads under a 1916 wartime railroad seizure law, which was still in effect. The secretary of the army took over the control of the roads, though leaving actual operation to railroad personnel. This arrangement continued for twenty-one months because no settlement was reached until the end of that period. A brief walkout by workers was ended by an army ultimatum to the workers to return or face dismissal and loss of seniority rights. A new contract was finally negotiated by the acting defense mobilizer, John R. Steelman, and the railroads were returned to private control.[41]

In March and April Congress's record was mixed. Housing, gas, rivers control, and foreign aid were among the subjects considered. In taking up housing for middle-income families, both chambers eliminated the provision for loans to housing cooperatives by majorities composed of Republicans and southern Democrats.[42] As for the Kerr bill exempting natural gas producers from regulation, Truman vetoed it and Congress let it die. Truman's substitute for a Columbia River Valley authority, a coordinated Army-Interior plan, was defeated by the army engineers' lobby and local interests. On foreign aid, there were battles in both houses in April, but the President won. In the House, a letter from the President helped eliminate an agricultural raid on the foreign aid funds, and Speaker Rayburn turned back an attack on the technical assistance program. In the Senate, the technical assistance provision was retained by a party vote.[43]

On the urging of Senator Estes Kefauver of Tennessee, the Senate voted to create the Special Committee to Investigate Organized Crime in Interstate Commerce, with Kefauver as chairman. Beginning in May, he held televised hearings in large cities across the country and attracted considerable attention. Truman wrote that he did not approve of Kefauver's methods. Actually, he was embarrassed by the revelations of corruption involving Democratic politicians in city machines.[44]

During this session the President submitted twenty-seven plans for reorganization of various departments and agencies. The Senate disapproved six of these and the House one. In general, the plans proposed increased power for the heads of agencies. The senators objected to the lessening of the powers of the general counsel of the National Labor Relations Board as specified in the Taft-Hartley Act. They also objected to the threatened independence of the comptroller of the currency and to the greater powers given to the heads of the Interstate Commerce Commission, the Federal Communications Commission, and the Department of Agriculture and the transfer of the RFC to the Department of Commerce. They again objected to the creation of a new department of health, education and security.[45]

During June, bills concerning basing-point prices, rents, and social security were disposed of. The basing-point pricing bill was adopted by the vote of Republicans and southern Democrats, but it was vetoed by Truman and Congress let the veto stand. Rent controls were renewed but only to the end of the year. A bill amending social security was passed and signed by the President, who requested that the crippling Knowland amendment be reconsidered in a later bill.[46]

IMPACT OF KOREAN WAR

After the outbreak of the Korean war on June 25, the legislative situation changed radically. The President concentrated on defense and emergency bills. Senate hearings of the small business program were discontinued. The selective service bill, which had been delayed, was passed without significant change. Restrictive amendments on foreign military aid were abandoned. In a message to Congress on July 19, Truman requested authority for a system of priorities and allocations for defense production.[47]

Truman's hopes for a stabilized economy were blasted by the Korean war and American intervention under the United Nation's auspices. As consumers started buying in large quantities in case of shortages, it was apparent that inflation would soon be a problem. There were sharp differences of opinion as to how serious the pressures would be. President Truman in his July 13, 1950, press conference, attempting to calm fears, said: "There is no prospect of any food shortage in this country at any time." In his message to Congress, he asked for only a $10 billion additional appropriation for defense.[48] He and his advisers did not contemplate large military effort such as took place in World War II. Then on July 26, Bernard Baruch, the self-styled elder statesman, miscalculating the impact of a limited war and underestimating the strength of the American economy, stampeded Congress into passing standby authority to control prices and wages. Senator Paul Douglas of Illinois, a professional economist, pointed out that $10 billion was only 4 percent of the national income and would not justify price control, but Baruch's views prevailed.[49]

President Truman's administration of the Defense Production Act was poor. His appointment of Allan Valentine, an educator with little business or political experience, as economic stabilizer on September 9, 1950, proved to be a mistake. Valentine was slow to get started and did not appoint Michael DiSalle, the former mayor of Toledo, as head of the Office of Price Stabilization until November 30. Seeing that Valentine's hope for voluntary price control was not being realized, Truman appointed Charles E. Wilson of General Electric as defense mobilizer with authority over Valentine. When Valentine turned down DiSalle's proposal for a thirty-day freeze of prices and wages, Wilson supported DiSalle, and Valentine resigned.[50]

As 1951 began, Wilson and DiSalle were ready to do battle for the consumers. Actually, however, the sudden rise in prices in December caused by panic buying following a defeat in Korea by Chinese Communists was not to last. The stalemate in the limited war in Korea produced only a slight rise in defense spending. Inflationary pressures were to subside.

While the Tydings committee investigating McCarthy's charges cleared the State Department, the Republicans and many Democrats were not satisfied. The spy trials of Dr. K. Fuchs, an English scientist who gave atomic secrets to the Soviet Union, of Judith Coplon, a clerk in the Department of Justice accused of espionage, of Harry Bridges, president of the Longshoreman's Union, convicted of perjury, and of others led Congress to consider the sweeping Internal Security Act. The President sent a message to Congress on August 8 on the subject, advocating the strengthening of existing laws on sabotage and espionage, but Congress passed the so-called McCarran Act requiring registration of all members of the Communist party and communist-front organizations, and it gave to the attorney general power to imprison suspected spies and saboteurs in time of emergency. In an eloquent defense of civil liberties and personal freedom, Truman vetoed this bill, but it was passed over his veto.[51]

Congress recessed from September 23 until November 27. When the lame duck session began, the Korean situation had worsened because of the massive intervention of the Chinese Communists. On December 15 the President declared a state of emergency. Congress passed an emergency war measure supplemental appropriation of nearly $20 billion for military and shipping needs. It set up the Civil Defense Administration and gave the President power to renegotiate contracts. A bitter battle was fought over $38 million in aid for relief of famine in Yugoslavia, but it was passed. An excess profits tax bill was also passed. This busy session found time also to extend rent control for ninety days, to extend union shop and check-off to railway unions, to strengthen the antitrust laws, and to ban interstate shipment of slot machines.[52]

Republican Senator James P. Kem of Missouri led an attack on the foreign policy of President Truman and Secretary Acheson. He introduced a resolution demanding that any agreements reached with the British during Prime Minister Attlee's visit be submitted to the Senate in the form of a treaty. The Senate Republican conference on December 15 called for Acheson's dismissal. Kem's resolution lost by a narrow vote. President Truman came to Acheson's defense in a vigorous statement on December 19.[53] On the Kem resolution, the party ranks held firm. In this Congress, Truman could count on party loyalty on most foreign policy issues and on a few domestic issues that did not affect the vital interests of the southerners.

In *Public Policy* for 1954, Richard D. Neustadt, a former Truman White House office aide, in somewhat too glowing terms asserted that the Eighty-first Congress was "the most liberal" since 1938, pointing out that it

enacted the comprehensive housing program, providing generously for slum clearance urban redevelopment, and public housing; the Congress that put through the major revision of social security. . . . This was the Congress that reformed the Displaced Persons Act, increased the minimum wage, doubled the hospital construction program, authorized the National Science Foundation and the rural telephone program, suspended the "sliding scale" on price supports, extended the soil conservation program, provided new grants for planning state and local public works and plugged the long-standing merger loophole in the Clayton Act. And it was principally this Congress that financed Truman's last expansions of flood control, rural electrification, reclamation, public power and transmission lines.[54]

Some of these laws encountered serious obstacles in their implementation. The housing program was actually inadequate to meet needs, and it was slow in getting under way. As Richard O. Davies observed, while the President "gave every appearance of staunch liberalism in his housing policies . . . in the day-to-day conduct of his housing agency he closely adhered to the real estate lobby's position."[55] Although the minimum wage was raised from forty to seventy-five cents an hour, Congress excluded a half-million workers previously covered. The reformed Displaced Persons Act was soon overshadowed by the restrictive McCarran-Walter Act. The amended Clayton Act was only invoked once. The electric power program contained loopholes that enabled private utilities to dominate the market. On some of Truman's major domestic proposals, such as civil rights, the Brannan plan, regional planning, medicare, and aid to small business, no action was taken.

chapter 35 | THE 1950 ELECTIONS

*The private organ of the Republican National Committee came out
with a clarion cry to enlist all good citizens in a crusade against the
"Reds." There was no particular Communist activity visible at our
horizon; it was simply a specialty of the organization functionary
who happened to be running the paper. This gave us the opportunity
to talk about a red herring drawn across the trail and otherwise to
jeer at windmill jousting.*

—Charles Michelson, *The Ghost Talks*

During 1950 President Truman was conscious of his position as leader of
the Democratic party. In the spring, he conducted a whistle-stop tour of the
country, making forty-seven speeches in explaining his program, praising
the local Democrats, and pointing out the benefits that the party had
brought or was trying to bring to the locality. In making these speeches, he
had the aid of Charles Murphy and his assistants.[1] The climax of the spring
campaign was his speech at the National Democratic Conference and
Jefferson Jubilee in Chicago on May 15. This event commemorated the one
hundred fiftieth anniversary of the election of Thomas Jefferson, the
founder of the Democratic party, and it marked the opening of the 1950
congressional campaign. In his address, Truman praised the party and its
leaders in Congress, especially Senator Scott Lucas, the majority leader,
who was up for reelection in Illinois. He also denounced the backward-
looking senators and congressmen who had tried to defeat every progressive
measure. Regarding them, he said, "Now I hope by next January that some
of the worst obstructionists will be removed." He was no more specific than
this. Since several of the obstructionists were Democrats, he was loath to try
a purge.[2] His attempted purge of Congressman Slaughter in his own congressional district in 1946 had ended in disastrous charges of vote frauds
and was still being used by Republican orators to denounce him and the
party.[3]

The Korean war, which began in June, kept Truman so busy that he did
not have time to continue his campaigning for Democratic victories in the
fall elections, and he left intensive barnstorming to Vice-President Barkley.

The only major effort he made in the fall was his address in Kiel Auditorium in St. Louis on November 4, three days before the election. The crowd kept yelling at him, "Give 'em hell, Harry!" He responded, "All right! I'm doing it." He accused the Republicans of being captives of the special interests and charged isolationist leaders with endangering the progress toward peace that had been made under the bipartisan foreign policy. On the farm issue, he declared, "Any farmer who votes for the Republican Party ought to have his head examined."[4]

The Republicans waged a strong campaign against the Democratic candidates in congressional, state, and local elections, making communism one of their central themes. They charged the Democrats with being soft on communism, appeasers of the Soviet Union, and infiltrated with communist spies, and they declared that such policies as "socialized medicine" and the "socialistic" Brannon farm plan were inspired by Marxists-Leninists-Stalinists in the Democratic ranks. Senator Joseph McCarthy of Wisconsin, one of the leaders in exploiting these themes, made dramatic charges of communist subversion throughout the country. He also raised funds to help Republican candidates in key states. The public—frustrated with inflation, rising taxes, and shortages and alarmed by Korean casualties, strikes and labor unrest, exposures of the connections between crime and politics by Kefauver, charges of corruption reaching to the White House staff, and news during the year of communist espionage against American atomic and military secrets—was looking for scapegoats. Truman and the Democratic Congress were conspicuous targets.[5]

A number of senatorial contests were of vital interest to Truman and proved to be of great significance in later presidential politics. These were in California, Maryland, and Illinois. In California, a young Republican congressman, Richard M. Nixon, was running against a young Democratic congresswoman, Helen Gahagan Douglas, for the Senate seat vacated by Sheridan Downey, a Democrat. Nixon's campaign was spirited and ruthless. He had gained a national reputation as the member of the House Committee on Un-American Activities that had trapped Alger Hiss, a former Department of State official on a perjury charge based on evidence furnished by admitted former Communist Whittaker Chambers to the effect that Hiss had furnished classified State Department documents for transmission to a Soviet agent in the 1930s. The second trial of Hiss for perjury ended in a conviction in 1950. Truman was linked with the case since he had been trapped into agreeing that the proceedings were a "red herring" and Acheson was involved for saying he would not "turn his back" on Hiss, whom he had known for some time.[6] Nixon continued to criticize Truman for his failure to reverse himself on Hiss.[7] In his campaign he attacked Douglas as a communist sympathizer, as being soft on communism, and charged that her votes in Congress were linked with the procommunist votes of Congressman Vito Marcantonio of New York. The strategy was devised by public relations expert Murray Chotiner, who was unscrupulous in his methods.[8]

The gubernatorial race in California was also of significance to Truman in that it marked a changed attitude on the part of Franklin Roosevelt's eldest son, James, the Democratic candidate, who was running against the Republican incumbent, Governor Earl Warren. Young Roosevelt had been active in the preconvention dump-Truman movement of 1948, but Truman's victory had convinced him of his error, and late in the 1950 campaign he made a desperate appeal for a Truman appearance on his behalf. Truman could not grant it, however, because of the Korean war and other international commitments.[9]

In Ohio, Senator Taft, co-author of the Taft-Hartley labor relations bill, so hated by labor leaders and the leader of the isolationists, was up for reelection. He was the target of an allout effort by organized labor and its political arms. Because Taft was one of the outstanding critics of the Acheson-Truman foreign policies, the Democratic party opposed him vigorously. Taft blamed the Democrats for the "loss of China" and the Korean war. Unfortunately for the Democrats, their candidate, Joe Ferguson, was not a strong contender against Taft. During the campaign, Taft said that the entire campaign against him had been blueprinted by convicted Communist Gus Hall.[10]

In Maryland, the Democratic incumbent, Senator Millard E. Tydings, was up for reelection. As the first major conservative leader to denounce Senator Joseph McCarthy of Wisconsin on the ground that McCarthy's allegations of communist leanings on the part of certain officials were unfounded, Tydings himself was subjected to pitiless misrepresentations. McCarthy and his associates raised a huge campaign fund from sources outside the state, which was used by a Chicago public relations man, Joe M. Jonkel, to publicize the relatively unknown Republican candidate, John Marshall Butler, and to discredit Tydings as head of the Senate investigating committee. Using all media, the McCarthyites accused Tydings of "whitewashing" the State Department officials charged by McCarthy with being Communists. A fake composite picture of Tydings and Earl Browder, a prominent Communist, was distributed in order to smear the senator.[11] After a Senate investigation of the campaign, Jonkel was indicted and fined for conducting a campaign without being a resident of the state and for violating the Maryland election laws regarding the reporting of campaign contributions and expenditures on time. Tydings relied upon a traditional party machine, while Jonkel was adroit in using mass media and appealing to prejudices. The report of the Subcommittee on Privileges and Elections of the Senate Rules and Administration Committee said: "The Maryland campaign was not just another campaign. It brought into sharp focus certain campaign tactics and practices that can best be characterized as destructive of fundamental American principles.'' It recommended that for future elections, rules be devised to prevent the use of defamatory literature and misleading composite pictures or voice recordings.[12] By the time of the Watergate investigations in 1972, this had not been done.

The Illinois senatorial campaign involved the Democratic majority leader, Senator Scott W. Lucas, who was challenged by former Congressman Everett McKinley Dirksen, who campaigned as a conservative and an isolationist. President Truman praised Lucas in his Jefferson Jubilee address, but his exacting obligations in Washington after the Korean war prevented him from doing more. Dirksen welcomed the support of Senator McCarthy and the Truman-hating *Chicago Tribune*, so the battle was clearly joined.[13]

The election was a setback for the Democrats. They suffered a loss of five seats in the Senate. Nixon won over Douglas in California by 680,947, Butler defeated Tydings in Maryland by 43,000, Dirksen won over Lucas in Illinois by 294,354. James H. Duff defeated Francis J. Myers in Pennsylvania by 126,324, and Wallace F. Bennett defeated Elbert D. Thomas in Utah by 21,229. The Democrats retained only nominal control of the Senate by two votes. In the House, the Democrats lost 28 seats, and its majority was reduced from 92 to 35. Because most of the southern Democrats were conservatives, there was no Fair Deal majority. Liberals up for election, such as Frank Graham of North Carolina, Claude Pepper of Florida, and Glen Taylor of Idaho, were defeated. [14] Among the explanations for the setbacks were the voters' alarm about communist subversion, their concern about the charges of corruption and cronyism in government, their feelings of uneasiness about the news of Chinese Communists' crossing the Yalu, their fear of a third world war, their resentment at the casualties, inflation, and rising taxes, and their dislike of the growing influence of organized labor.[15]

The 1950 congressional elections were a turning point in Truman's career and in American history. The Republicans failed to gain control of Congress, but they came close. They introduced new campaign methods in California, Ohio, Maryland, North Carolina, Florida, and other parts that some twenty-two years later culminated in the Watergate scandals. These new methods marked the decline of the old-fashioned party machines and the rise of the professional public relations and media experts who were skilled in publicity techniques and did not hesitate to resort to unfair and unprincipled campaign practices. The big Taft victory in Ohio put "Mr. Republican" on the way to his closest bid for the presidency and made him a formidable opponent to the Truman program for the next two and one half years. Dirksen's huge majority in Illinois put him on the road to Senate minority leadership and eliminated Lucas as a presidential contender in

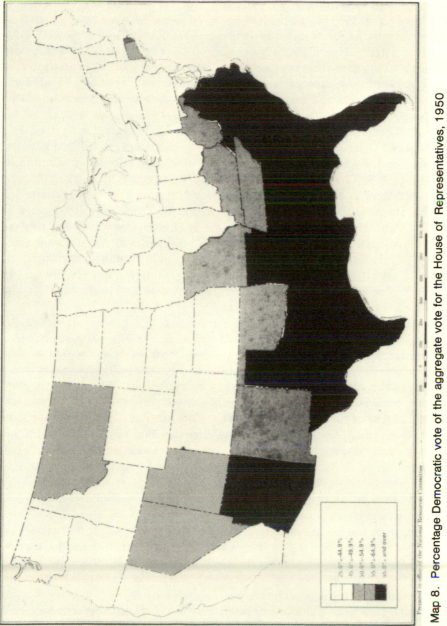

Map 8. Percentage Democratic vote of the aggregate vote for the House of Representatives, 1950

1952. It also paved the way for Lyndon Johnson of Texas to become minority leader in 1953. If Lucas had been reelected, he would have doubtless become the minority leader in 1953 when the Republicans took over Congress. Finally, Nixon's victory put him on his way to the White House. He was a young man from the second largest state in one of the fastest-growing regions with an impeccable anticommunist record; he was a tough campaigner and a prodigious investigator. According to the Republicans, the Democrats needed to be castigated and here was a man to lead in this endeavor. Nixon was to be a scourge to the Democrats during Truman's final two years in the White House. The Republican gains in 1950 paved the way for Eisenhower's victory in 1952. The combination of circumstances that enabled Truman to win in 1948 were fast fading.[16]

Ken Hechler made an analysis of the 1950 elections in which he contended that the results were not as discouraging to the Democrats as appeared at first sight. He pointed out that the loss of House seats was not as large as the average loss of seats by the party in power in midterm elections since 1914. Particularly noteworthy were the losses in the urban areas of Indiana, Ohio, and Illinois. Hechler's optimistic interpretation did not hold up in 1952. Map 8 shows that the Democrats did not do well in the Midwest, the Pacific Coast states, and the Northeast in 1950.[17]

The congressional elections were only one sign of the decline of the popularity of Truman and the Democrats. The public opinion polls also registered a downward trend in the number of voters who thought that Truman was doing a good job and that the Democratic party was taking better care of the interests of the voters than the Republicans. Truman's press blunders, his personal vindictiveness against a music critic who wrote an unfavorable review of his daughter's concert at Constitution Hall, and his apparent slowness in adopting measures to stabilize the economy contributed to his sagging reputation. Moreover, Truman's new speaking style, free and easy, without the use of a written manuscript, led to unfortunate mistakes. Comments on the atom bomb and its possible use in Korea made at his November 30, 1950, press conference led to misunderstandings abroad and created an international crisis.

Foreign newspapers misinterpreted Truman's remarks, and Prime Minister Attlee asked for a conference in Washington to discuss the matter. Truman and Acheson granted this request with no hesitation, but Congress was upset by the possible implications and obligations involved in this meeting. The crisis would have been avoided by more cautiously worded formal statements. The valiant press secretary, Charles Ross, tried to mend the damage, but he died a few days later.[18]

These problems occurred about the time of the Paul Hume affair involving Margaret Truman's debut as a concert singer in Washington. The music critic of the *Washington Post* did not like the concert and said so in his column. When Truman read the article, he wrote a personal denunciation of Hume and mailed it to him personally. Hume published the letter, and Truman was criticized for his intemperate language, his lack of dignity, and his lack of control. A father might have pride in his daughter's career, but this did not justify his lowering the prestige of the presidency by using vulgarity in his attack. Truman should have kept to channels until he was calmer. It is inconceivable that the correct correspondence secretary, Bill Hassett, would have allowed such a letter to go out.[19]

Truman's errors in the formulation and execution of economic and social policies depressed his public standing. The conservative farm bloc would have none of the Brannan plan. Organized labor was disappointed in the failure of the Eighty-first Congress to repeal the Taft-Hartley Act. Black organizations felt betrayed by the lack of progress in civil rights legislation. Veterans and low-income people felt their housing needs were not being met. Everyone to some extent suffered from the ill effects of inflation. The Republicans were shouting again "It's time for a change," as Truman's standing in the polls sank to the low twenties.

chapter 36 | KOREA AND JAPAN, 1950–1952

General Bradley said that General MacArthur's ideas on widening the conflict would involve us "in the wrong war, at the wrong place, at the wrong time and with the wrong enemy."
— U.S. Senate, *Military Situation in the Far East*, 1951

By 1950 a number of premises on which American foreign policy decisions had been made were rudely challenged. Truman and his advisers had assumed that the United States could rely upon its monopoly of atomic weapons to deter the Soviet Union from starting a war.[1] Since Truman had written in May 1948 that excessive military expenditures would endanger the domestic economy, a low budget ceiling was set for conventional military weapons.[2] The air force placed chief reliance upon strategic bombing, so Europe had a high priority because of its air bases. The discovery in September 1949 that the Soviet Union had exploded a nuclear device put an end to the American monopoly of the atom bomb. The victory of the Communists over the Nationalists in China in 1949 also changed the security position of the United States because China now had to be regarded as a possible foe. Secretary of State Marshall assumed in 1948 that the Soviet Union and its satellites were not likely to use open war to achieve their objectives.[3] Secretary of State Acheson assumed in 1950 that in the long run the Soviet Union and China would clash because they had conflicting interests.[4] Related to this was the view that the Truman doctrine should not be applied to China because the country was too vast and American resources were too limited. Therefore the civil war between the Nationalists and Communists had to run its course. The next probable step in this war would be a struggle between the Communists and Nationalists for Formosa. President Truman and Secretary Acheson held the view that the United States should not interfere in this struggle so that it did not become involved in a major Asian war. On January 5, 1950, Truman declared: "The United States will not pursue a course which will lead to involvement in the civil conflict in

China."[5] Secretary Johnson and General MacArthur, on the other hand, favored defending Formosa against a Chinese Communist invasion.

The concept of a limited war had not yet been developed in the United States. Four years later, some theorizing about limited war began. One limit was the nonuse of nuclear weapons. Another was the recognition of sanctuaries that should not be violated.[6] These concepts were utterly incomprehensible to General MacArthur, who had seen the successful use of atom bombs against Japan and who never became reconciled to the restraints on bombing Communist China when its troops were killing American soldiers.

THE KOREAN WAR

Since V-J Day, a Korean crisis had been building up gradually. At Cairo in November 1943, Roosevelt, Churchill, and Chiang Kai-shek had agreed that when Japan was defeated, Korea, which had been controlled by Japan since 1905, would be free and independent.[7] At Teheran a few weeks later, Stalin accepted this position regarding the future of Korea. He confirmed this view at Yalta and in his conversations with Harry Hopkins in 1945. In August 1945, both Ambassadors Pauley and Harriman recommended occupation of Korea by American forces before the Soviet Union made excessive demands.[8] The surrender terms, however, set forth in General Order 1, which the emperor of Japan issued at General MacArthur's instigation to Japanese troops, set the thirty-eighth parallel as an arbitrary dividing line in Korea; north of it the surrender was to be to the Russians and south to the Americans. Truman admitted in his *Memoirs* that when he approved this order, he did not realize its significance.[9] Two months later, reports from Korea indicated that the Russians had made the parallel a rigid boundary and were excluding South Koreans from crossing it, dividing Korea in a way that made both parts economically unstable. The industrial north had complemented the agricultural south. As in East Germany, the Russians proceeded to set up a communist regime with nationalized industries and strict controls.[10] Lieutenant General John R. Hodge, the American commander in Korea, lacked proper instructions and trained occupation forces. He had difficulty with the riots and opposition both from South Korean Communists and from extreme nationalists led by returned exile leader Syngman Rhee. He reported to the Joint Chiefs of Staff in December 1945 that the situation in South Korea was impossible and recommended joint withdrawal of American and Russian forces from the country. At the Moscow conference in December 1945, Secretary Byrnes and Molotov worked out an agreement for a joint commission to assist in formation of a provisional government for all of Korea. This commission was soon stalemated by Soviet demands.[11]

In June 1946 Ambassador Pauley, the presidential representative in reparations matters, reported to Truman on his trip to the Russian zone of Korea. He was convinced that Korea would be the testing ground between the two rival systems of control—that sponsored by the United States and that by the Soviet Union.

In 1947 General Hodge reported to the President on the political unrest in Korea, and another attempt was made to get the Joint Commission to work. When it failed, Truman instructed Secretary Marshall to place the issue before the U.N. General Assembly. The Soviet Union objected to this move and abstained from voting on a motion to establish a U.N. commission on Korea. The motion passed but the commission could hold elections only in South Korea as it was barred from the North by the Soviet commander.

After the establishment of the Republic of Korea (ROK) in the south with U.N. backing and the election of Syngman Rhee as president, in January 1949 the United States formally recognized this regime. The Soviet authorities had supported the proclamation of the Democratic People's Republic of Korea in the north and announced the withdrawal of their troops from North Korea by that time. In March 1949 General MacArthur reported to the National Security Council that American forces could be safely withdrawn because the South Koreans had developed their own security forces. President Truman agreed, and except for a small advisory group, American troops were withdrawn by the end of June. On January 6, 1950, a formal agreement under the National Defense Assistance Act was signed by the United States and the ROK, but congressional delay in passing the appropriation meant that little military supplies were available by June 25, 1950.[12]

President Truman regarded Korea as one of the trouble spots of the world. He did not like the dictatorial, reactionary, and repressive behavior of President Rhee, but he claimed there was no other anticommunist alternative. The National Security Council believed that the North Koreans would use subversion against the ROK rather than open aggression by armed forces.[13] However, in accordance with NSC 68, Truman and his advisers had been planning to build up American armed forces so as to be able to contain communist military advances should they occur in vulnerable places.

On June 24, 1950, when the North Koreans launched their attack on South Korea across the thirty-eighth parallel, Truman was in Independence, Missouri, spending the weekend with his family. Secretary Acheson told him the news over the telephone and suggested that the matter be referred to the U.N. Security Council. Truman agreed at once without asking that the consequences of such action be explored.[14] Eventually the use of the United Nations in defense of South Korea was to prove one of the limiting factors in America's freedom of action. The next day, Truman flew back to Washington, reflecting on the way that the situation was parallel to the events that had brought on World War II. He assembled his advisers, who interpreted the attack as part of a general offensive. In 1947 the Joint Chiefs of Staff had indicated that in a general war situation, Korea was not of strategic importance to the United States. Secretary Acheson had restated this position in his speech before the National Press Club on January 12, 1950, in which, however, he indicated that the defense of the ROK would be the responsibility of the United Nations.[15] When Truman called his civilian and military advisers together on June 25, the U.N. Security Council had already passed a resolution calling upon the North Korean forces to cease hostilities and pull back behind the thirty-eighth parallel. Truman, who hoped that the United Nations would be an effective organization for the maintenance of peace, had agreed to the presentation of the resolution to the U.N. Security Council.[16] At the time, the delegate of the Soviet Union was not present to veto the resolution, and it passed nine to zero, with Yugoslavia abstaining. The Soviet Union was boycotting the council because the Communist Chinese had not replaced the Nationalist Chinese on it.[17]

The group of advisers who met with Truman on June 25 included: from the State Department, Secretary Acheson, Under Secretary Webb, Assistant Secretaries Hickerson and Rusk, and Ambassador Jessup; from the Department of Defense, Secretary Johnson, Secretary of the Army Pace, Secretary of the Navy Mathews, and Secretary of the Air Force Finletter; and from the Joint Chiefs of Staff, Chairman General Bradley, General Collins of the army, Admiral Sherman of the navy, and General Vandenberg of the air force. Of these Truman relied most heavily on Acheson. Not included was Kennan from the State Department, whose divergent views on many questions were vindicated by later events.[18]

The group had to answer a number of serious questions. Should the United States interfere in a civil war on the Korean penninsula? Should the United States rely upon the United Nations to take a position on the question? Did the Korean crisis warrant any action in the Formosan Straits? In Indochina? In the Philippines? Truman's advisers answered these questions in the affirmative with no discussion of consequences or consideration of alternatives and without reference to the formal machinery of the National Security Council. The Soviet Union was soon to contend that in a civil war, no major power or the United Nations should interfere.[19] As for Formosa, the question was not placed before the United Nations. The United States was acting on its own initiative in reversing its stand on Formosa and in courting an unfavorable reaction by the Communist Chinese. This action was based on the assumption that the invasion of South Korea by the North Koreans was part of a worldwide conspiracy, and it had to be stopped in order to forestall communist armed attacks elsewhere. The domestic political situation in the United States supported this position. Republicans had bitterly criticized the Truman-Acheson China policy and strongly supported Chiang on Formosa.[20] Military considerations were also deemed important.

There was a consensus among Truman's advisers at this first meeting that the action taken by the U.N. Security Council should be strongly supported by the United States. The President agreed.[21] He mentioned the analogies of the League of Nations and the crises of the 1930s where appeasement had led to war. It must not happen again. It was assumed that the Soviet Union had worldwide aggressive intentions and might act the way the Nazis had if it was not stopped. Although there was no proof of direct Soviet involvement in the Korean crisis, it was assumed that the North Koreans were trained, armed, and encouraged by the Soviet Union to make the attack.[22]

Prior to June 25, American foreign and military policies had not been geared for limited warfare. Kennan, however, had vigorously advocated preparations for limited war.[23] American intelligence at the highest levels had not clearly anticipated an armed attack in this location. The South Korean military forces had not been properly trained and equipped to stop the North Koreans, who had been supplied with planes, tanks, and heavy artillery by the Russians. In addition, the American troops in nearby Japan had not been prepared for combat duty, and the United States did not have available a mobile combat force to meet such an emergency.[24]

George Kennan, called back but not consulted at the presidential level, did not regard the crisis as worldwide. He believed that the Soviet Union was alarmed at the American moves toward the negotiation of a separate peace treaty with Japan, to which the Soviet Union would not be a party, and which would be followed by a military alliance that left American troops in Japan. He also questioned the use of the United Nations to meet the crisis.[25]

Khrushchev Remembers states that Stalin and Mao Tse-tung approved the adventure of the North Koreans. The book alleges that the communists miscalculated. The North Koreans mistakenly thought that the South Koreans would rise up and revolt against Rhee; Mao thought that the United States would not interfere; and Stalin thought that the North Koreans were strong enough to win militarily.[26]

At the first conference on the war, Truman expressed the view that the Soviet leaders gambled that the United States would do nothing. He decided that American air and naval forces, staying south of the thirty-eighth parallel, should aid in evacuating Americans from Korea, that ammunition and equipment deemed necessary to prevent loss of the Seoul-Kimpo-Inchon area be sent to Korea, and that the Seventh Fleet be ordered to sail to Sasebo, Japan. These moves were directed primarily toward the safety of

American nationals in Korea. President Truman had decided, however, to take action deemed necessary to support the U.N. resolution. He had inquired on the readiness of the navy, the air force, and the army of occupation in Japan. The admirals and the air force generals argued that their forces would enable the South Koreans to stop the invasion, but the army generals expressed doubt about this, holding that only ground forces could turn back the North Koreans. There were two keys to the decision to back the ROK. One was the resolution adopted by the United Nations. The United States was not acting alone but as part of a world organization designed to maintain peace. The other was the nearness of Japan to Korea and the possibility of using American naval, air, and ground forces stationed nearby.[27]

Truman and his advisers hoped at first that the South Korean forces would be able to check the invaders and throw them back across the thirty-eighth parallel. If this had happened, the incident would soon have been over. Reports available at the time of the first conference indicated that the South Korean forces were holding. The next day, however, the reports were pessimistic. Some revisionist historians present the theory that the collapse and rapid retreat of South Korean troops was deliberately planned by President Rhee and General MacArthur in order to pressure the United States into furnishing men and supplies. But no proof is furnished for these inferences. The picture as presented by dispatches and news accounts is a confused one. Confusion is no proof of conspiracy.[28]

Reports from Rhee and MacArthur received June 26 were dismal. The South Koreans were said to be in headlong flight. MacArthur stated: "South Korean units unable to resist determined Northern offensive. Contributory factor exclusive enemy possession of tanks and fighter planes. South Korean casualties as an index to fighting have not shown adequate resistance capabilities or the will to fight and our estimate is that a complete collapse is imminent."[29]

At the second conference, held on June 26, Secretary Acheson proposed that the navy and air force give full support to the South Korean forces and that such support be limited to the area south of the thirty-eighth parallel. This was an important step beyond the mere evacuation of Americans, but no one seemed to have recommended the use of American combat ground forces at this time. The President and his advisers discussed the probable reaction of Soviet and Chinese communist leaders to the commitment of American naval and air units to the South Korean cause and concluded that it was possible but not probable that they would intervene. President Truman approved Secretary Acheson's recommendation, and orders were issued to American air and naval forces to operate against North Koreans south of the thirty-eighth parallel. He also approved the use of the Seventh Fleet to keep Formosa from military involvement and the furnishing of augmented military assistance to the Philippines and Indochina on the theory that the Communists might increase their efforts in these regions.[30]

On June 27, the U.N. Security Council met again and, in view of the flouting by the North Koreans of the previous decision calling for a cease-fire, in a resolution personally approved by President Truman, recommended that "members of the United Nations furnish such assistance to the Republic of Korea as may be necessary to repel the armed attack and to restore international peace and security in the area." This resolution was passed by a seven to one vote, with two abstentions, thus confirming action already taken by the United States.[31]

The first meeting of the National Security Council on the crisis was held on June 29. President Truman approved its directive, which authorized General MacArthur to extend his air and naval operations to North Korea, to employ army service forces for supply operations, and to commit a limited number of combat troops to protect the evacuation of American citizens. General MacArthur, on his own initiative, had already ordered the air force to attack targets in North Korea.[32] This same meeting considered the Soviet reply to the American note of June 27, which asked for Soviet cooperation in restraining the North Koreans. The Soviet government accused the South Koreans of provoking the incident and held that foreign powers should not interfere in the internal affairs of Korea and that the resolutions of the U.N. Security Council were illegal. Secretary Acheson interpreted the temperate tone of this reply as indicating that the Soviet Union did not want to be directly involved.[33] The Chinese Communists, on the other hand, were blatantly bellicose in their denunciations of the United States. On these developments, the President said, "That means that the Soviets are going to let the Chinese and the North Koreans do their fighting for them."[34]

After a trip to the front on June 28, General MacArthur reported that only the introduction of American ground combat forces could save the situation. His recommendation for the immediate commitment of a regimental combat team in the battle area and the buildup of two divisions for a counteroffensive did not reach Washington until June 30. Upon being informed of the recommendation by Secretary Pace, the President, who had previously hesitated about using American combat ground forces, authorized the regimental combat team immediately, but he deferred his final decision on the two divisions until he had consulted with his advisers. At the meeting of the top State and Defense officials, no objections were raised against the employment of American combat ground forces in Korea. This was a time when the objectives of the fighting should have been clearly defined. If the restoration of the status quo had been declared the limited aim, then later disasters might have been avoided.[35]

Truman and his advisers were faced with the question of whether the commitment of American forces in Korea would require congressional approval. Before Truman met with congressional leaders, Senator Connally advised him that as commander in chief and under the U.N. Charter, he had the right to act without the prior approval of Congress.[36] Republican leaders Taft and Wherry had questioned the President's powers to start a war, however, and had criticized severely the Truman-Acheson foreign policies, demanding the resignation of Secretary Acheson. Truman held meetings with congressional leaders on June 27 and 30. The President followed Senator Lucas's advice and did not ask for a joint resolution supporting his decisions.[37] The senator defended in the Senate the President's constitutional powers to take executive action. Senator Alexander Smith, however, suggested a congressional resolution approving the President's action, which now included the commitment of American ground forces. On July 3 at a conference of Truman's advisers, Senator Lucas, General Bradley, and Secretary Johnson opposed seeking such approval on the ground that it was unnecessary; the vast majority in Congress approved the actions, and a prolonged debate by the irreconcilable minority would be dangerous to national morale and to effective action. In view of subsequent events, the failure to try to secure legislative approval of executive action must be regarded as a mistake. The constitutional issue as to presidential powers was left moot. At this time there was strong support for what had been done. Later, when this support evaporated, the affair was called "Truman's war." At his press conference on June 29, Truman had slipped into a reporter's trap by agreeing that the United Nations was not at war in Korea but was engaged in a "police action."[38] This phrase was to haunt him later when heavy casualty lists came in. The meeting also considered the offer of thirty-three thousand Chinese Nationalist troops by Chiang Kai-shek. At first Truman was inclined to accept it, but he was persuaded not to by Secretary Acheson and the top military men, including General MacArthur. They argued that the presence of Chiang's troops in Korea would increase the probability of Chinese Communist intervention, that these poorly equipped and poorly trained troops were needed more in Formosa, and that the ships and planes needed to transport them could be better used in transporting American troops.[39]

General MacArthur's longstanding belief that the Far East was the most important area for American defense was bound to clash eventually with the Truman-Marshall-Acheson belief in the primacy of Europe. MacArthur had not been back to Washington for many years and was out of touch with the thinking in the Pentagon. Both MacArthur and Truman were stubborn, strong-willed men who believed that their views were right. Surrounded by admiring sychophants, the general had supreme confidence in his own ideas and refused to admit mistakes. He was bound to oppose the Truman-Acheson policy of avoiding heavy commitments in the Far East.[40]

On July 7, the U.N. Security Council authorized the United States to establish a unified command of U.N. forces in Korea. On the following day, General MacArthur was named U.N. commander in Korea.[41] Later events were to show that this appointment was a mistake; the general was no diplomat, he rejected negotiation, he was uncontrollable, and he was insensitive to the role of the President in military and foreign affairs and to the interests of other nations furnishing men and weapons for the command.

Upon the urging of Secretary Acheson, President Truman used the crisis to send a special message to Congress on July 19, followed by a radio and television address to the general public. He asked Congress for a $10 billion supplemental defense fund for Europe and the Far East and requested economic controls.[42]

The first clash between General MacArthur and the President came over the policy toward Formosa. While the Truman administration was trying to minimize its temporary role of defending and restraining Chiang, General MacArthur wanted a stronger pro-Chinese Nationalist policy. To this end, he went to Formosa on July 31 ostensibly to explain why the offer of Chinese Nationalist troops was not accepted but in fact to strengthen his ties with Chiang. This trip was not strictly in accord with his instructions, which urged him not to go there personally at that time. Both generals issued statements that alarmed Washington and allied capitals; they used such phrases as "all people in the Pacific should be free—not slaves" and "victory was assured."[43] Much concerned, Truman sent his special assistant, Averell Harriman, to Tokyo to brief General MacArthur on American foreign policy and the need for allied unity, which might be endangered by too strong support of Chiang. Harriman felt that MacArthur was unconvinced.[44] He was supported in this view by a harsh statement that MacArthur issued afterward virtually accusing his superiors in Washington of appeasement and defeatism. MacArthur's message to the Veterans of Foreign Wars meeting on August 28 was released to the press in advance. Its strong defense of Chiang and its implication that the United States should aid Nationalist control over Formosa were directly contrary to Truman's policies. The President considered relieving MacArthur of his Far East command but decided instead to have him withdraw his message to the VFW. At Secretary Acheson's urging, President Truman made a radio and television report to the American public explaining the limited aims in Korea and trying to reassure the Communist Chinese.[45]

This incident created a crisis with Defense Secretary Johnson, who was at first hesitant about transmitting the withdrawal order to MacArthur. For Truman, this was the last straw in a series of events involving his secretary of defense who had been feuding with Acheson on foreign policy matters, who had been resistant at first to NSC 68 policies, and who had become very unpopular with Congress and the public because of the army's unpreparedness. Truman demanded and secured Johnson's resignation on September 11. To replace him, the President turned to George C. Marshall, who agreed with the Truman-Acheson policy of placing Europe first.[46]

The next crucial decision grew out of military operations. While American efforts to stem the advance of the North Koreans were feeble at first—the available forces were small and lacked combat training and heavy weapons—a defensive line was established around the port of Pusan by the end of August when more men and supplies were on hand. General MacArthur proposed his bold plan for amphibious landings at Inchon behind the enemy lines on September 15. Truman's military advisers found many things wrong with the plan, but MacArthur was able to convince President Truman and the Joint Chiefs of Staff that he should go ahead. The plan succeeded beyond all expectations. Seoul was recaptured in eleven days. The U.N. forces broke out of the Pusan perimeter and closed the pincers. Only scattered remnants of the enemy forces managed to escape north. This brilliant victory greatly increased MacArthur's prestige and made him more difficult to manage. On September 27 President Truman approved the Joint Chiefs of Staff's instructions for MacArthur to advance north of the thirty-eighth parallel provided there had been "no entry into North Korea by major Soviet or Chinese Communist Forces, no announcement of such intended entry, nor a threat to counter our operations militarily in North Korea," and provided that only South Korean troops entered the provinces bordering the Soviet Union and Manchuria.[47] Since the Soviet delegate had returned to the U.N. Security Council where he could use the veto, it was necessary to use the U.N. General Assembly to secure the U.N. resolution of October 7 recommending that all appropriate steps be taken to ensure conditions of stability throughout Korea. The U.N. troops then crossed the thirty-eighth parallel. If the United States had been content with the original objective of restoring the status quo and not sought unification by force, it could have claimed victory and started negotiations for a cease-fire. The British and George Kennan of the State Department urged this policy, but Secretary Acheson turned it down.[48] George Marshall, who became secretary of defense on September 21, did not take a firm stand on what the crossing of the parallel meant. The Chinese Communists sent a shrill warning on October 3 that they would come to the assistance of the North Koreans if the parallel were crossed by non-Koreans, but this threat was discounted by Truman's top advisers. The President did not realize that he was endangering his European objectives at this point as the new Korean objective led to the intervention of the Communist Chinese. He could have justified MacArthur's moves north on grounds other than unification by force.[49]

President Truman was elated by General MacArthur's success, and he helped build up the latter's reputation by his praise of the victory and his insistence upon an October 15 personal meeting at Wake Island. The place and the circumstances did not add to the President's prestige. Why should he go so far to meet one of his generals? Secretary Acheson was suspicious of such a meeting and would not go along.[50] The President hoped to convince the general that the war was a limited one and that everything should be done to keep the Chinese Communists and the Soviet Union from entering it. But he failed to win over the general, who expressed the view that the Chinese Communists would not come in and that if they did, they would be slaughtered. Peking had already issued many explicit warnings of their intentions to assist the North Koreans, and American intelligence had indicated a concentration of Chinese Communist troops north of Korea. General MacArthur and his staff were guilty of colossal mistakes in interpreting these signs. At fault were the general's belief in his own infallibility, his contempt for the Chinese, and his lack of clear thinking and knowledgeable advisers who could stand up to him.[51] Truman did not help matters by his expression of apparent satisfaction with the outcome of the conference. At San Francisco, he said, "I also felt that there was pressing need to make it perfectly clear—by my talk with General MacArthur—that there is complete unity in the aims and conduct of our foreign policy."[52]

After the Wake Island conference, there were increasing signs of the building up of substantial Communist Chinese forces in North Korea. Prisoners captured on October 26, for example, were identified as Chinese. President Truman asked the Joint Chiefs of Staff to evaluate the situation. On November 4, General MacArthur still discounted the possibility of Chinese Communist intervention, but on November 6 he announced that he faced a new and fresh army, and he ordered a bombing mission to destroy bridges over the Yalu River in spite of his instructions not to invade the air space of Manchuria or Siberia. At this point the Chinese Communist forces broke contact with the U.N. forces pending possible "high level diplomatic moves." The British were anxious to start negotiations. Attempts by the United Nations, Acheson, and Truman to reassure the Chinese Communists that their territory was not in danger were failures. The meeting of the National Security Council on November 9 was the last opportunity Truman's advisers had to prevent the impending disaster by changing General MacArthur's directive to clear Korea and by attempting to start negotiations. Secretary Acheson later admitted that at this crucial moment he failed to serve Truman properly. Along with the President's other advisers, civilian and military, he later agreed that General MacArthur's instructions should have been changed and some real offer made to the Communist Chinese.[53] No one was willing to take the initiative, however. Secretary of Defense Marshall noted that the widely dispersed and thinly spread U.N. forces were running great risks, but neither he nor the Joint Chiefs of Staff were willing to overrule the theater commander. President Truman believed that he should back the general in the field. Secretary Acheson persuaded the British to hold up seeking a cease-fire resolution at the United Nations, and General MacArthur went ahead with his offensive on November 24.[34]

Although a Central Intelligence Agency summary made available on November 24 indicated that the Chinese possessed sufficient strength to force a withdrawal of U.N. forces, General MacArthur, in violation of his instructions regarding the use of non-Korean forces and of advances in the face of Chinese Communist intervention, pushed toward the Yalu with the Americans in front. Within four days, a strong Chinese counterattack had thrown the U.N. forces into confusion and panic. The United States and the United Nations suffered a disastrous defeat at the hands of a poorly equipped but numerous and well-led enemy. The optimism of MacArthur's earlier dispatches was now replaced by deep gloom and despair. His offensive to "end the war and bring the troops home by Christmas" had turned into "an entirely new war." He threatened complete disaster for his troops if the restrictions on retaliation against the Chinese on their home grounds were not lifted. He was a defeatist regarding the capability of his present forces of holding a defensive line near the thirty-eighth parallel. Secretary Acheson had completely lost confidence in MacArthur's judgment.[55]

The new problems did not cause Truman to lose his optimism and his self-confidence. He had no regrets, nor did he feel any sense of guilt regarding his Korean decisions. He had been misled by General MacArthur regarding Communist China's intentions and capabilities. He did not blame himself but strove calmly to solve the next problem. The war did not become his personal crusade, and he was willing to cut his losses.[56]

Truman and his advisers held many anxious conferences regarding the new crises. They argued that the kind of escalation that MacArthur was advocating might bring in the Soviet Union and lead to a world war, so they refused to accept his plans, directing him to make do with what he had. This order led MacArthur to desperate recriminations, trying to justify his actions and to place the blame on Washington for his defeat.

The other countries that had supported the stand to resist the aggression of the North Koreans were greatly alarmed. They did not want to become involved in a war with Communist China that might spread, and they thought that the United States might neglect its interest in Europe. President Truman made matters worse by his unrehearsed remarks about the possible use of the atom bomb in his press conference of November 30. When asked whether there was active consideration of the use of the atom bomb, he responded, "There has always been active consideration of its use." The press treated this offhand remark to mean that its use had been authorized and that Truman was leaving the final decision on how it would be used to General MacArthur. A subsequent White House press release tried to make it clear that only the President had the final decision and had given no authorization for its use in Korea.[57]

Prime Minister Attlee sought a conference with President Truman in early December. He was alarmed by the latter's press comments on the atom bomb, and he faced dissensions in his own party, which greatly distrusted General MacArthur's rashness and independence. The British sought a cease-fire in Korea at almost any price, including giving in on both Formosa and the Chinese seat in the United Nations, but Truman refused to negotiate on these terms. Acheson, advised by Kennan and Bohlen, insisted that the time was unfavorable for negotiations and convinced the British that fighting had to continue until the U.N. forces were in a stronger position. The final communique expressed agreement on resistance against aggression in the Far East, disagreement on recognition of the Chinese Communist government, and agreement on need to strengthen the Atlantic community.[58]

In order to justify his reverses and to bring pressure on Washington to accept his plans, General MacArthur engaged in a vigorous verbal barrage against his critics. His releases to the press charged that his setbacks were due to "extraordinary inhibitions . . . without precedent in military history." His reversal was a "tactical withdrawal" done "in a superior manner." He refused to accept any blame for what had happened and claimed that he would have won except for the fact that he was not allowed to have his way. Truman was upset by these public charges. In his *Memoirs* he wrote that he should have relieved MacArthur immediately but did not because he did not believe in going back on people when luck was against them. Instead he had the Joint Chiefs of Staff issue on December 5 an order that "no speech, press release, or other public statement concerning foreign policy should be released until it has received clearance from the Department of State." Although this order was a general one, it was aimed at MacArthur. His violation of it led to his dismissal.[59]

General MacArthur was quiet for a while, but his cause had been strengthened by Republican victories in the 1950 elections and was taken up by the Republicans in Congress led by Senator Robert Taft, who, upon the illness of Senator Vandenberg, became a leading spokesman of his party on foreign as well as domestic policies. President Truman used the Korean crisis as an occasion to request greatly increased defense expenditures, asking for approximately $50 billion for worldwide strategic plans, and he also declared a national emergency in order to bring about partial mobilization. These actions produced a large-scale debate on foreign policy. The Republicans attacked the limitations imposed upon General MacArthur and at the same time objected to the sending of four additional divisions to Europe. They demanded Secretary Acheson's dismissal, but President Truman stood firmly behind his secretary of state.[60]

When the Chinese Communists entered the Korean war, many of the nations that had supported the war against the North Koreans now sought an end to the hostilities because they did not want a general Far Eastern war. General MacArthur urged defiance of these nations and sought an allout war against the Chinese communists. Truman and his Washington advisers, however, wanted to preserve the cooperation of these nations, especially those in Europe. A bloc of Asian and Arab nations put through the U.N. Assembly a resolution establishing a three-man group to seek a cease-fire. The proposal of this group for a demilitarized zone north from the thirty-eighth parallel was rejected by Peking on December 21.[61]

In the meantime the military situation of the U.N. forces was improving. While General MacArthur had insisted in ever-more emphatic and dogmatic terms that there was no alternative between withdrawal and his allout war plans, General Walton Walker told General Collins early in December that he was confident he could defend most of South Korea. After General Walker was killed in a jeep accident, General Matthew B. Ridgway replaced him on December 26. Within a month, it was clear that what MacArthur said was impossible was being accomplished. General Ridgway bolstered the morale of the U.N. forces and led them on successful offensives that cost the Chinese heavily in casualties and helped restore the prestige of American military leadership.[62]

When the Joint Chiefs of Staff directed General MacArthur on January 9, 1951, to defend successive positions in Korea inflicting the maximum damage on the enemy, he replied that he had insufficient strength to hold a position in Korea. President Truman sent him a long message explaining why successful resistance in Korea was so essential to American foreign policy. On January 25, General Ridgway demonstrated that MacArthur was wrong in his estimate. The U.N. forces moved again toward the thirty-eighth parallel.[63]

During January, the negotiating team of the U.N. Assembly continued to seek a cease-fire. A proposal made on January 11 included a cease-fire prior to negotiations, the withdrawal of all non-Korean forces, steps toward a unified, independent, and democratic Korea, and the establishment of a body composed of British, American, Soviet, and Chinese Communist representatives to consider Formosa and the representation of China in the United Nations. Secretary Acheson, with Truman's approval, made the agonizing decision of supporting this resolution, an action that brought down upon him and the administration bitter criticism in Congress and the press. Peking, however, rejected the proposal, refusing to accept a cease-fire before negotiations. The United States then sought a resolution declaring Communist China an aggressor. It succeeded on February 1 in getting the General Assembly to pass a compromise resolution that condemned Chinese aggression but contained no specific sanctions against it.[64]

General MacArthur continued to explore ways of carrying out his ambition to win the war. According to General Whitney, he proposed a new plan that would close the enemy's lines of supply and communication by sowing a "defensive field of radioactive wastes" across northern Korea and by amphibious landings using new American divisions and troops from Formosa. Although General MacArthur later denied that he had recommended the use of the atom bomb, in his *Reminiscences* he mentions the plan for the radioactive wastes.[65]

General MacArthur was not satisfied with General Ridgway's recapture of most of South Korea. He called it an "accordion war" and on March 7 threatened a "military stalemate" unless certain "vital decisions" regarding Communist China were made. He was continuing his attack on the limitations on his freedom of counteroffensive action.[66]

The success of General Ridgway in pushing back to the thirty-eighth parallel led President Truman and his advisers to reexplore the possibilities of a cease-fire and the restoration of the status quo. On March 19 the President's advisers held a meeting to consider a State Department draft of a statement to be made by the President indicating, in diplomatic terms without threats or recriminations, that the United Nations was ready to discuss conditions of settlement in Korea. They were willing since they had already achieved the objective of repelling North Korean and Chinese Communist aggression against the South Korean Republic. General MacArthur was sent a copy of the draft and was asked whether he would need any particular authority to provide for the security of his troops and to maintain contact with the enemy. He replied that the current directive covered the situation quite well, but he asked that no additional restrictions be placed on his command. The prepared draft for the President was then submitted to the allied nations that had troops in Korea since their approval was being sought.[67]

General MacArthur, pursuing his own course of self-justification, sabotaged the plans of the Truman administration for negotiations at this time by issuing his own unauthorized and bombastic statement on March 24 that glorified his own achievements, which he referred to as "brilliant," and downgraded the "exaggerated and vaunted military power of Red China." He included an implied ultimatum in these words: "The enemy, therefore, must by now be painfully aware that a decision of the United Nations to depart from its tolerant effort to contain the war to the area of Korea, through an expansion of our military operations to its coastal areas and interior bases, would doom Red China to the risk of imminent military collapse." The general offered to confer in the field with the communist commander-in-chief at any time to find any military means to prevent further bloodshed. The tone of his statement was so different from that of the proposed presidential note that the allied governments were alarmed and confused about American foreign policy.[68] According to General Whitney, General MacArthur's statement thwarted a policy of appeasement that proposed giving Formosa and a seat on the U.N. Security Council to the Communist Chinese. The Senate hearings failed to reveal any such plot, however. While President Truman, Secretary Acheson, the service secretaries, and the Joint Chiefs of Staff regarded MacArthur as insubordinate, the general himself denied that he had disobeyed any orders.[69]

Truman was greatly upset and angered by this MacArthur "ultimatum." On March 24 he sent a warning directing the attention of the general to the December 5 order, hoping to prevent any further unauthorized statements. Apparently, the December 5 order was so general and its enforcement had been so lenient that MacArthur thought he could ignore it. The President in his *Memoirs* stated that he had already decided to relieve the general of his command because he could no longer tolerate the insubordination. He did not at this point, however, make known his decision because he wanted to get the firm backing of his advisers. His attempts to get the general to accept the idea of limited war and to withhold his overt criticisms of American foreign policy had failed. With his fondness for historical analogies, Truman reflected on the similarities between his situation and that of Lincoln in relations with General McClellan. Like Lincoln, he had been patient but finally felt compelled to relieve his top field commander. Some journalists thought that Truman did not have the courage to dismiss the distinguished MacArthur and face the outrage that would follow, but they miscalculated.[70]

The MacArthur controversy reached a climax on April 5 when House Minority Leader Joseph W. Martin released MacArthur's letter to him dated March 20 in which the administration's policy of limited war in Asia, especially the restraints on the use of Chinese Nationalist troops, was criticized. MacArthur concluded:

It seems strangely difficult for some to realize that here in Asia is where Communist conspirators have elected to make their play for global conquest, and that we have joined the issue thus raised on battlefield; that here we fight Europe's war with arms while the diplomats there still fight it with words; that if we lose the war to Communism in Asia the fall of Europe is inevitable, win it and Europe most probably would avoid war and yet preserve freedom. As you point out, we must win. There is no substitute for victory.[71]

Truman regarded this letter as a clear act of insubordination even though it was written prior to his March 24 warning to MacArthur. He conferred with Acheson, Marshall, Bradley, and Harriman several times. While Marshall hesitated at first to recommend drastic action, after he had read the exchanges with MacArthur over two years, he agreed with the rest that MacArthur had to be relieved. The Joint Chiefs of Staff concurred. General Bradley prepared the orders relieving General MacArthur of all of his commands—the American command in the Far East, the allied command in Japan, and the U.N. command in Korea.[72]

President Truman's dismissal of General MacArthur and the appointment of General Ridgway in his place were rougher than he intended them to be. He wanted the orders to be presented by Secretary of the Army Pace who was in Korea, but Pace could not be located, and Press Secretary Short, fearful of a news leak, sent the orders directly to Tokyo. Truman was afraid that MacArthur would resign before he had a chance to dismiss him. The precipitous character of the proceedings left no opportunity for the usual amenities, such as the ceremonies for the change of command, which added to the outcry against Truman's action.[73]

President Truman thought that his constitutional position as the nation's spokesman on foreign policy and as commander in chief of the military was at stake in his controversy with General MacArthur, and he tried to convince Congress and the public of this stance. He issued to the press the announcement of General MacArthur's relief, the order of December 5, the notification to MacArthur of the proposed presidential statement on negotiations, the reminder of March 24, and the exchanges between MacArthur and Congressman Martin. On April 11, he made a radio address explaining what the American objectives in Korea were and why he could not allow the Korean affair to become a full-scale war. MacArthur was not in sympathy with the decision to try to limit the war in Korea.[74]

The MacArthur dismissal polarized views regarding the general and regarding American Korean policies. Some newspapers called him the greatest living soldier, a martyred statesman, a national hero; others referred to him as a narrow-minded, egotistic, flamboyant, arrogant militarist who refused to recognize the limits of his power and responsibilities. While most of those who followed the events closely agreed that he had stepped beyond the bounds of his authority, there was a general feeling that it was a great tragedy to end a distinguished military career in this humiliating fashion. President Truman was denounced for his handling of the dismissal and was compared unfavorably with the general. A World War I captain had crossed swords with one of America's most celebrated generals.[75]

General MacArthur was now free to advocate his antiadministration policies from any forum he could obtain. In an address before Congress and in speeches around the country, he denied that he had been insubordinate and proclaimed that Communist China, not the Soviet Union, was the main enemy, that Europe should not have any special place in American strategy, that allies were not necessary, and that limited war was a species of appeasement. These were policies held by many prominent Republicans such as Taft, Wherry, Martin, and McCarthy, who continued to heap abuse upon Truman and Acheson, including a demand for impeachment. MacArthur's return was marked by great emotionalism, huge demonstrations, and burnings of Truman in effigy. The public was dismayed at a war that promised no victory, at the casualty lists, at the stepping up of the draft, at inflation, and at the imposition of controls, and they made Truman the scapegoat for their frustrations. MacArthur, whose reputation had been tarnished by his defeat in December by the Communist Chinese, was now a hero in the eyes of many. People failed to see that his policies calling for the escalation of the war would have made conditions worse. The paradox of MacArthur's bizarre popularity can be explained partially in terms of the national fear, which Senator Joseph McCarthy of Wisconsin succeeded in exploiting, that Communists were penetrating American government. It may also be understood as a reaction against the policy of containment, which had not worked well in the Far East and which, even in Europe, was contrary to American traditions of no entangling alliances.[76]

Senator Tom T. Connally told Truman, "National sympathy will be on MacArthur's side at first, even though his proposals would have plunged us headlong into World War III. After a while, however, national interest in the General will pall and the affair will blow over." This is what happened, but Truman had to pay for it in terms of his power, prestige, and influence in domestic affairs.[77]

The Republicans wanted open hearings on the MacArthur controversy regardless of what might be revealed to America's enemies in the communist bloc, but Senator Connally won for closed hearings with the daily release of unclassified material, a step that deprived the eloquent MacArthur of his platform. Two months of voluminous testimony amounting to more than two million words bored the public. MacArthur repeated all of his arguments against limited war and against a strategy that placed Europe first. The top officials of the Departments of State and Defense refuted MacArthur's claims and upheld the President.[78]

President Truman relied upon Senator Richard B. Russell of Georgia to keep the hearings in balance. The senator was chairman of the Committee on Armed Services and the Committee on Foreign Relations and saw to it that everyone's case was fairly treated. The Joint Chiefs contradicted MacArthur's testimony. The hearings were educational but costly to American foreign policy since they deprived Truman of the threat he might have made to expand the war. It thus reassured the enemy that he would not expand the war.[79]

President Truman was used to vacillations in his popularity, and he came valiantly to the defense of Secretary Acheson, who was also under violent attack. He was confident that his actions would be justified. The widely publicized hearings furnished the forum for his defense. It was surprising that the Republican senators failed to uphold the fundamental principle of the American Constitution that the civilian authorities were superior to the military. On the other hand, the top military men contradicted MacArthur's testimony that he had not been insubordinate. MacArthur, long absent from Washington, was completely out of touch with American military and political policies. The Chiefs of Staff insisted that the plans that MacArthur advocated were basically wrong. They held that blockading the whole Chinese coast and bombing Chinese bases would not end the war as soon as MacArthur claimed. Instead these actions might bring on a world war. The United States could not afford to alienate its allies, who were so essential to the defense of Europe.[80]

Some indication of the influence of the hearings on public opinion is to be found in the Gallup poll on the Truman-MacArthur controversy. Immediately after the dismissal, Truman's popularity dropped to 24 percent, but it rose to 31 percent a few weeks after the Senate hearings ended on June 25. This was still a low level of popular support and indicated that Truman had failed to explain the Korean crisis to the satisfaction of many.[81]

General James Van Fleet, who was appointed as a commander of the Eighth Army when General Ridgway replaced General MacArthur, dealt the Chinese and North Korean forces a stunning defeat in June 1951, thus removing the sting of earlier U.N. defeat and inflicting enormous casualties upon the Communists. Van Fleet proposed a combined amphibious and land operation toward Wonson, which he claimed would complete the rout, but the Joint Chiefs rejected the plan. Thus was lost a prime opportunity to destroy the communist forces and end the war.[82]

Truman and Acheson failed to take advantage of the military situation and revised their war aims (uniting Korea by force and destroying the enemy's potential was no longer an objective), and they sought to stop the fighting, giving the Communists time to regroup their forces. Acheson recalled George Kennan and had him sound out Soviet Ambassador Jacob Malik secretly on the possibilities of peace negotiations. The response was favorable, and on June 13 Malik appealed to the contending parties to start armistice negotiations. General Ridgway radioed an offer to negotiate with the Chinese and North Koreans, and it was accepted.[83]

The negotiations were long, tedious, frustrating, and exasperating. The Communists displayed extraordinary arrogance. Intermittent fighting continued during the Truman administration. The exchange of prisoners of war proved to be a stumbling block. Not all of the Chinese and North Korean prisoners indicated a wish to return to their homelands, and Truman did not want to force them to do so. Consequently a deadlock ensued on this issue, and the armistice was stalled. The mounting U.N. casualty lists (more than twelve thousand deaths in the two years) were not understood, and the undeclared war became unpopular. In addition to the shock resulting from the dead, wounded, and missing in action, there were the many domestic dislocations—a greatly increased national budget, higher taxes, inflation, and labor disturbances.[84]

The Korean war was a disaster for all concerned, especially for the

Koreans whose country was ravaged and population decimated. Could President Truman have avoided this war? Should Acheson have indicated in early 1950 that Korea was not strategic? Could Truman have prevented the escalation of the war? Did he and Acheson make full use of the opportunities for negotiation? Did they take advantage of the military situation in June 1951? Could Truman have lessened the damage the war did to his prestige, his foreign policy, and the fortunes of his party?

Truman and Acheson might have made clearer before June 25 that North Korean aggression would be firmly met. Truman might have changed his ideas on the need for economy in the defense budget sooner than he did. American armed forces were poorly prepared for the emergency. Greater speed could have been shown in getting authorized foreign aid to South Korea before June 1950. The Korean decisions were made in a hurry before there was time for opposing views to develop. Truman and his advisers did not explore carefully the possible consequences of different courses of action. Acheson should have listened to George Kennan's advice regarding the dangers of crossing the thirty-eighth parallel. Truman should have tried to obtain congressional approval of his actions in Korea at the beginning when the war was popular. General MacArthur should never have been made U.N. commander, and he should have been relieved—or at least curbed—sooner. His orders should have been changed on November 9, 1950, so as to eliminate the conquest of North Korea as an objective. Truman did not deliberately plan a confrontation with the Communist Chinese. In fact, he tried to avoid it, but he was caught by MacArthur's bad advice and by Acheson's inflexibility regarding negotiations. In June 1951 Truman and his advisers failed to take advantage of the demoralizing defeat the communists had suffered and gave them an opportunity to recover.

By means of the Korean war, Truman taught the communist bloc nations some hard lessons. The North Koreans, with the aid of Soviet weapons and Chinese Communist intervention, were not able to conquer South Korea. The Communists suffered far heavier casualties than did the U.N. forces. As for the Soviet Union, its relations with Communist China and North Korea were strained because of the inadequate aid it gave. Truman used the Korean crisis to build up European defenses, the last thing that Stalin wanted to happen.

Truman was a firm believer in the United Nations. Did he strengthen it by enlisting its support on behalf of the South Koreans? He took advantage of a peculiar situation, the absence of the Soviet delegate, which is not likely to happen again. If he had stopped at the thirty-eighth parallel, it would have been a victory for the United Nations. However, Truman and Acheson could not convince the United Nations that Communist China should be attacked, and most of the nations that had originally supported the Korean war backed away when the Chinese Communists entered in force. The result was that the United States found itself fighting mostly alone with allies that were seeking a way out. The U.N. participation in the Korean war took on too much the appearance of an American anticommunist crusade.

The long-range consequences of the Korean war are still in the process of being assessed. It is not likely that American troops will remain in South Korea indefinitely. The fears expressed at the time of a worldwide conflagration did not materialize. The changes in American Formosa policy led to the unrealistic stand toward Communist China for two decades. There were the beginnings of an Indochina policy that later led to war.

In the Korean crisis, Truman made many mistakes, but he showed calmness in not panicking at reverses, courage in dismissing MacArthur, wisdom in upholding the constitutional principle of the superiority of the civilian authorities over the military, and persistence in adhering to his main foreign policies, which were oriented toward Europe and toward avoiding another world war.

JAPAN

President Truman's experience with the Russians at Potsdam convinced him that it would be folly to share with the Soviet Union responsibility for the occupation of the Japanese islands. Once in position as in the Eastern European countries, Stalin and his cohorts did not let go, and they consolidated their power. In General MacArthur, Truman had a useful instrument with which to carry out a policy of sole American responsibility for the occupation of Japan. The imperious general did not like interference from the outside from any source in carrying out duties given to him. The Russians were frustrated in their efforts to gain a foothold in Japan. The Allied Council for Japan could not impose its will upon MacArthur. Blocked at every turn in their attempts to influence the occupation policies directly, the Russians had to fall back on propaganda, subversion, penetration of the Japanese labor movement, and the strengthening of the Japanese Communist party with its journals and youth organizations.

At the London conference of foreign ministers in September 1945 and later at a Moscow conference, the Russians and the Americans could not find a satisfactory formula for reconciling their interests in Japan. Meanwhile in Japan itself, General MacArthur was building up a successful regime. The Japanese, who had been fierce warriors before their defeat, proved to be cooperative under American leadership, which was forgiving, benign, and generous. In its peacetime assignment, the Supreme Command Allied Powers tried to win the confidence of the Japanese leaders and to rebuild the Japanese economy. President Truman supported these policies.

In 1947 the Department of State began work on a draft treaty of peace with Japan. The earlier versions were draconian in character, but General MacArthur differed with this approach and urged that a lenient peace be concluded as quickly as possible in order to relieve the United States of occupation costs. He felt that the demilitarization of Japan had been accomplished. It was soon apparent that the Soviet Union would not agree to the peace terms that the Americans were proposing.[85]

Secretary Acheson described the problem of preparing a Japanese peace treaty:

In planning content and method, four groups had to be reckoned with: the Communists, the Pentagon, our allies, and the former enemy. Of these, the Communists gave the least trouble. Their opposition to any tenable idea was predictable and irreconcilable. It could only be ignored. The most stubborn and protracted opposition to a peace treaty came from the Pentagon.[86]

The Pentagon wanted to prolong the occupation in order to keep unrestricted control of bases on Japanese territory. As a consultant to the State Department on Asian affairs, John Foster Dulles sought a briefing on the plans for a Japanese peace treaty. At the end of the meeting, he said, "You'll never get anything done unless you select someone in whom you have confidence, give him a job to do, and then hold him to results." Acheson was impressed with the comment and gave him the job. First, however, Truman's opposition to Dulles had to be overcome. Truman resented Dulles's bringing foreign policy into his 1949 campaign for the Senate, and he told Acheson that he would never appoint Dulles to any office again. But Acheson persisted and overcame Truman's objection. In a formal announcement on May 18, 1950, the President assigned Dulles to work on the treaty. Drawing upon a National Security Council paper approved by President Truman in November 1948, Dulles prepared a memorandum of his own that contended that any attempt to impose vengeful terms would be self-defeating and that the cold war made it necessary to align Japan with the free nations.[87]

Dulles's assignment brought him into the picture shortly before the beginning of the Korean war. In fact, he was in Korea when the hostilities started, and he sent his own reports back to Washington. He was aware of the seriousness of the situation before MacArthur was. The Korean war increased the urgency of a Japanese peace treaty. Dulles worked tirelessly and with great skill in negotiating terms acceptable to the Japanese and to the many allies, who had different ideas about war damages, reparations, the postwar economic position of Japan, and the extent of Japanese demilitarization. At the time of the dismissal of General MacArthur, President Truman summoned Dulles to the White House and asked him to go at once to Tokyo and reassure the Japanese that the departure of MacArthur would not mean any change in American plans regarding the treaty. In each of allied capitals, Dulles patiently ironed out the various differences.[88]

Truman elevated Dulles from consultant to ambassador in 1951 and elaborated his instructions. He was to go ahead without waiting for the end of the Korean war and was to indicate that the United States was willing to conclude mutual security treaties with Japan, the Philippines, Australia, New Zealand, "and perhaps Indonesia." In the battle with the Pentagon, Truman strongly backed Dulles and Acheson, and the objections of the military were overruled.

A conference to sign the Anglo-American draft peace treaty was set for September 4, 1951. The invitation to the 50 nations concerned stated that the sole purpose of the conference was to sign the Anglo-American draft in the form presented. No amendments would be allowed. Acheson wrote, "Never was so good a treaty so little loved by so many of its participants."[89] The Soviet Union sent delegates for the purpose of obstruction but they never solved the problem of the rules of procedure, and they left without signing. At a meeting in the White House on October 3, Truman extended his warm congratulation to Dulles for the work he had done in securing the treaty.[90]

Japan and Korea had been tied together by the proximity of the islands to the peninsula. Now Japan and part of Korea were under the American international security system for the Far East. Before World War II, China had been the center of America's policy in the Pacific. Now it was Japan, whose industrial strength was soon to become one of the principal features of the region.

chapter 37

MILITARY, ECONOMIC
AND SOCIAL
PROBLEMS,1951–1952

During the last two years of his presidency, Truman was faced with the problem of how to reconcile the conflicting goals of mobilization and economic stabilization. The Korean war was stalemated and was not demanding the scale of defense spending that Bernard Baruch had envisaged when he pressured Congress for controls. Defense expenditures rose from $20 billion to $50 billion during the period, but this was still only 15 percent of the gross national product as compared with defense spending of about one half of the gross national product at the peak of World War II.[1] On the guns versus butter issue, it was clear that the Americans would expect both. Much to the delight of the industrial-military complex, the fears of overstraining the economy were proving to be unfounded. The Office of Defense Mobilization did little to alarm the largest corporations. On the stabilization front, Truman faced a recalcitrant Congress, a critical business community, restless labor, farmers alarmed at even small drops in farm prices, and consumers greatly concerned with the continuing rise in prices.[2]

To meet these problems, Truman had a weakened administration. Some of his officials were under fire because of charges of corruption, and McCarthyism was undermining the morale of many public employees. To control the inflation that he thought was coming, the President sought higher taxes and the extension of controls. He did not have a united administration to back him in seeking these controls.

THE EIGHTY-SECOND CONGRESS, FIRST SESSION

In solving his many problems, Truman could hope for little help from the Eighty-second Congress. The overriding concern about the Korean war meant that he could count on congressional support for purely defense measures but not for much else. The key committees were dominated by men who were sympathetic toward the industrial-military complex but not toward the needs of the underprivileged. Although nominally the Democrats were in control of both houses, practical control had passed to the combination in the Senate of 42 Republicans and 22 conservative southern Democrats and a combination in the House of 199 Republicans and 102 southern Democrats. Thus the coalition had about a two-thirds majority in both houses, enough to override Truman's vetoes. Truman realized that he had little chance of getting favorable action on his domestic program, so he was willing to sacrifice some of it in order to obtain support for his foreign and defense policies.[3]

There was a slight change in congressional leadership. Although the House reelected Rayburn as Speaker and McCormack as majority leader and the Senate continued McKellar as president pro tempore, it elected Ernest McFarland to replace Lucas. The new Senate majority leader was not much help to Truman on domestic issues, and he found himself in difficulty with his own constituents in 1952. The Republican minority leaders, Martin in the House and Wherry in the Senate, remained as obstructionist as before.

A bad omen for Truman was the 243 to 180 (Democrats 91 to 137 and Republicans 152 to 42) vote in the House on the first day of the session to restore the power of the Rules Committee to smother bills by refusing to report them out for consideration of the floor. In setting aside the twenty-one-day discharge rule enacted earlier, the conservative combine lost no time in clamping a damper on Truman's domestic legislative plans.

In his annual message to Congress on the state of the union delivered in person on January 8, 1951, President Truman departed radically from the Fair Deal tone of his earlier messages.[4] It was like Franklin Roosevelt's "Mr. Win the War" speech in 1943. Truman concentrated on explaining the significance of the Korean war and the burdens it imposed, the need for implementing the NATO alliance, and the dangers of a Soviet world conquest if drastic steps were not taken to prevent it. As subsequent events were to show, he exaggerated the dangers of war. The speech was couched in lofty patriotic tones, and it urged the congressmen to put their country above partisanship. The recommendations for domestic legislation were all tied to the defense effort. The emphasis was on expansion of production, greater agricultural crops, stable labor-management relations, defense housing, and means for increasing the supply of trained medical personnel. The domestic program was put in the background at the suggestion of Leon Keyserling, chairman of the Council of Economic Advisers. In a qualifying statement made later, Truman insisted that he still supported the Fair Deal and the Democratic platform. He was only setting priorities. It might also be said that he was facing realities.

The President's economic report, a much more elaborate document than the state of the union message, showed clearly the influence of Leon Keyserling. The emphasis was on greater production—industrial and agricultural—the need for increasing defense spending, the requirement of civilian sacrifices, the recruitment of additional manpower for defense industries, the strengthening of health and educational services, and an economic stabilization program to provide for higher taxes, credit controls, and price and wage controls.[5]

The third message, containing the budget requests and the tax estimates, was the most technical. NATO defense requirements and the Korean war had boosted the defense requirements from $12 billion in fiscal year 1950 to $60 billion for fiscal year 1952. It was estimated that unless taxes were substantially increased, there would be a budget deficit of $16.5 billion for fiscal year 1952. Truman said he would shortly transmit recommendations for new revenue legislation in order to help balance the budget. He contended that sacrifices were necessary because the communist attack in Korea had served notice that the Soviet leaders were willing to risk world peace to carry out their ambitions. He defended the increase in military and economic assistance abroad from $4.6 billion in fiscal year 1950 to $10.6 billion in fiscal 1952 on the ground that united efforts were needed to prevent the Soviet rulers from dividing the free nations. Estimates for domestic programs were kept at existing levels or reduced except in the case of those programs needed for increased production.[6]

In carrying out the day-to-day relations with Congress, Truman relied upon the Bureau of the Budget, which, under director Lawton, continued the referral as well as a clearance system in the White House. Counsel Charles S. Murphy, in addition to drafting messages, kept in touch with the bureau, the President, and Congress on legislative matters.

The new economic stabilizer, Eric Johnston, a businessman who replaced Valentine, announced price stabilizer DiSalle's price-wage freeze on January 26, 1951, which proved to be unpopular with both organized labor and farmers. Consumers also complained that high prices were not rolled back. Labor boycotted the whole mobilization program for a period. DiSalle wanted to modify the parity principle for farm products, but Congress refused to do so.[7]

The fear of inflation brought to a head a longstanding dispute between Secretary of the Treasury Snyder and the federal reserve system over the support of government bond prices. Snyder wanted to keep interest rates low, but the board opposed the policy on the ground that it was inflationary. Truman, who backed Snyder, met with the board in January 1951 but got nowhere. He directed Snyder and chairman McCabe to settle their differences. This was done in an accord that eventually gave the board greater powers to put supposed brakes on inflation.[8]

As he had promised, President Truman sent a special message to Congress recommending a "pay as we go" tax program on February 2, 1951. He included a request for an immediate increase in the personal income tax, an increase in corporation income taxes, increases in selective excise taxes, and the closing of loopholes in the existing tax laws, such as the undertaxation of the oil and mining industries, the gaps in the estate and gift taxes, the undue preference granted to capital gains, the tax-exempt securities, and the tax status of organizations exempt from paying taxes. But Truman was disappointed in the Revenue Act of 1951 as passed since it provided only for $5.5 billion additional in a full year instead of $10 billion, and it did little to close the loopholes.[9]

The military situation in Korea seemed so desperate in 1951 that Truman did not have great difficulty in getting Congress to grant him the funds and powers he thought he needed to prosecute the war. The civil defense bill, the emergency presidential powers bill, and the mutual security appropriation bill were all passed by voice vote in both houses. The draft extension was passed by an overwhelming vote (339 to 41) in the House. Truman was, however, critical of the inflation control provision of the Defense Production Act amendment, comparing it to "a bulldozer, crashing aimlessly through existing pricing formulas, leaving havoc in its wake." By the fall of 1951 it was clear that the danger of a general war had passed and that the planned high levels of military expenditures would not be needed, so Truman decided to stretch out production and reduce defense estimates.[10]

Labor

In his various messages to Congress, President Truman had failed to come out explicitly for the repeal of the Taft-Hartley Act. Senator Taft's victory in Ohio had made it clear that the public was not hostile to the measure and thought that labor should learn to live with it.

In 1951 and 1952, strikes hit the railway industry, textile mills, copper mines, communications industries, lumber industry, the steel industry, oil companies, coal mines, and construction, involving 5,760,000 workers and 82 million man-days lost, but the percentage of estimated working time involved was less than in 1946. It was 0.23 percent in 1951 and 0.57 in 1952 as compared with 1.43 in 1946. It could hardly be said that Truman had improved his handling of labor disputes. The Taft-Hartley national emergency provisions were invoked in the case of the strikes of coal miners and copper miners. In the strike of railway workers, the government seized control of the companies under the 1916 wartime railroad act in order to settle the strike. A brief walkout of the workers was ended by army pressure, and the unions criticized Truman.[11]

Cartoon by Orr, 1951. Reprinted, courtesy of the *Chicago Tribune*.

By far the most important of the labor disputes from the standpoint of the presidency and Truman's reputation was the steel strike. Truman thought he was taking the steps needed to avoid the strike without encouraging inflationary tendencies. With the demands for steel created by the Korean war and the building up of European defenses ever increasing, Truman regarded a steel strike as a national calamity. With the contracts between the United Steelworkers and the steel companies expiring December 31, 1951, President Truman persuaded the men to continue working without a contract while he referred the dispute to the Wage Stabilization Board.[12] Such was the situation at the end of 1951.

Agriculture

The Korean war brought an end to the legislative consideration of the Brannan plan. As 1951 began, organized labor demanded the deletion of the farm parity provisions of the Defense Production Act, and the farmers opposed price stabilization. Actually, there was little need for price controls because defense spending in the limited war effort did not reach levels to justify them as soon as panic buying subsided. Truman and DiSalle did not note these changes soon enough and still acted as though inflation was imminent. DiSalle sought a freeze of parity, but Brannan argued that the farmers needed parity since the government was allowing cost of living wage increases and higher business profits. Congress agreed with Brannan, and no changes were made in parity.[13]

Both Brannan and DiSalle faced problems with the soaring price of cotton. With a bad crop in 1950 and heavy foreign and domestic demand after the Korean war started, the price of cotton soared from 26.5 cents a pound in January 1950 to 45 cents in January 1951. Brannan tried to impose export restrictions, but the congressmen from the cotton states protested so loudly that he retreated. In March 1951, DiSalle placed a ceiling on raw cotton at 45.39 cents per pound. Senator Burnet R. Maybank of South Carolina called this "the socialization of agriculture" and Congressman John E. Rankin denounced it as "communistic." A showdown never took place, though, because the price of cotton began to sag, and DiSalle suspended the order in May. He had alienated the cotton farmers for nothing. His mistakes reflected upon Truman's standing among farmers.[14]

Beef prices proved to be another stumbling block for Truman and DiSalle. Swollen demand boosted beef prices after the Korean war started. The freeze of January 1951 at the wholesale level did not satisfy consumers, and it was proving disastrous to legitimate slaughterers who were caught with soaring live cattle prices, which they were forbidden to pass on to consumers. Again, DiSalle took bold action and placed a ceiling on live cattle in

May 1951 with a 10 percent rollback. When he threatened additional roll-backs and used slaughtering quotas to combat black marketeering, the problem escalated. With the Defense Production Act expiring, the special-interest-minded congressmen removed the rollback and quota powers. Again, all sides lost. DiSalle lost his controls, Truman's popularity sagged, and overproduction produced a drop in beef prices in November.

In January 1951, Secretary Brannan began a review of department pro-grams bearing on the family farm. His working committee, including his own officials and representatives of all farm organizations and some reli-gious organizations, produced a report, *Farm Family Policy Review*, in July.[15] Shortly before the report was issued, however, the Farm Bureau withdrew and began attacking the project. To Allan Kline of the bureau, it smacked of the Brannan plan, and it challenged his claim to be the true spokesman for farmers. Brannan's grass-roots meetings were attacked and misrepresented. The conservative commercial farms of the bureau won out again.

Civil Rights

The new Democratic majority leader of the Senate, Ernest McFarland of Arizona, had been a strong opponent of FEPC, as had been the majority whip, Senator Lyndon Johnson of Texas, who at the time was hostile to civil rights legislation. In the House the situation was equally dismal as far as minority rights and interests were concerned because of the reversal of the twenty-one-day rule.

President Truman in his state of the union address asserted, "We must assume equal rights and equal opportunities to all our citizens," and in his budget message he recommended FEPC legislation to prevent discrimina-tion in interstate industries "during a period of defense mobilization," but he failed to follow this up with specific bills.[16]

Various civil rights leaders pressured Truman to issue an executive order to take the place of legislative action. On February 2, 1951, he issued execu-tive order 10210, which said, "There shall be no discrimination against any person on the ground of race, creed, color, or national origins, and all con-tracts hereunder shall contain a provision against discrimination." Mindful of the Russell amendment, which forbad funds for any FEPC not author-ized by Congress, Truman left out enforcement provisions.[17] But black leaders were not satisfied and pressed for an FEPC with enforcement powers. Bills for a strong FEPC were introduced in the Senate, but none reached the floor.

Meanwhile, President Truman vetoed a bill that attempted to authorize segregated schools on federal property. In his veto message, he stated:

We have assumed a role of world leadership in seeking to unite people of great cultural and racial diversity for the purpose of resisting aggression, protecting their mutual security and advancing their own economic and political development. We should not impair our moral position by enacting a law that requires a discrimination based on race. Step by step we are discarding old discriminations; we must not adopt new ones.[18]

President Truman issued on December 3, 1951, a new regulation, executive order 10308, establishing the Government Contract Compliance Committee, but this body lacked real authority, and black leaders termed it no "substitute for an FEPC." Southerners were concerned about its political implications.[19]

The implementation of Truman's 1948 executive order on the desegregation of the armed forces was given a great boost by General Ridgway in Korea. The desperate need for replacement troops led the general to make better use of black soldiers under his command. The belief had been widespread among top white officers that black men did not make as good combat troops as did white men. Ridgway demonstrated that when black soldiers were integrated into white units, this was not so. The experience in Korea influenced the integration of blacks in Europe and in other commands.[20]

End-of-Session Events

Economic aid to Europe was cut some $250 million by the conservative alliance in the Senate. The military aid provisions were not challenged.

Truman's domestic legislative proposals in general fared badly in this session. An exception was the $1.6 billion defense housing bill, but the seventy-five thousand new public housing units proposed in the budget were cut to five thousand by the House. The Senate, under urging by Truman in a letter to Senator Burnet R. Maybank, raised the number to fifty thousand, and the House relented.

The first session of the Eighty-second Congress ended without any action on President Truman's Fair Deal proposals, such as national health insurance, aid to education, and increased public health benefits.

THE SECOND SESSION

There were no significant changes in the Congress as it began its second session on January 8, 1952. It was controlled by the same coalition of Republicans and southern Democrats. Counsel Murphy continued his practice of holding sessions on key items with the congressional leaders.

In his annual message to Congress on the state of the union, President

Truman appealed for a bipartisan foreign policy for peace. After Vandenberg died in 1951, bipartisanship became a shambles. Truman felt that he had to insist that the nation faced a "terrible threat of aggression" and that "until the Soviet Union accepts a sound disarmament proposal, . . . we have no choice except to build up our defenses." He stressed the need for allies, indicating that "if the United States had to try to stand alone against a Soviet-dominated world, it would destroy the life we know and the ideals we hold dear." He defended the fighting in Korea on the ground that the "Communist aggression had to be met firmly if freedom was to be preserved in the world."

The President praised the beneficial results achieved in India, Iran, Paraguay, Liberia, and other countries by the technical missions under the point 4 program and requested more funds for this work, especially in the field of agriculture.

With regard to oppressed peoples behind the iron curtain, in spite of long-time opposition within Congress he urged the expansion of the activities of the Voice of America, which brought a message of hope and truth.

On the domestic side, he urged that attention be paid to the defense production program, the support of sound stabilization policies, and the passage of Fair Deal measures that would improve farm production, provide better housing and working conditions for defense workers, and improve education, health, and social security services. He urged the revision of the Taft-Hartley labor law, which even the sponsors admitted needed to be changed. Truman knew that this Congress would not repeal the act. He mildly backed action on civil rights, realizing that the stiff discharge rules left little chance for such legislation to get out of committees.[21]

The President's economic report submitted to Congress on January 16, 1952, provided for the following legislative recommendations: renewal and strengthening of the Defense Production Act, continued economic and military aid to free nations, aid to small business, provision for the St. Lawrence Seaway and other development projects, construction of defense housing, revision of labor-management legislation, revision of agricultural price support legislation, tax rate increases and elimination of tax loopholes, additional powers to the board of governors of the federal reserve system, higher social security benefits, federal aid to education, and federal aid to medical education and local public health services. Truman regarded many of these proposals as guides for future action by his successors.[22]

In his annual budget message to Congress, submitted on January 21, 1952, President Truman repeated his alarm at Soviet intentions: "Eighteen months ago, the unprovoked attack upon the Republic of Korea made it clear that the Kremlin would not hesitate to resort to war in order to gain its ends. In the face of this grim evidence, this nation and the other nations of the free world realized that they must rearm in order to survive."

The new budget called for the largest expenditure for any year since World War II, double the amount before the fighting in Korea but less than had been requested by the military services in their original estimates. More than three-fourths of the expenditures were for national security programs. As Herbert Feis put it, "Not mutual trust, but mutual terror, it was to be." The new requests were directed toward the rearming of Europe, the development of atomic weapons, and for the police action in Korea. The budget defenders insisted that the United States could afford both the needed expenditures for national security and for domestic prosperity. Domestic welfare programs requested were not as large as they might have been without the expanded military budget, but they were still substantial. At the end of his message, Truman stated, "It is my hope . . . that we can some day cast off the heavy burden of armaments and devote our full energies to fighting the only war in which all mankind can be victorious—the war against poverty, disease, and human misery."[23]

Among the special messages that President Truman sent to Congress during this session were those urging action on the St. Lawrence Seaway, the extension and strengthening of the Defense Production Act, reporting on the labor disputes in nonferrous metal industries, the Mutual Security Program, aid for refugees and displaced persons, provisions for voting by members of the armed forces, reorganization plans, a national system of flood disaster insurance, and the steel strike. In addition to special messages, the President sent letters to committee chairmen, to the Speaker, and to the president of the Senate on urgent legislative matters.[24]

Labor

The Wage Stabilization Board that Truman established toward the end of 1951 worked valiantly to come up with a solution for the threatened steel strike. While it was still hearing the case, the President talked the union into postponing the strike twice. Finally a strike was set for April 9, 1952. But on March 20 the board presented recommendations for a settlement. The terms were satisfactory to labor but not to the companies. The President felt that he could not disavow the proposals of the board without wrecking the machinery for wage stabilization.[25]

Director of Defense Mobilization Wilson took personal charge of the crisis. He wanted to make a price concession to the companies sufficiently high to get them to agree to a settlement before the strike deadline. He rushed to Key West where Truman was vacationing and expressed his dislike of "the very unstabilizing effects of the wage settlement." Truman admitted that he "agreed as to a possible necessity of allowing some price increase." Unfortunately, Wilson expressed his distaste for the wage terms in a press conference, thus alienating labor. Then the spokesmen for the steel industry asked for higher prices than Wilson was suggesting and made no promises to settle with the union. Next price director Ellis Arnall won support from Truman for a firmer stand on prices. Wilson resigned on March 29. In accepting Wilson's resignation, Truman expressed the view that the price demands of steel industry were not fair and equitable.[26]

Truman and his staff tried desperately to settle the strike before the deadline. His tactics had been careless and he had failed to consider alternatives. Mediation was attempted, but no settlement was secured. Truman did not want to invoke the Taft-Hartley emergency provisions because he thought that labor would not accept this solution. He did not want to give in to the steel companies on their price demands and thus undermine the stabilization programs. He fell back on the seizure plan, although he knew that the Smith-Connally Act had run out in 1947. Government attorneys argued that the seizure was justified because of the needs of national defense, and it could be defended under the President's power as commander-in-chief. When the President put Secretary of Commerce Sawyer in charge of the companies by executive order, labor accepted this solution and stayed on the job. Senator Taft said that Congress should consider impeaching the President for his usurpation of power. The companies took their case to the courts, contending that the seizure was unconstitutional.[27]

When the district judge on April 29 denied the President's authority to seize the industry except under express congressional legislation, the strike began. It stopped three days later when the government appealed the case. The Supreme Court upheld the district court and barred changes in wages by a decision of six to three, with seven opinions rendered, leaving some points of law in doubt. Only two of Truman's four court appointees supported him in this case. Truman was so provoked at Justice Clark for going against him that ten years later he told an interviewer that Tom Clark was his biggest mistake.[28]

President Truman turned the steel companies back to their owners, and the strike began. It lasted fifty-three days and might have been a national disaster if the Korean war had escalated or if hostilities had broken out elsewhere, as the military feared. Actually no serious steel shortages developed. Truman was attacked bitterly by the steel industry spokesmen, by the press, and by congressmen from both parties, and he lost favor among consumers and labor leaders. He tried to get Congress to pass a seizure law, but he could not move the conservative coalition of southern Democrats and Republicans. In the final settlement, both the workers and the steel companies got the major part of their demands.

The strike was a setback for any sweeping interpretation of presidential powers in an emergency not recognized by Congress, for the stabilization program, and for Truman's reputation. What went wrong? A friendly critic contends that it was Truman's lack of capacity for persuasion. He could have tried the emergency provisions of the Taft-Hartley Act, the Defense Production Act, or the Selective Service Act, but his lawyers regarded these provisions as unsuitable. He could have been more convincing in his arguments with the steel companies. He was let down by his legal counsel, the Department of Justice lawyers, and by Secretary Sawyer, who did not want to be responsible for the steel mills.[29]

Other Developments

Since the conservative Farm Bureau Federation continued to attack Truman's grass-roots meetings on behalf of family farmers, Secretary Brannan concentrated on securing high price supports. He also helped write the Democratic platform on farm policy.[30]

An illustration of the way in which the conservative coalition worked is furnished in the Senate vote on the tidelands oil bill. The conservative Democrats wanted to establish state rights to the submerged lands within state boundaries, and so did the Republicans. The bill was passed fifty-six to thirty-five. Republicans voted thirty-five to nine, Democrats twenty-one to twenty-five, and Independents zero to one, in an attempt to accomplish this transfer from federal government. Truman vetoed the bill as agreed to by the House, saying that it "makes a free gift of immensely valuable resources, which belong to the whole nation, to states which happen to be located nearest them." No action was taken to override the veto.[31]

Some of the northern Democrats were also conservative on certain issues. The immigration and naturalization bill (McCarran-Walter) produced a bitter controversy between the President and Congress. Truman wanted to liberalize the immigration laws and to have Congress authorize the entry of three hundred thousand additional immigrants over a three-year period in order to ease the refugee situation, but the conservatives in Congress did not. The McCarran-Walter bill perpetuated the quota system based on national origins of the U.S. population in 1920, which favored the northwestern European countries, which did not always use their quotas. It discriminated against the southern and eastern European countries. Truman vetoed the bill, charging it was "worse than the infamous Alien Act of 1978," and it "would perpetuate injustices of longstanding against many other nations of the world, hamper the efforts we are making to rally the men of East and West alike to the cause of Freedom, and intensify the repressive and inhumane aspects of our immigration procedures." Congressman Francis E. Walter charged that the veto message was "fictional and amateurish,'' and the House voted to override 278 to 113. The Senate followed suit.[32]

Congress passed appropriations of $80 billion and extended the life of controls over prices and wages. It also extended the farm price parity formula with a fixed 90 percent parity. No attempt was made to introduce the Brannan plan in this Congress. A $1.4 billion defense housing program was passed and also a thirty-five-thousand-unit public housing program.

Among the measures that failed to pass were familiar ones: universal military training, statehood for Alaska and Hawaii, restrictions on filibustering in the Senate, and a federal fair employment practices act. Truman's coalition-building and educational efforts on behalf of these measures would yield fruitful harvest only after he left office. Congress also failed to pass the bill that would have abolished the Reconstruction Finance Corporation, an organization that had bestowed many favors on congressmen in the past. It also took no action on a bill that would have provided appointments based on merit for postmasters, customs officials, and U.S. marshals, which had all been patronage jobs. Truman was thus blocked in some of his efforts to ensure honest government.[33]

After Congress adjourned on July 7, 1952, Truman had his last fling at the recalcitrant members of both houses. He signed certain measures but in so doing, criticized parts that he did not like and recommended future changes. He castigated Congress for reducing the funds for the atomic energy program, for civil defense, for anti-inflation controls, and for the mutual security program. He particularly deplored the cut in funds for agricultural development in India. He found many deficiencies in the amendment to the Federal Coal Mine Safety Act and in the amendments to the Social Security Act. He did not hesitate to denounce the lobby of the American Medical Association for the impairment of insurance protection for millions of disabled Americans.[34]

In this period, President Truman had miscalculated the forces of inflation, the power of the great corporations, the needs of the military, the strength of the conservative agricultural organizations, and the difficulties of overcoming conservative opposition to civil rights, liberal labor legislation, aids to small business, and welfare measures. The Korean war had helped the economy, stimulated inflation, and shown the defense budget to be woefully inadequate to meet the needs of American containment policies. Budget Director Webb, Treasury Secretary Snyder, and Defense Secretaries Johnson and Marshall had given the President poor advice on defense spending. Sounder advice had come from George Kennan, who before the Korean war had advocated funds for mobile armed forces for limited war, and from Nitze, who had contended the American economy could support a much larger defense budget. Kennan's plan would have reduced overall defense spending with some hopes of softening tensions. Nitze's plan, on the other hand, was calculated to please the industrial-military complex and to satisfy those who put the worst interpretaions on Soviet intentions.[35]

Revisionists have interpreted Truman's ambitious legislative programs as window dressing for campaign purposes and accused him of hypocrisy. But those who knew him best have testified as to his sincerity and explained that he was trying to consolidate the New Deal and the Fair Deal accomplishments and to plan for future action when conditions were more favorable. In the last two years of his administration, he was caught in a web of unfortunate circumstances in which he and his advisers made many mistakes. Nevertheless he did not lose his optimism and urge for activity.

chapter 38 | INVESTIGATIONS, SCANDALS, SECURITY, AND McCARTHYISM, 1947–1952

The choice of a prince's ministers is a matter of no little importance;
they are either good or not according to the prudence of the prince.
The first impression that one gets of a ruler and his brains is from
seeing the men that he has about him.
    —Machiavelli, *The Prince*

A terrible thing is the mob, when it has villains to lead it.
    —Euripides, *Orestes*

SCANDALS

President Truman, the beneficiary of a corrupt political machine, inherited a political system that was prone to abuse if the key administrators were not constantly on the alert to detect irregularities. Positions in certain key bureaus were filled by the patronage system. Recommendations for appointments were made by congressmen and state and local politicians, and the President, who wanted harmony in the party ranks, usually agreed. Internal revenue agents, customs agents, district judges and attorneys, federal marshals, and postmasters were included in this category. The persons who held such patronage posts were under obligation to the local party organization, which was anxious to please party campaign contributors and other friendly local interests. The pressures for favors were strong and ever present. Tax, customs, and special favors in the administration of justice were eagerly sought by businessmen and others. Responsible officials had to hold a firm rein over their subordinates to make sure that they were fair and impartial in the performance of their duties.[1]

In the Truman administration there was a running battle between the executive and legislative branches of the government, with Congress making extraordinary use of its investigating powers and the President countering the legislative attacks with his powers over executive agencies. Professors Thomas I. Emerson and David Haber in their study, *Political and Civil Rights in the United States*, concluded that "the modern legislative committee has become one of the most potent forces in American political life."

Truman should have known this from his own experience as chairman of an important special Senate committee during the war, but as President he seemed to show at times that he had not learned this lesson well. In 1947 both House and Senate committees of the Republican Eightieth Congress investigated scandals in connection with grain speculation. Caught in the net of the committees was General Wallace Graham, Truman's personal physician, whom Truman kept on in spite of his violating the law and lying about his activities.[2]

The Senate Committee on Expenditure in the Executive Departments created a sensation in 1949 with its disclosure of the activities of the so-called five-percenters—men who claimed that they had been influential in obtaining government favors in return for a five-percent commission. James V. Hunt, a former army officer, was one of the accused influence peddlers, who charged a stiff retainer plus 5 percent of any contract landed. The President's military aide, Harry Vaughan, Chemical Corps chief Alden H. Waitt, and Quartermaster General Herman Feldman were said to be the contacts. Vaughan was accused of helping to obtain scarce lumber for a racetrack, of helping to obtain a permit for scarce molasses, and of getting clearance for early postwar trips to Europe on army planes. It appears that Vaughan did not profit personally from these transactions. He did, however, receive a gift of a used deep freezer from one of Hunt's clients. He claimed that he performed no service for this gift. Vaughan was attacked vigorously in the press, but he won a libel suit against the *Saturday Evening Post*, which alleged the charges against him were true. Truman stood by Vaughan since he regarded the attacks as attempts by his enemies to get at him personally. Vaughan, who had been secretary to Senator Truman, thought that he was only doing what congressmen do all the time for their constituents. The report of the committee criticized Vaughan, Hunt, Waitt, and Feldman.[3]

The Bureau of Internal Revenue was in the Treasury Department. Secretary Snyder had the confidence of President Truman, but he was not the vigorous top administrator that the situation demanded. He did not act quickly and courageously enough to save Truman and the Democratic party from considerable embarrassment. On March 19, 1951, the Subcommittee on Administration of the Internal Revenue Laws of the House Ways and Means Committee began an investigation of irregularities in tax administration. It looked into charges of conflict of interest, bribes, shakedowns, negligence, false statements, and other abuses involving internal revenue agents. The subcommittee also investigated tax fraud cases that had been turned over to the Justice Department and had not been properly prosecuted.[4] In 1951, some 166 internal revenue officials were fired or forced to resign. In the following year, a former commissioner of internal revenue and his assistant were convicted of tax frauds. Theron Lamar Caudle, assistant attorney general in charge of the Tax Division, was fired in 1951, but he was still under investigation by Congress and later by the courts.

The Republicans used this investigation to discredit the Truman administration. Caudle was originally appointed district attorney for North Carolina by President Roosevelt. Tom Clark had brought him into the Department of Justice first as assistant attorney general in charge of the Criminal Division and then in charge of the Tax Division. McGrath had continued him in that capacity and said he held no brief for the "indiscretions" of Caudle, but added, "If ever a man had a right to depend or believe in a man, I felt I had a right to depend on Lamar Caudle." The Special Subcommittee of the House Judiciary Committee to Investigate the Justice Department found Caudle "an honest man who was indiscreet in his associations and a pliant conformer to the peculiar moral climate in Washington." The court, however, convicted him in 1956 of a conspiracy to fix a tax case, and he went to prison for a brief term. He was pardoned by President Johnson on August 18, 1965.[5]

The tax irregularities disturbed President Truman, his White House staff, the Bureau of the Budget, and Secretary of the Treasury Snyder. On October 30, 1951, David E. Bell, on Murphy's staff, wrote a memorandum on the scandals. He recommended J. Edgar Hoover as a special investigator, the appointment of a special assistant to the attorney general, the reorganization of the Bureau of Internal Revenue, and a special message on the subject.[6] On January 2, 1952, President Truman made a statement on the reorganization of the bureau. He declared the plan "part of a program to prevent improper conduct in the public service, to protect the Government from the insidious influence peddlers and favor seekers, and to expose and punish any wrong doers. It is one of a series of actions . . . to insure honesty, integrity, and fair conduct of all government business."[7] Plan no. 1 of 1952 on the Bureau of Internal Revenue was submitted to Congress on January 14, 1952. It substituted for the existing organization built around the offices of politically appointed collectors of internal revenue a single commissioner with full responsibility for running the entire office, which would be manned by a professional service selected under civil service rules. In addition, an assistant commissioner would be in charge of an inspection service responsible for detecting and investigating irregularities. This plan was hailed as a great step forward in the improvement of tax administration, and it went into effect on January 14 over the objections of thirty-seven patronage-minded senators.[8]

President Truman's handling of the scandals in the Reconstruction Finance Corporation (RFC) was not quite as skillful, especially in the beginning when he allowed personal grudges against two senators to cloud his judgment. A subcommittee of the Senate Banking and Currency Committee under the chairmanship of Senator J. William Fulbright of Arkansas scrutinized in early 1950 the lending activities and policies of the RFC. The first report of the subcommittee charged favoritism and influence in awarding RFC loans. It accused William E. Boyle, national Democratic chairman; Donald Dawson, presidential assistant; Congressman Joseph D. Casey (D-Mass.); and E. Merl Young, husband of a White House stenographer, of unduly influencing RFC loans.[9] In a press conference, Truman called the report "asinine."[10] He later referred to Senators Fulbright and Paul H. Douglas, who came to see him regarding the RFC hearings, as "overeducated sons of bitches." The Bureau of Internal Revenue investigated Douglas's tax returns and found nothing irregular. Fulbright was a Rhodes scholar who had a degree from Oxford, and Douglas had a doctorate in economics. Because he lacked a college degree, Truman was sensitive to criticism by intellectuals. Senator Fulbright had outraged him in 1946 when he suggested that Truman resign when the Democrats lost the congressinal elections. The President paid dearly for his outburst against these two able senators, who made him swallow his words about the investigations. His counter investigation of the relations of senators to RFC did not help him. He then rushed to reorganize the RFC in accordance with the committee's recommendations. The plan, sent to Congress on February 19, 1951, abolished the board of directors and made a single administrator the executive head of the corporation. The plan also provided for certain safeguards with respect to loan policy and loan applications. Stuart Symington, chairman of the National Security Resources Board who had a reputation for looking at the favorable side of events, was appointed to the new position of administrator on April 17. In the RFC scandals, Truman lost prestige in his defense of Boyle and Dawson. Boyle was forced to resign as Democratic national chairman, and although Dawson was kept on, he was a target for the Republicans and the critical press as an example of Truman's failure to "clean up the mess."[11]

The scandals in the Department of Justice resulted in some bizarre events. In 1951, Attorney General McGrath had not wanted to fire Caudle, the Tax Division head, but President Truman insisted. Truman told some of his friends that he had been "sold down the river" by trusted officials. In accordance with David Bell's recommendations, he tried to get Judge Thomas F. Murphy of the Federal District of New York to head up a special White House commission to study corruption in government, but the judge backed out at the last minute. Truman then announced that Attorney General McGrath would be in charge of the job. His announcement was greeted with derision by both Republicans and Democrats because McGrath himself was not above suspicion. Truman selected Newbold Morris, a liberal Republican lawyer who was former president of the New York City Council, to head the probe. McGrath appointed Morris, but Morris thought he was working for the President.[12]

A subcommittee of the House Judiciary Committee under chairman Frank Chelf investigated irregularities in the Department of Justice beginning in March 1952. It called McGrath, Caudle, Morris, some Kansas City vote fraud investigators, and others to testify. Full of enthusiasm, Morris asked for some help from the Bureau of the Budget. Harold Seidman, who had worked with Mayor La Guardia in New York, was assigned to work with Morris. He designed a questionnaire that he intended to be used only by the attorneys. The idea was that he could not always unearth a person's income, but he could get a good idea of how much the person was spending. Morris, whom Seidman regarded as "a bit of a dope who didn't want to make any decisions," took the questionnaire and planned to send it to everybody in Washington, including high officials and members of Congress. He wanted McGrath to fill it out, and McGrath, along with many others, rebelled as they explained to the Chelf committee. Morris thought he was working for the White House, but McGrath thought he was in charge and summarily dismissed Morris on April 3. President Truman then fired McGrath, leaving plans in great disarray. The committee called the episode "an awkward bungling attempt" that "failed ingoriously" to clean up corruption.[13]

President Truman then nominated James P. McGranery, a federal district judge, as attorney general. Senator Homer E. Ferguson of Michigan opposed the nomination on the ground that McGranery lacked "qualifications and capacity" and charged that he "refused to allow a clean-up in the Department" in 1945 when he was an assistant to the attorney general. Press reaction was unfavorable, but the nomination was confirmed by a vote of fifty-two to eighteen on May 20. All senators opposing were Republicans. Some commentators contended that McGranery was not the vigorous prosecutor called for in the situation.[14]

President Truman failed to get rid of some of his appointees who were accused of questionable conduct, among them his military aide, Harry Vaughan, and his administrative assistant, Donald Dawson, both of whom he held to be innocent of any wrongdoing. In his public announcements, Truman condemned dishonesty and favoritism in government. In his Jefferson-Jackson Day address of March 29, 1952, he said:

I hate corruption not only because it is bad in itself, but also because it is the deadly enemy of all the things the Democratic party has been doing all these years. I hate corruption everywhere, but I hate it most of all in a Democratic officeholder; because it is a betrayal of all that the Democratic party stands for.[15]

Truman's reforms of the Bureau of Internal Revenue and the Reconstruction Finance Corporation were sound administrative advances. If they had come earlier in his presidency, he would have been saved much trouble.

How serious were the Truman scandals? They certainly damaged Truman's reputation and the fortunes of the Democratic party. Citizens were alarmed at the tax irregularities, which were undermining their confidence in the tax system and affected them financially. The RFC had made some loans that went bad and cost taxpayers large sums of money. Scandals in the Department of Justice undermined faith in law enforcement. The Republicans made the most of these and many other mistakes, but General Eisenhower was to discover in a few years that it was not easy to keep an administration completely free from scandal. Truman was slow in perceiving the harm that some corrupt officials were inflicting upon his administration, and his remedial actions were tardy.[16]

SECURITY AND LOYALTY

During World War II, there were fears of Nazi subversion in the United States. Shortly after the end of the war, there developed almost pathological fears of communist subversion, and congressional investigating committees kept these fears alive. Commenting on Nazi and communist totalitarianism, while he was a senator, Truman had expressed a view unfavorable to both of these dictatorships. During the war, he followed President Roosevelt's leadership in accepting the Soviet Union as an ally in the efforts to defeat Nazi Germany. The day after he became president, he was informed of the uncompromising position the Soviet government was taking against applying the Yalta agreements to the liberated areas. In a little over a month, Truman was informed of the presence of classified American documents discovered in the office of the magazine *Amerasia*, which was under the control of communist supporters. He immediately told the FBI agent in charge of the case to pursue the prosecution promptly of the six persons arrested for conspiracy to violate the Espionage Act. Included among the arrested was John Service, a foreign service officer. Thus, early in his administration, Truman took a firm stand against alleged Soviet espionage activities. In 1946, a subcommittee of the House Judiciary Committee investigated "the disposition of charges of espionage and the possession of documents stolen from secret government files." Thus began a series of investigations of the *Amerasia* case. The subcommittee sharply criticized the lack of security and recommended stricter procedures in hiring personnel and classifying documents.[17]

Among the most active of the congressional committees investigating communist subversion was the House Un-American Activities Committee, which in its 1946 report dealt with communist activities of infiltration, propaganda, subversion, and collection of funds.[18] The disclosure in June 1946 of a Soviet spy ring in Canada with U.S. connections led Congress to try to strengthen the federal security program. In its annual appropriation bill, the State Department was given power to discharge any officer when deemed "necessary or advisable in the interests of the United States." In September 1946, Clark Clifford sent a report to the President on American relations with the Soviet Union, which included a detailed description of Soviet espionage and intelligence activities in the United States.[19] On November 25, 1946, President Truman appointed the temporary Commission on Employee Loyalty. The House Judiciary Committee authorized a continuing investigation of the *Amerasia* case involving some State Department employees. Democrats denounced the investigation as an attempt to smear the administration.[20]

President Truman made a determined effort to quiet criticism of the anti-communists, who were disturbed by what they thought was government laxness in weeding out communists who had allegedly penetrated federal offices. On March 21, 1947, he issued executive order 9835, establishing a loyalty program for all civilian employees in the executive branch. The order provided for the creation of the Loyalty Review Board, composed of twenty prominent citizens, to coordinate the loyalty policies of the various agencies that would have primary responsibility for the program and to serve as a board of appeal in loyalty cases. The order required loyalty investigations of all government employees and all applicants for government jobs. Disloyalty included espionage, sabotage, intentional disclosure of confidential documents, and, additionally, membership, affiliation, or sympathetic association with an organization designated by the attorney general as totalitarian, fascist, communist, or subversive, or as having advocated changing the form of government by unconstitutional means. In November, President Truman appointed Seth Richardson, a prominent Washington lawyer, as chairman of the board. But this order did not quiet Congress or please those interested in the protection of civil liberties.[21]

The House Un-American Activities Committee of the Republican Eightieth Congress continued its investigation of communist activities in 1947. It did not add anything that was not well known in the White House, but it kept alive public concern about communist espionage and subversion in the United States.[22] Not until 1948 did Congress and the President begin to confront each other openly on how the danger of Soviet spying in the United States should be met. The first clash came between the House Un-American Activities Committee and the President regarding Truman's refusal to release to the committee loyalty data on an atomic scientist whom the committee regarded as a security risk. The next sensation occurred when Elizabeth Bentley, a confessed wartime communist spy, testified in July that Lauchlin Currie, a wartime assistant to President Roosevelt, and Harry Dexter White, a former assistant secretary of the Treasury, had reportedly furnished information to spy groups allegedly headed by Nathan Gregory Silvermaster and Victor Perlo, former Department of Agriculture employees.

Bentley was followed by Whittaker Chambers, a former Communist, who claimed that Alger Hiss, a former director of special political affairs in the State Department and currently president of the Carnegie Endowment for International Peace, had been involved in a prewar underground communist group in Washington. Hiss denied this claim and filed a slander suit against Chambers. Accusations flew back and forth. Congressman Richard Nixon, a member of the committee, became well known by persisting in the investigation and getting Hiss to admit that he knew Chambers, who then produced secret State Department documents allegedly handed to him by Hiss for transmission to Soviet agents. On December 6 Nixon charged that Truman was more interested in concealing "embarrassing" facts than in finding out who had stolen the documents. In his press conference, three days later, Truman again characterized the investigation as a "red herring" and charged that the committee was only seeking headlines. This was a serious mistake on Truman's part and the phrase came back to haunt him.[23]

Liberals criticized Truman for his part in the 1948 prosecution and conviction of Communist party leaders for violating the Smith Act of 1940. Michal R. Belknap wrote: "I am convinced that American political justice does not exist and that the Smith Act prosecutions are a prime example of that phenomenon." Truman agreed with Attorney General McGrath's charges that the communist leaders had conspired to teach and advocate the overthrow of the government by force. Chief Justice Vinson in the *Dennis* case upheld the convictions. In his speeches Truman used the cases as proof of the vigor of his campaign against communist subversion.[24]

While 1948 brought many explosive charges of disloyalty on the part of present and former government employees, communism as an issue was not important in the presidential election. Henry Wallace, not Truman, was the candidate who was obviously "soft on communism." The most damaging evidence in the Hiss case was revealed after the election. Dewey, expecting to win, did not think a red scare campaign was necessary.

After the defeat of Dewey for president, the frustration of the Republicans was great, and they were ready to seize any issue that would help ensure that they did not lose in 1952. The communist issue was becoming more potent. The first Hiss trial for perjury for denying under oath that he had not turned over any documents to Chambers resulted in a hung jury on July 8, 1949. Feelings ran high over the trial. Chambers was denounced as a liar, a perjurer, a sick neurotic, and a holder of bitter grudges, and Hiss was regarded as proof that American setbacks—the loss of China to the communists, the stealing of the atom bomb secrets by Soviet spies, and the undermining of American security—were caused by traitors in the government. The hearings of the House Un-American Activities Committee intensified the concern about Soviet spying at American atomic bomb installations.[25]

In 1950 the exploitation of the communist issue reached a new high. After Hiss's conviction in his second trial on January 21, 1950, Secretary of State Dean Acheson said, "Whatever the outcome" of the appeal, he "would not turn his back" on Hiss. His Republican opposition regarded this remark as condoning Hiss's acts.[26] The man who capitalized on these events was the then little-known senator from Wisconsin, Joseph McCarthy, who on February 9, 1950, stated at a Republican rally, "I have here in my hand a list of 205 that were known to the Secretary of State as being members of the Communist party, and who nevertheless, are still working and shaping policy in the State Department."[27] At later meetings, McCarthy varied the numbers. The Senate authorized an investigation of the charges, including power to subpoena loyalty files. Senator Millard Tydings (D.-Md.) was appointed chairman of the subcommittee. In the final report, filed July 20, the Democratic majority said that no evidence was shown that the *Amerasia* principals were part of a spy ring. It found "no evidence to support the charge that Owen Lattimore is the top Russian spy." Each of the other nine cases submitted by McCarthy was also found to be without substantiation or was rejected because the person accused had never been an employee of the government. Senator Henry Cabot Lodge, a Republican minority member, dissented on the ground that a thorough job had not been done. President Truman allowed the loyalty files to be examined, but Lodge found them worthless.[28] Senator Margaret Chase Smith of Maine was disturbed by Senator McCarthy's methods and with six others denounced the exploitation of "fear, bigotry, ignorance and intolerance" to achieve political victory. The tide, however, was running against the Democrats, and in the fall elections, Tydings and other Democratic candidates were defeated in campaigns characterized by questionable political tactics and additional McCarthy charges. Even the usually fair-minded Taft said of McCarthy's reckless attacks, "If one case doesn't work, then bring up another." Taft apparently had little regard for maintaining the morale of public employees.

The battle between the McCarthyites and the Democrats raged on during 1951. The Subcommittee on Privileges and Elections of the Senate Rules and Administration Committee investigated the Maryland election, and its report characterized the campaign as a "despicable back street" one, "destructive of fundamental American principles" in which McCarthy and his staff were a "leading and potent force."[29] McCarthy replied that the report was a "smear" and said the issue was "one of Communists in government" and that the composite picture of Tydings and Browder showed the spirit of their collaboration. Tydings, McCarthy alleged, was responsible for deaths in Korea. When the President fired General MacArthur, Senator McCarthy declared, "The son of a bitch [Truman] ought to be impeached." The communist issue was kept alive by the House Un-American Activities Committee, the Internal Security Subcommittee of the Senate Judiciary Committee, the MacArthur hearings before the Senate Armed Services and Foreign Relations Committees, and the Senate Subcommittee on Privilege and Elections investigating the charges and countercharges made by Senator McCarthy and Senator William Benton (D.-Conn.) against each other.[30] The House report referred to "the dismal record compiled by this country in dealing with Soviet espionage."

In 1952 the investigations of Soviet espionage and the charges that government employees were involved continued. The McCarran committee of the Senate investigated communist activities of American citizens employed by the United Nations and recommended tighter security arrangements with that body.[31] The trial of Julius and Ethel Rosenberg for atomic espionage and their conviction and sentencing to death in 1951 were damaging to the Democrats. The McCarthyites interpreted the verdict as proof of the failure of the Truman administration to protect the security of the United States, and some liberals criticized the trial as a miscarriage of justice.

In a Boston address on October 17, 1952, President Truman presented his answer to McCarthyism. He defended his record in ferreting out subversives and declared that McCarthy had not uncovered a single Communist. He declared, "The low point in his hysteria was reached when they tried to besmirch the reputation—the honor and the integrity—of one of the finest, most honorable, and most patriotic soldiers and public servants we have ever had—General George C. Marshall. Now, my friends, the moral pygmies who assailed this truly great man were Senator Jenner of Indiana and Senator McCarthy of Wisconsin."[32]

Truman's effort to stem the tide were futile. McCarthy represented fundamental conservatism, which had been frustrated by the unexpected Democratic victory of 1948. His technique of prescriptive publicity had proved to be a formidable weapon. The Republican victory of 1952, however, was ultimately to bring the McCarthy era of hysteria to an end. Some revisionists have interpreted the McCarthy era as the result of Truman's shrill anticommunist rhetoric used in defending the Truman doctrine and other cold war policies. They allege that he scared the public regarding the dangers of communist subversion and then seemingly failed to keep communist spies from penetrating the government and stealing valuable secrets.[33] This theory greatly exaggerates the power of Truman's rhetoric, however. He was not the only one talking about the communist menace. It is generally agreed that anticommunism was not a main issue between the two major parties in 1948. McCarthyism fed upon events occurring after Truman's election. Soviet rhetoric, the fall of Nationalist China, the Soviet atom bomb, the unpopular Korean war, the firing of a famous general, the Hiss case, the Rosenberg trial, and the many congressional investigations helped create an atmosphere that Senator McCarthy exploited. Frustrated Republicans were willing to countenance the use of demagogic devices to discredit the Democrats and help bring about their own return to power.

chapter 39 | CANDIDATE ADLAI STEVENSON, 1952

I have not sought the honor you have done me. I could not seek it because I aspired to another office, which was the full measure of my ambition. And one does not treat the highest office within the gift of the people of Illinois as an alternative or as a consolation prize.

I would not seek your nomination for the Presidency because the burdens of that office stagger the imagination. Its potential for good or evil now and in the years of our lives smothers exultation and converts vanity to prayer.

I have asked the merciful Father of us all to let this cup pass away from me. But from such dread responsibility one does not shrink in fear, in self-interest, or in false humility.

So, "if this cup may not pass from me, except I drink it, Thy will be done."

—Governor Adlai E. Stevenson in accepting the Democratic presidential nomination, 1952

In his *Memoirs* Truman stated that he decided not to run again for the presidency on the day of his inauguration in 1949. On April 16, 1950, he put his thoughts on the subject in a memorandum:

I am not a candidate for nomination by the Democratic Convention.

My first election to public office took place in November, 1922. I served two years in the armed forces in World War I, ten years in the Senate, two months and 20 days as Vice President and President of the Senate. I have been in public office well over thirty years, having been President of the United States almost two complete terms. . . .

In my opinion eight years as President is enough and sometimes too much for any man to serve in that capacity.

There is a lure in power. It can get into a man's blood just as gambling and lust for money have been known to do.

This is a Republic. The greatest in the history of the world. I want this country to continue as a Republic. Cincinnatus and Washington pointed the way. When Rome forgot Cincinnatus, its downfall began. When we forget the examples of such men as Washington, Jefferson and Andrew Jackson, all of whom could have had a continuation in the office, then will we start down the road to dictatorship and ruin. I know I could be elected again and continue to break the old precedent as it was broken by F.D.R. It should not be done. That precedent should continue not by a Constitutional amendment, but by custom based on the honor of the man in the office.

Therefore, to re-establish that custom, although by a quibble I could say I've only had one term, I am not a candidate and will not accept the nomination for another term.[1]

Truman wrote that he read this memorandum to his White House staff at the Little White House in Key West in March 1951 and pledged the listeners to secrecy. Most remarkably this pledge was kept until March 29, 1952, when Truman made the following announcement at the annual Jefferson-Jackson Day dinner: "I shall not be a candidate for re-election. I have served my country long, and I think efficiently and honestly. I shall not accept a renomination. I do not feel that it is my duty to spend another four years in the White House."[2]

Having taken himself out of the running, Truman looked out for the fortunes of his party by grooming the strongest possible candidate for the Democratic nomination. The situation demanded a man who could hold together the diverse elements within the party and challenge a popular man, General Eisenhower, who appeared to be the probable Republican candidate.

Truman's first choice was Chief Justice Fred M. Vinson, who had legislative, executive, and judicial experience, having served as a congressman from Kentucky, associate justice of the U.S. Court of Appeals for the District of Columbia, chief judge of the U.S. Emergency Court of Appeals, director of the Office of Economic Stabilization, federal loan administrator, director of the Office of War Mobilization and Reconversion, secretary of the treasury, and chief justice of the Supreme Court. Truman had great confidence in Vinson's political and administrative abilities and felt that his successful campaigns for Congress qualified him on the electoral side. The abortive mission to Moscow was an indication of the great trust Truman had in him even in a field where he was not an expert. Vinson refused to become a candidate, however, because he felt that the Supreme Court should keep out of politics, and he thought that the state of his health was such that he should not risk assuming the tremendous burdens of the presidency.[3]

Truman also considered Senator Estes Kefauver of Tennessee, a New Dealer-Fair Dealer, foe of the conservative Senator McKellar of Tennessee, and conqueror of Boss Crump of Memphis. But Senator Kefauver in January criticized the Truman administration for not doing enough to stamp out corruption. Kefauver had won a good deal of attention by his conduct of the televised hearings of the Senate Crime Investigating Committee. In some cities these hearings had proved embarrassing to the local

Democratic organizations—which Truman as an organization Democrat found hard to forgive. Senator Scott Lucas of Illinois blamed his defeat in 1950 on the Kefauver committee. So the senator from Tennessee was crossed off Truman's list even though he did well in the public opinion polls and he was having astonishing success in the Democratic presidential primaries. The genial senator was making a valiant effort to win the nomination by the presidential primary route— a course later to be employed successfully by Senator John F. Kennedy, Senator George McGovern, and former Governor Jimmy Carter. Kefauver had increased his following by diligent personal campaigning. In the March New Hampshire primary, Kefauver handed Truman a stunning defeat and followed with victories in Wisconsin, Nebraska, Illinois, New Jersey, Massachusetts, and Maryland. Only in Florida did he lose and in that case to Senator Russell of Georgia, a conservative southerner who was regarded as the spokesman for the South. Kefauver's support of home rule for the District of Columbia and his opposition to the filibuster made him unacceptable to the South. But to the President, Kefauver was a man to be stopped. He was not impressed with Kefauver's skillful use of the primaries. The President lined up with the party leadership against the people's choice. He could have nominated Kefauver with little effort had he so chosen.[4]

Senator Robert Kerr of Oklahoma also sought the nomination. A former governor of his state, an effective speaker, and a wealthy man who could help finance his own campaign, he possessed definite assets, but these were offset by his close identification with the oil industry. Truman liked Kerr personally but felt that his oil connections disqualified him as a candidate.[5]

Senator Richard Russell of Georgia was the candidate of the South for the nomination. While Truman admired Russell's skill as a legislator, he felt that a southerner could not hold the various elements of the party together. Russell's stand on civil rights alienated blacks and the northern liberals. On practically all Fair Deal issues, Russell was to be found in the opposition. He could not hope for Truman's backing.[6]

Averell Harriman of New York was also under consideration. Going back to the early days of Franklin D. Roosevelt in the White House, he held many important posts in the National Recovery Administration, in the National Defense Advisory Commission, and in the Office of Production Management. During the war he was a special representative of the Office of Lend-Lease Administration, the War Shipping Administration, and other important boards serving Great Britain and the Soviet Union. Then President Roosevelt appointed him ambassador to the Soviet Union, and President Truman continued him in that post. Later he was appointed ambassador to Great Britain, secretary of commerce, U.S. representative in Europe for the Economic Cooperation Act of 1948, special assistant to the president, American representative on the North Atlantic Treaty Organization, and director of Mutual Security Agency. Thus he had excellent experience in both the domestic and foreign fields. Among the drawbacks to his candidacy were a lack of experience as a candidate for elective office and the absence of a firm political base in New York. In the presidential primary held in the District of Columbia, however, he defeated Senator Kefauver. In 1954 he was to be elected governor of New York.[7]

Governor Adlai Stevenson of Illinois was a strong possibility for the nomination. David Lloyd, one of President Truman's administrative assistants, was an early booster of the governor. He admired Stevenson's service for the Department of State at the San Francisco conference on the United Nations organization where he adroitly handled the public relations of the conference.[8] In the 1948 elections, Stevenson had carried Illinois by a plurality of 572,067, votes whereas Truman had squeaked by with a plurality of only 33,612 votes. As governor he had acquired an excellent reputation as an able administrator, a champion of honesty in government, and an articulate liberal leader.[9] He had not alienated the South, and he was popular with labor and minority groups. Early in January 1952 Truman urged Stevenson to become a candidate. As he described it in his *Memoirs:*

> When I talked with him, I told him what I thought the Presidency is, how it has grown into the most powerful and the greatest office in the history of the world. I asked him to take it and told him that if he would agree he could be nominated. I told him that a President in the White House always controlled the National Convention. Called his attention to Jackson and Van Buren and Polk. Talked about Taft in 1912, Wilson in 1920, Coolidge and Mellon in 1928, Roosevelt in 1936, 1940, 1944. But he said: No! He apparently was flabbergasted.[10]

But Stevenson said that he wanted to continue as governor of Illinois and was not interested in the presidential nomination in 1952. In the minds of the politicians, Governor Stevenson was the most available candidate. His excellent record as governor, the job he had done in Illinois, his moderate positions, his wit and eloquence, and his acceptability among the various groups that made up the Democratic party made him highly attractive.[11]

Following Truman's announcement on March 29 that he was not a candidate for renomination, newsmen pressed Governor Stevenson to indicate his intentions, but the governor still held off. Some of his friends, however, began to organize a draft-Stevenson movement. They felt that he would be better off if he did not appear as President Truman's handpicked candidate. They were anxious to divorce the governor from the Truman administration, which had become increasingly unpopular.[12]

In desperation Truman considered running again, but his White House advisers urged him not to. The decline of his popularity in the public opinion polls, his defeat in the New Hampshire primary, the outcry against his handling of the steel crisis, the great popularity of General Eisenhower, the frustration of the public at the stalemate in Korea, and the domestic crises (which included political scandals, growing stridency of McCarthyism, and many economic maladjustments) made the prospects of a repeat of the 1948 performance look dim. Bess Truman was also anxious to get rid of the White House duties as First Lady as well as to escape from anxieties following an attempted assassination of her husband.[13]

Two weeks before the convention opened, Truman amazingly turned to Vice-President Barkley, who, at the age of seventy-five, wanted to make a bid for the nomination. The President conditioned his support of Barkley on the approval of the labor leaders at the convention. This Barkley was unable to obtain, and he told Truman he was withdrawing.[14]

In the meantime the preparations for the convention in Chicago were intensified. Chairman Frank McKinney of Indiana, a successful banker and businessman and a former vice-president of the Democratic National Finance Committee, had had some convention experience, which he put to good use. Truman had complete confidence in him. Governor Paul A. Dever of Massachusetts was selected as temporary chairman and Speaker Rayburn as the permanent chairman. Contrary to usual practices, Governor Stevenson, a possible though not an avowed candidate, was asked to make a welcoming speech as the leading Democrat in the host state. His speech was so effective that it enhanced his chances for the nomination. The convention had a problem about seating three southern delegations who were unwilling to pledge support in advance to the candidates nominated by the convention. The Illinois delegation backed a compromise that seated these delegations in an attempt to win southern support for a Stevenson candidacy.[15]

The Draft Stevenson Committee selected Governor Henry F. Schricker of Indiana to nominate Stevenson. A poll of county and city chairmen revealed strong support for Stevenson above all others. The pressure became so great that on the second day of the convention, Stevenson agreed to run. He asked Truman if it would embarrass him if he, Stevenson, "allowed his name to be placed in nomination." Truman later wrote: "I replied with a show of exasperation and some rather vigorous words and concluded by saying to Stevenson, 'I have been trying since January to get you to say that. Why should it embarrass me?'"[16]

Truman said that it did not embarrass him, but in fact it did. His blessing on Stevenson's candidacy came so late that people could not say that the President made the nomination. From Stevenson's standpoint, this was an advantage since it would have been a liability for him to have been branded as Truman's candidate. This would have alienated the South and tied Stevenson too closely to the Truman record. But Truman was used to disappointments in politics. He watched the convention proceedings on television with avid interest. He was delighted when Stevenson in his welcoming address ridiculed the attempts of the Republicans to label twenty years of

Democratic administration as a failure. As in the case of Garfield in 1880 and Bryan in 1896, the Stevenson speech made him more attractive as a possible candidate. The following speech of Senator Paul Douglas of Illinois defending the policy in Korea was also a delight to Truman.[17]

National chairman McKinney invited Stevenson to dine with the President, but Stevenson declined; he did not want people to think that he was seeking the nomination. His supporters realized that Kefauver had a head start on them. The weakness of Kefauver's primary victories was that they were won against little opposition. None of the other candidates, including Stevenson, had wanted to travel the primary route. It was regarded as too expensive, time-consuming, exhausting, and futile. Truman had called the primaries "eyewash." The public opinion polls were more useful. They were nationwide samples and caused the candidates no trouble or expense except in those cases where a candidate or party sponsored a poll. The non-party-sponsored polls, such as the Gallup and Roper polls, carried much greater weight than the partisan polls, which were always suspect. In his June 1952 poll of potential Democratic voters, Roper found that 33 percent favored Kefauver, 10 percent Barkley, and only 9 percent Stevenson. When Stevenson became an avowed candidate on July 24, his supporters had a big job before them in publicizing their candidate's virtues and availability.[18]

The convention proceeded with its regular business, which included the reports of the Credentials and Resolutions Committees. A member of Truman's White House staff, Richard Neustadt, had submitted a draft of the platform. Truman naturally took pride in the platform adopted by the convention because it was a vindication of his record. It called for repeal of the Taft-Hartley Act, agricultural price supports, and preference for public as opposed to private agencies for the development of electrical power systems. On the sensitive civil rights issue, it retreated from the strong position taken in the 1948 platform, but this was consistent with Truman's behavior on the issue. He agreed that the South must be appeased if it was to be held in line for the party ticket. On foreign affairs, the platform stood for peace with honor, the United Nations, strong national defense, collective strength for the free world, encouragement of European unity, a free Germany, aid for victims of Soviet imperialism, collective security in the Pacific, a workable plan for disarmament, helping other people to help themselves under Truman's point 4 program, expansion of world trade, and upholding the principle of self-determination.[19]

The convention then came to the nomination of candidates for the presidency and the balloting for the nominees. As expected, Kefauver led on the first ballot. The count stood Kefauver, 340; Stevenson, 273; Russell, 268; Harriman, 123½; Kerr, 65; Barkley, 48½; Dever, 37½; and scattered votes for others. The second ballot did not change the order of the two leading candidates, but Stevenson's gains were much larger than Kefauver's—

Kefauver, 362½, and Stevenson, 324½. Truman sprang into action because he did not want a deadlocked convention. He and his cohorts persuaded Harriman and Dever to withdraw in favor of Stevenson on the third ballot, and the race to get on the bandwagon was on. The count stood Stevenson, 617½; Kefauver, 275½; and Russell, 261. Stevenson was then nominated by acclamation.[20]

The convention listened to Truman and Stevenson pledge to do their utmost in the coming campaign. Truman made a fighting speech that was reminiscent of 1948: "I am telling you now that Adlai Stevenson is going to win in 1952. We are going to win in 1952 the same way we won in 1948. And I pledge to you now that I am going to take my coat off and do everything I can to help him win." Stevenson and his advisers must have winced at this pledge; they were anxious not to associate too closely with the Truman crowd. The polished Stevenson presented a striking contrast to the earthy Truman. The delegates nevertheless must have been struck by the positive approach of their old and new leaders.[21]

The last piece of business for the convention was the nomination of a candidate for vice-president. A group made up of Truman, Stevenson, McKinney, and Sam Rayburn agreed upon Senator John J. Sparkman of Alabama as the nominee. The convention confirmed this choice by acclamation in an attempt to make sure that the party did not lose again the four southern states that went Dixiecrat in 1948. Black delegates were most unhappy with the nomination of Sparkman, however. As they bolted the convention, Congressman Adam Clayton Powell of New York said: "They cram a candidate down our throat but they cannot make us vote for him."[22]

Governor Stevenson's acceptance speech made it appear almost as if he did not want to assume the responsibilities of the presidency and may have been an element in his ultimate defeat by Eisenhower in the general election. The American people do not want to give power to someone who shrinks from the responsibility of making difficult decisions. The convention, however, had decided that Stevenson was the best available candidate, and it was up to the party to do all it could to see that he was elected.

chapter 40 | IKE: THE OPPOSING CANDIDATE

Under no circumstances will I ask relief from this assignment in order to seek nomination to political office and I shall not participate in the pre-convention activities of others who may have such an intention with respect to me.
> —Dwight D. Eisenhower, head of NATO forces in Paris, January 5, 1952.

The bitter disappointment of the Republican leaders with their defeat in 1948 left them united in their determination to win the presidency in 1952 but divided as to how it might be done and with whom. The right wing of the party blamed the defeat on the policy of Governor Dewey, who refused to attack the Fair Deal vigorously and who went along with the bipartisan foreign policy except in the Far East. Conservative Republicans wanted a slashing attack on foreign and domestic policies of Truman and the Democrats, and they sought a return to old-fashioned Republican principles that glorified individual enterprise, rejected deficit spending, and advocated a withdrawal from foreign commitments and a return to isolation. Their favorite candidate was "Mr. Republican," Senator Robert A. Taft of Ohio, who had been seeking the Republican nomination since 1940. With Truman's popularity declining, Taft looked upon 1952 as his year.[1] Following in his father's footsteps, he sought the nomination by gaining the votes of state delegations by negotiating with state party leaders. He gained control of the Republican National Committee and found in Republican National Chairman Guy George Gabrielson of New Jersey a sympathetic supporter. Gabrielson, a successful lawyer and businessman, had been speaker of the New Jersey House of Assembly and at the time of his selection as chairman in 1949 he was national committeeman from New Jersey. He definitely was not the choice of the titular leader of the party, the defeated candidate of 1948, Governor Thomas E. Dewey.[2]

The more moderate wing of the Republican party clung to the bipartisan foreign policy except on Far Eastern questions and held to the middle of the road on domestic policies on the ground that extremist positions would alienate many potential supporters. Governor Dewey was the leader of this wing, and he did not want a third nomination, but he was extremely anxious to stop Taft, whose foreign policies he rejected. Dewey led the search for a candidate who could overcome the lead Taft had built up and could win the election. Assisting him in this enterprise was Senator Henry Cabot Lodge, Jr., of Massachusetts, who felt that General Dwight D. Eisenhower was their man. General MacArthur was ruled out because ideologically he was the same as Taft. In addition, he was an austere, distant individual, who found it hard to identify himself with common folk. Ike, on the other hand, projected a father image, kindly, courteous, diplomatic, sincere with that magnificent smile, not too dogmatic, willing to listen to advice, flexible in his views, and dedicated to America's new role in world affairs. In 1948 Eisenhower stood first in the popularity polls among both Democrats and Republicans, and he maintained that high position during the subsequent four years.[3]

Military heroes have played an important role in American politics. We have already seen how in 1948 there was a movement to make Eisenhower the Democratic candidate even after Truman had announced his candidacy for renomination. The Eisenhower boom collapsed when the general made it clear that he would not accept such a nomination. Arthur Krock claims that Justice William O. Douglas told him that the President told the justice on November 6, 1951, that he, Truman, had sounded out General Eisenhower on his attitude toward accepting the Democratic nomination for president in 1952. Truman later denied that he had made any such advance.[4]

As soon as it became clear that Eisenhower was a Republican and would not accept a Democratic nomination, the relations between Truman and Eisenhower began to cool.[5] While still in Paris as Supreme Allied Commander of NATO forces, Eisenhower admitted in January that he was Republican.[6] Lodge, Dulles, and others had convinced him that if the Republicans selected Senator Taft as their candidate, the cause of American cooperation with other countries on behalf of peace and defense of the free world would be set back. They also persuaded him that another Democratic victory would endanger the two party system. When he agreed to run, the remnants of the Thomas Dewey organization came together to put over his nomination. The general was not enthusiastic about running in the presidential primaries, but by force of circumstances he was driven to enter some. His backers soon discovered that he did well in these tests of popularity, and they urged him to use them to maximum advantage to overcome the lead Taft had acquired by his early entrance into the battle for the nomination. Eisenhower defeated Taft in the New Hampshire primary in March, in the New Jersey, Pennsylvania, and Massachusetts primaries in April, and in the Oregon primary in May. Only in Nebraska and South Dakota did he fall slightly behind Taft. Eisenhower's managers kept him out of California and Ohio, where favorite sons were running. Ike's success in the primaries kept him before the public. His popularity in the polls also helped. Before he withdrew, Truman was defeated by Ike in the polls. Then the Gallup poll showed Ike defeating both Kefauver and Stevenson in hypothetical races, while Taft fell behind when matched against these Democrats. The Associated Press delegate polls of Republican presidential candidates showed Eisenhower gaining steadily on Taft right up to the opening of the convention. He resigned his NATO command in June, returned to the United States, and devoted full time to winning the nomination.[7]

The Taft forces thought that their control of the national committee had sewed up the nomination for their man, but they soon found that they were mistaken. The Eisenhower forces contested the pro-Taft delegations already selected in several states, charged irregularities in the selection of the pro-Taft delegates, and presented delegations of their own. As the convention opened, charges and countercharges flew back and forth, with accusations on each side that the other side was trying to steal delegate seats.

General MacArthur was selected to make the keynote address because his foreign policy positions were close to those of Senator Taft. In his address, the general challenged Eisenhower as well as Truman. He not only denounced high taxes, high governmental spending, tampering with the Constitution, Democratic weakness and indecision in foreign and military affairs, the discarding of victory as a military objective which condemned U.S. forces to a stalemated struggle of attrition, and the Korean armistice negotiations that allowed the enemy time to recoup, but also the withdrawal of American forces from hard-won territory in Europe at the end of the war and the permitting of the encirclement of Berlin by Soviet forces. These last two events had been made possible by decisions made by Eisenhower.[8]

The Republican platform charged the Democratic party with appeasing communism at home and abroad, encouraging bureaucracy and socialism, and undermining local self-government. It accused Truman and the Democratic leaders of corruption and even treason. On the positive side, it was ambiguous and vague, advocating less government at the national level and greater local autonomy, less government control over business, reduction of governmental spending and taxation, and a tougher anticommunist policy in national and international affairs. On civil rights, it was woefully weak. Taft's influence was apparent in the foreign policy planks. The Democrats were accused of abandoning friendly Eastern European nations to the Russians, of denying the Chinese Nationalists promised military aid and thus substituting a murderous enemy for an ally, of making tragic blunders at Potsdam, and of starting an unnecessary and undeclared war in Korea, which resulted in ignominious stalemate.[9]

In a bitter convention fight, the moderate forces behind Eisenhower won out over the hard-core isolationists backing Taft, even though the Credentials Committee backed the Taft-contested delegations. The Eisenhower managers accused the Taft forces of trying to steal the nomination, an unfair charge because the Eisenhower-contested delegations from the South had no greater claim to legitimacy than the Taft delegates had, but the accusations undermined the Taft strategy. Aided by a resolution passed by Republican governors and by a press barrage, the Eisenhower backers won enough of the disputed delegations to tip the balance in their favor. The convention reversed the Credentials Committee and seated enough pro-Eisenhower delegates to give the general the victory on the first ballot after shifts.[10]

The nomination of a candidate for vice-president was the next order of business. Herbert Brownell, Jr., of New York, one of Eisenhower's convention managers, presided over the conference of Republican leaders that rejected Senator Dirksen, Taft's candidate, and recommended Senator Richard M. Nixon of California for vice-president, one of Truman's harshest critics. Nixon was young and had acquired a national reputation for the vigor with which he had carried on anticommunist activities. Senator William F. Knowland of California put Nixon's name before the convention, and the nomination was made by acclamation.[11]

Eisenhower's speech accepting the nomination for president was not modest. He held that he had been summoned to lead a great crusade "for freedom in America and freedom in the world." Its aims were "to sweep from office an Administration which has fastened on every one of us the wastefulness, the arrogance and corruption in high places, the heavy burdens and the anxieties which are the fruit of a party too long in power." He was conciliatory toward his defeated opponents and urged the election of a Republican Congress to put through the Republican program.[12]

Nixon's acceptance speech for the nomination as Republican candidate for vice-president was a fighting partisan speech that emphasized even more than Eisenhower had the need for a Republican Senate and House of Representatives. He also made an urgent plea for the party workers to go out into the precincts and do everything possible to win a Republican victory.

After the convention, Eisenhower made valiant efforts to unite the various factions in the Republican party. He held conferences with Senator Taft and with the other prominent Republican leaders. As a man known for his goodwill and for his abilities as a reconciler of clashing interests, he went about this task with deftness.[13]

chapter 41 | SPEAKING FOR STEVENSON

*I'll talk about the burden of taxes and their dangers to a people's
initiative, but let me tell you—I'll be darned if anyone is going to talk
me into making any idiotic promises or hints about elect-me-and-I-
will-cut-your-taxes-by-such-and-such-a-date. If it takes that kind of
foolishness to get elected, let them find someone else for the job.*
            —Dwight D. Eisenhower, quoted by Emmet John Hughes,
            The Ordeal of Power

Stevenson appealed to the same groups that supported Truman in 1948,
but he did so through his own organization and methods and not through
close associates of the President. Over Truman's protests he replaced
national chairman McKinney with Stephen A. Mitchell, a Chicago lawyer,
who had helped him get started in Illinois politics. Stevenson appointed
Wilson Wyatt, an ADA leader, former mayor of Louisville and former
housing expediter, as his campaign manager, who conducted business out of
Springfield, Illinois. This made it difficult for the President to influence the
course of the campaign. Except for David Bell, a Truman assistant, Stevenson's speech writers were not the usual Truman types. Stevenson used intellectuals such as Arthur Schlesinger, Jr., the Pulitzer Prize-winning Harvard
historian, John Kenneth Galbraith, a Harvard economist and former head
of the Economic Division of OPA, and Willard Wirtz, a liberal lawyer and
former member of the War Labor Board. Stevenson was also one of his
own speech writers, and Truman soon discovered that the governor was an
intellectual like some of those around him.[1]

From Truman's point of view, the Democratic campaign got off to a bad
start. The division of responsibility between Springfield and Washington
led to confusion and loss of momentum. In mid-August, Stevenson fell into
a trap that enraged Truman. A Portland, Oregon, editor wrote Stevenson
asking him how he proposed to deal with "the mess in Washington."
Stevenson in his reply used the phrase, but he forgot to see that it was in
quotes. Truman thought that Stevenson had promised to "clean up" the
"mess," and he exploded. As he later wrote, "How Stevenson hoped he
could persuade the American voters to maintain the Democratic party in
power while seeming to disown powerful elements of it, I do not know."[2]

On August 12, the day before Truman and the nominee met to discuss strategy, Duke Shoop of the *Kansas City Times* wrote: "President Truman will be kept at arms length during the fall Presidential campaign by Governor Adlai E. Stevenson." After Stevenson, Sparkman, and Truman had met in a strategy conference, they gave no indication as to Truman's part in the campaign.[3]

On August 13 the White House and the Stevenson Springfield headquarters announced simultaneously that both Truman and Stevenson would deliver Labor Day speeches. The President's role afterward was not defined. In his press conferences, Truman kept insisting that his record was the central issue of the campaign. This delighted the Republicans, who thought the record was vulnerable, but it did not please Stevenson. The *New York Times* indicated that Stevenson's advisers intended to keep "the President relatively in the background" and to keep Stevenson "at the center of the campaign's focus, and especially the television focus."[4]

The President's scheduled Labor Day speech was in Milwaukee. On the way he made station stops at Pittsburgh, Pennsylvania, and Crestline, Ohio, and on the way back at Cincinnati, Ohio, and Parkersburg, Clarksburg, Grafton, Keyser, and Martinsburg, West Virginia. Enthusiastic crowds gathered everywhere, and the Stevenson managers were impressed. As William S. White put it, "It is felt among many of the party leaders that the President's brief tour was a big success and that more of this sort of thing will be needed particularly in industrial and metropolitan areas."[5]

In spite of Stevenson's lack of enthusiasm, on September 27 Truman undertook a fifteen-day western train trip of some eighty-five hundred miles, going into seventeen states, and making ninety-six speeches. On returning east, he toured New York and then campaigned in New England, the northeastern states, and the Midwest. Altogether he delivered 212 speeches and traveled eighteen thousand miles, slightly more than Stevenson made, who traveled for the most part by airplane and was not subjected to the inconveniences of train travel.

Large crowds came to hear the President and to see his wife and daughter as they had done in 1948. One reporter on the train wrote, "The President unquestionably was scoring a personal success on this latest personal appearance tour. Crowds numbering up to 10,000 turned out at railroad stations to hear him, and cheered his half grim, half humorous man-of-the-people approach."[6]

Truman's 1952 campaign efforts on behalf of Stevenson were important to him personally because he felt that he was fighting for his place in history. Doris Fleeson wrote: "An easy tendency exists to regard the current Truman campaign as merely more of 1948 with all of its over-simplification and name-calling. That is not true. Mr. Truman was fighting recklessly for office then; he is fighting now for his place in history and it is a much more careful and deeply felt effort."[7]

Cartoon by Jim Berryman, 1952. Reprinted courtesy of *The Washington Star*.

Truman's whistle-stop campaign tour in 1952 had a different crew than in his 1948 tour, but the methods used were similar. Charles Murphy had replaced Clark Clifford as the chief speech writer on the train. He was aided by Richard Neustadt, who specialized on the short whistle-stop speeches, by James Sundquist of the Bureau of the Budget, who worked on the main speeches, by David Lloyd, an ADA lawyer who worked on foreign affairs addresses, by Ken Heckler, specializing in local color, and by Joseph Short, his press secretary.[8] Sundquist, later with the Brookings Institution, recalls this incident:

I remember one evening I was typing away in my compartment when I felt someone behind me and looked over my shoulder and there was the President of the United States; he smiled at me benignly and said, "Don't get up. I just wondered what stuff you're planning to put in the President's mouth tomorrow?" And I assumed he wanted to know and started out to tell him, but he shushed me and said, "That's all right, young man, I'm sure that what you're coming up with is going to be a lot better than anything I could suggest."[9]

The crowds that came to hear and see Truman were not as orderly as those in 1948. Some reacted violently against counterdemonstrations by Republicans, and a few listeners heckled, booed, or pelted the President with eggs. This behavior reflected the decline in the President's popularity, the dislike of the dismissal of General MacArthur, and the alienation of parts of the public caused by the war in Korea, which could not be won or stopped.[10] The Republicans were alarmed at the vigor of Truman's attacks on Eisenhower and sent a four-man group called the "Truth Squad" to counter the presidential efforts by following him and answering his arguments.[11]

Both major party candidates agreed that the four main issues of the campaign were communism, Korea, corruption, and the national economy, but they differed as to priorities. Eisenhower put Korea first, and Stevenson put the economic record of the Democrats first. Nixon added a fifth issue, Truman.[12]

Joseph Harsh described Truman's strategy in this way:

One of the oldest rules in politics is to attack rather than defend. The Truman formula calls for a small amount of defending, but always concealed within the body of attack. In the first 40 whistle stops he defended once again the corruption charge, contending that the private banks have a worse record than the government, and once on the charge of slowness to anticipate the Communist threat. He contended that he had been leading the fight and never saw any Republicans out in front of him.[13]

The President's attack centered on the argument that the Republican party was the party of special privilege, that it was largely isolationist, that the Republican candidate lacked the qualifications for the presidency, and that Republican campaign tactics were unfair.

Outstanding in Truman's campaign speeches for Stevenson were his strong attacks on Eisenhower as a candidate for president. Truman argued that as a professional military man, Ike was deficient in training and background for the job, as Ike himself had admitted in earlier years; that he had surrendered to the conservatives and the isolationists; that by endorsing William Jenner and Joseph McCarthy, he accepted "despicable" methods of fighting communism; that he had gone back on his own principles; and that he lacked moral backbone because he had deserted his friends, including General George Marshall, who had been so vital to him and his military career. In his October 7 attack at Colorado Springs, Truman said:

What I thought were his deep convictions, turn out not to be convictions at all. He has betrayed the more liberal and responsible wing of the Republican party which supported him for nomination in the July convention. He has betrayed every principle about our foreign policy and our national defense that I thought he believed in. . . .

In a recent article, that newspaper [Columbia University student newspaper] said, "The great crusade, passing through the stage of great compromise, must now be called the great disenchantment."[14]

What disturbed Truman most was Eisenhower's deletion of a passage defending General Marshall in a speech delivered in Milwaukee on October 3 at the behest of the party managers who did not want to offend Senator McCarthy. At this action Truman's rage had no bounds. In the same Colorado Springs speech he said:

This great man [General Marshall] has been the subject of an infamous attack by two Republican isolationist Senators. Acting from purely partisan motives, these two moral pygmies have called this great American a "living lie," a "front for traitors" and the center of an infamous conspiracy. Nothing more contemptible has ever occurred in the long history of human spite and envy. It is unspeakable, and the authors of these slanders are unworthy of the company of decent men and women.

Now what do you think of a man who deserts his best friend when he is unjustly demned these two slanderers? Has he denounced their lies about his great friend and benefactor?

I'll tell you what he has done. He has endorsed them both for reelection to the Senate. One he has embraced publicly. . . .

Now what do you think of a man who deserts his best friend when he is unjustly attacked? What do any of us say about a fellow who joins hands with those who have tried to stab an honored chief, a friend and a benefactor, in the back? . . .

That kind of moral blindness brands the Republican candidate as unfit to be President of the United States.[15]

Truman spoke with such sincerity that his audience did not show any open resentment at the downgrading of a man who was a war hero. Truman also attacked Eisenhower's campaigning, charging that the general as a candidate was criticizing decisions he had no right to speak against since he himself had been involved in making them. The failure to ensure a safe corridor to Berlin and the withdrawal of American troops from Korea in 1949 could be laid at Ike's door, and it ill behooved him to try to blame the Democrats for these actions.[16] Ike's solution for the Korean stalemate brought a scornful reply from Truman. To pull the U.N. forces out of Korea and let the South Koreans fight the Chinese alone was cruel and deceitful. Eisenhower's promise, "I will go to Korea," was a hoax; he had no plan for ending the war with honor. The phrase had been put in his address by a speech writer and had not been checked by his military and foreign policy advisers.[17]

In answer to the charge that his administration had been "soft on communism," Truman explained in Boston on October 17 that the charge "was so contrary to the fact as to be preposterous. . . . Outside the lie-factory of the Kremlin itself, it would be hard to find a more fantastic perversion of the truth." Truman quoted General Walter Bedell Smith's statement to answer the Republican charge.

Any future President, Republican or Democrat, is going to have to work with the same security agencies now in existence. Both will have the same difficulties that we now encounter today. If either one of them, the Democrat or the Republican, does as well as President Truman in cooperation with the security agencies in ferreting out subversives, the American people can congratulate each other and will have little to worry about.[18]

Truman's speeches contained no eloquent phrases such as characterized Stevenson's efforts. His speech writers endeavored to make the language simple and to emphasize the ideas to be conveyed.[19]

Truman had little quarrel with Stevenson's campaign. The governor supported the Fair Deal program, criticized the McCarthyists, and defended Truman's cold war policies, NATO, and the military buildup in accordance with NSC 68. He rejected MacArthur's strategy of attacks on Communist Chinese mainland, insisted that Nationalist China could not have been saved by the United States, and reminded his listeners of Eisenhower's pro-Soviet statement made in November 1945—"Nothing guides Russian policy so much as desire for friendship with the United States"—which completely missed the true nature of Soviet intentions as later revealed. Stevenson and Truman both denounced Ike's "I will go to Korea" statement, and the governor pointed out that the general did not have a program for settling the impasse. The negotiations were stalled because the U.N. forces refused to agree to communist demands for forced repatriation of all prisoners of war. Would Ike agree with the Communists on this issue?[20]

Stevenson believed in the Woodrow Wilson liberal tradition of rationalism in politics. As he said in his acceptance speech, "Talk sense to the American people . . . tell them the truth, that there are no gains without pains. Better we lose the election than mislead the people." He charged that Eisenhower was a "captive candidate": "The Old Guard has succeeded in doing what Hitler's best generals could never do—they have captured General Eisenhower." The "reactionaries own the Republican party, hoofs, hide and tallow." To this Eisenhower replied, "No one has a claim on me . . . I am my own man . . . Stevenson has been taken over, body, boots and britches by the Administration."[21]

The Republican campaign contrasted sharply with the Democratic. First, it was far better financed. The Republican national-level campaign groups outspent the Democratic groups as a whole in a ratio of about fifty-five to forty-five, and this included national labor expenditures of the Democrats.[22] The Republicans placed more emphasis on emotional appeals devised by advertising and public relations people. Under Robert Humphreys, the public relations head of the Republican campaign, an elaborate campaign plan was prepared that outlined in great detail what the Republicans would have to do to win. First, Eisenhower would have to make peace with the Taft forces who represented the core strength of the Republican party. Next they had to agitate those who ordinarily would not vote. A crusading zeal could be inspired only by attacking the Democrats and their presidential candidate vigorously. The plan called for the use of all media, especially television, to "merchandise Eisenhower's frankness, honesty, and integrity, his sincere and wholesome approach." Ike's campaign tours were planned to the smallest details, and Ike himself made the television spots. The Democratic response to the spots was devastating. George Ball called the campaign "a super-colossal, multi-million dollar production designed to sell an inadequate ticket to the American people in precisely the same way they sell soap, ammoniated tooth paste, hair tonic or bubble gum."[23]

A Gallup poll was ordered by the Republicans to help them select the issues to be emphasized. Gallup recommended three themes: corruption, communism, and Korea. On foreign policy issues Eisenhower was influenced by John Foster Dulles, who was active in helping to work out the Japanese treaty. Dulles's influence is evident in the speech Eisenhower made on August 25, before the American Legion in New York City. Ike talked about the "liberation" of peoples behind the iron curtain, about the danger of Soviet "infiltration" in areas critical to the American economy, and about the need for strong military forces with "great retaliatory power," but he did not explain how these problems could be met.

On September 12 Eisenhower had a meeting with Taft at his residence in New York, at which he accepted Taft's statement as to their agreement on issues and the distribution of patronage. Some moderate Republicans denounced this agreement as a sell-out. The Democrats called it "the surrender of Morningside Heights."[24]

In the middle of campaign, the Republican master plan was nearly destroyed. A columnist revealed that a group of California businessmen had raised an $18,000 fund for Nixon's use between elections. Both Republicans and Democrats called for Nixon's resignation, and Ike's great crusade was at stake. Instead of asking Nixon to resign at once, the public relations men convinced the Republican leaders that they should give Nixon a chance to defend himself, and to that end they purchased air time for a television broadcast on September 23. Ike suspended his decision on the matter until after the broadcast. Tom Dewey urged Nixon to put it up to his listeners whether he should stay on the ticket. In the sentimental broadcast, Nixon declared that the fund was not secret, it was not used for him personally, and no favors were given in return for contributions. He recited his life history—how as a poor boy he worked his way through college and law school, served in the war, and upon returning was urged to run for Congress, which he did successfully. He referred to his happy marriage and to his wife's "Republican cloth coat." He laid bare his personal finances and in an emotional appeal defended keeping the dog, Checkers, a gift to his daughters. (He admitted that he thought he was copying Franklin Roosevelt's dog Fala speech.) The largest television audience recorded up to that time listened to the broadcast, praised as a masterpiece and denounced as "soap opera." He appealed to the people to determine his future by wiring or writing to the Republican National Committee. The response by the faithful was overwhelmingly in favor of keeping Nixon on the ticket. When Ike met him, he put his hand around his shoulder and in a fatherly way said, "You're my boy."[25]

President Truman used the Nixon fund incident to denounce Nixon's voting record: "And as for their Vice-Presidential candidate you have been hearing about his finances—personal finances, but what is more important to you is his voting record in Congress. And it's simply awful. . . . He has been against the little fellow all along the line."[26] A CIO executive charged that the businessmen who contributed had "earned handsome dividends," citing Nixon's vote for the oil depletion allowance, his vote against raising the capital gains tax, and his opposition to public housing and rent control.

Stevenson did not make much of the Nixon fund because it was revealed that he had a fund as governor, which he used to supplement the salaries of some state officials who had accepted state positions at personal sacrifice. The two funds were quite different, however—Nixon's votes in Congress had helped California interests—but to some people a fund was a fund.[27]

After the Nixon fund televised defense, interest in the subject died down, and Nixon returned to his slashing anticommunist theme. He was the most outspoken in using this theme. He called Stevenson "Adlai the appeaser" and a "Ph.D graduate of Dean Acheson's cowardly College of Communist Containment." He condemned Stevenson for his "satisfaction with the appeasing disaster-bent policy of 'containing' global Communism," for his "soft attitude toward the Communist conspiracy at home," and for his being "duped by Communist Alger Hiss" on whose behalf he had testified. In a nationwide broadcast, Nixon asked, "Can a man as Stevenson be trusted to lead our crusade against Communism?" Senator McCarthy went even further and accused Adlai, whom de called "Alger," of "conniving" with communists in 1943 and surrounding himself with procommunist advisers.[28]

In answer to Stevenson's sardonic quips, Eisenhower replied:

It would be very, very fine if one could command new and amusing language, witticisms to bring you a chuckle. . . . The subjects of which we are speaking these days . . . are not those that seem to me to be amusing. . . . Is it amusing that we have stumbled into a war in Korea; that we have already lost in casualties 117,000 of our Americans killed and wounded; is it amusing that the war seems to be no nearer a real solution than ever; that we have no real plan for stopping it?

Stevenson's answer to this speech was that the initials GOP must now stand for "Grouchy Old Pessimists."

Just before the election, Eisenhower reiterated his ten pledges:

1. Be President of "all the people" regardless of race, creed, or political party.
2. Take no steps to repeal "social gains" made by either party.
3. Restore "integrity and competence to government."
4. Fight inflation.
5. Eliminate wasteful government spending and take steps to reduce taxes.
6. Defend the workingman "against any action to destroy his union or his rights" and promote fuller employment and higher wages.
7. Support farm prices at present levels.
8. Work to make "equality of opportunity a living reality" for all Americans.
9. Engage in no "witch hunts or character assassinations" but strive to "prevent infiltration of Communists and fellow travelers" into government.
10. Make "peace in the world for ourselves and for all free people" the primary goal of foreign policy, and start by going to Korea.[29]

The campaign was wound up by the Republicans with a spectacular one-hour television show that cost $267,000. It included a "report" to Ike on his crusade, a speech by the candidate, and remarks by people from all parts of the United States and all walks of life.

The Democrats could not afford such a show. Instead Truman, Barkley, Stevenson, and Sparkman spoke over radio and television. Truman

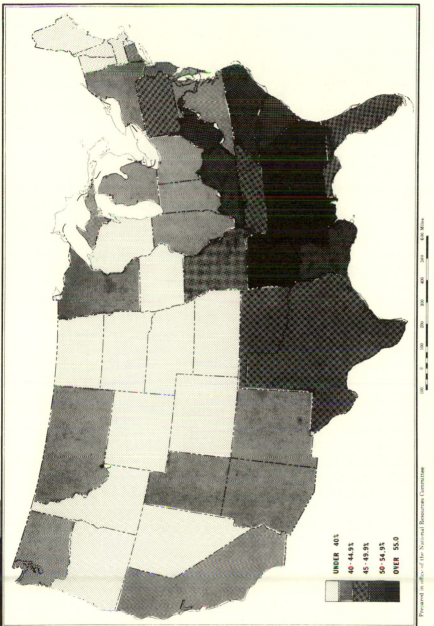

UNDER 40%

40 - 44.9%

45 - 49.9%

50 - 54.9%

OVER 55.0

100   0   100   200   300   400   500   600 Miles

Map 9.   **Percentage Democratic vote in the presidential election, 1952**

attacked the Republicans and a hostile press for playing politics with the sacrifices that Americans were making on the battlefield to protect freedom and peace. As for the importance of this election he said:

> This election may decide whether we shall go ahead and expand our prosperity here at home or slide back into a depression. It may decide whether we shall preserve and extend our civil rights and liberties, or see them fall before a wave of smear and fear. Above all, it may decide whether we shall finally achieve lasting peace or be led into a third world war.[30]

Frightened by their errors in 1948, the pollsters were cautious in predicting the outcome of the election in 1952. Their raw figures indicated an Eisenhower victory, but they were afraid to say so.

The election returns indicated an Eisenhower landslide, with the general taking 55.1 percent of the total vote and Stevenson only 44.4 percent. In absolute numbers, Ike received the largest vote any presidential candidate ever received, 33,936,234. And Stevenson received a record vote for a Democratic candidate, 27,314,992. The total vote cast for all candidates was an all-time high, 61,551,000.[31]

The electoral vote was much more one-sided than the popular vote. Stevenson carried only nine states, with eighty-nine electoral votes: the four Dixiecrat states (Louisiana, Mississippi, Alabama, and South Carolina), Arkansas, Georgia, North Carolina, Kentucky, and West Virginia. Eisenhower carried the rest of the South and all of the northern and western states. His margin was the thinnest in Massachusetts, Pennsylvania, Missouri, Tennessee, Oklahoma, Texas, and Florida, but even the loss of these states would not have changed the result. A characteristic of the election was the fact that Ike's popularity was far greater than that of the Republican party, whose candidates for Congress and state positions ran far behind the head of the ticket. The Republican percentage of the aggregate vote for congressmen was about 5 percent less than Ike's percentage of the presidential vote. Congress went Republican by the thinnest of margins.

Two public opinion analysts concluded that Eisenhower's personal popularity transcended the issues of the campaign and the strategy of the campaign managers. According to them, Eisenhower would have won the election four years earlier on either ticket when there was no Korean issue.[32] The general's popularity was based on his war record, his victories in the military crusade against the Nazis in Europe, and the favorable publicity he had received in the mass media over the past ten years. Polls taken in 1947 and 1948 clearly established the existence of his overwhelming popularity. Eisenhower was above politics. So deeply rooted were the feelings of admiration and pride in the accomplishments of the five-star general that the words of criticism heaped upon him by an angry president who had even greater admiration for General Marshall apparently had little effect.

Eisenhower's popularity extended to all elements of the American electorate. The Michigan Survey Research Center concluded that nearly one-quarter of the final vote for Eisenhower came from those who had voted for Truman in 1948. The newly enfranchised young voters, suburbanites, farmers, all income classes, Catholics, women, and many formerly indifferent voters supported Eisenhower strongly. Stevenson held the Democratic vote at traditional levels and did better only among blacks, trade unionists, and Italian-Americans.

Some pollsters found that the voters interviewed in 1952 placed the Korean war high on their list of important problems facing the nation. They were frustrated by the stalemate, the casualty lists, and the lack of victory. These respondents indicated that they thought Eisenhower could end the war sooner than Stevenson could.[33]

Other pollsters found that economic issues, corruption, and communism were bothering some voters, but these were not crucial. Eisenhower had removed many domestic welfare problems from politics by declaring that they were now rights and were no longer subject to political discussion. Farmers, low-income people, and skilled and unskilled workers who in 1948 thought that they might lose some benefits by voting Republican thought in 1952 that Ike would take care of them. Truman found that his attempted role of president maker was a failure, but he could take consolation in the fact that his strong defense of the New Deal—Fair Deal programs helped keep Eisenhower on a moderate course. The President elect did not want to turn the clock back.

chapter 42 | TRANSITION FROM TRUMAN TO EISENHOWER

> *If a man is acquainted with what other people have experienced at*
> *this desk it will be easier for him to go through a similar experience.*
> *It is ignorance that causes most mistakes. The man who sits here*
> *ought to know his American history, at least.*
> —Harry S. Truman, quoted in Hillman, *Mr. President*, 1952

With the election over, President Truman was anxious to facilitate as smooth a transition to the new administration as possible. He had been greatly disturbed at Eisenhower's failure to defend General Marshall, but now the campaign was over and he had to make peace with the President-elect. Truman had great respect for the office of president and vivid memories of how unprepared he was to fill it when it was suddenly thrust upon him in 1945. He would do everything he could to see that Eisenhower and his associates were as thoroughly briefed as possible.[1]

According to Richard Neustadt, Truman's general ideas about transition were these:

First, he wanted the new Administration informed to the point of action on issues, problems, policies and practices before it took office.

Second, he wanted the new Administration mechanically equipped to act—properly housed and serviced—as soon as it took office.

Third, he wanted the new Administration to understand what he was doing and why, in the interval between election and inauguration—though he neither expected nor desired his successors to share responsibility for his actions in that period.

And fourth, Truman wanted his own regime to wind up its affairs in a posture of dignity and good will, bowing out gracefully, neither cringing nor rancorous.[2]

While his intentions were good, Truman apparently could not refrain from a sly dig in his congratulatory telegram sent to Eisenhower from the train en route from Washington to Independence, Missouri:

Congratulations on your overwhelming victory. The 1954 budget must be presented to the Congress before January 15th. All the preliminary figures have been made up.

You should have a representative meet with the Director of the Bureau of the Budget immediately. The Independence will be at your disposal if you still desire to go to Korea.[3]

The telegram reflected Truman's residual anger at Eisenhower's using the Korean crisis for political advantage. Eisenhower was infuriated at Truman's telegam, but he responded politely:

I deeply appreciate your courteous and generous telegram. I shall try to make arrangements within the next two or three days to have a personal representative to sit with the Director of the Budget. I am most appreciative of your offer of the use of the Independence but assure you that any suitable transport plane that one of the services could make available will be satisfactory for my planned trip to Korea. With your permission I shall give the Secretary of Defense the earliest possible notice of my proposed date of departure.[4]

President Truman felt that he had been terribly handicapped when he took the oath of office and was confronted with a series of critical decisions without adequate briefing. He "thought it was an omission in our political tradition that a retiring President did not make it his business to facilitate the transfer of the government to his successor."[5]

It was twenty years since a Republican had been elected president, and transition of power from one party to the other had become much more complicated during that time. The depression, recovery, and two wars had increased the civilian bureaucracy fourfold and the military personnel sevenfold; the White House staff had grown from forty to over two hundred; and there were over a thousand employees in the Executive Office of the President, which included the Bureau of the Budget, the National Security Council, the National Security Resources Board, and the Council of Economic Advisers. Since World War II the United States had assumed a much larger role in world affairs, and international crises were always near.[6]

In addition to his telegram of November 6, Truman also sent a letter to General Eisenhower on the same day.

There are some really fundamental things pending before the United Nations that must be met in a positive manner. I wish you would suggest somebody, in addition to the person who is to talk to the Budget Director, to discuss these matters authoritatively with the Secretary of State, the Secretary of the Treasury and the Secretary of Defense.[7]

As far back as 1948, the Department of State and the Bureau of the Budget had considered the possibility of change in administration and the need for a smooth transition. As part of the bipartisan foreign policy, John Foster Dulles, Tom Dewey's adviser, was briefed on international questions and asked to serve as a delegate to a U.N. General Assembly. The Bureau of the Budget, in a June 15, 1948, working paper, considered how the budget and other presidential messages should be prepared in case the Republicans won.[8]

In 1952 the Bureau of the Budget again took the lead in planning for a change. The director, Frederick J. Lawton, a career officer, had been advised by President Truman to play down the role of the bureau in policy making and emphasize its technical, professional, and nonpartisan functions. Shortly after Truman announced that he would not run for president, the bureau staff began to prepare memoranda, such as "Adjusting to Change in the Presidency" and "Development of Briefing Materials for New President." Truman approved of these activities.[9]

The Policy Planning Staff of Secretary Acheson, under the chairmanship of Paul Nitze, also contributed a document on briefing candidates and the president elect. It recommended that everything be done to insure responsible conduct during the campaign and to step up the flow of information to the victor. Acheson and Truman agreed with the recommendations and followed them closely.[10]

During the campaign there was a hitch in this program. President Truman invited Stevenson to the White House for a briefing soon after he was nominated. At the same time he directed General Omar Bradley, chairman of the Joint Chiefs of Staff, to contact Eisenhower and offer him a general briefing. Bradley delayed in carrying out his assignment with Eisenhower, although he took part in the briefing of Stevenson. Ike, misunderstanding the entire situation, attacked Truman for having General Bradley participate in a Stevenson meeting, since it meant "a decision to involve responsible nonpolitical officers of our government . . . into a political campaign in which they have no part." Truman tried to repair the damage by inviting Ike to the White House for a briefing, but Ike turned down the invitation, proclaiming, "In my current position as standard-bearer of the Republican party and of other Americans who want to bring about a change in National Government, it is my duty to remain free to analyze publicly the policies and acts of the present Administration." In his press conference, Truman stated that arrangements had been made to brief Ike prior to the White House invitation. Ike denied this. Then General Bradley admitted his mistake in not carrying out his assignment promptly. At this point, Truman exploded in one of his famous letters:

Dear Ike:
I am sorry if I caused you any embarrassment. What I've always had in mind was and is a continuing foreign policy. You know that is a fact because you had a part in outlining it. Partisan politics should stop at the boundaries of the United States. I'm extremely sorry that you have allowed a bunch of screwballs to come between us.

You have made a bad mistake, and I'm hoping that it won't injure this great Republic.

There has never been one like it and I want to see it continue regardless of the man who occupies the most important position in the history of the world.

May God guide you and give you light.

From a man who has always been your friend and who always intended to be.[11]

Eisenhower replied with appreciation for Truman's intentions but still refused to come to the White House. The relations between the two had deteriorated greatly during the campaign, especially on the issue of McCarthyism, the defense of General Marshall, and the exploiting of the unpopularity of the Korean war.

After the election, Truman again invited Eisenhower to the White House. The President elect accepted but made it clear that he would not participate in any government decisions before taking office. Truman was anxious to have backing for an American resolution before the U.N. Assembly that would support the American negotiators in their insistence on the principle of nonforcible repatriation of prisoners of war in Korea.[12] While Eisenhower appointed Senator Henry Cabot Lodge, Jr., as his liaison with the State, Defense, and other departments, he directed him only to gather information and not to participate in any policy decisions. On budget matters, he selected Joseph M. Dodge, a Detroit banker who had been fiscal adviser to the military governments of Germany and Japan, to be his representative to the Bureau of the Budget. Before the meeting, Truman had some top-secret documents sent to Eisenhower by CIA director Walter Bedell Smith, who used to be Eisenhower's chief of staff, and by James Lay, secretary of the National Security Council. Included were basic NSC policy papers containing intelligence estimates of danger spots and plans for meeting emergencies.[13]

At the meeting, held November 18, 1952, Truman claims that he told Eisenhower privately that he thought the meeting was necessary to serve the best interests of the country. He had no purpose of setting any political trap or trying to shift any responsibility that was his as president. There might be some foreign policy issues that would not succeed unless other nations had assurance of the continuity of the policy under the new administration. This would be beyond his power to determine. He said, "We will tell you about these issues and would welcome concurrence if you want to give it. But we will not press for it. This is a matter on which you will have to make up your own mind on the basis of what is best for America."[14] Truman and Eisenhower then went into the cabinet room where they met with Acheson, Lovett, Snyder, Harriman, Lodge, and Dodge. The President explained again why the meeting was called, and he welcomed Lodge and Dodge. Acheson explained the pending problems in Korea, NATO, Iran, and Indochina. Snyder handed Eisenhower a memorandum on the financing of the federal government and foreign aid. Eisenhower and Truman agreed upon a joint statement after Lodge had suggested some alterations:

We have discussed some of the most important problems affecting our country in the sphere of international relations. Information with respect to these problems has been made available to General Eisenhower.

Under our Constitution the President must exercise his functions until he leaves office, and his successor cannot be asked to share or assume the responsibilities of the Presidency until he takes office.

We have worked out a framework for liaison and exchange of information between the present Administration and the incoming Administration, but we have made no arrangements which are inconsistent with the full spirit of our Constitution. General Eisenhower has not been asked to assume any of the responsibilities of the Presidency until he takes the oath of office. . . .

We believe, however, that the arrangements we have made for cooperation will be of great value to the stability of our country and to the favorable progress of international affairs.

We are confident that this meeting and that the arrangements we have made today for liaison and cooperation between the present Administration and the new Administration furnish additional proof of the ability of the people of the country to manage their affairs with a sense of continuity and with responsibility.[15]

The part that Lodge wanted omitted referred to the prisoners-of-war controversy in Korea. Acheson was concerned about a compromise offered by India. The United States was saved from embarrassment by the rejection of the Indian proposal by Communist China.[16]

Truman thought that Eisenhower was grim at this conference, "rather appalled at all that the President needs to know." One reporter wrote, "At least the President-elect seemed to observers to be a different and changed man when he came from the conference with President Truman. . . . His face wore a . . . startled look."[17]

Ten years later Merle Miller reported Truman as saying regarding this conference:

He came to see me. I invited him in not long after the election, and he didn't want to come; I think he didn't want to interrupt his golf game down in Florida or Georgia or wherever it was, but he finally did come. And he looked around a little, but I could see that nothing that was said was getting through to him. He got there mad, and he stayed mad. One of his troubles . . . he wasn't used to being criticized and he never did get it through his head that that's what politics is all *about*. He was used to having his ass kissed.[18]

General Eisenhower found that two weeks was all that he could spend in Augusta, Georgia. He had to handle the many messages from Truman and his advisers; he had to consider the selection of top officials; and he had to plan for his trip to Korea and for his inaugural.[19]

At his headquarters in the Hotel Commodore in New York City, Eisenhower organized his staff for taking over the presidency. Some of his advisers and fund raisers had engaged the management consulting firm of McKinsey and Company to make a study of executive recruiting. On November 20, he announced his choices of John Foster Dulles of New York for secretary of state; Charles E. Wilson, president of General Motors, for secretary of defense; Douglas McKay, governor of Oregon, for secretary of the interior; George H. Humphrey, chairman of M. A. Hanna and Co., for secretary of the treasury; Herbert Brownell, Jr., as attorney general; and Harold Stassen, former governor of Minnesota, for director of mutual security. A few days later he announced Ezra Taft Benson of Utah for secretary of agriculture; Arthur E. Summerfield, Republican national chairman, for postmaster general; Oveta Culp Hobby of Texas as administrator of the Federal Security Agency; and Sherman Adams, governor of New Hampshire, for the top White House post as the assistant to the president (the position held at that time by John Steelman, who was asked to stay on for a few weeks in order to ease the transition).[20]

All of the designated appointees except McKay reported to Eisenhower at the Commodore in a few days, received briefing documents on their duties from McKinsey and Company, and got in touch with their counterparts in the Truman administration in Washington. Wilson went to the Pentagon to see Lovett and others. Humphrey had some cordial talks with Snyder. Dulles, who was a familiar figure, had a number of conferences with Acheson and other State Department officials.[21]

Since administration reorganization had been a campaign issue, Eisenhower appointed a committee composed of former Assistant Secretary of State Nelson A. Rockefeller (as chairman), Arthur S. Fleming, president of Ohio Wesleyan University, and his own brother, Milton S. Eisenhower, who had had broad experience in government, to sift proposals and make recommendations. This committee relied extensively on the Hoover Commission appointed by President Truman.[22]

Before the end of November, additional choices for top positions were announced. Lodge was designated for chief delegate to the United Nations; Winthrop W. Aldrich, a New York banker related to the Rockefellers, for ambassador to Great Britain; Sinclair Weeks, a Boston businessman and campaign finance chairman, for secretary of commerce; and Martin P. Durkin, president of the Plumbers and Pipe Fitters Union and a registered Democrat, for secretary of labor. On the White House staff, James Haggerty would be press secretary, Gabriel Hauge, an administrative assistant, and General Milton B. Persons, the deputy assistant to the president. In making some of these appointments, the general, lacking political experience, offended some senators, especially Senator Taft who was not consulted about Humphrey from his own state and who regarded the appointment of Durkin as a personal insult.[23]

The Eisenhower trip to Korea was another source of friction between the President and the President elect. While Eisenhower admitted he had no panacea for ending the war, he wanted "to see it through." On his return, he consulted with secretaries-designate Dulles, Humphrey, and McKay, budget representative Dodge, and General Lucius Clay. Dodge brought bad news about the budget. From his consultations, he did not see how it could be balanced without raising taxes. Humphrey and Clay urged that economic controls be removed as soon as possible. During the trip, Eisenhower listened to General MacArthur's speech in New York in which he said, "I am confident there is a clear and definite solution." The two generals exchanged messages in which they agreed to meet and discuss the matter. Haggerty released these messages, and the fat was on the fire as far as Truman was concerned.[24]

At his press conference on December 11, 1952, Truman exploded about the proposed meeting between the two generals to discuss the Korean situation. If either Eisenhower or MacArthur had a solution, it was his duty to make it known to the President and the Defense Department. Truman was sure that MacArthur did not have anything new. He would merely repeat his plans for expanding the war into an allout attack on Communist China— a plan that had been rejected by the Joint Chiefs of Staff and by U.S. allies. Truman proved to be correct in this analysis. From his point of view, "The announcement of that trip was a piece of demagoguery, and then of course he had to make it after he had made the statement." Eisenhower was greatly offended and made no effort to see Truman again until the inauguration.[25]

Eisenhower's associates continued their contacts with the Truman officials. Adams visited the White House for a consultation with Steelman principally on housekeeping arrangements. Eisenhower's designated special assistant for national security affairs, Robert Cutler, a reserve brigadier general who had served with the Psychological Strategy Board, consulted officials of the State and Defense departments and the National Security Council. He and Dodge perhaps made the greatest use of their opportunities to learn and plan. Secretary of State Acheson saw that special briefing papers were prepared for Dulles. Secretary-designate Weeks visited the Department of Commerce, and Humphrey, with his top aides who had had considerable experience under the Truman administration, consulted with Treasury officials. Brownell and his chief assistant, William P. Rogers, got in touch with Attorney General McGranery. Wilson came again with his top aides to the Pentagon, but Lovett was disappointed that the consultations started so late. It was agreed that the assistant secretary of defense, Wilfred McNeill, a budget officer since Forrestal's day, would be continued in that capacity.[26]

Truman and his officials were sorry that greater use was not made of the arrangements for briefing the incoming administration. As Neustadt put it,

"In general, then, Truman threw the door wide open, but nobody came in, except to make physical arrangements for occupancy."[27]

In the final weeks of his presidency, Truman was subdued. There were no more outbursts like the one following Eisenhower's meeting with MacArthur. He tried to play the role of a good loser, confident of his place in history. He talked about the need for vigorous leadership in the White House and the importance of preserving the powers of the one representative of all the people.

A number of special reports and policy studies were wound up just before Truman left office, including Lovett's annual report on the problems of achieving civilian control of the military departments; the President's Advisory Committee on Management, which proposed permanent reorganization authority; the report of the National Security Resources Board on energy and scarce materials; the President's Commission on the Health Needs of the Nation; and the report of the Commission on Immigration and Naturalization.

In preparing his last three messages to Congress, President Truman could not use the formula that he had in previous years. It was not appropriate for the state of the union message to outline a legislative program, for the budget message to fix price tags on new programs, or for the economic report to explain and rationalize any changes proposed. It would be the duty of the new president to do these things. Consequently, the state of the union message, originally drafted by David Lloyd, Charles Murphy, and Richard Neustadt, was a moderate document, which reviewed the accomplishments of Truman's administration and some of the unsolved problems. After seven and a half years of diplomatic struggles with Stalin he warned of the communist danger, the Soviet menace to free institutions, and the Russian record of broken promises, subversive activities, and open aggression. The cold war came from "the distorted Marxist interpretation of history." He also warned against McCarthyism although he did not mention the senator by name:

But there are some things that could shift the advantage to their side. One of the things that could defeat us is fear—fear of the task we face, fear of adjusting to it, fear that breeds more fear, sapping our faith, corroding our liberties, turning citizen against citizen, ally against ally. Fear could snatch away the very values we are striving to defend.

Already the danger signals have gone up. Already the corrosive process has begun. And every diminution of our tolerance, each new act of enforced conformity, each idle accusation, each demonstration of hysteria—each new restrictive law—is one more sign that we can lose the battle against fear.[28]

The budget message did not provide for either revenue or expenditures that might result in new legislation. It was assumed that the authority for mutual security and certain defense production activities would be renewed. The budget in general provided for the continuation of existing programs at their current levels.

The economic report reviewed economic progress during the Truman presidency, an evaluation of the workings of the Employment Act of 1946, a statement of basic economic principles, and an optimistic forecast of American and foreign economic growth.[29]

During this time, President Truman's informal remarks at press conferences and groups of public employees received favorable attention. He was in a forgiving mood and was grateful for the favorable publicity that he had received in the past. At every opportunity he stressed the importance of the office he held and the need for firm leadership.[30]

While Truman said that he was leaving decisions to the new administration, he could not resist action that embodied his view on the tidelands oil question, which was at variance with that of Eisenhower. By executive order, he established a naval petroleum reserve in the offshore oil lands, which the Republicans had promised the coastal states would be ceded to them for private exploitation.

Eisenhower wanted his cabinet appointments confirmed on inauguration day. This required the cooperation of the Senate. Conservative Democrat Harry F. Byrd of Virginia objected on the ground that it was necessary to check the private holdings of the nominees in order to avoid any later conflict of interest charges. A compromise was worked out to have hearings in advance of the inauguration. If the committees agreed to the nominations, the Senate would take action by unanimous consent. These preinauguration hearings went smoothly until Charles E. Wilson came before the Armed Services Committee. He proposed to keep his stock in General Motors, and he apparently thought the conflict-of-interest laws were not important:

Senator Hendrickson: Mr. Wilson, you have told the committee, I think more than once this morning, that you see no area of conflict between your interest in the General Motors Corp. . . . and the position you are about to assume.

Mr. Wilson: Yes, sir.

Senator Hendrickson: Well now, I am interested to know whether if a situation did arise where you had to make a decision which was extremely adverse to the interests of your stock and General Motors Corp. in the interests of the United States Government, could you make that decision?

Mr. Wilson: Yes, sir. I could. I cannot conceive of one because for years I thought what was good for our country was good for General Motors and vice versa. The difference did not exist. Our company is too big. It goes with the welfare of the country. Our contribution to the Nation is quite considerable.[31]

Following this naive confession, there were meetings between Wilson, Eisenhower, and the Senate leaders. Wilson refused to sell his holdings, and the matter was not settled before inauguration.

The inauguration itself was not entirely harmonious. Truman was not pleased with the Eisenhower preference for a homburg over a top hat, and he was miffed when Eisenhower requested to be picked up at his hotel. Custom required the president-elect to pick up the retiring president at the White House. Eisenhower refused to come into the White House in violation of another tradition. Truman swallowed his pride and came out, and the two men sat grimly in silence for most of the trip from the White House to the Capitol. The general finally broke the silence by inquiring about who gave the orders for his son to come to the inaugural. Truman gladly confessed that he, the President, gave the order. As he recalled later, "If you think somebody was trying to embarrass you by this order then the President assumes full responsibility." Ten years later Truman still resented the way he was treated at the inaugural, and he characterized Ike as a "weak," "cowardly" "son of a bitch."[32]

Truman returned to Independence, Missouri, where he took up life as a private citizen, writing his *Memoirs*, talking to visitors at the Truman Library, lecturing to students, and dabbling, not always too successfully, in politics. His attempt to work out a smooth transition was only partially successful. Liaison between Lawton and Dodge regarding budget matters worked out well. Cutler did a good job in taking over functions at NSC. Durkin in the Labor Department took over without disruption. In other departments and in the Council of Economic Advisers, the going was rough. The council itself was saved by the intervention of Senator Taft.[33] Twenty years out of power, the Republicans were patronage hungry. Eisenhower did not follow Truman's idea of an active-positive presidency. Truman, of course, never used the phrase "active-positive presidency," a term coined by James Barber in his *Presidential Character*, but Truman's behavior fit the pattern. An active president is one who insists on making decisions and engaging in constructive activities. A positive president is one who is optimistic and refuses to look at things from a negative point of view. Barber placed Eisenhower in the passive-negative category.[34] During the transition, some of these qualities became evident. Eisenhower did not want to act on any suggestions coming from Truman because he resented Truman's criticisms. He wanted to make peace with Congress and to reconcile the various factions in the Republican party, including the Taft wing. Under these circumstances, he would not listen to Truman's advice regarding pending problems. Consequently, during the changeover period, many important governmental functions were disrupted.

chapter 43 | CHARACTER AND
CRISES

*Harry Truman . . . was an active-positive type, displaying high
self-esteem and continued enjoyment in the exercise of power. His
style was flexible and balanced: an aggressive, informal rhetoric; a
penchant for soaking up facts through study and deciding, without
much theory, between alternatives posed in either-or terms; a
personal relations style based on a strong sense of personal loyalty.
His world view was emphatically nonphilosophical—values were
simple for him, not a matter of great concern. He saw men as the
makers of history, character as the wellspring of behavior. From
his inner confidence and self-recognition he drew the strength to
grow in office, to develop through learning without anxiety, as a
person and as a President.*

—James David Barber, *The Presidential Character:
Predicting Performance in the White House*

Harry S. Truman was a highly controversial figure when he was in the
White House. He remained so after he left the presidency. Conflicting
myths began to grow about his character and his record. If anything, his
death on December 26, 1972, brought new clashes between the traditional-
ists, who early had claimed that Truman should be placed among the near-
great presidents, and the revisionists of various schools, who began to find
ways to downgrade the "little man" from Independence. On the other hand,
older historians still praise him, and journalists talk about the history of a
triumphant succession.

A 1977 survey of historians at a hundred colleges and universities found
that Truman ranked among the top eight who commanded more than half
of the votes as one of our greatest presidents. The other seven were Lincoln,
Washington, Franklin D. Roosevelt, Teddy Roosevelt, Jefferson, Wilson,
and Jackson.[1] Some admirers claim that although Truman lacked the usual
educational background called for in modern presidential nominees and a
distinguished prepresidential career, he showed great capacity for growth,
and he overcame his original handicaps by a fierce desire to serve his
country even at the expense of his own personal popularity.[2] On the other

hand, the revisionists denounce him vehemently as an incompetent who blundered from one error to another, who became the tool of the political bosses, the Wall Street financiers, and the military-industrial complex, who helped start the cold war, who missed many opportunities for a negotiated détente with the Soviet Union, and who promoted a selfish, nationalistic, international economic policy based upon the imperialistic extension of American capitalism and the suppression of all revolutionary movements wherever they might be found.[3]

In trying to evaluate a president's record, we sometimes forget that a president is not omniscient. We have come to demand too much of our presidents. They are expected to solve all problems—to steady the economy, to provide welfare for the poor, the sick, the unemployed, and the old, to see that our natural resources are conserved, to see that businessmen, workers, farmers, and others gainfully employed are getting their just dues, to see that consumers are satisfied with the price and quality of goods they desire, and to see that America's place in the world and its security against external attacks are maintained.[4] Among the expectations the American people hold for their president are two that James D. Barber has listed: "The President is king for a while and then shifts to being politician for a while, and back again. . . . A king who does not rule, a politician above politics, a man of action supremely serene—the President is expected to be all things to all men."[5] Truman never thought he was king. He did not seek power. He was just plain Harry from Independence, Missouri, with no illusions that he was the best man for the office. As Barber put it, "Truman put great store in maintaining the dignity of the office, but of course his strength was his fighting courage in the face of adversity."[6]

How does one rate a president? Can the performance of one president be usefully compared with that of another? Each president has had to face his own peculiar problems. Truman, unbriefed, unprepared for the awesome transition from the vice-presidency to the presidency, modest in rating his own gifts, stumbled a bit at first, but he kept on trying to find out what Roosevelt would have done under various circumstances.

Truman placed a great deal of emphasis on political loyalty. His Senate voting record shows that he was loyal to President Roosevelt. In some cases, his loyalty to persons who were once his superiors went too far. His standing by Tom Pendergast is a case in point. He did not need to go to the funeral of the notorious political boss; indeed his friends urged him not to go because this was his opportunity to repudiate all that the corrupt machine had stood for, but Truman remained fast in his loyalty to the person and went. From time to time, Truman also showed excessive loyalty to subordinates who were damaging his reputation. His military aide, General Harry Vaughan, got into trouble for accepting gifts from a contractor who had done business with the government. The President reassured

Vaughan that the attacks were purely political, aimed at embarrasing the White House, but the press did not accept this explanation.[7]

Another quality that sustained Truman in the White House was his incurable optimism. He always hoped for the best. In running for renomination as U.S. senator from Missouri in 1940, the press, his friends, and the opposition counted him out in advance. But Truman refused to think negatively and put together a winning combination. The same thing happened in 1948 when he ran for president in his own right. Some psychologists claim that such optimism is formed at a very early stage in the individual's development. It is called *oral optimism* since it develops as a fixation at the infant sucking age. The infant finds his mother's milk warm and satisfying. The close contact between the beloved mother and child is reassuring. As in the case of Franklin D. Roosevelt, Truman's infancy was of this character, and although his father had some financial problems, there was nothing in Truman's preadolescent and adolescent development to disturb his optimistic view of life. The Trumans were never in abject poverty, and the family life was happy. Remnants of Truman's oral tendencies were to be found in his fondness for good food, for drinking, and for talking and smiling. He was gregarious and liked meeting with his friends. He joined the Jackson County Farm Bureau, the Masons, the National Guard, the Old Trails Association, the American Legion, and many other organizations where he could drink and converse.[8]

What was the secret of Truman's standing up under the strain of nearly eight years in the White House, during which he was subjected to assassination attempts, bitter criticism, long hours of work, and ever-persistent crises? First, it is clear that he kept in good physical shape. Every afternoon he took a brief nap. Regardless of the pressure of his official duties, he took brisk morning walks and swam in the White House pool. Occasionally he would have a vigorous rubdown. He did not smoke. He also took periodic vacations on which he was able to relax completely and have fun playing poker and swapping stories. He did not worry and he had no regrets. The pressure of the presidency broke the health of six occupants in the White House in this century—Woodrow Wilson, Warren G. Harding, Franklin D. Roosevelt, Dwight D. Eisenhower, Lyndon B. Johnson, and Richard Nixon. Major party conventions and the voters have given too little attention to the physical fitness of aspirants for the presidency.[9]

Harsh criticisms of his performance in office did not depress Truman mentally. In the rough and tumble of Kansas City politics, there was no censorship of the rhetoric, and Truman had been called every name there is. The verbal lashings made no greater impression on him than a blast of hot air. He only lost his temper when he felt that Bess or Margaret were unjustly attacked. But in politics no one could dent his tough hide.

The Trumans had a highly developed sense of humor, and they immensely enjoyed a good joke. Regarding this trait, Crane wrote: "It is conceivable that his sense of humor frequently helped to lessen the tensions and to soften the austerity of the ardent advocates of both political parties, who came prepared for pitched battle but left in reasonable agreement.''[10] A former White House aide, now at Brookings Institution, relates: ''Another delightful incident was in Cincinnati. I had written a humorous takeoff on Taft for Taft's hometown as a change of pace after so many serious speeches. . . . Truman apparently liked it, too, because he hammed it up and adlibbed a great many additional lines that added punch and humor. . . Then he laughed so hard at his own wit—and pun—that he almost broke down and had us all breaking down with him. In short, he was a fine, relaxed, and enjoyable man to work for.''[11] A few excerpts will show why this happened. ''This is Bob Taft's hometown. . . . I thought the Republicans were going to nominate him for President this time—and he was my candidate. . . . If the American people had a chance to vote for Senator Taft, they would at least know what they are getting. . . . I don't believe the Republican Party can hide its record behind a new face.''[12] At Potsdam, Truman was greatly amused at the respect the Russians showed to his Jackson County friend, Fred Canfil, who was introduced as Marshal Canfil. (He was only a U.S. district court marshal with no military rank.) Truman wrote regarding Huey Long, who had just made a long speech of which he was proud, '' 'What did you think of my speech?' he asked. 'I had to listen to you,' I told him, 'because I was in the chair and couldn't walk out.' He never spoke to me after that.''[13]

Truman had a great time with the protocol officer and two reporter friends of his, whom he invited to get in the reception line with him. ''He [the President] grabbed me by one arm and Tony by the other and pulled us into the line with Stettinius. The protocol man coughed nervously and adjusted his tie. Stettinius roared with laughter.''[14]

Truman's humor with male companions sometimes took on a coarse and vulgar nature. Merle Miller in his *Plain Speaking* cites a number of examples. The vocabulary from Truman's jokes came from the saloon, the army barracks and latrines, the barnyards of the various farms he visited or worked on, and from the smoke-filled backrooms of the machine politicians.[15] His press secretary, Charlie Ross, saved him some salacious limericks. Justice William O. Douglas cited a good case in his autobiography *Go East, Young Man:*

Later as World War II approached, Truman headed the famous committee that investigated America's industrial plant. Two future Justices, whom he was to appoint, were on his committee—Harold Burton of Ohio and Shay Minton of Indiana. Burton, quiet and industrious and very conscientious, was the workhorse of the committee. Each endeared himself to Truman in many ways. For instance, on reaching a city, Shay would turn to Truman and say, ''Should we check into the hotel and leave our bags or go directly to the whorehouse.''[16]

Since Truman was most loyal to Bess, the only interpretation of this alleged incident is that Minton was trying to shock the prim Burton.

Truman was not known to have any nervous symptoms. In 1949 he dismissed as ridiculous Roger Sermon's story of a nervously disintegrated Truman on the day after the 1940 senatorial primary.[17] He may have had some inferiority feelings about certain things. He was excessively humble after being sworn in as president in 1945 because he was acutely aware of the gaps in his briefings, but as the information poured in, he bounded back. He may have had some slight tendency toward acquiring a persecution complex when the press emphasized some mistake he made, but all presidents tend to have such feelings toward the end of their term, and Truman's case was just a mild one.

There can be no doubts as to Truman's physical and moral courage. Pandemonium reigned on the afternoon when two men attempted to assassinate him. One man was killed and the other severely wounded. One guard was slain and two others were wounded, but Truman calmly left for a speaking engagement at Arlington Cemetery.[18] As to his moral courage, many examples could be cited. Admiral Leahy wrote regarding the Potsdam conference: "Truman had stood up to Stalin in a manner calculated to warm the heart of every patriotic American. He refused to be bulldozed into any reparations agreement that would repeat the history of World War I, which found the American taxpayer paying for German reparations."[19] Even the critical Sam Lubell admitted: "It took courage to order American troops into Korea. It also took courage to dismiss General MacArthur at a time when the Republicans were howling so furiously for Secretary of State Dean Acheson's English mustache."[20] In a letter to President Truman, Hoyt McAfee wrote: "I'm truly glad you're my President—because you're a fighting President; and one who will go down in history, I think, as a champion of social justice and humanitarian causes. A President with a HEART; and a President with GUTS."[21]

Truman was also noted for his tact, friendliness, gregariousness, and lack of putting on airs. Tristram Coffin wrote: "Harry Truman is probably the most friendly and democratic man in Washington. At the Jefferson Island outing of the Democrats, he has been seen arm in arm with Theodore (The Man) Bilbo, or joking good-naturedly with the club steward. He just likes people."[22] Truman was popular with the butlers and maids on the White House staff. Some noted a marked difference when the Eisenhowers moved into the White House and brought with them a semimilitary atmosphere.

Any estimate of the special skills of a president is frankly subjective, but it is better than a general, vague, impressionistic evaluation. Ideally a paired comparison system should be used, but this would apply most appropriately only to Franklin D. Roosevelt, who ran for the office four times and had four different opponents.

The preponderance of evidence seems to support the view that Truman had the capacity to make difficult decisions and make them promptly if the situation seemed to demand it. The President himself expressed the view that he was in a spot where he had to decide one way or other: "Being a President is like riding a tiger. A man has to keep on riding or be swallowed."[23] Admiral Leahy, his adviser on national security affairs, wrote that Truman "asked advice in regard to military matters and foreign relations as frequently as did his predecessor. He listened attentively to volunteered advice, and made positive decisions for which he assumed full personal responsibility."[24] Senator Vandenberg wrote: "But I liked the first decision Truman made—namely that Frisco should go on. Senator Connally immediately prophesied after FDR died that Frisco would be postponed. . . . Truman promptly stopped *that* mistake (which would have confessed to the world that there is an 'indispensable man' who was bigger than America)."[25] Many other examples of his ability to make decisions and stand by them can be cited: his decision to use the airlift to fight the Berlin blockade, his decision not to send Justice Vinson to Moscow when Secretary of State Marshall objected to the mission, and his decision to dismiss General MacArthur from his command posts in the Far East. Some said he made decisions too quickly without proper consideration of all the alternatives, and even Truman admitted that he made mistakes. When he did, he made another decision. He regarded the White House as a place where decisions were made. The motto on his desk read, "The Buck Stops Here."

The man from Missouri was a good interpreter of trends, both at home and abroad. At home he saw in 1948 that he had a chance to be reelected while most people had counted him out before the campaign began. Again, in 1952 he saw that Ike would be difficult to beat so he announced long before the Democratic National Convention met that he would not be a candidate. In 1948 he saw that Stalin and his cohorts did not want to start another world war for the sake of taking over Berlin. At a cabinet meeting he was asked to consider whether to stay in Berlin. He answered that we were staying, but the question was how. He foresaw that the Russians would not disturb the airlift. If they had, that might start general military activities. The risk was great—a straying Russian plane or missile could start a war. Soviet planes and missiles were not used. In 1949-1950 he saw that the Chinese Nationalist regime could not be saved. He was aware of the limits of American power in international affairs, and he strove to avoid actions that might start a world war.[26]

How was Truman as an administrator? Here there are many criteria that might be applied. For a time, Truman considered balancing the budget and piling up a surplus to pay off some of the national debt as a high priority, and he did just that. He established fine relations with his budget directors and the professional staff of the Bureau of the Budget. He sponsored a number of excellent reorganizations of the government, including the establishment of the National Security Council and its appendage, the Central Intelligence Agency, and the creation of the Council of Economic Advisers. His cabinet meetings were far more businesslike than Franklin Roosevelt's. He delegated powers to his cabinet officers and expected them to carry out their obligations. When they did not, he removed them, as in the case of Attorney General McGrath who mishandled wrongdoers in his department and in the Bureau of Internal Revenue. The White House staff was used efficiently and legally. He would not countenance any wire-tapping or bugging of his own men or of people he did not like. As to his attention to details, an assistant put it this way: "He pays conscientious attention to details. He plugs away very diligently." Jonathan Daniels, who worked under both Roosevelt and Truman, commented: "If Truman gave me an assignment, I wouldn't be fearful, as I might be under Roosevelt that he'd given it to two other fellows at the same time." Truman was always accessible to cabinet members and to his staff assistants.[27]

As a legislator, Truman brought ten years of experience in the Senate to his legislative responsibilities as president. He established working relations with the leaders of the Senate and the House. He had the excellent service of Charles Murphy, a skilled legislative draftsman. If necessary, he could prod key legislators with a message, a letter, a telephone call, or a summons to the White House for consultation. The Bureau of the Budget and the White House staff closely followed the course of legislation and made recommendations for signing or vetoing bills passed. Truman's annual messages contained the overall legislative programs. He was keenly aware of the limits of his powers to influence Congress, and he sometimes sacrificed domestic programs to secure support for his foreign policies.[28]

What rating should Truman get as a judge of men? On this subject, Truman himself wrote:

You have got to have a pretty good picture of the background and history of men, and what their connections have been, both in business and personal life. And then you have just got to be a judge of people. I am not very often mistaken in judgments I make of people, because I think I understand people pretty well. But you always take a chance when you put a fellow in a position of responsibility, because no matter how good he is, you cannot tell what he will do until he is tried.

Rex Tugwell and some of the revisionists took a dim view of Truman's appointment policies. Tugwell wrote in his *Chronicle of Jeopardy*: "For Mr. Truman even though he still protested his desire to implement Roosevelt's policies, had obviously been ridding himself of all those who could carry them on." Many criticisms have been made of his judicial appointments.[29] Looking over Truman's appointments as a whole, it must be admitted that though many—too many—of them were bad, some were good and a few were excellent—Dean Acheson, George C. Marshall, Oscar Chapman, Averell Harriman, Clark Clifford, Charles Murphy, Charles Brannan, and James Webb. Regarding Clifford, much has been written. In 1946 Tris Coffin wrote: "The handsome attorney stepped in to fill a White House need, as civilian chief of staff. . . . Soon he was giving Harry Truman the kind of firm instruction the President should have had all along. Clifford was polite, even unctuous, but he got results."[30] Regarding the less showy Murphy, one of his assistants declared: "Murphy impressed me at that time, and still does, as a man with about as sound a judgment as anybody I've ever known. He would take great pains to weigh all the angles of a question in order to come out with the right position from the viewpoint of the President."[31]

Regarding his success as a party organizer, it can be said that no other president in this century was more solidly a party organization man than Harry Truman, who did not mind telling an early biographer, "I owe my political life to the Pendergast organization. I never would have had an opportunity to have a career in politics without their support."[32] Truman began his political activities in his local precinct, and he ended up by naming several chairmen of the Democratic National Committee. After being elected to the Senate, his attendance at Democratic National Conventions was regular, and he served on the Resolutions Committee. He had to fight for his nomination for president in 1948, but when Eisenhower got out of the picture, he controlled the situation.[33] In his election campaign, he worked closely with the national and state party organizations.

In his conduct of foreign relations, Truman, relying upon George Marshall and Dean Acheson, made many important decisions, most of which turned out well. His circle of advisers, however, was not always wide enough to avoid certain pitfalls. Acheson screened out the advice of those opposing the crossing of the thirty-eighth parallel in Korea.

President Truman's techniques in the formulation and execution of domestic policies were controversial, but in spite of the adverse majorities in Congress made up of Republicans and southern Democrats, his strategy had merit. He was guarding existing gains and setting long-range goals.

As compared with President Roosevelt's press conferences, Truman's were not as brilliant, but they were sometimes more exciting, because no one knew what the plain-speaking man from Missouri might say next. Truman held regular press conferences, and he had able press secretaries who did not lie to the reporters. He did not have a rich voice, but he made his points over the radio.[34]

Harry dearly loved bull sessions, and he would lay aside the cares of the day to "strike a blow for liberty" and to exchange tall (or low) tales. He could be emphatic in his face-to-face conferences.

President Truman's speeches were not as literary as Roosevelt's or Stevenson's, but he had a way of making his points. His "Give 'em hell, Harry" style helped win the famous upset election of 1948.

President Truman made good use of the radio, but his style was amateur, though direct and factual. Walter Johnson wrote: "Truman lacked artistry in public relations. When he spoke, his gestures were as awkward as a penguin's waddle and his flat Middlewestern twang jarred radio loudspeakers." He lacked, Alistair Cooke has remarked, "musicianship, of knowing when to pause, when to paragraph, when to go slow and easy, and when to lift into the big sentence."[35]

Oratory has to fit the times. In 1948 Truman's style of speaking was exactly what was needed to attract organized labor alarmed by the Taft-Hartley Act, farmers concerned with the shortage of storage space, which meant economic disaster for them, Jews who were grateful for the recognition of Israel, blacks who saw him as a champion of civil rights, and others who had benefited from the New Deal and the Fair Deal. In 1952 Truman was not fighting for himself but for Stevenson, regarding whom he had some reservations. He was fighting for his place in history, but the times were against him. The defeat of the Chinese Nationalists by Mao's Communists, the Soviet explosion of a nuclear bomb, the entrance of the Chinese Communists in the Korean war, the dismissal of General MacArthur, inflation renewed by the Korean war, the revelation of Soviet espionage in the United States, the desperation of the Republicans (which led Senator Taft to embrace McCarthyism), and the mood of the public, who wanted a respite from experimentation and a return to old-fashioned values—all of these rendered his strenuous efforts to tear down General Eisenhower and build up Stevenson ineffective. On the other hand, they did help create the myth of Truman as "Give 'em hell, Harry," quite a different man from the humble and confused person who took the presidential oath in 1945.[36]

THE RECORD

During my study of the American presidency, I constructed for the 1949 edition of *The American Party System* a guide entitled "Characteristics of Successful and Unsuccessful Candidates for President," the purpose of which was to focus attention and sharpen the observation of the varying performance of American presidents as party leaders. Some of the criteria are relatively objective and refer to the overall performance of each president in terms of success in influencing legislation, in winning nominations and elections, and in securing a favorable verdict from a body of historians.[37]

How does a president stand up in a popularity contest? His percentage of the two-party vote could be one test. According to this measure, Warren G. Harding, who gained 63.8 percent of the two-party vote, comes out on top of the fourteen presidents in this century—this is not right. It was not

Harding's worth as a candidate that brought him out on top but rather the troublesome times, the reaction against Wilson's policies, and the letdown following the end of the war. All raters put Harding at the bottom of any presidential scale on other grounds. Next come Franklin D. Roosevelt in 1936, Lyndon B. Johnson in 1964, Richard M. Nixon in 1972, Theodore Roosevelt in 1904, Herbert Hoover in 1928, Dwight D. Eisenhower in 1956, William H. Taft in 1908, and Harry S. Truman in 1948. Woodrow Wilson in 1916, John Kennedy in 1960, Nixon in 1968, and Carter in 1976 were below Truman. Wilson in 1912 and Calvin Coolidge in 1924 could not be rated since there were big third-party votes in these years. Percentage of the popular two-party vote is not a satisfactory criterion since so many unique factors enter into each election.[38]

The public opinion polls might be a better criterion. Extensive public opinion surveys began in the 1930s. We can thus compare Truman with the other presidents since Hoover. Sample surveys are far from perfect as a measure of public opinion, however. Truman despised the polls and called them "sleeping pills designed to lull the voters into sleeping on election day." A striking characteristic of the measures of presidential popularity is the extraordinary range of their fluctuation. The polls on Truman had the greatest range of any president during this period. Harry had the highest and the lowest. What were the polls measuring? Gallup asked the question, "Do you approve or disapprove of the way Truman is handling his job as President?" In early 1945 when Truman had just assumed the arduous duties of the presidency, 87 percent answered "approve." In 1952 when the country was bogged down in Korea, when the newspapers were on the trail of the so-called Truman scandals, and when large elements of the population were still hysterical regarding the dismissal of General Mac-Arthur and Senator McCarthy's wild charges, only 23 percent answered "approve."[39] If Truman had been concerned only with his standing in the polls, he would have acted in a different manner. He did not follow Mac-Arthur's advice, "There is no substitute for victory," because he believed in a limited war under U.N. auspices. He did not keep the insolent and insubordinate general on because he believed it was his duty to defend the powers and prestige of the presidency regardless of the repercussions on his own reputation. He might have acted more promptly and more inclusively to purge the wrongdoers in his administration, but he believed every man should have his day in court before sentence should be passed on him. In 1945 American citizens wanted to see the war won as quickly as possible, and they were willing to give Truman the benefit of any doubts they had about his following so popular a president as Franklin D. Roosevelt. In 1952 the public blamed Truman for actions that were unpopular at the time but that were caused by circumstances largely beyond his control.[40]

A president's record may be judged by his success in securing a renomination for himself, by his influence in the choice of his successor, and by the success of his party in winning the presidency following the end of his term in office. In these respects, only the two Roosevelts and Andrew Jackson have perfect records. Truman secured his own renomination on the Democratic ticket in 1948 over determined opposition within his own party, which was thwarted by General Eisenhower's refusal to consider a Democratic nomination. No one knows what would have happened if Eisenhower had gone after the Democratic nomination in 1948. In 1952 Truman's success in choosing his successor was less than complete due to Stevenson's reluctance to become an avowed candidate. The Stevenson draft was started by amateurs, and Truman did not come into the picture until the last minute. At the convention itself, Truman was of some help in getting Harriman to switch his supporters to Stevenson in a block Kefauver movement.[41]

Another possible measure of presidential success in political matters would be how much better the candidate did in the election than the political commentators expected him to. The measure is related to the polls since extensive sample surveying began in the mid-1930s, but it existed long before that. According to this test, Truman did well in 1948. The political experts as well the pollsters had downgraded him before the election. In this century no other presidential candidate has so fooled the experts.

Truman's efforts to continue the Democratic party in power after he left the White House were destined to failure. The hero image that the press and other mass media had created regarding Eisenhower was so strong that Truman's most valiant efforts to tear it down came to naught in 1952. The Democrats had held the presidency for twenty years, and in that time they had disappointed many elements in the electorate. In a democracy you cannot please everybody. Roosevelt's mistakes and Truman's blunders came home to roost in 1952. A composite picture of the five Roosevelt and Truman elections is given in map 10, which shows that during the twenty-year period only Maine and Vermont remained Republican in all five presidential elections. The next area of some success for Republicanism was found in the plains states of the midwest—North Dakota, South Dakota, Kansas, and Nebraska—plus Indiana farther east. These areas looked like a small basis for a Republican comeback. Hovering near, however, were Iowa, Oklahoma, Pennsylvania, Delaware, New Hampshire, and Connecticut, all of which went Republican twice during the period. Disregarding the States' Rights defection in 1948, the solidly Democratic area swept from Maryland southwest across the country and up the West Coast, where Oregon was an exception. To this add the mountain states, Minnesota, Missouri, Illinois, Michigan, and Massachusetts, and the picture is complete. The swing of the pendulum in American politics forecast the return of the Republicans to power in the presidency. They had the popular issues and a charismatic war hero as a candidate.[42]

How does Truman's legislative record compare with that of other presidents? How can a legislative record be measured? One test would be to

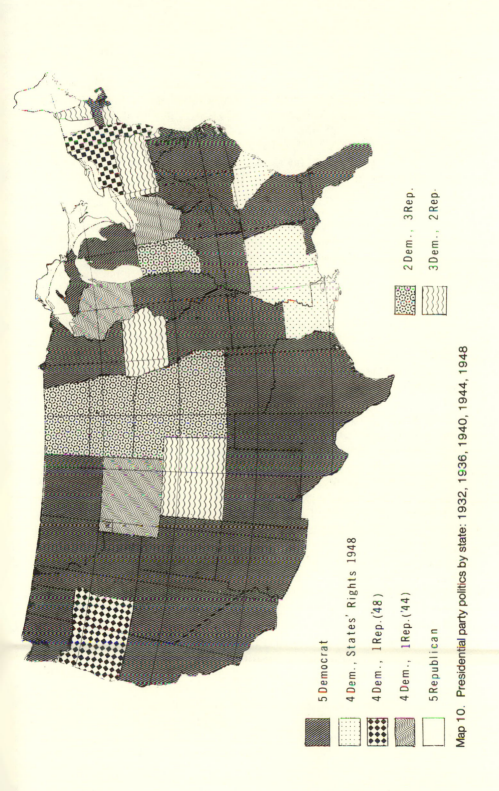

5 Democrat

4 Dem., States' Rights 1948

4 Dem., 1 Rep. ('48)

4 Dem., 1 Rep. ('44)

5 Republican

2 Dem., 3 Rep.

3 Dem., 2 Rep.

Map 10.   Presidential party politics by state: 1932, 1936, 1940, 1944, 1948

compare presidential legislative recommendations with bills passed. Another would be the number of vetoes and the proportion of vetoes that held. In recommending legislation to Congress, a president may genuinely push his proposals with the expectation that they will pass, or he may present them as future goals, realizing that they may not be achieved in the Congress he faces. Some revisionist historians have severely criticized Truman for making recommendations that he knew would not be favorably received by the sitting Congress.[43]

On Truman's use of the veto, his critics are without mercy. They claim that he had more vetoes overriden than any other president since Andrew Johnson. Congress generally repudiated his attempts to control its actions by means of the veto. There are several ways of looking at the use of the veto power. A timid president may not use it at all. Some eight presidents never did. It takes courage to exercise the veto power. A president must set his will against that of Congress. The three presidents who used the veto most were Franklin D. Roosevelt, Grover Cleveland, and Harry Truman. The five presidents who had the most vetoes overridden were Andrew Johnson, Harry Truman, Franklin D. Roosevelt, Grover Cleveland, and Woodrow Wilson. Truman did not need to be ashamed to be in this company. Many presidents refused to use the veto when they thought that they might be overridden. Truman was not afraid to face such a reverse. His vetoes of three tax reduction bills in 1948, the Taft Hartley Labor-Management Relations Act, and the McCarran-Walter Immigration and Nationality Act are examples of his courage in using the veto.[44]

Some revisionists interpret Truman's motives in his legislative actions as base in that he tried to attract votes among the electorate rather than to bring about fundamental changes in American life. The determination of motives is a difficult task. Charlie Ross made a sage remark about Truman: "Don't look for hidden meanings. Assume the obvious." Truman believed in these programs. His messages were prophetic, and they were also protective. He wanted to save the New Deal and the Fair Deal from Republican encroachments and he wanted to agitate for future action. President Lyndon Johnson recognized Truman's role in Medicare legislation and arranged for the signing of the bill at the Truman Library in Independence, Missouri.[45]

In pushing through domestic legislation, Truman was not always fortunate. During his entire administration, he faced a hostile majority in Congress made up of Republicans and southern Democrats. After 1937 President Roosevelt faced such a hostile majority, and his record in the domestic field was poor during his last seven years in office. Revisionists accuse Truman of playing politics with his domestic legislative programs, charging that they were nothing but campaign rhetoric designed to attract votes. A closer look is needed to arrive at a sound conclusion in this field.

The four Congresses concerned passed the Atomic Energy Act of 1946, the Employment Act of 1946, the Hospital Survey and Construction Act of 1946, the Federal Airport Act of 1946, the Legislative Reorganization Act of 1946, the National Security Act of 1947, the Hope-Aiken Price Support Act, a bill liberalizing housing credit terms, the extension of rent control, many public power, flood control and irrigation projects, reorganization of the RFC, and the Governmental Reorganization Act of 1949.[46]

In the foreign field Truman's legislative and displomatic record compares favorably with that of other presidents in the era. He was able to secure favorable congressional action on the ratification of the United Nations Charter, the Truman doctrine of aid to Greece and Turkey, the Marshall Plan for aid to Western Europe, the ratification of peace treaties with Italy, Hungary, Bulgaria and Rumania, NATO, Japan, the Inter-American Treaty of Mutual Assistance, and the Vandenberg Resolution.

Certain underlying conditions and assumptions influenced Truman's foreign policy decisions. During the period Stalin was still alive, the communist movement was assumed to be monolithic, although toward the end of the period, the Communist party of the Soviet Union was challenged as leader of the world communist movement by Yugoslavia and Communist China. It was assumed that the Communist party of the Soviet Union would continue its tactics, which involved probing for soft spots in the noncommunist world where advances might be made. It was also assumed that American young men were patriotic and willing to make sacrifices to support American policies. Perhaps a less rigid attitude toward the Soviet Union would have made possible more fruitful negotiations.[47]

DECISIONS ARISING OUT OF IDENTITY CRISES

The early decisions Truman had to make arose largely out of identity crises. What kind of profession did he wish to follow? What did he want to make out of his life? As he rose up the political ladder he had to decide what kind of political, social, and economic philosophy he wanted to follow. With what school of thought did he wish to be identified?

An early identity crisis concerned the role that music would play in his life. Encouraged by his mother, who found excellent piano teachers for him, he considered making a career as a concert pianist. He made progress by getting up early and practicing four hours a day, but by the age of fifteen he decided that he was not good enough to become a professional.[48] When he graduated from high school, he considered applying for West Point, but his weak eyes barred him from this course. However, upon becoming of age, he joined the Missouri National Guard. Although he was over draft age when World War I broke out, he rejoined the National Guard and saw service in France as an artillery captain. After the war, he became a reserve officer. As a senator he served on the Committee on Military Affairs and was chairman of his own committee to investigate the defense program. He applied for active military service in World War II, but General Marshall turned him down. His lifelong ambition for achievement in military affairs was finally satisfied when he became commander-in-chief.[49]

When the vision of a college education faded,[50] Truman had to decide what kind of a job he wanted. He chose a clerkship in a Kansas City bank and appeared to be doing well in this profession. His next occupational crisis was whether he should stick to banking as a career or become a farmer. He was doing well as a bank clerk, he liked living in the city, and his natural friendliness promised success in this field. His loyalty to his family, however, was so strong that he abandoned banking and moved to the family farm. He stuck to farming for ten years but it never satisfied him as shown by his side interests in a lead and zinc mine and in oil wild catting.

Mustered out of the army he decided to go into the haberdashery business. The enterprise looked prosperous for a while but the depression of 1921 changed all that. The business failed, and he lost his savings and his chances of making a go as a small businessman.

What should he do next? In his late thirties he found himself married and without a job or a profession. His friends urged him to enter politics. That he would be taking the first step toward the presidency never entered his mind. The elective county judgeship would be a meal ticket and he had no ambition or hope of rapidly ascending the political ladder.

Upon becoming a county administrator and a part of the Pendergast machine he found that he had to choose between being an honest or a corrupt elective official. Truman's personal honesty, ingrained by family training and example, enabled him to avoid taking advantage of the opportunities for graft and he acquired a reputation as an honest public servant which proved to be useful to the machine.[51]

Ten years on the county court gave Truman a taste for politics. The New Deal had started in Washington, and the lure of national politics beckoned. The offer to run for a seat in the United States Senate was beyond his fondest dreams, so when it came he seized it avidly even though the battle to win it would be a tough one.

Truman's first term in the Senate had been a little difficult. Some senators looked down upon him as the "senator from Pendergast," and he did not try to make a flashy record. Toward the end of his term he had to decide whether to seek another term or accept an offer of an appointed post on a federal regulatory commission. But his identity was involved. He would battle for the elective post even though he had no secure position to fall back upon if he should lose. The higher he went on the political ladder the more important it was for him to continue climbing.

In the Senate, Truman developed slowly but surely, and he came to feel that at last he had found his niche in life. His identity crisis had been met. This was where he felt he belonged. He did not aggressively seek the vice presidential on his own initiative in 1944. He would be willing to accept the nomination for vice president for the good of the party but he looked upon it as a personal sacrifice.[52]

Surely the most serious of Truman's identity crises was the decision whether to run for the presidency in 1948. A substantial portion of the party was against his renomination and was trying to get the popular General Eisenhower to challenge him in the convention. His record as president (by accident) was at stake, and he had to prove himself by becoming president in his own right.

Upon becoming president, Truman had to decide what philosophy of government he should espouse. He believed firmly in the American form of democracy set up under the Constitution of the United States with its separation of the executive, legislative, and judicial powers and its division of powers between central government and the states. He did not want to encroach on the powers of the other branches of the government and as a border politician he did not want to interfere with states' rights. He respected the presidency, but he did not think that it was imperial. On economic questions he adhered to the free enterprise system, free trade, personal freedom to choose one's own career, and a minimum of government regulation. Legislation against economic abuses was justified, but not interference with individual initiative. He was a New Dealer as his record in the Senate showed but he did not like the terms "liberal" or "progressive" and he preferred the term "forward-looking." Some of the professional liberals turned him off. While he put forward his own Fair Deal program, he was also sympathetic to the conservative business philosophy. He believed in a balanced budget, and fiscal responsibility. Deficit spending did not attract him although he had to do some during the Korean war. He preferred to meet economic problems by stimulating the growth of industry. His conservative views sometimes conflicted with his Fair Deal programs. Consistency did not bother him. He tried to meet each problem as it came.

Truman also had to decide what guiding philosophy to follow in the conduct of American foreign relations. As an admirer of Woodrow Wilson, he took the universalist approach. He believed in the United Nations as the means whereby freedom-loving nations could cooperate in a worldwide effort for the achievement of peace, plenty, and freedom. He was opposed to totalitarianism whether fascist or communist. He held that the popular front of the war years was dissolved by the aggressive actions of the Soviet Union. While at first he tried to preserve Allied unity, he soon lost hope in doing this and he openly attacked communism as warlike, a false philosophy characterized by "deceit and mockery, poverty and tyranny."[53]

DECISION CRISES

In his various positions, Truman had many decision crises to meet. He was noted for his ability to make decisions. Some accused him of deciding too quickly before adequate consideration could be given to the issues involved and before the consequences of alternative courses could be explored. This was true of some of the Korean decisions made in 1950.

Certain Truman decisions will be summarized briefly and an estimate presented as to whether they were wise under the circumstances in which they were made.

Prepresidential Decisions

When his haberdashery store failed in the early 1920s, Truman was faced with the problem of whether to go into bankruptcy as did his partner. He decided to pay off his debts, painful as that proved to be, and it took him some years. It was the moral thing to do, but it did not help him much politically because others (even his daughter) thought that he did go into bankruptcy.

As a county official, Truman had to decide whether to seek a referendum on a bond issue for road building and other construction work during the depression. Boss Pendergast thought the prospects for the passage of such a bond issue were slim, but he did not say that Truman should give up the idea. Truman went ahead, and the popular vote was favorable, making available many jobs and providing a much better road system. This was a sound decision.

During his first term as senator, Truman had to decide whether to use his power of senatorial courtesy against the renomination of Maurice Milligan as district attorney. Milligan had prosecuted Pendergast for bribery and evasion of the income tax. In accordance with President Roosevelt's wishes, Senator Truman did not exercise his power to block the nomination. This was the right decision. Mistaken was Truman's verbal attack on Milligan's integrity and his defense of the Kansas City vote thieves.

When Pendergast pleaded guilty of income tax evasion in the famous insurance bribery case, Truman should have cut his ties with the discredited and disgraced boss, but he failed to do so because he placed personal loyalty above loyalty to the city and state.

As chairman of the Senate Special Committee to Investigate the Defense Program, Truman had a number of crises to meet. One involved a top-secret project that his investigators discovered in Tennessee and Washington State —the atomic energy project. When Secretary of War Stimson asked him to call his investigators off, Truman agreed only after Stimson insisted for a second time. It was a wise decision at the time, although later as president, Truman had to know about the project.[54]

Crises in the Conduct of Foreign Relations

The biggest crisis Truman faced during his administration was how to treat the Soviet Union. Were the Russians friends or foes? World War II had left two great powers with widely different ideologies, aims, and methods facing each other over the ruins of Central Europe. During the war, President Roosevelt had maintained a friendly attitude toward the Soviet Union because its cooperation was needed to defeat Nazi Germany. But he failed to formulate a policy as to how the Soviet Union should be treated after the war. Just before he died, he was confronted with some Soviet actions that put a great strain on the relationships between the two countries. New crises were arising daily. How should the new President meet them? Nobody had briefed him. He could only take over the machinery of government as Roosevelt left it and ask the top administration officials to give him advice.

One of the first decisions that Truman made as president was to give instructions that the San Francisco conference of the United Nations organization should proceed as scheduled. This seemed at the time to be the correct decision, but later some thought that more time should have been spent to resolve some of the conflicts before the meeting took place. During the conference, there was considerable friction between the Soviet Union and the United States.

The decision to hold a summit conference at Potsdam was a controversial one. Truman was inexperienced and dreaded having to match wits with Churchill and Stalin and, later, with Attlee. Truman was deceived by Stalin's outward politeness, but he was alarmed by the Russians' demands and positions. Was the Potsdam conference a success? Truman thought so at the time. A modest Missouri farmer—a sharp contrast to his predecessor —held his own with the brilliant Churchill and the iron-willed Stalin, even though he was a little shaky at first. Relying heavily upon his briefings and upon his nimble secretary of state, he did his part in keeping the outward appearances of Allied harmony. Considering the clash between American and Soviet postwar aims and ideologies, this was about all that could be done. Bohlen contended that Roosevelt could not have done any better. No one could undo the mistakes that Roosevelt and Churchill had made during the war. Some revisionists contend that Truman did not want peace. Theirs is the burden of proof. It is overwhelmingly clear that Truman did not want to start another world war.[55]

The atom bomb decision is also controversial. Revisionists contend that it was not necessary to use the bomb, especially against a civilian population. They claim that the Japanese were ready to surrender, as indicated by their desperate diplomatic efforts carried on in Moscow. Besides, they claim that the bomb was not used primarily to bring the war with Japan to a close; it was exploded instead to intimidate the Russians and get them to be more amenable. Truman's official defense was that the bomb was dropped to save lives, Japanese as well as American. Amphibious landings on the Japanese islands would have involved millions of casualties. On the moral issues involved, Truman relied on Arthur Compton, a Nobel Prize winner. Truman claimed that the targets were selected because of their military importance. As for threatening the Soviet Union with the bomb, the revisionists have produced no evidence of this.

We now turn to the Truman policies regarding U.S. relations with particular countries and particular foreign problems.

Iran

One of Truman's greatest diplomatic successes was his handling of the Iranian crisis. He combined the proper amount of firmness at the United Nations with a veiled threat of the use of force and the right degree of naval display to persuade the Soviet Union to back down in its aggressive behavior toward Iran. The Russian military forces in Iran, which had stayed beyond the time of their promised withdrawal, were pulled back. The indigenous communist forces were not supported by the Russians when the Iranian regulars moved against them. Soviet demands for oil concessions were ignored by the Iranian government, which was relying on American assurances. American diplomats, psychological warriors, naval officers, and President Truman scored a great victory. The President is to be excused for exaggerating his role later on when he bragged about the ultimatum that caused the Soviet Union to back down. Actually there was no ultimatum, no brinksmanship, no threat of world war—just an adroit appeal to world opinion on moral grounds, a flexing of U.S. naval muscles, and a display of shrewd business sense. The United States got the oil concessions and an Iranian sense of gratitude, which was important much later when the Arabs imposed the oil embargo. Secretary Byrnes and the foreign service officers served Truman well on this occasion.[56]

Philippines

Truman's policy toward the Philippines was initially successful under Magsaysay. He carried out the Roosevelt policy regarding the Philippines faithfully. Full independence was granted to the islands on July 4, 1946. As in other parts of Southeast Asia, there was a strong Communist movement in the Philippines at the time, which was very adept at guerrilla warfare. Colonel Ed Lansdale of the U.S. Air Force skillfully spotted resistance fighter Ramon Magsaysay as a potential strong minister of defense. With U.S. aid and advice, the Philippine armed forces under the leadership of Magsaysay effectively had defeated the Huks by 1950. Magsaysay proved to be a popular leader, and he went on to be elected president in 1953. Here he built up confidence in the democratic process and in his own integrity among a people who had been somewhat cynical about their rulers. His death in an airplane accident in 1957 was a great tragedy.[57]

China

Some revisionists and some conservatives charge that the Truman administration "lost China," a ridiculous statement since China was never ours. Republican right wingers have claimed that the United States let Chiang Kai-shek down. Perhaps Roosevelt is more to blame for Chiang's collapse, for FDR undermined Chiang when he thought he was helping him. In 1945 Roosevelt refused to back General Stilwell in his attempt to reform the Chinese Nationalist armies, believing that he was defending Chinese sovereignty. But actually Chinese sovereignty under Chiang was an illusion because Chiang did not control large parts of Chinese territory. He and his cohorts were warlords whose main interest was not in fighting the Japanese but in holding onto their own bailiwicks. They expected the United States to win the war against Japan for them. After the war was over, they did not want to cooperate with Mao; they wanted to hold onto their fiefdoms and enrich themselves at the expense of the Americans and the other Chinese people. President Truman and General Marshall refused to become involved in an allout Asian war. When the Nationalist regime began to collapse in 1949, Secretary Acheson agreed that the United States should stay out of the Chinese civil war. Chiang was no Magsaysay, and he failed to win the loyalty of the Chinese people. Foreign service officers correctly predicted the triumph of the Chinese Communists, but for this they were persecuted by Hurley and the McCarthyites. Just when Truman and Acheson were inclining toward Mao, the Korean war broke out and destroyed any chance of a rapprochement with Mao for some twenty-two years.[58]

Indochina

President Truman was early faced with the question of whether to support Ho Chi Minh and his communist-dominated nationalistic Viet Minh or the French colonialists in Indochina. He ignored Ho's appeals for aid and at Potsdam agreed to have the Japanese surrender to the British in the southern part of Vietnam. The British brought back the French, who were soon at war with the Viet Minh. Secretary Acheson, in order to win French support for his European plans, backed them in Indochina with supplies and financial aid, which was increased after the Korean war started. Truman upheld Acheson's policies, which were based on assumptions that later led to American involvement in Vietnam. It was assumed that the Viet Minh Communists were part of a world strategy aimed against the free world and that their success in Indochina would seal the fate of Southeast Asia. These assumptions did not have to be followed, but unfortunately they were. Truman sent no troops to Vietnam.[59]

Korea

Was the limited war in Korea a mistake? Its limited character meant that it did not escalate into a world conflict, and it kept America's European allies. Under U.N. auspices, the original objective of preventing the North Koreans from taking over South Korea was accomplished. If Truman had had better advice, this war would not have been the depressant on his reputation that it became as it dragged into a stalemate. The two big errors in Korea were Secretary Acheson's assumption that the North Korean attack was a prelude to a general worldwide communist offensive and General MacArthur's assumption that the Chinese Communists would not enter effectively. At the time George Kennan pointed out that both of these assumptions were wrong. Stalin, Mao, and Kim Il-sung made some gross miscalculations of their own. They thought that Syngman Rhee's government would collapse, that his army would be defeated easily, and that the United States would stay out as it did in the Chinese civil war. To Stalin it was an opportunity to show his displeasure at American policy toward Japan. But everything went wrong for the Communists. The United States was about to let the Communists capture Taiwan. Now this move was blocked by the American fleet. The United States was about to support Communist China's bid for the U.N. China seat. Now this policy was changed and the fiction adopted that the legal sovereignty of China still rested with the defeated and discredited Chinese Nationalists in their island retreat. The communist threat to conquer all of Korea was thwarted. There is still a great need for South Korea to find its own effective leader.[60]

Japan

Truman learned his lesson about what happened when control of a defeated enemy was divided between the communists and the noncommunists; the Soviet zone of East Germany was soon shut off from the West. Truman did not want this to happen in Japan so the control of Japan was monopolized by the United States under the leadership of General MacArthur, who proved to be an able occupation administrator. Japanese friendship is the chief asset that the United States gained as a result of the war in the Pacific. This policy should be regarded as successful. A separate moderate treaty with Japan, which the Soviet Union refused to sign, was worked out skillfully by John Foster Dulles. It was one of the best examples of the bipartisan foreign policy system.[61]

Germany

After the war, Allies were faced with the problem of what to do with Germany. When Truman became president, he discovered that Roosevelt had not worked out a sound policy for Germany. A fatal error in solving the

German problem had been made when the zones of occupation were set up. These were altogether too favorable to the Soviet Union. American and British troops could have occupied most of Germany, but they were held back by the agreed zones of occupation. Churchill saw the mistake too late. He was one who had agreed to the zones. Once in possession of East Germany and East Berlin, the Russians clamped down their iron curtain and behind it set up a Sovietized East Germany and East Berlin. East Prussia was ruthlessly depopulated and annexed by the Soviet Union, which was soon to denounce military annexations by others. What could Truman do about this situation? A unified German administration was to be set up according to the Potsdam agreements, but the Russians refused to cooperate. The Western powers could shut off reparations to the Soviet Union from the Western zones of occupation, and they did just that. They could also set up a unified West Germany, and this was accomplished, although the French were not enthusiastically supportive. Truman's German policies have worked out well under the circumstances. The big mistakes were made by Churchill and Roosevelt.

Italy

Secretaries Byrnes and Marshall tried to secure a liberal peace treaty for Italy. Economic aid to a devastated Italy was granted in 1945 through the United Nations Relief and Rehabilitation Administration. When this relief came to an end, the United States granted a loan to Italy. The Italian peace treaty, effective September 15, 1947, had been held up by the Soviet Union, which sought by this means to secure concessions in the Balkan treaties. Postwar Italy has been a prime target for communist subversive activities and the Italian Communist party has been strong. Marshall Plan aid and encouragement to noncommunist political parties held back communist advances.

Greece

Revisionists claim that Stalin was not directly aiding the communist forces in Greece, that the Truman doctrine was altogether too broad and sweeping, that the oppressive Greek government bolstered by British troops was far from democratic, and that the British were far more heavily committed in Palestine than in Greece. The Greek communists were then supported by Tito, who at that time had not broken with Moscow. It was not necessary for Stalin to interfere directly. Truman's rhetoric was extreme because he was dealing with a Republican Congress, and Senator Vandenberg told him that it had to be emphatic or he would get no action from Congress. The Greek government was not ideal, but it was noncommunist. This was a chance to try to get the Greeks to adopt a more liberal government later. If the communists took over, that chance would be lost.

Turkey

Right after the war, the Soviet Union began making unreasonable demands on Turkey. The Russians wanted to take control of the straits. Truman ordered stiff notes to be sent to the Soviet Union and brought up naval units. The Russians backed down. Military aid to Turkey became part of the Truman doctrine, and Turkey became part of the European defense system.

Marshall Plan

At the end of the war, a crisis developed in the deteriorating economic and political stability in Western Europe. Responding to this situation, Secretary Marshall and his associates developed a plan for massive aid in the form of loans and grants for economic recovery. President Truman backed these efforts and played an important role in seeing the plan through Congress. The plan revived international trade and brought prosperity to Western Europe as measured by indexes of industrial production. It also brought greater political stability and closer political and military cooperation. Some revisionists, however, claim that it divided Europe and benefited capitalists more than the common man, especially in Western Germany.

The Berlin Blockade

In looking for soft spots, Stalin thought he had one in the divided city of Berlin, since General Eisenhower had failed to secure guaranteed ground access routes across East Germany. The airlift proved to be successful. Some American generals argued that the land route should be followed, but the risk of war was much greater that way because a direct confrontation was possible. Truman stuck to the air route, and the communists backed down.

Israel

Within the Truman administration, some elements strongly urged that nothing be done in Palestine to alienate the Arabs because of the importance of oil. Within the United States, the Zionist movement was strong and had an active lobby. The precipitous recognition of the new state of Israel in 1948 alarmed the pro-Arab group in the United States. There is still no answer as to where this decision will lead in the troubled Middle East.

NATO

The decision to establish the North Atlantic Treaty Organization marked a departure from the traditional American policy of no entangling alliances. NATO is still the bulwark of Western European defenses.

Point Four

The granting of technical aid to developing countries was immensely popular abroad, especially as far as the agricultural projects were concerned. The program never reached its full potential because of the death of Henry G. Bennett in 1951, who had brought energy, enthusiasm, and knowledge to the program, the switch toward Marshall Plan type of economic aid programs, and the subversion of an altruistic type of program by cold war and business considerations even before the Eisenhower administration took over.

DOMESTIC CRISES

A New Domestic Program

After six months in office, Truman was faced with the problem of whether to continue to rely upon Roosevelt's messages for program guidance or to present a program of his own. Conservatives within his administration warned him that a new statement of his objectives would disturb delicate labor-management relations and hold false hopes for those in need. But liberals in general welcomed a fresh statement, which would indicate that Truman was trying to carry out the New Deal. Concerned that the press was beginning to brand him as a conservative, the President issued his twenty-one point program, the start of what he later labeled the Fair Deal. Truman was unable to get Congress to accept many parts of it, but it anticipated many things that were accomplished later.

Civil Rights

Throughout his administration Truman was confronted with the problem of civil rights. What should be done about discrimination against minority groups in employment, education, voting, housing, police protection, criminal justice, restaurants, recreation facilities, amusement places, and in other matters? A crisis was created when World War II black veterans were brutally treated in the South. In response, Truman established the epoch-making Commission on Civil Rights, which rendered a forthright report, most of which Truman felt compelled to support in his messages to Congress. Revisionists have accused Truman of halfhearted support of the recommendations because of his desire to appease southern whites, but the fact remains that he advanced civil rights further than his predecessors did, including Roosevelt. Frustrated by filibusters and hostile majorities in Congress, Truman did what he could by executive orders and amicus curiae briefs.

Labor-Management Relations

In the labor-management field, Truman had less success than in some other fields. Reconversion involved many delicate adjustments. Some labor experts claim that Truman lifted the wartime controls too soon, and the result was a series of crippling strikes that delayed the return to a domestic economy. Regarded as a friend of labor in 1944, Truman antagonized his labor friends by his failure to champion their demands aggressively and his proposals to end the railroad strike. His battles with John L. Lewis did not make him popular with the miners. In 1947 he recovered some of his labor support by vetoing the Taft-Hartley Act, which helped him win the labor vote in the 1948 presidential election. His labor record thus was mixed.

Inflation Controls

Truman's record with regard to inflation controls was unsatisfactory. At first he backed Bowles, who was doing an excellent job explaining price controls and rationing to the public and Congress, but in a crucial showdown with the conservatives, he supported Snyder rather than Bowles. Confusion and greater inflation resulted. Truman found it hard to get satisfactory legislation from Congress in this field, and he did not act soon enough to stave off another wave of inflation during the Korean crisis.

Farm Policies

Truman's record in this field was indifferent. Secretary Anderson was more interested in protecting large commercial farmers than in safeguarding the interests of consumers here and abroad. The result was a shortage of food for export to starving millions abroad. Anderson also had a confrontation with Bowles, who wanted to hold down the prices of farm products and at the same time increase production for export. Anderson's higher prices policy won out, adding to the inflationary spiral. Secretary Brannan had the interests of the consumers and smaller farmers more at heart. The Brannan plan was an ingenious scheme for guaranteeing farmers' incomes and at the same time letting prices fall to their natural levels, which might help consumers. But conservative farm organizations would have none of this scheme and the old price supports were continued.

Scandals

Toward the end of his administration, Truman faced the problem of how to deal with irregularities in the Bureau of Internal Revenue, the Department of Justice, and the Reconstruction Finance Corporation revealed by Congressional investigations. Secretary Snyder had been looking into charges against internal revenue agents, most of whom were appointed by Roosevelt, but he had not acted soon enough, and the courts took over. Attorney General McGrath was not cooperative in cleaning up his department, so Truman demanded his resignation. A reorganization of the RFC was worked out but not soon enough. Truman's exchanges with the senators investigating the RFC did not add to his reputation.

Steel Mills Seizure

The steel mills seizure—done to prevent a strike in the steel industry and thus endangering the munitions factories turning out weapons for the Korean war—did not add to Truman's prestige and it weakened the powers of the presidency. He was given bad legal advice because his seizure was nullified by the U.S. Supreme Court. Secretary of Commerce Sawyer was not cooperative. As the Court pointed out, Truman should have invoked the provisions of the Taft-Hartley Act that were applicable. As it turned out, the strike was not long enough to endanger the munitions industries. Truman's popularity however, plummeted and prices rose. He was willing to sacrifice his popularity since he believed that continued production was necessary.

Transition

Although Truman was extremely bitter at General Eisenhower for failing to defend General Marshall, he was willing to forget the campaign after the election, and he wanted above everything else to work out a smooth transition that would preserve and protect the powers and prestige of the presidency. Eisenhower, still sensitive from Truman's campaign charges, did not cooperate well, but some of his subordinates took advantage of Truman's altruistic aims to serve his country. Thus the Truman presidency came to a close.

The journey from Lamar to the White House was truly an American saga. At many points on the way it might have been sidetracked. If Truman had stayed in banking, if his oil ventures had come through as they nearly did, if his haberdashery shop had not been hit by the 1921 depression, if he had not demonstrated his ability to lead men as a captain of artillery in World War I, if he had lost the 1922 primary election as candidate for judge of the Eastern District of Jackson County as he nearly did, if he had not won the renomination to the Senate in 1940, he would not have been on his way to the White House. His nomination for vice-president in 1944 was the product of Wallace's mistakes, Roosevelt's indifference and exhaustion, and his own reputation as chairman of the Truman committee, which became the watchdog of the Treasury during World War II. He was truly an accidental president who did not seek the post. His qualities of optimism, persistence, activism, and honesty kept him on the track moving from one point to the next on his ascent to power.

As an accidental president, he had many crises to meet. In a sense, these crises made his reputation because he was compelled to render many important decisions. The public generally felt that he tried to make these in the public interest. Even the unpopular Korean war did not develop the disorders that accompanied Vietnam. Truman made mistakes, but he was not a man to have regrets. There was always a new decision to make. He went forward to face the next crisis.

On becoming president in his own right, he had more serious crises to meet. Again he placed what he thought was for the good of the country above his own reputation. He could have kept General MacArthur on and either tolerated his insubordination or accepted the general's advice and expanded the war. He knew MacArthur's dismissal would be an unpopular decision with many, but he regarded the avoidance of another world war as more important than his own standing with the public. The unpopular decisions he made resulted in the decline in his personal popularity. Within a short time after his death, however, his qualities of greatness became more generally recognized in spite of the charges of revisionists. Truman was a tribune of the people, plain speaking, direct, courageous, and personally incorruptible. He rose above his questionable early political backing to carve for himself a place among the presidential near greats.

NOTES

When full citation of books is not given, complete information may be found in the selected bibliography. The following abbreviations are used:

CR	*Congressional Record*
DSB	*Department of State Bulletin*
EO	Executive Order
FDRL	Franklin D. Roosevelt Library
FR	*Federal Register*
FRUS	*Foreign Relations of the United States*
HSTL	Harry S. Truman Library
IE	*Independence Examiner*
JDP	Jonathan Daniels Papers, University of North Carolina
KCS	*Kansas City Star*
LC	Library of Congress
NA	National Archives
NYT	*New York Times*
OHC	Oral History Transcript, Columbia University
OHT	Oral History Transcript, Truman Library
PPR	*Public Papers: Franklin D. Roosevelt*
PPT	*Public Papers: Harry S. Truman*
SLPD	*St. Louis Post-Dispatch*
TM	*Truman Memoirs*, vol. 1: *Year of Decisions*, vol. 2: *Years of Trial and Hope*

CHAPTER 1
EARLY INFLUENCES

1. Articles on leadership can be found in *International Encyclopedia of the Social Sciences* (New York: Macmillan, 1969), 9:91-113; Richard D. Mann, "A Review of the Relationship between Personality and Performance in Small Groups," *Psychological Bulletin*, 56 (1959):241-270; James M. Burns, *Leadership* (New York: Harper and Row, 1978).

2. Oscar Chapman to Jonathan Daniels, January 17, 1950, JDP.

3. PPT, 1945, p. 150.

4. Daniels interview with Vivian Truman, JDP.

5. Daniels interview with Spencer Salisbury, JDP.

6. Van Sant to Daniels, 1949, JDP.

7. McGrath, *Power of the People*, p. 77.

8. Daniels interview with the Trumans of Grandview, JDP.

9. Gosnell, *Champion Campaigner: Franklin D. Roosevelt*, pp. 7-10.

10. J. F. Brown, *Psychology and the Social Order* (New York: McGraw-Hill, 1936), p. 321.

11. Karl Abraham, *Selected Papers, 1907-1925* (New York: Basic Books, 1953).

12. Hillman, *Mr. President*, p. 153.

13. TM, 1:113.

14. Hillman, *Mr. President*, p. 158.

15. PPT, 1945, p. 6.

16. Daniels, *The Man of Independence*, p. 49.

17. Ibid., p. 50.

18. Robert Alan Aurthur, "The Wit and Sass of Harry S Truman," *Esquire* (August 1971): 67.

19. Interview with Clark Clifford, January 24, 1974, Washington, D.C.

20. Interview with Congressman Richard Bolling, August 12, 1964, Washington, D.C.

21. Daniels, *Man of Independence*, pp. 58-59.

22. Hillman, *Mr. President*, p. 114.

23. NYT, July 27, 1947.

24. George and George, *Woodrow Wilson and Colonel House*; Sigmund Freud and William C. Bullitt, *Thomas Woodrow Wilson* (Boston: Houghton Mifflin, 1966).

25. Geoffrey Gorer, *The American People: A Study in National Character* (New York: Norton, 1948).

26. Hillman, *Mr. President*, p. 159.

27. Kornitzer, *American Fathers and Sons*, p. 93.

28. E. Victor Wolfenstein, "Some Psychological Aspects of Crisis Leaders" (paper presented to the American Political Science Association, 1966).

29. TM, 2:193.

30. Kornitzer, *American Fathers and Sons*, p. 12.

31. Daniels, *Man of Independence*, p. 48.

32. Hillman, *Mr. President*, p. 153.

33. Fenton, *Politics in the Border States*, chap. 7.

34. Margaret Truman, *Harry S. Truman*, p. 15.

35. W. Burlie Brown, "The Cincinnatus Image in Presidential Politics," *Agricultural History* 31 (January 1957): 25-29.

36. Truman, *Harry S. Truman*, pp. 526-527.

37. NYT, July 27, 1947.

38. Eric Severeid, *In One Ear* (New York: Knopf, 1952), p. 210.

39. Cabell Phillips, "Truman's Home Town Is 'Smalltown, U.S.A.,'" NYT *Magazine*, (July 1, 1945), pp. 13, 37-38.

40. OHT, Ethel Nolan.

41. Ibid., Henry W. Chiles.

42. Steffens, *Autobiography*, p. 373; Claude H. Wetmore and Lincoln Steffens, "Tweed Days in St. Louis," *McClure's Magazine* (October 1902).

43. Dorsett, *The Pendergast Machine*.

44. Daniels, *Man of Independence*, p. 82.

45. IE, September 21, 1919.

CHAPTER 2
ORIGIN OF POLITICAL INTERESTS, 1892-1922

1. Daniels interview with Ethel and Nellie Noland, SDP.

2. Margaret Truman, *Souvenir*, p. 16.

3. Daniels, *Man of Independence*, p. 39.

4. Truman, *Souvenir*, p. 16.

5. Steinberg, *Man from Missouri*, p. 247.

6. Allen and Shannon, *Truman Merry-Go-Round*, p. 10.

7. Kornitzer, *American Fathers and Sons*, chap. 1.

8. Joseph Short to Mrs. Lichty, January 14, 1952, HSTL.

9. TM, 1:116.

10. Daniels interview with Truman, November 12, 1949, JDP.

11. TM, 2:200.

12. Ibid., p. 20.

13. Daniels interview with Truman, August 30, 1949, JDP.

14. Ibid.

15. Alfred Henry Lewis, *Richard Croker* (New York: Life Publishing Co., 1901); Lincoln Steffens, "The Shamelessness of St. Louis," *McClure's Magazine* (March 1903); G. K. Turner, "The Thing above the Law," *McClure's Magazine* (March 1912); Walton Bean, *Boss Ruef's San Francisco* (Berkeley: University of California Press, 1952).

16. Jerome Beatty, "A Political Boss Talks about His Job," *American Magazine* (February 1933):113.

17. *Missouri Democrat*, October 21, 1927.

18. TM, 2:201.

19. Kornitzer, *American Fathers and Sons*, p. 20.

20. Reddig, *Tom's Town*, pp. 82-83; Dorsett, *Pendergast Machine*, chap. 3.

21. Daniels interview with Truman, August 30, 1949, JDP.

22. IE, July 18, 1922.

23. Dorsett, *Pendergast Machine*, pp. 68, 70.

24. Richard Rovere, "President Harry," *Harper's Magazine* (July 1948):29.

CHAPTER 3
THE EDUCATION OF HARRY TRUMAN, 1892-1901

1. Hillman, *Mr. President*, p. 159.

2. TM, 1:116.

3. *Jackson Examiner*, May 31, 1901.

4. Rogge's interview with Truman, cited in his "Speechmaking of Harry S. Truman," p. 20.

5. TM, 1:153.

6. Eugene E. White and Clair R. Henderlider, "What Harry S. Truman Told Us about His Speaking," *Quarterly Journal of Speech* (February 1954):39.

7. PPT, 1945, p. 17.

8. TM, 1:118.

9. Rogge's interview with Henry Bundschu, cited in his "Speechmaking of Truman," p. 22.

10. Robert M. Redding and Jimmie O'Brien, interview with Truman, June 25, 1963, Vertical File, HSTL.

11. OHT, Mize Peters, August 8, 1963, HSTL.

12. TM, 1:116, 118-121.

13. KCS, August 12, 1934.

14. Clemens, *Mark Twain and Harry Truman*.

15. Undated list in Vertical File, HSTL.

16. TM, 1:119.

17. KCS, August 12, 1934.

18. Karl Marx, *Das Kapital* (1867); Edward Bellamy, *Looking Backward* (Boston: Houghton Mifflin, 1888); Henry George, *Progress and Poverty* (Garden City: Doubleday, 1879, 1906).

19. OHT, Jonathan Daniels, October 4, 1963.

20. Neustadt, *Presidential Power*, p. 174.

21. OHT, Mize Peters, August 8, 1963.

22. TM, 1:115.

23. Daniels, *Man of Independence*, p. 57.

24. Daniels interview with Ethel and Nellie Noland, JDP.

25. Law School record, 1925, Truman Papers, Special Senatorial File, HSTL.

26. Truman told Daniels that all sorts of people followed him to school, even into the law library, about county matters. Interview, August 30, 1949, JDP.

27. TM, 1:119.

28. Arthur Krock, "The President: A New Portrait," NYT *Magazine*, (April 7, 1946), p. 46.

29. TM, 1:142.

30. Hillman, *Mr. President*, p. 90.

31. Krock, "The President: A New Portrait," p. 190.

32. Hillman, *Mr. President*, pp. 190, 217.

33. OHT, Harry S. Vaughan.

34. Max Lowenthal to Daniels, JDP.

35. President Truman's best line to Ivy League graduates was through Dean Acheson, who went to Yale and Harvard.

CHAPTER 4
LEARNING FARMING, 1905–1917

1. McNaughton and Hehmeyer, *This Man Truman*, p. 25.

2. *Missouri Agriculture* Bulletin 701, University of Missouri Agricultural Experiment Station, May 1958.

3. TM, 1:125.

4. Daniels interview with Truman, November 12, 1949, JDP.

5. Hillman, *Mr. President*, pp. 166, 191.

6. McNaughton and Hehmeyer, *This Man Truman*, p. 34.

7. KCS, August 12, 1934.

8. Samuel R. Guard, "From Plowboy to President," *Breeder's Gazette* (June 1945), p. 20.

9. Steinberg, *Man from Missouri*, p. 34.

10. IE, September 22, 1919.

11. Daniels, *Man of Independence*, p. 76.

12. McGrath, *Power of the People*, p. 80.

13. McNaughton and Hehmeyer, *This Man Truman*, p. 34.

14. Daniels, *Man of Independence*, p. 78.

CHAPTER 5
BUSINESS AND ACCOUNTING SKILLS, 1898–1935

1. McNaughton and Hehmeyer, *This Man Truman*, p. 19.

2. TM, 1:123.

3. Hillman, *Mr. President*, p. 164.

4. Roy Roberts (of the *Kansas City Star*) to Daniels, October 20, 1949, reporting that the records had been checked, JDP.

5. Steinberg, *Man from Missouri*, p. 31. Steinberg interviewed Arthur Eisenhower.

6. TM, 1:125.

7. Hillman, *Mr. President,*, p. 193.

8. David Morgan to Daniels, November 25, December 23, 1949, JDP. *Kansas City Directory 1916* has an advertisement for this company.

9. J. K. Brelsford's memorandum in regard to President's biography sent to Daniels in 1949, JDP.

10. Facts prepared by David H. Morgan in 1949, JDP.

11. Herbert Hoover, *The Memoirs of Herbert Hoover: Years of Adventure* (New York: Macmillan, 1951).

12. Stone, *They Also Ran*, pp. 307-308.

13. Daniels interview with Eddie Jacobson, 1949, JDP.

14. Soule, *Economic Forces in American History*, p. 468.

15. Hillman, *Mr. President*, p. 173.

16. McNaughton and Hehmeyer, *This Man Truman*, p. 59; *Washington Times Herald*, April 20, 1945, quoting Ed Meisburger.

17. Bundschu to Daniels, August 25, 1949, JDP.

18. Margaret Truman, *Harry S. Truman*, p. 89.

19. TM, 1:135.

20. Daniels interview with William Southern, September 26, 1949, JDP.

21. 1930 Report of the Missouri Building and Loan Supervisor, and October 5, 1949, memorandum to Mr. LaRoque from Rehabilitation and Recovering Division, JDP.

22. Memorandum by J. R. Fuchs of telephone conversation with Howard Bennett, April 30, 1962, HSTL.

23. KCS, October 25, 1940.

24. IE, April 23, 1926, stated that Truman's Community Savings and Loan Association had grown so rapidly that it was thought best that the officials sever connections with the banking business.

25. IE, August 9, 14, 21, October 31, 1926, April 17, 1929.

26. Roosevelt, *An Autobiography*, p. 55.

CHAPTER 6
MILITARY EXPERIENCES, 1905–1919

1. Hillman, *Mr. President*, p. 190.

2. Ibid., p. 104.

3. Alfred Adler, *Study of Organ Inferiority and Its Psychical Compensation* (New York: Nervous and Mental Disease Monograph Series No. 24, 1907 and 1917), Johnson Reprint.

4. The Democratic National Committee in *The Story of Harry S. Truman* (1948) published a panel that said: "Hey that looks like Harry Truman. I wonder how he passed the sight test to get into the National Guard?" "They tell me he memorized the eye chart just to get in!"

5. Hillman, *Mr. President*, p. 192.

6. James A. Huston, "Artillery Captain to the White House," *National Guardsman* (February 1950).

7. He gave full credit to Sergeant Jacobson. See *Chicago Sun*, April 19, 1945.

8. Lee, *Artilleryman*, p. 32.

9. IE, May 23, 1929.

10. Hillman, *Mr. President*, p. 44.

11. Ibid., p. 192.

12. Harry H. Vaughan, "Whipping Boy—First Class," manuscript, 1954, HSTL.

13. Huston, "Artillery Captain," p. 3.

14. McNaughton and Hehmeyer, *This Man Truman*, pp. 41-42.

15. OHT, Edgar G. Hinde, March 15, 1962, HSTL.

16. Daniels interview with Truman, November 12, 1949, JDP.

17. Daniels, *Man of Independence*, p. 95.

18. Samuel Gallu, *"Give 'Em Hell Harry,"* (New York: Viking, 1975), p. 34.

19. Steinberg, *Man from Missouri*, p. 46.

20. TM, 1:130.

21. Lee, *Artilleryman*, p. 129.

22. TM, 1:131.

23. Daniels interview with William Southern, September 26, 1949, JDP.

24. McNaughton and Hehmeyer, *This Man Truman*, p. 52.

25. Hillman, *Mr. President*, p. 32.

CHAPTER 7
BESS TRUMAN

1. Daniels interview with William M. Southern, September 26, 1949, JDP.

2. Marianne Means, "What Three Presidents Say about Their Wives," *Good Housekeeping* (August 1963):192.

3. Interview with Margaret Woodson, July 27, 1965.

4. OHT, Ethel Noland.

5. Daniels, *Man of Independence*, p. 104.

6. Margaret Truman, *Souvenir*, p. 12.

7. TM, 1:129.

8. Ibid.

9. Edith Asbury, "Meet Harry's Boss, Bess," *Colliers* (February 12, 1949): 15.

10. IE, June 28, 1919.

11. Truman, *Souvenir*, p. 20.

12. Ibid., p. 21.

13. Prindiville, *First Ladies*, p. 278.

14. Means, "What Three Presidents Say," p. 184.

15. Steinberg, *Man from Missouri*, p. 264.

16. Asbury, "Meet Harry's Boss," p. 64.

17. IE, July 3, 1957.

18. Asbury, "Meet Harry's Boss," p. 64.

19. Prindiville, *First Ladies*, p. 271.

20. SLPD, July 26, 1944.

21. Asbury, "Meet Harry's Boss," p. 65.

22. Daniels interview with Truman, August 1949, JDP.

23. *Time*, February 5, 1945; Truman to Bess, Dec. 28, 1945: "If I can get the use of the best brains in the country and a little bit of help from those I have on a pedestal at home, the job will be done." PSF, Personal, Box 309, HSTL.

CHAPTER 8
FIRST CANDIDACY, 1922

1. TM, 1:139.

2. Frances Burns, "The Life Story of Harry S. Truman," *Boston Globe*, April 13, 1945.

3. Reddig, *Tom's Town*, pp. 266-267.

4. Harold Zink, *City Bosses in the United States* (Durham: Duke University Press, 1930).

5. Rogow and Lasswell, *Power, Corruption and Rectitude*, p. 54.

6. *Missouri Democrat*, October 21, 1927.

7. Dorsett, *Pendergast Machine*, p. 61.

8. Interview with William Southern, September 26, 1949, JDP.

9. Schauffler, *Harry Truman, Son of the Soil*.

10. George R. Collins to Truman, September 28, 1939, HSTL.

11. *Boston Globe*, April 13, 1945, citing Mayor Sermon.

12. IE, March 8, 1922.

13. Rogge's interview with Harry S. Truman, August 13, 1957, cited in his "Speechmaking of Harry S. Truman," p. 54.

14. IE, July 17, 1922.

15. Ibid., May 22, 1922.

16. *Lees Summit Journal*, July 6, 1922.

17. TM, 1:137.

18. IE, July 17, 1922.

19. Schauffler, *Harry Truman*, p. 61.

20. IE, August 1, 1922, the day of the primary election.

21. Hillman, *Mr. President*, p. 197.

22. IE, November 6, 1922.

23. Daniels interview with William Southern, September 26, 1949, JDP.

24. *Kansas City Times*, October 27, 1944.

25. KCS, October 27, 1944.

26. OHT, Edgar Hinde, March 15, 1962 and Hinde to Daniels, October 4, 1949, JDP.

27. IE, November 6, 1922.

28. KCS, November 6, 1922; IE, November 11, 1922.

29. Wilson to William Hirth, n.d. (probably January 1932), cited by Dorsett, *Pendergast Machine*, pp. 94-95.

CHAPTER 9
POLITICAL APPRENTICESHIP, 1923–1924

1. KCS, June 1924, cited in Daniels's notes, JDP.

2. Cited by Steinberg, *Man of Independence*, p. 75.

3. Barker, *Missouri Lawyer*.

4. IE, April 3, 1923.

5. Ibid., April 6, 1923.

6. TM, 1:138.

7. IE, August 12, 1922.

8. Daniels, *Man of Independence*, pp. 112-113.

9. TM, 1:137.

10. KCS, November 3, 1924.

11. IE, August 6, 1924.

12. Ibid., August 4, 1924.

13. Ibid., August 9, 1924.

14. *Lees Summit Journal*, October 30, 1924.

15. IE, August 9, 1924.

16. KCS, November 3, 1924.

17. Ibid., November 6, 1924.

18. OHT, Henry P. Chiles, November 1, 1961.

19. Dorsett, *Pendergast Machine*, p. 80.

20. Charles P. Taft, *City Management: The Cincinnati Experiment* (New York: Farrar & Rinehart, 1933).

21. *Kansas City's Public Affairs* discussed in OHT, Walter Matscheck.

22. White, *City Manager*, chap. 2, "Henry F. McElroy." White did not quite realize how bad the Kansas City government was, but he had strong misgivings about it.

23. OHT, Walter Matscheck, p. 10.

24. IE, May 29, 1926.

25. KCS, April 14, 1926.

26. *Kansas City's Public Affairs*, no. 18, 1926.

CHAPTER 10
CHIEF COUNTY ADMINISTRATOR, 1927–1934

1. *Kansas City Times*, October 30, 1926.

2. KCS, November 3, 1926, reported 77,680 votes for Truman and 61,466 for Stewart.

3. IE, January 3, 1927.

4. *Kansas City's Public Affairs*, March 24, 1927.

5. OHT, Walter Matscheck, p. 28.

6. IE, January 18, 1927.

7. *Kansas City's Public Affairs*, June 23, 1927.

8. IE, December 8, 1927.

9. Daniels interview with Truman, November 12, 1949, JDP.

10. Editorial opinion of the *Engineering News-Record*, "How the County Road Bonds Won," reprinted in *Kansas City Times*, September 3, 1928.

11. Daniels, *Man of Independence*, pp. 145-146.

12. IE, October 6, 1928.

13. Ibid., November 8, 1929.

14. Ibid., January 24, 1929.

15. Matscheck's charges are substantiated by Dorsett, *Pendergast Machine*, pp. 118-119.

16. *Kansas City Times*, May 26, 1930.

17. KCS, October 31, 1930.

18. Ibid., October 17, 1930.

19. *Kansas City Journal-Post*, October 31, 1930.

20. KCS, November 5, 1930.

21. Ibid., November 14, 1930.

22. Ibid., May 12, 1931.

23. Reddig, *Tom's Town*, p. 176.

24. Dorsett, *Pendergast Machine*, chap. 8, cites letters to Roosevelt from Ike B. Dunlap, Roosevelt's representative in Kansas City. On the other hand, Mitchell, *Kicked In and Kicked Out of the President's Little Cabinet*, claims that he and his associates were the ones who rounded up votes for Roosevelt.

25. Fenton, *Politics in the Border States*, p. 138.

26. Schmidtlein, "Truman the Senator," p. 56.

27. Reddig, *Tom's Town*, p. 203.

28. *Missouri Official Manual* (1933).

29. Reddig, *Tom's Town*, p. 195.

30. Ibid., pp. 257-259.

31. Milligan, *Missouri Waltz*, p. 103.

32. Mayerberg, *Chronicle of American Crusader*.

33. KCS, December 10, 1936.

34. *New York Sun*, September 12, 1944.

35. Roy Roberts to Daniels, September 11, 1950, JDP.

36. IE, September 7, 1934.

37. Schauffler, *Harry Truman*, pp. 71-72.

38. Margaret Truman, *Harry S. Truman*, p. 74.

CHAPTER 11
CANDIDATE FOR U.S. SENATE, 1934

1. Schmidtlein, "Truman the Senator," pp. 64-65.

2. Fenton, *Politics in the Border States*, chaps. 1, 6, 7.

3. KCS, May 14, 1934.

4. Dorsett, *Pendergast Machine*, pp. 112-113, citing G. H. Foree to Mitchell, June 19, 1934.

5. Marquis Childs, *I Write from Washington*, pp. 96-99; *Missouri Farmer*, August 1, 1934.

6. *Sedalia Democrat*, May 10, 1934.

7. KCS, May 14, 1934.

8. Ibid., May 8, 1934.

9. Ibid., May 13, 1934.

10. Schmidtlein, "Truman the Senator," pp. 60-62, citing Lozier.

11. KCS, May 8, 1934.

12. TM, 1:141.

13. IE, June 1, 1934.

14. Ibid., July 20, 1934.

15. Daniels, *Man of Independence*, p. 171.

16. Truman to Governor Park, June 6, 1934, cited by Rogge, "Speechmaking of Truman," p. 132.

17. IE, May 30, 1934.

18. Ibid., June 29, 1934.

19. Ibid., July 7, 1934.

20. Ibid., August 7, 1934.

21. TM, 1:141.

22. *Kansas City Times*, July 25, 1934.

23. Ibid., July 7, 1934.

24. Ibid.

25. Ibid., February 10, 1934.

26. KCS, July 22, 1934.

27. Daniels, *Man of Independence*, p. 174.

28. Schmidtlein, "Truman the Senator," p. 79.

29. IE, July 30, 1934.

30. Schmidtlein, "Truman the Senator." p. 80.

31. *St. Louis Star-Times*, July 24, 1934.

32. SLPD, August 9 and 27, 1934.

33. Cited by Schmidtlein, "Truman the Senator," p. 84.

34. IE, August 8, 1934.

35. Schmidtlein, "Truman the Senator," p. 89.

36. *Kansas City Times*, October 19, 1934.

37. KCS, August 24, 1934.

38. SLPD, October 4, 1934.

39. Ibid., November 1, 1934.

40. *Labor Herald*, August 3, 1934.

41. OHC, Roy Wilkins, 1962.

42. Fenton, *Politics in the Border States*, chap. 7.

43. *Maryville Daily Forum*, November 8, 1934.

44. Matthews, *U.S. Senators and Their World*, chap. 3.

CHAPTER 12
"THE SENATOR FROM PENDERGAST," 1935-1940

1. KCS, June 18, 1935.
2. Frances Burns in *Boston Globe*, April 25, 1945, citing interview with Victor Messall.
3. Truman Papers, box S.V. 226, memorandum dated May 1941, with clipping attached, HSTL.
4. Truman to L. T. Stayton, February 5, 1935, cited by Dorsett, *Pendergast Machine*, p. 116.
5. KCS, May 10, 1935.
6. Barrett Papers, notorized affidavit, September 16, 1936, cited by Dorsett, *Pendergast Machine*, p. 116.
7. Mitchell, *Kicked In and Kicked Out of the President's Little Cabinet*, p. 345; *Future*, June 21, 1935 (a weekly under the auspices of National Youth Movement, a reform group).
8. Farley, *Jim Farley's Story*, p. 134.
9. Wheeler, *Yankee from the West*, p. 313; Daniels, *Man of Independence*, p. 179; Steinberg, *Man from Missouri*, p. 144.
10. TM, 1:151.
11. Democratic National Committee, *Proceedings of the Democratic National Convention, 1936*, pp. 135, 331.
12. Daniels interview with Truman, July 28, 1949, JDP.
13. Ibid., November 12, 1949, JDP.
14. Powell, *Tom's Boy Harry*, pp. 80-81.
15. Daniels, *Man of Independence*, p. 23.
16. Cited by Reddig, *Tom's Town*, p. 288.
17. Helm, *Harry Truman*, p. 33.
18. For a fuller discussion of these frauds, see Reddig, *Tom's Town*, pp. 284-294; Dorsett, *Pendergast Machine*, pp. 121-124; Milligan, *Missouri Waltz*, pp. 144-166; Powell, *Tom's Boy Harry*, pp. 72-74.
19. CR, 75th Cong., 3d sess., pp. 1962-1964.
20. KCS, February 15, 1938.
21. SLPD, February 16, 17, 1938.
22. Reddig, *Tom's Town*, p. 326.
23. SLPD, June 7, 1935.
24. Ibid., April 7, 1939.
25. Milligan, *Missouri Waltz*, p. 201.
26. SLPD, April 8, 1939.
27. Dorsett, *Pendergast Machine*, chap. 9.
28. Ibid., p. 135.
29. OHT, Matscheck, April 30, 1963.
30. Dorsett, *Pendergast Machine*, p. 134.
31. Wheeler, *Yankee from the West*, p. 373.

CHAPTER 13
LEGISLATIVE ROLE

1. Matthews, *U.S. Senators and Their World*, p. 61, classifies senators as patrician politicians, amateur politicians, professional politicians, and agitators.
2. Helm, *Harry Truman*, p. 7.
3. Ibid., p. 64.
4. Daniels, *Man of Independence*, p. 194, cites a letter that Norris later wrote to Henry Wallace expressing a favorable view of Truman.

5. TM, 1:144.

6. Ibid., p. 149.

7. Steinberg, *Man from Missouri*, p. 125.

8. Frances Burns in *Boston Globe*, April 25, 1945.

9. OHT, Harry Vaughan, January 14, 1963.

10. TM, 1:147.

11. Wheeler, *Yankee from the West*, p. ix.

12. Hillman, *Mr. President*, p. 179.

13. Wheeler, *Yankee from the West*, p. ix.

14. PPR, 1935, pp. 238-241.

15. Senate Document No. 15, 74th Cong., 1st sess.; House Document No. 221, 74th Cong., 1st sess.

16. CR, 75th Cong., 3d sess., p. 6515.

17. NYT, May 15, 1939.

18. 2 Stat. 973 (1938); Rhyne, *Civil Aeronautics Act.*

19. NYT, July 18, 1938.

20. Frederick, *Commercial Air Transportation.*

21. TM, 1:156.

22. Lowenthal, *The Investor Pays.*

23. Daniels interview with Truman, November 12, 1949, JDP.

24. OHT, Jonathan Daniels, October 4, 1963.

25. Daniels interview with Lowenthal, August 31, 1949, JDP.

26. Lowenthal to Daniels, December 10, 1949, JDP.

27. *Railroad Hearings*, pt. 2, pp. 581-595; pt. 11, pp. 4714-4719, 76th Cong., 1st sess., Report No. 23.

28. Steinberg, *Man from Missouri*, p. 148.

29. OHT, Daniels.

30. CR, 75th Cong., 1st sess., pp. 5271-5275.

31. Ibid., 75th Cong., 2d sess., p. 1923.

32. Ibid.

33. Swaine, *The Cravath Firm and Its Predecessors*, pp. 418, 430, 546, 549.

34. CR, 76th Cong., 1st sess., pt. 6, pp. 5869, 5956; Senate Bill No. S-2009; Ralph L. Dewey, "Transportation Act of 1940," *American Economic Review* 31 (1941):16-19.

35. CR, 76th Cong., 1st sess., pp. 5945, 5949, 5998, 6135; Senate Report No. 433, pt. 1, p. 3.

36. NYT, May 9, 1940; *Christian Science Monitor*, July 26, 1939.

37. SLPD, March 2, 1935.

38. TM, 1:155, states that he voted against the bill because it was not in the right form. Helm, *Harry Truman*, p. 116, states that Truman opposed it on principle.

39. Fenton, *Politics in the Border States*, chaps. 6, 7.

40. Schmidtlein, "Truman the Senator," p. 132.

41. U.S. Department of Agriculture, Agricultural History Branch, *Century of Service*, p. 168.

42. CR, 74th Cong., 2d sess., pp. 4373-4374.

43. Agricultural History Branch, *Century of Service*, pp. 173-174.

44. CR, 76th Cong., 1st sess., p. 799.

45. "What the United States Senate Thinks of Harry S. Truman," Pre-Presidential Correspondence File, HSTL.

46. Berman, *Politics of Civil Rights in the Truman Administration*, pp. 7-8.

47. Gunnar Myrdal, *An American Dilemma* (New York: Harper, 1944), p. 488.

48. Lubell, *Future of American Politics*, p. 8.

49. CR, 76th Cong., 1st sess., pp. 1105-1107.

50. PPR, 1938, p. 192.

51. TM, 1:154-155.

52. *Congressional Quarterly Almanac for 1945*, p. 142, gives the party divisions on these measures. CR gives the Truman and Clark vote on these measures.

53. Senator Clark said that Truman was unavoidably absent and if present would have voted for the measure. CR, June 11, 1935, 74th Cong., 1st sess., p. 9065.

54. Matthews, *U.S. Senators and Their World*, p. 231.

CHAPTER 14
RETURNED TO THE SENATE IN 1940

1. TM, 1:143.

2. Schmidtlein, "Truman the Senator," pp. 208-209.

3. TM, 1:159. But on August 30, 1949, Truman told Daniels that FDR indicated to him that he did not think he had any chance of renomination but that he would appoint him to the Interstate Commerce Commission (JDP).

4. Helm, *Harry Truman*, p. 124.

5. OHT, Edgar Hinde, March 15, 1962.

6. Steinberg, *Man from Missouri*, p. 167.

7. KCS, May 13, 1939.

8. Ibid., September 15, 1939.

9. Steinberg, *Man from Missouri*, p. 167.

10. Farley, *Jim Farley's Story*, p. 134.

11. Byrnes, *All in One Lifetime*, p. 101.

12. KCS, March 28, 1940.

13. Milligan, *Missouri Waltz*, pp. 131-132.

14. KCS, January 7, 1940.

15. Milligan, *Missouri Waltz*, chap. 5.

16. *Kansas City Journal*, January 11, February 1, 1940.

17. Rogge, "Speechmaking of Harry S. Truman," p. 140.

18. SLPD, January 8, 1940.

19. KCS, April 3, 1940.

20. Daniels interview with Vic Messall, October 27, 1949, JDP.

21. Truman to Major George R. Collins, May 29, 1940, Pre-Presidential File, HSTL.

22. Daniels interview with Messall, JDP.

23. Frank Monroe to Daniels, September 29, 1949, JDP.

24. CR, 76th Cong., 3d sess., 3925.

25. Daniels interview with Messall, JDP.

26. OHT, Harry H. Vaughan, January 14, 15, 1963.

27. Byrnes, *All in One Lifetime*, p. 101; Coit, *Mr. Baruch*, p. 543; Lubell, *Future of American Politics*, p. 15.

28. Helm, *Harry Truman*, pp. 146-148.

29. SLPD, June 21, 1940.

30. Ibid., January 7, 1940.

31. Ibid., April 12, 1940.

32. Ickes, *The Secret Diary of Harold L. Ickes*, 3; 286.

33. SLPD, July 19, 1940.

34. KCS, July 23, 1940; Daniels interview with William Southern, September 26, 1949, JDP.

35. KCS, July 11, 1940.

36. Stark to W. W. Watson, July 19, 1940, FDRL.

37. KCS, July 18, 1940.

38. Delmar Dail to Daniels, September 26, 1949, JDP.

39. Memorandum, Edward Keating to Daniels, JDP (copy available in HSTL).

40. Telegram to R. A. Wadlow, July 30, 1940, FDRL.

41. TM, 1:161.

42. CR, 76th Cong., 3d sess., p. 4546.

43. Ibid., p. 5367.

44. KCS, August 4, 1940.

45. Daniels interview with William Southern, September 26, 1949, JDP.

46. Martin, *The Bosses*, p. 281.

47. KCS, August 4, 1940.

48. Daniels interview with William Southern, JDP.

49. Rufus Jarman, "Truman's Political Quarterback," *Saturday Evening Post*, March 2, 1946; KCS, August 7, 1940.

50. Carl A. Hatch to Daniels, January 2, 1950, JDP.

51. State of Missouri, *Official Manual, 1941–1943*, pp. 366-367.

52. T. H. Van Sant to Daniels, 1949, JDP.

53. Parrington to Daniels, September 12, 1949, JDP.

54. Senator Truman to workers, August 23, 1940, Pre-Presidential File, HSTL.

55. Berenstein to Roosevelt, August 9, 1940, FDRL.

56. Rogge, "Speechmaking of Truman," p. 144.

57. *Kansas City Times*, August 30, October 26, November 1, 1940.

58. SLPD, September 22, 1940.

59. Fenton, *Politics in the Border States*, p. 157.

CHAPTER 15
TREASURY WATCHDOG, 1941–1944

1. CR, 77th Cong., 1st sess., p. 4175.

2. U.S. Bureau of the Budget, *United States at War*.

3. Helm, *Harry Truman*, p. 152.

4. CR, 77th Cong., 1st sess., p. 830.

5. Riddle, *Truman Committee*, p. 13.

6. CR, 77th Cong., 1st sess., p. 138.

7. Byrnes, *All in One Lifetime*, p. 92.

8. CR, 77th Cong., 1st sess., p. 1615.

9. Lubell, *Future of American Politics*, p. 17.

10. M. Nelson McGeary, "Congressional Investigations: Historical Development," *University of Chicago Law Review* 18 (Spring 1951):425; Schlesinger and Bruns, *Congress Investigates*; Taylor, *Grand Inquest*.

11. Lewis Schwellenbach to Truman, January 23, 1942, HSTL.

12. Daniels, *Man of Independence*, p. 218.

13. Democratic National Committee, "Man from Missouri," 1944 release, p. 8.

14. Members and terms are listed in I. H. M. Maher, "Role of the Chairman of a Congressional Investigating Committee."

15. Riddle, *Truman Committee*, p. 21.

16. Maher, "Chairman of Investigating Committee," p. 282, citing interview with Hugh Fulton, November 2, 1960.

17. Daniels, *Man of Independence*, p. 224.

18. McNaughton and Hehmeyer, *This Man Truman*, p. 95.

19. For an example, see Fulton's Memorandum of Salient Points in Connection with the Testimony of Mr. Nelson, Committee Files, NA.

20. Truman address before the Brooklyn Chamber of Commerce, May 22, 1944, CR, 78th Cong., 2d sess., p. 2522.

21. Report 480, 5, p. 172, 77th Cong., 2d sess., January 15, 1942.

22. "Billion Dollar Watchdog," *Time*, March 8, 1943.

23. Truman to Lou Holland, May 1, 1944, HSTL.

24. Maher, "Chairman of Investigating Committee," p. 70.

25. Riddle, *Truman Committee*, pp. 33-34.

26. Nelson to Truman, June 16, 1942, Committee Files, NA.

27. Donald Nelson to Truman, January 4, 1943, CR, 78th Cong., 1st sess., p. 39.

28. Memorandum from Patterson to FDR, December 13, 1941, OF, FDRL.

29. CR, 78th Cong., 1st sess., p. 39.

30. Riddle, *Truman Committee*, p. 76, citing interview with Somervell.

31. Ibid., p. 172, citing Fulton to the effect that the charge was unfounded.

32. CR, 78th Cong., 1st sess., p. 39.

33. Annual Report of Committee Investigations, January 15, 1942, pt. 5 of Report No. 480, 77th Cong., 2d sess.

34. Ibid., pt. 1, "Aluminum."

35. Childs, *I Write from Washington*, p. 276.

36. Report No. 480, pt. 7, p. 57, May 26, 1942.

37. *Public Hearings*, pt. 22, September-December 1943, "Canol Project."

38. Report No. 10, pt. 14, "Canol Project," 78th Cong., 1st sess., December 21, 1943.

39. Riddle, *Truman Committee*, p. 118.

40. Second Annual Report, March 11, 1943, pp. 217-220. Senator Paul Douglas told the writer that the Truman committee made a tape recording of a Bureau of Ships conversation in which a plot was being laid to cause the Higgins landing boat design to fail its test. This tape was played before Secretary Knox, who then reorganized the bureau.

41. CR, 78th Cong., 1st sess., pp. 843, 1943.

42. Report No. 10, pt. 12, p. 5, November 5, 1943.

43. TM, 1:186.

44. Connally, *My Name Is Tom Connally*, p. 274; Steinberg, *Man from Missouri*, p. 195.

CHAPTER 16
POLITICS AS USUAL, 1941-1944

1. Milligan, *Missouri Waltz*, pp. 217-233; Fenton, *Politics in the Border States*, pp. 130-134; Redding, *Tom's Town*, pp. 272-275.

2. PPT, 1952-1953, pp. 1085-1086.

3. Rufus Jarman, "Truman's Political Quarterback," *Saturday Evening Post*, March 2, 1946; "Robert E. Hannegan," *Press Research*, April 23, 1945; OHT, Harry Vaughan, January 14, 1963.

4. In the Democratic primary, McDaniel received 323,395 votes and McReynolds, 252,441 votes. In the general election, McDaniel received 907,917 and Donnell 911, 530 votes. *Missouri Manual 1941-42*.

5. *Messages and Proclamations of the Governor of Missouri*, vol. 25; State ex rel. Donnell v. Osborn, 347 Mo. 469; State ex rel. Donnell v. Searcy, 347 Mo. 1052.

6. TM, 1:324.

7. OHT, Harry H. Vaughan.

8. Memorandum from Francis Biddle to President Roosevelt, June 25, 1943, FDRL.

9. Memorandum from Roosevelt to Biddle, June 30, 1943, FDRL.

10. Interview with Joseph P. Harris, September 7, 1962.

11. Riddle, *Truman Committee*, p. 151.

12. *Congressional Quarterly Almanac for 1945*, p. 142.

13. Matthews, *U.S. Senators and Their World*, pp. 164, 279.

14. *New Republic*, May 8, 1944, February 5, 1945.

15. Dean R. Brimhall and A. S. Otis, "Consistency in Congressional Voting," *Journal of Applied Psychology* (February 1948):1-15.

16. Pre-Presidential File, HSTL.

CHAPTER 17
COMPROMISE CANDIDATE FOR VICE-PRESIDENT

1. MacDougall, *Gideon's Army*, pp. 92-94, presents Wallace's views.

2. Elliott Roosevelt, ed., *F.D.R.: His Personal Letters*, p. 1499.

3. Tully, *F.D.R., My Boss*, chap. 10.

4. McIntire, *White House Physician*, p. 193; Bishop, *FDR's Last Year*, pp. 157-158, 201-202.

5. Letter to Robert E. Hannegan, NYT, July 20, 1944. This letter also appears in PPR, 1944-1945, p. 197.

6. MacDougall, *Gideon's Army*, pp. 497-504; Charles Michelson, *The Ghost Talks* (New York: Putnams, 1944), p. 197; Walker, *Henry A. Wallace*, pp. 54-55, 111.

7. Rosenman, *Working with Roosevelt*, p. 439.

8. Flynn, *You're the Boss*, p. 180.

9. Rosenman, *Working with Roosevelt*, p. 442.

10. Roosevelt, *F.D.R.: His Personal Letters*, p. 1047.

11. Frank Monroe to Truman, April 13, 1942, HSTL.

12. *Kansas City Times*, April 18, 1944.

13. Allen, *Presidents Who Have Known Me*, p. 125; Lord, *Wallaces of Iowa*, p. 527.

14. Jones and Angley, *Fifty Billion Dollars*, p. 310.

15. Memorandum from Ed Pauley to Daniels, December 5, 1949, JDP.

16. Ibid.

17. NYT, March 31, 1944.

18. Ibid., April 30, 1944.

19. SLPD, April 30, 1944.

20. Williams, *Rise of the Vice Presidency*, p. 202; Walker, *Henry A. Wallace*, p. 107.

21. *Washington Post*, May 14, 1944; NYT, May 24, 1944.

22. Daniels, *Man of Independence*, p. 242.

23. Flynn, *You're the Boss*, p. 180.

24. Daniels, *Man of Independence*, p. 243.

25. Flynn, *You're the Boss*, p. 181.

26. Ibid.

27. Memorandum from Pauley to Daniels, JDP.

28. Ibid.

29. Allen, *Presidents Who Have Known Me*, p. 128.

30. Rosenman, *Working with Roosevelt*, pp. 444-446.

31. NYT, July 4, 8, 1944.

32. *Official Proceedings of the Democratic National Convention, 1944*, p. 63; Walker, *Henry A. Wallace*, p. 112.

33. Byrnes, *All in One Lifetime*, pp. 216-230.

34. Rosenman, *Working with Roosevelt*, p. 449.

35. Mayor Kelly to Daniels, May 5, 1950, JDP.

36. KCS, July 18, 1944. See also Josephson, *Sidney Hillman*, p. 622.

37. Flynn, *You're the Boss*, p. 182.

38. KCS, July 19, 1944.

39. NYT, July 25, 1944. See also OHC, Krock, 1950.

40. NYT, September 12, 1944.

41. Daniels interview with Max Lowenthal, August 31, 1949, JDP.

42. Millis, *Forrestal Diaries*, p. 5.

43. McNaughton and Hehmeyer, *This Man Truman*, p. 151; TM, 1:191; Josephson, *Sidney Hillman*, p. 621; Rosenman, *Working with Roosevelt*, p. 448. Byrnes, *All in One Lifetime*, p. 227, claims that A. F. Whitney of the Brotherhood of Railway Trainmen argued with Hillman on Byrnes's behalf but without success.

44. NYT, July 19, 1944.

45. Copy in FDRL. The letter is reproduced in PPR, 1944-1945, p. 200.

46. Daniels interview with Truman, November 12, 1949, JDP.

47. *Washington Star*, July 20, 1944.

48. *Baltimore Sun*, July 20, 1944.

49. Josephson, *Sidney Hillman*, p. 623; Walker, *Henry A. Wallace*, p. 112.

50. Memorandum from Pauley to Daniels, JDP.

51. Farley, *Jim Farley's Story*, p. 367.

52. NYT, July 22, 1944.

53. *Washington Post*, July 22, 1944.

54. *Official Proceedings*, 1944, pp. 199-200.

55. Ibid., p. 256.

56. Ibid., p. 271.

57. *Sioux City Journal*, July 23, 1944.

58. Daniels interview with Truman, August 30, 1949, JDP; Daniels, *Man of Independence*, p. 253.

59. SLPD, October 6, 1949; Steinberg, *Man from Missouri*, pp. 209-218.

60. Byrnes, *All in One Lifetime*, p. 229.

61. Mark Ethridge to the President, July 25, 1944, JDP.

62. Lord, *Wallaces of Iowa*, pp. 539-540.

63. KCS, July 22, 1944.

CHAPTER 18
THE 1944 CAMPAIGN

1. PPR, 1944, p. 202.

2. Williams, *The Rise of the Vice Presidency*.

3. Robert E. Sherwood, *Roosevelt and Hopkins*, p. 820.

4. NYT, November 5, 1944.

5. SLPD, July 26, 1944.

6. *Chicago Tribune*, October 17, 1944.

7. NYT, October 3, 1944.

8. Ibid.

9. TM, 1:193.

10. KCS, August 28, 1944.

11. CR, 78th Cong., 2d sess., p. A3860.

12. *Philadelphia Evening Bulletin*, September 8, 1944.

13. Letter of resignation, CR, 78th Cong., 2d sess., p. 6721.

14. Speech, September 4, 1944, Senatorial and Vice-Presidential File, HSTL.

15. *Newsweek*, May 7, 1945.

16. Truman to Tom Evans, August 8, 1944, Senatorial File, HSTL.

17. McNaughton and Hehmeyer, *This Man Truman*, p. 182.

18. Price Wickersham to Senator Truman, n.d., Background Material, Senatorial and Vice-Presidential File, HSTL.

19. McNaughton and Hehmeyer, *This Man Truman*, p. 170.

20. Williams, *Rise of the Vice Presidency*, chap. 11.

21. McNaughton and Hehmeyer, *This Man Truman*, pp. 180-181.

22. Steinberg, *Man from Missouri*, pp. 225-226.

23. Speech, October 19, 1944, Senatorial and Vice-Presidential File, HSTL.

24. Allen, *Presidents Who Have Known Me*, pp. 143-144.

25. Speech at Butte, Montana, October 21, 1944, Senatorial and Vice-Presidential File, HSTL.

26. Wheeler, *Yankee from the West*, p. 374.

27. Speech, October 26, 1944, Senatorial and Vice-Presidential File, HSTL.

28. *Christian Science Monitor*, October 28, 1944.

29. *New York Journal-American*, October 31, 1944.

30. Hassett, *Off the Record with FDR, 1942-1945*, p. 290.

31. William P. Collins to Senator Truman, November 9, 1944, Senatorial File, HSTL.

32. KCS, November 5, 1944, quoted Truman: "In San Francisco the Hearst papers passed the word around I was a Jew. If I were I would be proud of it. I had a grandfather by the name Solomon Young."

33. NYT, November 1, 1944.

34. Speech, November 4, 1944, Senatorial and Vice-Presidential File, HSTL.

35. Margaret Truman, *Souvenir*, p. 72.

36. PPT 200, FDRL.

37. Ross, *Loneliest Campaign*, p. 247.

38. TM, 1:193.

39. Truman Papers, V. Camp. 2, HSTL.

40. PPR, 1944-1945, p. 290.

41. Frank Monroe to Daniels, September 29, 1949, JDP.

42. Speech, Seattle, October 19, 1944 and speech, Providence, R.I., October 30, 1944, Senatorial and Vice-Presidential File, HSTL.

43. Speech, Los Angeles, October 16, 1944, and speech, Minneapolis, October 23, 1944, Senatorial and Vice-Presidential File, HSTL.

44. Radio address, October 3, 1944, Senatorial and Vice-Presidential File, HSTL.

45. Hadley Cantril, "The Issues—As Seen by the American People," *Public Opinion Quarterly* (Fall 1944):346.

CHAPTER 19
EIGHTY-TWO DAYS AS VICE-PRESIDENT, 1945

1. Williams, *Rise of the Vice Presidency*, p. 156; Margaret Truman, *Harry S. Truman*, p. 101.

2. Daniels interview with Truman, November 12, 1949, JDP.

3. CR, 79th Cong. 1st sess., p. 1165.

4. TM, 1:195. Action on S. 375 given in CR, 79th Cong., 1st sess., p. 679.

5. Daniels interview with Truman, November 12, 1949, JDP.

6. Millis, *Forrestal Diaries*, pp. 33, 36-37.

7. Daniels interview with Victor Messall, October 27, 1949, JDP.

8. CR, 79th Cong., 1st sess., p. 3247: "The Vice President. On this question the yeas are 39 and the nays are 39. The chair votes 'nay' and the motion of the Senator from Ohio is lost."

9. *New York Sunday News*, February 11, 1945.

10. McNaughton and Hehmeyer, *This Man Truman*, p. 199.

11. Hassett, *Off the Record with FDR*, pp. 327-328.

12. TM, 1:5.

13. Margaret Truman, *Souvenir*, p. 83.

CHAPTER 20
THE ROOSEVELT-TRUMAN TRANSITION: 1945

1. Blum, *The Price of Vision*, p. 452.

2. Sherwood, *Roosevelt and Hopkins*, p. 881; Elmer E. Cornwell, "The Truman Presidency," in Richard Kirkendall, *The Truman Period as a Research Field* (Columbia: University of Missouri Press, 1967), pp. 240-241.

3. *Time*, April 23, 1945.

4. TM, 1:323-327.

5. Blum, *Price of Vision*, p. 448.

6. Rexford G. Tugwell, *The Democratic Roosevelt* (Garden City: Doubleday, 1957), pp. 332-335.

7. Record of Harold Smith's Conference with President Truman, May 21, 1945, FDRL.

8. Gene Smith, *When the Cheering Stopped: The Last Years of Woodrow Wilson* (New York: Morrow, 1964).

9. Francis Russell, *The Shadow of Blooming Grove: Warren G. Harding and His Times* (New York: McGraw-Hill, 1968), pp. 452-453.

10. EO 8248, September 8, 1939.

11. PPT, 1945, p. 8.

12. Rosenman, *Working with Roosevelt*, p. 515.

13. OHT, Jonathan Daniels, October 4, 1963, HSTL.

14. Richard E. Neustadt, "Notes on the White House Staff under Truman," June 1953, p. 31, HSTL.

15. Rosenman, *Working with Roosevelt*, p. 453.

16. PPT, 1945, p. 17.

17. Ibid., p. 9.

18. Ibid., pp. 16-17.

19. OHT, Jonathan Daniels, October 4, 1963, HSTL.

20. Pollard, *President and the Press*, p. 28.

21. Farrar, *Reluctant Servant*, p. 155.

22. Allen and Shannon, *The Truman Merry-Go-Round*, p. 53.

23. Hassett, *Off the Record with FDR*, p. 346.

24. Allen and Shannon, *Truman Merry-Go-Round*, p. 53.

25. Anderson, *President's Men*, pp. 105-106.

26. Neustadt, "Notes on the White House Staff," pp. 29-30.

27. Abels, *Truman Scandals*, pp. 40-42.

28. Anderson, *President's Men*, pp. 97-105.

29. Allen and Shannon, *Truman Merry-Go-Round*, p. 49.

30. OHT, Harry Vaughan, January 14, 16, 1963, and his typed manuscript, "Whipping Boy—First Class, 1954," HSTL.

31. Neustadt, "Notes on White House Staff," p. 41.

32. Anderson, *President's Men*, p. 88.

33. Leahy, *I Was There*, p. 349.

34. TM, 1:18.

35. Leahy, *I Was There*, p. 352.

36. Author's interview with R. R. Zimmerman, July 1, 1963.

37. Ibid.

38. Neustadt, "Notes on White House Staff," pp. 38-39.

39. TM, 1:58-59.

40. Record of Smith's conferences with Truman, April 18, 1945, FDRL.

41. Ibid.

42. Ibid., April 26, 1945.

43. Ibid.

44. Ibid., May 4, 11, 21, June 5, 8, 14, July 6, 1945.

45. Copy in HSTL.

46. OHT, Frederick J. Lawton, June 17, 1963.

47. Record of Smith's conference with Truman, August 10, 1945, FDRL.

48. Ibid., October 16, 1945.

49. Somers, *Presidential Agency*, pp. 210-213.

50. Millis, *Forrestal Diaries*, p. 43.

51. Record of Smith's conference with Truman, May 21, 1945, FDRL.

52. TM, 1:329-330.

53. Neustadt, "Notes on White House Staff," p. 44.

54. Walter Johnson, "Edward Stettinius, Jr., 1944-1945," in Graebner, *An Uncertain Tradition*, pp. 210-222.

55. Byrnes, *All in One Lifetime*, p. 280.

56. TM, 1:22.

57. Vandenberg, *Private Papers*, p. 225.

58. TM, 1:23.

59. *Newsweek*, July 9, 1945.

60. Stimson and Bundy, *On Active Service*, p. 656. During the war, Stimson had doubts about Truman. Stimson Diaries, Mar. 13, 1944.

61. Mills, *Forrestal Diaries*, biographical introduction, and Rogow, *James Forrestal*, p. 121.

62. Riddle, *Truman Committee*, pp. 156-157.

63. Rogow, *James Forrestal*, chap. 1.

64. TM, 1:554.

65. Ickes, *Autobiography of a Curmudgeon*.

66. Lord, *Wallaces of Iowa*; Dwight MacDonald, *Henry Wallace* (New York: Vanguard Press, 1948); Schmidt, *Henry Wallace*; Schapsmeier and Schapsmeier, *Henry A. Wallace of Iowa*; Blum, *Price of Vision*.

67. Truman to FDR, April 5, 1945, FDRL.

68. Daniels, *Man of Independence*, p. 306.

69. Helm, *Harry Truman*, p. 173.

70. TM, 1:325.

71. Dean Albertson, *Roosevelt's Farmer*; Matusow, *Farm Policies and Politics in the Truman Years*.

72. Report of Special Committee to Investigate Food Shortages, *House Report* no. 504, 79th Cong., 1st sess.

73. TM, 1:325.

74. Francis Biddle, *In Brief Authority*.

75. TM, 1:325.

76. Acheson, *Present at the Creation*, pp. 109-110.

77. Steinberg, *Man from Missouri*, p. 254.

78. Phillips, *Truman Presidency*, p. 146; TM, 1:325.

79. TM, 1:327; Steinberg, *Man from Missouri*, p. 254; John Morton Blum, ed., *From the Morgenthau Diaries: Years of War, 1941-1945* (Boston: Houghton Mifflin, 1967), 3:465-473.

80. PPT, 1945, pp. 170-171.

81. Somers, *Presidential Agency*, pp. 84-85.

82. Coffin, *Missouri Compromise*, pp. 36-37.

83. TM, 1:484.

84. U.S. Bureau of the Budget, *The United States at War*, p. 385.

85. Somers, *Presidential Agency*, p. 87.

CHAPTER 21
LEARNING DIPLOMACY, 1945

1. Geoffrey S. Smith, "'Harry, We Hardly Know You': Revisionism, Politics and Diplomacy, 1945-54, A Review Essay," *American Political Science Review* 70 (June 1976): 560-582.

2. Ulam, *Stalin*, pp. 561, 611, 627.

3. PPT, 1945, pp. 1, 4.

4. Arthur Schlesinger, Jr., "Origins of the Cold War," *Foreign Affairs* 46 (October 1967): 28-29.

5. TM, 1:14-16.

6. Millis, *Forrestal Diaries*, p. 40.

7. NYT, June 24, 1941.

8. Stimson and Bundy, *On Active Service*, p. 610.

9. David S. McLellan and John W. Reuss, "Foreign and Military Policies," in Kirkendall, ed., *Truman Period as a Research Field* (1967), p. 47.

10. FRUS, 1945, 6:568.

11. Ibid., p. 547.

12. Millis, *Forrestal Diaries*, p. 97.

13. Ibid., p. 89.

14. FRUS, 1945, 5:818, "Ambassador in the Soviet Union [Harriman] to the Secretary of State," April 4, 1945.

15. TM, 1:552.

16. FRUS, 1945, *Potsdam Papers*, 1:64-69, Joseph Davies's report re: Mission to London, June 12, 1945.

17. Leahy, *I Was There*, p. 388.

18. *Fortune*, "Mr. Truman's White House," February 1952, p. 78.

19. Feis, *Between War and Peace*, p. 60.

20. Daniels interview with Truman, November 12, 1949, JDP.

21. Grew, *Turbulent Era*, vol. 2.

22. FRUS, 1945, 3:277-278, memorandum by Grew to President Truman, May 5, 1945.

23. Grew, *Turbulent Era*, 2:1475.

24. FRUS, 1945, 5:258-259, President Truman to Stalin, April 23, 1945.

24. TM, 1:82.

26. Hillman, *Mr. President*, p. 114.

27. Eisenhower to Marshall, May 8, 1945, cited by Feis, *Between War and Peace*, p. 17.

28. Sherwood, *Roosevelt and Hopkins*, pp. 894-896.

29. Daniels, *Man of Independence*, p. 271.

30. TM, 1:227-229. See also George C. Herring, Jr., "Lend-Lease to Russia; The Origins of the Cold War, 1944-45," *Journal of American History* 56 (June 1969): 93-114.

31. Sherwood, *Roosevelt and Hopkins*, p. 913.

32. Feis, *Between War and Peace*, pp. 83-84.

33. Sherwood, *Roosevelt and Hopkins*, p. 913.

34. Kennan, *Memoirs, 1925-1950*, pp. 212-213.

35. Churchill, *Triumph and Tragedy*, p. 578.

36. TM, 1:281.

37. Churchill, *Triumph and Tragedy*, pp. 572-574.

38. TM, 1:282.

39. Walter Johnson, "Edward R. Stettinius, Jr.," in Graebner, *An Uncertain Tradition*, pp. 219-220.

40. Acheson, *Present at the Creation*, p. 111.

41. Richard D. Burns, "James F. Byrnes," in Graebner, *An Uncertain Tradition*, pp. 226-227.

42. Byrnes, *All in One Lifetime*, p. 303.

43. TM, 1:23.

44. Feis, *Between War and Peace*, pp. 160, 320.

45. TM, 1:338.

46. Feis, *Between War and Peace*, p. 160.

47. Churchill, *Triumph and Tragedy*, pp. 455-456.

48. Ibid., pp. 630, 634.

49. Moran, *Churchill*, p. 306.

50. TM, 1:340. See also Truman's notes on Potsdam, July 16, 1945, PSF, Personal, Box 322, HSTL.

51. Ibid., p. 342.

52. Daniels, *Man of Independence*, p. 218.

53. Feis, *Between War and Peace*, p. 319.

54. TM, 1:349. See also Truman's notes on Potsdam, July 18, 1945, HSTL.

55. PPT, 1945, pp. 179-195, Joint Report with Allied Leaders.

56. Feis, *Between War and Peace*, p. 184.

57. TM, 1:360.

58. Ibid., p. 385.

59. FRUS, 1945, *Potsdam*, 2:208. See also Truman's notes on Potsdam, July 25, 1945, PSF, HSTL.

60. FRUS, 1944, 1:140-154, memorandum by United Kingdom Delegation to European Advisory Commission, January 15, 1944.

61. FRUS, 1945, *Potsdam*, 2:893-897, Pauley to President Truman, July 28, 1945. Truman's notes on Potsdam, July 30, 1945, HSTL.

62. Barton J. Bernstein, "American Foreign Policy and the Origin of the Cold War," in Bernstein, *Politics and Policies of the Truman Administration*, p. 31.

63. Kennan, *Memoirs, 1925-1950*, p. 259.

64. Rostow, *United States in the World Arena*, p. 117.

65. PPT, 1945, pp. 203-214.

66. Bernstein, *Politics and Policies*, pp. 32, 66. At this time, Truman was anxious to cooperate with Stalin. See Truman's notes on Potsdam, July 18, 25, 1945, HSTL.

67. Fletcher Knebel and Charles W. Bailey, "The Fight over the Bomb," *Look*, August 13, 1963, pp. 19-23.

68. Donovan, *Conflict and Crisis*, p. 96, citing interview with George Elsey.

69. Churchill, *Triumph and Tragedy*, p. 639.

70. Feis, *Atomic Bomb*, p. 108.

71. TM, 1:431. See also Truman's notes on Potsdam, July 25, 1945, HSTL.

72. Feis, *Atomic Bomb*, p. 100.

73. Eisenhower, *Crusade in Europe*, p. 443.

74. Knebel and Bailey, "Fight over the Bomb."

75. Grew, *Trubulent Era*, 2:1421-1428.

76. Stimson and Bundy, *On Active Service*, p. 619.

77. Walter Millis, ed., "The Political Target under Assault," in *Japan's Struggle to End the War: The United States Strategic Bombing Survey* (Washington, D.C.: Government Printing Office, 1946), pp. 9-13.

78. Blackett, *Fear, War and the Bomb*.

79. Feis, *Between War and Peace*, p. 179.

CHAPTER 22
DEMOBILIZATION AND RECONVERSION, 1945–1946

1. Riddle, *Truman Committee*, p. 152.

2. Harold Smith's Notes on Conference with the President, April 26, 1945, FDRL.

3. Somers, *Presidential Agency.*

4. Barton Bernstein, "Economic Policies," in Kirkendall, *Truman Period as a Research Field* (1967), pp. 87-148.

5. Kennan, *Memoirs, 1925–1950*, pp. 265-266.

6. Matusow, *Farm Policies*, pp. 5-6.

7. Herbert Lehman to the President, June 15, 1945, HSTL, and White House press release, April 30, 1945, HSTL.

8. DSB, 12:860.

9. PPT, 1945, pp. 61-62.

10. Ibid., 1947, p. 14.

11. Bureau of the Budget, *United States at War*, p. 236.

12. Harvey Mansfield, *Short History of the O.P.A.* (Washington, D.C., Government Printing Office, 1947).

13. McClure, *Problems of Postwar Labor*, chap. 1.

14. TM, 1:484.

15. Neustadt, *Presidential Power*, p. 175.

16. KCS, April 14, 1945.

17. Hayek, *Road to Serfdom*; Goldman, *Crucial Decade*, p. 8.

18. Hamby, *Beyond the New Deal*, pp. 57, 297.

19. PPT, 1952-1953, p. 270, news conference of April 17, 1952.

20. Vandenberg, *Private Papers,* p. 138.

21. TM, 1:46.

22. Vandenberg, *Private Papers*, p. 167.

23. PPT, 1945, p. 3.

24. Ibid., p. 6.

25. NYT, April 17, 1945.

26. Dorough, *Mr. Sam*, p. 368.

27. CR, 79th Cong., 1st sess., p. 3596.

28. Ibid., p. 3359.

29. Catton, *War Lords.*

30. PPT, 1945, p. 28.

31. Congressional Quarterly, *Congress and the Nation,*, p. 344.

32. PPT, 1945, pp. 72-75.

33. Vinson to Senator Wagner, May 30, 1945, HSTL.

34. PPT, 1945, pp. 40-41.

35. CR, 79th Cong. 1st sess., p. 4164.

36. NYT, May 6, 1945.

37. TM, 1:15, 509.

38. Neustadt, *Presidential Power*, pp. 174-175.

39. Coffin, *Missouri Compromise*, pp. 13, 16; Allen and Shannon, *Truman Merry-Go-Round*, pp. 19-25; Lubell, *Future of American Politics*, pp. 10-12.

40. Daniels, *Man of Independence*, pp. 27-28.

41. TM, 1:482.

42. "Mr. Truman Faces It," *Fortune* 33 (January 1946), pp. 101-109, 233-242.

43. TM, 1:481.

44. Ibid., p. 483.

45. Ibid., p. 484.

46. Ibid., p. 483.

47. PPT, 1945, p. 18.

48. Millis, *Forrestal Diaries*, pp. 42-43, contains no entry referring to the twenty-one-point program.

49. Byrnes, *All in One Lifetime*, p. 313, contains no reference to the message.

50. Harold D. Smith, conference with the President, August 31, 1945, FDRL.

51. Street, "Truman as Legislative Leader," p. 124.

52. PPT, 1945, p. 264.

53. Ibid., pp. 266-309.

54. Dorough, *Mr. Sam*, p. 401.

55. "Mangement's Washington Letter," *Nation's Business* 33 (October 1945), p. 17.

56. CR, 75th Cong. 1st sess., p. 5271.

57. NYT, September 9, 1945.

58. Ibid.

59. Ibid.

60. PPT, 1945, p. 362.

61. Ibid., pp. 404-413.

62. Kelley, *Professional Public Relations and Political Power*, pp. 67-106.

63. PPT, 1945, pp. 516-521.

64. Ibid., pp. 546-560.

65. Bailey, *Congress Makes a Law*, p. 163.

66. Ibid., p. 162.

67. PPT, 1945, pp. 597-583.

68. Ibid., p. 569.

69. PPT, 1946, pp. 36-87.

70. Harold D. Smith, conference with the President, December 5, 1945, FDRL.

71. PPT, 1946, pp. 66-87.

72. Congressional Quarterly, *Congress and the Nation*, p. 388.

73. Schilling, *Strategy, Politics, and Defense Budgets*, p. 29.

74. PPT, 1946, p. 72.

75. Millis, *Forrestal Diaries*, p. 162.

76. Richard D. Burns, "James T. Byrnes, 1945-1947," in Graebner, *An Uncertain Tradition*, p. 232.

77. Somers, *Presidential Agency*.

78. Bowles, *Promises to Keep*, p. 139.

79. TM, 1:223, 489.

80. Hamby, *Beyond the New Deal*, p. 70.

81. Bowles, *Promises to Keep*, pp. 144, 154.

82. PPT, 1946, p. 319.

83. McClure, *Problems of Postwar Labor*, chaps. 1, 2.

84. Ibid., chap. 3.

85. EO 9599, August 15, 1945,

86. PPT, 1945, pp. 516-521.

87. EO 9672, December 15, 1945.

88. McClure, *Problems of Postwar Labor*, pp. 59-60, 68-69.

89. Millis and Brown, *From the Wagner Act to Taft-Hartley*.

90. PPT, 1945, p. 372.

91. EO 9739, October 4, 1945.

92. Neustadt, "Notes on the White House Staff," HSTL.

93. McClure, *Problems of Postwar Labor*, p. 148.

94. PPT, 1946, pp. 277-280.

95. Papers of Clark Clifford, Railroad speech, HSTL; Anderson, *President's Men*, pp. 114-115.

96. Daniels, *Man of Independence*, pp. 329-331.

97. PPT, 1946, p. 278.

98. Ross, memorandum of May 28, 1946, Ross Papers, HSTL.

99. Hamby, *Beyond the New Deal*, pp. 76-77.

100. NYT, May 27, 1946.

101. PPT, 1946, pp. 289-297.

102. Berman, *Politics of Civil Rights in the Truman Administration*, chap. 1.

103. Street, "Harry S. Truman, His Role as a Legislative Leader," p. 206.

104. PPT, 1945, p. 104.

105. Congressional Quarterly, *Congress and the Nation*, 1945-1964, p. 1615.

106. White, *A Man Called White*, pp. 331-332.

107. EO 9808, December 5, 1946.

108. Matusow, *Farm Policies*, pp. 16, 25, 55, 60.

109. Bowles, *Promises to Keep*, p. 156.

110. PPT, 1946, pp. 322-329.

111. Ibid., pp. 1-8.

112. Ibid., p. 52.

113. Bailey, *Congress Makes a Law*, pp. 163, 221, 237.

114. PPT, 1946, p. 125; TM, 1:493.

115. PPT, 1945, pp. 362-366.

116. Street, "Harry S. Truman," pp. 194-195.

117. Congressional Quarterly, *Congress and the Nation, 1945-1964*, p. 246.

118. PPT, 1946, pp. 105-106.

119. TM, 2:15, 294-295.

120. Ibid., 1:512-515.

121. Neustadt, "Congress and the Fair Deal," *Public Policy* 5 (1954): 355.

CHAPTER 23
TEAM CHANGES, 1946-1948

1. TM, 1: 46.

2. Harry Truman, "Our Armed Forces Must Be United," *Colliers*, August 26, 1944.

3. Schilling, *Strategy, Politics and Defense Budgets*, p. 11.

4. Millis, *Forrestal Diaries*, p. 63; Albion and Connery, *Forrestal and the Navy*, p. 263.

5. Ferdinand Eberstadt, *Report to James Forrestal, Secretary of Navy, on Unification of the War and Navy Departments*, printed for Senate Military Affairs Committee, October 22, 1945.

6. U.S. Senate, Military Affairs Committee, *Hearings of a Single Department of National Defense*, 79th Cong., 1st sess., 1945.

7. PPT, 1945, pp. 546-560.

8. TM, 2:49.

9. Albion and Connery, *Forrestal and the Navy*, p. 271.

10. PPT, 1946, pp. 303, 306; Millis, *Forrestal Diaries*, pp. 203-204.

11. National Security Act of 1947, 61 Stat. 495 (July 26, 1947).

12. Richard E. Neudstadt, "Approaches to Staffing the Presidency: Notes on F.D.R. and J.F.K.," *American Political Science Review* 57 (December 1963): 860.

13. Allen Dulles, *The Secret Surrender* (New York: Harper & Row, 1966).

14. Harold D. Smith conferences with the President, April 26, September 13, November 28, 1945, FDRL.

15. PPT, 1946, pp. 88-89; TM, 2:52, 57.

16. U.S. Senate, Select Committee on Intelligence Activities, *Final Report, 1976*, book 1, pp. 132, 144.

17. Margaret Truman, *Harry S. Truman*, p. 33.

18. Rogow, *James Forrestal*, pp. 235, 330.

19. Ibid., pp. 304-305.

20. Elmer E. Cornwell, "The Truman Presidency," in Kirkendall, *Truman Period as a Research Field* (1967), p. 225.

21. Ickes diaries, January 12, 20, February 10, 1946, LC.

22. PPT, 1946, p. 111.

23. TM, 1:554; NYT, February 13, 1946; Hamby, *Beyond the New Deal*, p. 73.

24. Allen and Shannon, *Truman Merry-Go-Round*, pp. 95-96.

25. Richard S. Kirkendall, "Fred M. Vinson," in Leon Friedman and Fred Israel, eds., *The Justices of the United States Supreme Court* (New York: Chelsea House, 1969).

26. Hamby, *Beyond the New Deal*, pp. 57, 81.

27. Blum, *Price of Vision*, pp. 612-632; Walker, *Henry A. Wallace*, pp. 149-150.

28. MacDougall, *Gideon's Army*, pp. 60-71.

29. TM, 1:557; PPT, 1946, pp. 426-427.

30. OHC, Arthur Krock; Walker, *Henry A. Wallace*, pp. 152-153.

31. Farrar, *Reluctant Servant*, p. 184.

32. Byrnes, *Speaking Frankly*, pp. 239-243, and his *All in One Lifetime*, pp. 371-377.

33. Vandenberg, *Private Papers*, pp. 300-302.

34. Farrar, *Reluctant Servant*, p. 184.

35. PPT, 1946, pp. 426-427, and White House press release, September 14, 1946.

36. TM, 1:560; Walker, *Henry A. Wallace*, pp. 156-158.

37. Daniels interview with Clifford, October 20, 1949, JDP.

38. Allen and Shannon, *Washington Merry-Go-Round*, pp. 66-68, 131.

39. Sawyer, *Concerns of a Conservative Democrat*.

40. Rufus Jarman, "Truman's Political Quarterback," *Saturday Evening Post*, March 2, 15, 1946.

41. *Official Proceedings of the Democratic National Convention*, 1948, p. 388.

42. Allen and Shannon, *Truman Merry-Go-Round*, pp. 110-114.

43. Matusow, *Farm Policies*, pp. 171-172.

44. Lapomarda, "Maurice Joseph Tobin."

45. Fenno, *President's Cabinet*, p. 43; Hamby, *Beyond the New Deal*, pp. 249-250; Neustadt, *Presidential Power*, pp. 171-178.

46. Neustadt notes on the White House staff, HSTL.

47. Anderson, *President's Men*, pp. 90, 113-132.

48. Neustadt notes on the White House Staff.

49. Ibid.; OHT, Charles Murphy; OHT, James L. Sundquist.

50. Clifford, "American Relations with the Soviet Union: A Report to the President," September 1946, reproduced in Krock, *Memoirs*, appendix A.

51. Anderson, *President's Men*, pp. 92-95.

52. Neustadt notes on the White House staff, pp. 5-13.

53. Allen and Shannon, *Truman Merry-Go-Round*, pp. 72-74; Abels, *Truman Scandals*, pp. 8, 83, 107-110.

54. OHC, Bernard Gladieux.

55. Smith conference with the President, February 8, 1946, FDRL.

56. Matusow, *Farm Policies*, chap. 2.

57. Neustadt, "Presidency and Legislation: The Growth of Central Clearance," *American Political Science Review* 48 (September 1954):560; OHT, Roger W. Jones.

58. James E. Webb notes on conference with the President, August 15, 1946, Webb Papers, HSTL.

59. Schilling, *Strategy, Politics and Defense Budgets*, pp. 135-155.

60. On the Council of Economic Advisers, see Nourse, *Economics and the Public Service*; Flash, *Economic Advice and Presidential Leadership*; and Silverman, *Presidential Economic Advisers*.

CHAPTER 24
RELATIONS WITH SECRETARY OF STATE BYRNES, 1945–1946

1. Curry, *James F. Byrnes*, p. 162.
2. Byrnes, *All in One Lifetime*, p. 310.
3. Acheson, *Present at the Creation*, chap. 14.
4. Burns, "James F. Byrnes," in Graebner, *An Uncertain Tradition*, p. 268; Smith, *Dean Acheson*, chap. 2.
5. Hoopes, *Devil and John Foster Dulles*, pp. 9-15, 60.
6. FRUS, 1945, 2:328.
7. DSB, October 6, 1945.
8. Burns, "James F. Byrnes," p. 232; Millis, *Forrestal Diaries*, p. 106.
9. FRUS, 1945, 2:815-822; Acheson, *Present at the Creation*, p. 135.
10. Hillman, *Mr. President*, p. 46; TM, 1:551-552.
11. Byrnes, *All in One Lifetime*, pp. 400-403; Acheson, *Present at the Creation*, pp. 195-196.
12. FRUS, 1946, 7:366, 368.
13. TM, 1:522.
14. Byrnes, *All in One Lifetime*, pp. 351-352; Jones, *Fifteen Weeks*, p. 55.
15. Feis, *From Trust to Terror*, p. 83.
16. PPT, 1952, pp. 291, 295.
17. FRUS, 1946, 7:340-342, 348, 365.
18. Ibid., pp. 388, 471.
19. PPT, 1946, pp. 171-172.
20. Jones, *Fifteen Weeks*, pp. 57-58.
21. Feis, *From Trust to Terror*, pp. 86-87.
22. PPT, 1945, p. 365.
23. Stimson and Bundy, *On Active Service*, pp. 642-646.
24. Millis, *Forrestal Diaries*, p. 95; Acheson, *Present at the Creation*, p. 124; TM, 1:525-527; Blum, *Price of Vision*, pp. 482-487.
25. Acheson, *Present at the Creation*, p. 123.
26. NYT, September 22, 1945; Walker, *Henry A Wallace*, pp. 123-125.
27. FRUS, 1945, 2:55-56; PPT, 1945, pp. 381-383.
28. PPT, 1945, pp. 472-475.
29. Vandenberg, *Private Papers*, p. 229.
30. Curry, *James F. Byrnes*, p. 163.
31. FRUS, 1945, 2:609-610.
32. Vandenberg, *Private Papers*, pp. 232-233.
33. U.S. Department of State, Committee on Atomic Energy, *A Report on the International Control of Atomic Energy* (1946); Acheson, *Present at the Creation*, pp. 152-153.
34. Acheson, *Present at the Creation*, p. 154.
35. TM, 2:7-10.
36. Acheson, *Present at the Creation*, pp. 155-156.
37. Blum, *Price of Vision*, pp. 581-582; MacDougall, *Gideon's Army*, pp. 71-72; Coit, *Mr. Baruch*, chaps. 20, 21; Feis, *From Trust to Terror*, pp. 148-149, 398-400; Walker, *Henry A. Wallace*, p. 143.
38. Clay, *Decision in Germany*.

39. Byron Price, *Report to President Truman on the Relations Between the American Forces of Occupation and the German People.*

40. Gimble, *American Occupation of Germany*, p. 61.

41. The formal agreement was signed December 2, 1946.

42. Byrnes, *Speaking Frankly*, pp. 187-191; Clay, *Decision in Germany*, p. 79.

43. TM, 2:66; letter of resignation in U.S. Department of State, *United States Relations with China*, pp. 581-584.

44. Davies, *Dragon by the Tail*, pp. 418-419.

45. Acheson, *Present at the Creation*, pp. 139-148, 208-211.

46. The Churchill speech is reproduced in Bernstein and Matusow, *Truman Administration*, pp. 215-219.

47. Raeburn Green to Daniels, October 26, 1950, JDP; Vaughan, ''Whipping Boy—First Class,'' HSTL.

48. PPT, 1946, p. 145.

49. Feis, *From Trust to Terror*, pp. 78-79.

50. Blum, *Price of Vision*, pp. 556-557; MacDougall, *Gideon's Army*, pp. 30-31, 94-95.

51. Byrnes, *All in One Lifetime*, p. 353-355; DSB, January 19, 1947; Curry, *James F. Byrnes*, p. 314.

CHAPTER 25
CHANGING POPULARITY AND THE 1946 ELECTIONS

1. Fenton, *In Your Opinion*, p. 50.

2. TM, 1:11-12.

3. Pollard, *Presidents and the Press*, pp. 27-28.

4. Examples of Truman's salty language can be found in Jonathan Daniels's notes of interviews with Truman, November 12, 1949, JDP, and in Miller, *Plain Speaking*, pp. 133, 151, 290.

5. Farrar, *Reluctant Servant*, pp. 163-164.

6. PPT, 1945, pp. 8-13.

7. OHT, Jonathan Daniels, HSTL; TM, 1:49.

8. Farrar, *Reluctant Servant*, pp. 175-176.

9. PPT, 1945, pp. 381-383.

10. Coffin, *Missouri Compromise*, p. 20.

11. PPT, 1946, pp. 383, 424.

12. Farrar, *Reluctant Servant*, pp. 177-178; CR, Adolph J. Sabath, ''Popularity of Harry S. Truman,'' 79th Cong., 2d sess., p. A2073.

13. Elmo Roper, *You and Your Leaders* (New York: William Morrow and Company, 1947), p. 127.

14. Farrar, *Reluctant Servant*, pp. 178-179.

15. PPT, 1946, pp. 350-351.

16. Powell, *Tom's Boy Harry*, p. 135.

17. PPT, 1946, p. 352.

18. Memorandum on election cases, Papers of Clark Clifford, 1947, HSTL; radio address by Senator James P. Kem of Missouri, CR, 80th Cong., 1st sess., p. A3906; Reddig, *Tom's Town*, pp. 375-376; *U.S. News and World Report*, June 20, 1947.

19. Public Opinion Quarterly, ''Polls July 1946'' (Fall 1946):434.

20. OHC, Roy Wilkins.

21. Millis, *Forrestal Diaries*, p. 203.

22. Republican National Committee, *Republican News*, August and October, 1946; Congressional Quarterly, *Congress and the Nation*, p. 3.

23. Election returns from *Congressional Directory*, 80th Cong., 1st sess., pp. 244-251; NYT, November 11, 1946; Ross, *Loneliest Campaign*, pp. 9, 16.

24. NYT, November 7, 1946; *New Republic*, November 18, 1946.

25. Daniels, *Man of Independence*, pp. 293-294; Margaret Truman, *Harry S. Truman*, p. 322.

26. Hamby, *Beyond the New Deal*, p. 138; Douglas, *In the Fullness of Time*, p. 222.

CHAPTER 26
BATTLING REPUBLICAN OPPOSITION, 1947–1948

1. Floyd M. Riddick, "The First Session of the Eightieth Congress," *American Political Science Review* (August 1948):677-679; Street, "Harry S. Truman: His Role as Legislative Leader," p. 238.

2. Martin, *My First Fifty Years in Politics*, p. 177.

3. Hartmann, *Truman and the 80th Congress*, p. 14; Goldman, *Crucial Decade*, p. 56.

4. Hartmann, *Truman and the 80th Congress*, pp. 10-11, 17-18.

5. Memorandum by Rowe to Clifford, December 1946, Clifford Papers, HSTL.

6. Millis, *Forrestal Diaries*, p. 218.

7. PPT, 1946, pp. 477-479.

8. Ibid., pp. 475-477.

9. Hartmann, *Truman and the 80th Congress*, pp. 11-16.

10. PPT, 1947, pp. 4-5; OHT, James L. Sundquist; Neustadt, "Congress and the Fair Deal: A Legislative Balance Sheet," *Public Policy* (1954): 360-361.

11. PPT, 1947, pp. 40-97.

12. NYT, February 28, 1947.

13. TM, 2:489.

14. Harris, *Advice and Consent of the Senate*, pp. 155-158.

15. *New Republic*, April 14, 1947.

16. PPT, 1947, pp. 130, 193, 195; NYT, May 16, 1947.

17. Hartmann, *Truman and the 80th Congress*, pp. 41-45; PPT, 1947, pp. 243-244.

18. OHT, Oscar Ewing.

19. PPT, 1947, pp. 250-252.

20. Ibid., pp. 279-281; Hartmann, *Truman and the 80th Congress*, p. 74.

21. PPT, 1947, pp. 288-297; George Elsey Speech File, on Taft-Hartley bill, Elsey Papers, HSTL; James Webb to M. C. Latta, June 19, 1947, Clifford Papers, HSTL; Millis, *Forrestal Diaries*, p. 280.

22. NYT, June 22, 1947.

23. PPT, 1947, pp. 309-310.

24. Ibid., pp. 342-344; Riddick, "First Session," pp. 682-683.

25. PPT, 1947, pp. 368-371; Hartmann, *Truman and the 80th Congress*, p. 97.

26. PPT, 1947, pp. 371-372, 379-380; George Elsey Speech File, Elsey Papers, HSTL.

27. PPT, 1947, pp. 475-479, 495-498.

28. Hartmann, *Truman and the 80th Congress*, pp. 123-135.

29. PPT, 1947, p. 467.

30. Ibid., p. 532.

31. Hartmann, *Truman and the 80th Congress*, p. 127.

32. Clifford Papers, Memorandum for the President, November 19, 1947, HSTL.

33. Ross, *Loneliest Campaign*, pp. 55-56, citing private papers of Elsey.

34. George Elsey Papers, HSTL; Street, "Harry S. Truman," pp. 380-381.

35. PPT, 1948, pp. 1-10.

36. Clifford memorandum, November 19, 1947, HSTL.

37. *New Republic*, January 19, 1948.

38. *New York Herald-Tribune*, January 8, 1948; NYT, January 11, 1948.

39. PPT, 1948, pp. 11-59, 186-90; Rogow, *James Forrestal*, p. 285.

40. Schilling, *Strategy, Politics and Defense Budgets*, pp. 41-46, 136, 144-145; Millis, *Forrestal Diaries*, pp. 431-432, 435-438; OHT, Lawton, HSTL.

41. NYT, March 10, 1948.

42. PPT, 1948, pp. 200-203.

43. Ibid., pp. 205-206, 354-355.

44. Hartmann, *Truman and the 80th Congress*, pp. 145-146.

45. PPT, 1948, pp. 330-332; NYT, June 17, 1948.

46. Street, "Harry S. Truman," pp. 384-385.

47. PPT, 1948, pp. 121-126; Speech on Civil Rights, Elsey Papers, HSTL; TM, 2:180-181; *Washington Post*, February 4, 1948.

48. NYT, February 21, 1948; Ross, *Loneliest Campaign*, pp. 63-64; Redding, *Inside the Democratic Party*, pp. 135-137.

49. Dalfiume, *Desegregation of the Armed Forces*, p. 175; Nash to Clifford, September 2, 1948, Clifford Papers, HSTL.

50. PPT, 1948, pp. 256-258.

51. Matusow, *Farm Policies*, pp. 139-144; PPT, 1948, pp. 399-400.

52. Matusow, *Farm Policies*, pp. 86, 90.

53. *Nation*, November 9, 1946.

54. PPT, 1947, pp. 309-310; OHC, Will Clayton, p. 217; Congressional Quarterly, *Congress and the Nation*, p. 194.

55. Matusow, *Farm Policies*, pp. 106-108.

56. U.S. Department of Agriculture, *Century of Service*, p. 356.

57. PPT, 1947, pp. 437-443, 494-498; Matusow, *Farm Policies*, pp. 171-172.

58. McClure, *Problems of Postwar Labor*, pp. 177, 180.

59. Memorandum for the President, July 29, 1948, Sam Rosenman Files, HSTL.

60. NYT, July 28, 1948; *Time*, July 26, 1948; TM, 2:28; Ross, *Loneliest Campaign*, pp. 134-136.

61. NYT, August 1, 1948; Nourse to Keyserling and Clark, July 18, 1948, Nourse Papers, HSTL; Hartmann, *Truman and the 80th Congress*, p. 195.

62. PPT, 1948, pp. 416-421; NYT, July 28, 1948.

63. CR, 80th Cong., 2d sess., p. A4671.

64. TM, 2:208-209.

CHAPTER 27
THE TRUMAN DOCTRINE, 1947

1. Jones, *Fifteen Weeks*, pp. 3-13.

2. TM, 1:15.

3. FRUS, 1946, 6:696-709, Kennan to Byrnes, February 22, 1946; Kennan, *Memoirs, 1925-1950*, pp. 541-559; Curry, *James F. Byrnes*, p. 202; Millis, *Forrestal Diaries*, pp. 135-140; Gaddis, *Origins of the Cold War*, pp. 302-304.

4. Kennan, *Memoirs, 1925-1950*, pp. 358-361; Gardner, *Architects of Illusion*, chap. 10.

5. Byrnes, *All in One Lifetime*, p. 369.

6. Krock, *Memoirs*, pp. 421-462.

7. Alexander De Conde, "George Catlett Marshall," in Graebner, *An Uncertain Tradition*, p. 247.

8. TM, 2:112.

9. NYT, January 22, 1947.

10. Ibid., January 8, 1947.

11. Jones, *Fifteen Weeks*, pp. 129-138.

12. Acheson, *Present at the Creation*, p. 213.

13. Kennan, *Memoirs, 1925–1950*, p. 345.

14. Hull, *Memoirs*, p. 1459.

15. Xydis, *Greece and the Great Powers*.

16. Acheson, *Present at the Creation*, pp. 217-219.

17. Churchill, *Triumph and Tragedy*, p. 227.

18. FRUS, 1945, 8:286, MacVeagh to Secretary of State, December 15, 1945; Acheson, *Present at the Creation*, p. 199; Murphy, *Diplomat Among Warriers*, p. 306.

19. FRUS, 1945, 5:633-637, Ethridge report; Acheson, *Present at the Creation*, p. 217.

20. Connally, *My Name Is Tom Connally*, p. 317; Jones, *Fifteen Weeks*, pp. 138-142.

21. Vandenberg, *Private Papers*, pp. 338-339; Goldman, *Crucial Decade*, p. 59.

22. TM, 2:103-104.

23. Millis, *Forrestal Diaries*, p. 251; William D. Leahy, diary, March 7, 1947, LC.

24. TM, 2:105; Bohlen, *Witness to History*, p. 261; Jones, *Fifteen Weeks*, p. 155; Kennan, *Memoirs, 1925–1950*, pp. 314-315, 319. This was Elsey's view also. Elsey to Clifford, March 8, 1947, Elsey Papers, HSTL.

25. PPT, 1947, pp. 178-179.

26. Bohlen, *Witness to History*, p. 271; Goldman, *Crucial Decade*, p. 60; *Center Magazine*, "Table Talk/Requiem for the Cold War" (September-October 1971):53.

27. Fenton, *In Your Opinion*, p. 59; Hillman, *Mr. President*, p. 132; Hartmann, *Truman and the 80th Congress*, p. 63; MacDougall, *Gideon's Army*, pp. 141-145.

28. Jones, *Fifteen Weeks*, p. 185.

29. Vandenberg, *Private Papers*, pp. 341-346.

30. Acheson, *Present at the Creation*, p. 225; NYT, March 21, 1947. Truman's earlier views on Chiang were too favorable. See memorandum for the President, November 9, 1945, Box 1, China Folder, Rosenman Papers, HSTL.

31. PPT, 1947, pp. 254-255.

CHAPTER 28
THE MARSHALL PLAN, GERMANY, ISRAEL, AND NATO, 1947–1948

1. Lippmann, *Cold War*, pp. 52-57; Bernstein, "Walter Lippmann and the Early Cold War," in Paterson, *Cold War Critics*, p. 44; Jones, *Fifteen Weeks*, pp. 227-232.

2. Millis, *Forrestal Diaries*, p. 263; Feis, *From Trust to Terror*, p. 237.

3. Acheson, *Present at the Creation*, p. 226; Gardner, *Architects of Illusion*, chap. 5.

4. Kennan, *Memoirs, 1925–1950*, pp. 325-326.

5. PPT, 1947, pp. 167-72.

6. Acheson, *Present at the Creation*, p. 227.

7. Jones, *Fifteen Weeks*, pp. 206-213.

8. Daniels interview with Dean Acheson, September 9, 1949, JDP.

9. DSB, May 18, 1947, pp. 991-994.

10. Acheson, *Present at the Creation*, pp. 228-229.

11. Kennan, *Memoirs, 1925–1950*, pp. 335-342, 353.

12. Jones, *Fifteen Weeks*, pp. 246-248; Feis, *From Trust to Terror*, p. 241.

13. Bohlen, *Witness to History*, p. 263.

14. DSB, June 15, 1947, pp. 1159-1160.

15. TM, 2:112-115; Neustadt, *Presidential Power*, p. 47.

16. Acheson, *Present at the Creation*, pp. 232-233.

17. Memorandum for the President, November 19, 1947, Clifford Papers, HSTL.

18. PPT, 1947, pp. 272-276, 307.

19. Acheson, *Present at the Creation*, p. 235.

20. Vandenberg, *Private Papers*, pp. 376-378.

21. FRUS, 1947, 3:253.

22. Price, *Marshall Plan*, pp. 26-29, 36-39.

23. Excerpts from Foreign Minister Molotov's speech of July 2, 1947, in Bernstein and Matusow, *Truman Administration*, p. 260; Arkes, *Bureaucracy, the Marshall Plan, and the National Interest*, chap. 3; Murphy, *Diplomat among Warriers*, p. 308; Feis, *From Trust to Terror*, pp. 246-249.

24. U.S. Department of State, *General Report of the Committee of European Economic Cooperation* (Washington, D.C.: Government Printing Office, 1947), 1:60.

25. PPT, 1947, pp. 438-440, 475-479.

26. George Elsey Papers, December 16, 1947, HSTL; PPT, 1947, pp. 515-29.

27. Feis, *From Trust to Terror*, p. 253; McDougall, *Gideon's Army*, p. 184.

28. TM, 2:241.

29. Kolko and Kolko, *Limits of Power*, pp. 397-398.

30. TM, 2:119.

31. Vandenberg, *Private Papers*, p. 394.

32. Clay, *Decision in Germany*, pp. 156-157.

33. Hoopes, *The Devil and John Foster Dulles*, p. 68.

34. Alexander De Conde, "George Catlett Marshall," in Graebner, *An Uncertain Tradition*, p. 252.

35. TM, 2:121.

36. Feis, *From Trust to Terror*, pp. 275-284.

37. DSB, September 7, 1947, pp. 468-472.

38. Millis, *Forrestal Diaries*, p. 387.

39. Murphy, *Diplomat among Warriors*, p. 313.

40. Feis, *From Trust to Terror*, pp. 335-340.

41. TM, 2:124.

42. Connally, *My Name Is Tom Connally*, pp. 329-330.

43. TM, 2:124.

44. Murphy, *Diplomat among Warriors*, p. 318.

45. Merkl, *Origin of the West German Republic*, p. 59.

46. David Golding, "U.S. Foreign Policy in Palestine, Israel, 1945-1949" (Ph.D. dissertation, New York University, 1961); Feis, *The Birth of Israel*.

47. TM, 1:68-69, 2:132-133; Truman, *Harry S. Truman*, p. 298.

48. PPT, 1945, pp. 467-470.

49. Acheson, *Present at the Creation*, pp. 172-173; PPT, 1946, pp. 442-444; TM, 2:154.

50. FRUS, 1948, 5, pt. 2, pp. 832-833; TM, 2:162.

51. Rogow, *James Forrestal*, pp. 180-190; Millis, *Forrestal Diaries*, pp. 323-324, 356-357.

52. Margaret Truman, *Harry S. Truman*, p. 386.

53. PPT, 1947, pp. 266-267; FRUS, 1948, 5, pt. 2, p. 546.

54. Daniels interview with Eddie Jacobson, September 27, 1949, JDP; TM, 2:160-162; Eban, *Autobiography*, pp. 102-103; FRUS, 1948, 5, pt. 2, pp. 749-750; Margaret Truman, *Harry S. Truman*, p. 388; Weitzman, *Trial and Error*, p. 472.

55. Daniels interview with Clark Clifford, October 26, 1949, JDP; PPT, 1948, pp. 190-193.

56. PPT, 1948, p. 258.

57. FRUS, 1948, 5, pt. 2, p. 993; Eban, *Autobiography*, p. 110; Lash, *Eleanor: The Years Alone*, pp. 133-134.

58. FRUS, 1948, 3:1010; Kennan, *Memoirs, 1935-1950*, pp. 397-398; Feis, *From Trust to Terror*, p. 296.

59. Kennan, *Memoirs, 1925–1950*, p. 400.

60. George Elsey Papers, Speech File, Speech of March 17, 1948, HSTL; PPT, 1948, pp. 184, 189.

61. Millis, *Forrestal Diaries*, pp. 423, 434.

62. Vandenberg, *Private Papers*, pp. 404, 407.

63. TM, 2:246.

CHAPTER 29
NOMINATION FOR A FULL TERM

1. David, Goldman, and Bain, *Politics of National Party Conventions*, p. 114.

2. Fenton, *In Your Opinion*, p. 51; *Public Opinion Quarterly*, "The Polls" (Summer 1951):395-396.

3. Ross, *Loneliest Campaign*, pp. 14-16.

4. Coffin, *Missouri Compromise*, pp. 13, 16.

5. KCS, April 26, 1945.

6. *Newsweek*, September 17, 1945, p. 26.

7. TM 2:170-174.

8. Ross, *Loneliest Campaign*, p. 21.

9. Memorandum for the President, November 17, 1947, Clifford Papers, HSTL.

10. Ross, *Loneliest Campaign*, pp. 171-172.

11. Redding, *Inside the Democratic Party*, pp. 97-100.

12. TM, 2:295-296.

13. *Official Proceedings of the Democratic National Convention, 1948*, p. 374.

14. Ross, *Loneliest Campaign*, p. 79.

15. PPT, 1948, pp. 221-224; transcript of informal remarks, April 17, 1948, HSTL; TM, 2:179.

16. An editorial in the *Washington Daily News*, May 8, 1948, praised the new style; Hillman, *Mr. President*, p. 135.

17. PPT, 1948, pp. 259-261.

18. NYT, May 15, 1948.

19. Memorandum by Oscar Chapman, February 17, 1948, Chapman Papers, HSTL.

20. *Washington Post*, June 4, 1948.

21. Telegram from Bert Andrews to Ross, June 9, 1948, OF, HSTL.

22. Ross, *Loneliest Campaign*, pp. 83-84.

23. Rigdon, *White House Sailor*, pp. 245-246. The speech is not in PPT, 1948.

24. Edward D. McKim to Chapman, May 21, 1948, HSTL.

25. PPT, 1948, p. 291.

26. Redding, *Inside the Democratic Party*, p. 178; Abels, *Out of the Jaws of Victory*, p. 45.

27. PPT, 1948, p. 329.

28. Memorandum to Clifford from Elsey, June 14, 1948, Elsey Papers, HSTL.

29. PPT, 1948, pp. 336-340.

30. Draft of speech, Speech File, June 12, 1948, Elsey Papers, HSTL.

31. Daniels interview with Truman, November 12, 1949, JDP.

32. *Los Angeles Times*, June 15, 1948.

33. Draft of speech, June 14, 1948, Elsey Papers, HSTL.

34. PPT, 1948, pp. 348-353.

35. Ibid., p. 360.

36. *Denver Post*, June 14, 1948; *Washington Daily News*, June 2, 1948.

37. John Gunther, *Eisenhower: The Man and the Symbol* (New York: Harper and Brothers, 1951), p. 133.

38. Eisenhower, *Crusade in Europe*, p. 444.

39. Memorandum for the President, November 19, 1947, Clifford Papers, HSTL.

40. Phillips, *Truman Presidency*, p. 197.

41. "The Quarterly Polls," *Public Opinion Quarterly* (Spring 1948):167.

42. Gunther, *Eisenhower*, p. 136.

43. Brock, *Americans for Democratic Action*, p. 88.

44. Marquis Childs, *Witness to Power* (New York: McGraw-Hill, 1975), pp. 63-64, cites interview showing Eisenhower as a conservative.

45. Millis, *Forrestal Diaries*, pp. 404-405.

46. Abels, *Out of the Jaws of Victory*, p. 81.

47. *Time*, April 19, 1948.

48. Abels, *Out of the Jaws of Victory*, p. 79.

49. NYT, July 3, 6, 1948.

50. Ibid., July 10, 1948.

51. Statement in OF, July 19, 1948, HSTL.

52. NYT, July 10, 1948.

53. Ibid., July 12, 1948.

54. Ibid., July 5, 1948.

55. *Public Opinion Quarterly* (Spring 1951): 175.

56. Ibid. (Fall 1948): 560-561.

57. Barkley, *That Reminds Me*, p. 200.

58. *Official Proceedings*, p. 245.

59. Ibid., p. 42.

60. Box 9, Speech File, July 15, 1948, Elsey Papers, HSTL.

61. *Official Proceedings*, p. 176.

62. Ibid., p. 181.

63. Ibid., p. 192.

64. Ibid., pp. 202-210.

65. TM, 2:182.

66. *Official Proceedings*, p. 239.

67. Ibid., p. 247.

68. Ross, *Loneliest Campaign*, p. 118.

69. Barkley, *That Reminds Me*, p. 202; TM, 2:190-191.

70. TM, 2:191-204.

71. Memorandum of July 14, 1948, Speech File, Elsey Papers, HSTL; "Speech Material," Box 7, Ross Papers, HSTL.

72. PPT, 1948, pp. 406-410; *Official Proceedings*, pp. 300-306.

73. Jennings Randolph, "Harry Truman," *Quarterly Journal of Speech* (October 1948):302.

74. Evan Treharne to President Truman, July 16, 1948, OF, HSTL.

75. Coit, *Mr. Baruch*, p. 625; Lubell, *Future of American Politics*, p. 15.

CHAPTER 30
THE OPPOSITION: DEWEY, THURMOND, AND WALLACE

1. Richard S. Kirkendall, "Election of 1948," in Schlesinger and Israel, *History of American Presidential Elections* (New York: Chelsea, 1971); Ross, *Loneliest Campaign*, pp. 29-35.

2. Memorandum for the President, November 17, 1947, Clifford Papers, HSTL.

3. Roscoe Drummond, "The Case for Stassen," *Life*, March 1, 1948.

4. White, *Taft Story*.

5. MacArthur, *Reminiscences*, p. 319.

6. *Chicago Tribune*, June 11, 1948.

7. Ross, *Loneliest Campaign*, pp. 38-39.

8. Vandenberg, *Private Papers*, chap. 22.

9. Martin, *My First Fifty Years in Politics*, p. 164.

10. Parmet, *Eisenhower and the American Crusade*, p. 21.

11. Ross, *Loneliest Campaign*, p. 41.

12. Ibid., pp. 42-44.

13. NYT, April 8, 1948.

14. James W. Davis, *Presidential Primaries: Road to the White House* (New York: Thomas Y. Crowell, 1967), p. 296.

15. Ross, *Loneliest Campaign*, p. 46.

16. NYT, May 6, 1948.

17. Davis, *Presidential Primaries*, p. 296; *Public Papers for Thomas E. Dewey of 1948* (Albany, New York).

18. *Official Proceedings of the Twenty-fourth Republican National Convention, 1948*, p. 186.

19. Ibid., pp. 53-60.

20. Ibid., pp. 275-278; Bain, *Convention Decisions*, p. 271.

21. *Official Proceedings*, pp. 279-282.

22. Ross, *Loneliest Campaign*, pp. 101-102, based on interviews with Halleck and Dewey's advisers.

23. PPT, 1948, pp. 121-126.

24. V. O. Key, *Southern Politics in State and Nation* (New York: Knopf, 1949), pp. 329-344.

25. Congressional Quarterly, *Politics in America*, pp. 8, 98.

26. MacDougall, *Gideon's Army*, p. 134.

27. PPT, 1947, p. 203.

28. Josephson, *Sidney Hillman*, p. 661.

29. MacDougall, *Gideon's Army*, p. 128.

30. Ibid., p. 236, citing Wallace's broadcast of December 29, 1947; Walker, *Henry A. Wallace*, pp. 182-183.

31. MacDougall, *Gideon's Army*, chap. 15.

32. Ibid., pp. 323-325.

33. Hamby, *Beyond the New Deal*, pp. 218-219; Walker, *Henry A. Wallace*, p. 186.

34. Tugwell, *Chronicle of Jeopardy*, pp. 131-136, 160; *Public Opinion Quarterly* (Winter 1948-1949):767.

35. Abels, *Out of the Jaws of Victory*, pp. 114-115, 118; MacDougall, *Gideon's Army*, pp. 571-76.

36. PPT, 1948, p. 559.

CHAPTER 31
UPSET ELECTION OF 1948

1. Hamby, *Beyond the New Deal*, chaps. 8, 9, 10.

2. Helen Fuller, "The Funeral Is Called Off," *New Republic*, July 26, 1948; David Lloyd, *ADA World*, August 7, 1948.

3. Dan Williams to McGrath, September 19, 1948, HSTL.

4. Vandenberg, *Private Papers*, p. 448.

5. NYT, November 4, 1948.

6. Memorandum of July 27, 1948, "Dewey's Strategy vs. the President," OF, HSTL.

7. Ross, *Loneliest Campaign*, p. 169.

8. Ibid., p. 168.

9. *Washington Post*, July 7, 1948.

10. Daniels to Connelly, October 1, 1948, JDP.

11. Redding, *Inside the Democratic Party*, pp. 203, 223, 216, 262.

12. The booklet is discussed in NYT, October 10, 1948; *Time*, October 18, 1948; Redding, *Inside the Democratic Party*, pp. 237-238; Ivan Hinderacker, *Party Politics* (New York: Holt, 1956), pp. 565-566.

13. Redding, *Inside the Democratic Party*, pp. 246-254.

14. Ibid., pp. 228, 232; Lash, *Eleanor: The Years Alone*, p. 153.

15. Hillman, *Mr. President*, p. 39; Daniels, *Man of Independence*, pp. 358-359.

16. Jones and Angley, *Fifty Billion Dollars*, p. 310.

17. *Christian Science Monitor*, March 8, 1949; *Time*, March 14, 1949; Millis, *Forrestal Diaries*, pp. 548-554; Rogow, *James Forrestal*, pp. 313-316.

18. Congressional Quarterly, *Congress and the Nation*, p. 1536.

19. John Dreiske, "The Morning After," *Chicago Sun-Times*, October 27, 1948; *Newsweek*, November 8, 1948.

20. Max D. Danish, *The World of David Dubinsky* (Cleveland: World Publishing Co., 1957), p. 179.

21. Redding, *Inside the Democratic Party*, pp. 52-53.

22. Eugene H. Roseboom, *A History of Presidential Elections* (New York: Macmillan, 1970).

23. Margaret Truman, *Souvenir*, pp. 225-226.

24. Daniels, *Man of Independence*, pp. 359-360; interview with Oscar Chapman, September 24, 1962; memorandum to Clifford from William M. Batt, August 11, 1948, Clifford Papers, HSTL.

25. PPT, 1948, p. 728.

26. Ibid., pp. 463, 475.

27. Ibid., p. 477.

28. Phillips, *Truman Presidency*, p. 233.

29. "Political Plans of Unions," *U.S. News and World Report*, September 3, 1948.

30. NYT, September 18, 1948.

31. PPT, 1948, p. 506.

32. NYT, September 13, 25, 1948; Wesley McCure, "Farmer in Politics," *Annals of the American Academy of Political and Social Science* (September 1948):46; Redding, *Inside the Democratic Party*, pp. 211-212.

33. PPT, 1948, pp. 517-522.

34. Ibid., pp. 550-551.

35. Ibid., pp. 555-559.

36. Ibid., pp. 568-569.

37. Margaret Truman, *Harry S. Truman*, p. 34; Ross, *Loneliest Campaign*, pp. 201-202.

38. PPT, 1948, pp. 609-615.

39. Ibid., p. 660; Ross, *Loneliest Campaign*, p. 240.

40. NYT, October 13, 1948; *Time*, September 27, 1948.

41. SLPD, October 13, 1948.

42. PPT, 1948, p. 828.

43. NYT, August 3, October 1, 1948.

44. Redding, *Inside the Democratic Party*, pp. 62, 151.

45. Daniels interview with Clifford, October 26, 1949, JDP.

46. TM, 2:215.

47. Farrar, *Reluctant Servant*, p. 200; Connally, *My Name Is Tom Connally*, p. 331; Vandenberg, *Private Papers*, p. 456; TM, 2:216; Daniels, *Man of Independence*, pp. 361-362.

48. Hoopes, *Devil and John Foster Dulles*, pp. 72-73.

49. NYT, October 11, 12, 31, 1948.

50. Ross, *Loneliest Campaign*, pp. 214-215.

51. PPT, 1948, p. 817.

52. *New Republic*, October 25, 1948.

53. Abels, *Out of the Jaws of Victory*, p. 204.

54. DSB, 17:1163; FRUS, 1948, 5, pt. 2, pp. 1366-1369, 1415.

55. TM, 2:155; FRUS, 1948, 5, pt. 2, p. 1430; PPT, 1948, pp. 843-844.

56. PPT, 1948, p. 678.

57. Ibid., p. 711.

58. Thomas W. Walsh to Chapman, October 14, 1948, HSTL.

59. TM, 2:210; Jim Mackin to Connelly, October 14, 1948, HSTL.

60. PPT, 1948, p. 743.

61. Ibid., pp. 787-92; Speech File, Box 13, October 14, 1948, Elsey Papers, HSTL.

62. PPT, 1948, p. 839; KCS, October 24, 1948.

63. PPT, 1948, p. 848.

64. Ibid., p. 883.

65. Ibid., p. 913.

66. Ibid., pp. 923-925.

67. Ross, *Loneliest Campaign*, pp. 215, 235.

68. NYT, September 3, 1948; John Dreiske, "Shabby Treatment of a Grand Old Workhorse," *Chicago Sun-Times*, October 3, 1948.

69. Interview with Oscar Chapman, September 24, 1962; Marquis Childs, in *Washington Post*, November 5, 1948.

70. Mosteller, *Pre-Election Polls of 1948*, p. 59.

71. Ibid., p. 17.

72. OHC, Arthur Krock, 1950; NYT, October 31, 1948; *Newsweek*, November 8, 1948; *Time*, November 8, 1948.

73. PPT, 1948, p. 864.

74. Ross, *Loneliest Campaign*, p. 221.

75. Cummings memorandum, August 15, 1948, Clifford Papers, HSTL; speech by William M. Boyle, Jr., December 7, 1948, CR, 81st Cong., 1st Sess., p. A872.

76. Hugh Scott, report to Republican National Committee, August 4, 1949, in CR, 81st Cong., 1st sess., pp. A5172-A5174.

77. NYT, October 31, 1948; *Time*, November 8, 1948; *Baltimore Sun*, October 17, 25, 1948.

78. KCS, October 14, 1948; *Des Moines Register*, October 18, 1948.

79. Photograph in Gies, *Harry S. Truman*, p. 110; *Washington Post*, November 5, 1948.

80. Mosteller, *Pre-Election Polls of 1948*, pp. 290-315.

81. NYT, November 4, 1948.

82. Berelson, *Voting*, p. 53; Samuel J. Eldersveld, "The Influence of Metropolitan Party Pluralities in Presidential Elections since 1920," *American Political Science Review* (1949): 1189-1206.

83. Jules Boegholt to McGrath, November 20, 1948, McGrath Papers, HSTL; Matusow, *Farm Policies*, pp. 185-88; W. H. Lawrence, "Farm Vote Cost Dewey Presidency," NYT, November 29, 1948.

84. Conrad Clark to Ross, November 5, 1948, HSTL; Berelson, *Voting*, p. 76; Levy and Kramer, *Ethnic Factor*, pp. 42, 103.

85. Angus Campbell, *American Voter* (New York: Wiley, 1964), pp. 274-275.

86. *World Almanac, 1949*, p. 48.

87. Roper, *You and Your Leaders*, p. 112.

88. Harold F. Gosnell and Robert E. Martin, "The Negro as Voter and Office Holder," *Journal of Negro Education* (Fall 1963):419; Walker, *Henry A. Wallace*, p. 198.

89. Vandenberg, *Private Papers*, p. 460.

CHAPTER 32
THE FINAL TEAM, 1949-1952

1. Barber, *The Presidential Character*, p. 292.

2. Neustadt, *Presidential Power*, pp. 5-6. See also his "The Constraining of the President," *NYT Magazine*, October 14, 1952.

3. NYT, December 26, 1952.

4. Ferrell, *George C. Marshall*.

5. Smith, *Dean Acheson*, pp. 54-59.

6. Congressional Quarterly, *Congress and the Nation*, p. 104a.

7. TM, 2:428-430; Acheson, *Present at the Creation*, pp. 283, 730; Margaret Truman, *Harry S. Truman*, p. 404.

8. Rogow, *James Forrestal*, pp. 262-268.

9. Truman, *Harry S. Truman*, pp. 407-408.

10. Marquis Childs in SLPD, March 5, 1949.

11. Rogow, *James Forrestal*, pp. 313-314.

12. Ibid., p. 351.

13. CR, 81st Cong., 1st sess., pp. 2973, 3035.

14. Allen and Shannon, *Truman Merry-Go-Round*, pp. 443-484.

15. Schilling, *Strategy, Politics and Defense Budgets*, pp. 321-325.

16. CR, 81st Cong., 2d sess., pp. 14914-14917.

17. Congressional Quarterly, *Congress and the Nation*, pp. 261-262.

18. NYT, September 23, 1951; *Time*, September 24, 1951; *Newsweek*, September 24, 1951; *Current Biography* (1951), pp. 378-380.

19. Allen and Shannon, *Truman Merry-Go-Round*, p. 96.

20. Harold Ickes, "Farewell, Secretary Krug," *New Republic*, November 28, 1949; PPT, 1949, pp. 563-564; Steinberg, *Man from Missouri*, p. 370.

21. NYT, February 14, 1946; *Current Biography* (1949), pp. 101-104; "Triumph of the Empire Builders," *Fortune* (February 1952):110-117; R. Moley "Cabinet Hot Spot," *Newsweek*, November 17, 1952.

22. Interview with Senator Paul H. Douglas; *New Republic*, August 15, 1949; Abraham, *Justices and Presidents*, p. 229; Kirkendall, "Justice Clark," in L. Friedman and F. Israel, *Justices of the United States Supreme Court* (New York: Chelsea, 1967).

23. Miller, *Plain Speaking*, chap. 37.

24. Minority Report on S. Res. 116 by Senator Ferguson, CT, 81st Cong., 1st sess., p. 11708.

25. Congressional Quarterly, *Congress and the Nation*, pp. 1711-1712; PPT, 1952, p. 230.

26. Koenig, *Truman Administration*, pp. 21-22; Fenno, *President's Cabinet*, pp. 36, 43, 48-49, 112, 154, 164, 219.

27. Neustadt, "Notes on White House Staff," HSTL.

28. Walter Lippmann, "The Campaign and the Crisis," *New York Herald-Tribune*, October 4, 1948; Lubell, *Future of American Politics*, pp. 5, 12, 25, 219, 254.

29. Alexander George, "The Case for Multiple Advocacy in Making Foreign Policy," *American Political Science Review* (September 1972):pp. 772-777; Kennan, *Memoirs, 1925-1950*, pp. 487-496.

30. Joe Goulden, "Super Clark," *Washingtonian* (December 1971):66, and his *The Superlawyers*; OHT, Charles Murphy.

31. Neustadt, "The Constraining of the President"; OHT, Sundquist.

32. OHT, Charles S. Murphy; Neustadt, "Notes on White House Staff," HSTL.

33. Anderson, *President's Men*, pp. 92-95.

34. Farrar, *Reluctant Servant*, pp. 233-235; Pollard, *Presidents and the Press*, pp. 31-32; OHT, Roger Tubby; OHT, Charles S. Murphy.

35. TM, 2:449; OHT, Charles S. Murphy; Margaret Truman, *Harry S. Truman*, pp. 515-516; Miller, *Plain Speaking*, p. 305.

36. OHT, Roger Tubby; OHT, Irving Perlmeter.

37. OHT, Harry Vaughan; Vaughan, "Whipping Boy—First Class," 1954, HSTL; Neustadt, "Notes on the White House Staff," HSTL.

38. Neustadt, "Constraining of the President."

39. Phillips, *Truman Presidency*, p. 164.

40. OHT, Oscar Ewing; OHT, Leon Keyserling.

41. OHT, Fred Lawton; OHT, Roger Jones; OHT, James I. Sundquist; "Frank Pace," *Current Biography* (1950), p. 435; "Frederick Lawton," *Current Biography* (1951), p. 366.

42. Congressional Quarterly, *Congress and the Nation*, pp. 266, 270, 275-276; TM, 2:33.

43. OHT, Leon Keyserling; Hamby, *Beyond the New Deal*, p. 172.

44. PPT, 1949, p. 494.

CHAPTER 33
NATO, GERMANY, AND CHINA, 1949-1952

1. Acheson, *Present at the Creation*, p. 735.

2. Ibid., pp. 278-279; Kennan, *Memoirs, 1925-1950*, p. 411; Vandenberg, *Private Papers*, p. 477; PPT, 1949, p. 184; Smith, *Dean Acheson*, chap. 3.

3. PPT, 1949, p. 184; Smith, *Dean Acheson*, p. 71.

4. PPT, 1949, pp. 206-207.

5. U.S. Senate, Committee on Foreign Relations, *Hearings on North Atlantic Treaty*, 81st Cong., 1st sess., pp. 4-78.

6. PPT, 1949, pp. 570-571.

7. U.S. Senate, Committee on Foreign Relations, *Documents Relating to the North Atlantic Treaty*, 81st Cong., 1st sess., 1949; Feis, *From Trust to Terror*, p. 381.

8. PPT, 1949, pp. 395-400.

9. Kennan, *Memoirs, 1925-1950*, pp. 410-412, 463.

10. Truman's comments on U.S.-Soviet relations, June 7, 1949, Clark Clifford Papers, HSTL; Acheson, *Present at the Creation*, p. 347.

11. PPT, 1949, p. 570.

12. Clay, *Decision in Germany*, chaps. 19, 20; Stalin's statement in NYT, January 31, 1949; Robert Murphy, *Diplomat among Warriors*, chap. 22; Kolko and Kolko, *Limits of Power*, pp. 488-498; Gaddis Smith, "The Berlin Blockade through the Filter of History," *NYT Magazine*, April 29, 1973.

13. DSB, February 13, 1949, pp. 192-194; Smith, *Dean Acheson*, p. 84; PPT, 1949, p. 223; Acheson, *Sketches from Life*, pp. 175-180.

14. Smith, *Dean Acheson*, p. 94.

15. PPT, 1949, p. 324.

16. Ibid., pp. 438, 483, 485, 500-501; DSB, December 5, 1949, p. 863.

17. PPT, 1950, p. 626; TM, 2:254; Acheson, *Present at the Creation*, pp. 439-440.

18. PPT, 1950, pp. 750, 753-755; CR, 8; CR, 82d Cong., 1st sess., pp. 54-61.

19. PPT, 1950, p. 751.

20. Acheson, *Present at the Creation*, p. 493.

21. Kennan, *Memoirs, 1925-1950*, pp. 410-411; Marshall Schulman, *Stalin's Foreign Policy Reappraised* (Cambridge: Harvard University Press, 1963), pp. 13-17; Gardner, *Architects of Illusion*, chap. 9.

22. Acheson, *Present at the Creation*, pp. 493-495.

23. PPT, 1952, pp. 302-303; Parmet, *Eisenhower and the American Crusade*, p. 58.

24. PPT, 1952-1953, pp. 183, 395-398; TM, 2:254, 380; Acheson, *Present at the Creation*, p. 435.

25. Tuchman, *Stilwell*, pp. 202-203; Feis, *China Tangle*; U.S. Department of State, *U.S. Relations with China*, 1949 (China white paper, cited as CWP).

26. Tsou, *America's Failure in China*, pp. 111-122; Feis, *China Tangle*, chap. 19; CWP, pp. 68-71.

27. CWP, pp. 260-261; Davies, *Dragon by the Tail*.

28. Wedemeyer report, CWP, pp. 764-814; Tsou, *America's Failure in China*, pp. 454-462; Acheson, *Present at the Creation*, pp. 304-305.

29. General David Barr's report, CWP, pp. 325-338.

30. PPT, 1948, pp. 144-146, 385-386.

31. CWP, p. 984.

32. Ibid., p. 1054.

33. Vandenberg, *Private Papers*, p. 526.

34. U.S. Senate, Committee on Foreign Relations, *Hearings on the Nomination of Dean G. Acheson to Be Secretary of State*, 81st Cong., 1st sess., January 13, 1949.

35. Vandenberg, *Private Papers*, p. 529.

36. Ibid., pp. 526, 532; Phillips, *Truman Presidency*, pp. 286-287.

37. Acheson, *Present at the Creation*, p. 306.

38. Smith, *Dean Acheson*, pp. 113-114.

39. Tsou, *America's Failure in China*, pp. 510-511.

40. Vandenberg, *Private Papers*, p. 535.

41. CWP, p. xvi.

42. McLellan, *Dean Acheson*, p. 213.

43. PPT, 1949, pp. 408-409.

44. U.S. Senate, Committee on the Judiciary, *Hearings on the Institute of Pacific Relations*, 82d Cong., 1st and 2d sess., 1951-1952, pt. B, 4770.

45. Ibid., pt. 13, exhibit 752, p. 4533.

46. *U.S. News and World Report*, October 1, 1954.

47. Committee on the Judiciary, *Institute of Pacific Relations*, pt. 3, p. 923.

48. Kolko and Kolko, *Limits of Power*, chap. 20.

49. PPT, 1949, p. 520.

50. Smith, *Dean Acheson*, pp. 125-126, 128.

51. PPT, 1950, pp. 10-11.

52. Smith, *Dean Acheson*, p. 132.

CHAPTER 34
LIBERAL LEANINGS THWARTED, 1949–1950

1. David Truman, *Congressional Party*, chap. 2.

2. Congressional Quarterly, *Congress and the Nation*, pp. 337-357.

3. OHT, Charles S. Murphy.

4. Dorough, *Mr. Sam*, pp. 412-413.

5. Truman, *The Congressional Party*, p. 18.

6. Memorandum for Clark Clifford from George Elsey, November 14, 1948, Clifford Papers, HSTL.

7. PPT, 1949, pp. 1-7; Hamby, *Beyond the New Deal*, pp. 297-302; OHT, Leon Keyserling.

8. PPT, 1949, pp. 13-26.

9. Ibid., pp. 356-367.

10. Ibid., pp. 112-116; TM, 2:230-234; Clark Clifford to Herbert Feis, July 16, 1963, Clifford Papers, HSTL; Acheson, *Present at the Creation*, pp. 266-267.

11. PPT, 1949, pp. 118-119.

12. Matusow, *Farm Policies*, chap. 9.

13. U.S. Department of Agriculture, Agricultural History Branch, *Century of Service*, p. 355.

14. Congressional Quarterly, *Congress and the Nation*, pp. 689-692; U.S. House of Representatives, *Hearings on General Farm Program*, 81st Cong., 1st sess., April 7, 1949.

15. PPT, 1949, pp. 464-469; ibid., 1950, p. 8.

16. Matusow, *Farm Policies*, p. 219.

17. Congressional Quarterly, *Congress and the Nation*, pp. 586-587, 623.

18. Lash, *Eleanor: The Years Alone*, p. 162; Alfred Steinberg, *Mrs. R.: The Life of Eleanor Roosevelt* (New York: Putnams, 1958), pp. 341-342.

19. Kelley, *Professional Public Relations*, pp. 70-82.

20. NYT, March 4, 1949; PPT, 1949, pp. 158-159.

21. NYT, January 13, 1949.

22. *Washington Post*, July 13, 1949.

23. NYT, October 4, 1949.

24. PPT, 1950, pp. 2-11.

25. Ibid., pp. 18-31; OHT, Leon Keyserling.

26. PPT, 1950, pp. 44-106; Paul Y. Hammond, "NSC-68: Prologue to Rearmament," in Schilling, *Strategy, Politics and Defense Budgets*, pp. 271-318; NSC 68 is found in FRUS, 1950, 1:126-292.

27. PPT, 1950, p. 120.

28. Ibid., pp. 120-128; Truman, *Congressional Party*, p. 36.

29. PPT, 1950, p. 115.

30. NYT, January 26, 1950.

31. Ibid., February 24, 1950; *Chicago Defender*, March 10, 1950.

32. PPT, 1950, p. 253.

33. Memorandum for the President from Murphy and Spingarn, July 3, 1950, Stephen Spingarn Papers, HSTL; Truman, *Congressional Party*, p. 33.

34. OHT, Charles S. Murphy.

35. Memorandum for Clifford from Spingarn, November 22, 1949, Spingarn Papers, HSTL; Berman, *Politics of Civil Rights*, p. 292.

36. Shelly v. Kramer, 334 U.S. 1.

37. Davies, *Housing Reform*, p. 125.

38. McLaurin v. Oklahoma State Regents, 339 U.S. 637; Sweat v. Painter, 339 U.S. 629; Plessy v. Ferguson, 163 U.S. 537.

39. Henderson v. U.S., 339 U.S. 816.

40. Hamby, *Beyond the New Deal*, pp. 342-344.

41. PPT, 1950, pp. 516-518, 597; EO 10155.

42. Davies, *Housing Reform*, p. 120.

43. Truman, *Congressional Party*, p. 33.

44. TM, 2:494; U.S. Senate, Special Committee to Investigate Organized Crime in Interstate Commerce, *Hearings*, 81st Cong., 2d sess., Congressional Quarterly, *Congress and the Nation*, pp. 1700-1701.

45. Congressional Quarterly, *Congress and the Nation*, p. 1461.

46. PPT, 1950, pp. 600-601.

47. Ibid., pp. 527-537.

48. Ibid., pp. 522-524.

49. OHT, Leon Keyserling, p. 88; Congressional Quarterly, *Congress and the Nation*, p. 357.

50. Hamby, *Beyond the New Deal*, pp. 417-418, 447.

51. PPT, 1950, pp. 645-653.

52. Ibid., pp. 741-746; Truman *Congressional Party*, pp. 39-40.

53. PPT, 1950, p. 751.

54. Neustadt, "Congress and the Fair Deal," *Public Policy* 5 (1954):366-367.

55. Davies, *Housing Reform*, p. 135.

CHAPTER 35
THE 1950 ELECTIONS

1. Memorandum of May 14, 1950 by Kenneth Hechler, Elsey Papers, HSTL.

2. PPT, 1950, pp. 409-413; OHT, Charles S. Murphy.

3. Woodruff of Michigan, May 24, 1950, in CR, 81st Cong., 2d sess., p. A3943; Senator Kem cited by *Kansas City Star*, July 20, 1950.

4. PPT, 1950, pp. 699-703; OHT, Charles S. Murphy.

5. Senator Ferguson's denunciation of Truman, May 9, 1950, in CR, 81st Cong., 2d sess., p. 6699; Latham, *Communist Controversy in Washington*, pp. 269-272.

6. Truman's "red herring" comment PPT, 1948, p. 433; Acheson's comment in *Present at the Creation*, p. 360.

7. Nixon, *Six Crises*, p. 64.

8. Mazo, *Richard Nixon*, chap. 6; Kelley, *Professional Public Relations*, p. 107.

9. James Roosevelt to President Truman, September 28, 1950, and President Truman to James Roosevelt, October 10, 1950, OF, HSTL.

10. Lubell, *Future of American Politics*, pp. 155, 189-195; Kelley, *Professional Public Relations*, chap. 4.

11. U.S. Senate, Subcommittee of the Committee on Rules and Administration, *Hearings on the Maryland Senatorial Election of 1950*, 82d Cong., 1st sess.

12. U.S. Senate, Committee on Rules and Administration, *Report on Maryland Senatorial Election of 1950*, 82d Cong., 1st sess.

13. Douglas, *In the Fullness of Time*, pp. 561-563.

14. Congressional Quarterly, *Congress and the Nation*, pp. 71, 74-75.

15. Lubell, *Future of American Politics*, pp. 137, 207, 229.

16. Roper, *You and Your Leaders*, pp. 44-46; Fenton, *In Your Opinion*, pp. 89-94.

17. Kenneth Hechler, The 1950 Elections, November 15, 1950, Ross Papers, HSTL.

18. PPT, 1950, p. 727; Farrar, *Reluctant Servant*, p. 226; OHT, Charles S. Murphy.

19. Miller, *Plain Speaking*, pp. 87-88.

CHAPTER 36
KOREA AND JAPAN, 1950–1952

1. Millis, *Forrestal Diaries*, pp. 50-51.

2. PPT, 1948, p. 255.

3. Schilling, *Strategy, Politics and Defense Budgets*, p. 144.

4. DSB, January 23, 1950.

5. PPT, 1950, p. 11.

6. Bernard Brodie, *War and Politics* (New York: Macmillan, 1973), p. 63.

7. DSB, December 4, 1943.

8. TM, 1:433-434.

9. Ibid., pp. 444-445; Schnabel, *Policy and Direction*, pp. 8-11.

10. U.S. Department of State, *Korea 1945 to 1948*, Washington, 1948.

11. TM, 2:320-323.

12. Schnabel, *Policy and Direction*, pp. 26-36.

13. TM, 2:329.

14. Paige, *Korean Decision*, p. 98; Alexander George, "The Case for Multiple Advocacy in Making Foreign Policy," *American Political Science Review* (September 1972):773.

15. DSB, January 23, 1950, p. 116.

16. Paige, *Korean Decision*, pp. 95-98, 116-121, 125-141.

17. TM, 2:332-234.

18. George, "Case for Multiple Advocacy," p. 776.

19. Spanier, *Truman-MacArthur Controversy*, p. 37.

20. TM, 2: 334.

21. Paige, *Korean Decision*, p. 125.

22. PPT, 1950, p. 610.

23. Schilling, *Strategy, Politics and Defense Budgets*, pp. 212, 287.

24. Schnabel, *Policy and Direction*, chap. 5.

25. Kennan, *Memoirs, 1950–1963*, p. 39, and *Memoirs, 1925–1950*, p. 498; Paige, *Korean Decision*, p. 132.

26. Khrushchev, *Khrushchev Remembers*, pp. 367-368.

27. Schnabel, *Policy and Direction*, pp. 68-69; FRUS, 1950, 7:178.

28. Paige, *Korean Decision*, pp. 104, 110, 142, 165; I. F. Stone, *Korean War*, chap. 14; Kolko and Kolko, *Limits of Power*, p. 589; Hoopes, *Devil and John Foster Dulles*, pp. 100-104; Warren F. Kimball, "Cold War Warmed Over," *American Historical Review* (October 1974):1122.

29. TM, 2:337.

30. Paige, *Korean Decision*, pp. 164, 178.

31. FRUS, 1950, 7:211; Department of State, *Guide to UN in Korea*, 1951, p. 13.

32. TM, 2: 341; Schnabel, *Policy and Direction*, p. 77.

33. U.S. Department of State, *U.S. Policy in Korean Crisis* (Washington, 1950), p. 64; Smith, *Dean Acheson*, p. 190.

34. FRUS, 1950, 7:248; Paige, *Korean Decision*, p. 248, citing Beverly Smith in *Saturday Evening Post*, November 10, 1951.

35. FRUS, 1950, 7:290; Acheson, *Present at the Creation*, p. 412; TM, 2:343; Neustadt, *Presidential Power*, pp. 123-124; Schnabel, *Policy and Direction*, pp. 77-79.

36. Connally, *My Name Is Tom Connally*, p. 349; Paige, *Korean Decision*, pp. 149, 187, 262.

37. Acheson, *Present at the Creation*, p. 414.

38. PPT, 1950, p. 504.

39. TM, 2:342-343.

40. MacArthur, *Reminiscences*, pp. 334-335; William Manchester, *American Caesar: Douglas MacArthur, 1880–1964* (Boston: Little, Brown, 1978), p. 551.

41. FRUS, 1950, 7:329.

42. PPT, 1950, pp. 520, 527-542.

43. TM, 2:354; Acheson, *Present at the Creation*, p. 422; MacArthur, *Reminiscences*, p. 340.

44. TM, 2:349-353; W. Averell Harriman, in Francis H. Heller, *The Korean War: A 25-Year Perspective* (Lawrence: Regents Press of Kansas, 1977), p. 233.

45. TM, 2:354-356; PPT, 1950, pp. 599, 602, 609-614; Acheson, *Present at the Creation*, pp. 423-424; Spanier, *Truman-MacArthur Controversy*, pp. 73-77.

46. PPT, 1950, pp. 632-633; Acheson, *Present at the Creation*, p. 441; Margaret Truman, *Harry S. Truman*, pp. 478-480.

47. Schnabel, *Policy and Direction*, pp. 154, 181-182; TM, 2:359.

48. Kennan, *Memoirs, 1925–1950*, pp. 487-496; Acheson, *Present at the Creation*, pp. 454-455; Smith, *Dean Acheson*, p. 208.

49. FRUS, 1950, 7:904; Neustadt, *Presidential Power*, pp. 124-125.

50. TM, 2:363-370; Acheson, *Present at the Creation*, p. 456; Rovere and Schlesinger, *General and the President*, pp. 253-262.

51. FRUS, 1950, 7:953, 974; Neustadt, *Presidential Power*, p. 144.

52. PPT, 1950, pp. 672-673.

53. Acheson, *Present at the Creation*, p. 466; TM, 2:376-380; FRUS, 1950, 7:1138; Schnabel, *Policy and Direction*, pp. 252-256.

54. TM, 2:384; Acheson, *Present at the Creation*, p. 467; Neustadt, *Presidential Power*, pp. 145-146.

55. FRUS, 1950, 7:1237; Acheson, *Present at the Creation*, pp. 471-472; Schnabel, *Policy and Direction*, pp. 274-284.

56. Barber, *Presidential Character*, pp. 282-286; *U.S. News and World Report*, December 8, 1950.

57. PPT, 1950, p. 727; TM, 2:393, 395-396; Schnabel, *Policy and Direction*, p. 288.

58. Acheson, *Present at the Creation*, pp. 476-477, 480-485; TM, 2:396-413; Smith, *Dean Acheson*, pp. 223-230; FRUS, 1950, 5:1392, 1431.

59. TM, 2,384; U.S. Senate, *Military Situation in the Far East*, 82d Cong., 1st sess., *MacArthur Hearings*, pp. 3532-3535.

60. Spanier, *Truman-MacArthur Controversy*, pp. 152-164; PPT, 1950, pp. 746, 749, 751.

61. Smith, *Dean Acheson*, pp. 263-264.

62. Schnabel, *Policy and Direction*, pp. 305-310, 327-328; Ridgway, *Korean War*, chap. 5; FRUS, 1950, 7:1469.

63. TM, 2:435-436; Schnabel, *Policy and Direction*, pp. 333-340.

64. Acheson, *Present at the Creation*, p. 513; *MacArthur Hearings*, pp. 3513-3514.

65. Willoughby, *MacArthur*, p. 408; MacArthur, *Reminiscences*, p. 384; TM, 2:438-440.

66. William Manchester, *American Caesar, Douglas MacArthur, 1880–1964*, (Boston: Little, Brown, 1978), p. 633.

67. Spanier, *Truman-MacArthur Controversy*, pp. 199-200.

68. TM, 2: 440-442; Acheson, *Present at the Creation*, p. 519.

69. MacArthur, *Reminiscences*, p. 392; Whitney, *MacArthur*, pp. 467-468.

70. TM, 2:441-443; Rovere and Schlesinger, *General and the President*, p. 174; Margaret Truman, *Harry S. Truman*, p. 513.

71. TM, 2:445-446; Bernstein and Matusow, *Truman Amdinistration*, pp. 454-455, reproduces the letters.

72. TM, 2:447-448; Schnabel, *Policy and Direction*, pp. 375-376.

73. Manchester, *American Caesar*, pp. 642-644; TM, 2:449-450.

74. PPT, 1950, pp. 222-227, 287-288.

75. Roper, *Your and Your Leaders*, pp. 161-162.

76. *MacArthur Hearings*, pp. 2553-2558.

77. Steinberg, *Man from Missouri*, p. 399.

78. Spanier, *Truman-MacArthur Controversy*, pp. 221-222.

79. Hamby, *Beyond the New Deal*, p. 443.

80. *MacArthur Hearings*, pp. 731-732.

81. George Gallup, *Public Opinion News Service*, January 12, 1953.

82. Maxwell D. Taylor, *Swords and Plowshares* (New York, Norton, 1972), pp. 135-136; Clark, *From the Danube to the Yalu*, pp. 316-317.

83. Smith, *Dean Acheson*, pp. 276-279.

84. TM, 2:460-461; Wilber W. Hoar, "Truman," in Ernest R. May, ed., *The Ultimate Decision* (New York, Braziller, 1960), pp. 208-210.

85. TM, 1:431-433, 2:366, 432; Reischauer, *The Japanese* (Cambridge: Harvard University Press, 1977), p. 48.

86. Acheson, *Present at the Creation*, p. 428; Hoopes, *Devil and John Foster Dulles*, pp. 89-91.

87. PPT, 1950, pp. 713; W. Walton Butterworth, in John Foster Dulles Oral History, Princeton University Library.

88. Hoopes, *Devil and John Foster Dulles*, pp. 97-100.

89. Acheson, *Present at the Creation*, pp. 542-549.

90. PPT, 1951, pp. 504-508.

CHAPTER 37
MILITARY, ECONOMIC, AND SOCIAL PROBLEMS, 1951-1952

1. Congressional Quarterly, *Congress and the Nation*, p. 390.

2. Fenton, *In Your Opinion*, p. 92.

3. Hamby, *Beyond the New Deal*, pp. 441-443; Neustadt, "Congress and the Fair Deal," *Public Policy* (1954): 374.

4. PPT, 1951, pp. 6-13; Congressional Quarterly, *Congress and the Nation*, p. 12.

5. PPT, 1951, pp. 27-47.

6. Ibid., pp. 47-106.

7. NYT, January 27, 1951; Matusow, *Farm Policies*, pp. 225-226; Marcus, *Truman and the Steel Seizure Case*, pp. 14-15; OHT, Frederick J. Lawton.

8. Congressional Quarterly, *Congress and the Nation*, pp. 358-359; Bernstein, "Economic Policies," in Kirkendall, *Truman Period as a Research Field* (1967), p. 119.

9. PPT, 1951, pp. 134-138, Congressional Quarterly, *Congress and the Nation*, p. 412.

10. PPT, 1951, p. 436; Snyder, in Schilling, *Strategy, Politics and Defense Budgets*, p. 387.

11. Congressional Quarterly, *Congress and the Nation*, pp. 567, 599, 623; Bernstein, "Economic Policies," pp. 112-113.

12. Marcus, *Truman and the Steel Seizure Case*, pp. 59-60; Neustadt, *Presidential Power*, pp. 13-14.

13. Matusow, *Farm Policies,* p. 229-230.

14. Ibid., p. 232; NYT, March 5, 1951.

15. U.S. Department of Agriculture, *Century of Service*, p. 371.

16. PPT, 1951, pp. 12, 80.

17. Bernstein, *Politics and Policies of the Truman Administration*, pp. 298-300.

18. PPT, 1951, pp. 616-617.

19. Berman, *Politics of Civil Rights*, p. 170.

20. Ibid., p. 169.

21. PPT, 1952-1953, pp. 9-17.

22. Ibid., pp. 35-54.

23. Ibid., pp. 64, 117; Feis, *From Trust to Terror*, p. 412.

24. Floyd M. Riddick, "The Eighty-Second Congress; Second Session," *Western Political Quarterly* (March 1953):619-634.

25. Marcus, *Truman and the Steel Seizure Case*, pp. 64-68; Hamby, *Beyond the New Deal*, pp. 454-458.

26. PPT, 1952-1953, p. 226; Neustadt, *Presidential Power*, pp. 13-16, 21-25, 28-29, 31.

27. PPT, 1952-1953, pp. 246-250; TM, 2:465-274; Marcus, *Truman and the Steel Seizure Case*, pp. 85-101.

28. Youngstown Sheet & Tube Co. v. Sawyer, 343 U.S. 579 (1952); Sawyer, *Concerns of a Conservative Democrat*, pp. 255-277.

29. Marcus, *Truman and the Steel Seizure Case*, chap. 10; Bernstein, "Economic Policies," pp. 129-130; Mary K. Hammond, "The Steel Strike of 1952," *Current History* (November 1952): 285-290.

30. Matusow, *Farm Policies*, pp. 240-243.

31. PPT, 1952-1953, pp. 379-384.

32. Ibid., pp. 441-447; Congressional Quarterly, *Congress and the Nation*, p. 12.

33. Neustadt, "Congress and the Fair Deal," pp. 378-381; OHT, Charles S. Murphy; OHT, Roger Jones.

34. PPT, 1952-1953, pp. 478-480, 486-488.

35. Schilling, *Strategy, Politics and Defense Budgets*, pp. 212, 323.

CHAPTER 38
INVESTIGATIONS, SCANDALS, SECURITY, MCCARTHYISM, 1947–1952

1. Congressional Quarterly, *Congress and the Nation*, pp. 1679-1712; Phillips, *Truman Presidency*, pp. 402-414; Schlesinger and Bruns, *Congress Investigates*.

2. U.S. House, Select Committee to Investigate Transactions on Commodity Exchanges, 80th Cong., 1st sess., *Hearings*, December 27, 1947.

3. U.S. Senate, Committee on Expenditures in the Executive Departments, 81st Cong., 1st sess., *Report*, January 18, 1950; OHT, Harry Vaughan.

4. U.S. House, Ways and Means Committee, Subcommittee on Administration of Revenue Laws, 82d Cong., 2d sess., *Final Report*, December 25, 1952; Abels, *Truman Scandals*, pp. 158-170.

5. U.S. House, Special Subcommittee of the Judiciary Committee to Investigate the Justice Department, *Hearings*, 82d Cong., 2d sess., pp. 1159-1386; OHT, Charles S. Murphy.

6. David E. Bell memorandum, October 20, 1951, Murphy Papers, HSTL.

7. PPT, 1952-1953, pp. 1-2.

8. Murphy to the President, January 23, 1952, Murphy Papers, HSTL; PPT, 1952-1953, pp. 27-31, 177, 197-198.

9. U.S. Senate, Subcommittee of Banking and Currency Committee on Reconstruction Finance Corporation, *Report*, 82d Cong., 1st sess., February 5, 1951.

10. PPT, 1951, p. 145.

11. Ibid., pp. 158, 175, 233, 454-458; Douglas, *In the Fullness of Time*, pp. 222-224; Hamby, *Beyond the New Deal*, p. 461; Abels, *Truman Scandals*, pp. 70-122.

12. Hamby, *Beyond the New Deal*, p. 464.

13. Subcommittee to Investigate the Justice Department, *Report*, 82d Cong., 2d sess., September 28, 1952; Murphy to the President, April 1, 1952, HSTL; OHT, Harold Seidman; Morris, *Let the Chips Fall*.

14. Congressional Quarterly, *Congress and the Nation*, p. 106a; Hamby, *Beyond the New Deal*, pp. 465-466.

15. PPT, 1952-1953, p. 224.

16. Congressional Quarterly, *Congress and the Nation*, p. 1463; Parmet, *Eisenhower and the American Crusades*, p. 32.

17. Latham, *Communist Controversy in Washington*, p. 210; U.S. House, Judiciary Committee, Subcommittee IV, 79th Cong., 2d sess., *Report 2732*, October 23, 1946.

18. U.S. House, Special Committee on Un-American Activities, *Annual Report*, 79th Cong., 2d sess., *Report 2233*, June 7, 1946; Congressional Quarterly, *Congress and the Nation 1945-1964*, p. 1690.

19. Report to the President on American Relations to the Soviet Union, September 1946, in Krock, *Memoirs*, pp. 472-475.

20. PPT, 1946, p. 532.

21. Ibid., 1947, pp. 489-491.

22. U.S. House, Committee on Un-American Activities Committee, *Report*, April 1, 1947, 80th Cong., 1st sess.

23. U.S. House, Committee on Un-American Activities, *Hearings*, July 31-December 14,

1948, 80th Cong., 2d sess.; Latham, *Communist Controversy in Washington*, pp. 185-194; Nixon, *Six Crises*, pp. 1-71; Smith, *Alger Hiss*, pp. 158-176; PPT, 1948, pp. 432-433, 959.

24. Michal R. Belknap, *Cold War Political Justice: The Smith Act, the Communist Party, and American Civil Liberties* (Westport, Conn.: Greenwood Press, 1977), p. x.

25. Hamby, *Beyond the New Deal*, p. 385; House Committee on Un-American Activities, *Report*, April 26, 1950; Latham, *Communist Controversy in Washington*, p. 422.

26. Acheson, *Present at the Creation*, p. 360.

27. CR, 81st Cong., 2d sess., pp. 2043-2071, 2104-2110, 2168-2169.

28. U.S. Senate, Committee on Foreign Relations, Special Subcommittee to Investigate State Department Employees [Tydings committee], *Report*, July 20, 1950, 81st Cong., 2d sess.; Congressional Quarterly, *Congress and the Nation*, pp. 1701-1704.

29. U.S. Senate, Rules and Administration Committee, Subcommittee on Privileges and Elections, *Report*, August 8, 1951, 82d Cong., 1st sess.

30. U.S. Senate, Committee on Rules and Administration, *Report* on Investigation of Senators McCarthy and William Benton, January 2, 1953, 83d Cong., 1st sess.

31. U.S. Senate, Judiciary Committee, Internal Security Subcommittee, *Interim Report*, January 2, 1953, 83d Cong., 1st sess.

32. PPT, 1952-1953, p. 858.

33. Theoharis, *Seeds of Repression*.

CHAPTER 39
CANDIDATE ADLAI STEVENSON, 1952

1. TM, 2:488-489. A handwritten copy of this statement is in the Charles S. Murphy Papers, HSTL.

2. PPT, 1952-1953, p. 225; "President Truman Should Withdraw," *New Republic*, February 4, 1952. Actually, the Key West meeting took place in November 1951. Murphy to Truman, November 23, 1951, PSF, Personal File, HSTL.

3. TM, 2:489-491; Bernstein, "Election of 1952," in Schlesinger, ed., *Coming to Power*, pp. 405-407; Steinberg, *Man from Missouri*, p. 409.

4. David et al. *Presidential Nominating Politics in 1952*, pp. 35-41, 55-65; TM, 494; Myron Harris to President Truman, July 4, 1952, praising Kefauver, OF, HSTL; Davis, *Presidential Primaries*, pp. 60-61.

5. Bernstein, "Election of 1952," pp. 405-406; David, *Presidential Nominating Politics in 1952*, p. 37; TM, 2:494.

6. Bain, *Convention Decisions*, p. 286; Martin, *Adlai Stevenson*, pp. 554, 564.

7. Hamby, *Beyond the New Deal*, p. 485; Bernstein, "Election of 1952," pp. 406-407.

8. OHT, Charles S. Murphy.

9. Davis, *Prophet in His Own Country*, p. 381; Martin, *Adlai Stevenson*, pp. 418-419.

10. TM, 2:492.

11. Leo G. Gabriel to President Truman, February 5, 1952, OF, HSTL; James E. Poley to President Truman, May 19, 1952, OF, HSTL; Davis, *Prophet in His Own Country*, pp. 388-390.

12. Johnson, *How We Drafted Stevenson*; Martin, *Adlai Stevenson*, pp. 555-564; Davis, *Prophet in His Own Country*, pp. 390-394.

13. OHT, Charles S. Murphy.

14. Barkley, *That Reminds Me*, p. 230; TM, 2:495; David et al., *Presidential Nominating Politics in 1952*, p. 64; Bernstein, "Election of 1952," p. 407.

15. Democratic National Committee, *Official Proceedings of the Democratic National Convention, 1952*, pp. 8-11; Stevenson, *Major Campaign Speeches*, pp. 3-6; Bain, *Convention Decisions*, pp. 287-89; Martin, *Adlai Stevenson*, pp. 585-587.

16. TM, 2:496; Davis, *Prophet in His Own Country*, p. 403.

17. *Official Proceedings*, pp. 11-25.

18. PPT, 1952-1953, p. 132; Roper, *You and Your Leaders*, p. 212; David et al., *Presidential Nominating Politics in 1952*, p. 65.

19. *Official Proceedings*, pp. 253-275; OHT, Charles S. Murphy; Bain, *Convention Decisions*, pp. 289-290.

20. *Official Proceedings*, pp. 406, 457, 538; Martin, *Adlai Stevenson*, pp. 598-599; Bain, *Convention Decisions*, pp. 291-292.

21. *Official Proceedings*, pp. 539-550.

22. TM, 2:497; Bernstein, "Election of 1952," pp. 409-410; David et al., *Presidential Nominating Politics in 1952*, pp. 155-156.

CHAPTER 40
IKE: THE OPPOSING CANDIDATE

1. Parmet, *Eisenhower and the American Crusades*, p. 74; NYT, February 24, 1952; Fenton, *In Your Opinion*, pp. 95-113; Roper, *You and Your Leaders*, chap. 9; Bernstein, "Election of 1952," pp. 390-95.

2. Hugh A. Bone, *Party Committees and National Politics*, rev. ed. (Washington, D.C.: University of Washington, 1968), p. 7.

3. Bernstein, "Election of 1952," pp. 394-397; Roper, *You and Your Leaders*, p. 97; Bain, *Convention Decisions*, pp. 279-280.

4. Eisenhower, *Crusade in Europe*, p. 444; NYT, November 8, 1951; Krock, *Memoirs*, pp. 268-269; TM, 2:187; PPT, 1951, p. 629.

5. Miller, *Plain Speaking*; for Truman's low opinion of Eisenhower ten years after leaving the White House, see pp. 28, 130, 134, 259, 337, 342-344, 406.

6. *New York Herald Tribune*, January 8, 15, 1952.

7. Davis, *Presidential Primaries*, pp. 60-61; Dwight Eisenhower, *Mandate for Change* (Garden City: Doubleday, 1963), pp. 19-22; Bernstein, "Election of 1952," pp. 398-399; Parmet, *Eisenhower and the American Crusades*, pp. 54, 65-66.

8. Republican National Committee, *Official Proceedings of the Twenty-Fifth Republican National Convention, 1952*, pp. 67-76.

9. Ibid., pp. 309-324.

10. David et al., *Presidential Nominating Politics in 1952*, 3:330; NYT, July 13, 1952; Bain, *Convention Decisions*, p. 285; Eisenhower, *Mandate for Change*, pp. 38-40.

11. Mazo, *Richard Nixon*, pp. 94-97; Nixon, *Six Crises*, pp. 75-78; Bernstein, "Election of 1952," p. 403; Parmet, *Eisenhower and the American Crusades*, pp. 92-94.

12. *Official Proceedings*, pp. 432-434.

13. Parmet, *Eisenhower and the American Crusades*, pp. 107-112; Bernstein, "Election of 1952," pp. 410-412.

CHAPTER 41
SPEAKING FOR STEVENSON

1. Davis, *Prophet in His Own Country*, p. 408; OHT, Charles S. Murphy; Martin, *Adlai Stevenson*, pp. 623-625; Bernstein, "Election of 1952," pp. 420-421.

2. NYT, August 2, 1952; TM, 2:499-500; Davis, *Prophet in His Own Country*, p. 415; Martin, *Adlai Stevenson*, p. 644.

3. *Kansas City Times*, August 12, 14, 1952.

4. NYT, August 22, 1952; OHT, Charles S. Murphy.

5. PPT, 1952-1953, pp. 541-595; NYT, September 6, 16, 1952.

6. Rogge, "Speechmaking of Harry S. Truman," pp. 302-304; *Kansas City Times*, September 30, 1952.

7. *Kansas City Times*, October 7, 1952.

8. Charles S. Murphy Papers, HSTL.

9. OHT, James Sundquist.

10. OHT, Charles S. Murphy; *Kansas City Times*, October 6, 11, 23, 30, 1952; KCS, October 16, 1952.

11. NYT, October 2, 1952.

12. Ibid., November 2, 1952.

13. *Christian Science Monitor*, October 2, 1952.

14. PPT, 1952-1953, p. 738; OHT, Roger Tubby; Bernstein, "Election of 1952," p. 421; Rogge, Speechmaking of Harry S. Truman," pp. 334-337.

15. PPT, 1952-1953, p. 740; OHT, Charles S. Murphy; Parmet, *Eisenhower and the American Crusades*, pp. 131-132; Dwight D. Eisenhower, *Mandate for Change* (Garden City: Doubleday, 1963), p. 318.

16. PPT, 1952-1953, p. 710; Rogge, "Speechmaking of Harry S. Truman," p. 337.

17. PPT, 1952-1953, p. 992; Parmet, *Eisenhower and the American Crusades*, p. 143; TM, 2:501.

18. PPT, 1952-1953, p. 856; Rogge, "Speechmaking of Harry S. Truman," pp. 341, 352.

19. OHT, James Sundquist.

20. Davis, *Prophet in His Own Country*, p. 421; Bernstein, "Election of 1952," p. 424.

21. *Proceedings of the Democratic National Convention, 1952*, p. 550; NYT, November 2, 1952.

22. Alexander Heard, *Costs of Democracy* (Chapel Hill: University of North Carolina Press, 1960), p. 20.

23. Weisbord, *Campaigning for President*, pp. 153-154; Kelley, *Professional Public Relations and Political Power*, p. 151; Eisenhower, *Mandate for Change*, chap. 3; Parmet, *Eisenhower and the American Crusades*, pp. 123-124.

24. Bernstein, "Election of 1952," p. 412.

25. NYT, September 24, 1952; Nixon, *Six Crises*, pp. 73-129; Parmet, *Eisenhower and the American Crusades*, pp. 135-141; Martin, *Adlai Stevenson*, pp. 685-703.

26. PPT, 1952-1953, pp. 612, 729.

27. Davis, *Prophet in His Own Country*, p. 419; Bernstein, "Election of 1952," pp. 414-415.

28. Weisbord, *Campaigning for President*, pp. 161-162; Nixon, *Six Crises*, p. 125.

29. Weisbord, *Campaigning for President*, pp. 164-165.

30. PPT, 1952-1953, p. 1047.

31. Congressional Quarterly, *Congress and the Nation*, p. 40; Bernstein, "Election of 1952," p. 428.

32. Herbert Hyman and Paul B. Sheatsley, "The Political Appeal of President Eisenhower," *Public Opinion Quarterly* (Winter 1953-1954):443-460.

33. Campbell et al., *The Voter Decides*, chap. 5; Samuel Lubell, *The Revolt of the Moderates* (New York: Harper, 1956), pp. 264-266.

CHAPTER 42
TRANSITION FROM TRUMAN TO EISENHOWER

1. TM, 2:504.

2. Neustadt, "Notes on White House Staff; Appendix, Notes on Truman's Arrangements for Transition to Eisenhower," p. 50, HSTL.

3. TM, 2:505.

4. NYT, November 6, 1952; Dwight D. Eisenhower, *Mandate for Change* (Garden City: Doubleday, 1963), p. 86.

5. TM, 2:506-508.

6. Henry, *Presidential Transitions*, p. 458; Parmet, *Eisenhower and the American Crusades*, p. 162.

7. TM, 2:507.

8. Henry, *Presidential Transitions*, p. 469.

9. Ibid., pp. 470-472.

10. Memorandum for the President from Dean Acheson, January 12, 1953, Murphy Papers, HSTL; Acheson, *Present at the Creation*, p. 714; Parmet, *Eisenhower and the American Crusades*, p. 103.

11. Henry, *Presidential Transitions*, pp. 473-476.

12. TM, 2:507.

13. Henry, *Presidential Transitions*, pp. 482-483.

14. TM, 2:514-545; PPT, 1952-1953, pp. 1048-1049; Eisenhower, *Mandate for Change*, pp. 84-85.

15. PPT, 1952-1953, p. 1051.

16. Donovan, *Eisenhower*, pp. 16-17; NYT, November 22, 25, 1952.

17. *Washington Star*, November 19, 1952.

18. Miller, *Plain Speaking*, p. 344; TM, 2:514-521.

19. Parmet, *Eisenhower and the American Crusades*, p. 158; Henry, *Presidential Transitions*, p. 488.

20. Eisenhower, *Mandate for Change*, pp. 86-92.

21. Acheson, *Present at the Creation*, pp. 711-713.

22. Henry, *Presidential Transitions*, p. 497.

23. OHT, Roger Tubby; Parmet, *Eisenhower and the American Crusades*, chap. 19.

24. Eisenhower, *Mandate for Change*, p. 96; Henry, *Presidential Transitions*, pp. 499-504.

25. PPT, 1952-1953, p. 1073; OHT, Roger Tubby; OHT, Roger Jones; OHT, David K. E. Bruce.

26. Henry, *Presidential Transitions*, pp. 505-511.

27. Neustadt, "Notes on White House Staff," HSTL; Acheson, *Present at the Creation*, p. 707.

28. PPT, 1952-1953, p. 1127.

29. Memorandum for Keyserling from Neustadt, January 2, 1953, Murphy Papers, HSTL; PPT, 1952-1953, pp. 1179-1189.

30. OHT, James L. Sundquist.

31. U.S. Senate, Committee on Armed Services, *Hearings*, 83d Cong., 1st sess., 1953, pp. 25-26.

32. Henry, *Presidential Transitions*, pp. 529-530; Miller, *Plain Speaking*, p. 342.

33. OHT, Leon Keyserling; OHT, William Salant.

34. Barber, *Presidential Character*, pp. 156-173.

CHAPTER 43
CHARACTER AND CRISES

1. Henry Commager, "Our Greatest Presidents," *Parade*, May 8, 1977.

2. Rossiter, *American Presidency*, pp. 146, 172; Arthur M. Schlesinger, Sr., *Paths to the Present* (New York: Macmillan, 1946), pp. 105-106; Freidel, *America in the Twentieth Century* (New York: Knopf, 1965), p. 503; Link, *American Epoch*, pp. 667-668.

3. Cochran, *Truman and the Crisis Presidency*, pp. 396-399; Bernstein, *Politics and Policies of the Truman Administration*, pp. 3-14.

4. Cronin, *State of the Presidency*.

5. James D. Barber, "The Presidency: What Americans Want," *Center Magazine* (January-February 1971): 2-6.

6. Barber, *Presidential Character*, p. 292.

7. Daniels, *Man of Independence*, p. 257; OHT, Harry Vaughan; Barber, *Presidential Character*, pp. 289-291; Steinberg, *Man from Missouri*, pp. 229-230.

8. Bailey, *Presidential Greatness*, p. 164; Daniels, *Man of Independence*, pp. 22, 129, 154, 158: Barber, *Presidential Character*, pp. 263-264.

9. Acheson, *Present at the Creation*, p. 730; Bailey, *Presidential Greatness*, appendix B.

10. John M. Crane, *The Pictorial Biography of Harry S. Truman*, American Historical Series (Washington, D.C.: 1948), p. 29; Truman, *Souvenir*, pp. 107-108, 118, 251, 255.

11. OHT, James Sundquist.

12. PPT, 1952-1953, p. 548.

13. Steinberg, *Man from Missouri*, p. 257; TM, 2:145-146.

14. Smith, *Thank You Mr. President*, p. 227.

15. Miller, *Plain Speaking*, pp. 230, 406.

16. Douglas, *Go East, Young Man*, p. 416.

17. Daniels interview with Truman, November 12, 1949, JDP.

18. Acheson, *Present at the Creation*, pp. 459-460; Truman, *Souvenir*, p. 311.

19. Leahy, *I Was There*, p. 427.

20. Lubell, *Future of American Politics*, p. 10.

21. Hoyt McAfee to President Truman, October 9, 1952, OF, HSTL.

22. Coffin, *Missouri Compromise*, p. 14.

23. TM, 2:1; Acheson, *Present at the Creation*, p. 731.

24. Leahy, *I Was There*, p. 4.

25. Vandenberg, *Private Papers*, p. 168.

26. Bailey, *Presidential Greatness*, p. 323; TM, 2:122-124; Millis, *Forrestal Diaries*, pp. 454-455.

27. Hillman, *Mr. President*, p. 16; Bailey, *Presidential Greatness*, p. 216; OHT, Jonathan Daniels.

28. Hartmann, *Truman and the 80th Congress*, p. 212; Neustadt, "Congress and the Fair Deal," *Public Policy* (1954):351-381.

29. Hillman, *Mr. President*, pp. 16-17; Tugwell, *Chronicle of Jeopardy*, p. 48; Abraham, *Justices and Presidents*, pp. 224-225.

30. Goulden, *Superlawyers*, chap. 2; Coffin, *Missouri Compromise*, p. 42.

31. OHT, James Sundquist.

32. Steinberg, *Man from Missouri*, p. 230.

33. Richard S. Kirkendall, "Election of 1948," in Schlesinger and Israel, eds., *History of American Presidential Elections*.

34. OHT, James Sundquist; Pollard, *President and the Press*, chaps. 2, 3; Neustadt, *Presidential Power*, p. 53; Bailey, *Presidential Greatness*, p. 200.

35. Johnson, *1600 Pennsylvania Avenue*, p. 223.

36. Rogge, "Speechmaking of Harry S. Truman," pp. 554-570.

37. Merriam and Gosnell, *American Party System*, appendix; Bailey, *Presidential Greatness*, pp. 93, 265; Arthur Schlesinger, Sr., in NYT, August 11, 1962.

38. Congressional Quarterly, *Congress and the Nation*, p. 62.

39. PPT, 1948, p. 864; Fenton, *In Your Opinion*, pp. 44-73; Roper, *You and Your Leaders*, pp. 142-150.

40. Neustadt, *Presidential Power*, p. 96.

41. David, Goldman, and Bain, *Presidential Nominating Politics in 1952*, pp. 53-54.

42. Ross, *Loneliest Campaign*, chap. 11; Abels, *Out of the Jaws of Victory*, chap. 14; Bernstein, "Election of 1952," in Schlesinger, ed., *Coming to Power*, pp. 406-409, 428-436.

43. Bailey, *Presidential Greatness*, pp. 236-238; Neustadt, "Congress and the Fair Deal," *Public Policy* (1954); Hartmann, *Truman and the 80th Congress*, pp. 211-217.

44. Congressional Quarterly, *Guide to Congress*, p. 583.

45. Bernstein, "Economic Policies," in Kirkendall, *Truman Period* (1967), p. 106.

46. Kirkendall, "Harry Truman," in Borden, *America's Eleven Greatest Presidents*, pp. 276-277.

47. Clifford Memorandum for the President on American Relations with the Soviet Union, September 1946, in Krock, *Memoirs*, appendix A.

48. Hillman, *Mr. President*, pp. 199-203.

49. Madison, *Leaders and Liberals* pp. 460-462.

50. Daniels interview with Ethel and Nellie Noland, September 25, 1949, JDP; Steinberg, *Man from Missouri*, p. 405.

51. Truman, *Harry S. Truman*, pp. 74-75.

52. Schmidtlein, "Truman the Senator," pp. 316-332.

53. Kirkendall, "Harry Truman," in Borden, *America's Eleven Greatest Presidents*, pp. 259-260.

54. TM, 1:10-11.

55. Bohlen, *Witness to History*, p. 239.

56. Feis, *From Trust to Terror*, chap. 13.

57. Lansdale, *In the Midst of Wars*.

58. Edwin O. Reischauer, *Beyond Vietnam: The United States and Asia* (New York: Knopf, 1968), pp. 164-64.

59. New York Times Staff, *The Pentagon Papers* (1971), pp. 3-36.

60. Wilber W. Hoare, "Eisenhower and After," in Ernest R. May, ed., *The Ultimate Decision* (New York: Braziller, 1960), pp. 208-210.

61. Reischauer, *Beyond Vietnam*, pp. 112-139.

BIBLIOGRAPHY

Abels, Jules. *Out of the Jaws of Victory*. New York: Holt, 1959.
_____. *The Truman Scandals*. Chicago: H. Regnery Co., 1956.
Abraham, Henry A. *Justices and Presidents*. New York: Penguin Books, Inc., 1975.
Acheson, Dean Gooderham. *The Pattern of Responsibility*. Boston: Houghton Mifflin Co., 1952.
_____. *A Democrat Looks at His Party*. New York: Harper & Row Pubs., Inc., 1955.
_____. *Sketches from Life of Men I Have Known*. New York: Harper & Row Pubs., Inc., 1961.
_____. *Present at the Creation: My Years in the State Department*. New York: Norton, 1969.
Agar, Herbert. *The Price of Power: America Since 1945*. Chicago: University of Chicago Press, 1957.
Albertson, Dean. *Roosevelt's Farmer: Claude R. Wickard in the New Deal*. New York: Columbia University Press, 1961.
Albion, Robert Greenhalgh, and Connery, Robert H. *Forrestal and the Navy*. New York: Columbia University Press, 1962.
Alinsky, Saul David. *John L. Lewis: An Unauthorized Biography*. New York: Putnam's, 1956.
Allen, George Edward. *Presidents Who Have Known Me*. New York: Simon Schuster, Inc., 1950.
Allen, Robert Sharon, and Shannon, William V. *The Truman Merry-Go-Round*. New York: Vanguard Press, Inc., 1950.
Almond, Gabriel. *The American People and Foreign Policy*. New York: Harcourt, Brace, 1950.
Alperowitz, Gar. *Atomic Diplomacy: Hiroshima and Potsdam*. New York: Simon and Schuster, Inc., 1965.
Ambrose, Stephen. *The Military and American Society*. New York: Free Press, 1972.
American Library in London. *An Introductory Anthology of President Truman*. London: OWI, 1945.
Anderson, Patrick. *The President's Men*. Garden City, N.Y.: Doubleday, 1968.
Andrews, Bert. *Washington Witch Hunt*. New York: Random House, 1948.
Appleman, Roy E. *South to Naktong, North to the Yalu: United States Army in the Korean War*. Washington, D.C.: Government Printing Office, 1961.

Arkes, Hadley. *Bureaucracy, the Marshall Plan and the National Interest.* Princeton: Princeton University Press, 1972.

Asbell, Bernard. *When FDR Died.* New York: Holt, 1961.

Bailey, Stephen Kemp. *Congress at Work.* New York: Holt, 1952.

_____. *Congress Makes a Law.* New York: Vintage, 1950.

Bailey, Thomas A. *Presidential Greatness.* New York: Appleton-Century-Crofts, 1966.

Bain, Richard C. *Convention Decisions and Voting Records.* Washington, D.C.: Brookings, 1960.

Baker, Ray Stannard. *Woodrow Wilson, Life and Letters.* Garden City, N.Y.: Doubleday, 1927-1939.

Baldwin, Frank. *Without Parallel: The American Korean Relationship Since 1945.* New York: Pantheon, 1973.

Ballou, M. E. *Jackson County, Missouri: Its Opportunities and Resources.* Rural Jackson County Chamber of Commerce, Independence, Mo., 1926.

Barber, James David. *The Presidential Character.* Englewood Cliffs, N.J.: Prentice-Hall, 1972.

Barghoorn, Frederick C. *The Soviet Image of the United States.* Port Washington, N.Y.: Kennikat, 1950.

Barker, John Tull. *Missouri Lawyer.* Philadelphia: Dorrence, 1949.

Barkley, Alben. *That Reminds Me.* New York: Doubleday, 1945.

Barth, Alan. *Loyalty of Free Men.* New York: Viking, 1951.

Belknap, Michal R. *Cold War Political Justice: The Smith Act, the Communist Party, and American Civil Liberties,* Westport: Greenwood Press, 1977.

Bell, Jack. *The Splendid Misery: The Story of the Presidency and Power Politics at Close Range.* Garden City, N.Y.: Doubleday, 1960.

Bendiner, Robert. *White House Fever: An Innocent's Guide to Principles and Practices, Respectable and Otherwise, Behind the Election of American Presidents.* New York: Harcourt, Brace. 1960.

Bentley, Elizabeth. *Out of Bondage.* New York: Devin-Adair, 1951.

Berelson, Bernard R.; Lazarsfeld, Paul F.; and McPhee, William N. *Voting: A Study of Opinion Formation in a Presidential Campaign.* Chicago: University of Chicago Press, 1955.

Berle, Beatrice Bishop, and Jacobs, Travis Beal, eds. *Navigating the Rapids, 1918–1971: From the Papers of Adolph A. Berle.* New York: Harcourt, Brace, 1973.

Berman, William C. *The Politics of Civil Rights in the Truman Administration.* Columbus: Ohio State University Press, 1970.

Bernstein, Barton J., "Economic Policies." In Richard S. Kirkendall, *The Truman Period as a Research Field.* Columbia: University of Missouri Press, 1967.

_____. "The Election of 1952—The Republicans Return." In Arthur M. Schlesinger, Jr., ed., *The Coming to Power.* New York: Chelsea House, 1972.

_____, ed. *Politics and Policies of the Truman Administration.* Chicago: Quadrangle Books, 1970.

_____. *Towards a New Past: Dissenting Essays in American History.* New York: Pantheon, 1968.

_____. *Twentieth-Century America: Recent Interpretations.* New York: Harcourt, Brace, 1972.

_____, ed. *The Atomic Bomb: The Crucial Issues.* Critical Issues in American History Series. Boston: Little, Brown, 1976.

Bernstein, Barton J., and Matusow, Allen J., eds., *The Truman Administration: A Documentary History.* Ithaca: Cornell University Press, 1966.

Biddle, Francis. *The Fear of Freedom.* Garden City, N.Y.: Doubleday, 1952.

_____. *In Brief Authority.* Garden City, N.Y.: Doubleday, 1962.

Bishop, Jim. *FDR's Last Year, April 1944–April 1945*. New York: Morrow, 1974.

Blackett, Patrick M. S. *Fear, War and the Bomb*. New York: McGraw-Hill, 1949.

Blum, John Morton, ed. *The Price of Vision—The Diary of Henry A. Wallace, 1942–1946*. Boston: Houghton Mifflin, 1973.

_____. *From the Morgenthau Diaries: Years of War, 1941–1945*. Boston: Houghton Mifflin, 1967.

Bohlen, Charles E. *Witness to History, 1929–1969*. New York: Norton, 1973.

Bontecou, Eleanor. *The Federal Loyalty Security Program*. Ithaca: Cornell University Press, 1953.

Borden, Morton, ed. *America's Eleven Greatest Presidents*. Chicago: Rand McNally, 1971.

Bowles, Chester. *Promises to Keep: My Years in Public Life*. New York: Harper & Row Pubs., Inc., 1971.

Brock, Clifton. *Americans for Democratic Action*. Washington, D.C.: Public Affairs Press, 1962.

Brown, Andrew Theodore. *The Politics of Reform: Kansas City's Municipal Government, 1925–1950*. Kansas City: Community Studies, 1958.

Brown, John Mason. *Through These Men: Some Aspects of Our Passing History*. New York: Harper & Row Pubs., Inc. 1952.

Brzezinski, Zbigniew. *The Soviet Bloc: Unity Conflict*. Cambridge: Harvard University Press, 1971.

Bundschu, Henry A. "Harry S. Truman, the Missourian." *Kansas City Star*, December 26, 1948.

Burns, Francis. "The Life Story of Harry S. Truman, 32nd President of the United States." *Boston Daily Globe*, April 13, 1945.

Burns, James MacGregor. *Roosevelt: Soldier of Freedom*. New York: Harcourt Brace, 1970.

Byrnes, James Francis. *Speaking Frankly*. New York: Harper & Row Pubs., Inc., 1947.

_____. *All in One Lifetime*. New York: Harper & Row Pubs. Inc., 1958.

Cadogan, Sir Alex. *The Diaries of Sir Alex Cadogan, 1938–1945*. Edited by David Dilks. New York: Putnam's, 1972.

Caldwell, George S. *Good Old Harry*. New York: Hawthorn, 1966.

Campbell, Angus, et al. *The Voter Decides*. Evanston: Row, Peterson, 1954.

Campbell, Angus, and Kahn, R.L. *The People Elect a President*. Ann Arbor: Institute for Social Research, 1952.

Caraley, Demetrios. *The Politics of Military Unification: A Study of Conflict and Policy Process*. New York: Columbia University Press, 1966.

Caridi, Ronald. *The Korean War and American Politics: The Republican Party as a Case Study*. Philadelphia: University of Pennsylvania Press, 1968.

Carr, Albert H. Z. *Truman, Stalin and Peace*. Garden City, N.Y.: Doubleday, 1950.

Carr, Robert. *Federal Protection of Civil Rights*. Ithaca: Cornell University Press, 1947.

Catton, Bruce. *The War Lords of Washington*. New York: Harcourt, Brace, 1948.

Chambers, Whittaker. *Witness*. New York: Random House, 1952.

Childs, Marquis. *I Write from Washington*. New York: Harper & Row Pubs., Inc., 1942.

Churchill, Winston. *Triumph and Tragedy*. Boston: Houghton Mifflin, 1953.

Clark, Mark W. *From the Danube to the Yalu*. New York: Harper & Row Pubs., Inc., 1954.

Claude, Inis. *Swords into Ploughshares*. New York: Random House, 1956.

Clay, Lucius. *Decision in Germany*. Garden City, N.Y.: Doubleday, 1952.

Clemens, Cyril. *The Man from Missouri*. Webster Groves: International Mark Twain Society, 1945.

_____. *Mark Twain and Harry Truman*. Webster Groves: International Mark Twain Society, 1950.

Cochran, Bert. *Harry Truman and the Crisis Presidency*. New York: Funk & Wagnalls, 1973.

Coffin, Tristram. *Missouri Compromise*. Boston: Little, Brown, 1947.

Coit, Margaret C. *Mr. Baruch: The Man, the Myth, the Eighty Years*. Boston: Houghton Mifflin, 1957.

Collins, J. Lawton. *War in Peacetime: The History and Lessons of Korea*. Boston: Houghton Mifflin, 1969.

Committee on Foreign Relations. *U.S. in World Affairs*. New York: Harper & Row Pubs., Inc., 1945-1952.

Congressional Quarterly. *Congress and the Nation, 1945-1964*. Washington, D.C.: Congressional Quarterly, 1965.

_____. *Guide to Congress*. Washington, D.C.: Congressional Quarterly, 1971.

Connally, Tom. *My Name Is Tom Connally*. New York: Crowell, 1954.

Cook, Fred J. *The Nightmare Decade: The Life and Times of Senator Joe McCarthy*. New York: Random House, 1971.

Cornwell, Elmer J. *Presidential Leadership in Public Opinion*. Bloomington: Indiana University Press, 1965.

Corwin, Edward Samuel. *The President, Office and Powers, 1787-1957: History and Analysis of Practice and Opinion*. New York: New York University Press, 1957.

_____. *The Constitution and What It Means Today*. Princeton: Princeton University Press, 1954.

Cronin, Thomas E. *State of the Presidency*. Boston: Little, Brown, 1975.

Curry, George. *James F. Byrnes*, in *American Secretaries of State and Their Diplomacy*, vol. 14. New York: Cooper Square, 1965.

Dalfiume, Richard. *Desegregation of the Armed Forces*. Columbia: University of Missouri Press, 1969.

Daniels, Jonathan. *The Man of Independence*. Philadelphia: J. B. Lippincott, 1950.

Darilek, Richard E. *A Loyal Opposition in Time of War: The Republican Party and the Politics of Foreign Policy from Pearl Harbor to Yalta*. Westport: Greenwood Press, 1976.

David, Paul, et al., *The National Story*, vol. 5: *Presidential Nominating Politics in 1952*. Baltimore: Johns Hopkins University Press, 1954.

David, Paul T.; Goldman, Ralph M.; and Bain, Richard C. *The Politics of National Party Conventions*. Washington, D.C.: Brookings Institution, 1960.

Davies, John Paton, Jr. *Dragon by the Tail: American, British, Japanese, and Russian Encounters with China and One Another*. New York: Norton, 1972.

Davies, Richard O. *Housing Reform During the Truman Administration*. Columbia: University of Missouri Press, 1966.

Davis, David Brien, ed. *The Fear of Conspiracy: Images of Un-American Subversion from the Revolution to the Present*. Ithaca: Cornell, 1972.

Davis, Kenneth S. *A Prophet in His Own Country: The Triumphs and Defeats of Adlai E. Stevenson*. Garden City, N.Y.: Doubleday, 1957.

Davis, Lynn Etheridge. *The Cold War Begins: Soviet-American Conflict Over Eastern Europe*. Princeton: Princeton University Press, 1974.

Dayton, Eldorous L. *Give 'em Hell Harry: An Informal Biography of the Terrible Tempered Mr. T*. New York: Devin-Adair, 1956.

Deane, John R. *The Strange Alliance: The Story of Our Efforts at Wartime Co-operation with the Russians*. New York: Viking, 1947.

Democratic National Committee. *Official Proceedings of the Democratic National Conventions 1944, 1948, 1952*.

Dille, John. *Substitute for Victory*. Garden City, N.Y.: Doubleday, 1954.

Divine, Robert A. *Foreign Policy and U.S. Presidential Elections*. New York: Watts, 1974.

Dizard, Wilson P. *Strategy of Truth*. Washington, D.C.: Public Affairs Press, 1961.

Donahoe, Bernard T. *Private Plans and Public Dangers: Story of Franklin D. Roosevelt's Third Term Nomination*. South Bend: University of Notre Dame Press, 1965.

Donovan, Robert J. *Eisenhower: The Inside Story*. New York: Harper & Row Pubs., Inc. 1956.

_____. *Conflict and Crisis: The Presidency of Harry S. Truman, 1945-1948*. New York: Norton, 1977.

Dorough, C. Dwight. *Mr. Sam*. New York: Random House, 1962.

Dorsett, Lyle W. *The Pendergast Machine*. New York: Oxford University Press, 1968.

Douglas, Paul. *In the Fullness of Time: The Memoirs of Paul H. Douglas*. New York: Harcourt Brace, 1971.

Douglas, William O. *Go East, Young Man*. New York: Random House, 1974.

Druks, Herbert. *Harry S. Truman and the Russians, 1945-1953*. New York: R. Speller, 1967.

Dulles, John Foster. *War or Peace*. New York: Macmillan, 1950.

Eaton, Richard, and Hart, La Valle. *Meet Harry S. Truman*. Washington: Dumbarton House, 1945.

Eban, Abba. *An Autobiography*. New York: Random House, 1977.

Eberstadt, Ferdinand. *Report to James Forrestal, Secretary of the Navy, on Unification of the War and Navy Departments*. Printed for Senate Committee on Naval Affairs, October 22, 1945.

Eden, Anthony. *The Reckoning*. Boston: Houghton, Mifflin, 1965.

Edwards, India. *Pulling No Punches: Memoirs of a Woman in Politics*. New York: Putnam's, 1977.

Eisenhower, Dwight D. *Crusade in Europe*. Garden City, N.Y.: Doubleday, 1948.

Ellis, Howard Sylvester. *The Economics of Freedom: The Progress and Future of Aid to Europe*. New York: Harper & Row Pubs., Inc., 1950.

Emmerson, Thomas I., and Haber, David. *Political and Civil Rights in the United States*. Buffalo: Dennis, 1952.

Ernest, Morris L., and David, Loth. *The People Know Best: The Ballots vs. the Polls*. Washington, D.C.: Public Affairs Press, 1949.

Faber, Doris. *Mothers of American Presidents*. New York: New American Library, 1968.

Fairbank, John King. *The U.S. and China*. Cambridge: Harvard University Press, 1971.

Farley, James. *Jim Farley's Story: The Roosevelt Years*. New York: McGraw-Hill, 1948.

Farrar, Ronald T. *Reluctant Servant: The Story of Charles G. Ross*. Columbia: University of Missouri Press, 1969.

Feis, Herbert. *Between War and Peace: The Potsdam Conference*. Princeton, N.J.: Princeton University Press, 1960.

_____. *The Atomic Bomb and the End of World War II*. Princeton, N.J.: Princeton University Press, 1966.

_____. *The China Tangle*. Princeton, N.J.: Princeton University Press, 1953.

_____. *The Birth of Israel*. New York, Norton, 1969.

_____. *Contest over Japan*. New York: Norton, 1967.

_____. *From Trust to Terror: The Onset of the Cold War, 1945-1950*. New York: Norton, 1970.

Fenno, Richard F. *The President's Cabinet: An Analysis in the Period from Wilson to Eisenhower*. Cambridge: Harvard University Press, 1959.

Fenton, John H. *Politics in the Border States*. New Orleans: Hauser, 1957.

_____. *In Your Opinion*. Boston: Little, Brown, 1960.

Ferrell, Robert A. *George C. Marshall*. In *American Secretaries of State and Their Diplomacy*. Vol. 15. New York: Cooper Square, 1966.

Fesler, James W., et al. *Industrial Mobilization for War*. Washington, D.C.: Government Printing Office, 1947.

Flash, Edward S. *Economic Advice and Presidential Leadership*. New York: Columbia University Press, 1965.

Fleming, Denna Frank. *The Cold War and Its Origins, 1917–1960*. Garden City, N.Y.: Doubleday, 1961.

Flynn, Edward J. *You're the Boss*. New York: Viking, 1947.

Flynn, George Q. *The Mess in Washington: Manpower Mobilization in World War II*. Westport: Greenwood Press, 1979.

Fogelman, Edwin. *Hiroshima: The Decision to Use the A-Bomb*. New York: Scribner's, 1964.

Forrestal, James. *The Forrestal Diaries*. Edited by Walter Millis with E. S. Duffield. New York: Viking, 1951.

Foster, James C. *The Union Politic: The CIO Political Action Committee*. Columbia: University of Missouri Press, 1975.

Frederick, John H. *Commercial Air Transportation*. Chicago: Irwin, 1942.

Freeland, Richard M. *The Truman Doctrine and the Origins of McCarthyism*. New York: Knopf, 1971.

Fried, Richard M. *Men Against McCarthy*. New York: Columbia University Press, 1976.

Friedrich, Carl J., and Galbraith, J. Kenneth, eds., *Public Policy*. Cambridge: Harvard Graduate School of Administration, 1954.

Furer, Howard, ed. *Harry S. Truman 1884—Chronology, Documents, Bibliography*. Dobbs Ferry: Oceana, 1969.

Futrell, R. Frank. *Air Force in Korea, 1950–53*. New York: Duell, Sloan & Pearce, 1961.

Gaddis, John Lewis. *The United States and the Origins of the Cold War*. New York: Columbia University Press, 1972.

Galbraith, Kenneth. *Money: Whence It Comes*. Boston: Houghton Mifflin, 1975.

Gardner, Lloyd C. *Architects of Illusion: Men and Ideas in American Foreign Policy, 1941–1949*. Chicago: Quadrangle, 1970.

_____. ed. *The Korean War*. New York: Quadrangle, 1972.

Garson, Robert A. *The Democratic Party and Politics of Sectionalism, 1941–1948*. Baton Rouge: Louisiana State University Press, 1974.

Garwood, Darrell. *Crossroads of America*. New York: Norton, 1948.

George, Alexander, and George, Juliette. *Woodrow Wilson and Colonel House*. New York: John Day, 1956.

George, Alexander, et al. *Deterrence in American Foreign Policy*. New York: Columbia University Press, 1974.

Gerson, Louis L. *American Secretaries of State and Their Diplomacy*, vol. 16: *John Foster Dulles*. New York: Cooper Square, 1967.

Gilbert, Amy. *Executive Agreements and Treaties, 1946–1973*. New York: Endicott, 1973.

Gimbel, John. *The American Occupation of Germany*. Stanford: Stanford University Press, 1968.

_____. *The Origins of the Marshall Plan*. Stanford: Stanford University Press, 1976.

Giovannitti, Len, and Freed, Fred. *The Decision to Drop the Bomb*. New York: Coward-McCann, 1965.

Goldman, Eric Frederick. *The Crucial Decade: America, 1945–1955*. New York: Knopf, 1956.

Goodrich, Leland M. *Korea: A Study of U.S. Policy in the United Nations*. New York: Council on Foreign Relations, 1956.

Goodwin, Craufurd D., ed. *Exhortation and Control: The Search for a Wage and Price Policy*. Washington, D.C.: Brookings, 1975.

Gosnell, Harold F. *Champion Campaigner: Franklin D. Roosevelt*. New York: Macmillan, 1952.

Goulden, Joe. *The Superlawyers*. New York: Dell, 1973.

_____. *The Best Years, 1945–1950.* New York: Atheneum, 1976.

Graebner, Norman A. *Cold War Diplomacy.* Princeton, N.J.: Princeton University Press, 1962.

_____, ed. *An Uncertain Tradition: American Secretaries of State in the Twentieth Century.* New York: McGraw-Hill, 1961.

Grew, Joseph C. *Turbulent Era.* Boston: Houghton Mifflin, 1952.

Griffith, Robert. *The Politics of Fear: Joseph R. McCarthy and the Senate.* Lexington: University of Kentucky Press, 1970.

Griffith, Robert, and Theoharis, Athan, eds. *The Spector: Original Essays on Cold War and McCarthyism.* New York: Watts, 1974.

Groves, Leslie R. *Now It Can Be Told: The Story of the Manhattan Project.* New York: Harper & Row Pubs., Inc., 1962.

Gunther, John. *Roosevelt in Retrospect.* New York: Harper & Row Pubs., Inc., 1950.

Haines, C. Grove, ed. *The Threat of Soviet Imperialism.* Baltimore: Johns Hopkins University Press, 1954.

Halle, Louis J. *The Cold War as History.* New York: Harper & Row Pubs., Inc.,: 1967.

Halperin, Morton. *Limited War.* Cambridge: Harvard Center for International Affairs, 1962.

Hamby, Alonzo L. *Beyond the New Deal: Harry S. Truman and American Liberalism.* New York: Columbia University Press, 1973.

Hammond, Paul Y. *Organizing for Defense.* Princeton, N.J.: Princeton University Press, 1961.

Hansen, R. Joseph, and Cannon, Mark W. *The Making of Public Policy.* New York: McGraw-Hill, 1965.

Harper, Alan D. *The Politics of Loyalty: The White House and the Communist Issue, 1946–1952.* Westport, Conn.: Greenwood Press, 1969.

Harris, Joseph P. *Advice and Consent of the Senate.* Berkeley: University of California Press, 1953.

Hartmann, Susan M. *Truman and the 80th Congress.* Columbia: University of Missouri Press, 1971.

Hassett, William D. *Off the Record with FDR, 1942–1945.* New Brunswick: Rutgers University Press, 1958.

Hayek, Friedrich A. *The Road to Serfdom.* Chicago: University of Chicago Press, 1944.

Haynes, Richard F. *The Awesome Power: Harry Truman as Commander in Chief.* Baton Rouge: Louisiana State University, 1973.

Helm, William Pickett. *Harry Truman, a Political Biography.* New York: Duell, Sloan and Pearce, 1947.

Henry, Laurin L. *Presidential Transitions.* Washington, D.C.: Brookings Institution, 1960.

Herring, George C., Jr. *Aid to Russia: Strategy, Diplomacy, the Origins of the Cold War.* New York: Columbia University Press, 1973.

Hersey, John. "Mr. President." *New Yorker,* April 7, 14, 21, 28, 1951.

Herz, Martin F. *Beginnings of the Cold War.* Bloomington: University of Indiana Press, 1966.

Hewlett, Richard G., and Anderson, Oscar E. *A History of the United States Atomic Energy Commission: 1939–1946.* University Park: Pennsylvania State University Press, 1962.

Higgins, Trumbull. *Korea and the Fall of MacArthur: A Precis in Limited War.* New York: Oxford University Press, 1960.

Hillman, William, ed. *Mr. President.* New York: Farrar, Straus, 1952.

Hoopes, Townsend. *The Devil and John Foster Dulles.* Boston: Little, Brown, 1973.

Horowitz, David. *The Free World Colossus: A Critique of American Foreign Policy in the Cold War.* New York: Hill & Wang, 1961.

Hughes, Emmet J. *The Living Presidency: The Resources and Dilemmas of the American Presidential Office.* New York: Coward, 1972.

_____. *The Ordeal of Power.* New York: Atheneum, 1963.

Hull, Cordell. *The Memoirs of Cordell Hull.* New York: Macmillan, 1948.

Huthmacher, J. Joseph, ed. *The Truman Years.* Hinsdale, Ill.: Holt, 1972.

Ickes, Harold L. *Autobiography of a Curmudgeon.* New York: Reynal and Hitchcock, 1943.

_____. *The Secret Diary of Harold L. Ickes.* New York: Simon & Schuster, 1954.

Jackson, John Hampden. *The World in the Postwar Decade, 1945-1955.* Boston: Houghton Mifflin, 1956.

James, D. Clayton. *The Years of MacArthur, vol. 3:1941-1945.* Boston: Houghton Mifflin, 1975.

Janeway, Eliot. *The Struggle for Survival.* New Haven: Yale University Press, 1951.

Jessup, Philip C. *The Birth of Nations.* New York: Columbia University Press, 1974.

Johnson, Walter. *How We Drafted Adlai Stevenson.* New York: Knopf, 1955.

_____. *1600 Pennsylvania Avenue.* Boston: Little, Brown, 1960.

Jones, Jesse H., and Angley, Edward. *Fifty Billion Dollars.* New York: Macmillan, 1951.

Jones, Joseph Marion. *The Fifteen Weeks, February 21-June 5, 1947.* New York: Viking Press, 1955.

Josephson, Matthew. *Sidney Hillman: Statesman of American Labor.* Garden City, N.Y.: Doubleday, 1952.

Kahn, E. J., Jr. *The China Hands: American Foreign Service Officers and What Befell Them.* New York: Viking, 1975.

Kelley, Stanley. *Professional Public Relations and Political Power.* Baltimore: Johns Hopkins, 1956.

Kennan, George F. *Memoirs, 1925-1950.* Boston: Little, Brown, 1967.

_____. *Memoirs, 1950-1963.* Boston: Little, Brown, 1972.

Khrushchev, Nikolai. *Khrushchev Remembers.* Boston: Little, Brown, 1970.

Kirkendall, Richard S. *The Truman Period as a Research Field.* Columbia: University of Missouri Press, 1967.

_____. *The Truman Period as a Research Field: A Reappraisal, 1972.* Columbia: University of Missouri Press, 1974.

_____. "Harry Truman." In Morton Borden, ed., *America's Eleven Greatest Presidents.* Chicago: Rand McNally, 1971.

Knebel, Fletcher, and Bailey, Charles W. *No High Ground.* New York: Harper & Row Pubs., Inc., 1960.

Koenig, Louis W., ed. *The Truman Administration: Its Principles and Practice.* New York: New York University Press, 1956.

Kolko, Joyce, and Kolko, Gabriel. *The Limits of Power.* New York: Harper & Row Pubs., Inc., 1972.

Kornitzer, Bela. *American Fathers and Sons.* New York: Hermitage House, 1952.

Krock, Arthur. *Memoirs: Sixty Years on the Firing Line.* New York: Funk & Wagnalls, 1962.

Kucklick, Bruce. *American Policy and Division of Germany: The Clash with Russia over Reparations.* Ithaca: Cornell University Press, 1972.

LaFeber, Walter, *America, Russia, and the Cold War 1945-1967.* New York: Wiley, 1971.

Lamont, Lansing. *Day of Trinity.* New York: Atheneum, 1965.

Lansdale, Edward G. *In the Midst of Wars: An American Mission to Southeast Asia.* New York: Harper & Row Pubs., Inc., 1972.

Lapomarda, Vincent Anthony. "Maurice Joseph Tobin, 1901-1953." Ph.D. dissertation, Boston University, 1968.

Laquer, Walter. *History of Zionism.* New York: Holt, 1972.

Lash, Joseph P. *Eleanor: The Years Alone.* New York: Norton, 1972.

Latham, Earl. *The Communist Controversy in Washington From the New Deal to McCarthy.* Cambridge: Harvard University Press, 1966.

Leahy, William D. *I Was There.* New York: Whittlesey House, 1960.

Lee, Jay M. *Artilleryman.* Kansas City, Mo.: Press and Spencer Printing Co., 1920.

Lee, R. Alton. *Truman and Taft-Hartley*. Lexington: University of Kentucky Press, 1966.

Leopold, Richard W. *The Growth of American Foreign Policy*. New York: Knopf, 1962.

Lerche, Charles O., Jr. *The Cold War and After*. Englewood Cliffs, N.J.: Prentice-Hall, 1965.

Levy, Mark, and Kramer, Michael S. *The Ethnic Factor: How America's Minorities Decide Elections*. New York: Simon & Schuster, 1972.

Lilienthal, David E. *The Journals of David E. Lilienthal*. New York: Harper & Row Pubs., Inc., 1964.

Link, Arthur S. *American Epoch: A History of the U.S. Since the 1890's*. New York: Knopf, 1958.

Lippmann, Walter. *The Cold War: A Study in U.S. Foreign Policy*. New York: Harper & Row Pubs., Inc., 1947.

Long, Luman. "Rise of Pendergast's Protege." *Congressional Record*, 78th Cong., 2d sess., pp. A4215, 4253, 4310.

Longaker, Richard P. *The Presidency and Individual Liberties*. Ithaca: Cornell University Press, 1961.

Lord, Russell. *Wallaces of Iowa*. New York: Reynal and Hitchcock, 1947.

Lowenthal, Max. *The Investor Pays*. New York: Knopf, 1933.

Lubell, Samuel. *The Future of American Politics*. Garden City, N.Y.; Doubleday, 1956.

Lukacs, John A. *A New History of the Cold War*. New York: Anchor, 1966.

MacArthur, Douglas. *Reminiscences*. New York: McGraw-Hill, 1964.

McClure, Arthur F. *The Truman Administration and the Problems of Postwar Labor*. Rutherford: Fairleigh Dickinson University Press, 1969.

McConnell, Grant. *The President Seizes the Steel Mills*. University: University of Alabama Press, 1960.

McCoy, Donald, and Knetten, Richard T. *Quest and Response: Minority Right and the Truman Administration*. New York: Regents, 1973.

McDonald, James G. *My Mission to Israel, 1948–1951*. New York: Simon & Schuster, 1951.

Macdougall, Curtis D. *Gideon's Army*. New York: Marzani and Munsell, 1965.

McGrath, James Howard. *The Power of the People*. New York: J. Messner, 1948.

McIntire, Ross T. *White House Physician*. New York: Putnam's, 1946.

McLellan, David S. *Dean Acheson*. New York: Dodd, Mead, 1976.

McNaughton, Frank, and Hehmeyer, Walter. *This Man Truman*. New York: McGraw-Hill, 1945.

McNeill, W. H. *America, Britain and Russia: Their Cooperation and Conflict*. London: Oxford University Press, 1953.

McReynolds, Edwin C. *Missouri—A History of the Crossroads State*. Norman: University of Oklahoma Press, 1962.

Maddox, Robert J. *The New Left and the Origins of the Cold War*. Princeton, Princeton University Press, 1973.

Madison, Charles Allan. *Leaders and Liberals in the Twentieth Century*. New York: Ungar, 1961.

Maher, I.H.M. "The Role of the Chairman of a Congressional Investigating Committee: A Case Study of the Special Committee of the Senate to Investigate the National Defense Program, 1941-1948." Ph.D. dissertation, St. Louis University, 1962.

Marcus, Maeva. *Truman and the Steel Seizure*. New York: Columbia University Press, 1977.

Markowitz, Norman D. *The Rise and Fall of the People's Century: Henry A. Wallace and American Liberalism, 1941–1948*. New York: Free Press, 1973.

Martin, Joe. *My First Fifty Years in Politics*. New York: McGraw-Hill, 1960.

Martin, John Bartlow. *Adlai Stevenson of Illinois*. Garden City, N.Y.: Doubleday, 1976.

Martin, Ralph C. *President from Missouri: Harry S. Truman*. New York: Messner, 1964.

_____. *The Bosses*. New York: Putnam's, 1954.

Mason, Frank. *Truman and the Pendergasts*. New York: Regency, 1964.

Matthews, Donald R. *U.S. Senators and Their World*. Chapel Hill: University of North Carolina Press, 1960.

Matusow, Allen J. *Farm Policies and Politics in the Truman Years*. Cambridge: Harvard
University Press, 1967.

May, Ernest. *The Truman Administration and China*. Philadelphia: Lippincott, 1975.

Mayerberg, Samuel Spier. *Chronicle of American Crusader*. New York: Bloch Publishing Co.,
1944.

Mazo, Earl. *Richard Nixon: A Political and Personal Portrait*. New York: Harper & Row
Pubs., Inc., 1959.

Means, Marianne. *The Women in the White House: The Lives, Times and Influence of twelve
Notable First Ladies*. New York: Random House, 1963.

Mee, Charles L., Jr. *Meeting at Potsdam*. New York: Dell, 1976.

Merkl, Peter H. *The Origin of the West German Republic*. New York: Oxford University
Press, 1963.

Merriam, Charles E., and Gosnell, Harold F. *The American Party System*. New York: Macmillan, 1949.

Miller, Merle. *Plain Speaking: An Oral Biography of Harry S. Truman*. New York: Putnam's,
1973.

Milligan, Maurice M. *The Inside Story of the Pendergast Machine by the Man Who Smashed
It*. New York: Scribner's, 1948. *Missouri Waltz* is an earlier title of this book.

Millis, Harry, and Brown, Emily. *From the Wagner Act to Taft-Hartley*. Chicago: University
of Chicago Press, 1950.

Millis, Walter, ed. *The Forrestal Diaries*. New York: Viking, 1951.

Mitchell, Ewing Young. *Kicked in and Kicked out of the President's Little Cabinet*. Washington, D.C.: Andrew Jackson Press, 1936.

Moran, Lord. *Churchill: The Struggle for Survival, 1940–1965*. Boston: Houghton Mifflin,
1966.

Morris, Newbold. *Let the Chips Fall*. New York: Appleton, 1955.

Morris, Richard Brandon. *Great Presidential Decisions: State Papers That Changed the Course
of History*. Philadelphia: Lippincott, 1960.

Mosley, Leonard. *Dulles*. New York: Dial Press, 1978.

Mosteller, Frederick, et al. *The Pre-Election Polls of 1948*. New York: Social Science Research
Council, 1949.

Murphy, Robert. *Diplomat among Warriors*. Garden City, N.Y.: Doubleday, 1964.

Nelson, Donald M. *Arsenal of Democracy*. New York: Harcourt, Brace, 1946.

Neumann, William L. *After Victory: Churchill, Roosevelt, Stalin and the Making of the Peace*.
New York: Harper & Row Pubs., Inc. 1967.

Neustadt, Richard E. *Presidential Power: The Politics of Leadership*. New York: Wiley, 1960.

––––––. "Congress and the Fair Deal: A Balance Sheet." In Carl J. Friedrick and J. Kenneth
Galbraith, eds., *Public Policy*. Cambridge: Harvard Graduate School of Administration, 1954.

––––––. "Notes on the White House Staff Under President Truman." June 1953. HSTL.

Nevins, Allan. *Herbert H. Lehman and His Era*. New York: Scribner's 1963.

Nixon, Richard M. *Six Crises*. Garden City, N.Y.: Doubleday, 1962.

Norris, George W. *Fighting Liberal: An Autobiography*. New York: Macmillan, 1945.

Nourse, Edwin G. *Economics in the Public Service*. New York: Harcourt, Brace, 1953.

Osgood, Robert E. *NATO: The Entangling Alliance*. Princeton, N.J.: Princeton University
Press, 1962.

Page, Bruce; Leitch, David; and Knightley, Phillip. *The Philby Conspiracy*. Garden City,
N.Y.: Doubleday, 1968.

Paige, Glenn D. *The Korean Decision, June 24–30, 1950*. New York: Free Press, 1968.

Parks, Lilian. *My Thirty Years Backstairs at the White House*. New York: Fleet, 1961.

Parmet, Herbert S. *Eisenhower and the American Crusades*. New York: Macmillan, 1972.
_____. *The Democrats: The Years after FDR*. New York: Macmillan, 1976.
Paterson, Thomas G. *Soviet-American Confrontation: Postwar Reconstruction and the Origins of the Cold War*. Baltimore: Johns Hopkins University Press, 1973.
_____, ed. *Cold War Critics*. Chicago: Quadrangle Books, 1971.
Patterson, James T. *Mr. Republican: A Biography of Robert A. Taft*. Boston: Houghton Mifflin, 1972.
Pearson, Drew. *Diaries, 1949–1959*. New York: Holt, 1974.
Phillips, Cabell. *The Truman Presidency*. New York: Macmillan, 1966.
Pogue, Forrest C. *George C. Marshall: Ordeal and Hope, 1939–1942*. New York: Viking, 1966.
_____. *George C. Marshall: Organizer of Victory*. New York: Viking, 1973.
Pollard, James E. *The President and the Press*. Washington, D.C.: Public Affairs Press, 1964.
Pomper, Gerald. *Nominating the President: The Politics of Convention Choice*. New York: Norton, 1966.
Powell, Gene. *Tom's Boy Harry*. Jefferson City, Missouri: Hawthorn Publishing Co., 1948.
Price, Byron. *Report to President Truman on the Relations Between the American Forces of Occupation and the German People*. Washington, D.C.: Government Printing Office, 1947.
Price, Harry Bayard. *The Marshall Plan and Its Meaning*. New York: Cornell University Press, 1955.
Prindiville, Kathleen. *First Ladies*. New York: Macmillan, 1954.
Reddig, William M. *Tom's Town, Kansas City and the Pendergast Legend*. Philadelphia: Lippincott, 1947.
Redding, John M. *Inside the Democratic Party*. Indianapolis: Bobbs-Merrill, 1958.
Reedy, George. *Twilight of the Presidency*. New York: New American Library, 1971.
Rees, David. *Korea*. New York: St. Martin's Press, 1964.
Reitzel, William, et al. *United States Foreign Policy, 1945–1955*. Washington, D.C.: Brookings Institution, 1956.
Rhyne, Charles S. *Civil Aeronautics Act Annotated*. Washington, D.C.: National Law Book Company, 1939.
Riddle, Donald H. *The Truman Committee*. New Brunswick: Rutgers University Press, 1964.
Ridgway, Matthew. *Korean War*. Garden City, N.Y.: Doubleday, 1967.
Rigdon, William M. *White House Sailor*. Garden City, N.Y.: Doubleday, 1962.
Rinn, Fauneil Joyce. "President Meets the Press." Master's thesis, University of Chicago, 1954.
Rogge, Edward Alexander. "The Speechmaking of Harry S. Truman." Ph.D. dissertation, University of Missouri, 1958.
Rogow, Arnold A. *James Forrestal: A Study of Personality, Politics and Policy*. New York: Macmillan, 1963.
Rogow, Arnold A., and Lasswell, Harold D. *Power, Corruption and Rectitude*. Englewood Cliffs, N.J.: Prentice-Hall, 1963.
Roosevelt, Elliott, ed. *F.D.R.: His Personal Letters, 1928–1945*. New York: Duell, Sloan and Pearce, 1950.
Roosevelt, Theodore. *Theodore Roosevelt: An Autobiography*. New York: Scribner's 1920.
Roper, Elmo. *You and Your Leaders*. New York: Morrow, 1957.
Rose, Lisle A. *Dubious Victory: The U.S. and End of World War II*. Kent: Kent State University Press, 1973.
Rosenman, Samuel I. *Working with Roosevelt*. New York: Harper & Row Pubs., Inc., 1952.
_____, ed. *Coming to Power: Critical Presidential Elections in American History*. New York: Harper & Row Pubs., Inc., 1950.
Rositzke, Harry. *CIA's Secret Operations: Espionage, Counterespionae and Covert Action*. New York: Reader's Digest Press, 1977.

Ross, George Edward. *Know Your Presidents and Their Wives*. Chicago: Rand McNally, 1960.

Ross, Irwin, *The Loneliest Campaign: The Truman Victory of 1948*. New York: New American Library, 1968.

Rossiter, Clinton Lawrence. *The American Presidency*. New York: Harcourt, Brace, 1956.

Rostow, W.W. *The United States in the World Arena*. New York: Harper & Row Pubs., Inc., 1960.

Rovere, Richard Halworth, and Schlesinger, Arthur M. *The General and the President, and the Future of American Foreign Policy*. New York: Farrar, Straus, 1951.

Sachar, Howard M. *Europe Leaves the Middle East, 1936-1954*. New York: Knopf, 1972.

Sawyer, Charles. *Concerns of a Conservative Democrat*. Carbondale: Southern Illinois University Press, 1968.

Schapsmeier, Edward L., and Schapsmeier, Frederick H. *Henry A. Wallace and the War Years, 1940-1965*. Ames: Iowa State University Press, 1970.

Schauffler, Edward R. *Harry Truman, Son of the Soil*. Kansas City: Schauffler Publishing Co., 1947.

Schilling, Warner R., et al. *Strategy, Politics and Defense Budgets*. New York: Columbia University Press, 1962.

Schlesinger, Arthur M., Jr. *The Imperial Presidency*. Boston: Houghton Mifflin, 1973.

————, ed. *Coming to Power: Critical Presidential Elections in American History*. New York: New York: Chelsea, 1971.

————. *Coming to Power: Critical Presidential Elections in American History*. New York: Chelsea, 1971.

Schlesinger, Arthur Jr., and Bruns, Roger, eds. *Congress Investigates: A Documented History*. New York: Chelsea, 1975.

————, and Israel, Fred, ed. *History of American Presidential Elections*. New York: Chelsea, 1971.

Schmidt, Karl M. *Henry Wallace: Quixotic Crusade, 1948*. Syracuse: Syracuse University Press, 1960.

Schmidtlein, Eugene F. "Truman the Senator." Ph.D. dissertation, University of Missouri, 1962.

Schnabel, James F. *Policy and Direction: The First Year, U.S. Army in the Korean War*. Washington, D.C.: Government Printing Office, 1972.

Sebald, William J. *With MacArthur in Japan*. New York: Norton, 1965.

Service, John Stewart. *The Amerasia Papers: Some Problems in the History of U.S.-China Relations*. Berkeley: University of California Press, 1971.

Sherwin, Martin J. *A World Destroyed*. New York: Knopf, 1975.

Sherwood, Robert E. *Roosevelt and Hopkins*. New York: Harper & Row Pubs., Inc., 1948.

Silverman, Corrine. *Presidential Economic Advisers*. University, Ala.: University of Alabama Press, 1959.

Smith, A. Merriman. *Thank You Mr. President: A White House Notebook*. New York: Harper & Row Pubs., Inc., 1946.

————. *A President Is Many Men*. New York: Harper & Row Pubs., Inc., 1948.

Smith, Gaddis. *American Secretaries of State and Their Diplomacy*, vol. 16: *Dean Acheson*. New York: Cooper Square, 1972.

Smith, Jean Edward, ed. *The Papers of General Lucius D. Clay: Germany, 1945-1949*. Bloomington, Ind.: Indiana University Press, 1975.

Smith, John Chabot. *Alger Hiss: The True Story*. New York: Holt, 1976.

Smith, John Malcolm. *Powers of the President During Crises*. Washington, D.C.: Public Affairs Press, 1960.

Smith, R. Harris. *OSS*. New York: Delta, 1972.

Snetsinger, John T. *The Jewish Vote and Creation of Israel.* Stanford: Hoover Institute, 1974.

Solberg, Carl. *Riding High: America in the Cold War.* New York: Mason and Lipscomb, 1973.

Somers, Herman Miles. *Presidential Agency, the Office of War Mobilization and Reconversion.* Cambridge: Harvard University Press, 1960.

Soule, George. *Economic Forces in American History.* New York: Dryden Press, 1950.

Spanier, J. W. *The Truman-MacArthur Controversy.* Cambridge: Harvard University Press, 1959.

Stallings, Laurence. *The Doughboys: The Story of AEF, 1917-1918.* New York: Harper & Row Pubs., Inc., 1963.

Steffens, Lincoln. *The Autobiography of Lincoln, Steffens.* New York: Harcourt, Brace, 1931.

Stein, Herbert. *The Fiscal Revolution in America.* Chicago: University of Chicago Press, 1969.

Steinberg, Alfred. *The Man from Missouri: The Life and Times of Harry S. Truman.* New York: Putnam's, 1962.

Stephens, Oren. *Facts to a Candid World.* Stanford: Stanford University Press, 1955.

Stettinius, Edward R., Jr. *Roosevelt and the Russians: The Yalta Conference.* Edited by Walter Johnson. Garden City, N.Y.: Doubleday, 1949.

Stevenson, Adlai. *Major Campaign Speeches.* New York: Random House, 1953.

Stimson, Henry L., and Bundy, McGeorge. *On Active Service in Peace and War.* New York: Harper & Row Pubs., Inc., 1947.

Stone, Isidor F. *The Truman Era.* New York: Monthly Review Press, 1953.

———. *The Hidden History of the Korean War.* New York: Monthly Review Press, 1952.

Stone, I. G. *They Also Ran.* Garden City, N.Y.: Doubleday, 1943.

Strauss, Lewis, L. *Men and Decisions.* Garden City, N.Y.: Doubleday, 1962.

Street, Kenneth W. "Harry S. Truman: His Role as Legislative Leader, 1945-1948." Ph.D. dissertation, University of Texas, 1963.

Swaine, Robert T. *The Cravath Firm and Its Predecessors, 1819-1948.* New York: Private Printers at Ad Press, 1946-1948.

Taylor, Telford. *Grand Inquest.* New York: Simon & Schuster, 1955.

Theoharis, Athan. *The Yalta Myths: An Issue in U.S. Politics, 1945-1955.* Columbia: University of Missouri Press, 1970.

———. *Seeds of Repression: Harry S. Truman and the Origins of McCarthyism.* Chicago: Quadrangle, 1971.

Toland, John. *The Rising Sun: The Decline and Fall of the Japanese Empire.* New York: Random House, 1970.

Tompkins, C. David. *Senator Arthur H. Vandenberg: The Evolution of a Modern Republican, 1884-1945.* East Lansing: Michigan State University Press, 1971.

Toulmin, Harry Aubrey. *Diary of Democracy: The Senate War Investigating Committee.* New York: R. R. Smith, 1947.

Truman, David. *The Congressional Party.* New York: Wiley, 1959.

Truman, Harry S. *Memoirs.* Garden City, N.Y.: Doubleday, 1955-1956. 2 vols.

———. *The Free World and Free Trade.* Dallas: Southern Methodist University Press, 1963.

———. *Freedom and Equality: Addresses.* Columbia: University of Missouri Press, 1960.

———. *Mr. Citizen.* New York: Geis Associates, Random House, 1960.

———. *The Truman Administration.* Edited by Louis W. Koenig. New York: New York University Press, 1956.

———. *The Truman Program: Addresses and Messages.* Washington, D.C.: Public Affairs Press, 1949.

———. *Truman Speaks.* New York: Columbia University Press, 1960.

Truman, Margaret. *Harry S. Truman.* New York: Morrow, 1973.

_____. *Souvenir: Margaret Truman's Own Story.* New York: McGraw-Hill, 1956.

Tsou, Tang. *America's Failure in China: 1949-50.* Chicago: University of Chicago Press, 1963.

Tuchman, Barbara. *Stilwell and the American Experience in China, 1911-1945.* New York: Bantam, 1972.

Tucker, Robert W. *The Radical Left and American Foreign Policy.* Baltimore: Johns Hopkins University Press, 1971.

Tugwell, Rexford. *The Brains Trust.* New York: Viking, 1968.

_____. *A Chronicle of Jeopardy.* Chicago: University of Chicago Press, 1955.

_____. *The Enlargement of the Presidency.* Garden City, N.Y.: Doubleday, 1960.

_____. *How They Became President.* New York: Simon & Schuster, 1964.

_____. *Off Course from Truman to Nixon.* New York: Praeger, 1971.

Tully, Grace. *F.D.R., My Boss.* New York: Scribner's, 1949.

Ulam, Adam B. *Expansion and Coexistence: The History of Soviet Foreign Policy, 1917-1967.* New York: Praeger, 1968.

_____. *The Rivals: America and Russia Since World War II.* New York: Viking, 1971.

_____. *Stalin: The Man and His Era.* New York: Viking, 1973.

United States. Bureau of the Budget. *United States at War.* Washington, D.C.: Government Printing Office, 1946.

_____. Congress. *Congressional Record.* 74th through 82nd.

_____. Congress. Senate. Committee on Foreign Relations. *A Decade of American Foreign Policy: Basic Documents, 1942-49.* Washington, D.C.: U.S. Government Printing Office, 1950.

_____. Department of Agriculture. Agricultural History Branch. *Century of Service: The First 100 Years of the United States Department of Agriculture.* Washington, D.C.: Government Printing Office, 1963.

_____. Department of State. *Bulletin.* 1935-1953.

_____. Department of State. *Foreign Relations of the United States.* 1935-1950.

_____. Department of State. *United States Relations with China.* Washington, D.C.: Government Printing Office, 1949.

_____. President. *Public Papers of the President—Harry S. Truman 1945-1952-53.* Washington, D.C.: Government Printing Office, 1961-1966. 8 vols.

Vandenberg, Arthur H., Jr. *The Private Papers of Senator Vandenberg.* Boston: Houghton Mifflin, 1952.

Walker, J. Samuel. *Henry A. Wallace and American Foreign Policy.* Westport: Greenwood Press, 1976.

Walker, Richard L., and Curry, George. *Edward Stettinius and James F. Byrnes, American Secretaries of State.* New York: Cooper Square, 1965.

Walker, Stanley. *Dewey: An American of This Century.* New York: Whittlesey, 1944.

Walton, Richard J. *Henry Wallace, Harry Truman and Cold War.* New York: Viking, 1976.

Warren, Sidney. *The President as a World Leader.* Philadelphia: Lippincott, 1964.

Weisbord, Marvin R. *Campaigning for President.* Washington, D.C.: Public Affairs Press, 1964.

Weitzmann, Chaim. *Trial and Error: An Autobiography.* New York: Schocken, 1966.

Weitzmann, Vera, with David Tutaev. *The Impossible Takes Longer.* London: Harper & Row Pubs., Inc., 1967.

Welles, Sumner. *Seven Decisions That Shaped History.* New York: Harper & Row Pubs., Inc., 1951.

Wellman, Paul I. *Stuart Symington.* Garden City: Doubleday, 1960.

West, J. V., with Mary Lynn Kotz. *Upstairs at the White House: My Life with the First Ladies.* New York: Coward, 1973.

Westerfield, H. Bradford. *Foreign Policy and Party Politics.* New Haven: Yale University Press, 1955.

Wheeler, Burton K. *Yankee from the West.* Garden City, N.Y.: Doubleday, 1962.

White, Leonard D. *The City Manager.* Chicago: University of Chicago Press, 1927.

White, Walter. *A Man Called White.* New York: Viking Press, 1948.

White, William S. *The Taft Story.* New York: Harper & Row Pubs., Inc., 1954.

Whitney, Courtney. *MacArthur: His Rendezvous with History.* New York: Knopf, 1956.

Wick, James L. *How Not to Run for President—A Handbook for Republicans.* New York: Vantage Press, 1952.

Williams, Irving, G. *The Rise of the Vice Presidency.* Washington, D.C.: Public Affairs Press, 1956.

Williams, William Appleman. *The Tragedy of American Diplomacy.* Rev. ed. New York: Dell, 1962.

Willoughby, Charles A., and Chamberlain, John. *MacArthur, 1941-1954.* New York: McGraw-Hill, 1954.

Wolfson, Victor. *The Man Who Cared: A Life of Harry S. Truman.* New York: Farrar, Straus, 1966.

Xydis, Stephen G. *Greece and the Great Powers, 1944-1947.* Thessaloniki: Institute for Balkan Studies, 1963.

Yarmolinsky, Adam. *The Military Establishment: Its Impact on American Society.* New York: Harper & Row Pubs., Inc., 1971.

Yarnell, Allen. *Democrats and Progressives: The 1948 Presidential Election as a Test of Postwar Liberalism.* Berkeley: University of California Press, 1974.

Young, Roland. *Congressional Politics in the Second World War.* New York: Columbia University Press, 1956.

Zinn, Howard. *Postwar America, 1945-1971.* Indianapolis: Bobbs-Merrill, 1974.

Zornow, William Frank. *America at Mid-Century: The Truman Administration, the Eisenhower Administration.* Cleveland: H. Allen, 1959.

INDEX

ABOUT THE AUTHOR

Harold F. Gosnell, one of the founders of modern American political science, retired in 1971 from a long career as a scholar and public official to devote himself to writing. His many books include *Boss Platt and His New York Machine* and *Grass Roots Politics*.

Contributions in Political Science
Series Editor: Bernard K. Johnpoll